The Lives of Ancient Villages

Our conception of the culture and values of the ancient Greco-Roman world is largely based on texts and material evidence left behind by a small and atypical group of city dwellers. The people of the deep Mediterranean countryside seldom appear in the historical record from antiquity, and almost never as historical actors. This book is the first extended historical ethnography of an ancient village society, based on an extraordinarily rich body of funerary and propitiatory inscriptions from a remote upland region of Roman Asia Minor. Rural kinship structures and household forms are analysed in detail, as are the region's demography, religious life, gender relations, class structure, normative standards, and values. Roman Hieradoumia is perhaps the only non-urban society in the Greco-Roman world whose culture can be described at so fine-grained a level of detail: a world of tight-knit families, egalitarian values, hard agricultural labour, village solidarity, honour, piety, and love.

PETER THONEMANN is Forrest-Derow Fellow and Tutor in Ancient History at Wadham College, Oxford. His books include *The Maeander Valley: A Historical Geography from Antiquity to Byzantium* (Cambridge, 2011), which won the 2012 Runciman Prize; *The Hellenistic World: Using Coins as Sources* (Cambridge, 2015); and *An Ancient Dream Manual: Artemidorus' The Interpretation of Dreams* (2020). He is currently Editor of the *Journal of Roman Studies*.

The Lives of Ancient Villages

Rural Society in Roman Anatolia

PETER THONEMANN

University of Oxford

CAMBRIDGE
UNIVERSITY PRESS

Shaftesbury Road, Cambridge CB2 8EA, United Kingdom

One Liberty Plaza, 20th Floor, New York, NY 10006, USA

477 Williamstown Road, Port Melbourne, VIC 3207, Australia

314–321, 3rd Floor, Plot 3, Splendor Forum, Jasola District Centre,
New Delhi – 110025, India

103 Penang Road, #05–06/07, Visioncrest Commercial, Singapore 238467

Cambridge University Press is part of Cambridge University Press & Assessment,
a department of the University of Cambridge.

We share the University's mission to contribute to society through the pursuit of
education, learning and research at the highest international levels of excellence.

www.cambridge.org
Information on this title: www.cambridge.org/9781009123211
DOI: 10.1017/9781009128452

First published 2022

Printed in the United Kingdom by TJ Books Limited, Padstow Cornwall

A catalogue record for this publication is available from the British Library.

Library of Congress Cataloging-in-Publication Data
Names: Thonemann, Peter, author.
Title: The lives of ancient villages : rural society in Roman Anatolia /
Peter Thonemann, University of Oxford.
Description: First Edition. | New York : Cambridge University Press, 2022.
| Series: Greek Culture in the Roman World | Includes bibliographical
references and index.
Identifiers: LCCN 2022016952 | ISBN 9781009123211 (Hardback) |
ISBN 9781009128452 (eBook)
Subjects: LCSH: Ethnology – Turkey. | Human ecology – Turkey. | Kinship – Turkey. |
Villages – Turkey. | BISAC: HISTORY / Ancient / General
Classification: LCC GN308.3.T9 T56 2022 | DDC 306.09561–dc23/eng/20220719
LC record available at https://lccn.loc.gov/2022016952

ISBN 978-1-009-12321-1 Hardback

Contents

v

Figures

Tables

Preface

This book is a historical ethnography of the rural communities of the middle Hermos valley in inland western Asia Minor during the first three centuries AD. Kinship and household structure are central concerns throughout, for reasons which will I hope become clear; I have also said something about the region's demography, land-tenure patterns, village politics, rural cults, and – more tentatively – the relationship between kin-groups and wider social organization. I hope that the book may be of use for the comparative study of non-urban societies in the ancient world, a field where a good deal remains to be done.

Much of this book is founded on other people's grief. Its primary raw materials are thousands of tombstones, set up by grieving parents for their children; by young husbands for their beloved wives; by women for their brothers, sisters, and friends. For the purposes of the present study, this ocean of personal sorrow has been reduced to a set of cold demographic data-points: a female who dies aged 16; a death on Day 20 of the month Apellaios; a tombstone erected by members of the nuclear family. I have tried always to remember that behind these data-points lie real people – people like Assklepiades and Glykeia, the father and mother of a much-loved daughter Ammias, who died aged sixteen on the twentieth day of Apellaios, autumn AD 210; father and mother, too, of a son named Assk-lepiades, who died aged sixteen on the thirteenth day of Apellaios, autumn AD 216. Assklepiades and Glykeia were sober and undemonstrative people, and the tombstone that they set up for their children strictly says noth-ing to prove that Ammias and her brother were 'much loved'. But I am sure they were.

Much of the research for this book was undertaken in 2013–2015, when I was the holder of a Philip Leverhulme Prize. I am grateful to the Lever-hulme Trust for their support and for their patience. Alain Bresson, Richard Duncan-Jones, and Kyle Harper commented helpfully on an early draft of Chapter 3, and Sally Humphreys and Karl Praust sharpened my thinking in Chapter 4. I am indebted to an anonymous external reader and to the Series Editors (particularly Jaś Elsner), for their acute and constructive comments on a first draft of the whole. Charles Crowther and Andrew Meadows were good-humoured travelling companions. Every author, I take it, writes with an ideal reader in mind; I hope that John Davis (1938–2017) would have approved. My greatest debt is to my own beloved *syngeneia*: my wife Sarah, and my children Alex and Sam.

Abbreviations

AD	*Archaiologikon Deltion*
AE	*L'Année épigraphique*
ANRW	*Aufstieg und Niedergang der römischen Welt*
BE	*Bulletin épigraphique*, annually in *REG*.
BMC Lydia	B. V. Head, *A Catalogue of the Greek Coins in the British Museum: Catalogue of the Greek Coins of Lydia*. London, 1902.
BMC Phrygia	B. V. Head, *A Catalogue of the Greek Coins in the British Museum: Catalogue of the Greek Coins of Phrygia*. London, 1906.
BNJ	I. Worthington (ed.), *Brill's New Jacoby Online*, Second Edition https://referenceworks .brillonline.com/browse/brill-s-new-jacoby-2
CGRN	*Collection of Greek Ritual Norms*. http://cgrn.ulg.ac.be
CIG	A. Boeckh, *Corpus Inscriptionum Graecarum* (4 vols). Berlin, 1828–1877.
CIRB	V. V. Struve, *Corpus Inscriptionum Regni Bosporani*. Moscow and Leningrad, 1965.
CNG	*Classical Numismatic Group* (auction catalogues)
Coll. Wadd.	E. Babelon, *Inventaire sommaire de la collection Waddington*. Paris, 1898.
DGE	*Diccionario Griego-Español*. Madrid, 1980–.
DPRR	*Digital Prosopography of the Roman Republic*. www.romanrepublic.ac.uk
EBGR	*Epigraphic Bulletin for Greek Religion*, annually in *Kernos*.
GM Winterthur	H. Bloesch, *Griechische Münzen in Winterthur* (2 vols in 4). Winterthur, 1987–1997.
HED	J. Puhvel, *Hittite Etymological Dictionary*. Berlin and New York, 1984–.

I.Amyzon	J. Robert and L. Robert, *Fouilles d'Amyzon en Carie I. Exploration, histoire, monnaies et inscriptions*. Paris, 1983.
I.Anazarbos	M. H. Sayar, *Die Inschriften von Anazarbos und Umgebung. IGSK* 56,1. Bonn, 2000.
I.Ancyra	D. H. French and S. Mitchell, *The Greek and Latin Inscriptions of Ankara (Ancyra)* (2 vols). Munich, 2012–2019.
I.Antioche de Pisidie	M. A. Byrne and G. Labarre, *Nouvelles inscriptions d'Antioche de Pisidie d'après les Note-Books de W. M. Ramsay. IGSK* 67. Bonn, 2006.
I.Apameia und Pylai	T. Corsten, *Die Inschriften von Apameia (Bithynien) und Pylai. IGSK* 32. Bonn, 1986.
IAph2007	J. Reynolds, C. Roueché and G. Bodard, *Inscriptions of Aphrodisias 2007*. www.insaph .kcl.ac.uk/iaph2007/
I.Arykanda	S. Şahin, *Die Inschriften von Arykanda. IGSK* 48. Bonn, 1994.
IBurdurMus	G. H. R. Horsley, *Regional Epigraphic Catalogues of Asia Minor V: The Greek and Latin Inscriptions in the Burdur Archaeological Museum*. Ankara, 2007.
I.Byzantion	A. Lajtar, *Die Inschriften von Byzantion I. Die Inschriften. IGSK* 58. Bonn, 2000.
I.Denizli	E. Miranda and F. Guizzi, *Museo Archaeologico di Denizli-Hierapolis. Catalogo delle iscrizioni greche e latine: Distretto di Denizli*. Naples, 2008.
I.Didyma	A. Rehm, *Didyma II. Die Inschriften*. Berlin, 1958.
I.Ephesos	H. Wankel, R. Merkelbach *et al.*, *Die Inschriften von Ephesos* (7 vols). *IGSK* 11–17. Bonn, 1979–1981.
IG	*Inscriptiones Graecae*
IGBulg	G. Mihailov, *Inscriptiones Graecae in Bulgaria repertae* (5 vols in 6). Sofia, 1958–1997.
IGR	R. Cagnat, *Inscriptiones Graecae ad Res Romanas Pertinentes* (3 vols). Paris, 1906–1927.
IGUR	L. Moretti, *Inscriptiones Graecae Urbis Romae* (4 vols). Rome, 1968–1990.
I.Iasos	W. Blümel, *Die Inschriften von Iasos* (2 vols). *IGSK* 28. Bonn, 1985.

I.Ilion	P. Frisch, *Die Inschriften von Ilion. IGSK* 3. Bonn, 1975.
I.Iznik	S. Şahin, *Katalog der antiken Inschriften des Museums von Iznik (Nikaia)* (2 vols in 4). *IGSK* 9–10. Bonn, 1979–1987.
I.Kaunos	Chr. Marek, *Die Inschriften von Kaunos.* Munich, 2006.
I.Keramos	E. Varinlioğlu, *Die Inschriften von Keramos. IGSK* 30. Bonn.
I.Kibyra	T. Corsten, *Die Inschriften von Kibyra I. IGSK* 60. Bonn, 2002.
I.Kios	T. Corsten, *Die Inschriften von Kios. IGSK* 29. Bonn, 1985.
I.Klaudiu Polis	F. Becker-Bertau, *Die Inschriften von Klaudiu Polis. IGSK* 31. Bonn, 1986.
I.Knidos	W. Blümel, *Die Inschriften von Knidos I. IGSK* 41. Bonn, 1992.
I.Konya	B. H. McLean, *Regional Epigraphic Catalogues of Asia Minor IV: Greek and Latin Inscriptions in the Konya Archaeological Museum.* Ankara, 2002.
I.Kyzikos	E. Schwertheim, *Die Inschriften von Kyzikos und Umgebung, Teil I: Grabtexte. IGSK* 18. Bonn, 1980.
I.Magnesia	O. Kern, *Die Inschriften von Magnesia am Maeander.* Berlin, 1900.
I.Manisa	H. Malay, *Greek and Latin Inscriptions in the Manisa Museum.* Vienna, 1994.
I.Milet	P. Herrmann, N. Ehrhardt and W. Günther, *Milet. Ergebnisse der Ausgrabungen und Untersuchungen seit dem Jahr 1899. Band VI: Inschriften von Milet* (3 vols). Berlin and New York, 1997–2006.
I.Miletupolis	E. Schwertheim, *Die Inschriften von Kyzikos und Umgebung, Teil II: Miletupolis, Inschriften und Denkmäler. IGSK* 26. Bonn, 1983.
I.Mylasa	W. Blümel, *Die Inschriften von Mylasa* (2 vols). *IGSK* 34–35. Bonn, 1987–1988.
I.Nordkarien	W. Blümel, *Inschriften aus Nordkarien. IGSK* 71. Bonn, 2018.

I.Oropos	B. Petrakos, *Οἱ Ἐπιγραφὲς τοῦ Ὠρωποῦ*. Athens, 1997.
I.Priene[2]	W. Blümel and R. Merkelbach, *Die Inschriften von Priene*. IGSK 69. Bonn, 2014.
I.Prusa ad Olympum	T. Corsten, *Die Inschriften von Prusa ad Olympum* (2 vols). IGSK 39–40. Bonn, 1991–1993.
I.Smyrna	G. Petzl, *Die Inschriften von Smyrna* (2 vols in 3). IGSK 23–24. Bonn, 1982–1990.
I.Stratonikeia	M. Ç. Şahin, *Die Inschriften von Stratonikeia* (2 vols in 3). IGSK 21–22. Bonn, 1981–1990.
I.Sultan Dağı	L. Jonnes, *The Inscriptions of the Sultan Dağı I*. IGSK 62. Bonn, 2002.
IvP	M. Fränkel, *Die Inschriften von Pergamon* (2 vols). Berlin, 1890–1895.
KILyk	G. Laminger-Pascher, *Die kaiserzeitlichen Inschriften Lykaoniens I*. Vienna, 1992.
LBW	P. Le Bas and W. H. Waddington, *Inscriptions grecques et latines recueillies en Asie Mineure* (2 vols). Paris, 1870.
Leu	*Leu Numismatik* (auction catalogues)
LfgrE	*Lexikon des frühgriechischen Epos*
LGPN	*Lexicon of Greek Personal Names*
Lindos II	C. Blinkenberg, *Lindos. Fouilles et recherches, 1902–1914*. Vol. II, *Inscriptions* (2 vols). Copenhagen and Berlin, 1941.
LSCG	F. Sokolowski, *Lois sacrées des cités grecques*. Paris, 1969.
LSJ	H. G. Liddell and R. Scott, *A Greek-English Lexicon*, revised by H. Stuart Jones and R. McKenzie.
LSS	F. Sokolowski, *Lois sacrées des cités grecques, Supplément*. Paris, 1962.
MAMA	*Monumenta Asiae Minoris Antiqua*
Michel, *Recueil*	C. Michel, *Recueil d'inscriptions grecques*. Brussels, 1900.
Naumann	*Numismatik Naumann* (auction catalogues)
OGIS	W. Dittenberger, *Orientis Graeci inscriptiones selectae* (2 vols). Leipzig, 1903–1905.

Pfuhl and Möbius	E. Pfuhl and H. Möbius, H. *Die Ostgriechischen Grabreliefs* (2 vols in 4). Mainz am Rhein, 1977–1979.
PIR2	*Prosopographia Imperii Romani*, second edition.
P.Mich.	*Michigan Papyri*, 1931–.
Ramsay, *Phrygia*	W. M. Ramsay, *The Cities and Bishoprics of Phrygia. Vol. I. Part I: The Lycus Valley and South-Western Phrygia. Vol. I. Part II: West and West-Central Phrygia.* Oxford, 1895–1897.
RECAM II	S. Mitchell, *Regional Epigraphic Catalogues of Asia Minor 2: The Ankara District: The Inscriptions of North Galatia.* Oxford, 1982.
Robert, *Hellenica*	L. Robert, *Hellenica. Recueil d'épigraphie, de numismatique et d'antiquités grecques* (13 vols in 12). Paris, 1940–1965.
Robert, *OMS*	L. Robert, *Opera Minora Selecta. Épigraphie et antiquités grecques* (7 vols). Amsterdam, 1969–1990.
RPC	*Roman Provincial Coinage* (https://rpc.ashmus .ox.ac.uk)
Sammlung Tatış	E. Schwertheim and N. G. Schwertheim, *Epigraphica der Sammlung Yavuz Tatış: Lydien, Mysien, Türkei.* İzmir, 2018.
Sardis II	G. Petzl, *Sardis: Greek and Latin Inscriptions Part II: Finds from 1958 to 2017.* Cambridge, MA.
Sardis VII 1	W. H. Buckler and D. M. Robinson, *Sardis Vol. VII: Greek and Latin Inscriptions. Part 1.* Leiden, 1932.
SEG	*Supplementum Epigraphicum Graecum*
SGO	R. Merkelbach and F. Stauber, *Steinepigramme aus dem griechischen Osten* (5 vols). Munich and Leipzig, 1998–2004.
SNG Von Aulock	*Sylloge Nummorum Graecorum, Sammlung Hans Von Aulock* (4 vols). Berlin, 1957–1968.
TAM	*Tituli Asiae Minoris*
TL	E. Kalinka, *Tituli Asiae Minoris I: Tituli Lyciae lingua Lycia conscripti.* Vienna, 1901.
TLL	*Thesaurus Linguae Latinae*

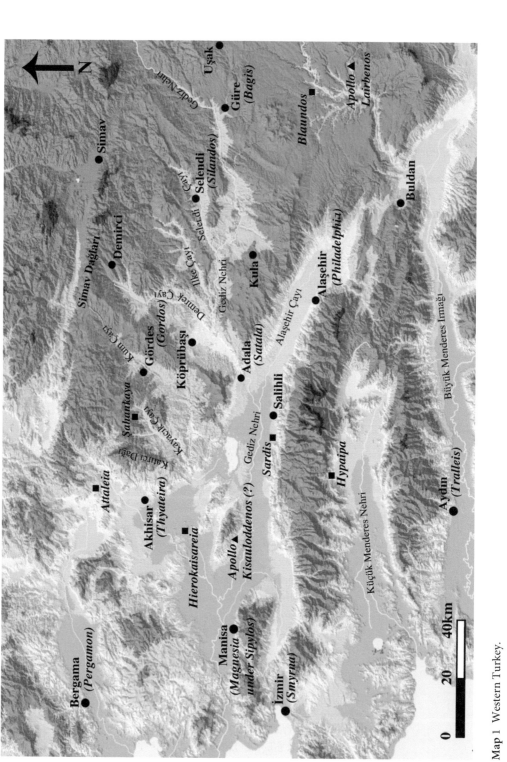

Map 1 Western Turkey.

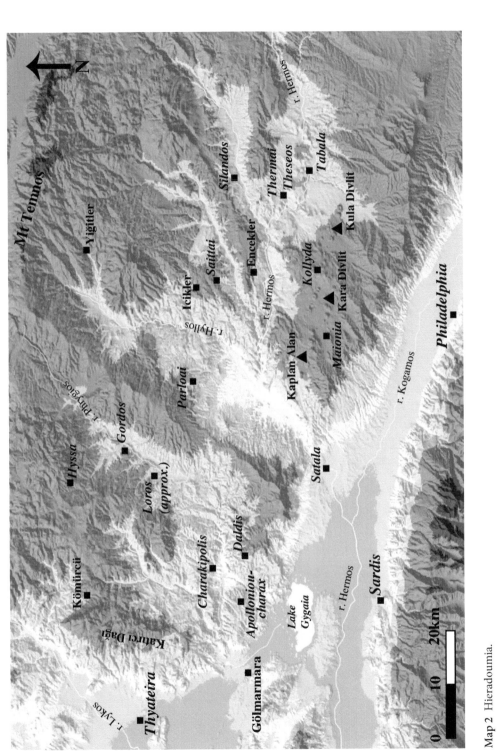

Map 2 Hieradoumia.

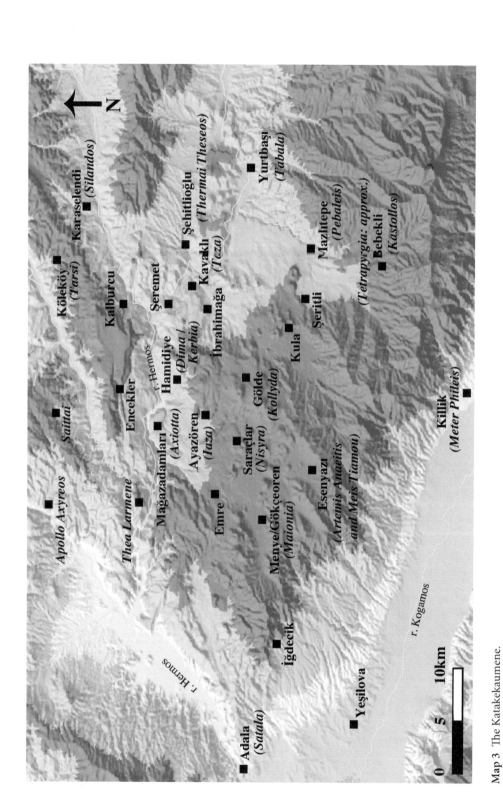

Map 3 The Katakekaumene.

1 | Hieradoumia

1.1 Hieradoumia: An Introduction

Hieradoumia (Maps 1 and 2) is an upland region in modern western Turkey, situated in the north-eastern part of Manisa province (*Manisa ili*), roughly corresponding to the modern districts (*ilçeler*) of Gördes, Köprübaşı, Demirci, Selendi, and Kula (*c.* 4,500 km²). Its modern-day population is around 145,000, just under half of which is concentrated in the five urban district capitals; Kula is today the largest town in the region, with a population of around 26,000. Most inhabited zones lie between 400 and 700 m above sea level, and the region has a temperate Mediterranean climate, with warm dry summers and mild wet winters. This book is about the culture and society of Hieradoumia in the Roman imperial period – that is to say, roughly the first three centuries AD, with fairly regular glances back into the first century BC, and occasionally earlier.

You could be forgiven for never having heard of Hieradoumia before. It is a made-up name – made up by me, for the purposes of this book. The use of an invented name is not frivolous.[1] It reflects the fact that in antiquity, this region was not a single political unit, was never (so far as we know) considered as a distinct cultural zone, and was not a primary focus of local identity. But the existence of a meaningful shared regional culture across time and space is not at all dependent on the conscious articulation of a shared identity on the part of that region's inhabitants, and so the fact that no one in antiquity ever had cause to assign this particular region its own special name is really neither here nor there.[2] Modern historians who have worked on this region have generally called it 'north-east Lydia'. This is not very satisfactory, since it implies that the region was culturally more closely linked to 'the rest of' Lydia to the west and south-west than it was to (say) Phrygia

---

[1] Compare the heuristic devices employed by Scott 2009, esp. 13–22 ('Zomia') and Purcell 2013 ('Tethys Corridor').

[2] Vlassopoulos 2007, 166–9; Roberts and Vander Linden 2011. The existence of non-random spatial and temporal association groups in the material record can be usefully separated from the second-order assumption that some of these association groups correspond to 'peoples' as self-conscious historical actors.

to the east or Mysia to the north, an implication that – as we will see – is problematic at best.[3] Others have preferred to refer to it as the 'middle Hermos', which is hydrologically correct (most of the region does indeed belong to the drainage basin of the middle Gediz Nehri, the ancient River Hermos) but gives an undue prominence to the Hermos river, which was not, so far as I can tell, particularly central to the human ecology of the region.[4] My choice of the name 'Hieradoumia' is almost arbitrary, but not quite.[5]

Why should you care about Roman Hieradoumia – assuming, that is, that you are not one of the dozen or so people with a professional interest in this obscure backwater of the ancient world? No important events ever occurred here. I cannot, with any conviction, praise the aesthetic quality of its art, the sophistication of its poetry, or the intellectual distinction of its inhabitants (though I do have a soft spot for the dream-interpreter Artemidorus of Daldis, half-Hieradoumian on his mother's side).[6] The case for Hieradoumian history rests on quite different grounds.

The people of the deep Mediterranean countryside appear very seldom in the historical record from antiquity, and almost never as historical actors. We can, of course, infer their existence from the vast incomes accumulated by large landowners (who in the Greco-Roman Mediterranean, as in all pre-modern societies, made up the overwhelming majority of the rich and very rich); we find them stereotyped, disparaged, and occasionally romanticized in the poetry and imaginative prose of the elite. But as agents they are desperately elusive, and we have, for the most part, literally no idea whether they shared the values of the elite. Inner Anatolia is the only part

---

[3] Debord 1985; Herrmann 1985, 249–50; Lochman 2003, 204–5; Wörrle 2009, 437, n. 116. It is true that Pausanias once refers to a town to the far east of this region as belonging to 'upper Lydia' (Temenouthyrai, modern Uşak: Paus. 1.35.7); modern scholars in fact prefer to assign Temenouthyrai to 'Phrygia' (Drew-Bear 1979), a nice illustration of the haziness of cultural boundaries in this region (Strabo 12.4.4, 12.8.2–3, 13.4.10–11). The excellent overview of 'Lydian geography' in Roosevelt 2009, 33–58 (including our region) is based on a putative 'Greater Lydia' of the seventh and sixth century BC.

[4] Unlike at least one other west-Anatolian river basin (or so I have argued); see Thonemann 2011a, 1–49.

[5] The term *doumos* is a Phrygian word denoting a 'kinship-group' or 'family' (Neumann 1999, 2002, with Chaniotis, *EBGR* 2004, 98 and *SEG* 53, 1505). In our region, we find numerous examples of small-scale cultic associations designated as 'sacred *doumoi*' (ἱεροὶ δοῦμοι), all of which are probably kin-based groups: *TAM* V 1, 179 (Saittai), 449 and 483a (Iaza), 536 (Maionia); *SEG* 57, 1174 (Petzl 2019, no. 140: Iaza); *SEG* 57, 1186 (Petzl 2019, no. 146: Kollyda); see Harland 2014, 199–203, with bibliography. Sacred *doumoi* are not quite unique to this region, but they do neatly encapsulate what I take to be one of the most distinctive features of Hieradoumian social organization, the institutionalization of extended kin groups as 'segments' of village society; see Chapter 10, Section 10.4.

[6] Thonemann 2020.

of the Roman Empire to provide us with a sufficient density of texts and monuments produced by peasants to give us something resembling an 'insider's view' of the culture of the non-urban 95 per cent.[7]

Within the vast and varied corpus of rural epigraphy from Roman Anatolia, the inscribed monuments of rural Hieradoumia stand out, for three reasons. First, their extreme homogeneity. As we will see in Chapter 2, the funerary and religious monuments of Roman Hieradoumia take a highly distinctive physical form, with common decorative elements and a stereotyped textual structure. Not only does this allow for a regional study that is closely bounded in both space and time, but it also enables rigorous quantitative analysis of a kind that is quite impossible anywhere else in rural Anatolia. Second, their volubility. In most parts of Anatolia, inscribed monuments set up by farmers and shepherds are short and – to be blunt – not vastly informative ('Aurelius Meiros set up this memorial for his own sons Attas and Manes'; 'Babeis, on behalf of her children, to Zeus Alsenos, in fulfilment of a vow'). In Roman Hieradoumia, things were different. The distinctive local habit of 'familial commemoration' means that epitaphs often list dozens of family members and associates of the deceased, providing us with a remarkably 'thick' picture of Hieradoumian rural households and extended kin groupings; likewise, the propitiatory inscriptions set up in Hieradoumian rural sanctuaries (Chapter 2, Sections 2.5–2.8) offer us extended narratives of crises and conflicts within families and village communities, of a length and detail quite unparalleled elsewhere in the Greco-Roman world. And third – it is only fair to add – the inscribed monuments of Hieradoumia have been exceptionally well published and studied by a series of outstanding historians, among whom particular honour is due to Karl Buresch, whose pioneering work in the early 1890s marks the beginning of serious research on Hieradoumia and its monumental culture[8]; to Josef Keil and Anton von Premerstein, who undertook three extensive epigraphic journeys in the region in the years before the First World War[9]; to Peter Herrmann, whose magisterial 1981

---

[7] Mitchell 1993, I 165–97 remains incomparably the best synthesis of the culture of rural Anatolia in the first three centuries AD; the most important body of new evidence to have appeared since then is the corpus of peasants' and shepherds' votives in Drew-Bear, Thomas, and Yıldızturan 1999. Some of Mitchell's premises have been challenged, but not overturned, by Schuler 2012.

[8] Buresch 1898, based on three extensive epigraphic journeys of 1891, 1894, and 1895, prepared for publication by Otto Ribbeck after Buresch's premature death at the age of thirty-three. Note in particular his outstanding discussion of the term *doumos* (58–72, on *TAM* V 1, 179).

[9] Keil and Premerstein 1907, 1911, 1914 (epigraphic journeys of 1906, 1908, 1911).

Figure 1.1 Peter Herrmann (r.) at Akhisar, 1986.

corpus of Hieradoumian inscriptions is a model of concision and good judgement (Figure 1.1)[10]; and more recently, to Georg Petzl, Hasan Malay (1948–2022), and Marijana Ricl, who continue to publish new material from Hieradoumia at a fearsome rate.

In this book, I hope to persuade you of the extraordinary interest and importance of rural Hieradoumia for the historian of the Greco-Roman world. With the exception of parts of Roman Egypt, no other rural society in any part of the ancient Mediterranean is known to us in anything like this level of detail. Only here is it possible to reconstruct typical household forms and networks of extended kin in a non-urban setting (Chapters 4–6). Only here can we map out with any precision the structural relations between different levels of social organization: the family, the village, cult associations and worshipping groups, trade guilds, and the *polis* (Chapters 7 and 10). Only here, thanks to the admirable Hieradoumian habit of recording date of death and age at death on their tombstones, are we able to sketch the outlines of a rural demographic regime over time (Chapter 3). Only here can we hear peasants speaking for themselves – in

---

[10] *Tituli Asiae Minoris* V 1, *Regio Septentrionalis ad Orientem Vergens* (1981), preceded (and followed) by a host of other superb studies on the epigraphy and topography of the region, a selection of which are reprinted in Herrmann 2016, chapters 1–20; see also Habicht 2003 and Petzl 2003.

the propitiatory inscriptions, almost literally 'speaking', in the first person –
on the matters that concerned them most: livestock, intra-familial relations,
vendettas between neighbours, theft, sickness (Chapters 8–9). Only here, in
short, are we able to describe an ancient rural *culture* on a level above the
superficial and anecdotal – its shared normative standards and values; its
structural tensions and contradictions; its distinctive gender relations and
class structure; its *Weltanschauung*.

Geographically, Hieradoumia falls into two unequal parts (Map 2), lying
to the north (*c.* 3,500 km²) and south (*c.* 1,000 km²) of the narrow valley
of the Gediz Nehri, the ancient river Hermos, which winds through the
region from the east to the south-west (Figure 1.2). On the right bank of
the Gediz Nehri, to the north, the land slopes gradually upwards towards
the formidable Simav Dağları mountain range (the ancient Mt Temnos),
which today serves as the boundary between the provinces of Manisa (to
the south) and Balıkesir and Kütahya (to the north); for the purposes of
this book, I treat the Simav Dağları as the northern limit of Hieradoumia.[11]
South of the Simav Dağları watershed, several small perennial rivers drain
southwards into the Gediz basin – from east to west, the Selendi Çayı, İlke
Çayı, Demrek (Demirci) Çayı, Kum Çayı, and Kayacık Çayı, all running
roughly parallel to one another from the north-east to the south-west
(Map 1). These five river valleys and the rolling hill country between them
supported a number of small urban centres in antiquity, some of which
enjoyed *polis*-status in the Roman imperial period: Silandos, on the lower
Selendi Çayı; Saittai, with an enormous dependent territory between the
İlke Çayı and Demrek Çayı; Gordos, on the upper Kum Çayı; Loros, south
of Gordos on the middle Kum Çayı; Daldis, between the lower Kum Çayı
and the Gediz Nehri.[12] Many of these towns – particularly Saittai – are

---

[11] The ancient Makestos valley, immediately north of the Simav Dağları, has produced virtually
no examples of the two characteristic epigraphic genres of Roman Hieradoumia, 'familial'
epitaphs and propitiatory inscriptions (Chapter 2); conversely, the funerary 'doorstones' characteristic of Phrygia and Galatia are absent from Hieradoumia, but frequently found in the
Makestos valley (Waelkens 1986, 35–7). However, the gabled funerary *stēlai* of the Makestos
valley do closely resemble those of Hieradoumia in their physical form, if not their epigraphic
content: Naour 1981, 15; *MAMA* X, xviii–xix, xxxi. For the cultural affiliations of Kadoi, east
of the Simav Dağları, see Nollé 2010, 72–90.
[12] For the vast territory of Saittai, see Robert, *OMS* I, 433–5; it is now known to have extended
to the south-west as far as Satala, on the edge of the plain of Sardis (*TAM* V 1, 604–17; Kolb
1990 [*SEG* 40, 1063]; Malay and Ricl 2019, 47 n. 6). For the location of Loros, see Ricl and
Malay 2012, 78–9; for the correct form of the name (Loros or Loron), see Petzl 2018. On the
character of these urban centres, see Chapter 10, Section 10.1.

Figure 1.2 The Hermos valley near Thermai Theseos.

known to have been significant ancient centres for the production of wool
and linen cloth, and fine textiles continued to be the chief export product
of the towns of post-antique Hieradoumia (Gördes, Kula, Demirci) down
to the later Ottoman period.[13] This northern segment of Hieradoumia is
naturally bounded to the west by the Katırcı Dağı mountain range, whose
western flanks drop down into the lowland valley of the Gördük Çayı, the
ancient river Lykos.

South of the Gediz Nehri rises the plateau known in antiquity as the 'burnt
country', the Katakekaumene (Map 3; Figures 1.3 and 1.4).[14] This region is
described in some detail by the Augustan geographer Strabo (13.4.11):

> After this [the Kogamos valley] comes the so-called Katakekaumene region,
> 500 stadia in length and 400 in breadth, which one may call either Mysia
> or Maionia, for both names are in use. The whole region is treeless, except
> for the vine which produces the wine called Katakekaumenite, inferior in

[13] Textile production at Saittai: Chapter 7, Section 7.2; for the late Ottoman rug industry in the
region, see Quataert 1993, esp. 134–60.
[14] See Robert 1962, 287–313, with numerous modern travellers' accounts, and a discussion of the
rich Greco-Roman mythology of the Kula volcanic field, especially the remarkable account in
Nonnus, *Dionysiaca* 13.471–97; see now also Rojas 2019, 82–8.

Figure 1.3 Lava field north-east of Kula; note the sharp edge between the β4 lava flow and the fields in the upper part of the image.

Figure 1.4 Cinder cones near Kula, looking north over the Hermos.

quality to none of the famous wines.[15] The plains have an ashy appearance, and the mountainous and rocky parts are black, as if they had been scorched. Some suppose that this phenomenon was the result of lightning bolts and breaths of flame, and they do not hesitate to situate here the myth of Typhon; Xanthos also speaks of a certain Arimous as king of this region.[16] But it is not plausible that so large a region could have been burned up all at once by such events; rather, it must have been caused by some fires under the earth, whose springs are now exhausted. Also pointed out in this region are three craters, which they call 'bellows', around 40 stadia distant from each other. Above them lie rocky hills, which were probably heaped up out of the blazing matter blasted out of the earth. That soil of this kind is good for vines can also be inferred from the soil of Katana, which was formed from heaped-up ash and now produces a great deal of excellent wine.

There can be little doubt that Strabo had seen the Kula volcanic field for himself. He provides a vivid and accurate description of the most distinctive landmarks of the plateau south of the Gediz Nehri, the three sombre cinder cones (Kula Divlit, Kara Divlit, and Kaplan Alan; see Map 2) that dominate the region. The Kula volcanic field, extending from Adala (ancient Satala) in the west to Kula in the east, is the youngest volcanic field in western Turkey, and the most recent basalt lava flows may date to historic times (eruption phase β4, ending perhaps as late as *c.* 600–400 BC).[17] The basalt boulders left by these youngest β4 flows are still today largely bare of vegetation, aside from the toughest maquis (Figure 1.3), and no vines could conceivably have been grown on them in antiquity; Strabo's vineyards must have been located on the ashy soils left behind by the much earlier eruption phase β3, which probably ended around 9,000 BC (Figure 1.5).[18] In antiquity, the Katakekaumene seems to have been much

---

[15] For viticulture in the region, see also e.g. Strabo 14.1.15; *SEG* 34, 1207 (Hamidiye); *SEG* 34, 1212–13 (Pereudos, near Saittai: Petzl 1994, nos. 17–18); *TAM* V 1, 318 (near Kula: Petzl 1994, no. 69); *SEG* 35, 1164 (near Kula: Petzl 1994, no. 71); *TAM* V 3, 1556 (Hayallı); Malay and Petzl 2017, no. 199 (vineyards near Kula). In funerary reliefs, the deceased and their commemorators are often depicted with bunches of grapes and vine-pruning knives: see e.g. *TAM* V 1, 36, 131, 207, 385 (here, Chapter 5, Figure 5.1), 477 (illustrated *I.Manisa*, Figure 124); *SEG* 39, 1294 (Uşak); *I.Manisa* 181.

[16] Xanthos of Lydia, *BNJ* 765 F13b, with A. Paradiso's commentary; Strabo alludes to the same passage of Xanthos in 12.8.19 (*BNJ* 765 F13a). On this interpretation, the Katakekaumene was the site of the battle between Zeus ('lightning bolts') and the fire-breathing giant Typhon ('breaths of flame'). Homer claimed that the 'couch of Typhon' was located in the land of the Arimoi (*Il.* 2.783), a tradition that underlies Xanthos' reference to an alleged Lydian king 'Arimous'.

[17] Heineke, Niedermann, Hetzel, and Akal 2016.

[18] Not coincidentally, the largest β3 lava flow extends over a broad stretch of land between the modern villages of Menye, Sandal, and Gölde in the south and the Gediz Nehri in the north, a region which we know to have been particularly densely settled in the Roman imperial period.

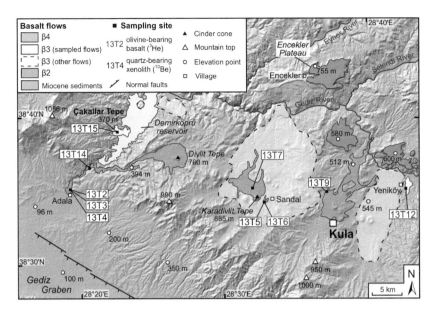

Figure 1.5 The Kula volcanic field.

more densely settled than the zone to the north of the Hermos river; although only two settlements south of the Hermos possessed *polis*-status in the Roman imperial period (Maionia and Kollyda), we know of numerous small villages and rural sanctuaries in this region, several of which have left remarkably rich epigraphic records (Nisyra, Iaza, Axiotta, and Taza, among many others).[19] The Katakekaumene region is bounded to the south by the rim of hills overlooking the lowland valley of the Alaşehir Çayı, the ancient river Kogamos.

1.2 Hieradoumia before Rome

No large-scale excavations or surveys have yet been conducted in Hieradoumia, and the history of human settlement in the region in the earlier first millennium BC is very poorly known. The great rock of Şahankaya, west of Gordos, seems to have served as a fortress and cult centre in the Achaemenid period.[20] A handful of inscriptions in Lydian and Aramaic

---

[19] Nisyra: *TAM* V 1, 425–38. Iaza: *TAM* V 1, 446–86; Thonemann 2019, nos. 3–7. Axiotta (Mağazadamları): Malay and Petzl 2017, 135–54. Meter Tazene and Meis Petraeites at Taza (Kavaklı): Malay and Petzl 2017, 175–87.

[20] Foss 1987, 81–91; Roosevelt 2009, 118–21.

are known from the vicinity of Maionia and Saittai, and there are several *tumulus* burials dating between the sixth and fourth centuries BC scattered throughout the region.[21] A major Persian royal road followed the course of the Hermos river eastwards, on its way from Sardis towards the Anatolian plateau, close to the route of the modern İzmir–Ankara highway; a spectacular group of Lydian chamber tombs (*c.* 500 BC), with artefacts of a strongly Persianizing character, were situated close to this road, near modern Güre (ancient Bagis) in the far east of Hieradoumia.[22]

For us, the human geography of Hieradoumia only really comes into focus in the second century BC, when the Attalid kings of Pergamon promoted the large-scale settlement of both Mysian and Greco-Macedonian soldiers throughout the region (Figure 1.6).[23] These colonists seem typically to have been settled at or near existing Lydian villages, no doubt on royal land.[24] In late Hellenistic documents, they are generally described as 'the settlers (*katoikoi*) at *x*', where *x* is typically an indigenous Anatolian toponym (Lyendos, Tamasis, Atetta, Morei, Adrouta, Kapolmeia).[25] By the end of the Hellenistic period, the population of Hieradoumia must have been a mixture of long-established Lydian and Phrygian population groups, immigrant soldiers and their families from Mysia (the wooded highlands north and west of the Makestos River), and Greek and Macedonian settlers from lands far off to the north and west (for more on this, see Section 1.3).[26]

---

[21] Roosevelt 2009, 240–9 (catalogue); 2019, 145–50. For a Lydian-period settlement at Daldis, see Meriç 2018 (*non vidi*).

[22] Özgen and Öztürk 1996. The relative absence of evidence for Iranian settlement in Hieradoumia contrasts strongly with the abundant testimonia for an Iranian diaspora in the lower Hermos, north and west of Sardis: Sekunda 1985; Robert 1987, 329–35; Klingenberg 2014.

[23] Evidence for Seleukid interest in Hieradoumia is very scanty: there seems to have been a Seleukid military settlement at Gordos already under Antiochos III (*TAM* V 1, 689), and the cult of Zeus Seleukeios at Nisyra (*TAM* V 1, 426; cf. *TAM* V 2, 1306) may have been of Seleukid origin (Robert, *Hellenica* VI, 24–6; de Hoz 1999, 63–4). For 'Macedonian' settlers in Hieradoumia, e.g. *TAM* V 1, 221 (*TAM* V 3, 1423: Kobedyle, under Eumenes II); *TAM* V 3, 1669 (Adrouta); Robert, *Hellenica* VI, 22–4; Mitchell 1993, I 180 n. 142; de Hoz 1999, 5; Mitchell 2018.

[24] For royal land in Hieradoumia, note the 'royal folds' (βασιλικαὶ μάνδραι) near Kula in Malay and Petzl 2017, no. 199 (first century BC?) and a 'village of the kings' near Satala (*TAM* V 1, 609).

[25] Lyendos: *TAM* V 1, 1 (second century BC); Tamasis: *TAM* V 1, 156 (65/4 BC; cf. *SEG* 40, 1063, 1104); Atetta: *TAM* V 1, 543 (157/6 or 136/5 BC); Morei: *SEG* 57, 1219 (45/44 BC); Adrouta: *TAM* V 3, 1429 (25/4 BC); Kapolmeia: *TAM* V 3, 1432 (2/1 BC) and 1435 (AD 42/3). Terminology: Schuler 1998, 33–41.

[26] de Hoz 1999, 8–9, assumes that the population of Roman Hieradoumia remained 'almost entirely' indigenous.

Figure 1.6 Epitaph of a cavalryman, from Yiğitler (late second century BC).
The deceased is honoured by four *dēmoi*, Lakemas, Ankyra Sidera, Odos, Mokada.
SEG 33, 1004 (Manisa Museum).

There is no sign that any settlements in Hieradoumia had *polis* status
during the second or first century BC. None of the later *poleis* of the middle
and upper Hermos valley (Gordos, Maionia, Daldis, Saittai, Silandos, Kadoi,
etc.) struck coins or passed civic decrees in the pre-imperial period, and it
is a striking fact that no settlements in the region took their names from

Seleukid or Attalid kings or queens. In this respect, Hieradoumia forms a stark contrast with both lowland Lydia to the west and highland Phrygia to the east, where new *polis* foundations by the Seleukid and Attalid kings are widespread.[27] For reasons that escape us, the Hellenistic kings decided not to re-organize this upland region on a *polis*-based model. As we will see in later chapters, this decision would go on to have very dramatic consequences for the social organization of Hieradoumia deep into the Roman imperial period.

Instead, the Attalid kings seem to have chosen to organize the human population of Hieradoumia into two large and sprawling regional polities corresponding to the regions south and north of the Hermos river: the '*koinon* of the Maionians in the Katakekaumene' to the south and the '*dēmos* of the Mysoi Abbaitai' to the north. Neither of these polities was centred on a single urban settlement, and both seem to have been loose federal associations of dispersed military *katoikiai*, possessing common laws and administrative institutions.[28] Whether indigenous village communities were included within these polities is unknown.

The earliest evidence for this 'decentralized' form of political organization in Attalid Hieradoumia derives from an inscription from İğdecik in the Katakekaumene, not far from the later *polis* settlement of Maionia. This inscription, dated to regnal Year 7 of Attalos II of Pergamon (153/2 or 152/1 BC), is an honorific decree for an Attalid royal appointee (his precise function unknown), 'resolved by the *koinon* ("commonality") of the Maionians in the Katakekaumene, whose [*katoikiai* (?)] are the ones written below'.[29] The force of the term 'Maionians' here is uncertain: it may signify 'ethnic Lydians' or simply 'persons resident in the region known as Maionia'. This Attalid-period *koinon* clearly encompassed several different settlements (*katoikiai*) in the Katakekaumene; its chief officials seem to have been a college of four *stratēgoi* ('generals'), attested on a boundary stone from İğdecik of the second or first century BC.[30] Apparently the individual

---

[27] Phrygia: Thonemann 2011a, 170–7; Thonemann 2013b, 17; Mitchell 2018. Lydia: Cohen 1995, 195–242 (Philadelphia, Apollonis, Thyateira, Attaleia, Stratonikeia on the Kaikos); Thonemann 2013a, 27–30; Roosevelt 2019, 155–61. The contrast is rightly highlighted by Ma 2013b, 71 ('saturation of the connective landscape with military settlements, rather than foundation of large fortified cities').

[28] In the late Republican Roman province of Asia, these associations were probably formally classed as *ethnē* (Latin *gentes*): Drew-Bear 1972a, 448–9; Mitchell 1999, 31.

[29] Malay and Ricl 2019, 45–53, no. 1, lines 2–4: [ἔ]δοξεν τῶι κοινῶι τῶν κατὰ τὴν Κατακεκαυ[μένη]ν Μαιόνων ὧν εἰσὶν αἱ ὑποτεταγμέναι [κατοικίαι]. The list of settlements is missing.

[30] Malay and Petzl 2017, no. 21 (*Sardis* II 432): a boundary stone of a sanctuary of Artemis erected by a college of four *stratēgoi*. Two of the four *stratēgoi* bear the personal name *Ilos*, which may be of Lydian origin (*SEG* 36, 1011, line 23 [Sardis, IV BC]; *Sardis* VII 1, 1, lines I.4 and I.10 [Lydian toponyms]); the name is cautiously taken as Greek by Masson 1987, 234.

stratēgoi had responsibility for particular clusters of military settlements in the Katakekaumene; this is suggested by a votive inscription from Maionia dating to the final stages of the war against Aristonikos (129 BC), which shows the mobilization of a group of three *katoikiai* that are described as having been 'formerly under Diokles the *stratēgos*'.[31] A lavish tombstone from the ancient village of Iaza, not far from Maionia, commemorates a *stratēgos* by the name of Mogetes, who may well have died in the course of the same war; no doubt Mogetes was the *stratēgos* of a cluster of military *katoikiai* around Iaza, which must certainly have belonged to the *koinon* of the Maionians in the Katakekaumene.[32] It may well have been this *koinon* that was responsible, in 61/0 BC, for passing a decree in honour of a 'citizen' (τῶν πολειτῶν) by the name of Ploutarchos; this decree was found at Menye, the site of the later *polis* of Maionia, but Maionia seems not to have possessed *polis* status until the Augustan period.[33]

The more northerly of the two Attalid regional polities, the *dēmos* ('people') of the Mysoi Abbaitai, sprawled over a large zone extending from the right bank of the river Hermos northwards to the river Makestos (Simav Çayı).[34] The precise geographic extent of this northern network of Attalid *katoikiai* is unknown, but it certainly included the later *poleis* of Kadoi, modern Gediz, near the headwaters of the Hermos river[35]; Silandos, modern Karaselendi, on the north bank of the Selendi Çayı[36]; and Gordos, modern Gördes, in the upper Kum Çayı valley.[37] Further groups of 'Mysian' settlers are found throughout the region north of the Hermos in the second century BC, and it is likely enough that most or all belonged to the larger *dēmos* of the Mysoi Abbaitai.[38] It is usually assumed, surely correctly, that the 'Mysians' of Hieradoumia were installed in this region as

---

[31] *TAM* V 1, 528, with Herrmann 1962, 5–7: dedication by the *hēgemōn* and *stratiōtai* of the
   [- -]ηνῶν καὶ Χοιρομε[- -]των καὶ Ταρσιανῶν τῶν πρότε[ρ]ον ὑπὸ Διοκλῆν στρατηγόν.
   I assume that Diokles was the Attalid-period *stratēgos* of this particular group of villages,
   whose post may have been vacant at the time of this dedication.

[32] *TAM* V 1, 468b (*SGO* I 04/19/01, Ayazören), with the discussion of Petzl 1978b, 269–73.
   For the name Mogetes, see further below.

[33] *TAM* V 1, 514: ἔδοξεν τῶι δήμ[ω]ι· ἐ[πεὶ] Πλούταρχος Ἑρμογένου τοῦ Πλουτάρχου τῶν
   πολιτῶν, κτλ. Thus already P. Herrmann, *TAM* V 1, p. 165 (Maionia not yet a *polis*).

[34] Debord 1985, 348–50; Nollé 2010; Thonemann 2013a, 27–30; Ma 2013b, 65–73.

[35] *OGIS* 446: dedication of a statue of Chromios by the *dēmos* of the Μυσῶν Ἀββαειτῶν
   (Nollé 2010).

[36] *SEG* 53, 1357: decree of the *boulē* and *dēmos* of the Μυσῶν Ἀβαΐτῶν.

[37] *SEG* 34, 1198: decree of [τοῖς ἐν] Γόρδῳ Μυσοῖς Ἀββαειταῖς in honour of a *stratēgos* of the
   σύμπας δῆμος of the Mysoi Abbaitai (Boulay 2014, 211–12); note also *TAM* V 1, 690
   (183–159 BC): a ἡγεμὼν Μυ[σῶν] at Gordos.

[38] E.g. *SEG* 57, 1150, with Thonemann 2011b (*SEG* 61, 982: Apollonioucharax, *c.* 165/4 BC:
   'Mysian' settlers at Kadoi and Kornoubeudos); *SEG* 40, 1062 ('Mysians' at Emoddi, near

military settlers by deliberate policy of the Attalid kings, rather than having arrived as part of a spontaneous Mysian 'Völkerwanderung' southwards over the Simav Dağları towards the Hermos.[39] In a letter of the mid-160s BC to a community of military settlers at Apollonioucharax (near Daldis), Eumenes II refers to his intention 'to move the Mysians living in this place to Kastollos, since fresh land certainly exists there in an uncultivated condition'; Kastollos is firmly located at the modern village of Bebekli, in the Katakekaumene south-east of Kula.[40] 'Mysian' settlement in Hieradoumia was an essentially state-driven and state-directed project.

However, as with the 'Maionians' of the Katakekaumene, there is no way of judging what proportion of the 'Mysians' of Hieradoumia were in fact ethnically or culturally Mysian.[41] At Kadoi, sometime in the second or first century BC, the *dēmos* of the Mysoi Abbaitai dedicated a statue of the Homeric Mysian hero Chromios as their 'forefather' (*propatōr*), and the inhabitants of Kadoi later placed images of the Mysian heroes Chromios and Ennomos on their coins.[42] Numerous individuals with good Greek or Macedonian names are described as 'Mysians' in Greek inscriptions from Hieradoumia and elsewhere; however, we know so little about Mysian indigenous onomastics (which may well have been entirely Hellenized by the later Hellenistic period) that we cannot say with confidence that these men were definitely *not* of ethnically or culturally Mysian origin.[43]

Two extant inscribed decrees are explicitly attributed to the *dēmos* of the Mysoi Abbaitai, one from Gordos (dating shortly after the conclusion of the war with Aristonikos, *c.* 130 BC) and the other from Silandos (probably

---

Saittai, 162/1 BC). The four *dēmoi* of SEG 33, 1004 (Yiğitler: Lakemas, Ankyra Sidera, Odos, Mokada; here, Figure 1.6) surely belonged to the Mysoi Abbaitai (Debord 1985, 349; *contra*, J. and L. Robert, *BE* 1984, 385), since Strabo describes Ankyra Sidera as Ἀγκύρας τῆς Ἀβαειτίδος (12.8.11). For the toponym 'Mysia Abbaitis', cf. SEG 44, 867 (Bargylia, late second century BC), Μυσίας τῆς καλουμένης Ἀββαϊτίδος.

[39] Ma 2013b, 65–73.

[40] SEG 57, 1150, with the corrections of Thonemann 2011b (SEG 61, 982), lines A2–5: τοὺς δ' ἐν τούτωι τῶι τόπωι κατοικοῦντας Μυσοὺς [ἐπενόου]ν εἰς Καστωλλὸμ μετάγειν, ἐπεὶ καὶ[νὴ γῆ (?) παν]τελῶς [ὑ]πάρχει ἐκεῖ περισσή. For Mysians at Kastollos, see IG II² 9977 (Athens), Ἀπολλώνιος Ἀσκληπιάδου Μυσὸς ἀπὸ Καστωλοῦ. For the location of Kastollos, TAM V 3, 1415, with Petzl's commentary.

[41] The Epiktēteis, the inhabitants of Phrygia Epiktetos in north-west Phrygia (apparently also a regional polity of Attalid origin), seem to have been Greco-Roman military settlers, rather than Phrygians, but the evidence is exiguous: Thonemann 2013b, 25; Michels 2019, 34.

[42] OGIS 446, with Robert, OMS VII, 419–20, and above all Nollé 2010, 103–9.

[43] Masson 1993; Catling 2004–2009, 399. 'Mysians' with Greek names in Hieradoumia: e.g. TAM V 1, 444 (Karaoba), Μενεκράτης Τιμάρχου Μυσός; SEG 41, 1037 (SGO I 04/13/01: Yiğitler, late second century BC), Ἀσκληπιάδης Γλαύκου Μυσός; SEG 49, 1722 (unknown provenance), Μῆνις Δημητρίου υἱοὶ Διογένης καὶ Ἀπολλώνιος Μυσοί; IG II² 9977 (Athens, quoted above, n. 40).

late second or early first century BC).[44] These two decrees show that the *dēmos* of the Mysoi Abbaitai was organized in a *polis*-like structure, with a federal *boulē* and *dēmos*, a federal *stratēgos*, their own constitution (*politeia*), laws (*nomoi*), magistrates (*archai*), and contests (*agōnothesiai*); individual members were known as 'citizens' (*politai*), and the federal state was considered as their 'homeland' (*patris*).[45] Just as with the *koinon* of the Maionians in the Katakekaumene, the Mysoi Abbaeitai may have had a 'college' of *stratēgoi*, each responsible for a group of military settlements in the wider *koinon*; this is the natural implication of a late Hellenistic honorific inscription from the Demrek Çayı valley, north of the Hermos, erected by the *katoikoi* at Odos and Parloai in honour of 'their *stratēgos*'.[46] The Mysoi Abbaitai also minted their own bronze coins, which unfortunately cannot be dated with any precision; these too may well postdate the establishment of the Roman province of Asia.[47]

We do not know at what point these two regional polities, the *dēmos* of the Mysoi Abbaitai and the *koinon* of the Maionians in the Katakekaumene, ceased to function, or indeed whether their 'break-up' into their constituent smaller communities occurred at a single moment or gradually over a longer period of time. Certainly the *dēmos* of the Mysoi Abbaitai was still in existence in the mid-70s BC, when the Mysoi Abbaitai and the Epiktēteis (a rather similar regional organization in northern Phrygia) voted honours for a Roman legate, C. Salluvius Naso, who had protected them during the war with Mithradates.[48] One or other of the two Hieradoumian regional polities was still in existence in 64/3 BC, to judge from a decree found at the site of the later *polis* of Tabala, in the Hermos valley east of

---

[44] Gordos: *SEG* 34, 1198 ([ἔδοξε τοῖς ἐν] Γόρδῳ Μυσοῖς Ἀββαείταις – that is to say, a local sub-unit of the wider *dēmos*); Silandos: *SEG* 53, 1357 (ἔδοξεν Μυσῶν Ἀβαίτων τῇ βουλῇ καὶ τῷ δήμωι). Other documents explicitly mentioning the Mysoi Abbaitai as a political collective: *OGIS* 446 (Kadoi: ὁ δῆμος ὁ Μυσῶν Ἀββαειτῶν); *OGIS* 445 (Nemi, shortly after 74/3 BC: Μυσοὶ Ἀββαειῖται).

[45] *Boulē* and *dēmos*: *SEG* 53, 1357, lines 1–2; federal *stratēgos*: *SEG* 34, 1198, lines 16–17 (στρα[τηγὸς] ... τοῦ σύνπαντος δήμο[υ]); *politeia, nomoi, archai, agōnothesiai*: *SEG* 34, 1198, lines 24–25 and 14; *politai* and *patris*, *SEG* 53, 1357, lines 3 and 10 (also *SEG* 34, 1198, lines 23–24). The term *politēs* need not imply the existence of a *polis*: cf. *TAM* V 3, 1423.

[46] *TAM* V 1, 184, with the corrections of Malay and Tanrıver 2016, 172–3. The three 'joint' decrees passed by the *dēmoi* of Gordos and Loros in the early Julio-Claudian period (*TAM* V 1, 702–3; *SEG* 62, 917) may perhaps reflect an administrative 'grouping' of the two communities in the earlier *koinon* of the Mysoi Abbaitai.

[47] Coins: *BMC Phrygia* xx–xxi, 1–2 nos. 1–10 (three bronze denominations, probably of the late second or first century BC, legend Μυσῶν Ἀβαίτων); cf. *BE* 1984, 384 pp. 486–7.

[48] *OGIS* 445 (Nemi, shortly after 74/3 BC: voted by the Μυσοὶ Ἀββαειῖται καὶ Ἐπικτητεῖς); see Wörrle 2009, 436–7.

Figure 1.7 The site of Tabala, modern Yurtbaşı, with the Hermos river in the foreground.

Kula (Figure 1.7). This decree, for a 'citizen' (τῶν πολ[ιτῶν]) whose name is lost, is clearly the product of a *polis* or quasi-*polis* community: 'Resolved by the *boulē* and the *dēmos*, on the motion of the *stratēgoi* and the *grammateus* of the *dēmos*'.⁴⁹ But it is quite impossible to believe that an independent *polis* of Tabala was already in existence in 64/3 BC. Tabala is first attested as a self-governing community (not necessarily yet a *polis*) in the Flavian *conventus* list from Ephesos, did not mint coins until the reign of Antoninus Pius, and produced nothing else resembling a civic decree until AD 140/1.⁵⁰ It is certainly preferable to attribute the Tabala decree to either the *dēmos* of the Mysoi Abbaitai or the *koinon* of the Maionians in the Katakekaumene (geographically both are equally possible).⁵¹

⁴⁹ *SEG* 49, 1694 (improved text, *SEG* 53, 1360), dated [ἔτο]υς κβ′ = 64/3 BC (*sic*; 63/2 BC *SEG*).
⁵⁰ Flavian *conventus* list: *I.Ephesos* 13, I 23 (not necessarily a *polis*: Habicht 1975, 67; Mitchell 1999, 31). Coins: *RPC* IV.2, 2859 and 11013 (temp.). Civic institutions: *TAM* V 1, 194 (AD 140/1: ἡ Ταβαλέων γερουσία). The fragmentary late Hellenistic decree *I.Manisa* 517, from the vicinity of Tabala, may well also have been passed by one of the two Hieradoumian regional polities.
⁵¹ The phraseology of the Tabala decree is similar both to the undated decree of the *boulē* and *dēmos* of the Mysoi Abbaitai from nearby Silandos and to the decree of (I presume) the Maionians in the Katakekaumene of 61/0 BC: *SEG* 53, 1360 (Tabala), lines 3–6: ἐπ[εὶ - -]νίου τῶν πολ[ιτῶν ἀνὴρ καλὸς καὶ ἀγ]αθὸς καὶ γένο[υς ἀεὶ τὰ συμφέροντ]α τῷ δήμῳ πεπο[ιηκότος];

The earliest unambiguous evidence for the emergence of *poleis* on the former territories of the *dēmos* of the Mysoi Abbaitai and the *koinon* of the Maionians in the Katakekaumene dates to the Augustan period.[52] The clearest case is the *polis* of Maionia, south of the Hermos at modern Menye. Maionia certainly possessed *polis* status by the early Augustan period, as we learn from a long honorific decree for a certain Kleandros son of Mogetes dating to summer 16 BC (Figure 1.8).[53] This decree begins with an elaborate dating formula, referring both to the provincial high priest of the imperial cult and to two eponymous civic priests, one described as 'stephanēphoros and priest of Roma' and the other as '(priest of) Zeus Olympios'. The decision formula is identical to that of the decree of 64/3 BC from Tabala ('Resolved by the *boulē* and the *dēmos*, on the motion of the *stratēgoi* and the *grammateus* of the *dēmos*'), suggesting that the civic institutions of the new *polis* of Maionia may have been closely modelled on those of the old *koinon* of the Maionians in the Katakekaumene. The grant of *polis* status to Maionia probably occurred not long before the decree for Kleandros; an honorific inscription for a certain C. Iulius [Quadratus] Machairion, 'high priest and *stephanēphoros*', was set up around the turn of the era by 'those inhabiting the *polis* of Maionia' – a very unusual turn of phrase, surely indicating that the grant of civic status was relatively recent.[54]

A similar pattern can be seen at Gordos, which had received *polis* status by the reign of Tiberius at the latest, to judge from her use of the dynastic name 'Iulia Gordos' (first attested in spring AD 37).[55] Civic decrees of Gordos of the first century AD were invariably introduced by a college of three *stratēgoi* and the *grammateus* of the *dēmos*, again perhaps modelled

SEG 53, 1357 (Silandos), lines 2–4: ἐπεὶ Φιλόμηλος Ὀφ[έ]λα τῶν πολειτῶν ἀνὴρ καλὸς καὶ ἀγαθὸς καὶ γένους πρώτου; *TAM* V 1, 514 (Maionia), lines 1–4: ἐ[πεὶ] Πλούταρχος … τῶν πολιτῶν, ἀνδρὸς καλοῦ καὶ ἀγαθοῦ καὶ γένους πρώτου κτλ.

[52] Debord 1985, 352–3. There is no way of telling when the final bronze coin issues of the Mysoi Abbaitai were struck: some could, in principle, have been produced as late as the reign of Augustus (cf. the chronology of the late Hellenistic bronze coinage of Akmoneia: Thonemann 2010, 168 and 173 n. 34).

[53] SEG 57, 1198. A few years later, in 9 BC, a copy of the edict of Paulus Fabius Maximus on the calendar of the Roman province of Asia was inscribed on stone at Maionia: *TAM* V 1, 516 (on this edict, see now Thonemann 2015). Pliny describes Maionia as an independent *polis* (HN 5.111).

[54] *TAM* V 1, 544, with *BE* 1970, 520: [οἱ ἐν Μαι]ονίᾳ τῇ πό[λει κατοικ]οῦντες. Other C. Iulii in Hieradoumia at this period: C. Iulius C.f. Rufus (SEG 49, 1597, summer 36 BC [?]: honorific inscription set up by ὁ δῆμος ὁ ἐγ Ζευγωνος, near Maionia); C. Iulius C.f. Theodotos (*TAM* V 1, 688: *grammateus* of the *dēmos* at Gordos, AD c. 25–50). For the full restoration of Machairion's name, see further Chapter 10, n. 72.

[55] *TAM* V 1, 702 (Xandikos, AD 37); cf. also Ricl and Malay 2012, no. 1 (SEG 62, 917) and *TAM* V 1, 688, both probably dating to the first or second quarter of the first century AD.

Figure 1.8 Decree for Kleandros, from Maionia. *SEG* 57, 1198 (Manisa Museum).

on the internal organization of the old *dēmos* of the Mysoi Abbaitai.[56] Kadoi also seems to have been granted *polis* status around the turn of the era.[57] For many other towns of the region, our earliest evidence for

---

[56] *TAM* V 1, 687 (AD 75/6) and 688; *SEG* 62, 917 and 918 (AD 69/70). A college of Roman businessmen (οἱ παρ' ἡμῖν πραγματευόμενοι Ῥωμαῖοι) appears in the decrees of AD 69/70 and 75/6; they are absent from documents of the earlier Julio-Claudian period.

[57] Strabo 12.8.12.

the grant of *polis* status comes from civic bronze coinage: Kadoi started striking civic bronzes under Claudius, Ankyra and Maionia under Nero, Daldis (renamed Flavia Caesarea Daldis) under Vespasian, Gordos, Silandos, and Bagis under Domitian, and Saittai under Hadrian.[58]

By the turn of the first–second centuries AD, it seems likely that the majority of the smaller villages and rural sanctuaries of the region were formally subordinated to one or other of these new *poleis* for administrative purposes; a few large villages maintained an intermediate status as autonomous *dēmoi*, not subject to the authority of any other political community but lacking the developed institutions and offices of the new *poleis* of the region.[59] It is extremely hard to say how much difference this new and largely artificial administrative geography made to the settlement patterns and day-to-day life of the inhabitants of Hieradoumia (see Chapter 10). None of the urban centres of the region have been excavated, though some at least had a modest monumental infrastructure (notably Saittai).[60] The extent of the various *polis* territories is largely a matter of conjecture, particularly on the Katakekaumene plateau south of the Hermos, where several large villages cannot be attributed to a particular *polis* territory with any confidence.[61]

There is little sign of any emergent demographic or social divide between cities and villages in Hieradoumia during the Roman imperial period. As we will see in Chapter 10, the institutions of civic life do not seem to have been especially developed: public epigraphy is rare throughout the region, and at Saittai, virtually all of the inscriptions not erected by individuals and families were set up by a range of private associations (friendly societies, trade guilds, cultic associations, neighbourhood clubs).[62] Just as in the uplands of Phrygia to the east, patterns of settlement and social organization in Hieradoumia

---

[58] Kadoi: *RPC* I 3062–3065. Ankyra: *RPC* I 3108–3115. Maionia: *RPC* I 3011–3015. Daldis: *RPC* II 1324–1326. Gordos: *RPC* II 1384–1385. Silandos: *RPC* II 1350–1355. Bagis: *RPC* II 1356–1358. Saittai: *RPC* III 2543–2544, with the additional Hadrianic issues in *RPC* online (2543A–B, 2544A–D: Thonemann 2017b, 190). See Chapter 10, Section 10.1.

[59] Autonomous *dēmoi* in Roman Hieradoumia: Habicht 1975, 67, 71–7; Schüler 1998, 41–5. The best attested case is the *dēmos* of Loros, discussed further in Chapters 7 and 10.

[60] Saittai: Hamilton 1842, II 143–4 (discovery of the site, June 1837); Robert, *OMS* I, 424–5; Herrmann 1962, 12–14; Umar 2001, 291–9, with photographs. A large stadium is partially preserved, with reserved seating for the city's various tribes (Kolb 1990), where gladiatorial combats took place (*TAM* V 1, 138–40).

[61] The superb map produced by Peter Herrmann for *TAM* V 1 has been superseded only in minor details; further discussions of the *polis* territories of the region in Naour 1981, 1983, 1985; Malay and Tanrıver 2016; Malay and Petzl 2017.

[62] Discussed further in Chapter 7, Section 7.2.

were scarcely affected by the administrative reorganization of the region in the early imperial period. Hieradoumia remained – as it had no doubt been in the Attalid and pre-Attalid periods – a homogeneous, face-to-face rural society, decentralized and autarkic, structured around the family, neighbourhood, and village rather than around the city, tribe, or social class.[63]

1.3 Lydians, Mysians, Greeks

'As it had no doubt been in the pre-Attalid period' – well, or maybe not.

The cultural history of the Anatolian peninsula in the first millennium AD is beset by the problem of 'fossilized taxonomies' – names for peoples and places created at a time when there really were meaningful differences between neighbouring culture zones, but which then persisted *as names* into periods when those cultural differences had been largely erased by migration, acculturation, or both. In the late Iron Age, Asia Minor was home to several culturally and linguistically distinct population groups: Phrygians, Lydians, Karians, Lykians, Mysians, and others. Greek authors often named these population groups' primary regions of habitation after them: 'Phrygia', 'Lydia', and so on. These geographic designations had exceptionally long afterlives, in some cases persisting deep into the second millennium AD (e.g. the Byzantine *themata* of Paphlagonia and Cappadocia), when all cultural and linguistic distinctions between these Iron Age culture zones had long since disappeared.[64] The Roman imperial period poses particularly delicate problems for the cultural historian, as the key period of transition between Lykia (or wherever) 'as distinct culture zone' (still true in the Hellenistic period) and Lykia 'as pure geographic expression' (certainly true by the end of Late Antiquity). In the first three centuries AD, these regional culture terms still had very wide currency, both as administrative units (the 'Roman province of Karia') and – at least in some places – as markers of local identity.[65] But there is a persistent danger of overstating

---

[63] Urbanization without urbanism in Roman Phrygia: Thonemann 2013b, 31–9.

[64] Regional patterning in material culture certainly persisted in inner Anatolia well into Late Antiquity and beyond (e.g. Niewöhner 2007, 2013; Mitchell, Niewöhner, Vardar, and Vardar 2021), and these local traditions are sometimes described as 'Phrygian', 'Galatian', and so forth; but this is geographic shorthand, not an argument for the survival of 'The Phrygians' as a meaningful culture group in Late Antiquity.

[65] Local identity: Mitchell 2010 (Paphlagonia); Spawforth 2001 (Lydia); Hallmannsecker 2022 (Ionia); Kelp 2015 (Phrygia). For regional survival patterns of local non-Greek languages into the imperial period (and in a handful of cases beyond), see Mitchell 1993, I 172–5.

the real cultural differences which persisted between, say, 'Roman Karia' and 'Roman Lykia' in the first three centuries AD – or, more insidiously, of assuming that genuine regional disparities in cultural forms can all be explained by reference back to the Iron Age cultures of these regions (the common trope of 'indigenous survivals').

As we have seen, by the end of the Hellenistic period, the inhabitants of Hieradoumia included long-standing populations of Lydian and probably Phrygian origin, as well as large immigrant groups of Mysians, Macedonians, and Greeks.[66] How sharp were the cultural and linguistic distinctions between these different population groups, and how long did these distinctions persist? The short answer is that we have no way of telling. Every surviving written text from Hieradoumia from the third century BC to the fourth century AD is in ordinary *koinē* Greek or (in a very few cases) Latin; Greek grammar and orthography are sometimes deeply idiosyncratic, but never (so far as I know) in a manner that suggests 'interference' with non-Greek languages.[67] If people in remote Hieradoumian hill villages were still speaking Lydian in the second century AD, they have left no evidence of it. 'Indigenous survivals' of non-Greek vocabulary in the region's written language are very few: the only clear cases are the kinship term *kambdios* ('grandchild') and the Phrygian word *doumos* ('household', 'cult association').[68] Plenty of indigenous Lydian toponyms survived deep into the Roman period, but placenames are remarkably resilient – indeed some of them survive today in the region's modern Turkish toponymy (Gordos–Gördes, Silandos–Selendi, Iaza–Ayazören).

Personal names might in principle have helped us to detect the presence of Lydian (or Phrygian, Mysian, Macedonian) 'substrates', but in practice, we have little to go on. By the time that the first epigraphic documents from Hieradoumia start to appear in the later Hellenistic period, the onomastics of the region were already almost entirely Greco-Macedonian.[69]

---

[66] The settler population may (but need not) have been predominantly male; direct evidence for mixed marriages between immigrant soldiers and local women in the Hellenistic world is remarkably scanty (Chaniotis 2002; Fischer-Bovet 2014, 247–51).

[67] Brixhe 2001; conspectus of linguistic peculiarities of the propitiatory inscriptions in Petzl 2019, 91–5.

[68] *kambdios*: Chapter 3, Section 3.2. *doumos*: above, n. 5. In neither case can we in fact be quite certain that we are dealing with local 'survivals' (rather than, say, Mysian imports): the term *kambdios* (with various different orthographies) is attested in other parts of Anatolia, and the term *doumos* also appears in Thrace and Macedonia.

[69] E.g. *TAM* V 1, 677 (Charakipolis, second century BC): sixty-eight men's names, all of Greek or Macedonian origin (cf. Catling 2004–2009, 405–7, on the names Ἀττίνας, Δαιμένης);

Of the thousands of personal names attested in Hieradoumian inscriptions of the Roman imperial period, very few indeed fall outside the normal range of the Greek onomastic *koinē*.[70] Women do fairly often carry Lallnamen ('baby names') and other 'simple names' such as Tatas, Nanas, Ammias, Apphias; but such names are very widespread throughout inner Anatolia and beyond, and certainly ought not to be taken as indices of residual cultural 'Lydianness'.[71] Demonstrable cases of indigenous onomastic survivals in late Hellenistic and imperial Hieradoumia are very few. The most striking example known to me is the name Mōgetēs, carried by several elite men in the region of Maionia in the second and first century BC, including a man who served as a general (*stratēgos*) of the *koinon* of the Maionians in the Katakekaumene around 130 BC (see above).[72] The name Mōgetēs is not Greek, and is otherwise strongly characteristic of Kibyra and the Kabalis, a region which is said by ancient authors to have been settled by the Lydians at some point in the pre-Classical period; the name can thus reasonably be taken as a rare Lydian 'survival'.[73] But very few analogous cases fall to hand.[74]

cf. *SEG* 49, 1623 (Nisyra, 48/7 BC). In second-century documents from the sanctuary of Apollo Pleurenos (*Sardis* II 317, 323, 441), members of the hereditary priestly lineage carry Lydian names (Καδοας, Πληρι), but virtually all of the *mystai* have ordinary Greek names.

[70] Robert 1963, 209–10 (onomastics of the remote village of Kömürcü, north-west of Gordos, surely far from any centres of Greco-Macedonian colonization); cf. 320–2, on the Hellenization of Lydian onomastics: 'il ne restait rien comme noms indigènes ou presque rien … [l]es noms grecs sont pour la plupart d'une extrême banalité et se retrouvent dans tous les pays grecs.'

[71] Lallnamen: e.g. Curbera 2013, 111–12, and Robert, *Hellenica* VI, 90 ('En Anatolie même, l'extension de ce genre des noms de peut donner aucun indice sur le caractère indigène ou hellénique d'une famille'). The greater use (or 'persistence') of indigenous names among women has been observed elsewhere in Hellenistic and Roman Anatolia, notably in Phrygia (Brixhe 2013) and Lykia (Colvin 2004, 54–7; Schuler 2019, 206–7, 212); there is no sign of this phenomenon in Hieradoumia.

[72] *LGPN* V.A, s.v. Μωγέτης (six instances from the vicinity of Maionia, plus one from Sardis).

[73] Robert and Robert 1954, 76–7 (collecting literary traditions on 'Maionians' in the Kabalis); Petzl 1978b, 270–1. The Roberts also noted (77 n. 5) the epichoric woman's name Ενα(ς), twice attested in the area of Maionia in the late Hellenistic/early imperial period (*TAM* V 3, 1735; *SEG* 54, 1212), which is likewise strongly characteristic of Kibyra and the Kabalis (*LGPN* V.C, s.v. Ενα, Ενας).

[74] The indigenous Lydian name Γαμερσης appears in *SEG* 46, 1542 (Hellenistic: unknown provenance), alongside the woman's name Δοτδους, also found (in the form Δοδδους) in a handful of other late Hellenistic inscriptions from the region: *TAM* V 1, 775 (Loros, 46/5 BC); *SEG* 57, 1212 (Saittai); *SEG* 57, 1145 (Charakipolis). The man's name Διδας (*TAM* V 1, 707: Gordos, AD 70/1) may be Lydian; on the name Αριους, see Thonemann 2019, 123. The common Hieradoumian name Deskylos (*LGPN* V.A, s.v. Δεσκυλίς, Δεσκύλος) is not a Lydian survival but an 'epichoric' reminiscence of the legendary Lydian king Daskylos (Gibson 1981, 216); cf. Κροῖσος in *I.Manisa* 266 and *SEG* 49, 1603.

In the religious sphere, deities of non-Greek origin (Meis, Agdistis, Meter) were certainly widely worshipped in Roman Hieradoumia, and some of them carry what appear to be non-Greek cultic epithets (Meis Tiamou, Meis Labanas).[75] But it is very difficult to detect any unambiguously 'Lydian' elements in the actual religious practices of the region in the Hellenistic and Roman imperial periods. Purity regulations of the second century BC from sanctuaries at Maionia (the goddess Meter) and Thyateira (an unnamed goddess) show no local idiosyncrasies; even the propitiatory practices that are so distinctive a feature of the religious epigraphy of Hieradoumia can in fact be widely paralleled elsewhere in the Greek world (it is the commemorative habit, not the rituals themselves, which is unusual).[76]

In summary, there is no sign that the varied historic origins of the inhabitants of Roman Hieradoumia translated into a culturally differentiated social order. By the Roman imperial period at the latest, the various local and immigrant populations of the region seem (so far as we can tell) to have been integrated into a single, culturally homogeneous whole.[77] The qualification 'so far as we can tell' is of course critical, since we can only access Hieradoumian society through their representational practices – the things they chose to write and depict on stone inscriptions. Still, speculation about what they might have chosen *not* to tell us is unlikely to bear much fruit. It may well be that some of the idiosyncratic features of Hieradoumian kinship terminology, family structures, religious practices, and social organization are 'relics' of Lydian, Phrygian, Mysian, or indeed Macedonian cultural practices; we simply have no way of knowing.

Perhaps we ought not to obsess too much about origins. Arguably a more urgent methodological problem is how, in the absence of generalizing statements about 'Hieradoumian society' in ancient texts, we can move from observable peculiarities in the representational practices of this tightly bounded region to broader hypotheses about the region's social structure. The problem is strictly parallel to the famous art-historical problem of the relationship between stylistic transformations in artistic production and

[75] de Hoz 1999, 28–62; but there is no reason to categorize gods who take their epithet from a non-Greek toponym (e.g. Zeus Masphalatenos) as 'Anatolian deities'. On the cultic epithet Τιαμου, see Parker 2017, 117 n. 19.
[76] Purity regulations: *TAM* V 1, 530 (*CGRN* 211: Maionia, 147/6 BC); Malay and Petzl 2017, no. 1 (Thyateira, II BC), with Parker 2018; see Chapter 8, n. 8. Rituals of confession and propitiation: e.g. Chaniotis 2009a, esp. 142–8. For the historiographic shift away from the idea that the propitiation inscriptions represent a 'relic' of Anatolian religious practices, see above all the exemplary study of Potts 2019; also Rostad 2020, 41–53; Schuler 2012, 67, 83–4. For an extreme example of primordialism, see Ricl 1997, 36 n.16 (Hittite continuity); cf. Ricl 2003, 81.
[77] Cf. Scott 2009, 265–70.

contemporary changes in society, religion, politics, mentalities, and so forth.[78] Without the heuristic crutch of 'indigenous survivals' (which are at best unprovable), how do we move from a series of individual monuments to meaningful generalizations about the distinctive local morphology of 'Hieradoumian culture'? The necessary starting point is to treat the commemorative monumental practices of Roman Hieradoumia as a cultural phenomenon *in their own right*, independent of their putative evolutionary origins; this is what I will attempt to do in Chapter 2.

---

[78] The bibliography is stupendous in both bulk and quality. The best starting points remain Riegl 1901 (with Panofsky 1981 and Elsner 2006), Panofsky 1939 (with Elsner and Lorenz 2012), and Gombrich 1960, 99–125 (with Ginzburg 1989).

2 | Commemorative Cultures

As we saw in Chapter 1, the historical and institutional development of Hieradoumia in the late Hellenistic and early Roman imperial periods was in many ways unlike that of other parts of inland western Asia Minor. Large-scale migration into the region in the later Hellenistic period created an ethnically and culturally mixed society, in which it is effectively impossible to distinguish 'indigenous' Lydian and Phrygian elements from 'imported' Greek, Macedonian, and Mysian cultural forms. As a result of the settlement policies of the Seleukid and Attalid kings, urbanism in the region during the Hellenistic period was minimal, in terms both of settlement agglomeration and *polis*-institutions; instead, the late Hellenistic *koina* of the region (the Mysoi Abbaitai; the Maionians in the Katakekaumene) seems to have served as a functional alternative to organization by *poleis*. The scattered villages of the region were, eventually, lumped together into *poleis*, but this development was (or so I will argue in Chapter 10) late and marginal. The result of this combination of trajectories, by the turn of the era, was a region which possessed a highly distinctive shared culture, but lacked a strong focus of collective identity.

Nonetheless, the strongest argument for treating Roman Hieradoumia as a distinct and meaningful culture zone is *not* the region's particular historical and institutional development between, say, 200 BC and AD 200. It is, instead, a case based on material culture – more specifically, the emergence in this region of two highly idiosyncratic and instantly recognizable local commemorative practices, the familial epitaph and the propitiation-*stēlē*. It is almost entirely from these two categories of epigraphic monument that our knowledge of the social structure of Hieradoumia derives. The aim of the present chapter is to introduce these two categories of monument, to describe their distribution in time and space, and to indicate some of the ways in which they can be used to reconstruct the particular statics and dynamics of Hieradoumian society. As we will see, although the two kinds of monument were set up in different places and to very different ends, they in fact bear close resemblances in both physical appearance and – more surprisingly – in textual content.[1] As these formal similarities suggest, both commemorative practices should be seen as ways of expressing a single distinctive Hieradoumian cultural 'outlook' on the world. In Alois Riegl's famously knotty formulation, they are different facets of a single *Kunstwollen* or 'artistic volition' – the expression in diverse artistic and textual genres of a single distinct worldview, specific to a particular place and time.[2]

It is, of course, hardly surprising that the inscribed monuments of one region look different from those of another region. Microregional diversity in epigraphic practice (particularly the funerary sphere) is characteristic of much of the ancient Greek world, both at the level of the individual city and its territory, and at the level of cultural regions as a whole; inner Anatolia is no exception.[3] Nonetheless, the geographic clarity and definition of the Hieradoumian 'material culture zone' is striking and significant, and it maps with satisfying precision onto that stretch of the middle Hermos valley which underwent the peculiar pattern of historical and institutional development described above. As I will argue throughout this book, there is good reason to think that the distinctive *Kunstwollen* of the rural communities of the middle Hermos valley, as expressed in their two chief commemorative cultures, may reflect real differences between the social structure of this region and other parts of inland western Asia Minor. If so, that is perhaps rather exciting, and might even be methodologically consequential.

2.1 Familial Epitaphs in Roman Hieradoumia: Overview

Between the first and third century AD, the men and women of Hieradoumia regularly commemorated their dead with a highly distinctive local type of epitaph. Here is a characteristic example, from a village on the territory of Saittai, dated to early AD 167:[4]

---

[1] It is infuriating that – to the best of my knowledge – not a single one of the thousands of inscribed monuments from the region was discovered *in situ*. We do not know what a Hieradoumian village graveyard looked like, nor how propitiatory *stēlai* were disposed within rural sanctuaries (although see Chapter 8, Section 8.2).

[2] Riegl 1901, 209–18, esp. 215, with Ginzburg 1989, 45. As it happens, my own large cultural generalizations derive primarily (though not only) from close formalist analysis of the textual content of the monuments rather than their decorative features; but the analogy stands. More on this in Chapter 10.

[3] Thonemann 2013b, 36–7; Kelp 2013, 2015.

[4] *TAM* V 1, 175, from Hacı Hüseyn Damları, in the far south-east of the territory of Saittai, near Kalburcu (Map 3).

ἔτους σνα΄, μη(νὸς) Δύ-
στρου ηι΄.
Ἡρακλείδης β΄ καὶ
Φλ. Σωφρόνη Σωφρό-
5 νην τὴν ἑαυτῶν θυγα-
τέρα καὶ Εὔδοξος ὁ ἀνὴρ
καὶ Δημόφιλος καὶ Νύσα οἱ
ἑκυροὶ καὶ Ἡρακλείδης ὁ υἱὸς
καὶ Δημόφιλος ὁ δαὴρ καὶ οἱ ἴδι-
10 οι πάντες ἐτείμησαν ζήσα-
σαν ἔτη κϛ΄.

Year 251, Day 18 of the month Dystros. Herakleides, son of Herakleides, and
Fl(avia) Sophrone (honoured) Sophrone their daughter, and Eudoxos her husband
(honoured her), and Demophilos and Nysa her husband's parents, and Herakleides her son, and Demophilos her husband's brother, and all her own people (*idioi*)
honoured her, having lived for 26 years.

Around a thousand epitaphs of this basic type are known, almost all of
them dating between the mid-first and the mid-third century AD.[5] The
'Hieradoumian' epitaph type is characterized by four distinctive features:

(1) *Physical form and decoration.* The monuments typically take the form
    of a thin trapezoidal marble *stēlē* tapering towards the top, terminat-
    ing in a triangular pediment with akroteria, with a rough *tenon* below
    for fixing to the ground. The upper part of the shaft generally carries
    a depiction of a vegetal wreath, incised or in low inset relief, either
    above the inscribed text or – as in the example depicted in Figure 2.1 –
    between the date and the remainder of the text. In a minority of cases,
    instead of a wreath, the upper part of the shaft bears a sculptural depic-
    tion of the deceased (who may be accompanied by one or more other
    figures), either in a recessed niche or in low relief projecting forward
    from the face of the shaft.

(2) *Date and age.* The overwhelming majority of epitaphs either begin or
    conclude with a date in the form Year – Month – Day (more rarely,
    Year – Month, or Year alone), indicating – as we will see shortly – date

[5] Figure 2.7 below shows only the chronological distribution of the 781 epitaphs from Hieradoumia and neighbouring regions which are precisely datable to the year; around a hundred
further dated epitaphs cannot be assigned to a particular year, either through uncertainty as
to the era in use (Sullan or Actian: see below), or through damage to the stone. If one were to
include undated and fragmentary 'Hieradoumian-type' epitaphs, the total number of extant
texts of this basic type from the region would be significantly over 1,000.

Figure 2.1 Epitaph of Sophrone, from Hacı Hüseyn Damları. *TAM* V 1, 175.

of death. Age at death is indicated in around 30 per cent of cases, as in the example quoted here.[6]

(3) *Grammatical structure.* The name of the deceased is invariably given in the accusative case, followed or preceded by the name(s) of at least one commemorator, always in the nominative. The act of commemoration is almost always indicated by means of the verb τ(ε)ιμᾶν, 'to honour', in the aorist tense (ἐτείμησεν in the singular, ἐτείμησαν in the plural). We very occasionally find other verbs used, such as στεφανοῦν, 'wreathe', μνησθῆναι, 'commemorate' (with the genitive), or καθιερῶσαι, 'consecrate'.[7] The verb is sometimes omitted, leaving a simple 'accusative of the deceased' and 'nominative(s) of the honourer(s)'.

(4) *Familial commemoration.* Most epitaphs feature a more or less extended list (in the nominative case) of the relatives who joined in commemorating the deceased, most commonly consisting of around four to six persons, but sometimes running into the dozens. These relatives are sometimes accompanied by acquaintances and friends from outside the deceased's immediate kin-group, and/or by corporate bodies of one kind or other (trade guilds, cult associations).[8]

Not all of these features are found on every monument, but together they make a sufficiently distinctive 'package' that there is in practice no real difficulty in identifying and classifying marginal cases. Figures 2.2–2.5 illustrate some of the kinds of variation found within the basic Hieradoumian monument type. Figure 2.2 is a 'standard' Hieradoumian epitaph from the territory of Saittai, with virtually the full complement of typical textual and iconographic features (lacking only the day of the month and the age of the deceased).[9] Figure 2.3, from Silandos, includes all the same formal features,

---

[6] See Chapter 3, Section 3.4. Broux and Clarysse 2009, 32 note that the age of the deceased is less frequently found on epitaphs antedating *c.* AD 140.

[7] στεφανοῦν: *TAM* V 1, 775 (Loros, 45 BC); *SEG* 57, 1212 (Saittai: Hellenistic); *SEG* 40, 1077 (Uşak: imperial period). ἐμνήσθη/-ησαν: *TAM* V 1, 133 (Saittai); *SEG* 29, 1161 (Daldis); *TAM* V 3, 1773, 1783 (Philadelphia). καθιέρωσεν/-αν: *TAM* V 1, 177 (Saittai); *TAM* V 1, 298 (Kula); *SEG* 38, 1232 (unknown provenance); *SEG* 40, 1077 (Uşak); *TAM* V 3, 1784 (Tetrapyrgia), with bibliography; cf. *TAM* V 1, 285 (Kula), where the deceased appears to be 'consecrated' to Zeus Ktesios. The verb ἀνατίθημι is occasionally found: *SEG* 35, 1235 (Saittai: with the dative); *TAM* V 1, 682 (Charakipolis: with the accusative). The formula in *SEG* 49, 1673 (Saittai: στήλην θῆκαν, with the dative) is anomalous.

[8] For the various corporate groups of non-kin that appear in Hieradoumian epitaphs, see Chapter 7.

[9] *TAM* V 1, 102 (Çayköy): ἔτους ρϙϛ', μη(νὸς) Ξανδικοῦ. Ἀπολλωνιὰς Ἀσκληπιάδου Ἀπολλώ|νιον τὸν ἑαυτῆς ἄνδρα καὶ οἱ | υἱοὶ αὐτοῦ Ἑρμογένης, Γάϊος |(5) καὶ Βρόμιος ὁ συμβιωτὴς αὐ|τοῦ ἐτείμησαν ('Year 196 [AD 111/12], month Xandikos. Apollonias daughter of Asklepiades (honoured) Apollonios her husband, and his sons Hermogenes and Gaios and his *symbiōtēs* Bromios honoured him').

Figure 2.2 Epitaph of Apollonios, from Çayköy. *TAM* V 1, 102 (Manisa Museum).

but is visibly of much cruder workmanship: both pediment and wreath are asymmetric, and the lettering is far less professionally executed.[10] By contrast, Figure 2.4, from the ancient village of Taza, is at the very top end of the scale for technical quality; it commemorates two individuals, a husband and wife (the latter still living at the time the monument was erected), and carries a relief depiction of the couple instead of a wreath.[11] Finally, Figure 2.5 is an epitaph now in the Uşak Archaeological Museum, of uncertain provenance,

---

[10] *SEG* 57, 1225 (Karaselendi): ἔτους ρνγ΄, μη(νὸς) Δύσ|τρου π(ροτέρᾳ). | Ἀτικὸς καὶ Γάμος καὶ | Θάλ⟨α⟩μος ἐτείμησαν |(5) Παπαν τὸν πατέραν | καὶ Νύνφη ἡ σύνβιος αὐ|τοῦ ('Year 153 [AD 68/9], on the penultimate day of the month Dystros. Atikos and Gamos and Thalamos honoured their father Papas, as did his wife Nynphe'). Note the various orthographic and phonetic peculiarities, absent from the more 'professional' text from Saittai quoted above.

[11] *SEG* 34, 1200 (Kavaklı): ζῇ. | ἔτους ροθ΄, μη(νὸς) Δαισίου α΄. | Ζεῦξις ὁ καὶ Γάϊος καὶ Ἀντίο|χος καὶ Φιλέρως ἐτείμη|(5)σαν Μηνόφιλον τὸν | [π]ατέρα καὶ Μελ⟨τί⟩νην | [τὴν] μητέρα ('Year 179, day 1 of the month Daisios. Zeuxis, also known as Gaios, and Antiochos and Phileros honoured their father Menophilos and their mother Meltine'.) The single word ζῇ, 's/he is living', is inscribed immediately below the feet of the female figure in the relief, indicating that Meltine was still alive when the monument was set up; the date therefore reflects the date of death of her husband Menophilos (see further Section 2.2).

Figure 2.3 Epitaph of Papas, from Karaselendi (Silandos). *SEG* 57, 1225 (Manisa Museum).

but certainly from Hieradoumia (probably somewhere in the eastern part of the region). The inscribed text is of the normal Hieradoumian type (date, ἐτείμησαν-formula, etc.), but the upper part of the *stēlē* carries an unusually elaborate relief depiction of the deceased woman, standing within a 'bower' of curling vine branches loaded with grapes, flanked by decorative pilasters with capitals supporting an archivolt with two fascias.[12]

In terms of their overall geographic distribution, 'Hieradoumian-type' epitaphs are almost exclusively confined to the middle and upper Hermos valley. The westernmost boundary of the Hieradoumian 'epitaphic zone' can be drawn very sharply along the western flank of the Katırcı Dağı mountain range, the dividing line between the territories of Gordos and

---

[12] *SEG* 39, 1294: ἔτους τμα', μη(νὸς) Δίου δ'. | Ἀφφιὰς Βάσσαν τὴν θυγατέ|ρα καὶ οἱ ἀδελφοὶ αὐτῆς | καὶ ὁ σύνβιος αὐτῆς Ἀμιανὸς |(5) ἐτείμησαν μνίας χάριν ('Year 341 [AD 256/7], day 4 of the month Dios. Apphias (honoured) Bassa her daughter, and her brothers and her husband Amianos honoured her, for memory's sake').

Figure 2.4 Epitaph of Menophilos and Meltine, from Kavaklı (Taza). *SEG* 34, 1200 (Manisa Museum).

Loros to the east and the territories of Thyateira and Attaleia to the west (Maps 1 and 2).[13] To the west and south-west, the cities of the lower Hermos valley (Sardis, Magnesia under Sipylos) and the Lykos plain (Thyateira, Apollonis, Attaleia, Hierokaisareia) have produced virtually no epitaphs of this type. West-Lydian epitaphs generally take a quite different form: dated epitaphs are very rare, and epitaphs were typically erected (κατασκευάζειν, ποιεῖν) by a *single* individual for *several* family members, whose names are listed in the dative case.[14] To the south and south-east, Hieradoumian-type familial epitaphs do appear in the hill country north of Philadelphia, but

---

[13] West of the Katırcı Dağı, Hieradoumian-type epitaphs appear at Sarılar (*TAM* V 2, 840A-B), Görenez (*TAM* V 2, 1128), Hacıosmanlar (*TAM* V 2, 1059, 1095, 1156, 1213), and Akçaalan (*TAM* V 2, 1062 and 1064); all these villages lie in the far east of the territories of Thyateira and Attaleia, on the fringe of the Hieradoumian culture zone.

[14] Numerous examples in *TAM* V 2, 831–854 (Attaleia), 1044–1156 (Thyateira), 1371–1392 (Magnesia). Epitaphs of the west-Lydian 'dative' type also predominate at Gölmarmara, in the western part of the territory of Daldis (*TAM* V 1, 653–670); *SEG* 57, 1157 is a notable exception.

Figure 2.5 Epitaph of Bassa, uncertain provenance. *SEG* 39, 1294 (Uşak Museum).

very seldom in the plain of the Kogamos river itself.[15] No epitaphs of Hieradoumian type are known at Blaundos, in south-east Lydia. To the north,
Hieradoumian-type epitaphs remain dominant up to, but not beyond, the
Simav Dağları mountain range (ancient Mt Temnos). Two epitaphs of
Hieradoumian type have been found at the modern village of Yassıeynehan,
in the upper Selendi Çayı valley (probably the far north-east of the territory
of Silandos); beyond Mt Temnos, only a single example is known from the
territories of Synaos and Ankyra Sidera, in the plain of Simav.[16]

    Within the Hieradoumian culture zone, sub-regional variation is relativ-
ely slight. Most of the longest examples of Hieradoumian-type epitaphs, listing

---

[15] Hieradoumian-type epitaphs in the northern part of the territory of Philadelphia: *TAM* V 3,
1700 (Yeşilova), 1732 (Hayallı), 1734 (Kastollos), 1736 (Sarı Sığırlı), 1745 (Toygarlı), 1775
(Kastollos), 1776 (near Şeritli), 1845 (Bebekli), 1894 (Yeşilova). At Philadelphia itself, only
TAM V 3, 1722, 1744, 1772, probably all brought to Alaşehir from villages to the north.

[16] Yassıeynehan: *SEG* 58, 1359 and 1360. Among the numerous epitaphs from the plain of Simav
published in *MAMA* X, nos. 359–483, only one is of Hieradoumian type (*MAMA* X 458, from
Savcılar).

dozens of separate family members, derive from the western part of the region (Gordos, Daldis, Apollonioucharax), although there are exceptions.[17] Most of the earliest dated examples seem also to derive from the west, particularly from the towns of Gordos and Loros. It therefore seems reasonable to suppose that this particular commemorative habit originated in the western part of the region in the late Hellenistic period, before gradually being adopted in towns and villages further up the Hermos valley to the east over the course of the first two centuries AD. Conversely, in the north-eastern part of Hieradoumia (in particular on the large territory of Saittai), epitaphs tend to be relatively short, typically only listing half a dozen relatives or (more often) fewer. Saittai was also home to a distinctive 'non-familial' variant of the Hieradoumian epitaph type, in which individuals (usually, but not always, adult males) are commemorated by a trade association or other corporate body rather than by their kin; epitaphs of this 'guild' type are all but unknown elsewhere in the Hieradoumian culture zone.[18]

It is particularly striking that the characteristic funerary practices of late Hellenistic and Roman Sardis seem to have left virtually no influence at all on the middle Hermos region. At Sardis, the most common form of funerary monument is the inscribed cinerary chest (usually bearing the deceased's name in the nominative, with no relatives mentioned), a monumental type which is all but unattested in Roman Hieradoumia.[19] The absence of Sardian influence on Hieradoumian commemorative culture is particularly striking in light of the abundant evidence for members of the Sardian elite owning large estates in rural Hieradoumia (see Chapter 10, Section 10.2).

2.2 Familial Epitaphs in Roman Hieradoumia: Dating and Chronology

The overwhelming majority of gravestones from Roman Hieradoumia record the date of death, either at the beginning or at the end of the epitaph, and usually in the form Year – Month – Day. This is one of the most

---

[17] Lengthy examples from Gordos and neighbouring towns: *TAM* V 1, 701–707, 710–714, 725, 764–765, 768–769 (Gordos); *SEG* 57, 1156, *I.Manisa* 521 (Apollonioucharax); *TAM* V 1, 624–625 (Daldis). Extended lists of relatives elsewhere in Hieradoumia: *TAM* V 1, 432–433 (Nisyra); *TAM* V 1, 483a (Iaza); *SEG* 40, 1070, *SEG* 49, 1657 and 1660 (Saittai).

[18] See Chapter 7, Section 7.2.

[19] Alexandridis 2018. The Sardis-style cinerary chest does seem to have been in limited use in the area around Daldis–Charakipolis in the early Julio-Claudian period (*I.Manisa* 465, 467; *SEG* 57, 1147–1149), but it evidently did not catch on. Inscribed epitaphs on Sardian cinerary chests do often bear dates of death (usually the name of the annual Sardian eponym, month + day), and it is possible that this influenced dating practices on Hieradoumian funerary *stēlai*.

idiosyncratic features of the epitaphs of this region compared to other parts of the Greek East: the inclusion of dates of any kind on epitaphs is exceptionally rare in the ancient Greek-speaking world at any period. Here is a typical dated Hieradoumian epitaph from the city of Saittai[20]:

> ἔτους σϞζ′, μη(νὸς) Ξανδικοῦ ι′.
> Αὐρ. Βάσσος ὁ σύνβιος καὶ
> Αὐρ. Ἀσκληπίδης καὶ Αὐρ.
> Βασσιανὸς οἱ υείοὶ καὶ Αὐρ.
> 5   Φρούγιλλα ἡ ἐγγόνη Βάσ-
> σαν καλῶς βιώσασαν ἔτη
>   να′ ἐτείμησαν.

Year 297, (Day) 10 of the month Xandikos. Aur(elius) Bassos her husband, and Aur. Asklepides and Aur. Bassianos her sons, and Aur. Frugilla her granddaughter honoured Bassa, who lived creditably for 51 years.

This particular tombstone, like most dated epitaphs from Roman Hieradoumia, carries the 'full' threefold dating by year, month, and day (Figure 2.6). Epitaphs dated by year and month alone are also widely found in the region; tombstones dated by year alone are distinctly less common.[21] The year of death is generally reckoned according to either the Sullan era (85 BC) or the Actian era (31 BC), or in a few cases both. Although the Sullan era was by far the more widely used of the two, some towns in the region did use the Actian era (e.g. Daldis), and hence Hieradoumian-type epitaphs which lack a firm provenance cannot always be dated with confidence.[22] The epitaph of Bassa is firmly attributed to the vicinity of Saittai, a city which is known to have used the Sullan era, and the text can thus be securely dated to AD 212/213.[23] In fact, in this particular case, the use of the Sullan era is neatly confirmed by internal evidence; 10 Xandikos of Year 297 of the Sullan era corresponds to early spring AD 213, very shortly after the *constitutio Antoniniana*. In the epitaph, the four surviving members of the family all bear the *nomen* 'Aurelius' (unattested in earlier inscriptions from Saittai), while the deceased does not.[24] It is therefore highly likely

---

[20] *TAM* V 1, 122 (İcikler).
[21] Broux and Clarysse 2009, 33: 'in about 14% of this type of stelae a month is given without any day indication'.
[22] There are also several cases of funerary *stēlai* which have migrated *within* Hieradoumia in recent years: Thonemann 2015, 132 n.55; Thonemann 2019, 132 no. 8.
[23] Herrmann 1972, 526–9; Leschhorn 1993, 301–35, esp. 318–21.
[24] Adoption of the *nomen* 'Aurelius' by families in Asia Minor immediately after AD 212: Robert, *Hellenica* XIII, 232–4; *MAMA* XI 201; Kantor 2016, 49–50. Another Hieradoumian example: *SEG* 57, 1230 (Thermai Theseos), a dedication to the river Hermos erected by Μᾶρκος Αὐρ[ή]λιος Ἄνβεντος, dated 18 Loos, Year 297 (Sullan era, mid-summer AD 213).

Figure 2.6 Epitaph of Bassa, from İcikler. *TAM* V 1, 122 (Manisa Museum).

that the *constitutio Antoniniana* took effect in Hieradoumia in the interval between Bassa's death and the erection of her tombstone.

781 epitaphs from Hieradoumia and neighbouring regions can be dated to the year with reasonable confidence.[25] Their chronological distribution, grouped by ten-year bands, is presented in Figure 2.7. Dated epitaphs of the first century BC and of the Julio-Claudian period are relatively few in number, with a slow rising trend across the first sixty years of the first century AD. Epitaphic production rises sharply in the Flavian period (after AD 70) and reaches a peak in the later Antonine and early Severan period (160s–190s); it then drops off very sharply in the second half of the third century, and inscribed epitaphs cease altogether in the early fourth century; 90.3% of all dated epitaphs from the region (n = 705) date to the two

---

[25] This figure includes around 30 dated epitaphs from Philadelphia, and a small handful of dated epitaphs from Sardis and the Kaystros valley. On the overall chronology of the epigraphic habit in Roman Hieradoumia, see already MacMullen 1986; Broux and Clarysse 2009 (who collected 606 dated funerary monuments from the region).

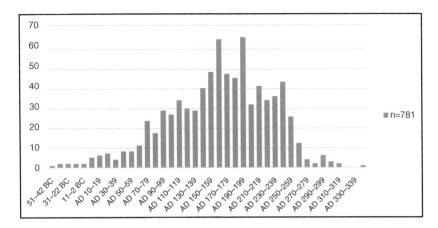

Figure 2.7 Chronological distribution of dated epitaphs from Hieradoumia and neighbouring regions (n = 781).

centuries between AD 70/1 and AD 269/70. As we will see later in this chapter, precisely the same overall trends can be seen in the chronological distribution of dated votive and propitiatory monuments from Roman Hieradoumia (Figure 2.17); dated public monuments from the region are too few for meaningful analysis.

Can we be certain that the dates on Hieradoumian tombstones represent the date of death, rather than (say) the date on which the tombstone was erected,[26] or even the date on which a copy of the epitaph was deposited in the city archives?[27] My view is that we can. In eight epitaphs – not, it is true, a particularly large number – the phraseology makes it all but certain that the recorded date does indeed reflect the date of death.[28] In one, highly

---

[26] The gap between these two dates could be a year or more: cf. *TAM* V 3, 1780 (Philadelphia): date of death, Year 178, Month XII Hyperberetaios 6 (late summer AD 148); tomb completed, Year 180, Month I Dios (early autumn AD 149).

[27] Explicit in several epitaphs from Thyateira (*TAM* V 2, 1051, 1075, 1080, 1084, 1144, 1149, probably 1150–1152); also at Blaundos, in south-east Lydia (Filges 2006, 340, no. 33). However, in all these cases, the deposition of a copy in the city archives is connected to the stipulation of a fine to the city treasury for illicit use of the tomb, and provisions of this kind are all but unknown in Roman Hieradoumia.

[28] (1) *TAM* V 1, 95 (Saittai: τελευτήσαντα ἔτους ρξβ΄); (2) *TAM* V 1, 218, lines 5–7 (Tabala: τελευ[τ]ᾷ δὲ ἡ Ἄπφιον ἔτους σϞζ κτλ.); (3) *TAM* V 1, 289 (Kula: ἔτους τα΄, μη(νὸς) Ἀπελλαίου Ἀσκληπιάδης τελευτᾷ ιγ΄, ἐτῶν ις΄); (4) *TAM* V 1, 546 (*SGO* I 04/22/02, Maionia: ἔτους Ϙ΄ καὶ γ΄, μη(νὸς) Ὑπερβερταίου ε΄ ἀπιούσ[η], μετήλαξεν Ἄρτεμις); (5) *TAM* V 1, 631 (Daldis: ἔτους τϛι΄, μη(νὸς) Λῴου δ΄, ἐτελεύτησεν ὀνόματι Εὐκάρπη); (6) *SEG* 34, 1227 (Saittai: τελ(ευτήσαντι) ἔτ(ους) σπα΄ κτλ.); (7) *SEG* 40, 1090 (unknown provenance: ἔτ(ους) σλθ΄, μηνὸς πρώτου, ζήσας ἔτη εἴκοσι τελευτᾷ); (8) *SEG* 55, 1308 (unknown provenance: ἔτους σνγ΄, μη(νὸς) Αὐδναίου ιε΄, Ἕρμιππος τελευτᾷ ἐτῶν η΄). Cf. Robert, *Hellenica* VI, 102.

anomalous case, a certain Dionysios of Saittai is honoured with *two* separate tombstones, erected by different corporate groups, both dated to 19 Peritios, AD 167/8; this date must surely reflect Dionysios' actual date of death.[29] Moreover, in a few cases where two or more individuals are commemorated by the same epitaph, separate dates are given for each deceased individual: in such instances, the two (or more) dates must surely reflect their actual dates of death.[30] More problematic are the numerous epitaphs which commemorate two or more individuals, but where only a single date is given; in such instances, I take it that the date probably reflects the most recent date of death, or the fact that one or more of the individuals commemorated is in fact yet to die.[31] In only a very small number of cases does the recorded date demonstrably *not* represent the date of death.[32] In the absence of strong arguments to the contrary, it therefore seems safe to assume that the dates recorded on Hieradoumian Lydian epitaphs do

---

[29] Thonemann 2017b, 192–4, on *TAM* V 1, 91 and *SEG* 33, 1018. We have no way of knowing whether the two *stēlai* originally stood side by side above a single tomb: compare the case of the two 'epitaphs' of Antonia of Sardis, Herrmann 1959, 7–8 (*Sardis* II 669–670), discussed further below.

[30] *TAM* V 1, 95 (three deceased, with a gap of seven years between the first and last deaths); *TAM* V 1, 289 (two deceased, with a gap of six years); *SEG* 60, 1291 (two deceased, with a gap of two years); *TAM* V 1, 704 (two deceased, with a gap of one month). This last example is a *post mortem* honorific decree of the city of Gordos, and we can thus infer that the dates on other such *post mortem* decrees (e.g. *TAM* V 1, 701–2, 705, 775; perhaps *TAM* V 1, 687) also reflect date of death, not the date on which the decree was voted. In a few cases, a second date is subsequently added to the tombstone in a separate hand, to reflect the burial of a second individual in the same tomb: *TAM* V 1, 218, 811; *TAM* V 2, 840; *SEG* 35, 1258; *SEG* 49, 1561; *SEG* 57, 1148; *I.Manisa* 241.

[31] *TAM* V 1, 35 (two *tethrammena*), 57 (parents), 61 (wife and daughter), 104 (two children), 167b (parents), 174 (parents), 191 (father and daughter), 198 (two sons), 212 (two daughters), 216 (parents), 434 (two siblings), 472 (husband and son), 480 (parents), 511 (two children), 547 (two sons), 591 (mother and son), 705 (wife's brother, parents, sister), 714 (two sons), 737 (parents), 803 (parents), 811 (son and grandson); *SEG* 32, 1216 (wife, son and *threptē*); *SEG* 32, 1235 (two daughters and a male child); *SEG* 33, 1015 (parents); *SEG* 35, 1270 (father, sister and brother); *SEG* 40, 1101 (two daughters); *SEG* 49, 1619 (wife and another female), *SEG* 49, 1727 (daughter and son-in-law); *SEG* 52, 1165 (parents); *SEG* 54, 1211 (five individuals); *SEG* 55, 1286 (husband and daughter-in-law); *SEG* 55, 1305 (two sons); *SEG* 55, 1306 (son and daughter); *Sardis* II 666 (husband and son); *I.Manisa* 376 (parents); Thonemann 2019, no. 1 (parents and son). In a few cases, one or more 'honoured' individuals are explicitly described as still living at the time the tombstone was erected: *SEG* 31, 1009 (= *SEG* 49, 1628); *SEG* 34, 1200 (see above, n.11); *SEG* 40, 1085; cf. *SEG* 53, 1341.

[32] In an epitaph from Koloe, in the eastern Kaystros valley, the date clearly reflects the completion of the monument: *SEG* 56, 1322 (ἐτελέσθ⟨η⟩ ἔ⟨τ⟩ου⟨ς⟩ σκζ', μη⟨νὸς⟩ Πανήμου, Ἀπολλώνιος λατύπος); the same may be true of *Sardis* VII 1, 139 (lines 9–12, ἐποίησε μνίας ἕνεκα, ἀνθυπάτου Σιλβανῷ, μη⟨νὸς⟩ Ξανδικοῦ γι') and Filges 2006, 342, no. 34 (Blaundos). The character of the date in *TAM* V 1, 741 (Gordos) is unclear; it *could* reflect the date of death of the (unnamed) wife of the tomb builder.

indeed generally represent the (or at least a) date of death; as we will see in Chapter 3, patterns in the seasonal distribution of recorded dates provide strong *prima facie* support for this assumption.

Of development over time in the Hieradoumian familial epitaph – evolution, refinement, decadence, decline – there is none. In both their physical form and their textual conventions, the last extant epitaphs, from the very early fourth century AD, are, to all intents and purposes, indistinguishable from those of the Julio-Claudian period.[33]

2.3 Familial Epitaphs in Roman Hieradoumia: Families

It is of course quite normal for Greek and Latin tombstones to be erected by close kin of the deceased. But the epitaphs of Roman Hieradoumia typically list not just one or two close family members, as is standard elsewhere, but family groupings which may run to dozens of individuals. In one extreme case, a deceased eighteen-year-old priest at the village of Nisyra was commemorated by no fewer than thirty-two named relatives, teachers and friends, plus seven unnamed spouses, and an uncertain number of children.[34] All of these kinsmen and friends are precisely located in the deceased's family tree: paternal and maternal uncles and aunts, brothers- and sisters-in-law, step-kin, foster-siblings, and so forth.

The form of self-representation of familial groups in the epitaphs of Roman Hieradoumia is very much *sui generis*: there is nothing else quite like this in the vast corpus of funerary epigraphy from the Greco-Roman world.[35] The only remotely meaningful analogies that I know of come from Rhodes and neighbouring parts of coastal Asia Minor (the Rhodian Peraia, Xanthos), where, in the second and first century BC, there was a short-lived trend for private honorific statues to be erected by large extended families – up to twenty-one relatives, including uncles and aunts, cousins, nephews and nieces, and kinsmen by marriage.[36]

---

[33] Three centuries separate *TAM* V 1, 152 (Ariandos, AD 8/9) from *SEG* 49, 1741 (region of Kula, AD 309/10); but you wouldn't know it.

[34] *TAM* V 1, 432 (Nisyra). The interest of this text is highlighted by Robert, *OMS* V, 692–4.

[35] Although, as we will see, there are some close connections with the funerary epigraphy of northern Phrygia, particularly the Upper Tembris valley.

[36] Fraser 1977, 58, 147–8 nn. 323–5; Rice 1986, 209–33; Kontorini 1993 (*SEG* 43, 527: a particularly elaborate example, listing twenty-one relatives); Ma 2013a, 160–3, 203–5. Rhodian Peraia: e.g. Bresson 1991, no. 3 (Kedreai). Xanthos: e.g. *SEG* 55, 1502. The verb

However, unlike in Roman Hieradoumia, these late Hellenistic Rhodian 'family monuments' were not tombstones; only in a very few cases can we be sure that the honorand was deceased at the time the statue was erected.[37] Nor is there any reason to think that this short-lived Rhodian familial 'statue-habit' exercised any direct influence on the commemorative practices of Roman Hieradoumia, and I suspect that we are dealing with entirely independent developments.

As a result of the commemorative practices of Roman Hieradoumia, we know more about family and kinship structures in this small region than in almost any other part of ancient western Eurasia.[38] As we will see in Chapter 4, thanks to these familial epitaphs, the kinship terminology of Roman Hieradoumia is known to us in extraordinary detail. We can reconstruct large extended families with absolute precision and can say something about how those families chose to represent themselves. Even if not all the individuals listed on an epitaph literally co-habited in the same dwelling, the fact that they (and not others) all joined in commemorating a deceased relative clearly tells us *something* about family forms in the region (see Chapter 5). Finally, we can start to say something about distinctive interfamilial strategies in Roman Hieradoumia: marriage, adoption, fosterage, and so forth.

The relationship of the 'honouring' individuals to the deceased seems generally to have been recorded as precisely as possible. The relevant kinship term can either appear in the nominative, describing the honourer (Μᾶρκος ὁ πατὴρ ἐτείμησεν Γλύκωνα, 'Marcus, the father, honoured Glykon'), or in the accusative, describing the deceased (Μᾶρκος ἐτείμησεν Γλύκωνα τὸν υἱόν, 'Marcus honoured Glykon, his son'). Similarly, if a man's brother's wife dies, he can either describe himself as her δαήρ ('husband's brother') or describe her as his ἰανάτηρ ('brother's wife'). In some epitaphs, kinship terms appear in the nominative throughout; in others, the accusative is consistently preferred, and sometimes we find a mixture of the two.[39]

ἐτείμησεν/ἐτείμησαν is not used on statue bases of this type: the verb is generally omitted altogether. Elsewhere in the Hellenistic world, inscriptions associated with private honorific statues typically name one or two family members of the honorand, almost always from his/her immediate nuclear family unit (parents, siblings, spouses, children: Ma 2013a, 155–239).

[37] E.g. *TAM* II 370 (Xanthos), a small funerary altar, where the honorand is described as ἥρωι (line 10).

[38] Robert, *Hellenica* VI, 94–8.

[39] Nominatives: e.g. *TAM* V 1, 210, 379. Accusatives: e.g. *I.Manisa* 521, 524. Mixture: e.g. *SEG* 40, 1044; *I.Manisa* 525.

The choice of one or the other 'grammatical perspective' was not entirely random. In describing cross-generational kinship relationships, there seems to have been a general preference for marking the elder generation: so the terms for 'grandfather/-mother' are far more common than the terms for 'grandson/-daughter'. Furthermore, individuals seem always to have tended to gravitate towards the most precise kinship term available. As we will see in Chapter 4, the inhabitants of Roman Hieradoumia had a very rich and specialized kinship terminology for different categories of uncle and aunt (the mother's brother, the father's brother, the father's brother's wife …), but no distinct terms for the nephew and niece. Hence when an uncle chose to honour his deceased nephew, he almost always opted to use the nominative (Γλύκωνα ἐτείμησεν Μᾶρκος ὁ πάτρως, 'Marcus, the uncle, honoured Glykon'), while when a nephew chose to honour his deceased uncle, he generally opted to use the accusative (Γλύκωνα ἐτείμησεν Μᾶρκος τὸν πάτρως, 'Marcus honoured Glykon, his uncle').[40] In cases where the terminology would have been equally precise either way (e.g. siblings, cousins), the choice between the two possible grammatical perspectives seems to have been more or less arbitrary.

It is very difficult indeed to say what determined the length of the list of relatives in any given text (although, as we have seen, there is a distinct concentration of longer texts in the western half of the region). At the village of Nisyra, in autumn AD 120, a certain Hipponeikos was commemorated by his mother and his brother alone; at the same village, in winter AD 183, a boy called Dionysios, who died nine days short of his tenth birthday, was commemorated by his father and mother, brother and sister, paternal uncle, maternal aunt, two unspecified kinsmen, grandfather, maternal uncle, six slaves, four friends, and three foster-parents.[41] Can we conclude from this that Hipponeikos lived in a tight-knit nuclear family and that Dionysios belonged to a sprawling multigenerational household? Or simply that Dionysios' family was

---

[40] So in *TAM* V 1, 625 (Daldis), nephews and nieces indicate their relationship with the deceased with the accusative τὸν πάτρως … τὸν μήτρως (lines 8–10), while his uncles and aunts use the nominative οἱ μήτρως … [ἡ τ]ηθεῖς (lines 13–14). The various Greek terms for 'uncle/aunt' appear *c.* 120 times in Hieradoumian epitaphs, while the Greek terms for 'nephew/niece' are effectively absent altogether (only six certain examples, plus perhaps an uncertain number of ἀδελφιδεῖς, relatives 'through the brother': see Chapter 4, Section 4.5).

[41] *TAM* V 1, 431 (Hipponeikos) and 433 (Dionysios): βιώσαντα ἔτη ι΄, παρὰ ἡμέρας θ΄. For this 'sentimental precision', see Robert, *OMS* V, 312–14; *TAM* V 3, 1780 (an adult woman); likewise e.g. *SEG* 43, 817 (Ephesos), *IG* V 1, 801 (Sparta), *SEG* 26, 1193 (Rome) (small children in each case).

rich, and Hipponeikos' family was poor? It is better to confess that we simply do not know.

Nor can we be certain in any given case that the list of relatives honouring the deceased represents the complete register of those to be found around the family dinner table on Sundays (as it were). On occasion, the deceased is honoured by very small children, who cannot conceivably have been conscious actors in the commemorative process.[42] In at least two instances, individuals listed among those honouring the deceased were demonstrably already dead themselves (!).[43] In some cases, all the honouring relatives are recorded by name; in others, large parts of the family are listed in summary form, as in an epitaph for a brother and sister (perhaps twins) from Nisyra, who were commemorated by the brother's two children, the woman's husband and son, 'their paternal uncles and paternal aunts, their cousins, their foster-siblings, their relatives, their private association, and their homeland'.[44] In very many inscriptions, however, long or short the list of named kinsmen may have been, the register of those honouring the deceased is rounded off with a general summary phrase such as '... and all the relatives, acting in common' (καὶ οἱ συγγενεῖς πάντες κατὰ κοινόν), apparently a catch-all formula for those relatives who are not listed by name.[45] All this

---

[42] *TAM* V 2, 841 (Yeniceköy), erected by a one-year-old girl; *TAM* V 1, 105 (Saittai), a twenty-year-old mother honoured by her husband and infant son; *SEG* 39, 1280 (Saittai), a father honoured by, among others, a son less than three years old.

[43] *SEG* 52, 1165 (uncertain provenance), ἐτίμησαν οἱ υἱοὶ ... ἡ νύνφη καὶ οἱ προάξαντες ὑπὸ ζόφον εἰερόνεντα; *SEG* 55, 1286 (uncertain provenance), Ἄφφιον Ἀνδρέαν τὸν ἑαυτῆς ἄνδρα ζήσαντα ἔτ(η) μ', ἐνοῦσα καὶ αὐτή, ἐτείμησε (see Petzl 2010). Cf. also perhaps *TAM* V 1, 494 (*SGO* I 04/22/03: Hamidiye), τειμὴν ἔλαβα ὑβὸ πατρός, [κ]εῖμαι δαὶ μετὰ αὐτοῦ, although here the father could merely be indicating his intention to be buried in the same tomb.

[44] *TAM* V 1, 434 (*SGO* I 04/20/01, Nisyra): οἱ πάτρως καὶ ἑ πάτραι, οἱ ἀδελφιδεῖς, οἱ σύντροφοι, οἱ συγγενεῖς, ἡ συνβίωσις, ἡ πατρὶς ἐτείμησαν.

[45] καὶ οἱ συγγενεῖς πάντες κατὰ κοινόν: e.g. *SEG* 56, 1293 (Hierokaisareia); sometimes in the form καὶ οἱ λοιποὶ συγγενεῖς, 'and the other relatives', as in *TAM* V 1, 725 (Gordos), and frequently. For the phrase κατὰ κοινόν, cf. e.g. *SEG* 29, 1164 (Gölmarmara); *I.Manisa* 427 (Daldis?); *I.Manisa* 521 and 525 (Apollonioucharax). The family is sometimes described with the noun ἡ συγγένεια: *TAM* V 1, 824 (Kömürcü); *I.Manisa* 533 (Daldis: a line missing from the transcription), καὶ ἡ συγγένεια ἐτείμησαν κατὰ κοινόν. In an inscription from Kavakalan (*TAM* V 1, 777 [*SGO* I 04/10/04]), nine individuals are described collectively as οἱ ἴδιοι καὶ προσήκοντες; it is not clear whether these two terms carry distinct meanings (e.g. 'consanguines and affines'?). For the phrase οἱ προσήκοντες, cf. *TAM* V 2, 1341 (Hyrkanis), οἱ προσήκοντες μητρόθεν γένους σου, 'belonging to your family on the mother's side'; cf. *TAM* V 1, 625 (Daldis), οἱ πατρὸς καὶ μητρὸς συγγενεῖς. Foster-kin (θρεπτοί, σύντροφοι) were not considered to be part of the συγγένεια: e.g. *I.Manisa* 292 (Saittai: οἱ ἴδιοι vs. οἱ σύντροφοι), *TAM* V 1, 777 (Kavakalan: οἱ ἴδιοι καὶ προσήκοντες vs. ὁ σύντροφος), *TAM* V 2, 1062 (Thyateira: οἱ συγγενεῖς vs. τὰ θρέμματα); *TAM* V 1, 626 (Daldis: οἱ συγγενεῖς vs. τὰ τεθραμμένα).

makes it difficult or impossible to use the funerary epigraphy of Roman Hieradoumia as hard statistical evidence for the size and shape of the extended family in the region: the list of named relatives provided in any given text seems not to have been governed by any firm rules or norms, but simply to have reflected the whim of the particular family concerned.

Nonetheless, the mere fact that we have so many epitaphs from the small towns and villages of Roman Hieradoumia listing so many members of the deceased's extended family and social circle is a significant and profoundly startling social phenomenon in its own right. Nowhere else in the Greek-speaking world (with the partial exception of late Hellenistic Rhodes) did people choose to commemorate their kin in this remarkable manner – why did they do so here? As we will see in Chapter 4, this commemorative habit in fact goes hand-in-hand with a far richer and more precise terminology of kinship than we find anywhere else in the Greek world. Hieradoumian funerary practices in the first three centuries AD therefore reflect a culture in which kinship relations were not just more visibly commemorated, but were actually *more finely defined*, than in any other part of the Roman Empire. And as I will argue in Chapters 5 and 6, although Hieradoumian epitaphic practice does not allow us to 'see' familial structures in a direct and straightforward way, recurring patterns in the ways in which extended kin groups chose to commemorate themselves can nonetheless tell us a very great deal about the characteristic forms of familial groups in the region.

2.4 Familial Epitaphs in Roman Hieradoumia: 'Honour'

A final distinctive feature of Hieradoumian epitaphs is the conception of the tombstone as an 'honour' paid by living relatives to the deceased, as seen most clearly in the ubiquitous epitaphic formula ὁ δεῖνα ἐτείμησεν τὸν δεῖνα, '*x* honoured *y*', a usage which is almost entirely confined to Hieradoumia and immediately neighbouring regions.[46] This 'honour' was primarily conceived as residing in the erection of an inscribed *stēlē* to mark the place of burial, rather than the act of formal burial *per se*. This is made

---

[46] The same usage is also found in neighbouring regions of north-west Phrygia, particularly the Upper Tembris valley: Robert, *OMS* II, 1344–6; *Hellenica* VI, 92; *BE* 1971, 603.

explicit in a few cases, as for instance in a verse epigram for a youthful doctor from Saittai[47]:

τὸν νέον εἰητῆρα | κασιγνήτη Διόφαν|τον
τείμησε στήλ|λῃ ξεστῇ κὲ γράμ|(5)μασι τοῖσδε
Τειμα|ῖς κὲ τῆσδε πόσις | Πραξιανὸς ἀμύμων.

The young doctor Diophantos – his sister Teimais honoured him with a carved *stēlē* and with this inscription, as did her husband, blameless Praxianos.

Several Hieradoumian epitaphs lay particular emphasis on the making and erection of the *stēlē* as the primary honour conferred on the dead, by singling out those relatives who took on the specific responsibility for the construction of the funerary marker. So, for instance, in a verse epitaph from the village of Iaza in the Katakekaumene (Figure 2.8), the deceased was 'adorned and buried' by all his (unnamed) kin and 'honoured with a *stēlē* and noble inscription' by his (named) foster-father and wife:[48]

ἐνθάδ' ἐγὼ κεῖμαι Τρόφιμος ὁ τραφεὶς | εἰς ἄστυ Γολοίδων
κἀμὲ κάλυψε γῆ | ὡς Μοῖρ' ἐπέκλωσ' ἐν Ἰάζοις·
τὸν ἴδιον | κόσμησαν ἔθαψαν ἅπαντες,
τεί|(5)μησαν δ' ἄρ' ἐμὲν στήλῃ καὶ γράμ|μασι σεμνοῖς
θρεπτὸν ἐὸν Χροίσα[ν]|θος, ἄνδρα Ἑρμιόνη τὸν ἑαυτῆς.|
τοῦτο γέρας θνητοῖς, μνήμη δὲ | ἐώνιός ἐστιν.
ἔτους τζι', | (10) μηνὸς Ἀρτεμισίου.

Here I lie, Trophimos, who was reared in the city of Kollyda, and the earth covered me in Iaza, as Fate assigned. All my kin adorned and buried me, their kinsman; and Chrysanthos honoured me, his *threptos*, with a *stēlē* and noble inscription, as did Hermione, for her husband. This is the honour (*geras*) due to the dead, and my memory is everlasting. Year 317 (AD 232/3), month Artemisios.

[47] *SEG* 29, 1203 (*SGO* I 04/12/05); cf. *SEG* 27, 785 (uncertain provenance, ἐτείμησεν στήλλῃ); *SEG* 40, 1065 (Saittai: τείμης γράφες = ἐτείμησε γράφαις); *TAM* V 1, 96 (Saittai: ἐτείμησαν ... στήλλῃ μαρμαρίνῳ); *Sammlung Tatış* 36 (uncertain provenance, στήλλῃ τίμησέ με τῆδε); *TAM* V 3, 1896 (*SGO* I 04/24/14, Philadelphia: βωμῷ τειμήσας). The metaphorical τειμή of a funerary monument was of course undesirable: *TAM* V 1, 550 (*SGO* I 04/22/04, Maionia), ἐτείμησαν ἐμὲν ἣν οὔποτε ἤλπισα τειμήν.

[48] *TAM* V 1, 475 (*SGO* I 04/19/04, Iaza). The relief depicts Trophimos with a staff in his left hand, leading two mules by the reins with his right hand; on mules in the region, Robert, *Hellenica* VI, 106–7. In *SEG* 31, 1020 (Saittai), the deceased's son-in-law is singled out as having made the *stēlē* himself (ὁ ποήσας τὴν στήλλην); likewise, in *TAM* V 1, 191 (Saittai), the son of the deceased constructed the tomb from his own resources ([κατ]εσκεύασεν τὸ ἡρῷ[ον ἐκ τῶν ἰδί]ων πόρων καὶ ἐτεί[μησεν]), while the rest of the family simply 'honoured' the deceased. Cf. also *TAM* V 1, 117 (Saittai: one individual singled out as having constructed the tomb); *TAM* V 1, 190 (Saittai: the *stēlē* erected by the deceased and her husband, with the rest of her family συντειμησάντων); perhaps also *TAM* V 2, 840B (Sarılar); *TAM* V 1, 682 (Charakipolis). Cf. *I.Ancyra* 287, a tombstone carved by a professional stonemason (λιθουῦργος) for his friend and his friend's wife.

Figure 2.8 Epitaph of Trophimos, from Ayazören (Iaza). *TAM* V 1, 475 (Manisa Museum).

A still more extreme example of conceptual separation of the burial proper from the 'honour' conferred by the inscribed *stēlē* derives from the city of Sardis where, at some point in the second century AD, a certain Apollophanes constructed a familial tomb for his deceased wife Antonia, for himself, and for other individuals specified in his will. The chief funerary inscription was inscribed on the front face of the tomb itself, which probably took the form of a monumental sarcophagus: 'Apollophanes son of Apollophanes, of the tribe Asias, constructed the memorial (τὸ μνημῖον κατεσκεύασεν) while still living for himself and for his deceased wife Antonia, daughter of Diognetos, etc'. But alongside this tomb structure, Apollophanes also set up a pedimental *stēlē* depicting his wife in low relief, with the simple inscription 'Apollophanes son of Apollophanes, of the tribe Asias, honoured her (ἐτείμησεν)'. This 'honorific' *stēlē* was only one element in a larger package of burial rituals, and its full significance would only have been apparent to the viewer in the context of the wider tomb complex: indeed, the *stēlē* did not even carry Antonia's name.[49]

Explaining *why* the inhabitants of a particular region might originally have adopted a given set of epitaphic formulae is necessarily going to be speculative (assuming that 'why' is even a meaningful question in this context). But the honorific 'colouring' of Hieradoumian epitaphs does strongly suggest that this epitaph type might have originated in a kind of 'generic transferral' of the conventions of civic honorific epigraphy. The notion that the form and language of Hellenistic inscribed honorific decrees might have influenced the shape of funerary commemoration in Hieradoumia is not as implausible as it might seem at first sight. Across large swathes of inland Asia Minor, the habit of inscribing (Greek-language) texts on stone begins only in the second or first century BC; in very many places, the *earliest* inscribed texts known to us are civic honorific decrees.[50] For many communities in inner Anatolia, the practice of inscribing written texts of any kind on stone may well have begun with 'public' honorific decrees, and only subsequently been extended to 'private' texts like tombstones, making the idea of generic transplantation of honorific conventions into the funerary sphere less peculiar than it might intuitively appear.

The argument for 'generic transferral' can in fact be made more strongly than this. Among the earliest inscribed texts from Hieradoumia, dating to the late Hellenistic and early Julio-Claudian periods, we find a distinctive and unusual group of hybrid public/private monuments which blur together the genres of 'civic honorific' and 'private epitaph'.[51] In this group of 'hybrid' monuments, elite individuals are honoured after their death both by the local *dēmos* and by their grieving relatives. This genre seems to have been particularly popular at the small towns of Loros and Gordos, neighbouring communities in the valley of the Kum Çayı (the ancient river Phrygios), between the mid-first century BC

---

[49] Herrmann 1959, 7–8; *Sardis* II 669–670.

[50] E.g. Apameia (*MAMA* VI 173 and *SEG* 61, 1140, with Bresson 2012); Akmoneia (Chin and Lazar 2020); Aizanoi (Günther 1975), Synnada (Wilhelm 1911, 54–61), Themisonion (Michel, *Recueil* 544, with Wilhelm 1921, 45–8); Sala/Apollonia (*SEG* 63, 990: attribution uncertain); see further Thonemann 2013b, 25–8. Several of these texts are in fact posthumous honorifics, as at Sala/Apollonia, Aizanoi and Synnada.

[51] The earliest example perhaps *TAM* V 1, 468b (*SGO* I 14/19/01: Iaza, *c*. 130 BC): the *stratēgos* Mogetes honoured by the *dēmos*; wife, mother, and brother mentioned in the accompanying epigram. Cf. also the early hybrid text *TAM* V 3, 1894 (*SGO* I 04/24/12, Yeşilova: perhaps first century BC).

and the mid-first century AD.[52] Here is a typical example, from Gordos, dated to spring AD 37[53]:

> [ἔ]τους ρ′ καὶ κα′, μη(νὸς) Ξανδικοῦ α′.
> ὁ δῆμος ὁ Ἰουλιέων Γορ-
> δηνῶν καὶ ὁ Λορην⟨ῶ⟩ν δῆ-
> μος ἐτίμησεν Νέωνα Μη-
> 5   τροφάνου.
>   *wreath*
> Μητροφάνης Νέωνα τὸν
> υἱόν, Ἀπφιας καὶ Μέναν-
> δρος τὸν ἀδελφόν, Θυνεί-
> της τὸν πενθεριδῆ, Ἀλκὴ
> 10 τὸν πρόγονον, Ἀρτεμίδω-
> ρος καὶ Ἀμμιας τὸν ἀδελ-
> φιδοῦν, οἱ συνγενεῖς καὶ
> οἰκέται χρυσῷ στεφάνῳ.

Year 121 [AD 36/7], day 1 of the month Xandikos. The *dēmos* of the Ioulieis Gordenoi and the *dēmos* of the Lorenoi honoured Neon son of Metrophanes. Metrophanes (honoured) Neon his son, Apphias and Menandros (honoured) their brother, Thyneites (honoured) his wife's brother, Alke (honoured) her step-son, Artemidoros and Ammias (honoured) their cousin (?), the kinsmen and slaves (honoured him) with a golden wreath.

These hybrid public/private monuments, which served simultaneously as a record of public honours and as a private tombstone, seem to be a local peculiarity of Hieradoumia (Figure 2.9). Naturally, monuments of this kind would only ever have been set up for members of the local elite.[54] But it is, I hope, fairly easy to see how they could have served

---

[52] *TAM* V 1, 701–705, 775; *SEG* 57, 1157 (Gölmarmara) and 1176; Ricl and Malay 2012, nos. 1 and 2 (*SEG* 62, 917–918). The earliest example dates to 45 BC (*TAM* V 1, 775), the latest to AD 76 (*TAM* V 1, 704). In each case, the *dēmos* had presumably voted some concrete posthumous honours to the deceased (a public funeral, bronze or marble portrait statues, a painted portrait, etc.): see also *TAM* V 1, 687–688 (posthumous honorific decrees from Gordos); on public funerals, Herrmann 1995, 195–7. See further Chapter 7, Section 7.3.

[53] *TAM* V 1, 702, found at Gördes; for the location of Loros, either near Tüpüler (immediately south-west of Gordos) or further downstream near Eğrit/Korubaşı, see Ricl and Malay 2012, 78–9; for the toponym, Petzl 2018. The precise scope of reference of the term *adelphidous* (lines 11–12) is unclear (see Chapter 4, Section 4.5): here it could signify 'cousin', 'nephew', or even conceivably 'step-brother'.

[54] Likewise, the earliest purely 'private' epitaphs from Hieradoumia are very clearly elite monuments: *SEG* 35, 1166 (*SGO* I 04/22/07, Maionia, late second or early first century BC); *SEG* 41, 1037 (*SGO* I 04/13/01, with Ma 2013b, 66–8: Yiğitler, late second century BC):

Figure 2.9 Epitaph of Neon, with posthumous honours conferred by the *dēmoi* of Iulia Gordos and Loros. *TAM* V 1, 702 (Gördes).

as a kind of 'intermediary stage' between Hellenistic civic honorific decrees and the ordinary sub-elite familial epitaphs of Roman-period Hieradoumia.

Various other elements of Hellenistic honorific practice similarly became 'fossilized' in the Roman-period funerary epigraphy of the region. On the most formal level, the use of the tapered pedimental *stēlē* as the typical form of gravestone in Hieradoumia – rather than (say) the sarcophagus, *bōmos*, *cippus* or doorstone – may well have been

Πατροκλείδης Ἀττάλου Ἀσκληπιάδην τὸν γαμβρὸν κα[ὶ] Στρατονίκην τὴν ἀδελφὴν φιλοστοργίας ἕνεκεν τῆς πρ[ὸς αὐ]τούς, χαίρετ[ε], 'Patrokleides son of Attalos (honoured) his brother-in-law Asklepiades and his sister Stratonike, for the sake of his affection towards them, farewell', followed by a twelve-line epigram. Although the verb ἐτείμησεν does not appear in the Yiğitler text, the 'accusative of the deceased' and 'nominative of the honourer' are already present.

Figure 2.10 Epitaph of Servilius, from Gordos. *TAM* V 1, 705 (Gördes).

influenced by the widespread usage of pedimental *stēlai* for the inscribing of honorific decrees in the Hellenistic period. Perhaps most striking
of all is the vegetal wreath which we find depicted on the overwhelming
majority of Hieradoumian grave-*stēlai*, either incised or (more often)
in low inset relief. This iconographic feature is certainly a direct imitation of the visual repertoire of Hellenistic inscribed honorific decrees,
which often feature schematic depictions of vegetal wreaths, reflecting
the common practice of crowning civic benefactors with gilded wreaths.
On the funerary *stēlai* of Roman Hieradoumia, the Hellenistic 'honorific wreath' takes on a complex and baroque visual life of its own: we
find wreaths integrated into abstract decorative patterns (Figure 2.10);
wreaths with a portrait of the deceased at their centre, looking out as if
through a circular window (Figure 2.11); and giant, intricately carved
wreaths with the entire epitaph inscribed within (Figure 2.12).[55]

---

[55] Abstract patterns: *TAM* V 1, 705 (Gordos, AD 57/8). Wreath surrounding portrait of the
     deceased: *TAM* V 1, 13 (Aktaş, AD 94/5). Wreath surrounding the epitaph: *TAM* V 1, 823

Figure 2.11 Epitaph of Oinanthe, from Aktaş. *TAM* V 1, 13 (Uşak Museum).

It is a delicate question whether the wreaths depicted on Roman-period Hieradoumian epitaphs should be understood as reflecting a 'real-life' practice of honouring the dead with wreaths, or whether this is simply a conventional visual shorthand for the respectful grief felt by relatives for the deceased. In favour of the first hypothesis, we can point to a substantial cluster of Hieradoumian epitaphs in which the standard verb of 'honouring' is expanded to the more explicit phrase 'honour *x* with a golden wreath' (τειμᾶν χρυσῶι στεφάνωι), as in the epitaph for Neon of Gordos quoted above.[56] When Greek cities honoured their benefactors with public

(*SGO* I 04/07/02: Kömürcü, AD 241/2). This last type is closely paralleled in a painted tomb inscription at late antique Sardis (*Sardis* II 693); the date alone is sometimes inscribed inside the wreath, as in e.g. *SEG* 57, 1154 (Taşkuyucak, AD 184/5 or 238/9). Note also *TAM* V 1, 682 (Charakipolis), the epitaph of a married woman, in which the wreath surrounds a depiction of a wool basket, as if it were the woman's domestic virtues being honoured.

[56] Explicit mention of family members honouring the deceased with a 'gilded wreath': *TAM* V 1, 775 (Loros: 46/5 BC); *SEG* 57, 1176B (Loros, AD 5/6); *TAM* V 1, 13 (Aktaş, AD 94/5), οἱ συγγενεῖς καὶ φίλοι πάντες ἐτείμησαν χρυσοῖς στεφάνοις; *TAM* V 1, 470a (Iaza, AD 96/7); *SEG* 57, 1175 (Iaza, AD 164/5); *TAM* V 1, 483a (Iaza, undated: a minimum of twelve gilded wreaths).

Figure 2.12 Epitaph of Hesperos, from Kömürcü. *TAM* V 1, 823 (Bursa Museum).

burial in the late Hellenistic period, the funerary honours conferred by the *dēmos* often included a golden or gilded wreath, which was placed on the deceased in the course of his/her funeral;[57] this practice probably underlies the incised wreaths surrounding the words ὁ δῆμος ('the *dēmos*') which often appear on late Hellenistic funerary *stēlai* from Smyrna and other parts of western Asia Minor.[58] In an early Hieradoumian-type epitaph from Saittai, a woman explicitly says that she has wreathed her husband 'with the

---

[57] Cic., *Flacc.* 75; Günther 1975 (Aizanoi, 49/48 BC); *I.Smyrna* 515 (*SGO* I 05/01/38: second century BC); Debord and Varinlioğlu 2001, 108–10, no. 4 (Pisye); Herrmann 1995, 196–7. In *I.Priene²* 67, lines 290–293 (decree for Krates, shortly after 90 BC), it is envisaged that Krates will be wreathed with a golden wreath at his funeral (ὅταν δὲ μεταλλάξῃ τὸν β[ίον], στεφα[νῶσαι] αὐτὸν [ἐπὶ τῆς ἐκφορᾶς στεφάνωι χρυσέωι]), and that anyone else who wishes will be permitted to add their own wreath ([ἐξεῖναι δὲ καὶ ἐπὶ τῆς ἐκφορᾶς τῶν] λοιπ[ῶν τὸν β]ουλόμενον στεφανοῦν Κράτητα).

[58] Robert, *OMS* III, 1411; Zanker 1993, 214; Herrmann 1995, 196 n.34. In Hellenistic Hieradoumia, note e.g. *SEG* 33, 1004 (Yiğitler, late second century BC: Chapter 1 above, Figure 1.6): epitaph of a cavalryman with four wreaths in inset relief, each 'conferred' by a different local *dēmos*; *TAM* V 1, 700 (Gordos: first century BC?), with Robert, *Hellenica* VI, 89–91: posthumous honours for a married couple, with seven incised wreaths associated with different parts of the citizen body, no doubt reflecting wreaths conferred at a public funeral. For public funerals in Roman-period Hieradoumia, cf. *Sammlung Tatış* 36 (uncertain provenance): the 'whole *polis*' participates in the funeral of a three-year-old (πᾶσα πόλις δὲ θανόντα προπέμψατο).

Figure 2.13 Votive dedication to Hekate, from Menye. *TAM* V 1, 523 (Manisa Museum).

wreath depicted above'; on a late Hellenistic gravestone from Maionia, a relief depiction of the deceased and his parents is surrounded by four small holes, probably for fixing a metal wreath to the front of the *stēlē*.[59]

All this seems strongly to imply that the wreaths depicted on Hiera-doumian grave-*stēlai* represent real wreaths employed in funerary ritual. But some caution is required, since vegetal wreaths, either incised or in low relief, also appear in monumental contexts where we can be pretty certain that no 'real-life' wreaths were involved. Most notably, we have several examples of votive dedications to various deities inscribed on pedimental *stēlai* bearing images of vegetal wreaths (Figure 2.13).[60] In no case is there

[59] *SEG* 57, 1212 (Saittai: late Hellenistic): ἐστεφάνωσεν τῷ προκιμέν[ῳ] στεφάνῳ (which I take to mean the wreath 'lying before' the inscription on the *stēlē* itself); *SEG* 35, 1166 (SGO I 04/22/07, Maionia).

[60] *TAM* V 1, 523 (*SGO* I 04/22/01: Hekate: Maionia, second century AD; here, Figure 2.13); Malay and Petzl 2017, nos. 16 (Zeus Kananeirenos: 149/8 or 148/7 BC), 30–31 (Meter Anaeitis: early imperial), 39 (Meter Anaeitis and Meis Tiamou: 3/2 BC); 211 (Theos Hypsistos: early imperial). Cf. also *I.Manisa* 176 (genre unclear).

any indication that the votive *stēlē* serves even incidentally to 'honour' persons either alive or dead. The conclusion seems inescapable that on these votive dedications, we are dealing with an irrational transferral of a standard decorative schema into an epigraphic genre where it *no longer bears any representational meaning.* We therefore cannot rule out the possibility that on some, or many, of the hundreds of tombstones which bear an image of a wreath, the same may be true.

2.5 Propitiation-*stēlai* in Roman Hieradoumia: Overview

To turn from the epitaphs of Roman Hieradoumia to the propitiation-*stēlai* erected at the rural sanctuaries of the region is not just to move from one genre of evidence to another; it is to enter what appears to be a completely different moral universe. On their tombstones, in formulaic prose or sober and dignified verse, the peasants and small farmers of the region showed off the impeccable virtues of the deceased, and the honour dutifully paid to them by the large and tight-knit familial units to which they belonged. Yet when one opens the pages of Georg Petzl's extraordinary corpus of *Die Beichtinschriften Westkleinasiens* ('The confession-inscriptions of Western Asia Minor', almost all of which derive from Roman Hieradoumia), one is instantly plunged into a colourful world of theft, sexual promiscuity, impiety, witchcraft, and interpersonal violence, much of it conducted *within* those very same tight-knit family groups which represented themselves with such grave decency in their epitaphs.[61]

The sense of wild disjunction between the Dr Jekyll of the epitaphs and the Mr Hyde of the propitiatory inscriptions is only heightened by the remarkably close physical and formal similarities between the two epigraphic genres. In both cases, we are typically dealing with small tapering white marble *stēlai* with triangular pediments topped with palmette acroteria, often with a sculptured image in low relief at the top of the shaft; both categories of text typically begin or end with a date, in the format Year – Month – Day. The *stēlai* were evidently produced by the same workshops, and it looks very much as though the region's lapidary workshops produced generic 'blanks', which could be used equally for tombstones or for propitiatory inscriptions (or other dedications or votives).

What actually is a 'propitiatory inscription'? In the most schematic terms, it is an inscribed *stēlē* erected in a sanctuary, bearing a narrative

---

[61] Petzl 1994, with the supplement in Petzl 2019.

Figure 2.14 Propitiatory inscription of Claudia Bassa. *SEG* 33, 1012 (Petzl 1994, no. 12).

of a private moral or religious transgression which was subsequently punished by the gods (typically in the form of the death or illness of the perpetrator or a family member). The text usually goes on to narrate the way in which the perpetrator propitiated the god's anger (generally by the very act of inscribing and erecting the *stēlē* itself); many texts conclude with a short eulogy of the god's power. Here are two fairly characteristic examples, from a rural sanctuary of 'Zeus from the Twin Oaks' on the territory of ancient Saittai (Figures 2.14 and 2.15):

Διὶ ἐγ Διδύμων Δρυῶν· Κ. Βάσσα κο-
λασθῖσα ἔτη δ' καὶ μὴ πιστεύους-
α τῷ θεῷ, ἐπ⟨ι⟩τυχοῦσα δὲ περὶ ὧ-
ν ἔπαθα, εὐχαριστοῦσα ⟨σ⟩τήλλην
5   ἀνέθηκα, ἔτους τλη′, μη(νὸς) Περιτίου ηι′.

To Zeus from the Twin Oaks. I, C(laudia) Bassa, having been punished for four years and having no faith in the god, having been successful concerning my sufferings, I dedicated the *stēlē* in gratitude, Year 338 [AD 253/4], day 18 of the month Peritios.[62]

μέγας Ζεὺς ἐ⟨γ⟩ Δεδύμων
Δρυῶν· Ἀθήναιος κολασ-
θεὶς ὑπὸ τοῦ θεοῦ ὑπὲρ
ἁμαρτείας κατὰ ἄγνοι-
5   αν ὑπὸ ὀνείρου πολλὰς
κολάσεις λαβὼν ἀπητή-
θην στήλλην καὶ ἀνέγρα-
ψα τὰς δυνάμις τοῦ θεοῦ.
εὐχαριστῶν ἔσστηλο-
10   γράφησα ἔτους τμη′,
μη(νὸς) Αὐδναίου ηι′.

Great is Zeus from the Twin Oaks! I, Athenaios, was punished by the god on account of my error, because I was unaware; and having received many punishments, I had a *stēlē* demanded of me in a dream, and I wrote up the powers of the god. I inscribed the *stēlē* in gratitude in Year 348 [AD 263/4], day 18 of the month Audnaios.[63]

---

[62] Robert 1987, 364–7 (*SEG* 33, 1012; Petzl 1994, no. 12); it is not clear whether Bassa's 'lack of faith' is conceived as the original cause of her punishment. The relief sculpture above the text depicts (I assume) Bassa herself at top right, placing an uncertain object (incense?) on a small altar; the bearded male figure at top left, carrying a wreath in his right hand, is presumably a priest (likewise in Figure 2.15); the two smaller figures with raised right hands in the lower register perhaps represent the 'crowd' who witnessed Bassa's public propitiation at the sanctuary (see Chapter 10, n. 94). The imagery is strikingly disconnected from the textual content of the inscription; I do not know what the ritual significance of the gesture above the altar or the priestly wreath-bearing might have been.

[63] Robert 1987, 360–4 (*SEG* 33, 1013; Petzl 1994, no. 11). On the phrase 'because I was unaware' (κατὰ ἄγνοιαν), see further below. The specification that the order to erect a *stēlē* was delivered in a dream is atypical, but compare Petzl 1994, no. 1 (the god appears to Meidon 'in his sleep'); Petzl 1994, no. 106 (the god appears in a dream); perhaps Petzl 2019, no. 143; Potts 2019, 100. The 'angel' who delivered the commands of Meis Axiottenos (Petzl 1994, nos. 4 and 38; Cline 2011, 60–5) may well have done so in dreams.

Figure 2.15 Propitiatory inscription of Athenaios. *SEG* 33, 1013 (Petzl 1994, no. 11).

As will be clear, a fair amount of variation is possible even between near-contemporary texts from the same sanctuary (which are probably the work of the same stonemason, at that). Physically, one has a pediment, the other does not; one begins with an acclamation of the deity ('Great is Zeus!'), the other with the name of the deity in the dative (indicating that the *stēlē* is formally a dedication *to* the god); one bears an account of the god's 'demand' for a *stēlē* by way of propitiation ('I had a *stēlē* demanded of me'), the other does not – and so on. In light of this pervasive variation in form and structure, it is unclear how hard a line we can legitimately draw between these 'propitiatory *stēlai*' (a category which is, after all, a modern scholarly construct) and other votives and dedications from Roman Hieradoumia. Take, for instance, the following dedication from the sanctuary of Zeus from the Twin Oaks, dated around a generation earlier than the two texts quoted above (Figure 2.16)[64]:

μέγας Ζεὺς ἐγ Διδύ-
μων Δρυῶν Ποπλιανῷ
παρέστη καὶ ἀπήτησεν
αὐτὸν στήλλην, ἣν ἀπο-
5   δίδει μετὰ τῆς συνβίου
εὐλογῶν καὶ εὐχαρισ-
τῶν τῷ θεῷ. ἔτους σϘ-
δ', μη(νὸς) Ἀπελλαίου.

Great Zeus from the Twin Oaks appeared to Poplianos and demanded a *stēlē* of him, which he gives along with his wife, with praise and gratitude to the god. Year 294 [AD 209/10], in the month Apellaios.

Formally speaking there is very little indeed to distinguish this monument from the *stēlai* of Claudia Bassa and Athenaios quoted above: their physical form is extremely similar; the god 'demands' a *stēlē* from Poplianos in a dream, exactly as he would later do for Athenaios; all three dedicators speak of their 'gratitude' (εὐχαριστέω) to the god; all three texts end with the date of erection of the *stēlē* in the format Year – Month – Day.[65] In short, the category of propitiatory inscriptions is a 'fuzzy concept': a fairly easily recognizable subgroup within the larger category of Hieradoumian votive and dedicatory *stēlai*, characterized by certain loose affinities of theme (a concern with divine punishment and propitiation), but lacking hard definitional boundaries.[66]

[64] *SEG* 57, 1224; for the generic similarity to propitiatory inscriptions from the sanctuary, Chaniotis, *EBGR* 2007, 300, no. 66.

[65] Likewise, one might compare the propitiatory *stēlē* of Claudia Bassa with e.g. *TAM* V 1, 455 (Kula): [θεῷ ἐπηκ]όῳ Μηνὶ Ἀξιτη|[νῷ Τ]ροφιμος εὐξάμε|[νος] καὶ ἐπιτυχὼν εὐχα|[ρισ]τῶν ἀνέθηκα. |(5) [ἔτους ..., μ]η(νὸς) Δίου βι', 'To Meis Axiottenos, the god who listens; I, Trophimos, made a vow and was successful, and I dedicated this in gratitude. Year [-], Day 12 of the month Dios'. Both Bassa and Trophimos speak in sequence of their 'success' (ἐπιτυγχάνω), 'gratitude' (εὐχαριστέω), and 'dedication' of the monument (ἀνατίθημι)

[66] Further examples of marginal cases abound (Chaniotis 2009a, 117–18; Potts 2017). There is little distinction between Malay and Petzl 2017, no. 53 (a man is cured from illness, is grateful, and makes a dedication to Artemis Anaeitis and Meis Tiamou) and Malay and Petzl 2017,

Figure 2.16 Votive dedication of Poplianos. *SEG* 57, 1224 (collection of Yavuz Tatış, Turkey, inv. 2122).

2.6 Propitiation-*stēlai* in Roman Hieradoumia: Structure

As one would expect, the textual structure of the propitiatory inscriptions varies a great deal. Nonetheless, some standard (or at least recurrent) features can be identified. The inscriptions often begin with a short acclamation of the god to whom the *stēlē* was erected, in the form 'Great is Meis Artemidorou who possesses Axiotta and his power!'.[67] The 'narrative' part of the text frequently begins with the conjunction ἐπεί, 'since, whereas', a feature which is otherwise almost unknown in Greek votive and dedicatory inscriptions, and

no. 55 (Petzl 2019 no. 154: a woman is punished in her eyes, is saved, is grateful, and makes a dedication to Artemis Anaeitis and Meis Tiamou). Conversely, one might quibble about the classification of *TAM* V 1, 453 (Petzl 1994, no. 61) which features neither transgression nor punishment; or *SEG* 53, 1344 (Petzl 2019, no. 56), in which a man praises Meis at length for rescuing him from imprisonment at the hands of his nephew.

[67] Petzl 1994, no. 79: μέγας Μὶς Ἀρτεμιδώρου Αξ[ιο]ττα κατέχων καὶ ἡ δύναμις αὐτοῦ. The basic form is completely standard for Greek acclamations of deities: Chaniotis 2009b, 203–6; Potts 2019, 105.

which presumably should be taken as an imitation of the typical structure of Greek honorific decrees ('Since *x* has been a good man …'). The texts then proceed through a set of four fairly conventional 'narrative stages', not all of which are found in all inscriptions[68]:

(1) Almost all of the texts begin with at least some minimal description of the act which incurred the gods' wrath. In many cases, only context-specific vocabulary is used ('I swore a false oath'; 'I entered the sanctuary while in a state of ritual impurity'; etc.), but when the action is described in generic terms, the most common word used is (ἐξ-)ἁμαρτάνω, 'err', and the act itself is a ἁμαρτία or ἁμάρτημα, 'error'.[69] *Hamartia* is one of the most controversial terms in Greek ethical vocabulary, but it is widely accepted that the term does not connote 'sin', so much as a 'mistake of fact', a broad concept which may in Greek thought encompass both moral failing and ignorance of the true state of affairs.[70] Similarly, in Roman Hieradoumia, *hamartia* is demonstrably conceived primarily as an act of 'ignorance' rather than 'sin'. This is clear from the terms used as synonyms for ἁμαρτάνω: we regularly find people describing their actions in terms of 'unawareness' (ἀγνοέω) or 'forgetting' (λανθάνομαι).[71] This does not signify that they did not know that they were doing anything wrong, but rather – or so I take it – that they were 'unaware' of the gods' willingness to impose fearful punishments for what they themselves conceived as venial rule bending.[72]

[68] For various views on the number of discrete narrative stages in the propitiation inscriptions (three, four, six), see Belayche 2012, 321. On the vocabulary, de Hoz 1999, 114–24.

[69] ἁμαρτάνω and cognates appear in some seventeen texts in total: Petzl 2019, 77 and 81, Index *s.v.* ἁμαρτάνω, ἁμάρτημα, ἁμαρτία, ἐξἁμαρτάνω.

[70] The bibliography is vast: e.g. Bremer 1969; Stinton 1975; Belfiore 1992, 166–70.

[71] 'Unawareness': Petzl 1994, no. 10 (Stratoneikos cut down a sacred oak 'because he was unaware', διὰ τὸ ἀγνοεῖν αὐτόν); no. 34 (Hermogenes swore a false oath 'being unaware', ἀγνοήσας); no. 76 (Aur. Stratoneikos cut trees from a sacred grove 'in unawareness', κατὰ ἄγνοιαν); Petzl 2019, no. 155 (Trophimos laid hands on something 'in unawareness', κατὰ [ἄγ]νυαν). 'Forgetting': Petzl 1994, no. 6 (Pollio 'forgot' and crossed a boundary when impure, με ἔλαθεν); no. 112 (Eutychis entered the sanctuary when impure: 'I forgot', λημόνησα); no. 115 (a person 'forgot' and entered when impure, ἔλαθέ [με]). The concepts of *hamartia* and 'unawareness/forgetting' are sometimes combined: so in Petzl 1994, no. 11 (quoted above), Athenaios was punished 'on account of my error, because I was unaware' (ὑπὲρ ἁμαρτείας κατὰ ἄγνοιαν); in no. 95, Ammias was punished 'on account of her error, having spoken a word and having been forgetful' (δι' ἁμαρτίαν λόγον λαλήσασ[α] καὶ λαθαμένη – apparently a false oath).

[72] Chaniotis 1997, 360 (followed by Gordon 2004, 193; also Chaniotis 2004a, 24–6) takes these terms to be mitigating considerations introduced by the guilty parties to minimize their culpability (i.e. an insistence that they 'did not realise what they were doing'); this seems to me less likely (I do not see how one could be unaware one was swearing a false oath). See further Potts 2019, 114–22.

(2) The act of *hamartia* is then followed by a description of the divine punishment, again sometimes described with context-specific vocabulary ('the god slew him/her'), but most commonly indicated with the verb κολάζω and/or the noun κόλασις, or with the near-synonyms νεμεσάω and νέμεσις.[73] In light of this punishment, the perpetrator of the 'error' is compelled to acknowledge the power of the gods. The term used for this is ἐξομολογέομαι, 'recognise/acknowledge (the gods' power)', and the 'recognition' generally follows close after the act of punishment. The term ἐξομολογέομαι has in the past often been taken to mean 'confess (one's sin)', but this is certainly incorrect: the sense 'acknowledge the power of the gods' is explicit in one case, and in other texts, this sense is clearly preferable to 'confess'.[74]

(3) The gods then typically demand propitiation or redress, sometimes in response to a direct enquiry from the perpetrator as to what he/she needs to do to appease the gods' anger.[75] The technical term for the 'demand' made by the gods is ἐπιζητέω, sometimes with the form of redress explicitly specified (e.g. ἐπεζήτησε ὁ θεὸς στήλην, 'the god demanded a *stēlē*'); a few texts use instead a clause introduced by the verb κελεύω.[76] The act of propitiating or appeasing the god is indicated with the verb (ἐξ-)ἱλάσκομαι, in place of which we occasionally find the verb (ἐκ-)λυτρόομαι, 'pay a ransom', particularly in cases where the act of propitiation involves a payment of

[73] κολάζω/κόλασις appear in some 94 texts; for νεμεσάω/ νέμεσις, see Petzl 1994, nos. 3, 15, and 59; that the terms are effectively synonyms emerges from Petzl 1994, no. 57, ἐκολάσετο αὐτήν … καὶ ἐκέλευσεν στηλλογραφηθῆναι νέμεσιν, 'he punished her … and ordered her to inscribe the punishment on a *stēlē*'.

[74] 'Acknowledge the power of the gods': Petzl 2019, no. 146, ἐξομολογούμενον τὰς δυνάμις τῶν θεῶν. In Petzl 1994, no. 111, ἐξομολογοῦμε κολασθεὶς ὑπὸ τοῦ θεοῦ means effectively 'I recognise that I was punished by the god'. For other examples, see Petzl 1994, nos. 3, 43, 109, 112, 116; Petzl 2019, no. 144. The verb is mistranslated by Petzl as referring to 'confession' (e.g. Petzl 1994, no. 3, ἐξωμολογήσατο, 'er tat ein Geständnis'), followed by many others (e.g. Belayche 2008, 181; Rostad 2020, 8). People do occasionally 'admit' to a criminal act in the propitiatory inscriptions, but the verb used is always ὁμολόγεω (Petzl 1994, nos. 68, 100, 106; Petzl 2019, no. 141). For the terms ὁμολόγεω and ἐξομολογέομαι, see further Potts 2019, 28–41.

[75] Indicated with the verb ἐρωτάω (9 texts): see, most explicitly, Petzl 2019, no. 146, ἐρωτῶντες τοὺς θεοὺς … ἵνα ἐλέου τύχωσιν, 'asking the gods … so that they might be pitied'.

[76] Petzl 2019, no. 125. The verb ἐπιζητέω is used in some 33 texts, with various different constructions (but always with the god as the implied subject: Belayche 2012, 330); it sometimes takes the 'error' as its direct object, as in Petzl 1994, no. 4, ἐπεζήτησεν … τὸ ἁμάρτημα, 'demand (propitiation for) the error' (similarly Petzl 1994, no. 40). The verb can be used in the passive, of a person who 'has redress demanded of them', as in e.g. Petzl 1994, no. 89 ([ἐπ]ειζητηθεῖσα ἀνέθ[ηκεν]); in a few cases, the verb is active in form but apparently passive in meaning, as in Petzl 1994, no. 75 (ἐπιζητήσασα ἀν[έθ]ηκεν), and probably in nos. 73 and 74 (ἐπεζήτησεν ἱεροπόημα, which I take to mean that the perpetrator 'had a ritual offering demanded of him').

cash or other goods to the deity.[77] The most common form of propitiation is the simple act of erecting an inscribed *stēlē*, often described with a phrase like 'writing up on a *stēlē* the power of the gods' (στηλ(λ)ογραφῆσαι τὰς δυνάμεις τῶν θεῶν).[78]

(4) Finally, texts often conclude with an expression of 'gratitude' to the gods (usually with the verb εὐχαριστέω), and/or a statement that in future the perpetrator and his family 'will praise the gods from now on' (ἀπὸ νῦν εὐλογοῦμεν and similar). The idea of 'bearing witness' (μαρτυρέω) to the gods' powers appears in the concluding lines of several texts; at the sanctuaries of Apollo Lairbenos and Zeus from the Twin Oaks, this act of 'bearing witness' is expressed in a standardized formula, 'I proclaim that no-one should despise the god, since s/he will have this *stēlē* as an exemplar' (παραγγέλλω μηδένα καταφρονεῖν τοῦ θεοῦ, ἐπεὶ ἕξει τὴν στήλην ἐξεμπλάριον).[79]

There is clearly some room for debate about what the 'central' function of these texts might be, depending on whether we choose to lay the emphasis on the original transgressive act ('confession-inscriptions'); the propitiation of the gods' anger ('propitiation-inscriptions'); or the act of praising and bearing witness to the gods' power ('exaltation-inscriptions'). To my mind, the accent ought to lie firmly on the latter two aspects, not the first. The transgression itself often not mentioned at all, or is described in only the vaguest of terms – sometimes no more than the simple statement that 'I erred' (ἡμάρτησα).[80] As we have seen, the concept of 'confession' is seldom explicitly articulated in these texts, and it is far from clear that the texts reveal any real conception of 'sin' or 'sinfulness'. No less important,

---

[77] The verb (ἐξ-)ἱλάσκομαι appears in some 21 texts; for the verb λυτρόομαι and cognates, see Petzl 1994, p.XI; Chaniotis 1997, 373; Chaniotis 2004a, 37–8; that straightforward cash payments were sometimes involved is clear from e.g. Petzl 2019, no. 133, where the λύτρον is divided equally between the gods, the village community, and the priests. A 'successful' propitiation is sometimes marked with the verb ἐπιτυγχάνω.

[78] Sometimes the act of erecting the *stēlē* is emphasized, with the verb (ἀν-)ίστημι, 'set up', or ἀνατίθημι, 'dedicate'; sometimes the act of writing is highlighted, with the verb ἐγγράφω or (more often) στηλ(λ)ογραφέω (thirty-two instances).

[79] 'Bearing witness': e.g. Petzl 2019, no. 159, εὐχαριστῶ Μητρὶ Θεῶν Λαρμηνῇ καὶ μαρτυρῶ αὐτῇ τὰς δυνάμεις, 'I am grateful to Meter Theon Larmene and I bear witness to her powers'; likewise Petzl 1994, nos. 8, 17, and 68. 'I proclaim … exemplar': e.g. Petzl 1994, nos. 106–7, 109–112, 117, 120–121; Petzl 2019, no. 150 (Apollo Lairbenos); Petzl 1994, nos. 9 and 10 (Zeus from the Twin Oaks). The word ἐξεμπλάριον is a Latin loan-word. Broadly similar in function is the 'proclamation-formula' in Petzl 2019, no. 146, μή τίς ποτε παρευτελίσι τοὺς θεούς, 'Let no-one ever belittle the gods!'.

[80] No transgression mentioned: Petzl 1994, nos. 38, 41, 51, 53, 75, 83–4, 89, 94; Petzl 2019, nos. 125, 133, 147, 154, 156, 169. Vague references to 'error': Petzl 1994, nos. 11, 24, 66 (ὑπὲρ ὧν ἁμαρτοῦσα ἐπέτυχεν), 73, 74 (ἐπεὶ ἡμάρτησεν … ἐπεζήτησεν ἱεροπόημα), 109.

the generalizing statements with which the texts conclude – the 'lessons learned', if you like – only very seldom refer back to the details of the transgression.[81] Instead, the take-home messages generally focus solely on the appropriate attitude to be adopted towards the gods and their powers: 'I proclaim that no-one should despise the god'; 'I shall praise the god from now on'; 'I have written up the powers of the god on a *stēlē*'. These formulaic phrases strongly suggest that the problem was not so much the original transgression itself, but rather the underlying contempt for the gods that these transgressions demonstrated.

It therefore seems to me – and I am certainly not the first to say so – that to call these texts 'confession inscriptions' is positively misleading. It focuses on a relatively incidental part of the narrative (the description of the original transgression which revealed the perpetrator's contempt for the gods); it also introduces inappropriately Christianizing categories ('sin' and 'confession') which are largely absent from the texts themselves. The point of these texts is rather to bear witness to the power of the gods (as manifested in the punishment) and to encourage readers to adopt an appropriately respectful attitude towards the gods and their powers. Several modern scholars have therefore preferred to refer to the texts as 'propitiatory inscriptions'; although I am not sure this quite captures their primary function, it is certainly better than the alternative, and I have no appetite for inventing yet another name.[82]

2.7 Propitiation-*stēlai* in Roman Hieradoumia: Chronology and Geography

Given the difficulty of drawing clear dividing lines between propitiatory inscriptions and other private votives and dedications, it would be somewhat misleading to tabulate the chronological distribution of propitiatory inscriptions alone. Figure 2.17 therefore gives the overall distribution over time of all dated 'private' religious texts from Hieradoumia (propitiatory inscriptions, votives, dedications: n = 219). Sixty-one of these dated texts are classed as 'confession-inscriptions' by Petzl and are indicated in dark

---

[81] For exceptions, see *TAM* V 1, 179b (Petzl 1994, no. 10): 'I proclaim that no one should belittle the god's powers and cut an oak' (παραγγέλω δὲ, αὐτοῦ τὰς δυνάμις μή τις κατευτελήσι καὶ κόψει δρῦν); Petzl 1994, nos. 27 (no one should swear unjust oaths), 110; Petzl 1994, no. 123 (no one should eat goat meat that has not been offered in sacrifice).

[82] See e.g. Belayche 2008, 181, 193; Chaniotis 2009a, 116–18; Gordon 2016, 227 n.2; Hughes 2017, 151; Rostad 2020, 8–9.

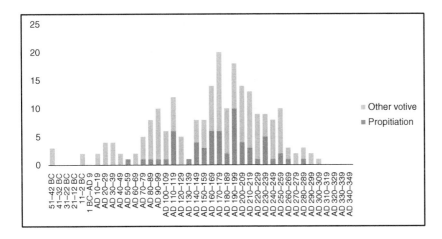

Figure 2.17 Chronological distribution of dated propitiatory inscriptions and other private religious texts from Hieradoumia and neighbouring regions (n = 219).

grey. As one might have hoped, the overall distribution is pleasingly similar to that of dated epitaphs from the region (compare Figure 2.7 above). We see the same paucity of dated private religious inscriptions in the late republican and Julio-Claudian periods (40s BC–60s AD); as with dated epitaphs, we see a sharp rise in the Flavian period (70s–90s), a peak in the later Antonine and early Severan periods (160s–190s), and a dramatic drop-off in the second half of the third century, with production of dated propitiatory and other private religious *stēlai* ending around AD 300; 87.2% of the dated propitiatory inscriptions and other private religious texts from the region (n = 191) date to the two centuries between AD 70/1 and AD 269/70; the comparable figure for epitaphs is 90.3%.

It will quickly be seen that the distribution of propitiatory inscriptions is broadly in line with that of other private religious texts, at least in the second and third century AD. However, the genre does not really emerge until the turn of the first/second century AD. The two earliest dated texts in Petzl's corpus of 'confession-inscriptions' are both in fact generically 'marginal' cases. The earliest dated text (AD 58) is an extended series of acclamations of Meis Axiottenos, with a narration of the help provided by the god in freeing the dedicator from custody; no 'error' or propitiation is involved.[83] The next dated text (AD 72) is the only known propitiatory inscription in verse (five elegiac couplets); the content fits well into the main run of propitiatory inscriptions (a man vows to erect a *stēlē* if he recovers from illness, fails to do

[83] *SEG* 53, 1344 (Petzl 2019, no. 56), with Chaniotis 2009a, 115–21, on the text's genre.

so, has further tortures imposed on him, and finally dedicates a more lavish *stēlē*), but the idiosyncratic use of verse may suggest that the generic 'norms' of propitiatory *stēlai* were not yet fully established.[84] We should probably see the later Julio-Claudian and Flavian periods as a transitional phase, during which the regionally specific Hieradoumian practice of monumentalizing acts of propitiation was gradually emerging out of older and more conventional votive and dedicatory practices. I will offer a tentative explanation for this chronology in the final pages of Chapter 9 below.

When we turn to look at the geographic distribution of propitiatory *stēlai*, we find some interesting similarities and differences with the distribution of the Hieradoumian-style familial epitaph. The geographic 'core zone' of both epigraphic practices is identical: the middle Hermos valley between Satala in the west and Tabala in the east, with dense concentrations of relevant texts on the left bank of the Hermos in the Katakekaumene (Maionia, Kollyda, and the villages to the north: Map 3) and on the right bank of the Hermos in the large territories of Saittai and Silandos (Map 2). By my count, 138 of the 175 texts in Petzl's corpus (78.9%) can be certainly or very plausibly attributed to this 'core zone'.[85] A further seven texts derive from closely neighbouring regions: one from Buldan, south-east of Philadelphia near Apollonia–Tripolis, and six from Sardis.[86] Eight monuments derive from various parts of western and central Phrygia, but in each case, their classification as propitiatory *stēlai* is questionable at best.[87] Twenty-one of the remaining twenty-two texts derive from the remote rural sanctuary of Apollo Lairbenos, some distance to the south-east of the main Hermos cluster, on the left bank of the Maeander in the modern Çal ovası (Map 1).[88] One final outlier is said to derive from Akçaavlu, in the upper Kaystros valley north-east of Pergamon; but since the text refers to a cult of Zeus Trosou, a deity whose sanctuary is known to have been located near the sanctuary of Apollo Lairbenos at modern Akkent, it is quite possible that this *stēlē* has 'migrated' northwards from the Çal ovası in modern times.[89]

---

[84] Malay and Petzl 2017, no, 188 (Petzl 2019, no. 171).

[85] Petzl 1994, nos. 3–97; Petzl 2019, nos. 125–142, 144–149, 154–172. This count includes fifteen texts from the territory of Philadelphia (Petzl 1994, nos. 83–97), almost all of them dedications to Meter Phileis, whose sanctuary was located near Killik on the northern flank of the Kogamos valley, on the fringe of the Katakekaumene (Malay 1985; *TAM* V 3, 1557–1618).

[86] Petzl 1994, no. 98 (Buldan); nos. 99–101 and Petzl 2019, 173–175 (Sardis).

[87] Petzl 1994, nos. 2, 102–105; Petzl 2019, nos. 151–153. Only two of these texts refer to 'punishment' (nos. 104 and 151) and none describe acts of propitiation.

[88] Petzl 1994, nos. 106–124; Petzl 2019, nos. 143 and 150.

[89] Petzl 1994, no. 1 (*I.Manisa* 55); for the sanctuary of Zeus Tros(s)ou at Akkent, see Akıncı Öztürk, Baysal and Ricl 2015.

Two features of this geographic spread are of particular interest. First, the total *absence* of propitiatory texts from the westernmost part of the Hieradoumian culture zone, west of the Demrek (Demirci) Çayı: we have not a single propitiatory inscription (and, for that matter, very few votive and dedicatory texts of any kind) from the territories of Gordos, Loros, Daldis, or Charakipolis, all of which have produced substantial numbers of Hieradoumian-type epitaphs. Second, the *presence* of a substantial group of propitiatory *stēlai* from the rural sanctuary of Apollo Lairbenos, far to the south-east of the main Hieradoumian culture zone, located in a region which has produced no epitaphs of the distinctive Hieradoumian type. There is nothing particularly disturbing about these geographic 'mismatches': it would, indeed, be startling if the spatial distribution of two distinct groups of cultural artefacts *ever* mapped onto one another with absolute precision. It is worth noting that the 'outlying' group of propitiatory inscriptions from the sanctuary of Apollo Lairbenos does in fact show some minor but consistent differences from the 'main' Hieradoumian group: none of the *stēlai* from the sanctuary of Apollo Lairbenos bear dates, and none of them include acclamations of the deity.

In short, the distribution of propitiatory *stēlai* in both time and space, while not identical to that of Hieradoumian-type epitaphs, is certainly close enough to suggest that the two monumental practices can usefully be treated as different aspects of a single distinctive regional culture.

2.8 Epitaphs and Propitiations: Towards a Cultural History of Roman Hieradoumia

This final point can in fact be pushed one step further. As we have seen, in formal terms, there are very strong overlaps between the propitiatory inscriptions and the epitaphs of Roman Hieradoumia: their physical form is more or less indistinguishable (pedimental *stēlai* with a decorative feature on the upper part of the shaft), and both categories of text typically begin or end with a date in the form Year – Month – Day. But the affinities between the two groups of texts in fact go further than that. One of the most striking recurrent features of the propitiation-*stēlai* is the conception of the immediate family unit as a single 'moral entity' which bore collective responsibility for the errors of its members. When an individual committed a *hamartia*, his or her closest relatives were considered to be implicated in the act in various ways: the god's punishment often fell not on the perpetrator, but on one or more close kinsmen or -women, and it was very often other family members who ended up performing the formal act of propitiation (sometimes, but not always, after the perpetrator's death). Here, for example, is a propitiatory *stēlē* from a sanctuary of Meis Labanas and Meis Petraeites (almost certainly at the village of Pereudos), in which divine vengeance fell on the perpetrator's son and granddaughter, who are depicted alongside the penitent man in the relief panel (Figure 2.18)[90]:

μέγας Μεὶς Λαβανας καὶ Μεὶς
Πετραείτης. ἐπὶ Ἀπολλώνιος
οἰκῶν ἐ⟨ν⟩ οἰκίᾳ τοῦ θεοῦ παραν-
γελλομένῳ αὐτῷ ὑπο τοῦ θε-
5   οῦ, ἐπὶ ἠπίθησεν, ἀπετελέ-
σετο αὐτοῦ Εἰούλιον τὸν υἱὸν
καὶ Μαρκίαν τὴν ἔκγονον αὐτοῦ,
καὶ ἐστηλογράφησεν τὰς δυνά-
μ⟨ις⟩ τῶν θεῶν, καὶ ἀπὸ νῦν συ
10   εὐλογῶ.

Great are Meis Labanas and Meis Petraeites! Since Apollonios – when a command was given to him by the god to reside in the house of the god – (5) when he disobeyed, (the god) slew his son Iulius and his grand-daughter Marcia, and he inscribed on a stele the powers of the gods, and from now on (10) I praise you.

This collective responsibility seems generally not to have extended very far within the family group. We have no examples of persons being punished for the sins of their uncles or aunts, brothers-in-law, or sisters-in-law. Instead, as is clear from a glance at Table 2.1, divine punishment generally fell either on the perpetrator or on his/her children alone; we have single instances of punishment being extended to the perpetrator's father, daughter-in-law, son-in-law, and granddaughter, and a solitary example where the perpetrator's 'whole household' was made 'close to death'.[91] It may be significant that we have no certain cases of a

---

[90] *SEG* 35, 1158 (Petzl 1994, no. 37): perpetrator at left, granddaughter at centre, son at right, all making the same gesture (raised right hand), which presumably represents acknowledgement of the god's power. The *stēlē* lacks a firm provenance, but the gods Meis Labanas and Meis Petraeites are known to have been worshipped together at Pereudos (*SEG* 34, 1219). For Apollonios' refusal to 'reside in the house of the god', see Chapter 8, Section 8.5.

[91] 'Whole household … close to death': *TAM* V 1, 179b (Petzl 1994, no. 10), with Chaniotis, *EBGR* 2004, 98 (*SEG* 53, 1505): ὁ θεὸς … αὐτὸν κατέθηκεν ὁλοδουμε⟨ὶ⟩ ἰσοθανάτους; for a possible link between this text and the Antonine Plague, see Chapter 3, Section 3.6. In a couple of instances (Petzl 1994, nos. 34 and 113), punishment fell on the perpetrator's livestock. Clearly collective responsibility is not at issue here; I take it that livestock were regarded as 'extensions' of a man or woman's person just as his/her children were, but as (say) his/her brother generally was not.

Table 2.1 Persons said to have been punished for a relative's *hamartia* in Hieradoumian propitiatory inscriptions

Petzl no.	Perpetrator	Person(s) punished (*killed*)	Person(s) depicted on relief
1994, no. 10	Male	Perpetrator and 'whole household'	Perpetrator
1994, no. 62	Female	Father	Victim
1994, no. 7	Male (?)	Son	Perpetrators and victim
1994, no. 64	Male	Two sons	None
1994, no. 69	Female	*Perpetrator and son*	None
2019, no. 127	Male	*Son and daughter-in-law*	None
1994, no. 37	Male	*Son and granddaughter*	Perpetrator and victims
1994, no. 34	Male	*Daughter, ox and donkey*	None
1994, no. 45	Male	Daughter	None
2019, no. 168	Female	Daughter	None
1994, no. 71	Male	Female relative	None
2019, no. 160	Male	Female relative	None
1994, no. 28	Male (?)	Son-in-law (?) and others (?)	None
1994, no. 113	Male	Ox	None

Figure 2.18 Propitiatory inscription of Apollonios. *SEG* 35, 1158 (Ödemiş Museum).

spouse or a sibling being punished: the underlying conception seems to
be that divine anger tends, as a general rule, to travel 'vertically down-
wards' within the perpetrator's family lineage. In fact, this fits rather nicely
with wider local conceptions of the 'heritability' of guilt: epitaphs from
Roman Hieradoumia (and other parts of inland Asia Minor) often include
a curse-formula stating that the gods' anger will pursue tomb robbers 'to
their children's children', and in a propitiatory inscription from the village
of Perkon, a penitent man likewise claims to have 'appeased the gods, to
my children's children and my descendants' descendants'.[92] As it happens,
we have no examples of foster-children (*threptoi*) being punished for their
foster-parents' transgressions, but we do find the children of two women
who have committed a *hamartia* of some kind collectively propitiating the
goddess 'on behalf of their children and foster-children', indicating that it
was seen as a realistic possibility that the goddess' anger might fall on either
their natural children or their *threptoi*.[93]

When it came to the propitiation of the gods, we find a somewhat wider
range of family members taking on responsibility for appeasing the gods'
wrath, although still very seldom extending far beyond the immediate
nuclear family group: the evidence is collected in Table 2.2.[94] Once again,
the perpetrator's sons and daughters are by far the most heavily represented,
although we also find spouses, siblings, grandchildren, foster-children,
and – in a case where the offenders seem to have been children – parents.[95]

The underlying conception of the workings of divine punishment and
propitiation is not in itself distinctive: as readers of Greek tragedy will be
well aware, the concepts of 'ancestral fault' and 'inherited guilt' had a long

---

[92] Curse-formula (εἰς/διὰ τέκνα τέκνων and similar): Robert, *Hellenica* XIII, 96–7; Robert, *OMS*
V, 282–3; Strubbe 1994, 73–83; Thonemann 2019, 131. Appeasement: *SEG* 39, 1279 (Petzl
1994, no. 6: AD 239), lines 19–21: ἱλασάμην τοὺς θεοὺς διὰ τέκνα τέκνων, ἔγγον' ἐγόνων.

[93] *TAM* V 1, 322 (Petzl 1994, no. 70, with addendum in Petzl 2019, p.19): εἱλασαμένυ ... ὑπὲρ
τέκνων καὶ θρεμμάτων, where (*pace* Petzl) the term θρέμμα must mean 'foster-child', not 'livestock'. In *SEG* 38, 1229 (Petzl 1994, no. 4), two *tethrammenai* propitiate the god for a *hamartia*
committed by their foster-father.

[94] In the fragmentary text *TAM* V 1, 180 (Petzl 1994, no. 13) at least four family members are
involved in some way (a man, his mother, his wife, and his sister). Several brothers seem to
be associated in both transgression and propitiation in the fragmentary *TAM* V 1, 527 (Petzl
1994, no. 80); cf. *TAM* V 1, 466 (Petzl 1994, 28: several brothers, perhaps in the context of an
inheritance dispute); *SEG* 54, 1225 (Petzl 2019, no. 125: two sisters). The family relationships
in *SEG* 41, 1039 (Petzl 1994, no. 38) cannot be determined.

[95] Parents: *SEG* 37, 1737 (Petzl 1994, no. 22); it is not clear whether the perpetrators (a boy and
a girl) are siblings. 'Underage' persons did not set up their own propitiatory *stēlai*: note *SEG*
37, 1000 (Petzl 1994, no. 58), in which a husband propitiates the god for his wife's false oath,
'because she was not yet of age' (μήπω οὖσα ἐνῆλιξ).

Table 2.2 Persons responsible for seeking appeasement on a relative's behalf in Hieradoumian propitiatory inscriptions

Petzl no.	Perpetrator	Person(s) responsible for appeasement	Person(s) depicted on relief
1994, no. 8	Unknown	'The family' (*syngeneia*)	None
1994, no. 22	Male and female	Parents	None
1994, no. 9	Male	Son	None
1994, no. 46	Male	Three sons	None
1994, no. 74	Female	Son	None
2019, no. 135	Female	Son	None
1994, no. 39	Male	Perpetrator and son	None
1994, no. 24	Male	Son and two grandsons (by a different son)	None
2019, no. 142	Male	Son and daughter's daughter	None
1994, no. 54	Male	Daughter	None
2019, no. 143	Male	Daughter and son	None
2019, no. 151	Female	Perpetrator and daughter	None
1994, no. 70	Two females	Daughters and sons	Perpetrators (breasts/leg)
1994, no. 36	Female	Heirs (*klēronomoi*)	None
1994, no. 69	Female	Daughter's daughter and her three brothers	None
1994, no. 44	Female (and her *threptos*)	Grandson	None
1994, no. 58	Female	Husband	None
1994, no. 102	Female	Husband	None
2019, no. 141	Male	Wife	Perpetrator (leg)
1994, no. 15	Male	Wife	None
1994, no. 68	Male	Wife, child and brother 'with the children'	None
1994, no. 34	Male	Wife (?), three sons and one daughter	None
1994, no. 72	Male	Brother	None
1994, no. 18	Male	Brother, heirs, brother-in-law (?)	Perpetrator
1994, no. 4	Male	Two foster-daughters (*tethrammenai*)	Perpetrator

prehistory in Greek thought.[96] What is unusual and striking is the decision of so many Hieradoumian families to place all the mortifying details of these familial catastrophes on public display, at what was no doubt a serious cost to familial honour. In short, just as with the familial epitaphs of Hieradoumia,

---

[96] E.g. West 1999; Sewell-Rutter 2007; Gagné 2013, especially 22–54 (theological justifications offered by Proclus and Plutarch); the Hieradoumian material offers a rare opportunity to observe the belief system in practice.

the propitiatory inscriptions of the region also served as a form of *familial self-representation*, underlining in both words and images – even in this most reputationally damaging of contexts – the solidarity of the family unit as the basic 'building-block' of Hieradoumian rural society.

As will by now be abundantly clear, the propitiatory inscriptions of Roman Hieradoumia are of immense value for our understanding of religious mentalities, ritual practices, and (thanks to their extensive descriptions of divine 'punishments') the social history of illness in Roman Asia Minor. Over the past generation or so, the texts have attracted a large body of first-rate scholarship coming from one or more of these perspectives.[97] For us, though, the primary interest of these texts lies elsewhere, in their status as a highly localized cultural epiphenomenon, the product of a particular rural society located very precisely in space (the middle Hermos valley) and time (the first three centuries AD). Indeed, as we have seen, one of the most remarkable things about the propitiatory inscriptions is how closely they map on to the geographic and chronological contours of the Hieradoumian 'familial' epitaphic habit. The two monumental genres can usefully be treated – as they will be in this book – as the two halves of a local diptych, speaking to us about a single, largely rural village culture. Put crudely, the epitaphic half of the diptych tells us about *social norms*: the ways in which individuals, families, and corporate groups wished ideally to be seen and remembered by their peers. The accent throughout is on honour, sentiment, familial and corporate solidarity, and the exemplary virtues of the deceased. The propitiatory half of the diptych tells us about moments of *social dysfunction* – moments when a member of Hieradoumian rural society has deliberately or (less often) inadvertently transgressed that society's collective norms. The epitaphs reflect the mechanisms of *solidarity* within peasant society; the propitiatory texts give us a series of brief but sometimes brilliant glimpses into the subterranean *tensions* of that society, when the interests of one family member rub up hard against those of another, or when one household ends up locked in a vendetta with another, or when an individual chooses to put him- or herself at odds with the wider community. Neither aspect of Hieramounian culture – neither the static nor the dynamic – can be properly understood without the other.

---

[97] The bibliography is ample (Petzl 2019, 4–7). I have learned most from Belayche 2006, 2008, 2012; Chaniotis 1995, 1997, 2004a, 2004b, 2009a, 2012; Hughes 2017, 151–86; Petzl 2011a; Potts 2019 (the best discussion of confessional practices in the wider Greco-Roman world); Rostad 2020. For the propitiatory inscriptions as evidence for the local cultural history of Roman Hieradoumia, see in particular Petzl 1995; Ricl 2003; Gordon 2004; Gordon 2016 (these last two of particular quality and interest). To the best of my knowledge the propitiatory *stēlai* have never been systematically set in dialogue with the region's epitaphs.

In the chapters that follow, I shall attempt to trace the outlines of the society that produced these two remarkable bodies of cultural artefacts. This society was, I will argue, a fundamentally *kin-ordered* one, in which laterally and vertically extended kin groups played a central role in the organization of social life. The forms and functions of kinship in Roman Hieradoumia will be described in three lengthy chapters (Chapters 4–6), dealing in turn with kinship terminology, household structure, and the circulation of children between households ('fosterage'). In Chapter 7, we will look at the extra-familial corporate groupings (friends and neighbours, cultic and trade associations, political communities) who appear alongside kin groups in commemorative contexts. Chapter 8 turns to the role played by the village sanctuaries of Hieradoumia in the organization of rural society, with a particular focus on land and labour. Chapter 9 draws on the narratives recorded in the propitiatory *stēlai* to evoke some of the inter- and intra-familial dynamics of village life in Roman Hieradoumia. Chapter 10 attempts to draw some of these threads together into a coherent picture of the social structure of Hieradoumia in the first three centuries AD. Before all that, though, we ought to begin with a few words about the region's underlying demographic regime.

3 | Demography

3.1 Epitaphs and Mortality in Roman Hieradoumia

The epitaphs of Roman Hieradoumia provide us with a magnificent body of data for the study of mortality patterns in inland western Asia Minor during the first three centuries AD. Thanks to the habitual recording of the date of death in the form Year – Month – Day (Chapter 2, Sections 2.1 and 2.2), we are able to chart the overall seasonality of death in the region with some confidence. Since age at death is often recorded and since the sex of the deceased is almost always known, it is possible to break down this seasonal mortality pattern by sex and age. Finally, unexpected 'bulges' in the distribution of epitaphs over time potentially allow us to discern large-scale mortality events, such as plagues and pandemics.

Virtually, all dated Hieradoumian epitaphs indicate the month of death. Throughout the region, the twelve months of the year are usually designated with the standard Macedonian month names (Dios, Apellaios, Audnaios, Peritios, Dystros, Xandikos, Artemisios, Daisios, Panemos, Loos, Gorpiaios, and Hyperberetaios); in a handful of epitaphs, the month is numbered rather than named ('Month 1', 'Month 2', etc.). The day of the month is specified in around four-fifths of cases. The first twenty days of the month are usually designated simply 'Day 1' to 'Day 20'; the first day of the month ('Day 1') is occasionally described as the 'New Moon' (*noumēnia*) and is rather more often given the name 'Sebaste'. The final day of the month is always called 'Day 30', and the penultimate day of the month is always called 'Penultimate' (Greek *protera*). The intervening days (Days 21–28 in 30-day months, Days 21–27 in 29-day months) are generally counted off with numerals descending from 'Day 10 Waning' to 'Day 3 Waning' (in 30-day months) or 'Day 9 Waning' to 'Day 3 Waning' (in 29-day months).[1]

We do not know for certain which calendar was in use in the towns and villages of Hieradoumia during the first three centuries AD. In 9/8 BC, an

---

[1] 'Waning' = ἀπιόντος or ἀπιούσῃ, usually abbreviated to ἀ() or ἀπι(); so μηνὸς Δίου ι′ ἀ. is 21 Dios, and μηνὸς Δίου γ′ ἀ. is 28 Dios (in a 30-day month) or 27 Dios (in a 29-day month).

official solar calendar was introduced for the Roman province of Asia, with New Year's Day on September 23 (Augustus' birthday). With the exception of Month I Dios (now renamed Kaisar), the twelve months of this new calendar continued to carry the old Macedonian month names. But each month was now assigned a fixed length (between 28 and 31 days), pegged to the Julian calendar, such that each Asiatic month began on the ninth day before the Kalends of a Julian month.[2]

However, as I have argued in detail elsewhere, the epitaphs of Roman Hieradoumia seem generally not to have been dated according to this solar 'calendar of Asia'.[3] Instead, there are strong reasons to think that the inhabitants of this region continued to use a lunisolar calendar throughout the Roman imperial period, with months of either 29 or 30 days determined by first observation (or, more likely, advance calculation) of the crescent moon.[4] If so, the inhabitants of the region must have inserted intercalary months on a regular cycle, in order to keep the calendar roughly in step with the solar year. This is most likely to have been the nineteen-year cycle employed by the Seleukid monarchy (intercalary Xandikos in years 3, 6, 8, 11, 14, and 19; intercalary Hyperberetaios in year 16), although there is no way of demonstrating this with certainty.[5] It would, of course, be immensely interesting to know whether this retention of a lunisolar calendar was a local peculiarity of Roman Hieradoumia, or whether the same was true in other parts of the Greek East; unfortunately, due to the near-total absence of precisely dated inscriptions from other parts of the Greek world in the Roman period, we simply have no way of knowing.

A further oddity in the Hieradoumian 'epitaphic calendar' deserves emphasis. Although there is no necessary reason to expect that dates of death should be evenly distributed *within* any given month (in principle, mortality could have been far higher in late July than in early July), any

---

[2] Laffi 1967; Stern 2012, 274–84.

[3] Thonemann 2015. I take the opportunity to note three errors in my catalogue of testimonia for the 'calendar of Asia' after 9–8 BC (125–9), kindly pointed out to me by Sacha Stern: T10, last line, for '19 July' read '20 July'; T12, second line, for '17 July' read '18 July'; T23, last line, for 'twenty-eighth' read 'twenty-ninth'.

[4] For an additional argument in favour of the continued use of a lunisolar calendar in Roman Hieradoumia (the significance of Day 12 in the cult of Meis), see further Section 3.3.

[5] Intercalary Xandikos in Hellenistic Lydia: *Sardis* II 603 (II/I BC), Ξανδικοῦ ἐμβολίμου ιγ΄; *Sardis* II 612 (I BC), ἐμβολίμο[υ Ξανδικοῦ] ζ΄ ἀπιόντος (the restoration of the month name seems guaranteed by the line-length); cf. *Sardis* II 595 (II/I BC), μηνὸς ἐνβολίμο[υ (*name*) (*numeral*)]. *TAM* V 2, 1094 (Thyateira, AD 233/4) is dated μη(νὸς) ε Ξανδικοῦ ζ΄; but Xandikos is in fact Month VI, not Month V, and it is therefore possible that we should understand μη(νὸς) ἐ(μβολίμου) Ξανδικοῦ ζ΄.

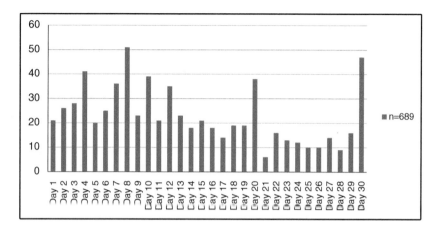

Figure 3.1 Frequency chart of attested days of death in Hieradoumian epitaphs
(n = 689).

given day of the month ought to be roughly equally represented across
the *entire* sequence of twelve months (since there is no reason to expect
that people systematically avoided dying on, say, the fifth of the month).
However, the dates recorded on Hieradoumian epitaphs in fact show a
strikingly uneven distribution across the 30 days of the month. This une-
venness is presented visually in Figure 3.1, a frequency chart of all known
attestations of the day of death in epitaphs from the region (689 data points
in total).[6]

The most striking feature of this chart is what appears to be the systematic
under-representation of dates between the 21st and the 29th of the month,
and the sharp over-representation of the 20th and 30th days of the month.[7]
As should be obvious, this 'avoidance' of Days 21–29, and 'favouring' of
Days 20 and 30, is exceptionally unlikely to reflect actual mortality patterns
(more people dying on the 20th and 30th days of the month *every month*?).
It hence seems likely that some 'date-rounding' tended to occur in the last

---

[6] The raw data (n = 689) is as follows: Day 1 (21), Day 2 (26), Day 3 (28), Day 4 (41), Day 5 (20),
Day 6 (25), Day 7 (36), Day 8 (51), Day 9 (23), Day 10 (39), Day 11 (21), Day 12 (35), Day 13
(23), Day 14 (18), Day 15 (21), Day 16 (18), Day 17 (14), Day 18 (19), Day 19 (19), Day 20 (38),
Day 21 (6), Day 22 (16), Day 23 (13), Day 24 (12), Day 25 (10), Day 26 (10), Day 27 (14), Day
28 (9), Day 29 (16), Day 30 (47). These figures are slightly different from those in Thonemann
2015, Fig. 2, since I have here included epitaphs antedating 9/8 BC, and epitaphs from Sardis
and Philadelphia. For the sake of simplicity, I have recorded all descending-count dates as if for
a 30-day month.

[7] As I have argued elsewhere (Thonemann 2015, 136), the particularly sharp under-
representation of Day 21 probably reflects the alternation of 29- and 30-day months in a
lunisolar calendar: this day would have been omitted in (roughly) every second month.

ten days of the month: that is to say, if an individual died on 22 Xandikos (μηνὸς Ξανδικοῦ θ′ ἀπιούσῃ), the date on his or her tombstone had a pronounced tendency to be 'rounded up' to 20 Xandikos (μηνὸς Ξανδικοῦ κ′).

However, this alone does not sufficiently account for the under-representation of dates between the 21st and the 29th of the month. It is possible that Days 21–29 had a greater than usual tendency to be recorded by month name alone: that is to say, if we imagine two individuals dying on the 12th and 22nd of the month Xandikos respectively, the tombstone of the first would tend to carry the full and accurate date μηνὸς Ξανδικοῦ ιβ′ ('12 Xandikos'), while that of the second would tend to carry simply μηνὸς Ξανδικοῦ ('Month Xandikos') rather than μηνὸς Ξανδικοῦ θ′ ἀπιούσῃ ('22 Xandikos'). Moreover, since certain days early in the month (especially Days 4, 7, 8, and 10) are distinctly over-represented in Hieradoumian epitaphs, one wonders whether 'descending-count' dates (Days 21–28) were from time to time inaccurately recorded as if they were in fact 'ascending-count' dates: that is to say, if an individual died on 23 Xandikos (μηνὸς Ξανδικοῦ η′ ἀπιούσῃ), the date on his or her tombstone may occasionally have been mis-recorded as 8 Xandikos (μηνὸς Ξανδικοῦ η′).

Be all that as it may, it is evident that many inhabitants of Roman Hieradoumia (or their stonecutters) were unaccustomed to or uncomfortable with using the ἀπιόντος/ἀπιούσῃ 'descending-count' formula for the days between the 21st and 29th of the month, and hence dates falling in that range were not always precisely recorded on epitaphs. We thus cannot be confident that the dates given on Hieradoumian epitaphs provide us with an accurate picture of mortality rates *within* any given month. In the remainder of this chapter, therefore, I shall be concerned solely with the month of death.

3.2 Seasonal Mortality in Roman Hieradoumia

Our evidence for the overall seasonal distribution of mortality in Hieradoumia in the late Hellenistic and early Roman imperial periods is summarized in Table 3.1. This table is based on a total dataset of 874 discrete indications of the month of death in epitaphs from Hieradoumia and neighbouring regions.[8] Since the inhabitants of western Lydia and western

---

[8] The dataset is somewhat larger than that used for Figure 2.7 in Chapter 2 (overall chronological distribution of Hieradoumian epitaphs, n = 781): several epitaphs dated to the month cannot be assigned with confidence to a particular year, due to uncertainty over the era in use.

Table 3.1 Monthly distribution of deaths in
Roman Hieradoumia and neighbouring
regions (n = 874)

Dios	93
Apellaios	87
Audnaios	76
Peritios	83
Dystros	49
Xandikos	71
Artemisios	47
Daisios	57
Panemos	64
Loos	73
Gorpiaios	86
Hyperberetaios	88
Total	(874)

Phrygia did not generally date their epitaphs, the dataset has fairly clear
'natural' boundaries to the west and east. The overwhelming majority of
data points derive from Hieradoumian epitaphs of the first three centuries
AD, but I have included three small clusters of texts deriving from towns
immediately to the west and south of our 'core' region: sixty-five late Hellenistic and early imperial dated epitaphs from Sardis, twenty-seven dated
epitaphs from Philadelphia, and nine dated epitaphs from the Kaystros valley. I have excluded dated Christian epitaphs of the fifth and sixth century
AD, which are at any event very few in number.[9]

As we saw in Section 3.1, the months of the Hieradoumian calendar
did not correspond precisely with the Julian months. Since the twelve
Hieradoumian months were lunar in character, they must have cycled
backwards and forwards *vis-à-vis* the Julian months year on year. Month
I Dios would generally have begun in the early autumn, in principle on
or around 23 September; as we have seen, there is some reason to think
that the months Xandikos and Hyperberetaios were intercalated on a regular nineteen-year cycle (six intercalations of Xandikos, and one intercalation of Hyperberetaios). In order to establish the actual seasonality
of death in Roman Hieradoumia, we therefore need to re-calibrate the
raw data to take account of these regular intercalations, since the months
Xandikos and Hyperberetaios will otherwise be over-represented in the

---

[9] E.g. *TAM* V 1, 227, 438; half a dozen epitaphs from Philadelphia dating to the sixth century
AD: *TAM* V 3, 1882–1887.

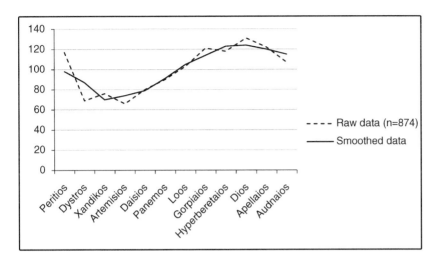

Figure 3.2 Seasonal mortality in Roman Hieradoumia, raw data re-calibrated for intercalary months (n = 874) and smoothed data (three-month moving averages).

proportions 25/19 and 20/19 respectively, compared to the other ten months of the year.[10]

Figure 3.2 is a visual representation of the data after re-calibration. The data for each month is presented as a proportion of the mean number of deaths per month across the entire year (=71.05 mean deaths p. m. after re-calibration): in other words, 100 on the y axis reflects the 'anticipated' number of monthly deaths in any given year. Figure 3.2 shows both the real monthly distribution of the re-calibrated raw data and the same data converted into three-month moving averages ('smoothed data'), in order to highlight the major patterns of seasonal change.[11] I have presented the months as running from Peritios to Audnaios, to mirror as closely as possible the familiar sequence January–December: in fact, Peritios runs roughly from late December to late January and Loos roughly from late June to late July, varying slightly year on year.

Figure 3.2 presents us with a pleasingly clear picture of a unimodal annual oscillation in overall mortality rates in Roman Hieradoumia: a sustained period of low mortality in late winter and spring (V Dystros to VIII

[10] The re-calibrated figure for Xandikos is 53.96 deaths per month; for Hyperberetaios, 83.60 deaths per month. This gives us a mean of 71.05 deaths per month allowing for intercalation.

[11] If the inhabitants of Roman Hieradoumia were in fact using the solar calendar of Asia introduced in 9/8 BC (which I do not believe to be the case), then the raw data would show a much sharper 'peak' in the month Xandikos, and no 'dip' in the month Hyperberetaios, but the overall shape of the graph would not be substantially altered.

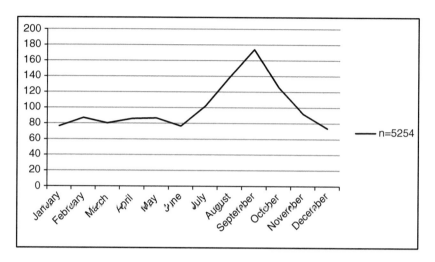

Figure 3.3 Seasonal mortality in late antique Rome (n = 5254), data courtesy of Kyle Harper.

Daisios, roughly late January to late May), and a period of elevated mortality in summer and autumn (X Gorpiaios to IV Peritios, roughly late July to late January), with peak mortality in early autumn (Dios, late September to late October).

This overall seasonal profile makes for illuminating comparisons and contrasts with those other parts of the Roman world for which we have good evidence for the contours of seasonal mortality. (In fact, it is worth emphasizing that the Hieradoumian dataset is our *only* substantial body of data illuminating seasonal mortality in the high Roman imperial period: other large datasets all derive from Late Antiquity.) By far the largest and best-known body of evidence derives from dated Christian epitaphs from the city of Rome between the fourth and sixth century AD, with a particular concentration in the latter half of the fourth century AD.[12] At Rome, as Figure 3.3 vividly illustrates, there was a similarly unimodal annual oscillation in mortality rates, with a very pronounced rise in mortality in the late summer and early autumn (August to October). The amplitude of variation between high-mortality and low-mortality months is considerably greater in late antique Rome than in first- to third-century Hieradoumia (a 'sharper' late summer peak), which no doubt reflects the far greater impact of infectious diseases in a densely settled urban area (Rome) as compared to a largely rural region (Hieradoumia). The particular pathogens at work in late

---

[12] Shaw 1996, esp. 115, Fig. 5; Harper 2015; Harper 2017, 81–4. Note also the smaller datasets collected and analysed by Shaw 2006.

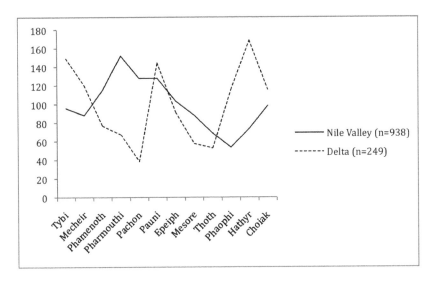

Figure 3.4 Seasonal mortality in Roman and Coptic Egypt and Nubia, raw data (source: Scheidel 2001b, 5, Table 1.1; 20, Table 1.4).

antique Rome have been much discussed: the formidable late summer peak at Rome points towards a cocktail of gastroenteric diseases (typhoid, dysentery) contracted through contaminated food and water, probably compounded by sporadic outbreaks of malaria in late summer and autumn.[13]

The Hieradoumian pattern shows both similarities and differences with that of late antique Rome. Mortality rates in Hieradoumia peaked at around the same time as in Rome (September), but they did not see the same sharp 'drop-off' in the autumn and winter months that can be observed in the data from Rome; in Hieradoumia, mortality rates remained elevated throughout October, November, and December.[14] Either the dominant pathogens in the middle Hermos valley were different or the seasonality of those pathogens differed.

The contrast is even sharper with seasonal mortality in Roman and Coptic Egypt and Nubia (Figure 3.4).[15] In the Nile valley, mortality rates rose sharply in the later spring months (April to June, a period when infectious diseases were particularly rife in the region), but declined in the autumn, with a mortality 'trough' in October, the very time when Hieradoumian

---

[13] On the impact of malaria, see e.g. Shaw 1996, 133; Sallares 2002, esp. 201–34; Scheidel 2003; Harper 2017, 84–8.

[14] Northern Italy in Late Antiquity seem to show a similar trend of continued elevated mortality through the autumn and early winter (Shaw 1996, 125–7).

[15] Scheidel 2001b, 4–10 (Nile valley), 19–25 (delta), 51–117 (determinants).

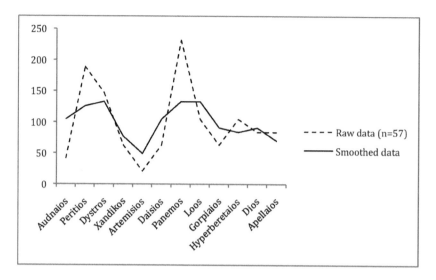

Figure 3.5 Seasonal mortality at Anazarbos, raw data (n = 57) and smoothed data (three-month moving averages).

mortality rates were at their peak. In the Nile delta, the pattern is different again: peak mortality occurs in late autumn and early winter (November to January), with a secondary early summer mortality spike (June), caused almost entirely by the deaths of children and teenagers.

Within the Anatolian peninsula, we have virtually no statistically meaningful dataset with which to compare the Hieradoumian evidence. The only other part of the peninsula to provide any kind of concentration of dated epitaphs is the city of Anazarbos in Smooth Kilikia, which furnishes a modest total of fifty-seven epitaphs dated by year and month (fifty-two from Anazarbos itself, five from neighbouring Kilikian towns and villages). All the dated epitaphs from Anazarbos itself are concentrated in a narrow eighty-year period, between AD 65/6 and 145/6. The calendar of Roman Kilikia is poorly known: it is a reasonable guess that, as in the neighbouring province of Syria, the calendar of Anazarbos ran in step with the Julian calendar, but with Macedonian month names and an autumn new year, perhaps around the time of the autumn equinox.[16] Unfortunately, no clear pattern of seasonal mortality at Anazarbos can be made out (Figure 3.5).[17]

---

[16] Calendar of Roman Antioch/Syria: Stern 2012, 284–5. Autumn new year in Kilikia (and era of Anazarbos): Ziegler 1993, 21–2, 67–8.

[17] The raw data is as follows: Dios/November (4); Apellaios/December (4); Audnaios/January (2); Peritios/February (9); Dystros/March (7); Xandikos/April (3); Artemisios/May (1); Daisios/June (3); Panemos/July (11); Loos/August (5); Gorpiaios/September (3); Hyperberetaios/October (5).

The data seem to suggest mortality spikes in late winter (Peritios–Dystros, roughly February–March) and again in high summer (Panemos–Loos, roughly July–August), but the sample size is too small for much weight to be placed on this.

The value of these three comparative cases, then, is primarily to indicate the *local specificity* of the pattern of seasonal mortality in Roman Hieradoumia. The seasonality of death in the middle Hermos valley was not the same as the seasonality of death in Rome, Egypt, or Smooth Kilikia. Local conditions, whether social, climatic, or epidemiological, created a distinctive Hieradoumian pattern of seasonal mortality.

3.3 Rhythms of Ritual Activity in Roman Hieradoumia

The relatively large number of dated propitiatory inscriptions and other private religious texts (votives and dedications) from Roman Hieradoumia allows us to explore seasonal patterns of religious activity in the region. Just as with epitaphs, the majority of votives and propitiatory inscriptions are dated by year, month, and day, giving us a crude proxy for the distribution of ritual activity within each year. As in Section 3.2, I have recalibrated the raw data on the assumption that the inhabitants of Roman Hieradoumia employed a lunisolar calendar with periodic intercalation of Xandikos and Hyperberetaios. In Figure 3.6, the data for each month is presented as a proportion of the mean number of votives and propitiatory inscriptions per month across the entire year (both the raw data and three-month moving averages), with 100 on the *y* axis reflecting the 'anticipated' number of monthly inscriptions in any given year.

It will immediately be clear that the seasonal pattern of the erection of private religious monuments is – as we might have anticipated – completely different from that of epitaphs. Private religious activity is distributed fairly evenly through the late summer, autumn, and winter months, with a sharp and dramatic spike in votives and propitiatory inscriptions in late spring and early summer (VIII Daisios and IX Panemos, roughly late April to late June). It is hard to say what might have determined this striking unimodal annual pattern, since the reasons for the erection of propitiatory inscriptions and other private religious texts demonstrably varied very widely from case to case.

We are on rather firmer ground with the distribution of the days of the month recorded on propitiatory inscriptions, votives, and dedications. As with dated epitaphs, we might naturally have expected that any given

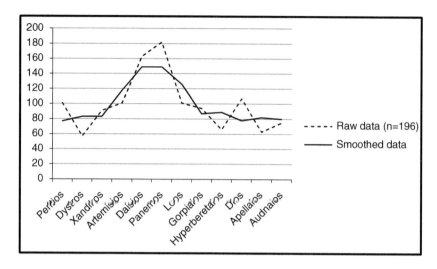

Figure 3.6 Seasonal distribution of private religious monuments in Roman Hieradoumia, raw data re-calibrated for intercalary months (n = 196) and smoothed data (three-month moving averages).

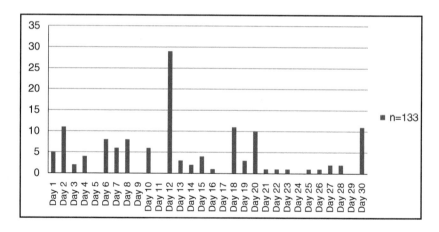

Figure 3.7 Frequency chart of attested days in Hieradoumian private religious monuments (n = 133).

day of the month would be roughly equally represented across the entire sequence of twelve months. This turns out to be emphatically not the case, as is vividly illustrated by Figure 3.7, a frequency chart of days of the month attested in dated Hieradoumian propitiatory inscriptions and other private religious texts.

Some features of this frequency chart echo what we saw for days of the month recorded in contemporary Hieradoumian epitaphs (see Figure 3.1).

Most notably, the sharp over-representation of Days 20 and 30, and equally sharp under-representation of Days 21–29, is a phenomenon already familiar from the epitaphic evidence (discussed further in Section 3.1). What is startling here, and finds no parallel in the funerary material, is the massive over-representation of the twelfth day of the month, which saw the erection of almost 22% of all votives and propitiatory inscriptions (29/133). We cannot account for this by reference to a single annual festival: multiple private religious monuments were erected on Day 12 of months falling in many different parts of the year (three in each of I Dios, II Apellaios, and III Audnaios; five in VI Xandikos; six in VIII Daisios; five in IX Panemos). Nor can it be wholly explained by reference to a specific cult, since private religious monuments dated to the twelfth day of the month were dedicated to a wide range of deities: Meis Artemidorou Axiottenos, Meis Gallenos, Apollo Axyreos, Meter Phileis, Meter Theon, Meter Motyllene, Zeus Sabazios, Zeus Batenos, Theos Dionysos, Theos Hypsistos.

Nonetheless, it is noteworthy that one of these deities, Meis Artemidorou Axiottenos, does seem to have had a particularly close association with the twelfth day of the month. Of twenty-two votives and propitiatory inscriptions erected for (or on the command of) Meis Artemidorou Axiottenos dated by day and month, over 50% (12 of 22) were erected on Day 12 of various months, strongly suggesting that the god Meis (or at least this specific cult of Meis) had particularly close associations with Day 12. In fact, in one particular case, we know that the god Meis Artemidorou specifically *ordered* that a transgressor must erect his propitiatory *stēlē* precisely on the twelfth day of the month. At the end of a long propitiatory inscription from the northern Katakekaumene, in which a certain Theodoros confesses to a series of sexual misdemeanours, the god Meis Artemidorou says 'I shall be merciful, if my *stēlē* is erected *on the day that I have ordained*' (εἵλεος εἶμαι ἀναστανομένης τῆς στήλλην μου ᾗ ἡμέρᾳ ὥρισα); the *stēlē* bears the date 'Month Panemos, Day 12', indicating that Day 12 was the day ordained by the god.[18] It is noteworthy that in at least two further propitiatory inscriptions (one to Meter Anaeitis and the other to Meis Axiottenos), dates were added after the completion of the rest of the

[18] *SEG* 38, 1237 (Petzl 1994, no. 5; translated in Chapter 8, Section 8.5), lines 22–24. The significance of the phrase is correctly highlighted by Chaniotis 2009a, 141–2 (cf. 120 n.27), without drawing the conclusions suggested here. The dates on propitiation-*stēlai* certainly reflect the date on which the monuments were set up: see e.g. *TAM* V 1, 179a (Petzl 1994, no. 9), ἀνέστησε δὲ τὸ μαρτ[ύ]ριον ἔτους σος΄, μη(νὸς) Δαισίου λ΄; similarly *SEG* 33, 1013 (Petzl 1994, no. 11).

inscription, indicating that the date of erection was not yet known at the time the *stēlē* was commissioned; this is at least compatible that the idea that a sinner might first have prepared the *stēlē* and then asked the god for guidance on the day of erection.[19]

Why should 'Day 12' have been particularly favoured by Meis (and perhaps other deities) for ritual activities in his honour? It is highly tempting to suppose that the explanation might lie in Meis' character as a lunar deity. His name (Μείς nom., Μηνός gen.) is of course semantically identical to the word for 'month'. As we have seen (Section 3.1), there is good reason to believe that the inhabitants of Roman Hieradoumia employed a lunisolar calendar, with the beginning of each month cued to the new moon, either on the basis of observation or calculation. It is therefore possible that Day 12 of the lunar month – *each and every* lunar month – had a particular significance in Hieradoumian cults of Meis precisely because this day marked a regular fixed point in the phases of the moon and hence tended to be the day specifically ordained by the god (and/or voluntarily chosen by worshippers) for the erection of votives and propitiatory texts.[20]

I tentatively suggest that Day 12 might have been conventionally treated as the day when the moon became 'full'.[21] There would be an obvious logic to this: human transgressions, prayers, expiatory acts, and rituals of exaltation could well have been conceived as particularly 'visible' to a lunar deity at the point when the moon's circle was at its fullest. I do not know of any other evidence for a particular association of Meis with the twelfth day of the month, although specific days of the (lunar) month were often regarded as sacred to particular deities in the ancient Greek world.[22] For the ritual significance of particular days of the month in Roman Hieradoumia, we might compare a propitiatory inscription from the hilltop sanctuary of Thea Larmene, in which a woman appears to be punished for 'having

---

[19] *TAM* V 1, 322 (Petzl 1994, no. 70: month Xandikos); *SEG* 57, 1158 (Petzl 2019, no. 137: Day 12 of the month Daisios). I have not noted any examples of dates on tombstones being added subsequent to the rest of the inscription.

[20] We might compare *IG* II² 1366 (*LSCG* 55), a set of imperial-period regulations for a sanctuary of Meis Tyrannos at Laureion in Attica, where there are specific regulations for those who offer sacrifices on the seventh day of the month (lines 16–18) and – more interestingly – between the new moon and the fifteenth day of the month (lines 18–20), that is to say during the period when the moon was 'waxing'.

[21] If the first day of the month was marked by the first observation of the lunar crescent, then the moon would indeed be practically full by the twelfth: West 1978, 354. See further Nilsson 1962, 35–44.

[22] Mikalson 1975, 13–24 (e.g. the seventh day of each month sacred to Apollo). A female name Dōdekatē ('twelfth') is attested in Roman Hieradoumia: *SEG* 31, 1040 (Saittai).

washed on Day 20'; of the five dated propitiatory *stēlai* set up to Zeus from the Twin Oaks, three are dated to Day 18, two to Day 30.[23]

I know of no relevant bodies of dated private religious texts from other regions to which the Hieradoumian material could be compared. It is therefore impossible to say how distinctive the seasonality and monthly rhythms of private ritual activity in Roman Hieradoumia might have been.

3.4 Sex- and Age-Specific Seasonal Mortality in Roman Hieradoumia

Let us return to Hieradoumian patterns of seasonal mortality (Section 3.2). The seasonality of death can vary considerably with sex and age. In late antique Rome, for instance, peak mortality for the elderly (50+) falls noticeably later in the year than for other age groups, no doubt indicating their greater acquired resistance to the gastroenteric diseases typical of high summer, and their relative vulnerability to the respiratory diseases characteristic of colder and wetter winter months.[24] Hence it is worth trying to establish whether the overall seasonal pattern observable in Hieradoumia was particularly acute for one or the other sex, or for one or more specific age groups.

A total of 785 dates of death attested in Hieradoumian epitaphs can be firmly associated with members of one or the other sex. We have 509 attested dates of death for males (65%) and 276 for females (35%), indicating that males were almost twice as likely as females to be commemorated with their own tombstone.[25] Figure 3.8 indicates the attested seasonal mortality patterns by month for both males (n = 509) and females (n = 276), plotted alongside the seasonal mortality profile for the entire population (n = 874).

It does not appear that sex was a primary determinant in seasonal mortality patterns in Roman Hieradoumia (a result which matches that for late antique Rome).[26] The annual mortality profile for males closely matches that of the Hieradoumian population as a whole. There is, though, some

[23] Thea Larmene: Malay and Petzl 2017, no. 159 (Petzl 2019, no. 159): κολασθεῖσα ὑπὸ Μητρὸς Λαρμηνῆς διὰ τὸ λούσασθε τῇ ἰκάδι. Zeus from the Twin Oaks: Petzl 1994, nos. 9–12; Petzl 2019, no. 125.

[24] Shaw 1996, 119–21; Harper 2015, 26–7.

[25] These figures are in one respect slightly misleading. They include a discrete body of 64 epitaphs from Saittai erected by corporate bodies (trade guilds and others) for their members, virtually all of whom (63 out of 64) were male: on this group of texts, see further Chapter 7, Section 7.2. If we omit this 'male only' group, and look purely at individuals buried by kin (n = 721), then the proportions are 62% male (446) and 38% female (275).

[26] Shaw 1996, 117.

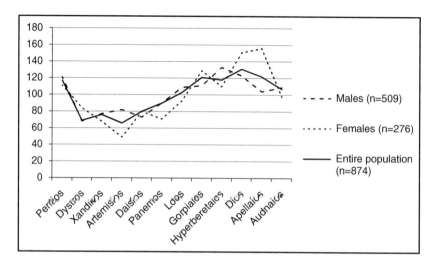

Figure 3.8 Seasonal mortality in Hieradoumia by sex, raw data re-calibrated for intercalary months (males, n = 509; females, n = 276).

indication that the high-mortality autumn months (I Dios and II Apellaios, roughly late September to late November) might have been even *more* perilous for females than for the rest of the population – that is to say, the pathogens that were prevalent in the cooler autumn months were more likely to be fatal for women than they were for men.

The situation is quite different for age-specific seasonal mortality. Around 29% of dated epitaphs (n = 252) from Hieradoumia also indicate the deceased's age at death.[27] Interestingly, men were no more or less likely than women to have their age recorded on their tombstone: the male-to-female sex ratio of those tombstones which include age at death is effectively identical to that of Hieradoumian funerary epigraphy as a whole (64% male and 36% female).[28]

[27] In fact, the original proportion of Hieradoumian epitaphs indicating age at death was probably somewhat higher than this. We have a large number of fragmentary tombstones from the region where only the upper part of the stone (including date of death) survives. Since the deceased's age at death was generally indicated at the *end* of the epitaph, it is usually impossible in such cases to determine whether the epitaph originally indicated the age at death. In the smaller sample of tombstones used by Broux and Clarysse 2009, 32, around 40% indicated age at death (206 of 503).

[28] The overall gender balance of epitaphs which include age at death and where the sex of the deceased can be determined (n = 251) is in fact 72.5% for males (182) and 27.5% for females (69). But once again, the dataset is skewed by the Saittan epitaphs erected by corporate groups (Chapter 7, Section 7.2), all but one of which were for males (61 out of 62). When one omits this group of 'male-only' non-familial epitaphs, the gender balance evens out considerably: among 'familial' epitaphs including age at death (n = 189), 64% were erected for males (121) and 36% for females (68).

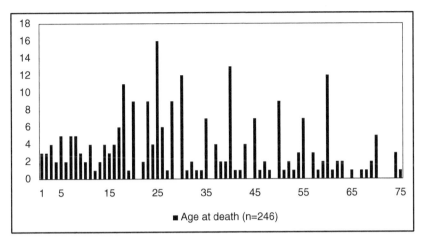

Figure 3.9 Recorded ages at death in Roman Hieradoumia, under 75s (n = 246).

It should immediately be noted that our data on age at death in Hieradoumia has a major inbuilt limitation, namely that the age of the deceased
shows a very strong tendency to be expressed in multiples of five: that is to
say, epitaphs from the region record a suspiciously large number of people
who died at the age of 30 (twelve), and suspiciously few who died at the age
of 29 or 31 (zero and one respectively). The magnitude of this bias can be
gauged, in a rough and ready kind of way, from a glance at Figure 3.9, which
tabulates all recorded ages at death of those aged 75 and under (n = 246).[29]
It will immediately be evident that age-rounding is particularly dramatic
among mature adults (those aged 30+); indeed, for those in advanced old
age, the rate of age-rounding rises to 100% (75 [1], 80 [1], 85 [1], 90 [2],
100 [1]). Age-rounding is also marked, though somewhat less so, for those
who died between the ages of 20 and 29; there is less sign of age-rounding
among the under-20s, although we might note the strikingly high number
of people recorded as having died aged 18.

The relative prevalence of age-rounding on tombstones from Roman
Hieradoumia seems be broadly consistent with that attested elsewhere in
the Roman provinces. Richard Duncan-Jones has collected a large quantity of evidence for age-rounding of mature adults (aged 23–62) in funerary records from different parts of the Roman Empire and has compared

[29] Six individuals are omitted from this graph (246/252): a man who died aged between 20 and
29 (*SEG* 48, 1459 [Saittai], ζήσαντα ἔτη κ[.]'), and five individuals who died in extreme old
age, all of them age-rounded (80, 85, 90 [x2], 100). For a rare instance where age-rounding is
explicit, see *TAM* V 1, 743 (Gordos: translated below, Chapter 5, Section 5.6): a man who died
'around 25' (ἐτέων ... ὡς εἴκοσι πέντε).

local rates of age-rounding through a simple index of deviation on a scale from 0 to 100 (0 = no age-rounding, 100 = all ages rounded to the nearest five years).[30] The index of deviation for Hieradoumia is 45.2 (n = 151), which is roughly in line with that attested for Mediterranean provinces (Italy outside Rome, 42.6; Gaul, 44.1; Rome, 47.0; Africa and Numidia, 51.4), and significantly lower than that attested for northern frontier provinces (Germany, 57.3; Dacia, 61.2; Pannonia, 64.8; Noricum, 85.4).[31] In short, although it would be perilous to take the overall levels of age-rounding as evidence of (e.g.) high levels of illiteracy or limited age awareness in Roman Hieradoumia, attributed ages at death in our data clearly need to be taken with at least a pinch of salt.[32]

It is unclear what determined the choice of whether or not to record the deceased's (rough) age at death. At some cities (e.g. Gordos), age at death was almost never recorded; at others (e.g. Saittai), it was recorded on the majority of tombstones.[33] In epitaphs erected by trade associations and other corporate groups at Saittai (discussed further in Chapter 7), age at death seems to be recorded in virtually every known instance (62 of 64 cases). Table 3.2 tabulates the 252 dated references to age at death in Hieradoumian epitaphs, grouped by ten-year age bands.

Taken as a whole, our 252 indications of date at death combined with age at death offer a broadly comparable profile of seasonal mortality to that of the entire population (874 indications of date of death). The similarity of profile is indicated by Figure 3.10, which compares the seasonal mortality profile of the entire dataset (n = 874) with the seasonal mortality profile of those individuals for whom age at death is indicated (n = 252). However, it is notable that the 'peak mortality period' in late summer and autumn is

[30] Duncan-Jones 1977, 337; Duncan-Jones 1990, 81–9. The percentage of ages divisible by 5 in each of the four decades from 23 to 62 is calculated, and the results averaged to produce an overall percentage for the sample. The quotient of 20% is subtracted from this, and the residual deviation is expressed on a scale running from 0 to 100 by multiplying by 1.25. Cf. also Scheidel 1992; Scheidel 1996, 58–61, 98–9.

[31] Duncan-Jones 1990, 87, with Scheidel 1991/1992 for Noricum. It would be interesting to compare the prevalence of age-rounding among men and women in Hieradoumia: elsewhere in the Roman world, women tend to be more prone to age-rounding than men. Unfortunately, not enough women between the ages of 23 and 62 have their ages recorded on their epitaphs (only 36 in total) to render the comparison statistically robust. Still, for what it's worth, the local indices of deviation by sex are 41.3% for females (n = 36) and 48.8% for males (n = 115).

[32] Scheidel 1996, 87–9; Laes and Strubbe 2014, 38–40. On literacy in Roman Hieradoumia, see de Hoz 2006.

[33] Gordos: age at death recorded in only one of 55 dated epitaphs (*TAM* V 1, 730). Sardis: age at death recorded in at least 31 out of 69 dated epitaphs. Saittai: age at death recorded in at least 130 out of 248 dated epitaphs.

Table 3.2 Monthly distribution of deaths in Hieradoumia, grouped by ten-year age bands (n = 252)

	0–9	10–19	20–29	30–39	40–49	50–59	60–69	70+	Total
Peritios	2	3	4	2	4	3	2	1	21
Dystros	1	0	4	1	4	0	1	0	11
Xandikos	2	1	7	0	2	7	2	1	22
Artemisios	0	2	2	4	1	1	2	0	12
Daisios	3	2	5	2	3	0	1	2	18
Panemos	0	1	2	1	2	1	1	1	9
Loos	3	4	5	5	2	1	3	0	23
Gorpiaios	4	3	6	3	3	2	2	1	24
Hyperberetaios	8	5	8	4	2	3	0	1	31
Dios	2	5	8	4	1	4	3	4	31
Apellaios	2	10	4	2	4	4	1	3	30
Audnaios	5	2	2	3	2	3	3	0	20
Total (n = 252)	(32)	(38)	(57)	(31)	(30)	(29)	(21)	(14)	(252)

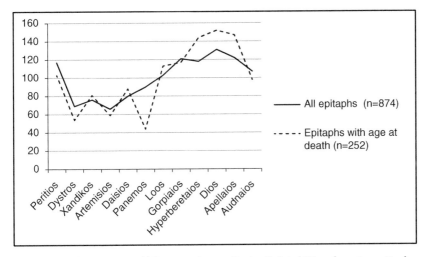

Figure 3.10 Comparison of (1) seasonal mortality in all dated Hieradoumian epitaphs (n = 874) with (2) seasonal mortality profile in dated Hieradoumian epitaphs which also indicate age at death (n = 252), raw data re-calibrated for intercalary months.

even more heavily represented in those epitaphs which include age at death (the peak on the right-hand side of the graph). It is therefore possible that individuals of one or more age bands were *both* more likely to die in late summer/autumn *and* more likely to have their age at death recorded on their tombstone than the population at large.

Table 3.3 Monthly distribution of deaths in
Hieradoumia, grouped into four broad age bands
(n = 252)

	0–15	16–29	30–49	50+
Peritios	4	5	6	6
Dystros	1	4	5	1
Xandikos	2	8	2	10
Artemisios	1	3	5	3
Daisios	4	6	5	3
Panemos	1	2	3	3
Loos	3	9	7	4
Gorpiaios	6	7	6	5
Hyperberetaios	9	12	6	4
Dios	6	9	5	11
Apellaios	5	11	6	8
Audnaios	6	3	5	6
Total (n = 252)	(48)	(79)	(61)	(64)

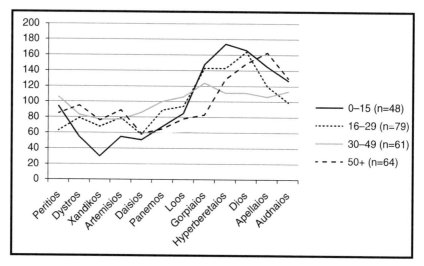

Figure 3.11 Seasonal mortality in Hieradoumia by age band (n = 252), re-calibrated
for intercalary months, smoothed data (three-month moving averages).

In view of the small sample size for each ten-year age band, in Table 3.3
I have grouped the age-specific mortality data into four larger age brackets:
sub-adults (0–15), young adults (16–29), mature adults (30–49), and the old
(50+). The monthly distribution of deaths for each age band (re-calibrated
for intercalary Xandikos and Hyperberetaios) is presented in Figure 3.11,
converted into three-month moving averages.

Despite the relatively small size of each age-banded dataset, several striking features emerge from this age-specific data. The seasonal mortality profile for men and women in middle age (ages 30–49) is relatively 'flat': late summer and autumn do not seem to have been significantly more perilous than other times of year for this age group. The other three age groups, sub-adults (ages 0–15), young adults (ages 16–29) and the old (50+), follow broadly the same unimodal seasonal trend which we have already observed for the entire population, albeit with some interesting variations. Perhaps most striking of all is the seasonal profile for the elderly (50+). For this age group, the mortality spike comes distinctly *later* than for other age groups, with peak mortality falling in the cooler mid- to late-autumn months (II Apellaios, roughly late October to late November). This pattern is very similar to that seen for the elderly in late antique Rome (see above). For young adults (16–29), peak mortality falls somewhat earlier in autumn (I Dios, roughly late September to late October), with a very steep decline in mortality through the late autumn months, when the old were dying in greatest numbers. Finally, seasonal variation in mortality seems to have been especially acute for sub-adults (0–15): the amplitude of variation between the spring 'trough' and the late summer/early autumn 'peak' is greater than for any other age group, and the summer 'peak' comes earlier than for any other age group (XII Hyperberetaios, roughly late August to late September). Once again, this pattern is echoed in the data from late antique Rome, where the amplitude of variation is likewise higher for under-15s than for any other age group.[34] The pathogens that caused increased mortality in Hieradoumia during the late summer and autumn months seem to have hit the young and very young harder than any other part of the population.

3.5 The Absent Infant

One major limitation in our data should be emphasized at this point. It is quite certain that deaths of infants and very young children are massively under-represented in Hieradoumian epitaphs. In our surviving data, children who died during their first year of life are effectively absent altogether: we have only a single certain case, an eleven-month-old boy, out of a total of 252 dated epitaphs listing age at death (0.4%).[35] Children who are recorded

---

[34] Harper 2015, 26–7.
[35] *TAM* V 1, 189 (Saittai). Note also *TAM* V 1, 201 (*SGO* I, 04/16/02, Tabala), a verse epitaph for a child who lived [*x*] months (perhaps 'three'?).

as having died between their first and fifth birthdays are also very thinly represented: only eleven dated tombstones in total (4.4%), and – perhaps significantly – no females under the age of three. Here is an example from the village of İcikler on the territory of Saittai, with a relief of the deceased boy holding a bird in his hands (Figure 3.12)[36]:

ἔτ(ους) σϙδ', μη(νὸς) Αὐδναίου γ'.
ἀρχόμενος βιότοιο μί|τοις Μοιρῶν ἔλιπον φῶς |
Ἀττικός, ὃν φίλεον πάν|(5)τες καὶ νήπιον ὄντα· |
τρὶς ἐτέων ζήσας 〚.〛 ἀρι|θμ{ν}οὺς κὲ τοὺς δύο μῆνας |
τοὺς ἰδίους λύπησα θα|νῶν γλυκερούς τε τοκῆας.

Year 294 [AD 209/10], Day 3 of the month Audnaios. At the beginning of my life, I, Attikos, departed the light of day, by the thread of the Fates – I whom everyone loved, although I was just an infant. I lived for three years and two months, and through my death I brought grief to my family and my sweet parents.

The proportion of extant epitaphs set up for infants and very young children is, needless to say, absurdly small compared with infant mortality rates in all attested pre-modern societies. The only possible conclusion is that the inhabitants of Hieradoumia did not, as a general rule, set up tombstones for small children. As a result of the minimal funerary representation of the very young, our picture of overall seasonal mortality in Hieradoumia is necessarily incomplete: we simply cannot say whether infant mortality followed the same seasonal pattern observable for other parts of the population.

Does the Hieradoumian data significantly misrepresent the actual age structure of the population in other respects? In Table 3.4, I provide a highly schematic comparison of the attested age-banded mortality rates in the region (expressed as a percentage of total mortality) with the anticipated age-banded mortality rates for a pre-modern Mediterranean population,

---

[36] *TAM* V 1, 135 (*SGO* I 04/12/03). Other cases: *TAM* V 1, 384 (Kollyda: a one-year-old boy), *SEG* 29, 1181 (Saittai: eighteen-month-old boy); *SEG* 38, 1316 (unknown provenance: a two-year-old child, name and sex not recorded); *SEG* 34, 1229 (Saittai: a two-year-old boy); *TAM* V 1, 126 (Saittai: a three-year-old boy); *TAM* V 1, 823 (*SGO* I 04/07/02, Kömürcü: a three-year-old boy); *SEG* 31, 1030 (Saittai: a three-year-old girl); *Sammlung Tatış* 58 (Saittai [?]: a four-year-old boy); *SEG* 53, 1341 (unknown provenance: a four-year-old girl). Cf. also *Sardis* II 598 (undated epitaph of a boy of one year and three months); *Sardis* II 663 (undated epitaph of a three-year-old girl); *Sammlung Tatış* 36 (undated verse epitaph of a boy of three years and two months). *SGO* I 05/01/65 (unknown provenance) is the verse epitaph of a male baby who was still breast-feeding, but age at weaning varied greatly in the Roman world (between five months and three years: Laes 2011, 80–1). Note the relatively high numbers of verse epitaphs for the very young, a phenomenon known from other parts of the Greek world.

Table 3.4 Age-banded mortality rates in Hieradoumia, expressed as a percentage of total mortality, compared with the predictions of (a) Woods 'South Europe' Model Life Table, $e(0) = 25$, and (b) Woods 'South Europe' Model Life Table, $e(0) = 20$.

Age	Hieradoumian epitaphs [n = 252 (240)]	Expected (a) [Woods 'South Europe', $e(0) = 25$]	Expected (b) [Woods 'South Europe', $e(0) = 20$]
0/(5)–9	12.7 (8.3)	45.6 (5.5)	54.2 (9.7)
10–19	15.1 (15.8)	6.0 (10.5)	6.4 (12.7)
20–29	22.6 (23.8)	10.5 (18.2)	10.4 (20.5)
30–39	12.3 (12.9)	9.4 (16.4)	8.3 (16.3)
40–49	11.9 (12.5)	7.6 (13.2)	6.2 (12.2)
50–59	11.5 (12.1)	6.7 (11.6)	5.0 (9.9)
60–69	8.3 (8.8)	7.7 (13.4)	5.4 (10.6)
70+	5.6 (5.8)	6.4 (11.2)	4.0 (8.0)

Note: Figures in brackets represent the same comparison, but this time excluding under-5s.

Figure 3.12 Verse epitaph of the three-year-old Attikos, from İcikler. *TAM* V 1, 135 (*SGO* I 04/12/03).

as derived from the high-mortality 'South Europe' Model Life Table constructed by Robert Woods.[37] I make no great claims for the scientific value
of this comparison: it is merely meant to indicate *by what order of magnitude* the Hieradoumian epitaphic record does, or does not, misrepresent
the likely age structure of the population of the region in antiquity.

A crucial variable here is the mean life expectancy at birth in Hieradoumia. For the entire Roman Empire, a mean life expectancy at birth of
25 ($e(0) = 25$) is a plausible guess, with the proviso that people in different Mediterranean environments are likely to have enjoyed significantly
higher or lower life expectancy, depending on local conditions.[38] We have
no idea whether the middle Hermos valley was a relatively safe or relatively hazardous environment by ancient Mediterranean standards. In the
second and third columns of Table 3.4, I have tabulated the Model Life
Table data generated by postulating a mean life expectancy at birth of 25
(Column 2, assuming that Hieradoumia was roughly typical of the Roman
Empire as a whole) and 20 (Column 3, assuming that Hieradoumia was
relatively hazardous by Roman standards).

Table 3.4 incorporates two discrete comparisons between the actual data
and the Model Life Tables, in order to mitigate the effects of the dramatic
under-representation of infants and young children (ages 0–4) in the Hieradoumian data. First, the entire dataset (Column 1, 252 data points, grouped
by ten-year age bands) is compared with the 'South Europe' Model Life Table,
calibrated both for a 'normal' and a 'low' mean life expectancy at birth (Column 2, $e(0) = 25$; Column 3, $e(0) = 20$). Second, since under-representation
of under-5s is so severe in the Hieradoumian data, I also compare the evidence for individuals who died at age 5+ (Column 1, 240 data points) with
the anticipated 'South Europe' mortality rates for over-5s, once again calibrated both for a 'normal' and a 'low' mean life expectancy at birth (Column
2, $e(5) = 36.9$; Column 3, $e(5) = 32.4$). This ought to provide us with a rough-
and-ready indication of whether any older age groups are also dramatically
over- or under-represented in the surviving data.

A glance across the first line of Table 3.4 suffices to show quite how
severely under-represented the very young must be in extant Hieradoumian epitaphs. Children who died before their tenth birthday make

---

[37] Woods 2007, 379. On the appropriateness of Woods' model life tables (and other recent
alternative models) for different parts of the Roman world, see Hin 2013, 109–23; Scheidel
2012a, 322, with further bibliography. For a similar comparison (Egyptian epitaphs and
mummy-labels), cf. Scheidel 2001b, 30–1.

[38] Scheidel 2001a, 25.

up only 12.7% of those commemorated (with age at death recorded) in Hieradoumia, whereas we would in principle expect such children to make up a full 50% or so of all those dying in any given year (45.6%, Column 2; 54.2%, Column 3). However, once we filter out the under-fives (the figures in brackets across all three columns), the age-banded mortality rates for all other age groups – *including* five- to nine-year-olds – appear to be roughly in line with what we would expect for an ancient Mediterranean population with life expectancy in the low- to mid-20s. There is some slight reason to think that teenagers and young adults (aged 10–29) might have been slightly 'over-commemorated' in epitaphs from Hieradoumia, and the old may similarly have been slightly 'under-commemorated', but naturally this depends entirely on the postulated mean age at death, which is – I emphasize again – completely conjectural.

We can therefore conclude that in Hieradoumia, children under 5, and particularly children who died before their first birthday, were (a) significantly less likely than other age groups to be commemorated with a tombstone which recorded their age of death and were (b) almost certainly far less likely to be commemorated with a tombstone *tout court*. There is, however, no good reason to believe that any other age group was significantly over- or under-represented in the epitaphic data available to us. We may therefore be reasonably confident that the seasonal mortality profiles depicted in Figure 3.2 and Figure 3.11 are in fact a fair reflection of real patterns of seasonal mortality in Hieradoumia (infants and very young children excepted).

3.6 The Impact of the Antonine Plague

Figure 3.13 is a frequency chart of dated epitaphs from Hieradoumia and neighbouring regions in the sixty-year period from AD 150/1 to AD 209/10 (n = 294). As Yanne Broux and Willy Clarysse remarked in an important paper on the dated epitaphs of the region (using a slightly smaller dataset than that employed here), the year AD 165/6 sees a sudden and striking jump in the annual number of surviving tombstones from the region, from around 4–5 per year to around 8–9 per year.[39] The number of extant epitaphs per year remains abnormally high through the late 160s (AD 165/6–170/1), and there are further anomalous spikes in the mid-170s (AD

---

[39] Broux and Clarysse 2009, 29–31.

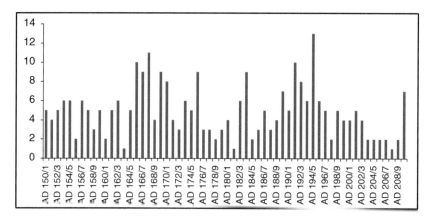

Figure 3.13 Chronological distribution of dated epitaphs from Hieradoumia and neighbouring regions, AD 150/1 to AD 209/10 (n = 294).

175/6) and mid-180s (AD 183/4). After what appears to be another period of intense tombstone production in the early 190s (AD 191/2–AD 194/5), the number of extant epitaphs per year drops back to a lower level in the late 190s and 200s.

The three decades from 165 to 195 can thus be seen as a period of great volatility in the production of epitaphs in Hieradoumia, with sporadic dramatic leaps in the rate at which tombstones were erected in the region. It is very unlikely to be a coincidence that the year AD 165 also saw the outbreak of the great Antonine Plague, most probably (but not certainly) a virulent smallpox epidemic.[40] Few parts of the Roman Empire were immune from the Plague, and it is known from both literary and epigraphic sources to have had a dramatic impact in western Asia Minor. Aelius Aristides describes a devastating outbreak of plague at Smyrna in (probably) summer AD 165, during which many of his neighbours and slaves perished.[41] Inscribed oracles of the Klarian Apollo offering advice on rituals to ward off plague are known from several cities in western Asia Minor (Pergamon, Ephesos, Kaisareia Troketta, Hierapolis), all of which have been plausibly attributed to the initial years of the Antonine Plague.[42]

---

[40] The modern bibliography on the Antonine Plague and its impact is vast. See, most notably, Duncan-Jones 1996; Lo Cascio 2012; C. Elliott 2016; Harper 2017, 98–118 (with Haldon et al. 2018, and the response of Harper 2018). The disease is usually identified as smallpox (Harper 2017, 102–7), but for doubts, see Flemming 2018, 225–40.

[41] Aelius Aristides, *Or.* 48.38–45.

[42] Faraone 1992, 61 4; Busine 2005, 32–40, 445–8; Oesterheld 2008, 43–231; Oesterheld 2014; Harper 2017, 100–2. A verse epitaph of a plague-victim from Phrygian Aizanoi (*MAMA* IX 79; *SGO* III 16/23/17) and an altar to the 'highest god' from Paphlagonian Amastris (*SEG* 50,

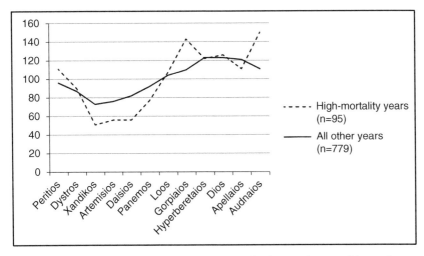

Figure 3.14 Seasonal mortality in Hieradoumia in 'high-mortality years' (n = 95), re-calibrated for intercalary months, smoothed data (three-month moving averages).

It is difficult not to see the sharp three-year 'spike' in the number of extant tombstones from Hieradoumia between AD 165/6 and AD 167/8 as reflecting the immediate effects of the outbreak of the Antonine Plague, and it is at least possible that the sporadic annual 'spikes' in epitaph production between the 170s and 190s reflect renewed outbreaks of the Plague. In particular, we have literary evidence for a dramatic revival of the Plague at Rome in AD 191, which is – suggestively – precisely the date at which the second extended period of increased tombstone production begins in Hieradoumia (AD 191/2–194/5).[43]

One potential way of testing this hypothesis of periodic Plague outbreaks in the middle Hermos valley in the late second century AD would be to consider whether seasonal mortality rates look different in apparent 'high-mortality' years. Figure 3.14 shows the seasonal mortality pattern for the ten discrete 'high-mortality' years between AD 165 and AD 195 (taking 8+ tombstones p. a. as the lower threshold): AD 165/6–167/8, 169/70–170/1, AD 175/6, AD 183/4, AD 191/2–192/3, and 194/5 (n = 95). Figure 3.14 also allows us to compare this pattern with that seen

---

1225; *SGO* II 10/03/01) can also be plausibly attributed to the initial outbreak of the Antonine Plague (see Thonemann 2021, on Lucian, *Alexander* §36), as can – less certainly – an oracle of the Didymaian Apollo from Apollonis (Malay and Petzl 2017, no. 3).

[43] Dio Cass. 73.14.3–4 (2,000 people dying each day at Rome); Herodian 1.12.1–2; Harper 2017, 111; Flemming 2018, 224–5.

in 'ordinary' years (i.e. all other years: n = 779). The data does suggest
that in years of elevated mortality, the characteristic Hieradoumian seasonal oscillation (low mortality in spring, high mortality in late summer/
autumn) might have been even starker than normal, with sharp mortality
spikes in both high summer and – very interestingly – in deep mid-winter
(III Audnaios). But the dataset is not large enough to demonstrate this
beyond reasonable doubt, and the seasonality of the Antonine Plague is
not otherwise known with any certainty (although it is noteworthy that
Galen describes a mid-winter outbreak of the Plague at Aquileia at the
end of AD 168).[44]

Naturally, we have no way of quantifying the impact of the Antonine
plague on the Hieradoumian population, but the mere fact of the visi-
bility of these mortality spikes in the region in the late 160s and thereaf-
ter suggests that it may have been very substantial. It is therefore worth
wondering whether the Plague might have left its mark on the *content* of
the funerary and votive epigraphy of Hieradoumia in this period. As we
have already seen, an inscribed oracle of the Klarian Apollo from Kaisareia Troketta, in the northern foothills of Mt Tmolos west of Sardis, offers
extensive guidance on how to ward off a devastating pestilence.[45] Another
inscribed Klarian oracle from Ephesos (but probably delivered to the Sar-
dians) advises that plague can be averted by means of the transfer of a
statue of Artemis from Ephesos to a Lydian sanctuary of Artemis in 'the
salty lands of Maionian Hermos', perhaps the Artemis-sanctuary at Koloe
on Lake Gygaia.[46] At an uncertain date, a certain Flaccus from the hill
country north of Gordos erected a votive *stēlē* to 'the divinity' to commemorate having 'escaped the terrible disease, along with his homeland
[i.e. the rest of his village?] and his loved ones'; clearly, Flaccus and the rest
of his village had found themselves miraculously untouched by a dreadful
epidemic of some kind.[47]

---

[44] Galen, *On His Own Books* 3.3: πλείστων ἀπολλυμένων οὐ μόνον διὰ τὸν λοιμὸν ἀλλὰ καὶ διὰ τὸ
μέσου χειμῶνος εἶναι τὰ πραττόμενα, 'most sufferers died, not only because of the Plague, but
also because these events occurred in mid-winter'. On the seasonality of smallpox, see Scheidel
2001b, 94–7; Nishiura and Kashiwagi 2009 (increased transmission in periods of low humidity).
[45] *SGO* I, 04/01/01; Malay and Petzl 2017, no. 13 (now in the Manisa Museum).
[46] *SGO* I, 03/02/01 (*SEG* 41, 981). An oracle of the Didymaian Apollo to Apollonis in north-west
Lydia (Malay and Petzl 2017, no. 3: second or third century AD) is similarly concerned with
the amelioration of a disastrous mass-mortality event, conceivably the Antonine Plague.
[47] *TAM* V 1, 761 (*SGO* I, 04/10/01, from the remote village of Tutluca): ἀργαλέην νοῦσον
προφυγεῖν σὺν πατρίδι καὶ φιλίοισι εὐξάμενος Θείῳ Φλάκκος ἔτευξα χάριν. There is no reason
to think (*pace* Keil *ap.* *TAM* V 1, 761) that Flaccus had to seclude himself *'in remota montium'*:
προφυγεῖν simply means 'escape'.

None of the texts mentioned in the previous paragraph can be closely dated, and hence in each case, the connection with the Antonine Plague is hypothetical (albeit fairly plausible). We are on somewhat firmer ground with a group of epitaphs and votive dedications which can be precisely dated to years when the Plague seems to have been rife in Hieradoumia. A single family at Charakipolis saw two deaths in fairly quick succession in late autumn 165 (an unmarried girl) and spring 168 (her father), commemorated on the same tombstone; both may well have been victims of the first wave of the Plague in western Asia Minor.[48] In the late summer of 176, apparently one of the worst plague years in the region (nine tombstones in AD 175/6), a certain Eutychis, *threptē* of C. Iulius Aniketos of Pergamon, erected a *stēlē* to Meis Axiottenos and the Mother of Meis in gratitude for her recovery from sickness.[49] In spring AD 183, the year of a significant mortality spike in the region, the village of the Odenoi, on the right bank of the Demrek Çayı, set up a collective dedication to the Greatest God (*Theios Megistos*) 'for their salvation'.[50] In the early summer of 195, one Stratoneikos of Saittai saw his entire household brought 'close to death', supposedly as the god's punishment for having cut down a sacred oak tree; in light of the fact that Hieradoumia saw a particularly terrible mortality spike in AD 194/5 (thirteen tombstones, the highest annual total), it is possible that Stratoneikos' family were in fact struck down by the Plague.[51] Finally, we have a pair of votive inscriptions from the rural sanctuary of Meter Tazene and Meis Petraeites, near modern Kavaklı on the south bank of the Hermos, dated to mid-winter 197/8 and spring 199 respectively.[52] The first is a private dedication by a woman who made a vow to Meis Petraeites at a time 'when the people were suffering from an intractable disease' (πασχόντων αὐτῶν δυσκώλῳ αἰσθενείᾳ) and fulfilled it after their collective recovery (ἐγερθέντων αὐτῶν τῶν ἀνθρώπων); the second is a dedication by an entire village community in commemoration of having successfully 'appeased the gods' (εἱλάσοντο [τοὺς] θεούς). In both cases, it is possible that we are seeing traces of the collective relief felt after the final departure of the Plague from western Asia Minor in the mid- to late-190s.

---

[48] Malay and Petzl 2017, no. 17.

[49] *SEG* 39, 1275 (unknown provenance): εὐξαμένη τῷ θεῷ ἀσθενοῦσα, εἰ μεταβολὴν σχῶ, στηλλογραφῆσαι, ἀκούσαντος τοῦ θεοῦ ἀπέδωκα τὴν εὐχήν, dated 2 Hyperberetaios, AD 175/6.

[50] *I.Manisa* 184.

[51] *TAM* V 1, 179b (Petzl 1994, no. 10): ὁ θεὸς … κατέθηκεν ὁλοδουμε⟨ὶ⟩ ἰσοθανάτους, καὶ σωθεὶς ἐκ μεγάλου κινδύνου εὐχαριστῶν ἀνέθηκεν, dated 18 Panemos, AD 194/5; see further the discussion in Chapter 8, Section 8.4. For the meaning of ὁλοδουμε⟨ὶ⟩, see Chaniotis, *EBGR* 2004, 98 (*SEG* 53, 1505).

[52] Malay and Petzl 2017, nos. 185 and 186 (dated 10 Peritios 197/8 and Artemisios 198/9).

3.7 Determinants of Seasonal Mortality in Roman Hieradoumia

The Antonine Plague aside, only a few tentative observations can be made about the possible determinants of the observed patterns of seasonal mortality in Roman Hieradoumia. We have effectively no direct evidence for 'normal' epidemiological conditions in ancient Hieradoumia: the rich osteological and written evidence that underlies Walter Scheidel's pioneering analysis of causes of death in Roman Egypt simply does not exist (so far) for inland western Asia Minor.[53] A tiny handful of inscriptions from Roman Hieradoumia do mention specific diseases, such as a thank-offering from Kula to the gods Holy and Just, set up in late summer AD 248 (8 Hyperberetaios, around the end of August) by a certain Alexandra, who had made a vow on behalf of her children 'because of the *peripnoia*'; Alexandra's children had clearly been suffering from a respiratory condition of some kind over the summer, from which they eventually recovered.[54] Self-evidently, single isolated texts of this kind cannot get us very far.

The climate of the middle Hermos valley is, by Mediterranean standards, relatively mild.[55] The hottest months of the year, July and August, see an average temperature of 25.8 degrees at Salihli (just east of Sardis) and 22.9 degrees at Kula (Katakekaumene). The coldest month is January, when average temperatures are around 7.2 degrees (Salihli) and 4.1 degrees (Kula); temperatures very seldom drop below freezing. The summer and early autumn months (July to September) are extremely dry, with average monthly precipitation of a mere 6–8mm in July–August at Salihli and 8–12mm at Kula; the water table is at its lowest in September. Most of the year's rain falls in heavy downpours between late October and March, with peak precipitation in December and January (at Salihli, 95–114mm; at Kula, 110–135mm).[56] Climatic variation is a major determinant of seasonal mortality patterns, and it is clearly no coincidence that overall mortality rates in Roman Hieradoumia were demonstrably at their highest during the hottest and driest months of the year. The months of peak mortality seen in the Hieradoumian epitaphic evidence (XII Hyperberetaios – I Dios, roughly late August to late October) correspond precisely to the period when the water table was at its lowest, shortly before the onset of the

---

[53] Scheidel 2001b, 51–117.   [54] *TAM* V 1, 247.
[55] Tac., *Ann.* 4.55 (*temperiem caeli*); praise of the Lydian climate also in *TAM* V 3, 1894.
[56] Hanfmann and Waldbaum 1975, 25.

autumn rains. We would naturally expect the prevalence of gastro-intestinal diseases to have been far higher during these months than at other times of year.

In the very recent past, the low-lying plain of Sardis, more particularly the area around Marmara Gölü (ancient Lake Gygaia), was notorious for malaria and other fevers. The American excavator of Sardis, Howard Crosby Butler, fifty years of age and otherwise in good health, contracted malaria in the early summer of 1922, 'in visiting a lake near Sardis' (prob-ably Marmara Gölü). In July, the disease abated, but it recurred at the start of August, and Butler eventually died in the American hospital at Paris on 13 August.[57] Almost a century earlier, Charles Boileau Elliott, who travelled along the north flank of the plain from Adala to Gölmarmara in the sum-mer of 1836, thought, rightly or wrongly, that 'malaria' (here simply 'bad air', rather than the specific disease) was the main cause of the depopula-tion of the Hermos plain around Sardis:

> At a distance of three hours from Adala, the road [to Akhisar], passing over a hill, enters a morass formed by the waters of the Gygaean lake, which sometimes overflow, and, then subsiding, leave it covered with a slimy deposit that feeds a noisome rush and engenders a pestilential miasma. This *malaria* has co-operated with a bad government to depop-ulate the country, and, extending to Sardis, has given rise to the prevalent dread of occupying a house on the site of the once famed capital of Lydia.[58]

The insalubrious character of the Hermos valley in high summer was also noted by William Hamilton, who travelled from Philadelphia to Sardis on 24 August 1837: he describes the plain around Salihli as 'a well-cultivated country for several miles intersected by numerous streams and pools of stagnant water, in consequence of which fever is very prevalent'.[59] Émile Le Camus, who visited the site of Sardis in 1896, has an even more vivid (and perhaps somewhat overdrawn) picture of the effects of 'fever', no doubt including malaria, on the local inhabitants:

> Two miserable houses roofed with branches, with a sort of terrace at the front, shelter the fifteen or twenty inhabitants who now represent the once enormous city [of Sardis]. It is melancholy to see these descendants of the ancient Lydians of Croesus, dressed in rags, consumed by fever, and fated to

---

[57] 'In memoriam Howard Crosby Butler', *BASOR* 7 (October 1922), 4.

[58] C. B. Elliott 1838, II 105–6; cf. II 71: 'The Turks now consider [the site of Sardis] pestilential, and have a saying that every man dies who builds a house at Sardis; consequently, not a single native Moslim resides there.'

[59] Hamilton 1842, II 377.

starve to death through unwillingness to shake off their incurable laziness. A woman busies herself in relieving her child from the vermin that devour him, while the men sleep with their feet in the shade and heads in the sun.[60]

Further to the north, the plain of Simav was rendered similarly unhealthy by the marshes around Simav Gölü. When Jeanne and Louis Robert visited the plain of Simav in September 1960, they found the lake in the process of being drained: although the inhabitants were thereby faced with the loss of their main livelihood (carp-fishing), they were nonetheless optimistic about the future:

> 'Our children will be more fortunate', they told us; 'there will be no more fevers, rheumatisms, or mosquitos.'[61]

Although drainage and irrigation works around Marmara Gölü may have been somewhat more effective in the Roman imperial period than in more recent times, it is likely enough that the ancient inhabitants of the towns and villages lying on the fringes of the plain of Salihli – Sardis, Philadelphia, Satala, Daldis – suffered from endemic malaria and waterborne diseases (typhoid, dysentery).[62] Which specific disease or diseases might have had the most significant effect on local mortality rates is impossible to say (and the answer may well have differed for different age groups).

It is, finally, worth returning briefly to the sharp discrepancy between observed seasonal mortality patterns for young adults (20–29) and mature adults (30–49), as represented in Figure 3.11. As we have seen, the late summer and early autumn months (Gorpiaios to Dios, roughly late July to late October) were far more perilous for young adults than for mature adults. Conversely, young adults (20–29) seem not to have died in especially large numbers in the late autumn months (Apellaios and Audnaios, late October to late December), which continued to be a period of danger for the very young (0–19) and, in particular, the very old (50+). One is therefore tempted to wonder whether seasonally specific pulmonary tuberculosis (a disease which falls particularly heavily on young adults) might have been a major cause of death for young adults in Roman Hieradoumia.[63] But in the current state of our knowledge, this can be little more than conjecture.

---

[60] Le Camus 1896, 219 (my translation).
[61] Robert 1987, 318 (my translation), with quotations from A. D. Mordtmann (315) and A. Philippson (317–18) on the insalubrious plain surrounding Lake Simav.
[62] Hanfmann 1983, 4 (decline of Roman irrigation systems around Sardis in late antiquity).
[63] Scheidel 2001b, 91–3.

4 | Kinship Terminology

The first step towards an analysis of the kinship system of Roman Hieradoumia is a proper understanding of the complex and distinctive kinship
classificatory system of the region. In this chapter, I collect the evidence for
kinship terminology in Hieradoumia, drawn almost entirely from the several hundreds of surviving 'familial' epitaphs of the first three centuries AD.
Individual kinship terms are catalogued and analysed in Sections 4.1–4.12,
including comparisons and contrasts with the kinship terminology of other
parts of the ancient Greek-speaking world where appropriate. The Hieradoumian kinship terminological system as a whole is presented in Figures
4.1 and 4.2, which will be found at the start of Section 4.13 (general discussion and comparanda). I make no apologies for the rather rebarbative
character of the analysis that follows. As will eventually become clear, I
believe that the kinship classificatory system of Roman Hieradoumia is in
fact wholly unique in the ancient Greco-Roman world; but demonstrating
this will, I fear, take a little time.

A word about the presentation of evidence in what follows. Several kinship terms attested in Hieradoumia are either extremely rare or completely
unattested elsewhere in the Greek world (καμβ(δ)ιος, πατρεία, ἰανάτηρ,
σύννυμφος); in other cases, common kinship terms are used in Hieradoumia
with a much more specific or idiosyncratic reference than seems to be the case
elsewhere (τηθείς, πενθερός, γάμβρος, ἀδελφίδης). In such cases, I have presented the Hieradoumian evidence in the fullest possible manner, using the
symbol * to denote instances where the precise sense of the term emerges with
certainty or a high degree of probability from the context. Certain very common kinship terms are employed in Hieradoumia in much the same manner
as in any other part of the Greek world (πάτηρ, μήτηρ, γυνή, ἀδελφός, etc.); in
such cases, I have not made a comprehensive collection of the material.

We begin with the terminology used for natal kin of various kinds:
primary kin (Section 4.1), grandparents and grandchildren (Section 4.2),
uncles and aunts (Section 4.3), uncles' and aunts' spouses (Section 4.4 –
in fact three-step affines, but treated alongside consanguineous aunts and
uncles for convenience), and nephews, nieces, and cousins (Section 4.5).
We next turn to the rich and complex terminology used in Hieradoumia

for various two-step affines: parents-in-law (Sections 4.6 and 4.7), the husband's and wife's siblings (Sections 4.8 and 4.9), the son's wife and brother's wife (Section 4.10), the daughter's husband and sister's husband (Section 4.11), and finally step-kin and adoptive kin (Section 4.12). The terminology of fosterage in Hieradoumia and elsewhere (θρεπτοί, σύντροφοι, etc.) will be treated separately in Chapter 6.

4.1 Primary Kin

The terminology used of primary kin in Hieradoumia shows no local peculiarities, and so can be treated very briefly. The ordinary terms for **father** and **mother** were πάτηρ and μήτηρ; these terms seem also to have been used of adoptive parents.[1] When both parents are referred to together, the usual term is οἱ γονεῖς, apparently never used in the singular.[2] In verse texts, parents are described with a variety of terms deriving from the verbs τίκτειν and γεννᾶν ('bear, beget').[3] In both prose and verse texts, the mother is sometimes referred to as ἡ τεκοῦσα (literally 'the bearer'), without any obvious distinction in context or tone from uses of μήτηρ.[4]

The usual terms for **husband** and **wife** were ἀνήρ and γυνή, although the gender-neutral term ὁ/ἡ σύμβιος also appears reasonably often. Verse epitaphs feature a much wider range of terms for spouses, most of them drawn from the rich spousal vocabulary of the Homeric epics (ἄλοχος, πόσις, παρακοίτης, etc.).[5]

---

[1] *TAM* V 1, 555 (Maionia), Θεοφίλα Φωκρίτου, φύσε[ι Μ]ητροφάνου, Φώκριτον τὸν ἀτῆς πατέρα.
[2] οἱ γονεῖς: *TAM* V 1, 383 (Kollyda), and often. οἱ γονῆς: *TAM* V 1, 123 (Saittai). τοὺς γονεῖς: *TAM* V 1, 95 (Saittai), and often. τῶν γονέων: *TAM* V 1, 231 (Kastoloupedion); *SEG* 52, 1165 (inc.). τοῖς γονεῦσι: *TAM* V 1, 653 (Daldis). τοῖς γονεῖσι: *TAM* V 1, 663 (Daldis).
[3] τίκτειν: *TAM* V 1, 636 (*SGO* I 04/08/02, Daldis: οἵ με τεκόντες); *TAM* V 1, 66 (*SGO* I 04/14/01, Silandos: [τοκῆε]ς); *TAM* V 1, 135 (*SGO* I 04/12/03, Saittai: τοκῆας); *TAM* V 1, 208a (*SGO* I 04/16/01, Tabala: τοκῆας); *SEG* 29, 1190 (*SGO* I 04/12/06, Saittai: τοκεῶνες). γεννᾶν: *TAM* V 1, 797 (*SGO* I 04/07/03, Hamit, (ὁ) γενέτης); *TAM* V 1, 1900 (*SGO* I 04/24/10, Philadelphia: γενέτης); *TAM* V 1, 701 (*SGO* I 04/10/03, Gordos, τὴν γεννήσασαν); *SEG* 35, 1166 (*SGO* I 04/22/07, Maionia, ὁ γεινάμενος).
[4] *TAM* V 1, 162 (Saittai, τὴν τεκοῦσαν); *TAM* V 1, 289 (Kula, ἡ τεκοῦσα); *TAM* V 1, 632 (Daldis, τεκούσης, in verse); *TAM* V 1, 805 (*SGO* I 04/07/04, Yeğenoba, τεκοῦσα, in verse); *TAM* V 1, 823 (*SGO* I 04/07/02, Kömürcü, ἡ τεκέουσα, in verse); *SEG* 41, 1073 (Kadoi, τεκοῦσα); *SEG* 57, 1201 (Maionia, τῆς [τ]εκούσης: votive); *TAM* V 3, 1813 (Philadelphia, τῇ τεκούσῃ); *TAM* V 3, 1813 (*SGO* I 04/24/98, Philadelphia, τεκοῦσα, in verse). See Robert, *Hellenica* XI/XII, 388–9; *MAMA* XI 123 (Akmoneia, with commentary).
[5] *TAM* V 1, 701 (*SGO* I 04/10/03, Gordos, ἄλοχον); *SEG* 40, 1037 (*SGO* I 04/13/02, Örücüler, ἄλοχος); *TAM* V 3, 1894 (*SGO* I 04/24/12: Yeşilova, ἀλόχου); *TAM* V 3, 1896 (*SGO* I 04/24/14:

The **son** and **daughter** are usually designated as υἱός (or ὑός) and θυγάτηρ. When more than one child is referred to, the usual term is τὰ τέκνα (cognate with τεκοῦσα, 'mother'), although the plural οἱ υἱοί is occasionally used with the sense 'sons and daughters'.[6] The singular τὸ τέκνον is rather less common, and often has an affectionate colouring, though it could be used of adult off-spring just as well as of young children.[7] The gender-neutral term ὁ/ἡ παῖς is very rare indeed in Hieradoumia, although there are several instances of the affectionate diminutive παιδίον, apparently always used of small children.[8]

The **brother** and **sister** are always referred to as ἀδελφός and ἀδελφή; there is a single case of an affectionate diminutive τὰ ἀδέλφια, 'little siblings'.[9] In a quasi-metrical epitaph from Gordos, the deceased's brother and sister are apparently designated as 'my closest kin' (ἄγχιστα γένους μου).[10] In verse texts, siblings are regularly referred to with the Homeric terms κασίγνητος and κασιγνήτη.[11]

Philadelphia, ἄλοχον); *SEG* 40, 1065 (Saittai, ἄλοχον); *SEG* 29, 1203 (*SGO* I 04/12/05, Saittai: πόσις); *TAM* V 3, 1798 (Philadelphia: πόσι, in prose); *SEG* 29, 1202 (*SGO* I 04/12/07, Saittai: ἡ σύνευνος ... σεῖο παρακοίτου); *TAM* V 1, 773 (*SGO* I 04/10/02, Gordos, τὴν [σ]υνευνέτιν); *TAM* V 1, 290 (Kula: [ὁ] σύνευνος); *TAM* V 1, 29 (*SGO* I 04/17/99, Akbulak: δάμαρτι). All these terms are common in verse epitaphs throughout the Greek world.

[6] οἱ υἱοί = 'sons and daughters': *SEG* 52, 1165 (inc.). In *I.Ephesos* 1590 A.2, two sons (τὰ τέκνα) are distinguished from a daughter (ἡ θυγάτηρ); the same distinction in *SEG* 28, 1156 (Eumeneia).

[7] Affection: *TAM* V 2, 851 (Attaleia, τῷ καταθυμίῳ τέκνῳ ἑνὶ καὶ μούνῳ; cf. Robert, *Hellenica* XIII, 215–16, n.1); *SEG* 41, 1042 (inc.: τὸ γλυκύτατον τέκνον). Age of τέκνα: *SEG* 38, 1316 (inc.: a two-year-old); *Sardis* II 663 (a three-year-old); *Sammlung Tatış* 58 (Saittai?: a four-year-old); *SEG* 35, 1235 (Saittai: a fourteen-year-old); *SEG* 35, 1272 (Salihli: an eighteen-year-old); *Sardis* II 662 (a twenty-one-year-old); *TAM* V 1, 295 (Kula: a twenty-three-year-old, τὸ γλ[υκύτα]τον τέκνον); *TAM* V 1, 743 (*SGO* I 04/10/05, Gordos: a twenty-five-year-old, τὸ καταθύμιον τέκνον); *TAM* V 2, 1139 (Thyateira: a twenty-nine-year-old); *TAM* V 3, 1838 (Philadelphia: a thirty-year-old).

[8] The restoration [οἱ παῖδες] αὐτοῦ in *SEG* 34, 1234 (Silandos) does not accord with Hieradoumian usage; restore instead [τὰ τέκνα] αὐτοῦ. παιδίον: *TAM* V 1, 206 (Tabala); *TAM* V 1, 597 (Maionia); *TAM* V 1, 248 (Kula); *SEG* 32, 1218 (Kula); *TAM* V 3, 1816 (Philadelphia); *Sardis* II 463; *SEG* 39, 1278 (inc.: a six-year-old); *SEG* 40, 1081 (inc.); *TAM* V 1, 317 (near Kula: a five-year-old); Naour 1983, 110; Gauthier 1989, 72. Elsewhere in Asia Minor, παῖς (unlike υἱός/θυγάτηρ) usually seems to indicate youthful age: cf. υἱοὶ παῖδες in *SEG* 43, 740 (Tralleis); τέκνοις πεδίοι[ς] in *SEG* 29, 1426 (Denizli).

[9] *TAM* V 1, 104 (Saittai), with Robert, *OMS* I, 423 n.82; Fıratlı and Robert 1964, 138; Drew-Bear 1984, 442–5.

[10] *TAM* V 1, 743 (*SGO* I 04/10/05, Gordos). The identification of the two individuals concerned (a man and a woman) as the deceased's siblings is not quite certain, but I do not see what other relationship could be referred to here.

[11] *SEG* 29, 1203 (*SGO* I 04/12/05, Saittai: κασιγνήτη); *TAM* V 1, 208a (*SGO* I 04/16/01, Tabala: κασιγνήτους); *SEG* 41, 1037 (*SGO* I 04/13/01, Yiğitler, late II BC, [α]ὐτοκασιγνάτωι); *TAM* V 1, 66 (*SGO* I 04/14/01, Silandos, κάσι [voc.]). In *TAM* V 1, 434 (*SGO* I 04/20/01, Nisyra), two siblings are referred to as δύω [ψ]υχαὶ φιλάδελφοι.

4.2 Grandparents and Grandchildren

The **grandfather** and **grandmother** are almost always known in Hieradoumia simply as πάππος (m.) and μάμμη (f.), without any terminological
distinction between paternal and maternal grandparents.[12] Married couples (grandfather and grandmother) are usually referred to as οἱ πάπποι
('grandparents'); two grandmothers are referred to as αἱ μάμμαι (i.e. both
the maternal and paternal grandmother).[13] The forms πάπος and μάμη (with
simplification of the geminate consonants -ππ- and -μμ-) are both widely
attested throughout the region.[14] The **great-grandparents** are referred to
only once in inscriptions from Hieradoumia, where they are called πάπποι
οἱ μεγάλοι, 'great-*pappoi*', a term which seems to appear nowhere else in
ancient texts.[15]

  In Hieradoumia, as everywhere else in the Greek world, the most
common terms for **grandson** and **granddaughter** were (ὁ) ἔγγονος and
(ἡ) ἐγγόνη. ἔγγονος is occasionally treated as a noun of common gender
(ἡ ἔγγονος), and there are a few examples of the neuter plural τὰ ἔγγονα
(on the model of τὰ τέκνα). As we will see, the term ἔγγονος could also
be used for the brother's child: see Section 3.5. The terms υἱδεῖς and

---

[12] The only exception known to me is Thonemann 2019, no. 6 (Iaza), where maternal and
   paternal grandmothers are distinguished (ἡ μάμμη/ἡ μήτηρ τοῦ πατρός). Elsewhere in
   Asia Minor, paternal and maternal grandparents are sometimes distinguished with phrases
   like ὁ πρὸς μητρὸς/πατρὸς πάππος: e.g. *SEG* 52, 1104 (Stratonikeia); *I.Byzantion* 320a;
   I.Smyrna 221; Balland 1981, 151–4, no. 62 (Xanthos); *I.Didyma* 345; Ramsay, *Phrygia* II
   658, no. 605 (Akmoneia). The very rare Greek terms νέννος ('maternal grandfather') and
   νίννη ('maternal grandmother') and variants (Bremmer 1983, 184–6) do not appear in
   Hieradoumia.
[13] οἱ πάπποι: *TAM* V 1, 705 (Gordos, τοὺς πάππους = 'paternal grandparents'); *TAM* V 1,
   747 (Gordos, οἱ πάππι, a man and a woman); *SEG* 33, 1016 (Saittai, οἱ πάπποι = 'maternal
   grandparents'). αἱ μάμμαι: *TAM* V 1, 550 (Maionia, ἐ ... μάμμε); *TAM* V 1, 769 (Gordos,
   Ἀφιάδες ἐ μάμμε, that is, two grandmothers, both called Aphia); Robert, *Hellenica* VI, 97 n.1.
[14] πάπος: *TAM* V 1, 98 (Saittai); *TAM* V 1, 681 (Charakipolis); *TAM* V 1, 764 (Gordos); *TAM*
   V 1, 811 (Dağdere); *SEG* 56, 1350 (Hasköy); *SEG* 57, 1249 (inc.); *I.Manisa* 360 (Zeytinliova).
   μάμη: *TAM* V 1, 723 (Gordos); *SEG* 32, 1223 (Saittai); *SEG* 33, 1016 (Saittai); *SEG* 35, 1271
   (inc.); *SEG* 40, 1044 (Gordos); *SEG* 48, 1433 = *SEG* 51, 1685 (*SEG* 56, 1249, inc.); *SEG* 48, 1443
   (Maionia). ὁ πάπος κὲ ... ἡ μάμη: *TAM* V 1, 126 (Saittai). The form μάμμης (nom.) appears in
   SEG 41, 1073 (Kadoi); cf. μάμης (nom.) in *I.Smyrna* 397.
[15] *TAM* V 1, 706 (Gordos); Robert, *Hellenica* VI, 95. Elsewhere in Asia Minor, the usual terms for
   great-grandparents are προμάμμη (e.g. Naour 1980, no. 30, Tyriaion; *TAM* II 916, Rhodiapolis;
   I.Arykanda 106) and πρόπαππος (e.g. *SEG* 57, 1235, Thyateira; *TAM* II 18, Telmessos); cf.
   πρόμαια in *I.Kaunos* 164 and perhaps προτήθην in Clinton 2005, no. 629 (Eleusis: apparently
   'great-grandmother'). A great-grandchild is an ἐξέκγονος in *SEG* 41, 1391 and 44, 1211 (Patara),
   and a προέκγονος in *IG* XII 6, 333 (Samos); *SEG* 43, 820 (Ephesos); *I.Ephesos* 1066; *Sardis* II
   401, lines 20–1; etc.

ὑ(ἱ)ωνός each appear once in the region with the sense 'grandchildren' and 'grandson' respectively.[16]

In addition, we find a highly distinctive local word for 'grandchild', namely καμβ(δ)ιος/καμβ(δ)ιον, a term of uncertain origin and etymology which appears four times in Hieradoumia.[17]

> ὁ κανβειος: *SEG* 31, 1031 (Saittai).
> τὸ καμβειν (acc.): *TAM* V 1, 706 (Saittai, ἡ μάμμη τὸ καμβειν).
> οἱ καμβδιοι: *SEG* 48, 1465 (Saittai).
> καμβδιου (gen.): *I.Manisa* 179 (inc.).

It is notable that each of the three texts from Saittai offers a slightly different orthography (κανβ-, καμβ-, and καμβδ-). Moreover, several further orthographic variants on the term are attested in different parts of Anatolia. Seven inscriptions from Karia include the kinship term κομβος/κομβιον; as in Hieradoumia, the sense 'grandchild' is securely attested in one instance and is likely enough in the others.[18] Two further inscriptions from Karia offer the variant form κονψος, which in each case could quite plausibly carry the sense 'grandchild'.[19] Finally, the form *κανψιον (with variants) appears in three inscriptions from Kilikia, with 'grandchild' a plausible sense in all three cases.[20]

It is quite clear that Hieradoumian καμβ(δ)ιος/καμβ(δ)ιον, Karian κομβος/κομβιον and κονψος, and Kilikian κανψιον are all regional variants on a single kinship term of non-Greek origin.[21] The term is completely absent from literary Greek texts and seems to be unattested outside Anatolia. To all appearances, we are dealing with a very ancient proto-Anatolian kinship term, preserved (with regional variants) in the spoken language of several different parts of Anatolia, and used interchangeably with a more 'cosmopolitan'

---

[16] ἡ ἔγγονος: *TAM* V 1, 162 (Saittai, ἡ ἔγονος); *TAM* V 1, 550 (Maionia, τὴν ἔγγονον); *SEG* 35, 1158 (Petzl 1994, no. 37: τὴν ἔκγονον). τὰ ἔγγονα: *SEG* 40, 1100 (inc.: τὰ ἔγονα); *I.Manisa* 377 (inc.: τὰ ἔγγονα, where the term signifies 'brother's children': see below). In *SEG* 33, 1030 (Silandos), it is not clear whether τῷ ἐγώνων (acc.) represents τὸν ἔγγονον (m.) or τὸ ἔγγονον (n.). υἱδεῖς: *TAM* V 1, 786 (Gordos). ὑωνός: *SEG* 33, 1016 (Saittai); cf. *Sardis* II 440 (ὑωνή, 'granddaughter').

[17] Robert, *Hellenica* VI, 96–8; Robert 1963, 327–8; W. Blümel, *I.Nordkarien* 225 (commentary).

[18] *SEG* 39, 1114 (Kildara, κομβια); *I.Stratonikeia* 1442 (Lageina, ἡ κομβης); *SEG* 59, 1251 (Stratonikeia, [τοὺ]ς κομβους); *I.Didyma* 349, with Robert, *OMS* III, 1632 (κομβο[ς], fem.); *I.Keramos* 26 (τῶν κομβων); Isager 2016, 121–3 no.1 (κομβοι); *I.Iasos* 394 (τὰ κομβια); Drew-Bear 1972b, 204–5.

[19] *I.Nordkarien* 225 (Alabanda, ὁ κονψος); *I.Stratonikeia* 449 (where read καὶ κονψου Μενεκλέου).

[20] *MAMA* III 745 (Korykos, τοῦ κανψη αὐτοῦ); LBW 1484 (Tarsos, τ[ῶν] κανψιων [αὐτοῦ]); *I.Anazarbos* 167 (τῷ καμψι). It is possible, but far from certain, that the term should also be restored in an epitaph from Uluağaç in Cappadocia (*SEG* 34, 1411, perhaps [κ]ανψιου); I am unconvinced by Merkelbach's restoration of [κο]μβον in *SEG* 48, 1801 (Komana).

[21] Neumann 1961, 61 (Hittite *kappi-*, 'small'); cf. Melchert 1994, 162, 330; *HED* 4.61–3, *s.v.* kappi.

Greek synonym (ἔγγονος). The only other absolutely clear example of a pre-Greek survival of this kind in the kinship terminology of Roman Asia Minor is Lykian πιατρα, 'son's wife', discussed further in Section 4.10. As we shall see, this Anatolian terminological 'relic' is of some importance for understanding the character of Hieradoumian kinship terminology as a whole (see Section 4.13).

4.3 Uncles (FB, MB) and Aunts (FZ, MZ)

We next turn to the terminology for the father's and mother's siblings (uncles and aunts). Throughout the greater part of the Greek world, the standard terms for an uncle and an aunt were ὁ θεῖος and ἡ θεία (or ἡ τηθίς) respectively, without any terminological distinction between the father's siblings (FB and FZ) and the mother's siblings (MB and MZ). When such a distinction was required, it was usually signalled with a phrase like ὁ πρὸς μητρὸς θεῖος, '*theios* on the mother's side' (MB).[22] From time to time, we find circumlocutionary phrases such as ὁ τοῦ πατρὸς ἀδελφός, 'the father's brother' (FB), and the self-explanatory genitival compounds *patradelphos/-ē* (FB/FZ) and *mētradelphos/-ē* (MB/MZ) appear in a handful of texts from Asia Minor, Thrace, and the Black Sea.[23]

It is all the more striking, therefore, to find that the terms θεῖος and θεία are all but completely absent from the inscriptions of Hieradoumia.[24] The inhabitants of this region preferred to use more precise classificatory terms for their parents' siblings and their spouses. Indeed, the people of

---

[22] E.g. *I.Amyzon* 34; Herrmann and Polatkan 1969, no. 1, lines 90–91 (Nakrason); *MAMA* VIII 375 (*I.Sultan Dağı* 604, Salır); *Sardis* II 401, lines 33–4. Note also the very rare terms νάννος, νάννη, and variants ('mother's siblings'), Wilhelm 1901, 56–7; Goody 1969, 240–52; Bremmer 1983, 184–6; Ma 2013a, 182.

[23] ὁ τοῦ πατρὸς ἀδελφός (FB): e.g. *IG* IV² 1, 234 (Epidauros); *I.Apameia und Pylai* 37. πατράδελφος (FB): *TAM* III 1, 124 and 131 (Termessos, τὸν πατράδελφον); *SEG* 57, 594 (Skaptopara, πατραδέλφῳ); Rhodes and Osborne 2003, no. 1 (Delphi, IV BC, πατραδελφεῶν). μητράδελφος/-αδέλφη (MB/MZ): *I.Sultan Dağı* 612 (Salır, τῇ μητραδέλφ[η]); *RECAM* II 28A (Yeniyurt, N Galatia: in lines 6–7, restore μητρα̣δ̣ε̣λ̣|[φη]); Bean and Mitford 1970, 144, no. 144 (Thouththourbia, μ[ητρ]αδέλφην); *CIRB* 753 (Pantikapaion, μητράδελφε). As Selen Kılıç Aslan kindly points out to me, the alleged instance of πατρόθειος, 'paternal uncle', in *I.Arykanda* 110 (not otherwise attested) must in fact be a misreading for πατρόθετος, 'adoptive father'.

[24] The sole exception known to me is the verse inscription *SEG* 29, 1190 (*SGO* I 04/12/06), from Saittai, where θεῖοι is used to refer collectively to all of the deceased's uncles and aunts. The term θεῖος appears twice in the funerary epigraphy of Thyateira: *TAM* V 2, 961 (*SGO* I 04/05/12); *TAM* V 2, 992. In *SEG* 31, 1004 (Saittai), lines 10–11, the restoration ὁ δε[ῖ]ος (i.e. = θεῖος) seems too short for the *lacuna*; I would prefer to restore ὁ ⟨ἀ⟩δε[λφ]ός. Naour 1985, 49 wished to restore the term θεῖον in *SEG* 35, 1245 (Saittai).

Hieradoumia seems to have possessed a more comprehensive terminology for denoting uncles and aunts on the paternal and maternal sides, and their respective spouses, then any other part of the ancient Greco-Roman world. Distinct terms are attested for six of the eight possible categories of uncle and aunt: the father's brother (FB) and sister (FZ), the mother's brother (MB) and sister (MZ), the father's brother's wife (FBW), and (perhaps) the mother's brother's wife (MBW).

The standard terms in Hieradoumia for the **father's brother** (FB) and the **mother's brother** (MB) were πάτρως/πάτρων and μήτρως/μήτρων respectively. In one instance, the term πάτρως seems to be used of the father's father's brother, the great-uncle of the deceased.[25] Each term existed in two distinct forms, one with a standard third-declension inflection (πάτρων/-ωνος and μήτρων/-ωνος), the other indeclinable (πάτρως and μήτρως).[26] These two different inflections were semantically interchangeable, and there is no sign of one coming to supersede the other over time; in two instances, πάτρως and μήτρων appear alongside one another in a single text.[27] Overall, across Hieradoumia, the indeclinable forms were favoured by a factor of about three to one: we have twenty-eight instances of μήτρως to ten instances of μήτρων, and forty-two instances of πάτρως to fifteen instances of πάτρων, along with a handful of anomalous forms.

> ὁ μήτρως (**1–11**): *TAM* V 1, 189 (Saittai); *SEG* 29, 1179 (Saittai); *TAM* V 1, 383 (Kollyda); *TAM* V 1, 432 (Nisyra); *TAM* V 1, 433 (Nisyra); *TAM* V 1, 633 (Daldis); *TAM* V 1, 706 (Gordos); *SEG* 35, 1257 (Silandos); *I.Manisa* 320 (inc.); *Sammlung Tatış* 36 (inc.); *Sammlung Tatış* 47 (Silandos).
>
> τὸν μήτρως (**12–24**): *TAM* V 1, 98 (Saittai); *SEG* 34, 1226 (Saittai); *SEG* 40, 1070 (Saittai); *TAM* V 1, 434 (*SGO* I 04/20/01, Nisyra); *TAM* V 1, 625 (Daldis); *TAM* V 1, 633 (Daldis); *TAM* V 1, 705 (Gordos); *TAM* V 1, 707 (Gordos); *SEG* 40, 1043 (Gordos); *I.Manisa* 548 (Charakipolis); *SEG* 57, 1156 (Apollonioucharax); *SEG* 49, 1620 (Maionia); *SEG* 56, 1259 (inc.).
>
> οἱ μήτρως (**25–27**): *TAM* V 1, 548 (Maionia); *TAM* V 1, 625 (Daldis); Thonemann 2019, no. 6 (Iaza).
>
> τῷ μήτρως (**28**): *Sardis* II 666 (inc.).

[25] *TAM* V 1, 432 (Nisyra), line 18, Λούκιος ὁ πάτρως. The deceased's father was called Λούκιος Θίουλος (lines 3–4), making it unlikely that Λούκιος ὁ πάτρως was the father's brother; furthermore, there is no sign in *TAM* V 1, 433 that Loukios Thioulos had a brother named Loukios. We do know, however, that Loukios Thioulos' own paternal uncle was named Λούκιος (*TAM* V 1, 433, lines 7–8).

[26] On these two different inflections, see Buresch 1898, 45; Wiegand 1905, 328; Michon 1906, 36; Petzl 1978a, 750; *BE* 2007, 452.

[27] *TAM* V 1, 477 (Iaza); *TAM* V 1, 769 (Gordos).

ὁ μήτρων (**1–3**): *TAM* V 1, 477 (Iaza); *TAM* V 1, 733 (Gordos); *TAM* V 1, 769 (Gordos).

τὸν μήτρωνα (**4–7**): *TAM* V 1, 288 (Kula); *TAM* V 1, 804 (Yeğenoba, apparently with the sense 'mother's *syntrophos*'); *SEG* 31, 990 (Iaza); *SEG* 56, 1285 (Charakipolis).

οἱ μήτρωνες (**8–9**): *TAM* V 1, 550 (Maionia); *SEG* 57, 1244 (inc.).

τῷ μήτρωνι (**10**): *TAM* V 1, 660 (Daldis).

ὁ πάτρως (**1–19**): *TAM* V 1, 152 (Saittai); *TAM* V 1, 295 (Kula); *TAM* V 1, 432 (Nisyra: 'great-uncle'); *TAM* V 1, 433 (Nisyra); *TAM* V 1, 473a (Iaza); *TAM* V 1, 477 (Iaza); *TAM* V 1, 623 (Daldis); *TAM* V 1, 680 (Charakipolis); *TAM* V 1, 706 (Gordos); *TAM* V 1, 730 (Gordos); *TAM* V 1, 743 (Gordos); *TAM* V 1, p.200 T6 (inc.); *SEG* 57, 1178 (Gordos); *TAM* V 1, 797 (Hamit); *SEG* 35, 1167 (Maionia); *SEG* 35, 1271 (inc.); *SEG* 40, 1085 (inc.); *SEG* 49, 1742 (inc.); *SEG* 56, 1262 (inc.).

τὸν πάτρως (**20–30**): *TAM* V 1, 483a (Iaza); *TAM* V 1, 625 (Daldis); *TAM* V 1, 681 (Charakipolis); *I.Manisa* 548 (Charakipolis); *SEG* 57, 1156 (Apollonioucharax); *TAM* V 1, 704 (Gordos); *TAM* V 1, 707 (Gordos); *TAM* V 1, 786 (Yayakırıldık); *SEG* 53, 1344 (Mağazadamları); *SEG* 64, 1158 (inc.); *Sammlung Tatış* 38 (inc.).

οἱ πάτρως (**31–41**): *TAM* V 1, 210 (Tabala); *TAM* V 1, 293 (?) (Kula); *TAM* V 1, 434 (*SGO* I 04/20/01, Nisyra); *TAM* V 1, 714 (Gordos); *TAM* V 1, 769 (Gordos); *SEG* 33, 1016 (Saittai); *SEG* 49, 1660 (Saittai); *SEG* 57, 1153 (Apollonioucharax); *SEG* 57, 1175 (Iaza); *SEG* 40, 1085 (inc.); *SEG* 56, 1259 (inc.).

τῷ πάτρως (**42**): *SEG* 32, 1230 (Saittai).

ὁ πάτρων (**1–5**): *SEG* 32, 1231 (Saittai); *SEG* 35, 1160 (Iaza?); *SEG* 41, 1073 (Kadoi); *SEG* 53, 1341 (inc.); *TAM* V 2, 840A (*SGO* I 04/06/02: Sarılar).

τὸν πάτρωνα (**6–10**): *TAM* V 1, 297 (Kula); *TAM* V 1, 630 (Daldis); *TAM* V 1, 764 (Gordos); *SEG* 31, 990 (Iaza); *I.Manisa* 377 (inc.).

οἱ πάτρωνες (**12–13**): *SEG* 57, 1244 (inc.); *SEG* 65, 1196 (inc.).

τῷ πάτρωνι (**14–15**): *TAM* V 1, 630 (Daldis); *IGR* IV 597 (Kadoi).

Anomalous forms: ὁ μήτωρ in *SEG* 48, 1433 = *SEG* 51, 1685 (*SEG* 56, 1249: inc.); οἱ πάτρω in *TAM* V 1, 811 (Dağdere); τὸν πάτρω in Sargın 2020, no. 3 (Gordos: twice); τὸν μήτρω in *Sammlung Tatış* 44 (?Gordos) and *TAM* V 2, 1062 (Akçaalan).

Similar inflectional variation is found elsewhere in Lydia, in northern Phrygia, and in Pisidia, where πάτρως/πάτρων (FB) and μήτρως/μήτρων (MB) were also widely used to denote paternal and maternal uncles.[28]

---

[28] The terms are very rare elsewhere in the Greek world. οἱ πάτρωνες, 'paternal uncles', appears in *I.Smyrna* 397, but the onomastics suggest that the deceased may have been of Hieradoumian origin (mother Τατης, grandmother Αμιας).

A selection only:

(ὁ) πάτρως: *Sardis* VII 1, 139; *Sardis* II 663; *MAMA* X 244 (Nuhören); *MAMA* X 308 (Ortaca: πάτρω[ς] or πάτρω[ν]); *MAMA* V 91 (Dorylaion); *I.Ephesos* 3719 (upper Kaystros valley).

τῷ πάτρω(ι): *CIG* 3846n (*MAMA* IX P251); *SEG* 52, 1253, 1262, 1286 (all Aizanoi).

(τῷ) μήτρωνι: *MAMA* IX 158 (Aizanoi); *SEG* 6, 204 (Eumeneia); *I.Kibyra* 265 (μήτρονι).

τῷ πάτρωνι: *MAMA* X 323 (Ali köy); *MAMA* X 512 (Tiberiopolis, Hisarcık); *SEG* 53, 1558 (Altıntaş); *SEG* 53, 1562 (Işıklar); Waelkens 1986, no. 225 (Kütahya); Bean 1971, 32 (Balboura: πάτρωνι ... πάτρωνος); *SEG* 57, 1640 (Kibyra: misunderstood by Horsley, *IBurdurMus* 226).

(τοῖς) πάτ[ρω]σι: *SEG* 53, 1557 (Upper Tembris valley).

(τοῖς) μήτρωσιν: *MAMA* X 240 (Gökçeler).

How this distinctive 'twin' inflection for πάτρως/πάτρων (FB) and μήτρως/μήτρων (MB) should have arisen is an open question. The forms πάτρως and μήτρως are widely attested in earlier Greek literature (the latter already appears in Homer), but in literary texts, they seem always to be equipped with a full declension (πάτρως/-ωος).[29] Why they should have become fossilized as indeclinable forms in parts of inner Anatolia is a mystery. The forms πάτρων/-ωνος (FB) and μήτρων/-ωνος (MB) may have been coined under the influence of the common Latin loan-word πάτρων = *patronus*, from which πάτρων = 'paternal uncle' (FB) is in fact morphologically indistinguishable; as we will see shortly, Latin forms may have influenced the Hieradoumian ἰανάτηρ ('brother's wife') and ὑκερός ('husband's father').

We now turn to the terms for the **father's sister** (FZ) and **mother's sister** (MZ). The **father's sister** (FZ) seems consistently to have been designated with the term πάτρα, attested seventeen times in inscriptions from Hieradoumia. As it happens, this precise meaning can only be demonstrated with absolute certainty in three texts, but it gives a perfectly plausible sense in the remaining fourteen texts from Hieradoumia in which the term appears. This term seems to be peculiar to Anatolian epigraphy; I have found only a handful of examples outside Hieradoumia, all from Phrygia.[30]

---

[29] E.g. Chantraine 1999, 698 (μήτρως), 864 (πάτρως); μήτρως already in Homer (*Il.* 2.662; 16.717). The etymology of both terms is controversial: Szemerényi 1977, 53–61; Mallory and Adams 2006, 214.

[30] Buresch 1898, 45. Other instances: *MAMA* X 392 (Synaos); *SEG* 28, 1136 (Eumeneia); *I.Denizli* 148 (Eumeneia: *MAMA* XI pp. 62–3, P146); cf. J. and L. Robert, *BE* 1959, 439.

ἡ πάτρα (**1–11**): *SEG 53, 1341 (inc.: the sense is guaranteed by SEG 52, 1165); *TAM* V 1, 706 (Gordos); *TAM* V 1, 714 (Gordos, ἡ πατ[ρα]); *TAM* V 1, 769 (Gordos); *TAM* V 1, 778 (Kavakalan); *TAM* V 1, 806 (Yeğenoba); *TAM* V 1, 477 (*SGO* I 04/19/02: Iaza); *SEG* 33, 1016 (Saittai); *I.Manisa* 525 (Apollonioucharax); *SEG* 56, 1262 (inc.); *TAM* V 2, 840A (*SGO* I 04/06/02: Sarılar).

τὴν πάτραν (**12–14**): *TAM V 1, 705 (Gordos); *TAM* V 1, 765 (Gordos); *I.Manisa* 426 (inc.).

αἱ πάτραι (**15–17**): *TAM V 1, 432 (Nisyra, αἱ πάτραι μετὰ τῶν συνβίων); *TAM* V 1, 434 (*SGO* I 04/20/01: Nisyra, ἑ πάτραι); *SEG* 56, 1333 (Saittai).

The **mother's sister** (MZ) is a more elusive figure. In nine inscriptions from Hieradoumia, female relatives are designated with the terms ἡ τήθη (four texts) or ἡ τηθείς/τειθείς (five texts). In no case does the precise meaning of the term emerge clearly from the context. However, in seven of these nine inscriptions, this female relative is listed alongside other aunts and uncles of the deceased, strongly suggesting that the terms τήθη and τηθείς are both being used to refer to an aunt of some kind.

ἡ τήθη: (**1**) *TAM* V 1, 608 (Ioudda: τῇ τείθι κὲ τῷ συμβίῳ αὐτῆς); (**2**) *TAM* V 1, 714 (Gordos: οἱ πάτρως, ἡ τήθη, ἡ πάτ[ρα]); (**3**) *TAM* V 1, 769 (Gordos: οἱ πάτρως, ἡ πάτρα, ἡ τήθη, ὁ μήτρων); (**4**) *SEG* 40, 1085 (inc.: ἡ τήθη, ἡ μάμμη, ὁ πάτρως, ἡ πατρεία).

ἡ τηθείς: (**5**) *TAM* V 1, 433 (Nisyra: ὁ πάτρως, ἡ τηθείς); (**6**) *TAM* V 1, 625 (Daldis: οἱ μήτρ[ως], [ἡ τ]ηθείς); (**7**) *SEG* 56, 1262 (inc.: ἡ τηθείς, ἡ πάτρα, ὁ πάτρως); (**8**) *SEG* 49, 1732 (inc.: ἡ τηθείς).

ἡ τειθείς/αἱ τειθείδες: (**9**) Thonemann 2019, no. 6 (Iaza: οἱ μήτρως, αἱ τειθείδες).

Elsewhere in the Greek world, the rare term τηθ(ε)ίς seems always to signify 'aunt', either the father's sister (FZ) or the mother's sister (MZ).[31] The term τήθη is rather more common and seems usually to have signified 'grandmother'.[32] However, τήθη certainly means 'mother's sister' (MZ) in

---

[31] τηθ(ε)ίς = 'mother's sister' (MZ): *Jannoray 1946, 254–9, no. 8 (Delphi: τηθίδα). τηθ(ε)ίς = 'father's sister' (FZ): Naour 1980, no. 30 (Tyriaion in Lykia: τηθίς); **I.Stratonikeia* 203 (τῆς τηθείδος). Uncertain meaning: *SEG* 6, 221 (Eumeneia: τειθείδι). The term is occasionally found in literary texts from the fourth century BC onwards (LSJ, *s.v.* τηθίς: Isaeus, Demosthenes, Menander, etc.), used indiscriminately of the father's sister and the mother's sister (Dem. 27.14 [FZ], 43.29 [MZ]).

[32] τήθη = 'grandmother': *Clinton 2005, no. 523 (Eleusis, τὴν τήθην = 'paternal grandmother'); *IGR III 1228 (Kanatha, τήθη = 'maternal grandmother'); *Lindos II 465, g3–6 (τῆθ[αν] = 'paternal grandmother'). The sense is uncertain in Clinton 2005, no. 223 (Eleusis, ἡ τήθη); Clinton 2005, no. 433 (Eleusis, τὴν τήθην); Clinton 2005, no. 629 (Eleusis, τὴν προτήθην); *IG* V 1, 594 (Sparta, τῆς τήθης); *IG* XII 9, 142 (Amarynthos, τὴν τήθην); Feissel 1983, no. 115 (Thessalonike, τήθη); *IG* X 2 1, 474 (Thessalonike, τήθη); *IG* XII 5, 923 (Tenos, τήθη[ν]); SEG

a Rhodian inscription of the first century BC, and the term is twice used with the sense 'father's sister' (FZ) in inscriptions from Stratonikeia in Karia.[33] In short, we know that τήθη and τηθείς *could* be used as synonyms, both meaning 'aunt'.[34] In Hieradoumia, the terms τήθη and τηθείς appear alongside ἡ πάτρα ('father's sister', FZ) in several texts and hence are very unlikely either to refer specifically to the father's sister or to be a general term for an aunt on either side of the family. I therefore tentatively conclude that both τήθη and τηθείς – at least in Hieradoumia – should be seen as technical terms for the mother's sister (MZ).[35]

4.4 Uncles' and Aunts' Spouses (FBW/MBW, FZH/MZH)

The four terms for uncles and aunts discussed so far (πάτρως/πάτρων [FB], μήτρως/μήτρων [MB], πάτρα [FZ], and τήθη/τηθείς [MZ]) appear only to have been applied to consanguine uncles and aunts (the parents' siblings), not to three-step affines (the wives and husbands of the parents' siblings). In an inscription from Nisyra, a certain Lucius was honoured after his death by, among others, 'his *metrōs* Theodoros along with his wife; his *patrai* Meltinē and Lucilla along with their husbands … his *patrōs* Lucius along with his wife and children and dependents'.[36] Lucius' consanguine aunts and uncles were designated with special terms and named in his epitaph; their various husbands and wives were left unnamed and described simply as 'the aunt's husband', 'the uncle's wife'.

55, 1368 (Nikomedeia, τήθη); *I.Smyrna* 640 (τήθην). In *IG* XII Suppl. 29b (Dardanos: for the provenance, see Robert 1966, 31 n.1), two brothers honour their τήθη for having reared them (ἐκτροφῆς ἕνεκεν). Ma 2013a, 175 understands the woman to have been their nurse; but she is a citizen, and so may well have been their grandmother (Robert, *Hellenica* XIII, 41 n.2) or aunt.

[33] τήθη = 'aunt': *SEG* 43, 527 (Kontorini 1993, 91–2, Rhodes, τᾶς τήθας = 'mother's sister', MZ); *I.Stratonikeia* 230a and 230b (τήθης = 'father's sister', FZ); *I.Stratonikeia* 206 (*SGO* I 02/06/10: τήθη = 'father's sister', FZ).

[34] Robert, *OMS* I, 429, upholds a distinction between τήθη ('grandmother') and τηθείς ('mother's sister', MZ), but note *I.Stratonikeia* 203 and *I.Stratonikeia* 206 (*SGO* I 02/06/10), where τηθείς and τήθη are used in contemporary texts of the same woman (cf. stemma p.90).

[35] In *TAM* V 1, 433 (Nisyra), the τηθείς Apphias is listed between the deceased's πάτρως Loukios and the συνγενεῖς Dionysios and Loukios (perhaps the sons of the πάτρως Loukios). The sequence suggests that Apphias might have been the father's brother's wife (FBW); but of course the brothers Loukios and Apollonios Thioulos might have married two sisters, as in *I.Ephesos* 1068 and apparently *SEG* 56, 1771 (Phellos), in which case Apphias would be both mother's sister (MZ) and father's brother's wife (FBW) to the deceased. The sense 'father's/mother's brother's wife' is excluded in *TAM* V 1, 608 and *SEG* 40, 1085.

[36] *TAM* V 1, 432 (Nisyra), ὁ μήτρως Θεόδωρος μετὰ τῆς συνβίου, etc. Cf. also *TAM* V 1, 730 (Gordos), Δημήτριος ὁ μήτρως μετὰ τῆς συνβίου; *TAM* V 1, 608 (Ioudda), Πώλλη τῇ τείθι κὲ τῷ συμβίῳ αὐτῆς Βεττηνιανῷ.

In fact, there do seem to have been special terms for at least one, and perhaps two of these more distant affine uncles and aunts: the **father's brother's wife** (FBW) and (less certainly) the **mother's brother's wife** (MBW). It stands to reason that it should be these two affines (rather than the father's sister's husband [FZH] and the mother's sister's husband [MZH]) who came to be designated with special terms. In a culture which practises patrilocal residence after marriage (see Section 5.6), the father's sister and the mother's sister would both become part of a different household at marriage, and hence their respective husbands would generally tend to be considered as more 'distant' kin than the wives of one's maternal or (particularly) paternal uncles.

The **father's brother's wife** (FBW) was designated in Hieradoumia by the extremely rare term πατρεία. This term seems not to be attested at all in Greek literary sources, and it is found in only five inscriptions, all from Hieradoumia. In the past, the term has been seen as a synonym for πάτρα, 'father's sister' (FZ), but this is clearly incorrect; in each of the five known cases from Hieradoumia, close attention to the context clearly demonstrates that the term must refer to the father's brother's wife (FBW).[37] I know of no distinctive term for the father's brother's wife anywhere else in the Greek world.

> In *SEG* 40, 1085 (inc.), Παπίας ὁ πάτρως καὶ Συντύχη ἡ πατρεία appear to be a married couple. Similarly, in *SEG* 57, 1175 (Iaza), two πατρεῖαι are paired with two πάτρως. In *SEG* 49, 1657 (Saittai: τὴν πατρείαν), the *patreia*'s niece (lines 14–15) is apparently the daughter of one of the *patreia*'s husband's brothers (lines 10–12), and in *SEG* 49, 1660 (Saittai: [τὴν] πατρ[εί]αν), the *patreia*'s nephew (lines 8–9) is apparently the son of the *patreia*'s *synnymphos* (lines 7–8). In *TAM* V 1, 782 (Yayakırıldık: τὴν πατρείαν), the individuals addressing the deceased woman as *patreia* seem to be the children of her *daērs*.

Finally, the **mother's brother's wife** (MBW) may perhaps have been designated with the feminine noun ἡ μήτρως, apparently attested only once, at Daldis in western Hieradoumia.[38] The sense of the term does not appear from the context, although it is clearly cognate with ὁ μήτρως, 'mother's brother' (MB). Realistically, there are only two possibilities for the meaning of ἡ μήτρως: 'mother's sister' (MZ, in which case the term would be a synonym for τήθη/τηθείς) and 'mother's brother's wife' (MBW, so that ἡ μήτρως

---

[37] Synonym for πάτρα (FZ): Keil and Premerstein 1911, no. 138, commentary; *MAMA* X 392, commentary; Malay 1999, 171–2, nos. 208–209 (*SEG* 49, 1657 and 1660); Brixhe 1999, 90–1.
[38] *TAM* V 1, 641 (Daldis: τὴν μήτρω).

is to ὁ μήτρως as ἡ πατρεία is to ὁ πάτρως). The latter seems to me the more economical explanation, but it cannot be taken as certain.

4.5 Nephews, Nieces, and Cousins

In stark contrast to the rich and precise Hieradoumian terminology for aunts and uncles, the vocabulary for **nephews**, **nieces**, and **cousins** is relatively limited and imprecise. In only half a dozen inscriptions from Hieradoumia do we find a niece or nephew unambiguously designated as such, always with a periphrastic phrase such as 'my brother's son' (ὁ τοῦ ἀδελφοῦ υἱός).[39] More surprisingly, in two epitaphs, neither with a known provenance, we find the term ἔγγονος (usually 'grandson') used in a context where it must necessarily mean 'nephew' or more precisely 'brother's son': in *I.Manisa* 377 (AD 257/8), τὰ ἔγγονα commemorate τὸν ἴδιον πάτρ[ω]να, and in *SEG* 65, 1196, οἱ πάτρωνες commemorate τὸν ἔγγονον.[40] This 'extension' of the semantic field of the term ἔγγονος is unexpected, and seems not to be found anywhere else in the Greek world; to all appearances, the word could be used in Hieradoumia as a classificatory term for a 'descendant', broadly conceived as two-step consanguineous kin in a younger generation (grandson or nephew). Given the small number of cases, we cannot be certain that the term was only used of the relationship between the *paternal* uncle and his nephews/nieces; however, the typical structure of the Hieradoumian household means that the paternal uncle would tend to have a closer relationship with his nephews than either the maternal uncle or the paternal/maternal aunt (see Chapter 5, Section 5.6).

The total number of cases where 'nephews' appear in the funerary epigraphy of Hieradoumia remains startlingly small, especially when set against the *c.* 130 instances of the various special terms for uncle/aunt. It is hard

---

[39] *I.Manisa* 521 (Apollonioucharax): τὸν τοῦ ἀδελφοῦ υεἱόν (lines 16–17: on this difficult text, see further below); *SEG* 39, 1309 (inc.), ἀδελφοῦ υἱῷ; *SEG* 53, 1344 (Mağazadamları), ἀδελφοῦ τέκνου; *SEG* 56, 1269 (inc.), ἀδελφῆς υἱός; *I.Manisa* 64 (Küpüler, sanctuary of Zeus Sabazios) τῶν τοῦ ἀδελφοῦ ... τέκνων; Waelkens 1986, no. 6 (Synaos), ἀδελφοῦ υἱῷ; cf. *TAM* V 2, 1084 (Thyateira), υὸν τῆς ἀδελφῆς. The very rare term ἀδελφότεκνον ('nephew') appears in two inscriptions from central Phrygia: *SEG* 28, 1148 (Eumeneia); Tabbernee 1997, 76–9, no. 6 (Waelkens 1986, no. 372; Uşak).

[40] It is true that the term πάτρων/πάτρως can mean 'great-uncle' (Section 4.3 above), but that is certainly not the case in *I.Manisa* 377, where the relationship paternal uncle/nephews is guaranteed by the context; in *SEG* 65, 1196 (certainly from Hieradoumia, as the formulae show), the relationship is effectively certain, despite the doubts of B. Puech in *AE* 2015, 1433.

to avoid the conclusion that epitaphs were usually consciously phrased in such a way as to avoid using the term 'nephew/niece' at all. Put another way, when uncle Marcus honoured his deceased nephew Glykon, he usually chose to describe their relationship in the form Γλύκωνα ἐτείμησεν Μᾶρκος ὁ πάτρως rather than Μᾶρκος ἐτείμησεν Γλύκωνα τὸν τοῦ ἀδελφοῦ υἱόν (Chapter 2, Section 2.3).

The standard terms for 'cousin' elsewhere in Roman Asia Minor were ἀνεψιός/-ά and ἐξάδελφος/ἐξαδέλφη. The word ἐξάδελφος seems to be unattested in Hieradoumia.[41] The terms ἀνεψιός (m.) and ἀνεψιά (f.) appear only in a tiny handful of texts from the region:

> τὸν ἀνεψιόν (**1–3**): *I.Manisa* 521 (Apollonioucharax, lines 18–19 and 20), *I.Manisa* 548 (Charakipolis).
> τὴν ἀνεψιάν (**4–5**): *SEG* 49, 1660 (Saittai); *SEG* 56, 1262 (inc.).

In none of these five cases is the relationship between the parties absolutely certain. Elsewhere in Roman Asia Minor, although the terms ἀνεψιός/-ά normally mean 'cousin', they do also occasionally carry the sense 'nephew/niece', and hence that meaning is a formal possibility in the examples from Hieradoumia also.[42] However, in three of the four inscriptions concerned, the individuals addressing the deceased as ἀνεψιός/-ά are grouped alongside other individuals who are specifically designated as the deceased's paternal or maternal aunts and uncles: it thus seems highly likely that in each case the term ἀνεψιός/-ά does indeed mean 'cousin'.[43]

---

[41] ἐξξα[δέλφου] has been tentatively restored in *TAM* V 1, 532 (Maionia): see *SEG* 33, 1008. The term is common across inner Anatolia (Phrygia, Galatia, Lykaonia, Pisidia, Lykia). For Phrygian examples, see e.g. *MAMA* VII 150 (Hadrianopolis: sense guaranteed); *I.Denizli* 148 (Eumeneia: *MAMA* XI pp. 62–3, P146); *MAMA* X 221 (Kepez); *SEG* 44, 1043 (near Dorylaion); *SEG* 53, 1533 (Saraycık); *MAMA* IX 143 (Aizanoi). The term occasionally signifies 'nephew' in literary texts (Robert, *Hellenica* XIII, 33–4), but I have not found an epigraphic instance; in *TAM* II 223 (Sidyma), ἐξάδελφον must mean 'first cousin once removed'.

[42] The sense ἀνεψιός/-ά = 'nephew/niece' is not recognized by LSJ, *s.v.*, or by *DGE* II 298. This sense is guaranteed e.g. in *MAMA* X 308 (Ortaca: πάτρω[ς ἀν]υψιῷ); *MAMA* X 85 (Altıntaş: ἀν[εψιοῖς], of the brother's children); *CIG* 3827p (Kotiaion: ἀνεψιῷ); *MAMA* VII 260a (near Yukarı Piribeyli: the brother's son); *MAMA* VII 543 (Insuyu: ἀνεψιοὶ … θείῳ); *SEG* 45, 1823 (Oinoanda: the sister's son). It is not clear to me what relationships are designated by the terms ἀδελφιδοῦς and ἀνεψιοῦ in *MAMA* VI 285 (Akmoneia).

[43] *SEG* 49, 1660 (Saittai): Μήθυμνος, Ἀπ[ολλώ]νιος οἱ πάτρως, Μήθυμνο[ς, - -]α τὴν ἀνεψίαν. *SEG* 56, 1262 (inc.): Ἀπολλώνιος τὴν ἀνεψίαν, Τατιας ἡ τηθείς, Τατιας ἡ πάτρα, Ἀρτεμίδωρος ὁ πάτρως. *I.Manisa* 521 (Apollonioucharax): Μένανδρος τὸν τοῦ ἀδελφοῦ υείόν, Ἀπολλωνίδης, Ἀθήναιος τὸν ἀνεψι[ό]ν, Μένανδρος, Ἕρμος, Ἀθή[ν]αιος τὸν ἀνε[ψ]ιόν. In this last case, it seems likely that Apollonides and Athenaios are the deceased's first cousins and that Menandros, Hermos, and Athenaios are his first cousins once removed. For the application of the term ἀνεψιός to first cousins of any degree of removal, see Rice 1986, 213–15 (inscriptions from Rhodes).

Can these four texts really be the only epitaphs from Hieradoumia in which cousins make an appearance? Given the numerous uncles and aunts attested in Hieradoumian epitaphs (almost 130 in total), it would be surprising to find cousins mentioned only in such a minuscule number of texts. This brings us to the highly problematic kinship terms ἀδελφίδης (m.) and ἀδελφίδισσα (f.), which appear in twenty texts from Hieradoumia (twenty-two attestations in total).[44]

> ὁ ἀδελφίδης (**1–4**): *SEG* 40, 1092 (inc.); *SEG* 49, 1561 (Daldis); *SEG* 53, 1341 (inc.); *Sammlung Tatış* 47 (Silandos).
>
> τὸν ἀδελφιδῆ (**5–9**): *TAM* V 1, 811 (Dağdere); *SEG* 40, 1099 (inc.); *SEG* 56, 1259 (inc.); *I.Manisa* 521, lines 15–16 (Apollonioucharax); *I.Manisa* 525 (Apollonioucharax).
>
> τὸν ἀδελφιδῆα (**10–11**): *TAM* V 1, 638 (Daldis); *I.Manisa* 521, lines 7–8 (Apollonioucharax).
>
> τὸν ἀδελφιδέα (**12–14**): *TAM* V 1, 707 (Gordos); *SEG* 56, 1263 (inc.); *SEG* 65, 1196 (inc.).
>
> τὸν ἀδελφιδοῦν (**15**): *TAM* V 1, 702 (Gordos).
>
> τῷ ἀδελφιδεῖ (**16**): *TAM* V 1, 12 (Lyendos).
>
> οἱ ἀδελφιδεῖς (**17–18**): *TAM* V 1, 434 (*SGO* I 04/20/01, Nisyra); *SEG* 35, 1247 (Saittai).
>
> τῶν ἀδελφιδαίων (**19**): *I.Manisa* 376 (inc.).
>
> ἡ ἀδελφίδισσα (**20–21**): *SEG* 53, 1341 (inc.); *SEG* 40, 1067 (Saittai, ἀδελφίδισα).
>
> τῇ ἀδελφιδί[σσῃ] (**22**): *TAM* V 3, 1796 (Philadelphia)

In both Greek literary texts and in inscriptions from other parts of the Greek world, the terms ἀδελφιδοῦς/-ίδης/-ιδεύς (m.) and ἀδελφιδῆ/-ίδισσα (f.) seem usually to signify 'sibling's son/daughter', 'nephew/niece'.[45] However, these are certainly not the only possible meanings of the terms. In an honorific inscription from Sardis of the early third century AD, the term ἀδελφιδ[οῦν] unambiguously means 'first cousin' (the father's

---

[44] In Hieradoumian texts, the masculine form is always rendered ἀδελφίδης in the nominative singular, with the accusative singular variously rendered as -ιδῆ, -ιδέα, and -ιδῆα. In Greek literary texts, and in epigraphy from other parts of the Greek world, the standard forms are ἀδελφιδοῦς (m.) and ἀδελφιδῆ (f.), inflections which are in fact very poorly attested in Hieradoumia (a single example of the masculine accusative -ιδοῦν). See P. Herrmann on *TAM* V 1, 811, and cf. the discussion of πενθερίδης below.

[45] LSJ, *s.v.*; *DGE* I 46; e.g. *I.Oropos* 431; *I.Ilion* 88; *SEG* 45, 791 (Philippoi); etc. In TL 25 (Tlos: IV BC), ἀδελφιδοῦς/ἀδελφιδῆ corresponds to the Lykian *tuhes*, 'nephew/niece': Brixhe 1999, 85–6. This meaning is usually assumed without argument for the Hieradoumian cases: e.g. P. Herrmann on *TAM* V 1, 811 ('fratris vel sororis filius'); H. Malay on *I.Manisa* 521 ('nephew'); Petzl 1990, 61 ('Nichte', comparing *SEG* 53, 1341); Malay and Ricl 2006, 65–6; G. Petzl on *TAM* V 3, 1796 ('Nichte'). For an exception, see Lajtar and Petzl 2003, 47 (translating 'Cousin/Cousine').

brother's son).[46] Still more striking is the use of the term ἀδελφιδοῦς on a late Hellenistic private honorific statue base from Xanthos in Lykia, where the term is twice used of a great-uncle, the father's father's brother (*sic*).[47] It appears that the term ἀδελφίδης and cognates could in principle refer to a whole range of natal kin related to one 'through a sibling'.

In no single one of the twenty-two Hieradoumian examples does the sense of the terms ἀδελφίδης (m.) or ἀδελφίδισσα (f.) emerge unambiguously from the context. The sense 'nephew/niece', 'sibling's son/daughter', is nowhere a necessary meaning for the term(s), and in several cases, it is unlikely or impossible.[48] At the same time, in five Hieradoumian epitaphs, ἀδελφιδεῖς of the deceased (or people describing the deceased as their ἀδελφίδης) are listed immediately after uncles or aunts of the deceased, which would have an obvious logic if the term signified 'cousin' (since cousins would then be listed immediately after their parents).[49] Indeed, the meaning 'cousin' gives a coherent and plausible family structure in all but one or two of the seventeen inscriptions from Hieradoumia and helps account for what would otherwise be a very curious *absence* of cousins in the funerary epigraphy of the region.[50] I therefore tentatively conclude that in Hieradoumia (as at Sardis: see above), the terms ἀδελφίδης (m.) or

[46] *Sardis* II 401, line 29: the honorand is the ἀδελφιδοῦς of C. Asinnius Rufus Nikomachos and C. Asinnius Lepidus, the sons of C. Asinnius Nikomachos, who is described as the honorand's 'paternal uncle' (lines 33–34, θεί[ου πρὸς πατ]ρός): Herrmann 1993, 255 (stemma).

[47] *SEG* 55, 1502 (Xanthos: ἀδελφιδοῦν, lines 10–11), with Baker and Thériault 2005, 358–60.

[48] In *TAM* V 1, 434 (*SGO* I 04/20/01, Nisyra), the deceased (a brother and sister) seem to have no other siblings, and hence οἱ ἀδελφιδεῖς (line 9) are very unlikely to be nephews. In *TAM* V 1, 707 (Gordos), if τὸν ἀδελφιδέα signified 'nephew', then Antiochos (line 11) would be a generation older than anyone else named in the inscription. In *SEG* 53, 1341 (inc.), the deceased is a four-year-old girl, and hence it would be surprising for her ἀδελφίδης and ἀδελφίδισσα (lines 15–17) to be her nephew and niece. See also the next note.

[49] *TAM* V 1, 434 (*SGO* I 04/20/01, Nisyra), οἱ πάτρως καὶ ἐ πάτραι, οἱ ἀδελφιδεῖς; *SEG* 53, 1341 (inc.), ὁ πάτρων Ἀγαθόπους κὲ ἡ πάτρα Ἰουλιανὴ κὲ ὁ ἀδελφίδης Δειογένης κὲ ἡ ἀδελφίδισσα ἡ Εὐγνωμονίς; *SEG* 56, 1259 (inc.), Κράτιππος, Ἀπολλώνιος οἱ πάτρως, Ἀπολλώνιος τὸν ἀδελφιδῆ; *I.Manisa* 525 (Apollonioucharax), Νεικόπολις ἡ πάτρα, Μελτίνη καὶ Γαλλικὸς τὸν ἀδελφιδῆ; *SEG* 65, 1196 (inc.), (three persons) οἱ πάτρωνες ἐτείμησαν τὸν ἔγγονον … (five persons) ἐτείμησαν τὸν ἀδελφι[δ]έα. In the last three cases, the sense 'nephew/niece' seems particularly unlikely: if the relevant persons were uncles/aunts of the deceased, why were they not so designated with a precise technical term (πάτρως, πάτρα etc.), like the other uncles and aunts listed? Cf. also *Sammlung Tatış* 47 (Silandos), Ἀλέξανδρος ὁ ἀδελφίδης, Γλύκων ὁ μήτρως (cousin listed before uncle?).

[50] In *I.Manisa* 521 (Apollonioucharax), a paternal uncle and five cousins are clearly designated as such (lines 16–20: Μένανδρος τὸν τοῦ ἀδελφοῦ υείόν, Ἀπολλωνίδης, Ἀθήναιος τὸν ἀνεψι[ό]ν, Μένανδρος, Ἕρμος, Ἀθή[ν]αιος τὸν ἀνε[ψ]ιόν), but three (perhaps five) men also address the deceased as their ἀδελφίδης (lines 6–8, Ἀθήναιος, Ἀρτεμίδωρος τὸν ἀδελφιδῆα; lines 14–16, Στράτιος, Ἀθήναιος, Ἀρτεμίδωρος τὸν ἀδελφιδῆα: perhaps an inadvertent repetition, as

ἀδελφίδισσα (f.) were generally used as synonyms for ἀνεψιός/-ά, 'cousin', albeit with the caveat that in some individual cases the terms may have been used of other relatively distant natal kin (nephews, nieces, great-uncles, etc.).

At any rate, by Hieradoumian standards, the terms ἀδελφίδης and ἀδελφίδισσα were evidently relatively blunt instruments, which served to designate only a general broad category of kin relationship (individuals related to one 'through a sibling'), rather than a specific relationship within a lineage.

4.6 Husband's Father and Husband's Mother

As in the Homeric poems – but in contrast to most post-Homeric Greek societies – the inhabitants of Hieradoumia drew a clear terminological distinction between the wife's parents and the husband's parents. In funerary inscriptions from the region, the husband's parents are referred to as ὑκεροί (ὑκερός HF, ὑκερά HM), while the wife's parents are denoted with the terms πενθερός (WF) and πενθερά (WM). This distinction was rigorously observed: there is not a single instance from Hieradoumia of the husband's parents being known as *pentheroi* or the wife's parents as *hykeroi*.

The **husband's father** (HF) and **husband's mother** (HM) are always referred to as ὑκερός and ὑκερά. These terms appear some thirty-two times in Hieradoumia, sixteen times in the masculine (*hykeros*, 'husband's father', HF), eleven times in the feminine (*hykera*, 'husband's mother', HM), and five times in the plural (*hykeroi*, 'husband's parents').

> ὁ ὑκερός (**1**): *TAM* V 1, 631 (Daldis: ὁ ἱκερός).
> τὸν ὑκερόν (**2–14**): *TAM* V 1, 704 (Gordos); *TAM* V 1, 764 (Gordos); *TAM* V 1, 771 (Gordos); *TAM* V 1, 774 (Gordos); *SEG* 40, 1043 (Gordos); *TAM* V 1, 784 (Yayakırıldık); *TAM* V 1, 796 (Hamit); *SEG* 31, 1007 (Saittai); *SEG* 57, 1156 (Daldis); *SEG* 49, 1629 (Nisyra); *TAM* V 1, 472 (Iaza); *SEG* 56, 1257 (inc.); *SEG* 57, 1249 (inc.).
> τῷ ὑκερῷ (**15–16**): *TAM* V 1, 657 (Daldis); *Sardis* II 666 (inc.).

apparently in *TAM* V 1, 706 [Gordos], the πάτρως and πάτρα). These three (or five) men are hence unlikely to be cousins to the deceased. They could be maternal uncles, but it is striking to find them listed (in lines 6–8) between the deceased's natural brother and sister: I wonder whether the term ἀδελφίδης might here signify step-brother or half-brother. Note also *SEG* 40, 1099 (inc.), where Philoxenos is ἐπίτροπος to his ἀδελφίδης, and hence perhaps more likely to be his uncle than his cousin. In *TAM* V 1, 12 (Aktaş), an ἀδελφίδῆς (bearing the same name as the deceased's father) acts as heir to the deceased: again, he may be the deceased's nephew.

ἡ ὑκερά (**17–19**): *SEG* 49, 1607 (Maionia); **TAM* V 1, 39 (Bagis); *Sammlung Tatış* 47 (Silandos: ἡ ἑκυρά)

τὴν ὑκεράν (**20–24**): **TAM* V 1, 765 (Gordos, line 7); *TAM* V 1, 765 (Gordos, lines 9–12, apparently of a husband's *threpsasa*); **TAM* V 1, 783+*SEG* 46, 1539 (Yayakırıldık); **TAM* V 1, 683 (Charakipolis); *I.Manisa* 522 (Apollonioucharax, of a husband's *threpsasa*).

τὴν ὑκερῆ (**25**): *SEG* 49, 1742 (Kula?).

τῆς ὑκερᾶς (**26**): Thonemann 2019, no. 6 (Iaza).

τῇ ὑκερᾷ (**27**): *I.Manisa* 325 (inc.).

οἱ ὑκεροί (**28–29**): **TAM* V 1, 825 (Kömürcü: [οἱ] ὑκαιροί); **TAM* V 1, 175 (Saittai: οἱ ἑκυροί).

τοὺς ὑκερούς (**30–32**): **TAM* V 1, 705 (Gordos: τοὺς ἑκυρούς); **TAM* V 1, 803 (Yeğenoba); **I.Manisa* 340 (Daldis).

As will be clear from the examples collected above, the correct form of the word in Hieradoumia was, without doubt, ὑκερ- rather than ἑκυρ- (twenty-nine instances of ὑκερός/-ά against three instances of ἑκυρός/-ά).[51] This 'Hieradoumian' orthography is all but unattested outside this small region: elsewhere in the Greek world, even in neighbouring parts of Phrygia, the 'correct' Homeric orthography ἑκυρός/-ά is overwhelmingly dominant (nineteen instances of ἑκυρός/-ά against one instance of ὑκερός/-ά).[52] This local peculiarity is of some socio-linguistic significance, since it shows that Hieradoumian ὑκερός/-ά was not simply a recondite Homeric 'borrowing', but was part of the living language in the region. How the form ὑκερός/-ά might have arisen is unclear: it is conceivably that we are dealing with linguistic cross-pollination between the original Greek ἑκυρός/-ά and the Latin *socer/socrus* (see further below, on Hieradoumian ἰανάτηρ and Latin *ianitrix*).[53]

The term ἑκυρός/-ά (HF/HM) appears fourteen times elsewhere in Asia Minor, almost always with its traditional 'Homeric' orthography. Seven examples derive from the parts of Phrygia immediately adjoining Hieradoumia to the north-east (Aizanoi, Kotiaion, Dorylaion, the Upper Tembris); there are also stray examples from eastern Phrygia (Vetissos and the Axylon), central Phrygia (Akmoneia), eastern Pisidia (Anaboura), and perhaps Mysia (Miletoupolis).

---

[51] Prevalence of ὑκερ- in Hieradoumia already noted by Robert, *Hellenica* VI, 103; treated as a simple 'métathèse graphique' in *BE* 1991, 501. The orthographic variation ε/υ is very rare in Roman Anatolia: Brixhe 1987, 46–61.

[52] The sole example of ὑκερ- anywhere outside Hieradoumia is *SEG* 35, 1289 (Miletoupolis), assuming that [ὑ]κεροί is correctly restored in line 2.

[53] The terms ἑκυρός/-ά (Gk) and *socer/socrus* (Lat) go back to IE **swéˆkuros*, **sweˆkrúh₂s*, 'father-in-law', 'mother-in-law' (Szemerényi 1977, 63–7).

Northern Phrygia (**1–7**): *MAMA IX 425 (Aizanoi: ἐκυρῷ, with misleading commentary); *MAMA V 22 (Dorylaion: read Κλαυδία Ἀμ[μ|ιο]ν τῇ ἐκυρᾷ); *Buckler, Calder and Cox 1925, 151–2, no. 137 (Kotiaion: understand Τατιανῆς ἐκυρᾷ, 'Tatianēs for her mother-in-law'); *MAMA X 104 (Tabbernee 1997, 258–61, no. 39, Alibeyköy: ἐκυροῖς); *Anderson 1906, 212–14, no. 10 (MAMA X 272, Aslanapa: read Ἄρδε[μ]ις κὲ Ἀμιας κὲ Τροφί[μη ἐκ]υροῖς κὲ δαέρι); *Anderson 1906, 225–6, no. 22 (SGO III 16/31/81, Aykırıkçı: ἐκυρός); SEG 28, 1098 (Tabbernee 1997, 271–7, no. 42, Altıntaş: ἐκυρᾷ).

Eastern Phrygia (**8–11**): *MAMA I 315 (Kolukısa: τῇ ἐκυρῇ); *MAMA VII 576 (Zengen/Özkent: τῇ ἐκυρῇ); *MAMA VII 321 (Vetissos: ἐκυρᾷ); *I.Konya 137 (Kelhasan: ἐκυρός).

Central Phrygia (**12**): *Michon 1906, 39–43 (Akmoneia: ἐκυροῖς).

Eastern Pisidia (**13**): *MAMA VIII 352 (I.Sultan Dağı 507, Karaağaç: τὸν ἐμὸν ἐκυρόν).

Mysia (**14**): SEG 35, 1289 (Miletoupolis: [ὑ]κεροί).

In all but one of these texts, ἐκυρός/-ά seems to carry its correct sense of 'husband's parent(s)' (HF/HM). The sole exception is an early Christian epitaph from the Upper Tembris, erected by three men and one woman for their ἐκυρά; apparently, in this text, the word carries a more general sense of 'spouse's mother'.[54] Outside Asia Minor, ἐκυρός/-ά is all but unknown; I can find only seven instances of the term in inscriptions from other parts of the Mediterranean world, four of them 'Homerizing' verse epitaphs. Significantly, in at least four of these texts ἐκυρός/-ά is incorrectly used to refer to the wife's father or mother, strongly implying that the term (at least with its technical meaning 'husband's parent') had ceased to be part of the living language in most parts of the Greek-speaking world.

(**1**) Thessalonike (IG X 2, 1 305: τῇ ἐκυρᾷ, sense unclear).

(**2**) Tegea (IG V 2, 20: ἐκυρός, apparently 'wife's father').

(**3**) Syrian Antioch (SGO IV 20/03/04: ἐκυρεῖ < ἐκυρεύς, 'wife's father').

(**4**) Hermoupolis Magna (Bernand 1999, no. 75: ἐκυράν distinguished from πενθεράν).

(**5**) Antinooupolis (Bernand 1969, no. 123: τὸν ἐκυρό[ν], 'wife's father').

(**6**) Rome (IGUR III 1209: ἐκυρήν, 'wife's mother').

(**7**) Tarraco (SEG 53, 1154: bilingual epitaph for a Jewish woman from Kyzikos, where *socera* = [ἐκυ]ρά).

---

[54] SEG 28, 1098 (Tabbernee 1997, 271–7, no. 42: Altıntaş).

4.7 Wife's Father and Wife's Mother

The proper terms for the **wife's father** and **wife's mother** are πενθερός (WF) and πενθερά (WM). These terms are attested some thirty-five times in Hieradoumia, nineteen times in the masculine (*pentheros*, 'wife's father', WF), and sixteen times in the feminine (*penthera*, 'wife's mother', WM). As it happens, the plural *pentheroi* ('wife's parents') seems not to be attested in Hieradoumia, but this is probably no more than a coincidence, since it is common enough elsewhere.

> ὁ πενθερός (**1**): **SEG* 40, 1095 (Maionia).
>
> τὸν πενθερόν (**2–18**): **TAM* V 1, 737 (Gordos); **TAM* V 1, 771 (Gordos); **SEG* 62, 917 (Gordos); **TAM* V 1, 704 (Gordos, of a wife's *threpsas*); **Robert, Hellenica* VI, no. 48 (Gordos?); **I.Manisa* 241 (Gündoğdu); *SEG* 57, 1156 (Daldis); **SEG* 31, 1021 (Saittai); **SEG* 35, 1241 (Saittai); **SEG* 40, 1070 (Saittai); **SEG* 40, 1093 (Saittai); **SEG* 49, 1620 (Maionia); **I.Manisa* 524 (Tabala); *I.Manisa* 360 (Zeytinliova); **Thonemann 2019, no. 1 (Kula); **SEG* 55, 1304 (inc.); **SEG* 56, 1257 (inc.).
>
> τῷ πενθερῷ (**19**): **SEG* 49, 1563 (Daldis).
>
> ἡ πενθερά (**20–21**): **TAM* V 1, 187 (Saittai); **TAM* V 1, 470a (Iaza).
>
> τὴν πενθεράν (**22–30**): **TAM* V 1, 717 (Gordos); **TAM* V 1, 736 (Gordos); **TAM* V 1, 737 (Gordos); **TAM* V 1, 768 (Gordos); **TAM* V 1, 812 (Dağdere); **I.Manisa* 522 (Apollonioucharax); **I.Manisa* 241 (Gündoğdu); **SEG* 56, 1294 (Iaza); **Thonemann 2019, no. 1 (Kula); **Sammlung Tatış* 46 (inc.).
>
> τῆς πενθερᾶς (**31–32**): **TAM* V 1, 318 (near Kula: propitiatory *stēlē*); **SEG* 32, 1215 (Kula: votive *stēlē*).
>
> τῇ πενθερᾷ (**33–34**): **SEG* 29, 1209 (Apollonioucharax); **TAM* V 1, 608 (Ioudda).

In contrast to *hekyros* and *hekyra*, the terms *pentheros* and *penthera* are very widely attested throughout Asia Minor and the rest of the Greek world. But in other parts of Asia Minor – as we should expect – the terms *pentheros* and *penthera* have a considerably broader sphere of reference ('parents-in-law') than they do in Hieradoumia ('wife's parents'). So the husband's parents are referred to as *pentheroi* in epitaphs from Laodikeia on the Lykos, the east-Phrygian steppe, Olympos and Idebessos in eastern Lykia, and Tyriaion in the Kabalis.[55] Three tombstones from the northern

---

[55] πενθερός/-ά of the husband's parents: *SEG* 54, 1349 (Laodikeia on the Lykos); *MAMA* VII 471 (Bulduk); *TAM* II 990 (Olympos); *TAM* II 866 (Idebessos); Naour 1980, no. 13 (Tyriaion). An inscription from rural north Galatia, Waelkens 1986, no. 621 (*RECAM* II 372: Kerpiç), reads

part of the Axylon were erected by men for their 'father and *penthera*'; in each case, it seems likely that *penthera* carries the sense 'step-mother'.[56]

The term for the reciprocal relationship between *hykeroi* and *pentheroi* – that is, between oneself and one's child's spouse's parents – is not, as it happens, directly attested in Hieradoumia. Indeed, to the best of my knowledge, the only document in which this relationship is described with a specific term is a fourth-century Christian epitaph from Aykırıkçı in the Upper Tembris valley, where a daughter's husband's parents are described as σύντεκνοι, 'persons with whom one shares a child'.[57] However, in the four Hieradoumian epitaphs where the term σύντεκνος appears, it seems to carry a somewhat different sense, further analysed in Chapter 6, Section 6.4.[58]

4.8 Husband's Brother (HB) and Husband's Sister (HZ)

We turn next to the **husband's brother** (HB) and **husband's sister** (HZ). The husband's brother (HB) is regularly referred to by the 'Homeric' term δαήρ, attested some thirty-one times in Hieradoumia.[59]

ὁ δαήρ (**1–3**): *TAM* V 1, 175 (Saittai); *SEG* 32, 1223 (Saittai); *Sammlung Tatış* 46 (inc.).

τὸν δαέρα (**4–19**): *TAM* V 1, 704 (Gordos); *TAM* V 1, 707 (Gordos); *TAM* V 1, 725 (Gordos); *TAM* V 1, 764 (Gordos); *TAM* V 1, 766 (Gordos); *SEG* 62, 918 (Gordos); *Sangın 2020, no. 3 (Gordos: twice); *TAM* V 1, 811 (Dağdere); *TAM* V 2, 1156 (Hacıosmanlar); *TAM* V 1, 680 (Charakipolis); *SEG* 35, 1247 (Saittai); *TAM* V 1, 548 (Maionia); *SEG* 34, 1208 (Palankaya, near Iaza); *SEG* 56, 1257 (inc.); *Sammlung Tatış* 44 (?Gordos).

Μυρτίλος καὶ Ὀλυμπιὰς Ἑρμεῖ πατρὶ καὶ πενθερῷ; it is not clear whether Hermes was the wife's or the husband's father. In *SEG* 52, 1418 (Onobara), the husband's mother is referred to as τῇ μητρὶ ἀνδρός μου; at Olympos (*TAM* II 1001), the wife's mother is referred to as μητρὶ τῆς γυναικός μου.

[56] Waelkens 1986, no. 632 (Kütükuşağı); Waelkens 1986, no. 644 (Kelhasan); Anderson 1899, 118, no. 111 (Kozanlı); cf. also perhaps Waelkens 1986, no. 599 (Sarıkaya), apparently for a *pentheros* (?= 'step-father') and mother.

[57] Gibson 1978, 76–9, no. 28 (*SGO* III 16/31/88), τοῖς συτέκνοις ... καὶ ... γανβρῷ; correctly interpreted by Tabbernee 1997, 394–401, no. 62; misunderstood by Thonemann 2013c, 135. The term seems to be otherwise unattested in this sense, but compare Hesych. Σ 2170 Hansen, συγκηδεσταί· οἱ τῆς νύμφης καὶ τοῦ γαμβροῦ γονεῖς, with Slater 1986 on Ar. Byz. F273.

[58] *TAM* V 1, 710, 712, 725 (all from Gordos); Thonemann 2019, no. 6 (Iaza). In Hieradoumia, σύντεκνος seems to denote the relationship between a natural parent and a foster-parent (Chapter 6, Section 6.4).

[59] Homeric Greek δαήρ, Latin *lēvir*, Sanskrit *devár-* < IE *daih₂wér, 'husband's brother'; Szemerényi 1977, 87–8; Chantraine 1999, 245–6.

τὸν δαίρα (**20–22**): *TAM* V 1, 472 (Iaza); *TAM* V 1, 483a (Iaza); *TAM* V 1, 56 (Silandos).

τὸν δααίρα (**23**): *SEG* 65, 1195 (inc.).

τὸν δέρα (**24**): *SEG* 64, 1158 (inc.).

(τοῦ) δαέρος (**25**): *SEG* 57, 1158 (near Kula: propitiatory *stēlē*).

τῷ δαέρι (**26**): *Sardis* II 666 (inc.).

τῷ δαίρι (**27**): *TAM* V 1, 660 (Daldis).

οἱ δαέρες (**28–29**): *TAM* V 1, 733 (Gordos); *TAM* V 1, 782 (Yayakırıldık).

(οἱ) δεέρες (**30**): *TAM* V 1, 810 (Dağdere);

οἱ δέρες (**31**): *TAM* V 1, 379 (Kollyda).

The term δαήρ is exceptionally rare elsewhere in Asia Minor, and seems not to be attested in Greek epigraphic texts outside the Anatolian peninsula. It appears five times in neighbouring parts of northern Phrygia (Aizanoi and the Upper Tembris valley), once in central Phrygia (Akmoneia), once in Bithynia (Kios), one in Paphlagonia (Kaisareia), and once in eastern Phrygia (Turgut, on the western fringe of the Axylon).

(**1**) MAMA IX 387 (Aizanoi: δαίερι);

(**2**) *SEG* 40, 1241 (Upper Tembris: δαήρ);

(**3**) *Anderson 1906, 225–6, no. 22 (*SGO* III 16/31/81, Aykırıkçı: δαήρ);

(**4**) *Anderson 1906, 212–14, no. 10 (*MAMA* X 272, Aslanapa: read Ἄρδε[μ]ις κὲ Ἀμιας κὲ Τροφί[μη ἐκ]υροῖς κὲ δαέρι);

(**5**) *SEG* 28, 1096 (Yalnızsaray: δαέρι);

(**6**) *Michon 1906: 39–43 (Akmoneia: δαέρι);

(**7**) *I.Kios* 53 (δῆρος);

(**8**) Marek 1993, 200, no. 51 (Kaisareia: δαέρος);

(**9**) *MAMA* VII 209 (Turgut: δαέρι).

Rarer still is the term for the **husband's sister** (HZ), who is designated with the 'Homeric' word γάλως in six inscriptions from Hieradoumia; the term seems to appear nowhere else in the post-Homeric Greek world.[60]

The sense 'husband's sister' is guaranteed in *TAM* V 1, 705 (Gordos: τὴν γάλω); it is effectively certain in *TAM* V 1, 765 (Gordos: τ[ὴν] γάλω) and *SEG* 56, 1258 (Gordos: τὴν γάλως); it is very likely in *TAM* V 1, 665 (Daldis: τῇ [γενομένη αὐτῆς γά]λῳ) and *TAM* V 1, 775 (Loros: τὴν γάλως); it is possible in *SEG* 31, 1004 (Saittai: ἡ γάλως).

---

[60] Homeric Greek γάλως, Latin *glōs*, Sanskrit *girí-* < IE *ˆgh₃- wos-, 'husband's sister' (Szemerényi 1977, 88–91). On the Homeric form, and a possible Attic variant (attested only in the grammarians), see Meissner 2006, 131–2. The alleged Phrygian term γέλαρος, 'brother's wife' (*sic!*) (Hsch. I 367 Latte) is not epigraphically attested.

Given the exceptional rarity (or non-existence) of the terms δαήρ (HB) and γάλως (HZ) outside Hieradoumia, the question arises of how people living in other parts of the Greek-speaking world referred to their husband's brother and husband's sister. Two inscriptions from Rhodes, one of the late Hellenistic period, the other dating to the reign of Titus, refer to the husband's brother (HB) simply as 'the husband's brother' (ὁ τοῦ ἀνδρὸς ἀδελφός), and seven inscriptions of the late Roman period from eastern Phrygia, Lykaonia and Isauria refer to the husband's siblings with descriptive genitival compounds, ἀνδραδελφός ('husband's brother', HB) and ἀνδραδελφή ('husband's sister', HZ).[61] The assumption must be that in the greater part of the Greek world, there were simply no distinctive kinship terms at all for one's husband's siblings (as of course is also the case in English).

4.9 Wife's Brother (WB) and Wife's Sister (WZ)

In documents from Hieradoumia, the **wife's brother** (WB) and **wife's sister** (WZ) are referred to as πενθερίδης and πενθερίδισσα respectively. Neither form is attested in Homer, and indeed, both are effectively unattested in Greek literary texts.[62] Both terms are regular patronymic formations from πενθερός, 'wife's father' (WF), with the suffixes -ίδης and -ίδισσα signifying 'son/daughter of'; we may compare the kinship terms *adelphidēs* and *adelphidissa*, formally (if not always in their actual usage: see above, Section 4.5) patronymic formations from *adelphos/adelphē*, 'sibling'.[63]

The term *pentheridēs* (WB) is used of the 'wife's brother' nineteen times in inscriptions from Hieradoumia; the female equivalent, *pentheridissa* (WZ), 'wife's sister', appears just twice.

ὁ πενθερίδης (**1–2**): *TAM V 1, 168 (Saittai); *SEG* 34, 1224 (=*SEG* 49, 1726, Saittai).
τὸν πενθερίδη (**3–13**): *TAM V 1, 705 (Gordos); *TAM V 1, 707 (Gordos); *TAM V 1, 711 (Gordos); *SEG 40, 1044 (Gordos); *TAM* V 1, 704 (Gordos,

---

[61] ὁ τοῦ ἀνδρὸς ἀδελφός (HB): *IG* XII 1, 72b; Segre and Pugliese Carratelli 1949–1951, no. 89. ἀνδραδελφός/-ή (HB/HZ): *MAMA* I 315 (Kolukısa), 324 (Gözlü), 363, 364, 369 (all Çeşmelisebil), *KILyk* 432 (Dorla); Bean and Mitford 1970, 143–4, no. 142 (Thouththourbia); Robert, *Hellenica* XIII, 33.

[62] Only in Epiphanius, *On Weights and Measures* 14 (Aquila, alleged πενθερίδης of the emperor Hadrian); Theodoret, *Quaestiones in Iudices* 4 (πενθερὸν δὲ αὐτὸν κέκληκεν, ὡς τῆς γαμετῆς ἀδελφόν· καὶ γὰρ νῦν πολλοὶ τοὺς τοιούτους πενθερίδας καλοῦσι).

[63] The correct nominative form seems to be πενθερίδης (P. Herrmann on *TAM* V 1, 707); in oblique cases, the noun declines as if from *πενθεριδεύς.

apparently of a wife's *syntrophos*); *TAM* V 1, 805 (*SGO* I 04/07/04, Yeğe-noba); **I.Manisa* 521 (Apollonioucharax); *TAM* V 1, 633 (Daldis); **I.Man-isa* 524 (Tabala, τὸ[ν πεν]θεριδῇ [ed. omits a line between ll. 9–10]); *SEG* 56, 1259 (inc.); **Sammlung Tatış* 44 (?Gordos).

τὸν πενθεριδέα (**14–17**): **TAM* V 1, 707 (Gordos); *TAM* V 1, 625 (Daldis); *SEG* 49, 1620 (Maionia); **SEG* 56, 1263 (inc.).

οἱ πενθεριδεῖς (**18–19**): **TAM* V 1, 701 (*SGO* I 04/10/03, Gordos); **SEG* 40, 1095 (Maionia).

τῇ πενθεριδίσσῃ (**20–21**): **SEG* 57, 1248 (inc.); *TAM* V 1, 65 (Silandos).

The term *pentheridēs* is attested a mere handful of times outside Hiera-doumia (*pentheridissa* does not appear elsewhere). Elsewhere in Asia Minor, πενθερίδης appears in western Lydia (Thyateira), northern Phrygia (the Upper Tembris valley), Bithynia (Kios), Pisidia (Kibyra), Isauria (Thouth-thourbia), and Galatia (Ankyra); outside Asia Minor, the term seems only to be attested at Serdica in Thrace and at Herakleia Sintike in Makedonia.

(1) **TAM* V 2, 1070 (Thyateira: [τῷ π]ενθεριδεῖ).

(2) **SEG* 30, 1462 (Adaköy: τοὺς πενδεριδεῖς).

(3) **I.Kios* 107 (τοῦ πενθεριδέος; Demetrios is Aur. Tryphon's father-in-law).

(4) *I.Kibyra* 268 (τῷ πενθερη[δ]ε̣ῖ).

(5) Bean and Mitford 1970, 143, no. 141 (Thouththourbia: τοὺς πενθεριδεῖς)

(6) **I.Ancyra* 233 (πενθεριδεῖ: apparently meaning 'wife's brother' [twice] and 'wife's sister's husband' [once]).

(7) **IGBulg* IV 2006 (Serdica: πενθεριδῖ).

(8) *SEG* 48, 801 (Herakleia Sintike: τῷ πενθερ⟨ι⟩δε⟨ῖ⟩).

Elsewhere in the Greek-speaking world, people seem largely to have done without special terms for the wife's siblings, as we have already seen to have been the case for the husband's brother and the husband's sister (see above). The circumlocution 'the wife's sibling' (ὁ/ἡ τῆς γυναικὸς ἀδελφός/-ή, WB/WZ) is found in inscriptions from Philadelphia in south-east Lydia, Phrygian Eumeneia, Rhodes, Aspendos in Pamphylia, and Xanthos and Olympos in Lykia.[64] The genitival compounds *gynaikadelphos* (WB) and *gynaikadelphē* (WZ) are attested across a wide swathe of Roman Asia Minor; I have found twelve examples, concentrated in Pisidia and eastern

---

[64] Philadelphia: *TAM* V 3, 1642 (AD 185/6: τῷ τῆς γυνα[ικό]ς μου ἀδελφῷ). Eumeneia: *SEG* 28, 1146 (Roman imperial period: τῇ ἀδελφῇ τῆς συνβίου). Rhodes: *SEG* 43, 527 (I BC: τὸν τᾶς γυναικὸς ἀδελφόν); *SEG* 41, 644 (Hellenistic: [τὸν τ]ᾶς γυναικὸς ἀ[δελφόν]); *AD* 21 (1966) Chron. P.447 a (Hellenistic: τὸν τᾶς γυναικὸς ἀδελφόν). Aspendos: *SEG* 38, 1351 (Roman imperial period: ἀδελφῷ τῆς γυναικός μου). Xanthos: *TAM* II 370 (first century BC (?): αὐτοῦ τῆς γυναικὸς ἀδελφῆς υἱόν). Olympos: *TAM* II 1017 and 1068 (Roman imperial period: ἀδελφὴ τῆς γυναικός μου, γυναικὸς ἀδελφοῖς).

Phrygia, but with outlying examples in Lykia, Bithynia, and Paphlagonia, and a single example from Tomis.[65]

4.10 Son's Wife (SW) and Brother's Wife (BW)

We now turn from the affines' natal kin to natal kin's affines, and in the first instance to the terminology used of women entering a household by marriage, the **son's wife** (SW) and the **brother's wife** (BW). The inhabitants of Hieradoumia used special terms for each of these persons, once again identical (or nearly identical) to terms found in the Homeric epics. The **son's wife** (SW) is designated with the Homeric term νυός in seven Hieradoumian inscriptions, all from the vicinity of Gordos and Charakipolis. The term is scarcely attested elsewhere in the Greek world; outside Hieradoumia, it seems only to appear at Kalindoia in the northern Chalkidike and at Arkadian Megalopolis.[66]

(**1**) *TAM* V 1, 703 (Gordos: τὴν νυόν).

(**2**) *SEG* 56, 1286 (?Gordos: τὴν νυόν).

(**3**) *TAM* V 1, 795 (Gökçeler, W of Gordos: τὴν ν[υ]όν).

(**4**) *TAM* V 1, 822 (Kömürcü, NW of Gordos: ἡ νεός).

(**5**) *TAM* V 1, 825 (Kömürcü, NW of Gordos: [οἱ] ὑκαιροὶ τῇ νυῷ).

(**6**) *SEG* 36, 1105 (Karayağcı, W of Charakipolis: τῇ γνησιωτάτη νυῶι).

(**7**) *TAM* V 1, 779 (Kavakalan, W of Gordos: τῇ νυῷ).

(**8 ?**) *TAM* V 1, 39 (Bagis: ἡ ὑκ[ερὰ τὴν] ἰδία[ν νυόν], a plausible restoration).

Elsewhere in Roman Anatolia, as we will see shortly, the son's wife was usually designated with the more general term νύμφη ('young woman who has entered a household by marriage'). Instead, outside Hieradoumia, only in Lykia do we find a special term for the son's wife in regular usage. The remarkable Greco-Lykian kinship term πιατρα/πιετρα, 'son's wife' (SW), is attested eleven times in Lykian epitaphs of the Roman imperial

---

[65] (**1**) Anderson 1899, 285, no. 178 (Çeşmelisebil, τῷ ἰδίῳ γυνε[καδέλφῳ]); (**2**) Ramsay 1888b, 255, no. 67 (Kadınhanı, γυναικαδέλφ⟨η⟩); (**3**) *MAMA* I 39 (Ladık, γυνεκαδάλφῳ); (**4**) *MAMA* I 212 (Kınık, τῆς γυνηκαδ[έλ]φης); (**5**) Kerpiç (*MAMA* VII 422 = *RECAM* II 385, γυνηκαδέλφῳ); (**6**) *KILyk* 308 (Alkaran/Yenisu, γυναικαδέλφῳ); (**7**) *TAM* II 986 (Olympos, γυναικαδέλφῳ); (**8**) Ramsay 1888a, 265, no. 5 (Gavur Ören, τὴν γυναικαδέλφην); (**9**) *I.Antioche de Pisidie* 85 (γυναικαδέλφῳ); (**10**) *I.Iznik* 557 (Nikaia, τῷ γυναικαδέλφῳ); (**11**) *SEG* 33, 1103 (Marek 1993, 196, no. 29: Hadrianopolis, γυναικαδέλφη); (**12**) Popescu 1976, 38 (Tomis, γυνεκάδελφος).

[66] Kalindoia: *SEG* 46, 756 (τῇ νυῷ αὐτῆς). Megalopolis: *IG* V 2, 465 (ἡ ἀδελφιδῆ καὶ νυός).

period.[67] This term is clearly linguistically cognate with the Lykian *pije-*, 'to give', a stem which also gave rise to a large range of Lykian personal names, the best-known case being the name *Natrbbijemi* ('Natr-given') in the Xanthos trilingual.[68] The original etymology of the Greco-Lykian kinship term πιατρα is probably something like 'given-daughter', as opposed to 'natural daughter' (*kbatra* in Lykian).[69] So far as we know, the term is unique to Lykia: an inscription from southern Lykaonia has sometimes been thought to offer a non-Lykian instance (in the variant form *πινατρα), but this is doubtful to say the least.[70] As we have already seen, this was not the only indigenous Anatolian kinship term to survive into the Roman imperial period; we may compare the closely analogous case of the kinship term καμβ(δ)ιος, 'grandchild', apparently of non-Greek origin, and attested in various different forms in Hieradoumia, Karia, and Kilikia (see Section 4.2 above).

Returning to Hieradoumia, the **brother's wife** (BW) is properly designated with another very rare word, ἰανάτηρ/ἐνάτηρ.[71] This term appears eight times in Hieradoumia, five times with the orthography (ε)ἰανάτ-, twice with the orthography ἐνάτ-, and apparently once in the form εἰνάτ-.

---

[67] *SEG* 54, 1454 (Tlos, τὴν πιατραν); *TAM* II 611 (Tlos, πιατρας); *TAM* II 385 (Xanthos, τῆ πιατρᾳ); *SEG* 55, 1490 (Phellos, τῆ πιατρᾳ); *SEG* 56, 1771 (Phellos, ταῖς πιατραις); *TAM* II 870 (Idebessos, πιατρις, i.e. πιατραις); *SEG* 62, 1450 (Limyra, πιατραις); *SEG* 62, 1456 (Limyra, πιᾳ[τραις]); *SEG* 62, 1464 (Limyra, πιατραις); *TAM* II 847 (Idebessos, πιετρᾳ); *TAM* II 848 (Idebessos, πιετρᾳ); Schuler 2005, 268. In the following notes I am much indebted to the learning and acuity of Karl Praust, who is preparing a detailed study of the term.

[68] Neumann 1979, N320 a4 and b3 (*Natrbbijemi* 'translated' as Ἀπολλόδοτος: *Natr-* corresponds to the god Apollo, *-pijemi* to -δοτος < δίδωμι). Names in Πια(τ)- are widespread across southern and inner Anatolia, but so far as I know, in no case is a fully convincing segmentation possible: see Zgusta 1964b, 93–102. E.g. Πιατηραβις (only at Termessos): *TAM* III 1, Index *s.v.* (twelve individuals; add *SEG* 41, 1258); Zgusta 1964a, 426 §1251–2; Neumann 1992, 32. Πιατερος (only at Laodikeia Katakekaumene): *MAMA* XI 265 (Ladık), Πιατερου; Ramsay 1888b, 263, no. 97 (Sarayönü), Πιατερ(ο)ς; Zgusta 1964a, 426 §1251–1; Brixhe 2013, 63–4.

[69] I.e. *pij(e)-atra*, with *-atra* transferred from *kbatra*, 'daughter' (Praust, *per litt.*). Schürr 1999 less convincingly takes the term to signify 'one who comes with a gift', i.e. 'one who brings a dowry' (cf. also Brixhe 1999, 89–91).

[70] *KILyk* 374 (Dorla/Aydoğmuş): Παπιας ἐκόσμησεν τὴν | πινατραν, with Schürr 1999, 29–30. However, a personal name Πινατρα is attested four times in Isauria and southern Lykaonia, rendering it very likely that we are also dealing with a PN here: *KILyk* 24 (Elmasun); Sterrett 1888, 123, no. 207 (Hacılar); Swoboda, Keil and Knoll 1935, 88, nos. 236 and 237 (Zengibar Kalesi). The only scholar to have seen the Dorla stone, W. M. Ramsay, could well have failed to indicate a possible lacuna at the end of line 1 or start of line 2, i.e. Παπιας ἐκόσμησεν τὴν [e.g. ἀδελφὴν]| Πινατραν.

[71] The brother's wife is occasionally referred to simply as ἡ τοῦ ἀδελφοῦ γυνή, as in *TAM* V 1, 625 (Daldis); *I.Manisa* 522 (Apollonioucharax).

(1) *SEG 49, 1660 (Saittai: τὴν ἰανάτερα).

(2) *TAM V 1, 682 (Charakipolis: τὴν ἰανάτερα).

(3) *TAM V 1, 754 (Gordos: τὴν ἰανάτερα).

(4) *TAM V 1, 775 (Loros: τὴν ἰανάτερα).

(5) *SEG 56, 1286 (?Gordos, τὴν ἐνάτεραν, line 10; in line 7, where the editors print τὴν *hed.* ἰ⟨ν⟩άταιραν, read instead τὴν θυ⟨γ⟩άταιραν).

(6) TAM V 1, 782 (Yayakırıldık: τὴν ἐνάτερα, either 'brother's wife' or 'husband's brother's wife').

(7) TAM V 1, 703 (Gordos: τὴν εἰαν[άτερα], either 'brother's wife' or 'husband's brother's wife').

(8) TAM V 1, 412 (Kollyda: [τ]ὴν εἰν[άτερα], sense unclear).

As with the term ὑκερός/-ά (see above), the orthography is significant, since Homer and other Greek authors use only the form εἰνάτ-. We should, therefore, recognize the forms ἰανάτ- and ἐνάτ- as distinctively Anatolian epichoric forms.[72] Just as with Hieradoumian ὑκερός/-ά and the Latin *socer/socrus*, it is conceivable that the Hieradoumian orthography ἰανάτηρ (BW) might reflect some cross-pollination with the related Latin term *ianitrix* (although see Section 4.13).[73]

The term ἐνάτηρ also appears in some seventeen texts from the Upper Tembris valley and neighbouring regions (Aizanoi, Synaos, Hadrianoutherai, Kotiaion), with a single stray example further to the east, in north Galatia.[74] In each of these non-Hieradoumian cases, the term appears in the form ἐνάτηρ; the form ἰανάτηρ seems to be restricted to Hieradoumia. The non-Hieradoumian evidence brings some clarification of the precise meaning of the term.

'Brother's wife' (BW): (1) *MAMA IX 188 (Aizanoi: ἐνάτρι); (2) *Waelkens 1986: no. 6 (Synaos: ἐνάτρι); (3) *MAMA X 287 (Kotiaion: ἐνάτρι); (4) *CIG 3827p (Kotiaion: ἐνάτρι); (5) *MAMA X 43 (Appia, Beşkarış: ἐνάτρι); (6) *MAMA X 85 (Appia, Altıntaş: ἐνάτρι); (7) *MAMA X 106 (Appia, Alibey: read [τὴν ἑ]αυτῶν ἐνάτερα); (8) *MAMA X 137 (SGO III 16/31/08, Appia, Karaağaç: ἐνάτρε[σ]ιν); (9) *Pfuhl and Möbius I, 478 (Upper Tembris valley: ἐνάτρι, τὴν ἐνάτερα); (10) *SEG 40, 1244 (Upper Tembris Valley: ἐν[ά]τρι).

---

[72] This suffices to dispose of Cameron's characterizsation (1939, 32 n.1) of Anatolian epigraphic usage of ἰανάτηρ/ἐνάτηρ as 'possibl[y] ... a literary affection': see further Section 4.13.

[73] Possible influence of Latin: Neumann 1987 (based on a very limited sample of documents); the parallel with *ianitrix* already drawn by Keil and Premerstein 1907, 78. Homeric Greek εἰνάτερες (< ἐνάτηρ, with metrical lengthening), Latin *ianitrices* and Sanskrit *yātár-* derive from IE *h₂yenh₂-ter-, '(husband's) brother's wife' (Szemerényi 1977, 92; Blažek 2001, 27; Kölligan 2012, 142–4).

[74] I omit a very uncertain Kilikian example, from the vicinity of Seleukeia on the Kalykadnos: Keil and Wilhelm 1915, 33–4 (καὶνετ[.]ραν = καὶ (ἐ)νέτ[ε]ραν?); cf. Hagel and Tomaschitz 1998, 364, Sel 82 (restoring καὶ ⟨μη⟩τ[έ]ραν). The alleged example of *ἐνάτειρα from Gerasa cited by Neumann 1987, 35, no. 5 (A. H. M. Jones 1928, 176, no. 51) is a simple misreading: see SEG 7, 903.

'Husband's brother's wife' (HBW): (**11**) *SEG 40, 1241 (Upper Tembris valley): Tateis' ἐνάτηρ is married to Tateis' δαήρ. (**12**) *SEG 49, 1846 (Upper Tembris valley): a dedication to Zeus Thallos or Zeus Ampeleites, erected by Ματεις καὶ Ἀμια ἐνάτερες; the two women were married to two brothers. (**13**) *SEG 53, 1548 (Upper Tembris valley): five ἐνάτερες, apparently married to five brothers.

'Brother's wife' (BW) and 'husband's brother's wife' (HBW): (**14**) *SEG 28, 1096 (Tabbernee 1997, 292–6, no. 47: Yalnızsaray), Αὐ[ρ.] Εὔτυχος ἀδελφῷ Κυρίλλῳ κὲ ἐνατρὶ Δόμνῃ κὲ Εὐτυχιανῆς δαέρι [Κ]υρίλλῳ κὲ ἐνατρὶ Δόμνῃ.

Sense uncertain: (**15**) SEG 53, 1536 (Upper Tembris valley: ἐνάτηρ); (**16**) I.Kyzikos 209 (Karaçaltı, E of Hadrianoutherai: ἐνάτρι); (**17**) RECAM II 27 (N Galatia, Aşağıığdeağacı: ἐνάτηρ).

In ten of these seventeen texts, the sense 'brother's wife' (BW) is certain. However, in a further three texts (all from the Upper Tembris valley), the term *enatēr* appears to carry the sense 'husband's brother's wife' (HBW), and in a Christian inscription from the Upper Tembris valley, the term signifies (in successive clauses) both 'brother's wife' (BW) and 'husband's brother's wife' (HBW).[75] This is not as problematic as it may appear at first sight. If we assume that the core sense of *enatēr* is not relational ('*my* brother's wife') but classificatory ('wife of *one of* the household's brothers'), then it is easy to see how the wives of two brothers could come to refer to one another with the term *enatēr*.

The two terms studied in the preceding paragraphs, *nyos* (SW) and *ianatēr/enatēr* ([H]BW), are both precise terms for describing one's relationship to a woman who has entered a household through marriage, 'son's wife' and '(husband's) brother's wife' respectively. However, neither term is anything like as common as the general classificatory term νύμφη, which is widely used throughout Asia Minor to denote both the **son's wife** (SW) and the **brother's wife** (BW).[76] In Hieradoumia, the term *nymphē* is used seventeen times of the son's wife, five times of the brother's wife, twice apparently of both the son's wife and the brother's wife, and four times with an indeterminable sense.

'Son's wife' (SW) (**1–17**): *TAM V 1, 733 (Gordos); TAM V 1, 773 (Gordos); *TAM V 1, 798 (Hamit); *TAM V 1, 176 (Saittai); SEG 31, 1004 (Saittai); *SEG 31, 1006 (Saittai); *SEG 31, 1020 (Saittai); *SEG 31, 1037 (Saittai); *SEG 34, 1224 (=SEG 49, 1726, Saittai); *SEG 36, 1081 (Saittai); *TAM V 1, 473c (Iaza); *TAM V 1, 480 (Iaza); *SEG 40, 1100 (Tabala: read κὲ ἑ νύνφ[ε], i.e. καὶ αἱ νύνφαι); *I.Manisa 352 (inc.: read αἱ νύνφε Τατιανὴ κὲ Μελίτη); *SEG 52, 1165 (inc.); *SEG 55, 1286 (inc.); *SEG 56, 1336 (=SEG 58, 1367; SEG 59, 1392, inc.).

---

[75] The twofold meaning of the term here is discussed (not entirely accurately) by Gibson 1978, 13–14.
[76] In the *Basilica*, νύμφη is a technical translation of the Latin *nurus*, 'son's wife': *Bas. Schol.* 45.3.2.4 = *Dig.* 38.10.4.6.

'Brother's wife' (BW) (**18–22**): *SEG* 40, 1067 (Saittai); *SEG* 49, 1657 (Saittai); *I.Manisa* 292 (Saittai, where the term seems to mean '*syntrophos*' wife'); *SEG* 49, 1616 (Maionia); *SEG* 34, 1208 (Palankaya).

Both 'son's wife' and 'brother's wife' (**23–24**): *SEG* 34, 1221 (Saittai: read ⟨τὴν νύν⟩φην in line 5); *TAM* V 1, 168d (Saittai: two men and one woman for their [ν]ύνφην).

Uncertain sense (**25–29**): *SEG* 57, 1205 (Maionia); *SEG* 49, 1742 (inc.); *SEG* 56, 1270 (inc.); *I.Manisa* 320 (inc.).

The precise range of reference of the term *nymphē* is rather difficult to determine. The word seems never to be used in the same text as *nyos* (SW) or *ianatēr/enatēr* ([H]BW), strongly suggesting that *nymphē* encompasses the meanings of both of those more precise terms (as *teknon*, 'child', encompasses both *hyios*, 'son', and *thygatēr*, 'daughter'). I have suggested elsewhere that the core sense of *nymphē* is 'a young woman who has entered a household by marriage'; I would now qualify this as 'a young woman who has entered a household by marriage (to someone other than myself)', since the term *nymphē* seems very seldom to be used in Anatolian texts with the sense 'wife, bride'.[77]

This 'classificatory' interpretation of the term *nymphē* helps to account for certain otherwise baffling usages of the term. In an epitaph from Tabala in eastern Hieradoumia, two paternal uncles (οἱ πατρώς, FB) are paired with two women described as *nymphai* (αἱ νύμφαι).[78] If the term *nymphē* really signified 'son's wife or brother's wife', then this apparent instance of 'father's brother's wife' (FBW) would be very puzzling indeed; the problem evaporates once we understand *nymphē* as a general term for any young woman who has entered a household by marriage. Similarly, in the east-Phrygian Axylon, three brothers set up a tombstone 'for our father Marcus and our *nymphē* Pribis and our grandmother Thekla': the natural reading of this text would suggest that Pribis was Marcus' wife, perhaps the three brothers' step-mother.[79] An epitaph from Gordos for a married woman named Tata begins with the single word *nymphē* in the accusative,

---

[77] Thonemann 2013c, 132–3. Despite what is claimed there, the sense 'one's own wife' is very poorly attested in Asia Minor. 'Wife' is certain in *TAM* V 3, 1910 (*SGO* I 04/24/07), and is a possible (but not certain) meaning in Ramsay, *Phrygia* II 662, no. 621 (Diokleia). In *SGO* III 16/31/82 (Zemme), the term is perhaps better understood as 'sons' wives'. The term μελλόνυμφος = 'fiancée' in *SGO* III 16/32/10 (Kotiaion).

[78] *TAM* V 1, 210 (Tabala).

[79] *MAMA* VII 578 (Zengen/Özkent): Αὐρ. Σίσιννος κὲ Κουέντος κὲ Μῖρος ἀνεστήσαμεν τῷ πατρὶ ἡμῶ[ν] Μάρκῳ κὲ νύνφη ἡμῶν Πριβι κὲ τῇ μάμμη ἡμῶν Θέκλῃ, κτλ. (wrongly interpreted by Calder 1910, 239, and by Thonemann 2013c, 132). Cf. perhaps *MAMA* VII 82 (Kındıras): Αὐρήλιοι Κυριακοῦ υἱοὶ Εὐπρεπούσῃ νύ[ν]φῃ γλυκυτάτῃ μνήμης χάριν.

serving as a kind of heading for the entire text: I assume that the term serves as a way of summing up Tata's status in her extended family.[80]

Finally, we have already seen that the term *ianatēr/enatēr* ([H]BW) can signify both 'brother's wife' and 'husband's brother's wife'. The term *nymphē* seems never to be used with the sense 'husband's brother's wife' (HBW). Instead, in Hieradoumia, this relationship can be described by the term σύννυμφος (HBW, six instances), which I would understand as meaning 'a woman who holds the joint status of *nymphē* in a household'.[81]

> 'Husband's brother's wife' (HBW): (**1**) *TAM V 1, 775 (Loros, τὴν σύννυμφον) and (**2**) *SEG 49, 1660 (Saittai, [τὴν] σύν[ν]υνφον), both distinguished from ἰανάτηρ = 'brother's wife' (BW); (**3**) *SEG 49, 1616 (Maionia, αἱ σύννυνφοι) and (**4**) *SEG 49, 1657 (Saittai, τὴν σύννυνφον), both distinguished from νύμφη = 'brother's wife' (BW); (**5**) **I.Manisa* 522 (Apollonioucharax, τὴν σύννυνφον), distinguished from ἡ τοῦ ἀδελφοῦ γυνή = 'brother's wife' (BW); (**6**) *TAM* V 2, 841 (Yeniceköy, [σ]ύννυμφος, sense unclear from context).

4.11 Daughter's Husband (DH) and Sister's Husband (ZH)

We next turn to another two relationships denoted by a single term, namely the **daughter's husband** (DH) and the **sister's husband** (ZH), both of whom are described in inscriptions from Hieradoumia by the single word γάμβρος.[82] This term fairly clearly means 'daughter's husband' in some nineteen inscriptions from Hieradoumia and signifies 'sister's husband' in some thirteen texts from the region; in four inscriptions, the term is used to refer both to the daughter's husband and the sister's husband. Exactly as with *nymphē*, we should understand the core meaning of *gambros* as 'a young man who has entered a family by marriage (to someone other than myself)'; this helps to account for two instances in which it appears to mean 'cousin's husband'.[83]

---

[80] *TAM* V 1, 703 (Gordos): the *nymphē* Tata is honoured by the *dēmoi* of Gordos and Loros, her parents, her husband, her mother-in-law, her two brothers, her husband's sister, and probably other relatives (the stone is broken below).

[81] The term is exceptionally rare elsewhere: I have found only Bean and Mitford 1965, no. 24 (Kilikia, Ayasofya).

[82] In the *Basilica*, it is used as a technical translation for the Latin *gener*, 'daughter's husband': *Bas. Schol.* 45.3.2.4 = *Dig.* 38.10.4.6. The daughter's husband is described as τῷ ἀνδρὶ τῆς θυγατρός in *TAM* V 2, 1100 (Thyateira).

[83] 'Cousin's husband' (?): *SEG* 40, 1067 (Saittai, line 10), assuming that ἀδελφιδίσσα (lines 9–10) means 'cousin'; *TAM* V 1, 707 (Gordos, line 12), assuming that ἀδελφιδέα (lines 11–12) means 'cousin' (see Section 4.5). For an alleged instance of *gambros* = 'granddaughter's husband', see *SGO* III 16/31/93, B verse 6 (Altıntaş). However, this interpretation is based on a false

'Daughter's husband' (DH) (**1–19**): *TAM* V 1, 725 (Gordos); *TAM V 1, 731 (Gordos); *TAM V 1, 768 (Gordos); *SEG 62, 917 (Gordos); *TAM* V 1, 190 (Saittai); *SEG 31, 1004 (Saittai); *SEG 31, 1009 (Saittai); *SEG 31, 1020 (Saittai); *SEG 31, 1031 (Saittai); *SEG 40, 1066 (Saittai); *SEG 32, 1226 (Saittai: both 'daughter's husband', line 6, and '*threptē*'s husband', line 9); *SEG 49, 1684 (Satala); *SEG 49, 1628 (Nisyra); *SEG* 58, 1360 (Silandos); *TAM V 1, 59 (Silandos); *SEG 40, 1100 (Tabala); *SEG 56, 1263 (inc.); *SEG* 48, 1432 (inc., apparently '*threptē*'s husband'); *I.Manisa* 426 (inc., apparently '*threptē*'s husband').

'Sister's husband' (ZH) (**20–33**): *TAM V 1, 763 (Gordos); *TAM V 1, 804 (Yeğenoba, apparently '*syntrophos*' husband'); *TAM V 1, 816 (Kömürcü); **I.Manisa* 241, lines 11–12 (Gündoğdu); *TAM V 1, 680 (Charakipolis); *TAM V 1, 660 (Daldis); *SEG* 33, 1024 (Saittai); *SEG 34, 1226 (Saittai); *SEG 40, 1067 (Saittai, line 8); *SEG 29, 1187 (Saittai, apparently '*syntrophos*' husband'); *TAM V 1, 470a (Iaza); *SEG 41, 1037 (*SGO* I 04/13/01, Yiğitler, late II BC); *SEG 56, 1269 (inc.); *TAM V 2, 850 (Musaca).

Both 'sister's husband' (ZH) and 'daughter's husband' (DH) (**34–37**): *TAM V 1, 701 (*SGO* I 04/10/03: Gordos, lines 7–8); *SEG 40, 1070 (Saittai: Apphias is the deceased's mother-in-law, and Alexandros, Attalos and Valerius are his brothers-in-law); *SEG 49, 1727 (inc., lines 5 and 10); perhaps *SEG* 32, 1226 (Saittai, lines 6 and 10, assuming that Helenē is the deceased's sister-in-law).

'Cousin's husband' (?) (**38–39**): *SEG* 40, 1067 (Saittai, line 10); *TAM* V 1, 707 (Gordos).

Uncertain sense (**40–48**): *TAM* V 1, 379 (Kollyda); *TAM* V 1, 664 (Daldis); *TAM* V 1, 743 (*SGO* I 14/10/05: Gordos); *SEG* 31, 989 (Iaza); *TAM* V 1, 814 (Kömürcü); *TAM* V 1, 168 (Saittai); *SEG* 40, 1066 (Saittai, lines 7–8); *SEG* 40, 1083 (inc.); *SEG* 40, 1093 (inc.).

The term *gambros* thus turns out to be perfectly parallel to the term *nymphē*, in that it serves as a general 'classificatory' term for any young man who has married into a family, without clearly indicating the precise relationship concerned. Unlike *nymphē*, though, *gambros* seems to lack any more precise synonyms for the various relationships it describes (contrast *nyos*, 'son's wife', SW, and *ianatēr/enatēr*, '(husband's) brother's wife', [H]BW). The parallel even extends to the existence of a term σύνγαμβρος (WZH) (compare σύννυμφος, HBW), describing the relationship between the husbands of two sisters ('wife's sister's husband').

---

restoration of the relevant verse (cf. critical note to *SEG* 6, 138, line 12); in fact, *gambros* here carries its usual sense of 'daughter's husband'. In *SEG* 31, 989 (Iaza), the *gambros* Graptos (lines 6–7) is probably the husband of an unnamed (deceased?) daughter, rather than husband of the named granddaughter.

'Wife's sister's husband' (WZH): *SEG* 40, 1066 (Saittai, τὸν σύνγαμβρον); *I. Manisa* 241 (Gündoğdu, τὸν σύνγαμβρον). The term is attested with the same sense in *SEG* 39, 1355 (Pontic Sebastopolis, οἱ σύνγαμβροι); *Marek 1993, 196, no. 29 (Hadrianopolis, συνγάμβρῳ); *MAMA* III 493a (Korykos: συνγάβρου).

Elsewhere in Asia Minor, the term *gambros* is occasionally used for a wider range of connections by marriage: I have found examples of it being used of the wife's brother (WB) and the husband's brother (HB).[84]

4.12 Step-Kin and Adoptive Kin

Although remarriage seems to have been fairly common in Hieradoumia, the terminology for step-kin does not show any locally distinctive features.[85] **Step-sons** and **step-daughters** appear in a handful of texts and are always referred to with the term ὁ/ἡ πρόγονος, a term which (confusingly) was also used to signify 'ancestor'.[86] The **step-father** was designated either by the word πατρωός, twice attested in Hieradoumia, or with the descriptive term πατροποίητος, found in a single inscription from the region. The **step-mother**, usually referred to in Greek inscriptions with the term μητρυιά, seems not to be attested in Hieradoumia.[87]

---

[84] Husband's brother: *TAM* II 866 (Idebessos). Wife's brother: Heberdey and Kalinka 1897, 33, no. 40 (Isinda). For its range of usage in literary texts, see Chantraine 1999, 208–9 (cf. Szemerényi 1977, 69–72).

[85] In addition to the texts cited below, see *TAM* V 1, 653 (Daldis: τῇ γυναικί ... τῇ γενομένῃ αὐτοῦ γυναικί), where the participle γενομένῃ = 'deceased', as in *TAM* V 1, 665 (Daldis: restored). Remarriage may also be attested in *SEG* 32, 1235 (inc.). The oddly emphatic phrase τῷ κυνῷ τέκνῳ in *SEG* 40, 1085 (inc.) might indicate that one or the other parent had children by a previous marriage. At first sight, the phrase οἱ υἱοὶ τῆς Κυίντας in *SEG* 40, 1095 (Maionia) appears to indicate remarriage, but the two sons carry the same names as Quinta's husband and father-in-law: might Quinta's second marriage have been to her first husband's brother?

[86] *TAM* V 1, 612 (Satala: τὸν πρ[ό]γονον); *TAM* V 1, 682 (Charakipolis: τὴν πρόγονον); *TAM* V 1, 702 (Gordos: τὸν πρόγονον); *TAM* V 1, 812 (Dağdere: οἱ πρόγονοι); *SEG* 34, 1222 (Saittai: προγόνου, misunderstood by ed. pr.); *SEG* 56, 1292 (Hierokaisareia: τῷ προγόνῳ). The ambiguity of the term is recognized by Artemidorus, *Oneirocritica* 3.27, πρόγονοι ... λέγω δὲ συγγενεῖς τοὺς πρὸ τῶν γονέων γεγονότας. Elsewhere in Asia Minor, πρόγονος = 'step-son' in Herrmann and Polatkan 1969, no. 1, lines 113–114 (Nakrason); *MAMA* VII 58 (Kındıras); *MAMA* VII 585 (Zengen/Özkent); *SEG* 6, 363 (Bilecik); *MAMA* I 146 (Osmancık); Naour 1980, no. 32 (Tyriaion, with a confused commentary); *TAM* II 370 (Xanthos); *SEG* 6, 667 (Attaleia); Woodward and Ormerod 1909/10, 116, no. 8 (Ouerbe); *SEG* 44, 1129 and 57, 1520 (both Termessos).

[87] πατρωός: *TAM* V 1, 786 (Yayakırıldık); *SEG* 56, 1259 (inc.). Elsewhere in Asia Minor: *I.Smyrna* 689, III.19 (a man from Thyateira, with a step-father from Tmolos); *TAM* II 130 (Lydai); *SEG*

Adoption seems to have been rather unusual in Hieradoumia, or at least was seldom recorded in funerary contexts. In an epitaph from Maionia, a certain Theophila, daughter of Phōkritos, natural (φύσει) daughter of Metrophanes, addresses her adoptive father Phōkritos simply as πάτηρ.[88] A difficult inscription from Charakipolis is best explained as a case of adoption of a boy by his much older sister and her husband; the difficulty of the text arises from the fact that both the natural father and the adoptive father simply refer to the boy as their υἱός.[89] A verse epitaph from Gordos seems to describe the adoption of orphaned children by a childless married couple (apparently relatives of the deceased father and mother), but it is not quite clear whether adoption or guardianship is at issue.[90] A votive inscription, perhaps from Sardis, was erected by (among others) a certain 'Menedemos, son of [- -]on, (son) by judgement of Menedemos' (κρίσι δὲ Μ[ε]νεδήμου); it is wholly unclear what this formula means.[91]

4.13 Kinship Terminology: Comparisons and Conclusions

The complete kinship terminological system of Roman Hieradoumia, as reconstructed in the preceding pages, is presented in visual form in Figure 4.1 and Figure 4.2 (omitting step-kin and adoptive kin). Consanguines and their spouses are presented in Figure 4.1, and affines are presented in Figure 4.2 (the husband and his relatives on the left, the wife and her relatives on the right).

55, 1502 (Xanthos, τὸν ἑαυτῆς πατρωιόν: misunderstood by Baker and Thériault 2005, 360). πατροποίητος: *SEG* 55, 1308 (inc.). Elsewhere in Asia Minor: *MAMA* VII 58 (Kındıras); *MAMA* VII 351 (Sülüklü); *RECAM* II 387 (Kerpiç); Waelkens 1986, no. 617 (Vetissos); *SEG* 42, 1267 (Laranda). μητρυιά, not attested in Hieradoumia: cf. *MAMA* IX 446 (Aizanoi); *I.Stratonikeia* 1201 (*SGO* I 02/06/12); *TAM* II 244. In the *Basilica*, πατρωός and μητρυιά translate the Latin *uitricus* and *nouerca*, and πρόγονος/προγόνη are used for the Latin *priuignus/priuigna*: *Bas. Schol.* 45.3.2.4 = *Dig.* 38.10.4.6. See also Artemidorus, *Oneirocritica* 3.26, 4.20.

[88] *TAM* V 1, 555, Θεοφίλα Φωκρίτου φύσε[ι Μ]ητροφάνου Φώκριτον τὸν ἀτῆς πατέρα; cf. *TAM* V 1, 166 (Saittai), Δημό[φιλ]ον Δ[η]μοφίλ[ου, φύ]σει δὲ Μενάνδρου, where the onomastics suggest that the younger Demophilos might have been adopted by his grandfather or paternal uncle. Adoption at Saittai also in *TAM* V 1, 166a.

[89] *TAM* V 1, 680, Διογένης ὁ γαμβρὸς καὶ Τατιας ἡ ἀδελφὴ ἐτείμησαν Ἀπολλώνιον τὸν ἑαυτοῦ υἱόν, Πάνομος τὸν τὸν υἱόν. Panomos, apparently a widower, has five sons (two of them already married) and a married daughter. I assume that he was unable to rear his youngest son Apollonios, and so gave him for adoption to his daughter Tatias and her husband. Adoption at Charakipolis also in *SEG* 57, 1149, discussed further in Chapter 5, Section 5.4.

[90] *SEG* 60, 1291, with Staab and Petzl 2010, 1–4.

[91] *Sardis* II 474 (*I.Manisa* 11): perhaps first century BC.

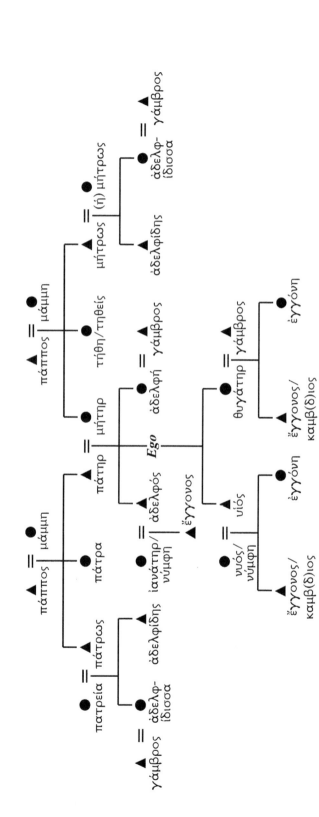

Figure 4.1 Consanguines.

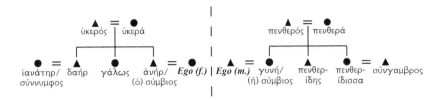

Figure 4.2 Affines.

As will have become clear from the preceding discussion, the kinship terminology of Roman Hieradoumia is considerably richer and more precise than that to be found almost anywhere else in the Greek-speaking world (or, for that matter, in the Latin West). So in most Greek communities, from the archaic period down to the end of antiquity and beyond, no terminological distinction was drawn between, for instance, aunts and uncles on the paternal and maternal side (indiscriminately θεῖος [m.] and τηθίς or θεία [f.]). Likewise, throughout most of the Greek world, the terminology for affines was very imprecise: the terms γαμβρός (m.), κηδεστής (m.), and πενθερός (m.) were used indiscriminately for all kinds of 'connections by marriage' (parents-in-law, the spouse's siblings, a sibling's spouse, etc.).[92]

In Roman Hieradoumia, as we have seen, things were very different. In particular, and most strikingly, the principle of bifurcation (distinction between two-step kin on the basis of the sex of the intermediary person), which had been almost entirely abandoned in Greek kinship terminology in the post-Homeric period, remained strongly in force in Roman Hieradoumia *and apparently nowhere else in the Greek-speaking world*.[93] In traditional anthropological classificatory terms, the inhabitants of Hieradoumia, apparently alone in the entire Greek-speaking world, employed a 'Sudanese' rather than 'Eskimo' kinship classificatory system, with rigorous distinctions between patrilineal and matrilineal relatives.[94] In the

---

[92] The phrase γαμβροί καὶ πενθεροί serves as an exhaustive listing of affines in Drako's homicide law (Osborne and Rhodes 2017, 183A, line 22, with Dem. 43.57), in the regulations of a Delphic phratry *c.* 400 BC (Rhodes and Osborne 2003, no. 1, C45–46), and in a second-century arbitration between Temnos and Klazomenai (*SEG* 29, 1130bis, B39).

[93] Wilgaux 2006, 217–20.

[94] In Latin, an up-to-date study of the chronology of the shift from a (partially) bifurcate to a lineal kinship terminology is much needed: see e.g. Goody 1983, 262–4; Godelier 2011, 180–1, 200–2.

final section of this chapter, I shall offer some very tentative thoughts on the origins and function of the highly distinctive kinship terminological system in use in this small corner of Roman Asia Minor. *Why* did the inhabitants of this remote rural district classify their kin with such rigorous precision? And why did they choose to refer to their kin with the particular terms that they did?

As has occasionally been noted in the past, the closest parallels for many elements of the Hieradoumian kinship terminological system are to be found in the language of the Homeric epics. In the two Homeric epics (particularly, as it happens, in the *Iliad*), we find a wide range of precise kinship terms, particularly for affines, which are all but completely unknown in the later Greek language (outside Hieradoumia, that is).[95] So Homer – unlike later Greek authors, but like the inhabitants of Roman Hieradoumia – distinguishes carefully between parents-in-law on the husband's side and on the wife's side, using *pentheroi* for the wife's parents, and *hekyroi* for the husband's parents.[96] This distinction largely disappears from the Greek language after Homer. With a few insignificant exceptions, the term *hekyros/-a* effectively dropped out of the post-Homeric Greek language altogether, and parents-in-law on both sides of the family came to be known indiscrimately as *pentheroi* (or, more vaguely, as *kēdestai*, 'connections by marriage').[97] Hellenistic grammarians found the Homeric distinction sufficiently noteworthy as to be worth explaining at length, as for instance in the lost *Syngenika* of Aristophanes of Byzantion (*c.* 200 BC, quoted in a marginal note to Eustathios' commentary on the *Iliad*)[98]:

> You should know that, in the *Syngenika* of Aristophanes the grammarian, a distinction is found between *hekyros* and *pentheros*. For he says that *pentheros* is the wife's father from the perspective of the bridegroom and

---

[95] Gates 1971.

[96] ἑκυρός/ἑκυρά: *Il.* 3.172, 22.451, 24.770 (*LfgrE* Band II, col. 511; *DGE* VII 1419). πενθερός: *Il.* 6.170; *Od.* 8.582 (*LfgrE* Band III, cols. 1147–8).

[97] The term ἑκυρός/-ά has a 'learned' Homerizing afterlife in verse texts: Corinna, F654, col. iii 46; Posidippus, *Epigr.* 25 (coupled with δαήρ); Ap. Rhod. *Argon.* 4.815 (coupled with νυός); *Orac. Sib.* 1.290 (coupled with δαήρ); Quint. Smyrn. 13.524; Nonnus, *Dion.* 17.294, 31.236, 44.302, 46.238. The term is used in prose by Plutarch (*Mor.* 143a11; *Comp. Lyc. et Num.* 3.7), Dionysius (*Ant. Rom.* 8.40.1), and Josephus (*AJ* 5.329–32). Note that Josephus incorrectly uses ἑκυρά of the wife's mother (!) at *BJ* 1.534. For the epigraphic evidence, see above, Sections 4.6 and 4.7.

[98] Ar. Byz. F264–72 Slater (Eust. 648.53–9, on *Il.* 6.365).

penthera is her mother, while *hekyros* is the husband's father from the perspective of the bride and *hekyra* is his mother, as, he says, Priam and Hekabe were to Helen. He also states that certain poets are often carried away even into using the word *gambroi* when they mean *pentheroi*.[99]

Roman grammarians and jurists were also interested in the Homeric distinction between *hekyroi* and *pentheroi*, which did not exist in Latin: parents-in-law on both sides are indiscriminately designated *socer* (m.) and *socrus* (f.).[100] Here is Modestinus' *Pandect* (AD *c.* 250), quoted in the *Digest* title *On Degrees of Cognate Relationships, Relations by Marriage, and their Names* (38.10):[101]

> The father of the husband and of the wife is called *socer*, and the mother of either party is called *socrus*. However, among the Greeks [in fact only in Homer], the husband's father is properly called *hekyros* and his mother *hekyra*, while the wife's father is called *pentheros* and her mother *penthera*.

None of this would have needed explaining to the inhabitants of Hieradoumia, who continued – apparently unlike any other Greek-speaking peoples – to employ the *hekyros–pentheros* distinction with absolute consistency throughout the Roman imperial period.

The author of the Homeric poems, like the inhabitants of Hieradoumia – but again unlike most Greek speakers in antiquity – also used special terms for various different categories of brothers- and sisters-in-law. In the *Iliad*, the husband's sister is designated with the term *galōs*, the husband's brother with the term *daēr*, and the wives of two brothers are referred to as *einateres* (only in the plural).[102] All three terms disappear from the living language after Homer: in post-Homeric literary texts, *galōs* and *einateres* appear only in Callimachus, as a learned reminiscence of Homer, and *daēr* is found only in Posidippus, the *Sibylline Oracles*, and Nonnus.[103]

[99] Aristophanes gives three examples (Ael. Dion. π 34 Erbse): Eur. F72 and F647 Kannicht (*gambros* for *pentheros*); Soph. F305 Radt (*pentheros* for *gambros*).

[100] The original IE terms for a father- and mother-in-law were **swéˆkuros, *sweˆkrúhₐs*, whence Homeric ἑκυρός/-ά and Latin *socer/socrus* (Szemerényi 1977, 63–7).

[101] Dig. 38.10.4.6 (Modestinus) = Schol. Bas. 45.3.2.4: *uiri pater uxorisque socer, mater autem eorum socrus appelatur, cum apud Graecos proprie uiri pater* ἑκυρός, *mater uero* ἑκυρά *uocitetur, uxoris autem pater* πενθερός *et mater* πενθερά *uocatur*.

[102] γάλως: *Il.* 3.122, 6.378, 6.383, 22.473, 24.769 (*LfgrE* Band II, col. 116; *DGE* IV 778). δαήρ: *Il.* 3.180, 6.344, 6.355, 14.156, 24.762, 24.769 (*LfgrE* Band II, col. 195; *DGE* IV 860). εἰνάτερες: *Il.* 6.378, 6.383, 22.473, 24.769 (*LfgrE* Band II, col. 469; *DGE* VI 1296–7).

[103] γάλως and εἰνάτερες: Callim. *Hymn* 3.135 (εἰνάτερες γαλόῳ τε). δαήρ: Posidippus, *Epigr.* 25; *Orac. Sib.* 1.290; Nonnus, *Dion.* 40.144. The reference to Menander (F135 Kock) in LSJ, *s.v.* δαήρ and in *DGE* IV 860 should be deleted (=*Dys.* 240; cf. Szemerényi 1977, 87 n.344).

Latin equivalents are found for all three terms (*leuir*, *glos*, *ianitrix), as Modestinus remarks[104]:

> The husband's brother is called *levir* [in Latin]. Among the Greeks he is called *daēr*, as is related in Homer, for Helen says to Hektor: 'you who are *daēr* to me, wicked scheming dog that I am' (*Il.* 6.344). The husband's sister is called *glos*, and *galōs* among the Greeks. The wives of two brothers are called *ianitrices*, and *einateres* among the Greeks. And the same Homer indicates this in a single verse: 'or some of her *galoōi* or fair-robed *einateres*' (*Il.* 6.378).

Despite what Modestinus says here, direct evidence for the use of the Latin terms *glos* and *ianitrix in either the literary or the spoken language is in fact very scanty indeed. Aside from glosses and the Latin grammarians, the term *glos* appears only in a fragment of Plautus and in Ausonius' learned *Technopaignion*; the term *ianitrix (attested only in the plural, *ianitrices*) is not found in literary or documentary texts at all.[105] Quite probably, as with Greek *galōs* and *einateres* after Homer, both terms had effectively become obsolete in Latin by the later republican period. Once again: it really does seem to have been only in Hieradoumia that these specific terms for particular categories of brother- and sister-in-law survived in common usage down to the third century AD.

How should we account for the early and rapid simplification of Greek kinship terminology – particularly the abandonment of bifurcation and simplification of terms for affines – almost everywhere in the Greek world in the post-Homeric period? No doubt part of the answer must lie in changes in the character of social organization in the Greek world after (say) the eighth century BC. As Moses Finley put it in *The World of Odysseus*[106]:

> Homer has a special word, *einater*, for a husband's brother's wife, to cite a clear-cut example, and that word soon disappeared from the ordinary vocabulary. The reason for the change is not hard to find. In a household like Nestor's there were half a dozen women whose relationship to one

---

[104] *Dig.* 38.10.4.6 (Modestinus) = *Schol. Bas.* 45.3.2.4: *uiri frater leuir. is apud Graecos* δαήρ *appellatur, ut est apud Homerum relatum: sic enim Helena ad Hectorem dicit:* δᾶερ ἐμεῖο κυνὸς κακομηχάνου ὀκρυοέσσης. *uiri soror glos dicitur, apud Graecos* γάλως. *duorum fratrum uxores ianitrices dicuntur, apud Graecos* εἰνάτερες. *quod uno uersu idem Homerus significat:* ἤ τινες γαλόων ἢ εἰνατέρων ἐϋπέπλων. The *Digest*, followed by the *Basilica*, here gives ἤ τινες κτλ. in place of Homer's ἤ πη ἐς κτλ.

[105] *glos*: Plaut. Fr. inc. sed. 62 Leo; Auson. *Technop.* 25.10.13: *Aeacidae ad tumulum mactata est Andromachae glos* (*TLL* VI, cols 2107–8). *ianitrices*: *TLL* VII col. 133. All three terms (*leuir*, *glos*, *ianitrices*) are discussed in Isid. *Etym.* 9.7.17.

[106] Finley 1977, 77–8.

another was that of husband's brother's wife. When that kind of extended family unit disappeared, when daughters went off to their husbands' homes and sons set up their own establishments while the father still lived, the fine distinction of *einater* became super-fine. The more general word *kedestes* for every in-law was then good enough.

There is clearly a great deal more to be said on the subject than that, but the general point will suffice for our purposes. The use of an unusually precise kinship terminological system by the inhabitants of Hieradoumia must surely reflect a fundamentally *different kind of social organization* from that found elsewhere in the Greek-speaking world (or at least the epigraphically productive Greek-speaking world), which made it more than usually important to be able to draw fine distinctions between different categories of affines – and, for that matter, between different categories of aunts and uncles.

All that said, Hieradoumian kinship structure was clearly not simply identical to that of the world of the Homeric poems. The rich Homeric terminology for affine kin is strikingly lop-sided: the *Iliad* and *Odyssey* offer us special terms for the husband's brother (*daēr*) and husband's sister (*galōs*), but not for the wife's brother or wife's sister; there are terms for the son's wife (*nyos*) and (husband's) brother's wife (*einateres*), but not for the daughter's husband or sister's husband (both designated in Homer with the non-specific term *gambros*).[107] This lop-sidedness is no accident. It results from the strongly patrilocal character of marriage in early Greek aristocratic society (and among the ancient Indo-Europeans more generally): since the wife generally came to live with her husband's family, kin relations between a woman and her husband's relatives needed to be defined much more precisely than those between a man and his wife's relatives.

In Roman Hieradoumia, matters were somewhat more complicated. Whatever the actual marital residence patterns may have been in Hieradoumia (see further Chapter 5), the inhabitants of the region frequently found the need for precise terms to refer to the wife's brother and the wife's sister. Lacking any inherited Proto-Indo-European terms for these individuals, they ended up using two distinctive patronymic formations derived from πενθερός ('wife's father'), *pentheridēs* (m.), and *pentheridissa* (f.), both of which are scarcely attested anywhere else in the Greek-speaking world.

---

[107] Gates 1971, 23–6; cf. Mallory and Adams 2006, 216 (the highly specific Homeric term *einateres* 'makes sense if the usual social unit was an extended family of parents and married sons'). This 'lop-sidedness' is true of Indo-European kinship terminology more generally: see e.g. Szemerényi 1977, 195–206; Gamkrelidze and Ivanov 1995, I 662–5; Aubrichs 2007, 151.

In other words, although several of the distinctive kinship terms found in Hieradoumia are otherwise scarcely attested outside the Homeric epics, the kinship terminology of the region is not purely and simply 'Homeric'.

This observation matters, because in the past, some historians have been tempted to wonder whether the rarer kinship terms in use in Roman Hieradoumia could have been artificially introduced to the vocabulary of the region on the model of Homeric usage. This was the opinion of Archibald Cameron, who suggested in 1939 that the kinship terminology of Hieradoumia might have been a matter of 'artificial archaizing':

> It is possible that the Greek terms [of relationship], some of which are archaistic, were adopted by a native [Lydian] population which had had previously a large vocabulary in this sphere and in which the feeling of family solidarity extended to a wider system of relations than was usual in more Hellenized communities ... It is perhaps unlikely that terms such as ἐνάτηρ and δαήρ had survived in ordinary usage. There is some evidence that in the Hellenistic period ἐνάτηρ had been replaced by σύννυμφος, and it is possible that its usage in the inscriptions is a literary affectation such as is known elsewhere.[108]

To my mind, this argument is extremely unlikely to be correct. If it were the case that terms such as γάλως, δαήρ, and εἰνάτηρ had been reintroduced 'artificially' to the language on the model of early Greek poetry – whether as a learned literary affectation, or as convenient Greek equivalents for putative indigenous Lydian or Mysian kinship terms – then we would expect these terms to take the same morphological form, and to carry the same meaning, as they do in Homer. But as we have seen, this is emphatically not the case. In Hieradoumia, Homeric εἰνάτηρ is generally rendered ἰανάτηρ (occasionally ἐνάτηρ), and Homeric ἑκυρός/-ά almost always appears in the distinctive local form ὑκερός/-ά. Furthermore, Anatolian ἰανάτηρ/ἐνάτηρ carries a slightly different range of meaning from Homeric εἰνάτηρ ('husband's brother's wife'): in Hieradoumia and neighbouring regions, ἰανάτηρ/ἐνάτηρ in fact usually means 'brother's wife', while the relationship 'husband's brother's wife' was generally designated with the non-Homeric term σύννυμφος. Homeric imitation is just not a credible explanation of the 'survival' of these rare kinship terms in Hieradoumia.

---

[108] Cameron 1939, 32–3. Cameron cites Eustathius (648.43) in support of the notion that ε(ι)νάτηρ was 'replaced' by σύννυμφος in the Hellenistic period; although the term σύννυμφος is used by ancient grammarians as a synonym for εἰνάτηρ (Ar. Byz. F271–2 Slater; Ael. Dion. ε 21 Erbse), the term σύννυμφος is in fact epigraphically unattested outside of Hieradoumia. The terms ἰανάτηρ and σύννυμφος appear side by side with different meanings ('brother's wife'; 'husband's brother's wife') in *TAM* V 1, 775 (Loros) and *SEG* 49, 1660 (Saittai).

The regionally specific Hieradoumian forms ἰανάτηρ and ὐκερός/-ά are in fact one of our more important pieces of evidence for the historical development of the kinship terminological system of Hieradoumia as a whole. As we have already seen, several scholars have tried to explain the form ἰανάτηρ (Homeric εἰνάτηρ) as arising from cross-pollination with Latin *ianitrix* (Section 4.10 above); I suggested above that a similar relationship could, in theory, be postulated for the Hieradoumian form ὐκερός/-ά (Homeric ἑκυρός/-ά) and the Latin *socer/socrus* (Section 4.6 above). But is this postulated Greek–Latin morphological 'interference' really any more historically plausible than the notion of learned Homeric imitation? The Latin term **ianitrix* (attested only in the plural, *ianitrices*) really was exceptionally rare: it is unattested in Latin documentary texts and appears only in glosses and the works of Roman grammarians. The earliest attested example of the Hieradoumian form ἰανάτηρ ('brother's wife') is found in an epitaph from Loros dating to 46/5 BC, one of the very earliest surviving inscriptions from Hieradoumia.[109] There is not the slightest sign of Roman or Italian influence in this particular epitaph; the twenty-odd personal names recorded in the text are all of Greek or Lydian origin. It is very hard to believe that a mere eighty-five years after the establishment of the Roman province of Asia, without any known settlement of Latin-speakers in Hieradoumia, that Latin *ianitrix* could have influenced the morphology of the ordinary Hieradoumian term for the brother's wife, *without* having similarly influenced the form of the north-Phrygian kinship term ἐνάτηρ (see Section 4.10).

On our present evidence, then, the hypothesis of direct Latin influence on the distinctive Hieradoumian forms ἰανάτηρ and ὐκερός/-ά remains, at best, unproven. Although they are not 'Homeric', neither form is particularly problematic in itself: both are perfectly plausible derivations from Proto-Indo-European $*h_1yenh_a\text{-}ter\text{-}$ and $*swé\hat{}kuros$ respectively. To my mind, there is no reason why ἰανάτηρ and ὐκερός could not be very ancient Greek morphological variants of the Homeric εἰνάτηρ and ἑκυρός, preserved down to the first century BC and beyond in some largely oral dialect of the Greek language.[110] In light of the character of Hieradoumia as a relatively remote rural backwater of the Greco-Roman world, it is obviously tempting to see the 'archaic' character of Hieradoumian kinship terminology as

---

[109] *TAM* V 1, 775. This text also includes the distinctive Hieradoumian kinship terms γάλως ('husband's sister') and σύννυμφος ('husband's brother's wife'). The earliest example of the form ὐκερός seems to be *SEG* 40, 1043 (Gordos: AD 59/60).

[110] Apparently the position of Wilgaux 2006, 215–16.

an example of the 'conservatism of peripheral zones' – an ancient kinship and familial system preserved in the deep Anatolian countryside since time immemorial.[111] This temptation ought to be firmly resisted. As we saw in Chapter 1, the population of Hieradoumia in the Roman imperial period was of very mixed origins: Lydian, Mysian, Greek, Macedonian, and probably others. It is perfectly plausible that much of the kinship terminology in use in Hieradoumia in the Roman imperial period could have been a late Hellenistic import from, say, Hellenistic Macedonia or Mysia, of whose kinship and familial systems we know almost literally nothing.

Finally, against the hypotheses of artificial 'Homerizing' or semi-conscious 'Latinizing' in the kinship terminology of Hieradoumia, we should remind our selves of the fascinating Hieradoumian kinship term καμβ(δ)ιος, 'grandchild' (Section 4.2). As we have seen, this kinship term appears in three slightly different forms in three distinct parts of Roman Asia Minor: καμβ(δ)ιος/καμβ(δ)ιον in Roman Hieradoumia, κομβος/κομβιον/κονψος in Karia, and κανψιον in Kilikia. We must surely be dealing with a very ancient kinship term of Hittite or (more likely) Luwian origin, which survived quite independently in the spoken language of three quite widely spaced parts of Anatolia (compare the indigenous Lykian kinship term πιατρα, 'son's wife', Section 4.10). The rich kinship terminology of Hieradoumia was thus demonstrably both a *linguistically mixed* one, with individual terms of both Greek and non-Greek origin (Greek ἔγγονος vs. Luwian [?] καμβ(δ)ιος), and a *regionally specific* one, with particular forms distinctive to the communities of the middle Hermos valley (Hieradoumian καμβ(δ)ιος vs. Karian κομβος; Hieradoumian ἰανάτηρ vs. N Phrygian ἐνάτηρ; Hieradoumian ὑκερός vs. Phrygian ἑκυρός).[112]

But perhaps – as I suggested already at the end of Chapter 1 – it is possible to get too hung up on the question of origins. After all, none of this provides much of an answer to the most interesting question of all: just why did the inhabitants of Hieradoumia feel the need to classify (some of) their kin relationships with such unusual precision? (Not all kin relationships were so classified: note the striking imprecision of the Hieradoumian terminology for cousins and nephews, Section 4.5.)[113] Clearly, the answer

---

[111] 'Conservatism of peripheral zones': Todd 2011, 23–9 (romantic fallacy, in my view).

[112] For non-Greek vocabulary in Hieradoumia, compare the use of the Phrygian term δοῦμος, 'kin-group', for kin-based cult associations: Chapter 1, n.5.

[113] In *TAM* V 1, 432 (Nisyra), where the deceased's parents, siblings, foster-parents and foster-siblings, uncles, aunts, and cousins are all precisely classified (lines 3–20), we also find a certain Dionysios (listed with his wife and children) described simply as the deceased's συγγενής (lines 23–25): presumably Dionysios was a kinsman for whom no precise term existed (e.g. a second cousin). For similar examples of individuals listed simply as 'kinsmen' (συγγενεῖς) in the midst of a list of precisely classified relatives, see e.g. *TAM* V 1, 433, 483a, 549, 623, 705, 812; *SEG* 49, 1732.

must lie in some distinctive aspect(s) of the social structure of Roman Hier-adoumia, which *also* led the inhabitants of the region to commemorate their dead in the highly idiosyncratic manner that they did, with lengthy epitaphs listing dozens of members of the extended kinship-circle of the deceased.

One can of course offer a banal description of the kind of social rela-tions that are likely to underlie the Hieradoumian kinship terminological system and epitaphic habit. So: in a relatively simple society such as that of Hieradoumia, in which political structures (notably the *polis* and its insti-tutions) were perhaps relatively 'weak' or socially unimportant (Chapter 10), kinship relations could well have tended to be of greater social impor-tance than in more structurally complex communities like, say, Classical Athens or Roman Ephesos. Fair enough: that last sentence is, I suspect, probably both true and important. But a moment's reflection shows that this cannot serve as an *explanation* of the extraordinary Hieradoumian kinship terminological system and epitaphic habit. After all, plenty of other parts of Roman Asia Minor (Phrygia, Pisidia, Galatia) were equally dom-inated by 'simple' village societies, and did not, so far as we know, feel the need to classify or commemorate their kin with the kind of rigorous care and precision employed by the inhabitants of Roman Hieradoumia. It is true that we know far less about the kinship terminologies in use in Gala-tia or Pisidia in the Roman imperial period *tout court*: it is theoretically possible (though I doubt it) that these regions also had a very precise and nuanced kinship terminological system, which happens to be concealed by local epitaphic practices.[114] But even if that were the case, we would still be left with the question of why the Hieradoumian 'habit' of extensive kin-commemoration emerged and persisted *here*, and not elsewhere.

In the next two chapters, I will make a first tentative attempt at a more sat-isfactory answer to this question. We will look first at household and family structure (Chapter 5), before turning to the distinctively Hieradoumian practice of circulation of children between households (Chapter 6). Only then will we move outside the household to consider the relation-ship between kin networks and wider social structures in the region (Chapters 7–10).

---

[114] Against this hypothesis, note e.g. the demonstrable fact that most Greek-speakers, in Asia Minor and elsewhere, did not distinguish systematically between the wife's parents and the husband's parents (Sections 4.6 and 4.7).

5 | Household Forms

5.1 Six Households at Late Roman Hypaipa

We have virtually no direct evidence for the make-up of households in Roman Hieradoumia, or indeed anywhere else in the Asia Minor peninsula. No 'hard' demographic data survives from Roman Asia Minor to compare with the census returns preserved from Roman Egypt; for the most part, the structures of families and households in Roman Asia Minor have to be inferred from the manner of their representation in the abundant funerary epigraphy of the peninsula.[1] The methodological problems associated with this are, to put it mildly, formidable.

Before turning to the funerary inscriptions of Hieradoumia, let us take a brief look at the sole category of hard evidence that we possess for household composition anywhere in Roman Asia Minor. At some point in the fourth century AD – either around 310 or in the 370s – several *poleis* in western Asia Minor and the Aegean islands took the extraordinary step of having complete registers of taxable persons and property under their jurisdiction inscribed on stone.[2] This is a truly bizarre thing for any city to have done. Even if a city's total tax liability was expected to remain stable for many years into the future, many of the details of these registers (e.g. the ages of individual taxable persons) would already have been out of date by the time the inscription was complete. Presumably, the cities were acting on the instructions of an over-enthusiastic Roman governor (the *vicarius* of the Asianic diocese), most likely in the early years of the new Diocletianic tax system (introduced in stages from AD 287 onwards).

The precise character of these census registers varies from city to city. Most important for our purposes is a very fragmentary register from the

---

[1] Roman Egypt: Bagnall and Frier 2006; Huebner 2013.

[2] Thonemann 2007 (AD *c.* 310); Harper 2008 (shortly after AD 371). Fragments survive from the Diocletianic provinces of *Caria* (Miletos, Mylasa), *Asia* (Hypaipa, Magnesia, Tralleis), and *Insulae* (Astypalaia, Chios, Cos, Mytilene, Samos, Thera). The mere existence of these outlandish documents is the strongest argument for an early date: it is hard to see why a Roman governor should have ordered the erection of these inscriptions once the new tax system had been in force for a generation or more.

small Lydian town of Hypaipa, in the middle Kaystros valley.[3] The Hypaipa register is organized by the individual taxpayer. Parts of eleven separate entries survive. The first six pertain to citizens of Hypaipa 'living in their own house', along with their dependants, taxable land, and livestock; the remaining five are concerned with non-residents, at least one of them a citizen of a different *polis*, who owned property at the village of Dideiphyta on the territory of Hypaipa.[4] Each entry is recorded in the first person, reflecting the wording of the census declaration made by the man (or, in one case, the woman) who was liable for tax payment on his or her household and property. So the shortest entry, the declaration of a single man with no dependants, taxable land, or livestock, reads simply:

Αὐρ. Συνόδιος Δρακοντίου Ὑπαιπ(ηνός)
οἰκ(ῶν) ἐν οἰκ(ίᾳ) ἰδίᾳ
ἐμαυτὸν   ἐτ(ῶν) κʹ.
        ὁ(μοῦ) αʹ.

Aur. Synodios, son of Drakontios, citizen of Hypaipa, living in my own house. Myself (*emauton*), 20 years old. Total: 1.

Only the first six tax declarations – those of the Hypaipene citizens 'living in their own house' – give us a clear sense of the shape of actual Lydian households. The five entries for non-resident landowners at Dideiphyta do not list the other members of the taxpayer's household, since these entries only describe their tax liabilities at Dideiphyta (the taxpayer and his/her immediate household lived elsewhere). The six relevant Hypaipene households are as follows.

(I)   The start of the first declaration is lost, and hence we do not know the name and age of the (male) head of the household. The names and ages of two of his dependents are preserved: his mother Tatia, aged 48, and his sister Mentoriane, aged 11. To all appearances, Tatia's husband has died, and her son has become head of the household unexpectedly early. We do not know whether this man was himself married at the time of the tax declaration. This man is the only one of the six declarants to have owned his own small plot of agricultural land: $3\,{}^1/_5$ *iugera*

---

[3] *I.Ephesos* 3804–3806; Déléage 1945, 164–9; Patlagean 1977, 147–50.

[4] Citizens of Hypaipa: *I.Ephesos* 3804. Non-resident property owners at Dideiphyta: *I.Ephesos* 3805 (indicated with the term ἐνκτήτωρ). So Aur. Metrodora (*I.Ephesos* 3805, I 1–9: in I 1, read Αὐρ. Μη[τ]ροδώρα) seems to be a citizen of Ephesos, resident in a village on Ephesian territory, while [Aur.] Andr[–] (*I.Ephesos* 3805, III 4–9: the restoration of the name is uncertain) seems to be a citizen of Hypaipa, resident at the Hypaipan village of K[–].

of vines (around 0.8 hectares), 4 $1/_6$ *iugera* of arable land (around one hectare), and an unknown number of olive trees, all in the vicinity of Hypaipa, along with some more olives near the village of P[.]st[.]s.[5]

(II)   The second declaration, as we have seen, was made by a single man, Aurelius Synodios, 20 years of age. Synodios was clearly old enough to set up house on his own, but had not yet married.[6]

(III)   The third declaration was made by a man named Aur. Hermolaos, aged 56. His household also included a 48-year-old woman called Kyriake, of uncertain status (but apparently not his wife); a son Moukianos, three years old; a daughter Meliton, probably younger than Mouki-anos, and a foster-child (*threptos*) also bearing the name Moukianos, of uncertain age. The character of the family unit is rather unclear. Hermolaos had clearly had children relatively late in life; his wife may have recently died, and been replaced in his household by a nurse or foster-mother. It is unlikely to be a coincidence that his son and his *threptos* carried the same name as one another (Moukianos). Perhaps his *threptos* Moukianos was the natural son of a close family member (e.g. Hermolaos' brother or sister), resident for a period in Hermolaos' household; declaration (VI) below provides a possible parallel.[7]

(IV)   The fourth declaration reflects a young nuclear family, headed by Aur. Dionysios, aged 34, along with at least one individual whose name and age is lost (probably his wife), and a 12-year-old child.[8]

(V)   The fifth declaration reveals another nuclear family, consisting of Aur. Eutyches, son of Eutyches (aged 40+), a man or woman called Eutyche or Eutyches (aged 30+), and a son aged 20+. Eutyches also owned a donkey and a pig, but apparently no land of his own. The most plausible reconstruction of this household would give us a husband and wife, aged 40-something and (say) 38 or 39 respectively, with a son in his early twenties who had not yet set up his own household (contrast II above).[9]

---

[5]   *I.Ephesos* 3804, I 1–8. For typical sizes of farms and estates in late Roman Asia Minor, see Thonemann 2007, 463–75. This farm is, relatively speaking, very small.

[6]   *I.Ephesos* 3804, I 9–12.

[7]   *I.Ephesos* 3804 I, 13–19. The woman Kyriake is described with a mysterious abbreviation, apparently *omicron* and *upsilon*. οὔ(ρου) (Déleage 1945, 165) is not otherwise found in documents of this type. For the *threptos* Moukianos, cf. Ricl 2009, 106.

[8]   *I.Ephesos* 3804, I 20–21, II 1–3.

[9]   *I.Ephesos* 3804, II 4–10. Patlagean 1977, 147 was puzzled by the apparent combination of a twenty-year-old son (ἐτ(ῶν) κ') and a thirty-year-old mother (ἐτ(ῶν) λ'), and wondered if we are dealing with a second marriage; but the age numerals are inscribed at the very edge of the block, and hence it is possible that some numerals have been lost (e.g. ἐτ(ῶν) λ[η'] or λ[θ']).

(VI) The sixth declaration consists of Aur. Kalochrotios, aged 30+, his wife Menophila, aged 30+, a son Onesimos (of uncertain age), a daughter Chryseon (aged either 1 or 4), and, most interesting of all, what appears to be 'a baby on his sibling's side', that is, his brother or sister's child, registered as being one year old.[10] Presumably this child's mother died in childbirth, and hence the baby was transferred to its uncle's household to be raised there (cf. III above). The fact that the child is not given a name (it is simply referred to as *paidion*) suggests that it may still have been very young – indeed, considerably less than a year old.[11] Kalochrotios also owned a pig.

Naturally, we have no way of knowing how representative this random group of six Hypaipene households might be, either of households at fourth-century Hypaipa or of households in Roman Asia Minor more generally.[12] But they do present at least three very striking features.

First, unless these households are wildly uncharacteristic, fosterage was evidently a very widespread social institution at Roman Hypaipa. Both of the two households with children under ten (III and VI) also included a 'foster-child': in one case (III) a *threptos* bearing the same name as his *syntrophos*, in the other (VI) the infant nephew or niece of the head of the household. A third *threptos* appears in a very suggestive context among the register of non-resident landowners at Dideiphyta. A certain Aur. [–]

---

[10] *I.Ephesos* 3804, II 11–19. As with the previous declaration, the age figures are inscribed on the edge of the stone, and hence there is no reason to think that Kalochrotios and Menophila were both thirty years old (ἐτ(ῶν) λ'); one could be up to nine years older than the other (ἐτ(ῶν) λ[θ']). In line 15, the sole extant copy of the stone leaves it unclear whether the son Onesimos was aged 10+ (ἐτ(ῶν) ι[.]') or 3 (ἐτ(ῶν) γ'); in line 16, the daughter Chryseon could be aged either 1 (ἐτ(ῶν) α') or 4 (ἐτ(ῶν) δ'). Line 17 apparently reads παιδίον πρὸς ἀδε̣λ(φοῦ/-φῆς) ἐτ(ῶν) α'.

[11] Children in Roman Anatolia were not named at birth: compare the nameless baby of the *threptē* Ammia, who lived 'for a few days', in an epitaph from the Upper Tembris valley (Waelkens 1986, 107–9, no. 252; Chapter 6, Section 6.1). Cf. also *SEG* 53, 1475 (Afyon Museum, restored by P. Thonemann in Masséglia 2013, 119), Ἀμία ἐπυ⟨ίσ⟩εν τῦ τέκνυ ἀώρυ{ς} χάριν μνήμης; *SEG* 62, 1063 (Hadrianopolis: an unnamed five-month-old boy); *MAMA* VII 234 (Turgut: a woman who died leaving two children, Δόμναν καὶ παῖδα σὺν αὐτῇ μεικρόν). At Rome, children were typically named eight or nine days after birth: Laes 2011, 65–6. In mainland Greece, tombstones for unnamed babies were sometimes marked simply with a *pi*, for *p(ais)*: Thonemann 2004, 218. Note also the near-total absence of epitaphs for infants in Hieradoumia (Chapter 3, Section 3.5), implying that 'social birth' in Roman inland western Asia Minor may have been relatively late.

[12] The contemporary census register of Thera describes five households of *paroikoi*, free rural labourers (Harper 2008, 101), as follows: (**I**) Theodoros (30), his wife Zosime (20), and a daughter Theodora (2) (Kiourtzian 2000, 142a, lines 18–19). (**II**) Neikasion (65), his wife (name and age missing), and four children, Dekimos (14), Zosime (12), Hermias (10+) and

son of Metrodoros, resident at the village of [–]aida, owned a plot of land
at Dideiphyta, on which he registered his foster-sibling (*syntrophos*), Metrodoros, aged 25. The coincidence of names (*x* son of Metrodoros; his *syntrophos* Metrodoros) strongly implies that the *syntrophos* Metrodoros was
a blood relative of the declarant, perhaps a cousin (cf. III and VI above)
or a bastard half-sibling. Apparently the farm at Dideiphyta was too far
from [–]aida to be worked directly by its owner, and hence he installed his
syntrophos there to look after the farm on his behalf.[13] We have no way of
knowing whether the *syntrophos* Metrodoros was formally of slave status,
but he clearly remained in a state of legal dependence on his foster-sibling,
at least for tax purposes.[14] As we will see in Chapter 6, the epitaphs of Hieradoumia likewise indicate that fosterage and the circulation of children
played a very important role in determining the makeup of typical households in the region.

Second, the picture that we get of the Hypaipan familial life cycle is
very varied. Men in their early twenties are found still living with their
parents (V) or having set up house on their own (II); one man seems to
have had his first child at the age of 22 (IV), another at an uncertain point
in his twenties (V), and a third man at the age of 53 (III). One (presumably
young) man has come into his inheritance tragically early and is left caring
for his widowed mother and his pre-teen sister (I). This is not to say that
there was no such thing as a 'typical' Hypaipan family, only that 'typicality'
is very much a matter of degree.

Finally, despite the varying composition of these six households, it is
striking that all are small in size (no more than five members). It would be
misleading to describe these as 'nuclear' families (at least without somehow
building the ubiquitous *threptos* into our concept of 'nuclearity'), but they

Sotion (6) (Kiourtzian 2000, 142d, lines 4–6). (**III**) Zosimos (60), his wife Epikteta (52), and
two children, Zosimos (age missing) and Eukleia (16) (Kiourtzian 2000, 142d, lines 7–8). (**IV**)
Dionysios (37) and his son Gelasios (11) (Kiourtzian 2000, 142d, line 9). (**V**) Gelasios (40) and
his wife Zosime (22) (Kiourtzian 2000, 142d, line 10). All are simple nuclear families, without
extended kin or *threptoi*. For the make-up of slave families at Thera (not attested at Hypaipa),
see Harper 2008, 106–16; Harper 2011, 74–6.

[13] Compare the absentee landlord Quadratus and his (slave?) bailiff Syneros in the contemporary
Magnesian census register (*I.Magnesia* 122, a14; Thonemann 2007, 441 n.26).

[14] *I.Ephesos* 3805, Col. II 9–13, Col. III 1–3. In Col. III line 1, the sole extant copy of the stone
reads Μητροδωρ[.]ν συντροφαν (*sic*); the noun *syntrophos* is otherwise always of common gender. The name could in theory be restored either Μητρόδωρ[ο]ν or Μητρόδωρ[α]ν. Another
epitaph from Hypaipa shows that at least some rearers (τεκέων τρέφοντες) and other foster-kin
(ἄνθρωποι θρεπτικοί) at Hypaipa were of unfree status: *SEG* 55, 1288; see further Chapter 6,
Section 6.2.

are certainly not sprawling multiple-family households either. Widowed mothers, adopted babies, and adult foster-siblings installed on outlying farms were all within the normal range of experience for households at Hypaipa; but there is no sign of (say) two married brothers living under the same roof, or of a young married couple still subject to the authority of the husband's father. The two relatively young fathers who appear in the Hypaipa tax declarations – Aur. Dionysios, aged 34 (IV), and Aur. Kalochrotios, aged 30+ (VI) – are both masters of their own households. Given the minuscule size of the sample, it would be dangerous to lay too much weight on this, but the contrast with the Egyptian census evidence (where multiple-family households were very common) is at least suggestive.[15]

5.2 Family Structure from Epitaphs: Methodological Problems

These half-dozen fourth-century Hypaipan households are a fragile foundation, to put it mildly, for any meaningful generalizations about family structure in inland western Asia Minor. For that we need a considerably larger body of evidence, ideally homogeneous in form, and ideally tightly defined in both space and time. This is precisely what the epitaphs of Roman Hieradoumia provide. As we saw in Chapter 2, one of the most distinctive features of the Hieradoumian epitaphic habit is the regular inclusion of a more or less extensive list of relatives who joined in 'honouring' the deceased – in some cases, only one or two close kin (parents commemorating a deceased child, or a wife commemorating her husband: Figure 5.1)[16]; in others, a dozen or more relatives of various kinds (parents-in-law, uncles and aunts, foster-siblings, etc.). At least in principle, the commemorative choices made by particular families can tell us a great deal about typical familial and household structures in Roman Hieradoumia.

'At least in principle' is very much the operative phrase. In practice, using these lists of commemorators as proxy evidence for family or household structure is very far from straightforward. We do not know what

---

[15] Bagnall and Frier 2006, 57–66.
[16] *TAM* V 1, 385 (Gölde): [ἔ]τους τμδ΄, μη(νὸς) Δείου. Λού|[κι]ος ὁ πατὴρ καὶ Ἐπείκτη|σις ἡ μήτηρ Λούκιον τὸν | υὸν ἐτείμησαν μνίας χάρ[ιν] ('Year 344 [AD 259/60], month Dios. Loukios the father and Epiktesis the mother honoured their son Loukios, in memory'). Note the vine-pruning knife and the bunch of grapes held by the elder and younger Loukios.

Figure 5.1 A nuclear family at Gölde (Kollyda). *TAM* V 1, 385 (Manisa Museum).

determined a family's choice to commemorate one of its members in limited ('nuclear') or comprehensive ('extended') fashion. Actual household structure is likely to have been only one of the determinants of this choice. 'Nuclear' commemoration is by definition cheaper than 'extended' commemoration, since long epitaphs require a large tombstone. If an epitaph includes only one commemorator (a wife for her husband or a father for his son), this may simply reflect the fact that the family – whatever its actual make-up – could not afford a larger tombstone. Similarly, it is likely enough that a large and lavish tombstone was a way of indicating social status. Some of the large 'extended' families that appear in Hieradoumian epitaphs may therefore not in fact have been meaningful social units at all: there is no necessary reason to think that the uncles and aunts and in-laws that appear on the longest epitaphs were co-resident (or even particularly intimate) with the deceased.[17]

---

[17] So, for instance, of the thirty-two named commemorators in *TAM* V 1, 432 (Nisyra: for an eighteen-year-old male), those listed towards the head of the epitaph (parents, brother, and

Direct evidence for co-residency is, in fact, almost completely lacking in Hieradoumia (as in most other parts of the Greek East). The various members of the large 'extended families' that appear in the Hieradoumian epigraphic evidence, although choosing to represent themselves as a single 'moral unit' in both funerary and propitiatory contexts, may in fact have resided in physically distinct nuclear family units.[18] It is also likely enough that the shape of households fluctuated over the course of the agricultural year, as is suggested by a dream recorded by Artemidorus of Daldis in the fifth book of his *Oneirocritica*, which seems reasonably likely to reflect conditions in rural Hieradoumia[19]:

> A man dreamt that stalks of wheat had grown out of his chest, and then someone came along and pulled them out as if they had no business to be there. The man had two sons, and they met with a cruel fate: they were living out on the farm (οἰκοῦσιν αὐτοῖς τὸν ἀγρόν), and a band of robbers attacked and killed them. The stalks of wheat signified his sons, and their removal signified the taking of his sons' lives.

The natural implication of this dream is that the two sons (perhaps as yet unmarried?) were temporarily co-resident on an outlying farm, away from their father's main household; this may well have been a normal arrangement at busy times of the agricultural year.

In recent years, Roman historians have expended some energy in debating whether we can legitimately use patterns of familial commemoration on tombstones as evidence for actual household and family structures in the Roman world.[20] In what proportion do nuclear-family relationships predominate among the hundreds of thousands of attested familial ties in Roman epitaphs? If an individual is commemorated only by members of his or her nuclear family – or erects a tombstone only for other members of his nuclear family – does that necessarily imply that he or she actually *resided* as part of a nuclear-family household? Local funerary epigraphic habits and norms may, in some regions, lead us to drastically overestimate the proportion of individuals who lived in nuclear-family households: I have argued elsewhere that the apparent overwhelming predominance

---

sisters) were surely co-resident with the deceased, and those listed towards the end (Tatianos the doctor; Apollonios, the deceased's friend) clearly were not; but what of the uncles, aunts, *syngeneis* and *idioi* listed in the central part of the epitaph?

[18] Thonemann 2013c, 129. On the problem of co-residency, see further Davis 1977, 174–6 (households as moral entities, sometimes but not always co-resident); Martin 1996, 50–1.

[19] Artemidorus 5.84 (trans. Hammond 2020).

[20] Short overview in Scheidel 2012b, 110–12.

of nuclear-family relationships in the funerary epigraphy of Apameia–Kelainai in Phrygia is an optical illusion of precisely this kind.[21]

There has also been some instructive disagreement about exactly how to gauge the 'nuclearity' or 'extendedness' of any given family grouping. In their 1984 study of familial commemoration in the western Roman provinces, Saller and Shaw focused on dyadic links between individual commemorators and the deceased.[22] Their conclusion (based on a data set of almost 6,000 discrete commemorative relationships in civilian epitaphs) was that the overwhelming majority of commemorators (between 75% and 90%) were 'nuclear' kin to the deceased, with 'extended' family commemorators making up less than 5% of the total. In 1996, Martin pointed out that by focusing on individual commemorative relationships, rather than commemorative groups as a whole, Saller and Shaw may have ended up overestimating the prevalence of nuclear family structures. To take a simple example, let us assume a deceased adult male is commemorated by his father, brother, wife, and daughter. Each of the four individual commemorative relationships is 'nuclear' in type, but the family structure as a whole is clearly better classified as 'extended'.[23] Martin's own study of funerary commemoration in Roman Asia Minor (focusing primarily on epitaphs from Olympos in Lykia, Termessos in Pisidia, and Nikomedeia in Bithynia) produced a very different picture: extended-family tombstones made up a full 75% of the total at Olympos, and 26% and 28% of the total at Nikomedeia and Termessos respectively.[24]

A further issue which Martin did not discuss, but which causes major problems when we try to compare typical family structures in Hieradoumia with any other part of the Asia Minor peninsula, is that of variation in the precise *type* of familial epitaph we are dealing with in any given region. In Hieradoumia (as in the western Roman Empire), epitaphs were typically small free-standing monuments set up for one individual only, more rarely for two individuals, very seldom for three or more; when the names of extended family members appear on the tombstone, they are almost always living relatives who joined in commemorating the deceased. By contrast, most of the 'familial' epitaphs studied by Martin (notably those from Olympos and Termessos) were large and expensive stone sarcophagi or 'house-tombs' erected

[21] Thonemann 2013c, 125–7.
[22] Saller and Shaw 1984, 134, 136, with the tables at 147–51.
[23] Martin 1996, 43–4. Note, however, that Saller and Shaw's statistics may not in fact be affected as much as one might expect: Edmondson 2005, 215–17.
[24] Martin 1996, 48, 59.

by a single individual for several family members, most of whom were yet to die (and in some cases were yet to be born!) at the time the tomb structure was built. That is to say, very many of the 'extended families' catalogued by Martin are in fact lists of those *hypothetical* descendants who will in future possess the right of burial in an existing family tomb ('my sons, their wives, my grandchildren …'). The length of these lists evidently need not necessarily tell us anything at all about actual family or household structures. In other words, when a man sets up a funerary *stēlē* for his granddaughter, we may reasonably infer the existence of a close affective relationship beyond the nuclear family; this kind of affective relationship cannot so easily be inferred when a man erects a familial sarcophagus or house tomb in which his future grandchildren have the right of burial.

For the purposes of this chapter, I have used a sample of 677 'familial' epitaphs from Hieradoumia erected for named individuals by one or more relatives (including foster-kin). This sample does not include epitaphs which give only the name of the deceased, without a list of commemorators; nor have I included tombstones set up for more than one individual (which pose intractable difficulties of classification), or tombstones erected by non-kin (e.g. by trade associations, friends, or other corporate groups).[25] When a tombstone includes among the commemorators a spouse, son, daughter, or grandchild of the deceased, I have assumed that the deceased is (or has been) married; when an individual is commemorated only by parents, siblings, foster-parents (*threpsantes*), or foster-siblings (*syntrophoi*), I have assumed that he or she is unmarried.[26] When a married individual is commemorated *only* by his or her spouse and/or children, I have classified this as a 'nuclear' family tombstone; similarly, when an unmarried individual is commemorated only by his or her parents and/or siblings, I have also classified the family as 'nuclear'. When any other individuals are included

---

[25] Epitaphs that give only the name of the deceased: particularly common at Sardis (e.g. *Sardis* VII 1, 112–133). Tombstones set up for more than one individual: e.g. *TAM* V 1, 770 (Gordos), an epitaph erected by Menandros for his mother and his daughter: should this be classified as a single extended three-generational family or as two nuclear relationships? Tombstones erected by non-kin (particularly common at Saittai): e.g. *TAM* V 1, 79–93 (*plateiai, synodoi, synbiōseis, philoi*, etc.; see further Chapter 7. For obvious reasons, I have only included tombstones that survive complete or nearly complete.

[26] In practice, of course, it is seldom easy to prove with certainty that an individual is unmarried (except when he or she is explicitly said to have died at, say, the age of eight or nine). Nonetheless, given the compendiousness with which the deceased's kin tend to be listed on Hieradoumian tombstones, the *absence* of a spouse or children among the commemorators of the deceased can reasonably be taken as an indication that they were unmarried. Of course, some such individuals may have been childless widows or widowers.

Table 5.1 'Familial' commemoration of individuals in Hieradoumia (n = 677)

	Commemorated by nuclear kin only	Commemorated by nuclear + extended kin	Commemorated by non-nuclear kin only	Total
Married (M)	86	104	1	191
Married (F)	83	109	3	195
Unmarried (M)	114	77	31	222
Unmarried (F)	46	14	9	69
All deceased	**329**	**304**	**44**	**677**

in the list of commemorators – foster-kin, grandparents, affines – I have classified the family as 'extended'.

The overall breakdown of this sample is summarized in Table 5.1. Just under half of all epitaphs for individuals, 329 in total (48.6%), were erected only by members of the deceased's immediate nuclear family. Most of the remainder, 304 tombstones in total (44.9%), were erected by members of the nuclear family plus one or more 'extended' kin (including foster-kin). The remaining 44 epitaphs (6.5%) were set up by non-nuclear kin only, in most cases by foster-kin alone (32 out of 44).[27] Of these 677 tombstones of 'familial' type, 191 (28.2%) were set up for married men, 195 (28.8%) for married women, 222 (32.8%) for unmarried (or apparently unmarried) males, and 69 (10.2%) for unmarried females. At first sight, we appear to have a stark gender imbalance among epitaphs erected for unmarried individuals: this apparent imbalance is discussed further in Section 5.3 below.

This body of epitaphs also allows us to gauge, at least in a rough and ready kind of way, the prevalence of fosterage in Hieradoumian society. Of 677 'familial' epitaphs for individuals from Roman Hieradoumia, 181 (26.7%) include at least one foster-relative (either a foster-child, a foster-sibling, or a foster-parent) in the register of those who joined in commemorating the deceased. But that statistic probably under-represents the proportion of individuals in Roman Hieradoumia who had close foster-kin of some kind. As we have seen, around half of all 'familial' epitaphs in the region (329, 48.6% of the total) were erected only by members of the deceased's immediate nuclear family; very many epitaphs for married men and women were erected by their spouses alone, and many epitaphs for unmarried males

---

[27] The four instances of married men and women commemorated by non-nuclear kin alone all appear to be cases of childless widows or widowers commemorated by their parents-in-law (*SEG* 40,1083; *TAM* V 1, 39; *TAM* V 1, 779; *SEG* 56, 1270).

and females were set up by one or both parents alone. If we omit these 'nuclear' tombstones from our data set, we are left with a total of 348 epitaphs set up by both nuclear and non-nuclear kin (or by non-nuclear kin alone), of which 182 (52.3%) include foster-kin among those commemorating the deceased.[28] It appears that fosterage was, if not quite universal, at least a completely normal feature of the Hieradoumian family, as at late Roman Hypaipa (see Section 5.1). At the most conservative estimate, we can reasonably infer that between a third and a half of all households in the region (and perhaps a considerably higher proportion than that) reared at least one *threptos* or *threptē*, whose sentimental relationship with his or her foster-family remained intimate enough for them to be named (either as commemorator or as deceased) on the family's tombstones. The character of fosterage in Roman Hieradoumia is explored further in Chapter 6.

In the following sections, I discuss various aspects of family and household structure in Hieradoumia as they emerge from the epitaphic evidence: differential commemoration of men and women and typical age at marriage (Section 5.3); marital preferences (Section 5.4); relations between married men and women and their pre-marital kin and post-marital affines (Section 5.5); the presence of uncles and aunts as 'extended' familial commemorators (Section 5.6), and – with all due caution – what we can conclude about the typical shape of extended family households in Roman Hieradoumia (Section 5.7).

5.3 Men and Women: Funerary 'Under-Representation' and Age at First Marriage

Overall, as we have seen, males were considerably more likely than females to be commemorated with their own tombstone in Hieradoumia; 61.0% of 'familial' tombstones for individuals (413) were set up for males of all ages, with a mere 39.0% (264) commemorating women of all ages.[29] However, this bare statistic conceals significant variation in commemorative practice over the life cycle. Among familial tombstones for the unmarried, males overwhelmingly predominate: of 291 epitaphs for the unmarried,

---

[28] Thirty-two of these are epitaphs set up by foster-kin only (i.e. a foster-parent for his/her foster-child, or a foster-sibling for his/her foster-sibling).

[29] This statistic only includes tombstones erected by family members. In fact, the *total* proportion of extant Hieradoumian epitaphs set up for men is even higher than this, since virtually all of the Saittan epitaphs erected by guilds and trade associations (not included in these figures) were for men (64 out of 65 examples: see further Chapter 7, Section 7.2).

Figure 5.2 Epitaph of Ammias and Assklepiades, from Kula. *TAM* V 1, 289 (Yale University Art Gallery, 1949.211).

222 (76.3%) are for males, and a mere 69 (23.7%) are for females. By contrast, almost exactly the same number of familial tombstones were set up for married men (191) and married women (195). At first sight, then, the evidence seems to suggest that married women were considerably more likely than unmarried females to be commemorated with their own tombstone.

There are some possible signs of sentimental 'undervaluing' of unmarried daughters in other aspects of the funerary epigraphy of Hieradoumia. An epitaph from Kula, with a relief sculpture depicting a young woman and a young man standing side by side (Figure 5.2), reads as follows[30]:

---

[30] *TAM* V 1, 289. The relief no doubt depicts the two deceased.

ἔτους σθε', μη(νὸς) Ἀπελλαίου κ'. Ἀμμιὰς
τελευτᾷ ἐτῶν ιϛ', Ἀσσκληπιάδης
ὁ πατὴρ, Γλυκεῖα ἡ τεκοῦσα τὴν θυγατέ-
ρα ἐτείμησαν. ἔτους τα', μη(νὸς) Ἀπελλαίου
5   Ἀσσκληπιάδης τελευτᾷ ιγ' ἐτῶν ιϛ',
Ἀσσκληπιάδης ὁ πατὴρ, Γλυκεῖα ἡ τεκοῦσα τὸν υἱὸν ἐτείμησαν.

Year 295 [AD 210/11], Day 20 of the month Apellaios. Ammias dies aged 16. Assklepiades her father, Glykeia her mother honoured their daughter. Year 301 [AD
216/17], in the month Apellaios, Assklepiades dies on (Day) 13 aged 16. Assklepiades his father, Glykeia his mother honoured their son.

   Assklepiades and Glykeia did not set up a tombstone for their daughter
when she died in early autumn AD 210; only when their son died six years
later was Ammias commemorated on stone alongside her younger brother.
If the younger Assklepiades had happened to live to adulthood, quite probably Ammias would not have received her own tombstone at all. Much
earlier, perhaps around 100 BC, an eighteen-year-old from Maionia by the
name of Menekrates, nicknamed Skollos ('top-knot'), was commemorated
in a prose epitaph by his parents, his five brothers, and his two sisters; in
the accompanying verse epigram, there is no mention of his sisters, and
Menekrates is simply said to have left 'five siblings (gnōtoi)'.[31] In another
epitaph from Maionia, an elderly man is commemorated by four sons and
a stepdaughter, and by six grandsons by his four sons. Perhaps none of
his sons happened to have female children; more likely his granddaughters
were simply omitted from the list of relatives, as being less worthy of note.[32]
   However, this apparent under-representation of unmarried females in
the epitaphs of Hieradoumia may well be illusory. A great deal depends
on what we take to have been the typical age at first marriage for men and
women. Let us assume, for the sake of argument, (i) that no children (or
almost no children) under the age of five were commemorated with their
own tombstone, and (ii) that women typically married aged around 16
and that men typically married aged around 30.[33] In that case, the apparent

---

[31] SEG 35, 1166 (SGO I 04/22/07). For the name Skollos, see Robert 1963, 267–70. For the
omission of unmarried daughters from the verse epigram accompanying a prose epitaph,
compare MAMA X 219 (SGO III 16/31/77), with Thonemann 2013c, 138–9.
[32] TAM V 1, 555.
[33] These assumptions are not arbitrary. For the under-representation of the very young in
Hieradoumian epitaphs, see Chapter 3, Section 3.5; for typical age at marriage,
see the discussion below.

under-commemoration of unmarried females would start to look much less stark, since the total population of unmarried females who might expect to receive their own tombstone would only consist of girls between the ages of 5 and 16, while the population of unmarried males who might expect to receive their own tombstone would consist of boys and young men between the ages of 5 and 30 – on any hypothesis, a considerably larger group.

We have seen that tombstones for unmarried males outnumber tombstones for unmarried females by around 3:1 (222 epitaphs for unmarried males, 69 epitaphs for unmarried females). Still working on the two assumptions made in the previous paragraph (no tombstones for under-5s; marriage for women around 16, marriage for men around 30), is this 'commemorative disparity' of the kind of magnitude that we would naturally expect? We can test this in a rough and ready kind of way by comparison with age-specific mortality rates for a typical pre-modern Mediterranean population.[34] In a Mediterranean population with mean life expectancy at birth of 20 ($e(0) = 20$), we would normally expect 7.46% of the population (both male and female) to die between the ages of 5 and 15, and 21.76% of the population to die between the ages of 5 and 30; in a population with life expectancy at birth of 25 ($e(0) = 25$), we would expect 5.47% of the population to die between 5 and 15, and 19.63% to die between 5 and 30. That is to say – still on the two assumptions of minimal funerary commemoration of under-5s and differential age at marriage (around 16 for women, around 30 for men) – unmarried females are not in fact under-represented on Hieradoumian epitaphs at all: we would naturally expect unmarried females to be outnumbered by unmarried males by a factor of around 3:1 or 4:1. In that case, we would be able to say that although women were *overall* less likely to receive their own tombstone than men were, there is no good reason to think that unmarried females are particularly under-represented in our evidence. If anything, it is *married* women who are likely to be significantly under-represented in our surviving epitaphs. It is a plausible enough supposition that married women were often buried in their husband's tomb, without the fact being recorded on his tombstone; differential age at marriage would have meant that, on the whole, husbands were likely to die before their wives.

Of course, this whole argument depends on an assumption about typical age at first marriage in Hieradoumia, to which we now turn. To the best of

---

[34] I here use the high-mortality 'South Europe' Model Life Table proposed by Woods 2007, 379. For further discussion of the use of Model Life Tables, see Chapter 3, Section 3.5.

my knowledge, in only a single case can we be absolutely certain of a woman's precise age at marriage (21).[35] In another two instances, dated epitaphs of both husband and wife allow us to reconstruct the age gap between the couple (six years and four years respectively).[36] In a group of epitaphs relating to a single family from Charakipolis around the turn of the era, we find two women who married in their late teens (one who had her first child at the age of 17, and another who died married at the age of 20), and a man who had his first son at the age of 29.[37] Of the six households described in the Hypaipa census declarations, four provide some evidence for age at marriage. Aur. Hermolaos (declaration III) seems to have had his first child at the age of 53, while Aur. Dionysios (declaration IV) had his first child at the age of 22. Aur. Eutyches and his wife (?) Eutyche (declaration V) were aged (at most) 29 and 19 respectively when their son was born; either or both could in fact have been some years younger than that. Finally, Aur. Kalochrotios and his wife Menophila (declaration VI), parents of two young children, were both in their thirties at the time that their tax declaration was made.

Isolated examples of this kind will clearly not get us very far. However, so long as we are willing to make a single simple and plausible assumption about Hieradoumian commemorative practices, a larger body of indirect evidence for typical age at first marriage can be brought into play. As we have seen, the characteristic 'familial' epitaphs of Hieradoumia typically list a number of individuals (ranging from one to more than thirty) who joined in commemorating the deceased. It seems reasonable to assume that if the deceased was married, then his or her spouse would normally be listed among the relatives listed on the tombstone. Hence the *absence* of a spouse or children from the list of those commemorating the deceased is an extremely strong indication that he or she was not in fact married at the time of his or her death.[38]

---

[35] *TAM* V 3, 1772 (Philadelphia), the epitaph of a woman who died at the age of 24, having been married for three years. Length of marriage (but without age at death) is recorded in e.g. *TAM* V 1, 631 (Daldis: five years), *TAM* V 1, 717 (Gordos: thirty-seven years); such indications usually reflect a tragically short or an impressively long marriage (Robert, *OMS* V, 314–15).

[36] *SEG* 52, 1163 and 1164 (uncertain provenance) record the deaths of a twenty-six-year-old wife (AD 195/6) and her seventy-two-year-old widower (AD 235/6). The husband was therefore some six years older than his wife; we do not know their actual ages at marriage. *TAM* V 1, 95 (Saittai) is the epitaph of a couple and their son, set up by a second surviving son. The husband died aged 85 in AD 77/8; the wife died aged 84 in AD 80/1; their son died aged 43 in AD 73/4. We thus learn that the husband was around four years older than his wife, and that one of their sons was born when the husband was 37 and his wife was 34.

[37] *TAM* V 1, 678–679; *SEG* 57, 1147–1149; see further Section 5.4.

[38] If it were the case that deceased individuals were typically commemorated either by their parents alone or by their spouse alone, then the assumption that the shift in commemorative

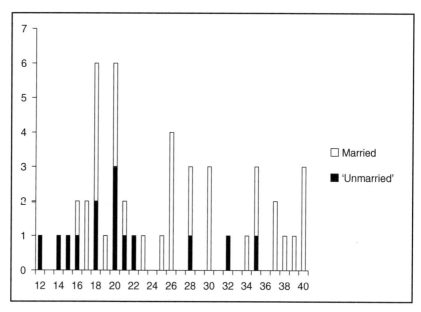

Figure 5.3 Spousal and non-spousal commemoration of women with recorded age at death (ages 12–40) in Hieradoumian epitaphs (n = 47).

The Hieradoumian evidence for spousal and non-spousal commemoration of men and women who died between the ages of twelve and forty is collected in Figure 5.3 (women: n = 47) and Figure 5.4 (men: n = 69).[39] Three of the relevant epitaphs for men are not included in Figure 5.4, since the age of the deceased is not precisely known: in each case, the deceased was in his twenties (20–29) and was commemorated by parents and siblings alone (i.e. can be presumed to have been unmarried).[40] Even though the total number of data points is relatively small, the overall patterns for men and (especially) women are clear. From the age of sixteen upwards, the overwhelming majority of women were commemorated by their husbands: of the seventeen women known to have died between the ages of sixteen and twenty, twelve were demonstrably already married. For men,

practice corresponded to a change in marital status would be no more than an assumption, albeit a plausible one (Scheidel 2007). But in fact, the case for a link between commemorative practice and marital status is vastly stronger in Hieradoumia than in other parts of the Greco-Roman world, precisely because of the large numbers of kin and affines regularly listed in Hieradoumian epitaphs.

[39] I have not included the abundant epitaphs from Saittai erected by guilds of various kinds (*synbiōseis, plateiai, synergasiai* etc.), since we have no way of knowing whether the individuals (usually men) commemorated in these texts were married or not.

[40] *TAM* V 2, 1326; *SEG* 48, 1459; *SEG* 49, 1681.

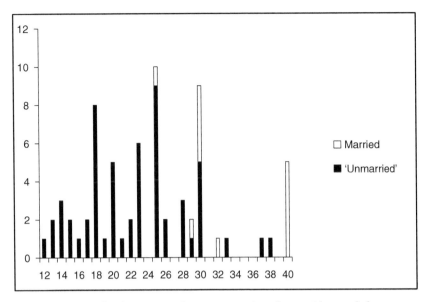

Figure 5.4 Spousal and non-spousal commemoration of men with recorded age at death (ages 12–40) in Hieradoumian epitaphs (n = 69).

the pattern is completely different. Our Hieradoumian epitaphic data provide not a single example of a man who is known to have married before the age of twenty-five.[41] The one man who can be seen to have been married by his mid-twenties seems to have been an only child, whose father was already dead: perhaps there was particular pressure on him to marry early.[42] In general, spouses and children start regularly to appear on tombstones for men only from the age of thirty upwards.[43] We should thus imagine a typical age gap between husband and wife in Roman Hieradoumia of around twelve to fifteen years.[44] This pattern fits well with evidence from the Latin-speaking western provinces (based on much larger data sets than

---

[41] Though recall the case of Aur. Dionysios at Hypaipa, who had his first child at the age of 22 (*I. Ephesos* 3804, I 20–21, II 1–3).

[42] *TAM* V 1, 743 (*SGO* I 04/10/05: Gordos).

[43] I have found very few examples of married men aged below 25 anywhere in Asia Minor. As we have seen, the Hypaipa tax declaration of Aur. Dionysios (*I.Ephesos* 3804, I 20–21, II 1–3) suggests that his first child was born when he was twenty-two years old. Marek 1993, 149, no. 44 (Pompeiopolis, AD 253) commemorates a man who lived fifty-four years, was married for thirty-two years, and left nine children (i.e. marital age of 22); cf. also *I.Kios* 54 (a married man who died at 21).

[44] For a substantially larger age gap, see e.g. Marek 1993, 207, no. 80 (*SEG* 43, 912: Kaisareia): a seventy-five-year-old man and his fifty-year-old wife (some age-rounding?).

that used here), where marriage in the late teens for women and in the late twenties for men seems to have been the norm.[45]

Elsewhere in the Asia Minor peninsula, women seem quite regularly to have married in their mid- to late-teens.[46] Women who must have married at the age of fifteen or sixteen are known from Apameia–Kelainai and Dionysopolis in southern Phrygia and at Dorylaion in northern Phrygia.[47] An inscription from Pontic Amaseia commemorates the death (apparently through the sudden collapse of her house) of a sixteen-year-old woman in the days immediately preceding her marriage.[48] At a remote village in the east Phrygian steppe, we have the tombstone of a married woman named Matrona, who died at the age of fifteen and a half while giving birth to a daughter.[49] In Paphlagonia, two epitaphs of the Antonine period commemorate married women who died at the ages of fourteen and fifteen respectively; the latter, a member of the upper crust of the local civic elite, was married to a man who seems to have been aged twenty-nine at the time of her death.[50] A third Paphlagonian epitaph, from Neoklaudiopolis, records the death of a twenty-year-old woman who had been married for five years.[51] A fourth Paphlagonian epitaph commemorates a fourteen-year-old who was apparently on the verge of marriage at the time of her death.[52] An even younger Paphlagonian wife appears in an extraordinary epitaph from Kaisareia, of uncertain date, recording the suicide of a girl (*korē*) named Domitilla who had been seized by Gothic raiders or pirates:

> Traveller, look on this tombstone that bears the evidence of great virtue. For the young girl (*korē*) Domitilla lies here in this tomb, she who gained the crown of prudence (*sōphrosynē*). For of all the girls (*kourai*) who were

---

[45] Shaw 1987 (women); Saller 1987 (men); Saller 1994, 25–41. A smaller age gap between husband and wife seems to have been typical in Roman Egypt: Bagnall and Frier 2006, 111–21.

[46] For wives who died in their late teens, cf. e.g. *I.Klaudiu Polis* 100 (died aged 18); *I.Kyzikos* 510 (*SGO* II 08/01/42: died in childbirth aged 18); *TAM* IV 1, 306 (Nikomedeia: died aged 19, having been married for fifteen months); *SEG* 42, 1137 (= *SEG* 39, 1731, Herakleia Pontike: died aged 19).

[47] Apameia: *MAMA* VI 205 (Dikici: an eighteen-year-old who had lived with her husband less than three years). Dionysopolis: *MAMA* IV 319 (Üçkuyu: a sixteen-year-old [?] who lived with her husband for five months). Dorylaion: *MAMA* V KB 3 (Eskişehir: a sixteen-year-old who died in childbirth, πρῶτα λοχευσαμέ[νη]).

[48] *SGO* II 11/08/04 (*SEG* 51, 1720: S. of Çorum).

[49] *MAMA* I 301 (*SGO* III 14/05/01: Atlantı).

[50] Fourteen-year-old: Marek 1993, 145, no. 31 (Pompeioupolis, AD 179). Fifteen-year-old: Marek 1993, 172, no. 55 (*SEG* 43, 907: Amastris, AD 184). For the high status of her husband's family (the Vibii of Amastris), see Marek 1993, 99.

[51] *SEG* 65, 1205.

[52] Marek 1993, 201, no. 53 (*SGO* II 10/02/09: Kaisareia).

carried off to be outraged by the men who came down from the sea by the anger of the gods and by fate, when they were all being violated at the hands of the barbarians, she alone did not hesitate to die instead of suffering hateful violence. Having given delight to her dear husband for a mere seven months, she departed her maiden's life (*parthenikon phōs*) at the age of fourteen.[53]

Domitilla must have married, at the latest, soon after her fourteenth birthday. Her epitaph describes her as still being a *parthenos* ('maiden'), here not necessarily an indication of her virginity, but perhaps simply the fact that she still belonged to the age class of 'young women'.[54] A still younger wife may be attested at Prusa in Bithynia, where a certain Soteris is said to have died at the age of twenty, having been married for seven years and given birth to three children.[55] The very youngest wife known to us from the Asia Minor peninsula is an unnamed woman from a remote Phrygian-speaking village on the territory of Amorion, who died in childbirth 'having seen her sixteenth year', after five years of marriage: she must therefore have married at the age of eleven or twelve.[56] This is the only certain case of pre-pubertal marriage in Roman Asia Minor; it is easy to see why her fatal (first?) pregnancy should have come only in her fourth or fifth year of marriage.

It is, finally, worth noting that girls in Roman Asia Minor could marry before they reached the formal 'age of majority' that existed in many cities of the peninsula.[57] A propitiatory *stēlē* from the Katakekaumene, dated to early summer AD 167, records how a woman named Sardion swore a false oath in the name of the goddess Tarsene. Since Sardion was 'not yet of age' (μήπω οὖσα ἐνῆλιξ), the goddess demanded only a minimal fine for Sardion's transgression (nine obols), which was paid by the woman's husband Eudoxos.[58] A Milesian epitaph from an earlier period (the second century

---

[53] *SEG* 34, 1271; Marek 1993, 197–8, no. 28 (*SGO* II 10/02/12); Matthews and Glatz 2009, 212–13. The identity of the 'men from the sea' is uncertain; the first editor (Kaygusuz 1984) thought that they were Goths and dated the text to AD 262 (cf. Goltz and Hartmann 2008, 276–7).

[54] Chaniotis 2016. This usage is to be distinguished from the common phrase γυνὴ παρθενική, which simply means 'woman who was a virgin at marriage': *BE* 1940, 83; Drew-Bear 1978, 101; *I.Ephesos* 3861; *I.Klaudiu Polis* 29, παρθενικῇ γυναικὶ ζησάσῃ ἔτη λη′.

[55] *SEG* 28, 1045 (*I.Prusa ad Olympum* 165). Soteris' recorded age at death (20) may have been rounded down to the nearest decade.

[56] *MAMA* VII 258 (*SGO* III 16/43/04: Aşağı Piribeyli); Thonemann 2013c, 135 n.42.

[57] For the 'age of majority', ἡ (ἔννομος) ἡλικία, for men and women, see e.g. *MAMA* VI 207 and 225 (Apameia–Kelainai); Ramsay, *Phrygia* II 391, no. 254 (Eumeneia); Thonemann 2013c, 125–6. Cf. Chankowski 2010, 69–71 (οἱ ἐν τῇ ἡλικίᾳ).

[58] *SEG* 37, 1000 (Petzl 1994, no. 58).

BC) goes so far as to describe a woman named Demetria as having been 'still a child (*pais*)' at the time of her first marriage.[59]

In summary, men in Hieradoumia tended to marry aged about 30, while women tended to marry twelve to fifteen years earlier, aged about 15–18. Although very many more epitaphs survive for unmarried males (222) than for unmarried females (69), there is no reason to think that unmarried females were significantly less likely to receive their own epitaph than unmarried males: this discrepancy can largely be explained through differential age at marriage. Overall, very many more tombstones were set up for men of all ages (413) than for women of all ages (264); aside from the very young, married women are the demographic group most likely to be significantly under-represented in our surviving epitaphic data.[60]

5.4 Marital Preferences

Aside from the 'normal' ten to fifteen-year age differential between spouses, the Hieradoumian evidence does not allow us to say much about marital preferences.[61] The family whose marital history is known to us in most detail is a close-knit kin group from the small town of Charakipolis, in the lower Kum Çayı valley in the far west of the region (Figure 5.5).[62] Shortly

---

[59] *I.Milet* (VI 2) 738 (*SGO* I 01/20/24). The woman's first husband was a certain Dionysios, 'who married me while I was still a *pais* (ἔτι παῖδα) and did not get to enjoy me in my bloom (ὥραν)' (although she did have his baby).

[60] Most likely these 'missing women' were interred alongside other relatives (e.g. their husband, if he had died first). *TAM* V 1, 218 is the tombstone of a certain Lucius, commemorated by his wife and two sons; twenty-nine years later, a couple of lines were added to the epitaph, to indicate that his wife had also been interred in the same tomb. Perhaps the practice was common, but not normally recorded on the epitaph.

[61] A propitiatory inscription from Sardis, dating to AD 160/1 (*Sardis* II 461; Petzl 1994, no. 101), was erected by a man who had made a vow to an unknown deity, which he promised to fulfil 'if he should get the wife whom I wish for' (ἐὰν λήψεται γυναῖκαν ἣν θέλω); he failed to fulfil the vow, and was punished accordingly.

[62] *TAM* V 1, 678–679; *SEG* 57, 1147–1149 (clearly all referring to the same family). In the stemma presented here (Figure 5.5), I have assumed that the Arkesilaos of *TAM* V 1, 678–679 (husband of a woman honoured, presumably late in life, in 10/9 BC) is identical to the Arkesilaos of *SEG* 57, 1148B (father of a girl born in 37/6 BC). The earliest known member of the family (probably born *c.* 110 BC) carries the surprising name Μηνόφιλος Τρεβώνιος. The name Trebonius is otherwise unattested in Hieradoumia (though note Μάνιος Τριβώνιος Διονύσιος in *SEG* 39, 1299, Uşak Museum), and no other member of the family carries a Roman name. One wonders whether Menophilos might have come to be nick-named Τρεβώνιος as a result of some relationship (in old age?) with C. Trebonius, proconsul of Asia in 44/43 BC (Broughton 1951–1986, II 330; *DPRR* TREB2336), or one of his ancestors.

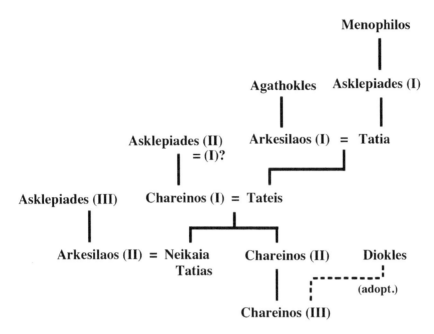

Figure 5.5 A family from Charakipolis.

before 20 BC, a woman in her mid-teens by the name of Tateis, daughter
of Arkesilaos (I), married a relative of hers, a certain Chareinos (I) son of
Asklepiades (II), perhaps her mother's brother. In 20/19 BC, Tateis, then
aged seventeen, gave birth to her first child, a girl called Neikaia; a son by
the name of Chareinos (II) was born five years later, in 15/14 BC, when
Tateis was twenty-two years old. On reaching adulthood, in her own mid-
to late teens, Neikaia married a man by the name of Arkesilaos (II) son of
Asklepiades (III) – clearly a close relative, perhaps Neikaia's cousin. The
marriage cannot have lasted more than a couple of years, since Neikaia
died in AD 1/2, at the age of twenty. Ten years later, in AD 11/12, her
mother Tateis was interred alongside her in the family tomb, having died
at the age of forty-seven.

   The younger Chareinos (II) seems to have married somewhat later
in life than his elder sister had done.[63] Not until he was twenty-nine
years old, in AD 15/16, did he see the birth of his first son, also named
Chareinos (III). Chareinos (II) died a mere six years later, at the age of

---

[63] Compare *TAM* V 1, 434 (*SGO* I 04/20/01: Nisyra, AD 194/5): the siblings Aristotelianos and
    Aristoteleia (perhaps twins) seem to have died around the same time; the sister is married, her
    brother unmarried.

thirty-five. The six-year-old Chareinos (III) was then adopted by another man, a certain Diokles.[64] Chareinos (III) died in AD 39/40, at the age of twenty-four, and was buried in the same tomb as his father, his aunt, and his grandfather and grandmother; there is no sign that he had married by the time of his death.

We have no way of knowing how characteristic this family history may have been. Nonetheless, two points of interest are worth drawing out. First, this family clearly followed the Hieradoumian 'norm' for optimal age at marriage: Tateis had her first child at the age of seventeen, and Neikaia was married by the time of her death at the age of twenty; Chareinos (II), by contrast, seems not to have had his first son until the age of twenty-nine. Second, and more suggestively, both Tateis and her daughter Neikaia clearly married close relatives. Tateis married a man whose father bore the same name (Asklepiades) as her maternal grandfather; Neikaia, whose paternal and maternal grandfathers were named Asklepiades and Arkesilaos respectively, married a man named Arkesilaos son of Asklepiades. Although we cannot say for certain what the precise relationships between Tateis and Neikaia and their husbands might have been, both women evidently married very close to home. It is tempting to suppose that Tateis might have married her mother's brother (MB/ZD); for Hieradoumian families practising close-kin marriage, the large age gap typically found between husband and wife may well have tended to favour marriages of this type, since a girl's mother's brother would often have tended to be around fifteen to twenty years older than her (a 'suitable' age differential).[65]

Close-kin marriage in Roman Hieradoumia can be inferred from onomastic evidence in a handful of further cases. In an epitaph from Kula dating to the late first century BC, we find a woman named Tatia, daughter of Hermogenes, married to a man called Hermogenes; the name Hermogenes is, however, very common in this region.[66] A more secure case comes from an epitaph of uncertain provenance (AD 110), in which a certain Ammin, daughter of Teimaios, was married to a man named Teimaios; the name Teimaios is relatively rare in Hieradoumia, rendering it likely that husband

---

[64] For other cases of adoption in Roman Hieradoumia, see Chapter 4, Section 4.12.

[65] MB/ZD marriage is not in fact widely attested elsewhere in Asia Minor: Thonemann 2017a (two Lykian instances). For a Rhodian instance, see Rice 1986, 217–20 (*Lindos* II 382). Several examples are known from Classical Athens: Humphreys 2018, I 107–34, e.g. 113 (the daughter of Apollodoros son of Pasion), 121 (Plato's mother), 127 (Lysias).

[66] Thonemann 2019, 122–3 no. 1 (15/14–7/6 BC). A still more uncertain case is found in *SEG* 53, 1344 (Petzl 2019, 17–18, no. 56): Glykon and his wife Myrtion, daughter of Glykon.

and wife were close kin.[67] An epitaph from Gordos (AD 189) was set up by
a certain Tatianos for his wife Polyneike; Tatianos' own mother also bore
the name Polyneike, and both Tatianos' brother and Polyneike's brother
(as well has her mother's brother) carried the name Menekrates, clearly
indicating that husband and wife were close relatives.[68]

It is very hard to say whether these cases of apparent close-kin marriage
are the visible tip of a large invisible iceberg of Hieradoumian marriages
between close kin. Numerous Hieradoumian epitaphs list relatives on both
the husband and wife's side of the family, and so it may in fact be significant that there are not *more* plausible cases of close-kin marriage; on the
other hand, the two close-kin marriages of Tateis and Neikaia of Charakipolis are only visible to us as a result of the (very unusual) circumstance that
we have several near-contemporary tombstones of several members of the
same family.

Second marriages were clearly quite standard in Hieradoumia, as
emerges from the relatively frequent appearance of stepparents and stepchildren among the commemorators of deceased persons: I have found
eight examples of women remarrying and five of men remarrying.[69] In most
cases, such marriages presumably resulted from the death of a spouse, but a
clear case of divorce is found in an epitaph from Charakipolis (AD 162)[70]:

```
     ἔτους ρϙβ′, μη(νὸς) Δαισίου
     τρίτῃ. Τατιας Ἀμμια-
     ν τὴν θυγατέρα ⟨ἀ⟩νέθηκε
     μνείας ἕνεκον, Ἀνθ-
  5  εστιανὸς τὴν γυν-
     αῖκα, Σώσανδρος τὴν π-
     ρόγονον, Ε⟨ὐ⟩καρπία τὴν σύ-
     ντροφον, Συλλᾶς τὴν ἰ-
     ανάτερα, Ἀπολλώνιος τὴ-
 10  ν θυγατέρα, καὶ οἱ συνγε-
     νεῖς ἐτείμησαν.
```

---

[67] *SEG* 39, 1303 (Uşak museum). The name Teimaios also in *TAM* V 1, 173 (Saittai) and *I.Mani-
     sa* 234 (inc.).

[68] *TAM* V 1, 733. The name Polyneike is otherwise attested five times in Hieradoumia: *TAM* V 1,
     711 and 713 (Gordos); *TAM* V 1, 168 and 191 (Saittai); *SEG* 40, 1100 (Tabala).

[69] Women remarrying: *TAM* V 1, 612 (Satala); *TAM* V 1, 682 (Charakipolis); *TAM* V 1, 786
     (Yayakırıldık); *TAM* V 3, 1700 (Yeşilova); *SEG* 34, 1222 (Saittai, misunderstood by ed. pr.);
     SEG 40, 1095 (Maionia); *SEG* 55, 1308 (inc.); *SEG* 56, 1259 (inc.). Men remarrying: *TAM* V 1,
     653 (Daldis); *TAM* V 1, 702 (Gordos); *TAM* V 1, 812 (Dağdere); *TAM* V 3, 1914 (Akrokastol-
     los); *SEG* 32, 1235 (inc.). Unclear: *SEG* 40, 1085 (inc.).

[70] *TAM* V 1, 682. The use of the verb ἀνατίθημι is deeply idiosyncratic.

Year 192, on the third day of the month Daisios. Tatias dedicated her daughter Ammia, for the sake of memory; Anthestianus (honoured) his wife, Sosandros his stepdaughter (*progonos*), Eukarpia her *syntrophos*, Sullas his brother's wife (*ianatēr*), Apollonios his daughter; and the (other) relatives honoured her.

Ammia's 'core' family group, listed at the beginning of the epitaph, consists of her mother, husband, and stepfather; her natural father is tucked away at the end, the last individual mentioned in the epitaph. Ammia had evidently been brought up by her mother and stepfather after her parents' divorce; her natural father was not, to all appearances, a very significant figure in her circle of relations.[71]

Almost nothing can be said about the social norms governing second marriages. In a tantalizing text from Maionia, we find a member of the civic elite, Tryphon son of Bithys, being commemorated by his wife Quinta, daughter of Achillas, and by 'the sons of Quinta', Bithys and Tryphon. The wording strongly suggests that the two boys Bithys and Tryphon were the sons of Quinta by a prior marriage. The onomastics show that Quinta must previously have been married to a close relative of her second husband; this may perhaps be a case of 'levirate marriage' whereby a man marries his brother's widow, a phenomenon attested elsewhere in Asia Minor.[72]

Relations between stepparents and stepchildren could be strikingly affectionate. A long and emotive verse epitaph of the fourth century AD from the village of Akrokastollos describes how a certain Damianos took as his second wife a young woman called Alexandra from the city of Kadoi, 80km to the north-east, who seems to have died fairly shortly after her marriage. Alexandra's verse epitaph – one of the longest and tenderest to survive from Hieradoumia – was composed and erected by her stepson, Damianos' son by his first marriage. The damaged final part of the inscription seems to describe the process by which the stepson went about calculating Alexandra's precise age at death (*x* years and four months). One wonders whether this young man might have been closer to his stepmother in both age and sentiment than his father was; such situations were certainly common enough in the Roman world.[73]

---

[71] Note the similar postponement of the father in the list of relatives honouring an unmarried man in *SEG* 56, 1269 (unknown provenance).

[72] *SEG* 40, 1095 (AD 211/212). For another likely case of a widow marrying her first husband's brother, see Debord and Varinlioğlu 2001, 118–19, no. 11 (Pisye, first century BC: a Rhodian family).

[73] *TAM* V 3, 1914 (*SGO* I 04/23/03). Young stepmothers and their stepsons: Watson 1995, 136–9 (the stereotype of the 'amorous stepmother'); Bradley 2000, 292–3.

5.5 Extended Families (1): Relations of Married Men and Women with Pre-marital and Affine Kin

As we have seen, almost half of all tombstones from Roman Hieradoumia (304 epitaphs, 44.9% of the total sample), were erected by members of the deceased's nuclear family plus one or more 'extended' kin (including foster-kin). When a nuclear family is 'extended' by the addition of one or more non-nuclear relatives as co-commemorators, in which direction or directions does this extension of the nuclear family group tend to occur? The answer ought to tell us something about typical family structures and significant sentimental or legal relationships in the Hieradoumian house-hold. If, for instance, we were to find that the epitaphs of unmarried boys and girls were regularly erected by the nuclear family plus paternal grand-parents, but seldom if ever included maternal grandparents, then that might indicate the existence in Hieradoumia of a 'stem' family structure, characterized by co-residence of the eldest son and his family with his par-ents after marriage.[74]

In this section, I shall try to draw out some characteristic patterns in the commemoration of married men and women (386 epitaphs in total, 191 for married men, 195 for married women). Table 5.2 is a summary tab-ulation of the kinship groups who commemorated these 386 individuals. Line I of the table gives the number of epitaphs in which a married man or woman is commemorated *only* by members of his or her nuclear family (spouse and/or children); the remaining four lines give the number of epi-taphs in which a married man or woman is commemorated *both* by his or her nuclear family *and* by one or more extended kin (parents and siblings, affines, grandchildren, foster-kin). Line II of the table gives the number of epitaphs in which a married man or woman is commemorated only by his/her nuclear family and by kin who are 'common' to both husband and wife (i.e. descendants and their spouses): grandchildren, foster-children, sons- and daughters-in-law, and so forth. Lines III and IV give the number of epitaphs in which a married man or woman is additionally commemo-rated by extended kin *only* on one or the other side of the family: either by

---

[74] In fact, this particular pattern is not prominent in the Hieradoumian evidence. We have a mere eight epitaphs for unmarried males and females erected by the nuclear family 'extended' by the addition of grandparents alone. Of these, two epitaphs include maternal grandparents (*TAM* V 1, 97 and 219), one epitaph includes the paternal grandfather (*TAM* V 1, 207), and in the remaining five cases it is unclear whether the grandparents are on the paternal or maternal side (*TAM* V 1, 747; *SEG* 35, 1246; *SEG* 39, 1302; *SEG* 49, 1659; *SEG* 56, 1293).

Table 5.2 Nuclear and extended 'familial' commemoration of married men and women in Roman Hieradoumia (n = 386)

	Married men	Married women
I: Commemorated by nuclear kin only	86	83
II: Commemorated by nuclear kin + common kin	38	28
III: Commemorated by nuclear/ common kin + pre-marital kin	53	52
IV: Commemorated by nuclear/ common kin + spouse's kin	6	14
V: Commemorated by nuclear/ common kin + pre-marital kin + spouse's kin	8	18
Total	191	195

the deceased's own natal/pre-marital family (parents, foster-parents, siblings, etc.: line III) or by his/her affines (spouse's parents, siblings etc.: line IV).[75] Line V of the table gives the number of epitaphs in which a married man or woman is commemorated *both* by his or her own natal/pre-marital extended kin (parents, siblings) *and* by his/her spouse's extended kin (parents-in-law, siblings-in-law).

Two points of interest immediately jump out from this data. First, tombstones for married women were just as likely to include members of their own pre-marital kin (parents, siblings, foster-parents and foster-siblings) among the list of commemorators as tombstones for married men were (Table 5.2, line III). As we will see in Section 5.6, there is good reason to think that patrilocal residence after marriage was common in Roman Hieradoumia – that is to say, that married women left their own household at marriage and joined their husband's father's household. Nonetheless, our epitaphic evidence clearly shows that married women retained close sentimental ties with their pre-marital kin, such that a woman's parents or siblings were still very likely to join in commemorating their daughter or sister even after her marriage.

Second, married women appear to have been significantly more likely than married men to be co-commemorated by their spouse's kin (Table 5.2, lines IV and V). We have thirty-two cases of women being co-commemorated

---

[75] I have included in the figures under row IV those very small numbers of persons – presumably childless widows and widowers – commemorated by the spouse's parents alone.

Table 5.3 'Primary commemorators' of married men and women in Roman
Hieradoumia, where the spouse is present (lines I–III) and absent (lines IV–VI)

	Married men	Married women
I: Spouse as p(rimary) c(ommemorator)	113	138
II: Sons, sons-in-law, *threptoi* as p.c. (spouse present)	28	4
III: Parents, brothers, *threpsantes* as p.c. (spouse present)	21	25
IV: Sons, daughters as p.c. (spouse absent)	28	23
V: Parents as p.c. (spouse absent)	0	2
VI: Parents-in-law as p.c. (spouse absent)	1	3
Total	191	195

by their husband's parents and siblings (16.4% of all tombstones for
married women), compared to a mere fourteen cases of men being co-
commemorated by their wife's parents and siblings (7.3% of all tombstones
for married men). In other words, although married women developed close
sentimental relationships with their husband's family, married men did not
tend to have such intimate relations with their wife's family.

Further evidence for the relationships between married men and women
and their extended families (both their own pre-marital kin and their
post-marital affines) comes from the sequence in which the deceased's relatives are listed on his or her tombstone. When a married man or woman
dies, which relative is listed first on his or her tombstone, as 'primary commemorator' of the deceased? The results are tabulated in Table 5.3.

In the overwhelming majority of cases, as we would expect, the primary
commemorators of married men are their wives (113 of 191), and the primary commemorators of married women are their husbands (138 of 195)
(Table 5.3, line I). Things get more interesting when we look at cases where
the spouse is *not* the primary commemorator of the deceased. In a total of 57
cases, the spouse is absent and can be presumed to have predeceased his/her
wife or husband (lines IV–VI). In the overwhelming majority of such cases
(51 of 57), as we would expect, the deceased's children take on responsibility
for the erection of the tombstone (line IV)[76]; in a handful of cases, the tombstone was set up by the deceased's parents or parents-in-law (lines V–VI).

In a total of 78 epitaphs, the spouse is listed among the relatives honouring the deceased, but is *not* the primary commemorator (lines II–III). In

---

[76] Usually a son or sons (forty-one epitaphs), in a few cases a daughter with her husband (six
epitaphs), in fewer cases still a daughter alone (four epitaphs).

28 cases, a man's son(s), son(s)-in-law, or male *threptoi* are listed first on his tombstone, ahead of his still living wife; by contrast, in only four cases are a woman's male descendants listed ahead of her still living husband (line II).[77] This presumably reflects a tendency for a tombstone to be erected by the household's most senior living adult male. If a deceased woman's husband is still living at the time of her death, he almost always takes primary responsibility for the erection of her tombstone (only four exceptions). But if a deceased's man's wife is still living at the time of his death, the man's tombstone can be erected *either* by his wife *or* by his (adult?) male son, son-in-law, or *threptos*.

Most interesting of all is the unexpectedly large number of epitaphs (46 in total) in which married men and married women are commemorated first by their own pre-marital kin – their parents, siblings, or foster-parents (*threpsantes*) – and only secondarily by their spouse (line III: 21 tombstones for married men and 25 for married women). In the great majority of such cases (33), the primary commemorators are the deceased's parents (14 tombstones for married men and 19 for women). In rather fewer instances, the foster-parents act as primary commemorators (three tombstones for men and five for women), and in a handful of cases tombstones are set up by the deceased's brother or brothers (four tombstones for men and one for a woman).[78]

It ought not to surprise us that a married man's tombstone should, on occasion, have been the primary responsibility of his parents or brothers rather than of his wife. As we have seen, there was a general tendency in Roman Hieradoumia for tombstones to be erected by the household's most senior living adult male. If it was indeed the case (as I shall suggest in Section 5.6) that many married couples in Hieradoumia were co-resident with the husband's parents and/or male siblings, then it is easy to see why a married man's close male relatives (father and brothers) should occasionally have been placed in a more prominent position on a 'familial' epitaph than the deceased's wife (who may have been just one of several junior females in her father-in-law's household).

[77] Usually a son or sons (25 epitaphs), occasionally one or more *threptos* (five epitaphs), very occasionally a daughter with her husband (two epitaphs), never a daughter alone.
[78] The sole example of an epitaph for a married woman where her siblings act as 'primary commemorators' is Sargın 2020, no. 2 (Yayakırıldık): brothers, mother, *threpsantes*, husband. I assume that the deceased woman was young and recently married, and her father was already dead. *TAM* V 1, 133 looks at first sight like a case in which a married woman was commemorated first by her sister, but her parents were probably mentioned in the lost first lines of the epitaph.

It is more surprising that so many married women (twenty-five in total) were commemorated with tombstones that foregrounded their relationship to their parents or foster-parents rather than to their husbands. Even if a woman generally left her parental household on marriage (as I assume she did), she clearly maintained sufficiently close sentimental relationships with her parents, foster-parents, and siblings that it was quite normal for her pre-marital kin to take primary responsibility for commemorating her after her death. Indeed, in a few cases, the husband seems to be a relatively marginal figure in the commemoration of his wife. So in a tombstone from the territory of Gordos, a certain Amachiane is commemorated (in this order) by her parents, her husband, her two grandmothers, her mother's brother, her sister, and six further named uncles and aunts.[79] Similarly, a woman by the name of Athenais was commemorated by her parents, her sister and brother, her daughter, her foster-father, her three foster-sisters, and – almost as an after-thought – her husband.[80] Occasionally, married women could even be buried in the same tomb (and commemorated with the same epitaph) as their married or unmarried brothers or sisters. At Nisyra, in AD 194/5, a brother and sister (perhaps twins?) were buried together by their parents, despite the fact that the sister was already married with a son; her husband and son appear only as 'secondary' commemorators.[81] In another three cases, we find a married woman being buried alongside her unmarried sister, with both their natal family and the married woman's husband and/or children sharing in the commemoration of the two sisters.[82] Evidently, even after marrying and bearing children of their own, women could be commemorated as if they remained an integral part of their parental household, even to the extent of being buried along with their unmarried siblings.[83]

---

[79] *TAM* V 1, 769. Amachiane appears to have died childless, and may well have been recently married.
[80] *SEG* 40, 1089. For other cases where the husband is tacked on at the end of a list of commemorators, cf. *TAM* V 1, 778 (parents, aunt, husband); *SEG* 29, 1187 (foster-mother, three sons, foster-sister, foster-sister's husband, husband); Sargın 2020, no. 2 (brothers, mother, *threpsantes*, husband).
[81] *TAM* V 1, 434: Aristotelianos and Aristoteleia, 'two sibling-loving souls' (δύω [ψ]υχαὶ φιλάδελφοι), commemorated by their parents, Aristoteleia's husband and son, and other unnamed relatives.
[82] *SEG* 32, 1235 (two sisters commemorated by their parents and grandmother, along with the husband, son and *syntrophos* of one sister); *SEG* 40, 1101 (two sisters commemorated by their mother and five brothers, along with the two sons of one sister: was her husband already dead?); *SEG* 57, 1248 (two sisters commemorated by the husband and sons of one sister, and by the parents and two brothers of both).
[83] Elsewhere in Roman Asia Minor, we occasionally find two married sisters buried together: e.g. *SEG* 39, 1355; *SEG* 41, 1117 (both from Pontic Sebastopolis); perhaps *SEG* 55, 1288 (Hypaipa).

Table 5.4 Co-commemoration of married women by the husband's kin in Roman Hieradoumia (n = 32)

Husband's parent(s)	12
Husband's parent(s) and brother(s)	4
Husband's parents, brother, and sister(?)	1
Husband's brother(s)	6
Husband's brother(s) and their wives	3
Husband's brother(s) and their wives and children	3
Husband's father/mother and sister	2
Husband's father or brother (uncertain)	1
Total	32

None of this should be taken to mean that Hieradoumian women typically remained in their parents' household after marriage, or that a woman's parents or brothers retained any legal authority over their daughter or sister after her marriage. But the epitaphic evidence from Hieradoumia does provide very strong support for the notion that married women retained intimate sentimental links with their own pre-marital kin.

Finally, as we have already seen, married women were much more likely than married men to be co-commemorated by their spouse's kin, whether or not their own pre-marital kin also appear as co-commemorators (Table 5.2, lines IV and V). So the husband's parents and siblings appear in 32 epitaphs for married women (16.4% of all tombstones for married women), while the wife's parents and siblings appear in a mere 14 epitaphs for married men (7.3% of all tombstones for married men). The 32 epitaphs for married women in which their husbands' kin appear can be broken down further as in Table 5.4.[84]

What is striking about this data is the near-total *absence* of the husband's sister from the commemoration of married women. The husband's brother(s) appear seventeen or eighteen times as co-commemorators of married women, six times accompanied by their wives and children; the husband's sister, by contrast, appears only twice, perhaps three times in total.

[84] Husband's parents only: *TAM* V 1, 39; 631; 773; 779; 795; 798; 825; *SEG* 36, 1105; 49, 1607; 56, 1336; 57, 1205; *Sammlung Tatış* 47. Husband's parents and husband's brothers: *TAM* V 1, 168d; 175; 733; *SEG* 34, 1221. Husband's parents, husband's brother and (?) sister: *SEG* 56, 1286 (unless Glykea is Menandros' wife). Husband's brothers only: *TAM* V 1, 107; 379; 682; 810; *SEG* 32, 1223; *Sammlung Tatış* 46. Husband's brothers and their wives: *TAM* V 1, 775; *SEG* 49, 1616; *I.Manisa* 522. Husband's brothers and their wives and children: *TAM* V 1, 782; *SEG* 49, 1657 and 1660. Husband's father/mother and sister: *TAM* V 1, 703 (incomplete); *SEG* 31, 1004. Husband's father or brother: *SEG* 56, 1270.

How should we account for this curious under-representation of the husband's sisters among affine commemorators of married women? It cannot be simply a matter of a general absence of women among affine commemorators, since the husband's mother and the husband's brother's wife appear on numerous occasions (sixteen and six or seven times respectively). In fact, it seems to me, this particular pattern of commemoration can most neatly be explained on the assumption that residence after marriage was normally patrilocal. A married woman would then regularly find herself co-resident with her husband's father, her husband's brother (δαήρ), and her husband's brother's wife (σύννυμφος); she would relatively seldom find herself co-resident with her husband's sister (γάλως).

Further evidence in support of this hypothesis will be found in Section 5.6; for the time being, let me illustrate the kind of extended household structure that would have resulted with a single concrete example. In early spring AD 167, a young married woman by the name of Sophrone died at the age of 26. Her tombstone (quoted and illustrated in Chapter 2, Section 2.1, Figure 2.1) was erected by her parents Herakleides and Fl. Sophrone, along with her husband Eudoxos, her husband's parents Demophilos I and Nysa, her young son Herakleides (named after his maternal grandfather), and her husband's brother Demophilos II.[85] In my view, the shape of this commemorating group reflects a social structure in which Sophrone would have moved into the household of her husband's parents at marriage – and was hence co-resident with her husband's brother, Demophilos II – but nonetheless retained close sentimental links with her own parents, who took on responsibility for erecting her tombstone. Five years later, in early autumn AD 172, Demophilos I died at the age of 67. His own tombstone was erected by his wife Nysa; by his two sons, Eudoxos and Demophilos II (both of whom were, in my view, still resident in their father's household); by his daughter-in-law Elpis (probably the wife of Demophilos II, but conceivably the second wife of Eudoxos – the tombstone does not tell us); by 'Herakleides, the son of Eudoxos', his only living grandson; and by three *thremmata* (two female, one male).[86] The actual patterns of residence of these various individuals cannot strictly be demonstrated. In theory, Eudoxos and Sophrone could have lived in the house of Sophrone's parents or could have set up their own *ménage* elsewhere. But the scenario proposed here seems to me to make far better sense of the particular pattern of funerary commemoration chosen by this extended family; and, of course, it

---

[85] *TAM* V 1, 175 (Saittai).   [86] *TAM* V 1, 176 (Saittai).

makes a perfect fit with the *wider* patterns of selective commemoration by the husband's kin discussed in the preceding paragraphs.

5.6 Extended Families (2): The Father's Brother and Patrilocal Marriage

We now turn to the commemoration of unmarried males and females. Unmarried males and females seem to have been more likely than married men and women to be commemorated by members of their nuclear family (parents and siblings) alone. 55.0% of epitaphs for unmarried males and females (160 of 291) were erected only by nuclear kin, compared with 43.8% of epitaphs for married men and women (169 of 386).

We find the nuclear families of unmarried males and females 'extended' in a wide variety of ways, through the addition of one or more set of grandparents, foster-parents or foster-siblings, uncles and aunts, and various more distant relatives. Saller and Shaw's comment that 'grandparents, uncles and other extended family members appear too infrequently as commemorators [in Latin epitaphs of the western empire] for us to believe that they were regarded as part of the core family unit' is emphatically not true of the funerary epigraphy of Hieradoumia.[87] In this section, I wish to highlight one particularly striking pattern which appears in 'extended' Hieradoumian familial epitaphs for unmarried males and females: the relative prominence of the father's brother.

In seven epitaphs, unmarried males are commemorated by their nuclear family (parents and siblings) 'extended' by the addition of the father's brother alone.[88] In one of these seven epitaphs, the father's brother is listed first, as the primary commemorator of the deceased, before the deceased's parents.[89] In another five epitaphs, unmarried males are commemorated

---

[87] Saller and Shaw 1984, 124.

[88] (**1**) *TAM* V 1, 152 (parents, two sisters, father's brother); (**2**) *TAM* V 1, 295, for a twenty-three-year-old (parents, brother, father's brother); (**3**) *TAM* V 1, 473a (parents, father's brother, brother); (**4**) *TAM* V 1, 623 (parents, four siblings, father's brother, five unspecified kin); (**5**) *TAM* V 1, 797 (*SGO* I 04/07/03), in verse, for an eleven-year-old (parents, father's brother: the boy is said to have been named after his father's brother); (**6**) *SEG* 39, 1309 (father's brother, parents); (**7**) *SEG* 57, 1153 (father, sister, father's brothers, *syntrophoi*). Cf. also *Sardis* VII 1, 139 (father, father's brother).

[89] *SEG* 39, 1309 (unknown provenance, AD 111/2). It may be significant that the father's brother seems to have been the only member of the family to have held Roman citizenship. Other cases where uncles act as primary commemorators: *SEG* 29, 1190 (*SGO* I 04/12/06), for a

by their nuclear family, their paternal grandparents, and their father's brother(s) – that is to say, by their nuclear family extended one generation 'upwards' on the father's side, including the father's male sibling(s).[90] We once find an unmarried male commemorated by his nuclear family (parents and siblings), three paternal uncles and a group of five cousins (presumably the children of his father's brothers),[91] and in a further six epitaphs (four for unmarried males and two for married men), the father's brother is the only uncle or aunt named among a longer list of extended kin.[92] We also find three examples of unmarried adult males being commemorated by their brother's sons.[93] In total, then, we have some twenty-two epitaphs in which the nuclear family group is 'extended' in such a way as to highlight the relationship between the father's brother(s) and his/their nephew(s).[94]

By contrast, there are only six Hieradoumian epitaphs which highlight the relationship between the mother's brother and his sister's sons.[95] In two

---

five-year-old boy (θεῖοι καὶ τοκεῶνες); *TAM* V 1, 189, for an eleven-month-old boy (mother's brother, father, and mother).

[90] (**1**) *TAM* V 1, 210 (mother, paternal grandparents, three father's brothers and two wives, a friend); (**2**) *TAM* V 1, 293 (parents, two *syntrophoi*, paternal grandparents, two father's brothers); (**3**) *SEG* 35, 1160, for a thirteen-year-old (parents, father's brother, and paternal grandfather); (**4**) *SEG* 41, 1073 (paternal grandparents, parents, and two father's brothers); (**5**) *SEG* 57, 1175 (parents, paternal grandfather, two father's brothers and their wives).

[91] *SEG* 65, 1196.

[92] (**1**) *TAM* V 1, 680 (brother-in-law and sister [the deceased's adoptive parents], father, four brothers, two brothers' wives, father's brother); (**2**) *TAM* V 1, 743, for a twenty-five-year-old (mother, wife, daughter [?], father's brother, two unspecified close kin, and wife's father); (**3**) *SEG* 32, 1230 (parents, *threpsasa*, sister and her husband, and father's brother); (**4**) *SEG* 32, 1231 (*threpsas*, brother, and father, father's brother); (**5**) *SEG* 35, 1167 (parents, *threpsasa*, *syntrophos*' son, brother, wife, four children, sister and brother, and father's brother); (**6**) *SEG* 56, 1259 (parents, wife, son, *threptos*, brother and sister, two father's brothers, cousin, sister's husband, sister's two sons, and two adoptive sons).

[93] *TAM* V 1, 297 (*threpsasa*, two brother's sons, and a *stratiōtēs*); *TAM* V 1, 630 (three brother's sons); *Sammlung Tatış* 38 (brother's son alone; the deceased uncle was a sacred official, probably unmarried). Note also *TAM* V 1, 681 (the brother's son added to a list of direct descendants and *threptoi*), and *I.Manisa* 377 (Ammianos commemorated by his brother and his brother's children).

[94] Note also four further cases in which the father's siblings (but not the mother's siblings) are included among those commemorating young males: *TAM* V 1, 434, for a brother and sister (οἱ πάτρως καὶ ἓ πάτραι); *TAM* V 2, 840A, for a twenty-three-year-old (parents, sister, father's sister, and father's brother); *SEG* 33, 1016 (paternal grandparents, parents, father's two brothers, father's sister, two *syntrophoi*, and maternal grandparents); *I.Manisa* 525, for a nine-year-old (parents, grandfather, father's sister and her two children).

[95] (**1**) *TAM* V 1, 189, for an eleven-month-old (mother's brother, father, and mother); (**2**) *TAM* V 1, 383, for a male described as *neos* (parents, mother's brother, and sister); (**3**) *TAM* V 1, 288, a man commemorated by his sister's sons 'for the sake of his devotion (*euphilia*) towards them'; (**4**) *SEG* 29, 1179 (mother, two brothers, and mother's brother); (**5**) *SEG* 48, 1433 (=51, 1685),

of these six cases, the father appears to be already dead, suggesting that the mother's brother may have tended to play a more prominent role in the life of young men who had lost their father. Perhaps in such cases the mother's brother took over responsibility for his sister's children: we have an instance of an uncle acting as his nephew's *epitropos* ('guardian'), although it is unclear whether he was the father's brother or the mother's brother.[96] Naturally, there are also cases in which both the father's and mother's siblings appear as part of a longer list of commemorators of young men: in such cases, the father's siblings are usually listed first.[97]

This differentiated pattern of avuncular commemoration is less clear for young women. As we have seen, many fewer epitaphs were erected for unmarried females (69) than for unmarried males (222): uncles and aunts appear among the commemorators of deceased females in thirteen cases, compared to some thirty-one appearances of uncles and aunts in epitaphs for males (a broadly similar ratio overall). In six of these thirteen cases, young married or unmarried females are commemorated by familial groups including aunts or uncles on the paternal side only; in another five cases, the mother's brother is the only uncle or aunt singled out in the list of family members. There is hence no good evidence that the father's siblings played a more prominent role than the mother's siblings did in the lives of young women.[98]

---

for a fifteen-year-old (mother, *threpsas*, mother's brother, *syntrophos*, and grandmother); (**6**) *Sammlung Tatış* 36, for a three-year-old (mother's brother takes primary responsibility for erecting tombstone). Text (**6**) is the only indication in the Hieradoumian evidence for the kind of intimate relations with the maternal uncle postulated by Bremmer 1983 (cf. Bremmer 2000) for the early Greek world.

[96] *SEG* 40, 1099.

[97] E.g. *TAM* V 1, 477 (father's brother and sister, mother's brother); *TAM* V 1, 706 (father's brother, mother's brother, and father's sister); *TAM* V 1, 714 (father's brothers, mother's sister, and father's sister); *SEG* 40, 1085, for a five-year-old (mother's sister [?], father's brothers); *SEG* 57, 1244, for a fifteen-year-old (father's brothers, mother's brothers). In *SEG* 31, 990, a man is commemorated by his brother's daughter and son, his sister's son, and his *threptē*.

[98] The father's siblings: (**1**) *TAM* V 1, 778, for a married woman (parents, father's sister, husband); (**2**) *SEG* 35, 1271 (parents, father's brother, and grandmother); (**3**) *SEG* 53, 1341, for a four-year-old girl (parents, siblings, father's brother, father's sister and children); (**4**) *SEG* 56, 1333 (father's sisters); (**5**) *SEG* 57, 1178 (parents, father's brother, and two sisters); (**6**) *TAM* V 1, p.200 T6 (parents and father's brother); cf. also *Sardis* II 663, for a three-year-old girl (parents, father's brother; the latter absent from the epitaph *Sardis* II 662, erected by the same parents for two other children). The mother's siblings: (**1**) *TAM* V 1, 550 (parents, brother, two mother's brothers, and two grandmothers); (**2**) *TAM* V 1, 730, for a five-year-old girl (parents, brothers, mother's brother and his wife); (**3**) *TAM* V 1, 733, for a married woman (the mother's brother included in a long list of commemorators); (**4**) *SEG* 35, 1257 (parents, sister, grandparents, mother's brother, and *syntrophos*); (**5**) *Sammlung Tatış* 47 (parents, *syntrophos*, husband, husband's mother, cousin, and mother's brother). Both father's and mother's siblings appear in *TAM* V 1, 769 (for a married woman) and in *SEG* 56, 1262 (for an unmarried woman).

How should we account for the relative over-representation of the father's brother in the 'extended-familial' commemoration of young men? Let us assume, for the sake of argument, that the prominence of the father's brother in Hieradoumian epitaphs, and the relative unimportance of either the father's sister or the mother's siblings, reflects real household composition – that is to say, that children were often co-resident with their father's male siblings, but relatively seldom lived under the same roof as their father's female siblings or their mother's siblings.[99] Households of this type will tend to be especially common in societies which favour patrilocal residence after marriage. In such societies, when a son marries, he remains in his father's household, along with his other married or unmarried brothers ('patriarchal family households'); when his father dies, he may then remain co-resident with his other married brothers and unmarried siblings ('*frérèche* households'). By contrast, when a daughter marries, she typically moves away from her parental home to her father-in-law's household. In a society of this type, one would naturally expect children to develop closer relations with their father's brother than with any of their parents' other siblings. Can we conclude, then, that patrilocal residence after marriage was indeed the norm in Roman Hieradoumia (as already suggested, for different reasons, in Section 5.5)?

Several further items of evidence do indeed point strongly in this direction. First, kinship terminology. As we saw in Chapter 4, the inhabitants of Hieradoumia had a very rich and precise vocabulary for describing the relationships between a married woman and her husband's family, with distinct terms for the husband's parents (*hekyroi*), the husband's brother and sister (*daēr* and *galōs*), and the husband's brother's wife (*synnymphos*, occasionally *ianatēr*). From the perspective of the husband's family, the woman who had 'married in' to the family could be described either with a precise relational term – son's wife (*nyos*) or brother's wife (*ianatēr*) – or with a classificatory term, 'young woman who has entered my household by marriage' (*nymphē*). By contrast, the vocabulary for describing the relationships between a married man and his wife's family was distinctly less precise: although there were distinct terms for the wife's parents and siblings (all cognates: *pentheroi*, *pentheridēs*, *pentheridissa*), the man who had married into a woman's family was denoted only with a single, very generic classificatory term, 'young man who has entered my household by marriage' (*gambros*). This terminological lop-sidedness suggests that there

---

[99] On the problem of co-residency, see Section 5.2.

was a need to define the relationships between a married woman and her husband's family considerably more closely than the relationships between a married man and his wife's family – that is to say, presumably, that a married woman typically became part of her husband's household, not *vice versa*. We might also note the significance of the curious (and distinctively Hieradoumian) usage of the term ἔγγονος both for a grandson and for the brother's son (Chapter 4, Section 4.5). This usage evidently makes perfect sense within a social context of *frérèche* households, since from the perspective of an elder male within a patriarchal family household, children in the household will necessarily fall into three categories: his own children, his grandchildren, and his brother's children. The term ἔγγονος can thus comfortably be seen as a classificatory term for the two latter categories ('descendant within my household who is not my own child').

Further supporting evidence comes from directly attested cases of co-residency of married men with their parents and (male) siblings. It is usually impossible to tell whether any given relatives listed on a tombstone physically resided in the same house as the deceased. A rare exception to this is an epitaph from Gordos, probably of the second century AD, commemorating a man by the name of Phaeinos, around twenty-five years old at the time of his death[100]:

> The *daimōn* snatched me from the house (*melathra*) of my father and mother before my time – I who was the *oikonomos* of the whole *polis* and of the greatest *boulē*. His homeland honoured Phaeinos (5), a most excellent man; his mother Basilia (honoured) her beloved child; his wife Hermione (honoured) her beloved husband, in memory, as did my dear Hermione. Young Phaeinos (10), your father's brother Stratoneikos honoured you, as did Kalligeneia and Praxiteles, my closest relatives; and Onesimos, for his *gambros*, in memory. The dead man lived for around twenty-five (15) years. Whoever violates my tomb, apart from my mother and wife, will pay 2,500 *denarii* to the imperial fisc. This is the end of living, the end-point of life. (20) Farewell.

---

[100] *TAM* V 1, 743 (*SGO* I 04/10/05): [δ]αίμων ἥρπασεν ἐκ μελάθρω[ν] | με πατρὸς καὶ μητρὸς ἄωρον. ο[ἰ]κονόμον πάσης πόλεως βουλῆ[ς] | ⟨τ⟩ε μεγίστης Φάϊνον τείμησε πα|(5)τρὶς τὸν ⟨ἄριστον⟩ ἐόντα, καὶ μήτηρ Βασιλί|α τὸ καταθύμιον τέκνον καὶ Ἑρμιόνη ἡ σύνβιος τὸν ἑαυτῆς ἄνδρ[α] | τὸν καταθύμιον μνείας χάριν καὶ Ἑρμιόνη μου ποθητή· Φάεινόν σε νέον |(10) τείμησε πάτρως Στρατόνεικος, | Καλλιγένεια καὶ Πραξιτέλης ἄν|χιστα γένους μου, καὶ Ὀνήσιμος | τῷ ἑαυτοῦ γανβρῷ μνίας χάριν. τῶν | ἐτέων πλήρωσε νέκυς ὡς εἴκοσι |(15) πέντε. ὃς ἂν τύνβον ἐμὸν συλήσει | χωρὶς μητρὸς καὶ γυνεκός, θήσι ἰς τὸ | ἱερώτατον ταμεῖον (δηνάρια),βφ΄. τοῦτ᾽ ἐσ|τὶν τὸ τέλος βιὀ τοῦ ζωῆ⟨ς⟩ τε | τελευτή. |(20) χαῖρε. The epitaph (partially in verse) switches awkwardly back and forth between the first-, second-, and third-person singular; for prose epitaphs with verse elements at Gordos, compare *TAM* V 1, 730, with Robert, *Hellenica* VI, 94.

In this epitaph, Phaeinos is commemorated by his mother Basilia, his wife Hermione, his young daughter (?) Hermione, his father's brother Stratoneikos, two 'close relatives' (Kalligeneia and Praxiteles), and a man named Onesimos (probably his wife's father). Phaeinos' father is clearly already dead, and there is no clear indication that Phaeinos has any living siblings, which may help to account for his unusually early marriage (see Sections 5.3–5.4: most men in Hieradoumia did not marry until around the age of thirty). The main point of interest here is the first clause of the epitaph, stating that death snatched Phaeinos 'from the house of my father and mother'. Assuming we can take this literally, the clause would seem to imply that Phaeinos was still living in his parental home, along with his widowed mother and his young wife and daughter (and perhaps with his father's brother, Stratoneikos). A household of a very similar kind is attested in the Hypaipa census register (Section 5.1, declaration I), where the head of the household (a young man, whether married or not is unclear) lives with his widowed forty-eight-year-old mother and his eleven-year-old sister. When a male patriarch died, it was clearly normal for his son to take over his household and to take on responsibility for caring for his widow.[101]

Finally, patrilocal residence after marriage, and consequent co-residence of children with their father's brother, can – with all due caution – be inferred from the manner in which the extended family group is presented in a handful of Hieradoumian epitaphs. A particularly clear example comes from two Hieradoumian tombstones which present the same extended family from different generational perspectives. In spring AD 296, three siblings joined together in burying their parents, Aurelius Diogenes and Aurelia Secunda. Their tombstone reads as follows[102]:

> Year 380 [AD 295/6], Day 8 of the month Xandikos. Aur. Diogenes and Aur. Secunda, the discoverers (5) of wisdom, who had splendid children, and were joined together in marriage by the will of the son of Kronos, were honoured by their children, Aur. Agathopous (10) and Aur. Iuliana, and by Aur. Trophime their daughter-in-law (*nymphē*), and by those who had already passed under the murky darkness, Aur. Diogenes, the blessed

---

[101] For similar households in Roman Egypt, see Huebner 2013, 111–18.

[102] *SEG* 52, 1165 (uncertain provenance): ἔτους τπʹ, | μη(νὸς) Ξανδικοῦ ηʹ. | Αὐρ. Διογένην κὲ Αὐρ. | Σικόνδαν τοὺς εὑ(5)ρετὰς τῆς σοφίας, | [τ]οὺς καλλιτέκνους, | [τ]οὺς ζευχθέντας ἐκ | βουλῆς Κρονίωνος ἐτίμησαν οἱ υἱοὶ Αὐρ. Ἀγ⟨α⟩θό|(10)πους κὲ Αὐρ. Ἰουλιανὴ κὲ Αὐρ. | Τροφίμη ἡ νύνφη κὲ οἱ προ|άξαντες ὑπὸ ζόφον εἰ⟩λερόεντα, Αὐρ. Διογένης | ὁ μακαρίτης κὲ Αὐρ. Καλαν|(15)δίων ὁ πᾶσι φίλος κὲ τὰ ἔγ|γονα κὲ οἱ συνγενεῖς κὲ Αὐρ. | Διογενειανός, ὃς χάριν | γονέων ἐώνεια φίλτρα ἐφύ|λαξιν· θαυμάζι δὲ πάτρη |(20) τὸν ἐπάξιον υἱὸν γονέων. | εἴ τις τούτοις παρααμαρ|[τ]ήσι, τῇ στήλῃ ἢ τῷ ἡρῴῳ, | ἕξξι τὸν Ἀξιττηνὸν | κεχολωμένον. For the family, Lajtar and Petzl 2003.

one, and Aur. Kalandion (15), who was dear to all, and by their grandchildren and their relatives, and by Aur. Diogenianos, who preserved eternal affection for the sake of his parents; his homeland marvels at him (20), a son worthy of his parents. If anyone violates this *stēlē* or this tomb, he shall meet with the wrath of (Meis) Axiottenos.

By the standards of Hieradoumian funerary inscriptions, this epitaph is unusually prolix. Diogenes and Secunda are characterized with three non-formulaic phrases: they were 'discoverers of wisdom' (whatever that means), were the parents of splendid children (five in total, three still living at this point), and were married by Zeus' will (whatever *that* means).[103] Two of their five children, Diogenes and Kalandion, were already dead by the time of their parents' burial, but are nonetheless anachronistically included in the register of family members honouring the deceased. The younger Diogenes and Kalandion are each described with a short affectionate phrase, 'the blessed one', 'he who was dear to all', reminding the reader of the sentimental relationships that bound this family together.[104] It is easy to see which family member was responsible for drafting this epitaph: one of the three surviving children, Diogenianos, holds a prominent place at the end of the list of relatives, where he is described as the 'marvel of his homeland' and a 'son worthy of his parents'.

Four years later, Diogenianos' own daughter died, and was commemorated with another lengthy tombstone (Figure 5.6), erected by what is to all intents and purposes the same extended family group. Diogenianos still cannot resist boasting to the reader about his own achievements (this time, his travels to Rome and Syria)[105]:

Year 384 [AD 299/300], Day 18 of the month Daisios. Aur. Diogenianos, son of Diogenes and of Aur. Secunda, who travelled to Rome and Syria, and Aur. Trophime, daughter of Glykon, constructed this tomb while still

---

[103] For the epithet καλλίτεκνος, cf. *SGO* III 16/31/10 B (Upper Tembris valley: καλλιτέκνῳ... ἣ ἔ{τε}τεκε καλὰ τέκνα); *MAMA* VII 57 (Kındıras); *I.Iznik* 1352 (*SGO* II 09/05/41).

[104] For μακαρίτης (usually Christian), cf. *MAMA* VIII 252b (*SEG* 31, 1319: Savatra); *MAMA* IX 75 (Aizanoi); for πᾶσι φίλος, e.g. *KILyk* 373, 409, 415 (Dorla [Aydoğmuş]); *MAMA* XI 303 (Konya); *I.Anazarbos* 122; *SEG* 51, 1710–1711 (Nikaia); Marek 1993, 145, no. 30 (*SGO* II 10/05/03: Pompeiopolis). For the addition of descriptive epithets of this kind, cf. e.g. *SEG* 29, 1202 (*SGO* I 04/12/07: Saittai).

[105] *SEG* 53, 1341 (uncertain provenance): ἔτους τπδ΄, | μη(νὸς) Δαισίου ηι΄. | Αὐρ. Διογενιανός, Διογένους | κὲ Αὐρ. Σικόνδας |(5) υειός, ἐκδημήσας | Ῥώμην καὶ Συρί|ας, καὶ Αὐρ. Τρο|φίμη Γλύκωνος | ζῶντες τῇ θυγατρὶ |(10) κὲ αὐτοῖς τὸ ἡρῷον | κατεσκεύασαν. ἐτείμη|σαν καὶ οἱ ἀδελφοὶ τὴν Γλυκωνίδα, Αὐρ. Ἰουλιανὴ καὶ Αὐρ. Τατιανός, καὶ ὁ πάτρων Ἀγαθόπους |(15) κὲ ἡ πάτρα Ἰουλιανὴ κὲ ὁ ἀδελφί|δης Δειογένης κὲ ἡ ἀδελφίδισ|σα ἡ Εὐγνωμονὶς κὲ οἱ λοιποὶ | συγγενεῖς μνήμης χάριν, | ζή(σασαν) ἔτ(η) δ΄. εἴ {ε} τις δὲ παραμαρ|(20)τήσι τῇ στήλῃ ἢ τῷ ἡρῴῳ, ἕξ|ξει τὴν Οὐρανείαν Ἑκάτην | κεχολωμένην. ταῦτα. χέρετέ | μοι, παροδεῖται.

Figure 5.6 Epitaph of Glykonis, unknown provenance. *SEG* 53, 1341 (National Museum in Warsaw, inv. 198813).

living for their daughter and for themselves. Glykonis was also honoured by her siblings, Aur. Iuliana and Aur. Tatianos, and by her father's brother (*patrōn*) Agathopous and by her father's sister (*patra*) Iuliana and by her cousin (*adelphidēs*) Diogenes and by her cousin (*adelphidissa*) Eugnomonis and by her other relatives, in memory; she lived for four years. If anyone violates this *stēlē* or this tomb, he shall meet with the wrath of Heavenly Hekate. Such is life. Hail, passers-by.

In this second text, the young Glykonis is commemorated by her parents, her two siblings, and by her father's brother and sister (and apparently by her father's brother's two children). If this reflects real household composition, then we would be dealing with a laterally extended household of the so-called *frérèche* type, with two male siblings and their families living together (in this case along with a female sibling, probably unmarried). In fact, as the earlier inscription implies, Glykonis' family had until very recently been organized as a 'patriarchal' family group, with the three siblings Diogenianos, Agathopous, and Iuliana (along with their own spouses and children) living in the household of their elderly parents Diogenes and Secunda.[106] Hence the prominence of the father's siblings in the funerary commemoration of Glykonis would reflect the historic organization of this family as a 'patriarchal' extended family household.[107] Whether in fact the married brothers Diogenianos and Agathopous continued to reside together after their father's death, or split off to create new households of their own, we cannot say.

A closely comparable case to the household of Diogenianos can be found at the village of Iaza in the Katakekaumene. Early in AD 211, a certain Eupelastos (I) commemorated his deceased wife Agrippina in concert with his two sons Apollonios and Eupelastos (II) and his daughter-in-law Flavia (presumably resident in her father-in-law's household). Three and a half years later, in autumn AD 214, Eupelastos (II) and his wife Flavia set up a tombstone for their thirteen-year-old son Trophimos, in concert with Trophimos' paternal uncle Apollonios and his grandfather Eupelastos (I). Precisely, the same family group act as commemorators in both cases, and it is hard not to conclude (as with the family of Glykonis, discussed earlier) that we are dealing with a genuine extended household unit, consisting of

---

[106] Note the separation of the married couple Diogenianos and Trophime in *SEG* 52, 1165; Trophime is instead grouped with her sister-in-law Iuliana. This 'irrational' sequencing makes more sense if both women belonged to the same household: cf. Thonemann 2013c, 128–9, on the 'irrational' sequencing of relatives in *SGO* III 16/31/33 (Çakirsaz).

[107] For this characteristic 'cycling' through different household forms, e.g. Davis 1977, 169, 176–97; Le Roy Ladurie 1978, 47–8.

the patriarch Eupelastos (I) and his two sons, one married and the other (at least at this point) unmarried.[108] The presence of the father's brother Apollonios in the later epitaph would then reflect the fact that Eupelastos (II) remained in his father's household after marriage.

Patrilocal residence after marriage is also implied by the epitaph of a young man called Deskylos (II) from the territory of Saittai, who was commemorated (in this order) by his paternal grandparents Deskylos (I) and Aphias, his parents Theon and Tatias, his father's two brothers and sister, two *syntrophoi*, and his maternal grandparents. Very unusually, even though the parents of Deskylos (II) were both still living, the primary commemorator on his tombstone was his paternal grandfather. Theon apparently remained in his father's household after his marriage, along with his two brothers and sister; even his own son's tombstone was taken care of by the household patriarch Deskylos (I).[109] Equally suggestive is an epitaph from Tabala for a certain Epaphrodeitos, who was commemorated by his mother Ammion, his grandfather Apollonios and grandmother Apphia, three paternal uncles, two women (both called Tatia) designated as *nymphai*, and a friend called Aelianus. The term *nymphē* usually means 'daughter-in-law' or 'sister-in-law', but that clearly cannot be the case here, since Epaphrodeitos has no male siblings. The two *nymphai* must therefore be the wives of two of the deceased's paternal uncles, described in terms of their relationship with the household patriarch Apollonios – even though Apollonios was not in fact the primary commemorator of the deceased. Ammion, Tatia, and Tatia were thus the wives of three brothers (one of them already dead), apparently living in a single multiple-family household dominated by the patriarch Apollonios.[110]

---

[108] *TAM* V 1, 473c (AD 210/11); *SEG* 35, 1160 (AD 214/5). The patriarch Eupelastos (I) died four years later, in AD 218/9, and was commemorated by his (elder?) son Eupelastos (II) alone (*SEG* 33, 1011); Eupelastos (II) and his wife Flavia reappear in AD 234/5 as co-commemorators of their former *threptē* (*TAM* V 1, 475a). The elder Eupelastos (I) and his own brother Apollonios appear in two slightly earlier propitiatory inscriptions from the region, *SEG* 34, 1212 and 1213 (Petzl 1994, nos. 17 and 18, the latter dated to AD 199/200, after Apollonios' death): see further Section 5.7. The name Εὐπέλαστος ('Approachable') is unattested elsewhere, and so *SEG* 33, 1009 (AD 190/1), *SEG* 40, 1083 (AD 222/3) and *SEG* 45, 1633 (AD 217/8) may well pertain to members of the same family.

[109] *SEG* 33, 1016 (AD 103/4). The patriarch Deskylos also appears, much earlier in life, in *SEG* 31, 1020 (AD 82/3). The name Δεσκύλος (and its feminine equivalent Δεσκυλίς) is only attested in Hieradoumia (*LGPN* V.A, *s.v.*). For a very similar case, cf. *SEG* 41, 1073 (Kadoi), in which a young man called Beroneikianos is commemorated by his paternal grandparents, his parents, and two paternal uncles (in that order).

[110] *TAM* V 1, 210 (AD 140/1). On this 'classificatory' usage of the term *nymphē*, see already Thonemann 2013c, 132–3.

In the light of all this, I think we can confidently conclude that the relative prominence of the paternal uncle in funerary commemoration of unmarried boys and girls in Roman Hieradoumia reflects the general practice of patrilocal residence after marriage, resulting in the creation of 'patriarchal' family households made up of an elderly male household head and his married sons. On the death of the head of household, such extended family groups may have persisted as *frérèche* households, or split into separate nuclear-family households. What proportions of households in Roman Hieradoumia took these forms is of course impossible to say. It is perfectly possible (as the fourth-century Hypaipa census declarations may suggest) that extended family households of all types were in fact numerically outnumbered by nuclear-family households; this is not incompatible with the assumption that the extended-family household was the ideal norm.[111] At a minimum, we can be certain that 'patriarchal' and *frérèche* households were at least *a* common household type in Roman Hieradoumia, and there is good reason to think that they were *the* typical extended-household type (whatever the real proportion of extended to nuclear households may have been).

As we saw in Section 5.5, we need not necessarily conclude from this that married couples always had a more intimate relationship with the husband's (often co-resident) parents and siblings than with the wife's (typically non-co-resident) parents and siblings. We have good evidence that married women did retain close sentimental relations with their parents, foster-parents, and siblings. But the evidence does seem to suggest that children, particularly male children, developed a far closer relationship with their father's parents and siblings than with their mother's parents and siblings; after all, they may well have spent their entire early life co-resident with their father's brothers.

Finally, this structural feature of Hieradoumian society sheds some welcome light on a remarkable inscribed 'eulogy', dating to spring AD 58, erected at the sanctuary of Meis Artemidorou at Axiotta, on the left bank of the Hermos in the northern Katakekaumene[112]:

---

[111] Davis 1977, 168–76, distinguishing 'ideal' and 'statistical' norms; similarly Martin 1996, 48 n.34 ('Even in those cultures which are categorized as "extended family" cultures, the actual percentage of extended family structures compared to nuclear structures is seldom a majority').

[112] *SEG* 53, 1344 (Petzl 2019, no. 56), with Chaniotis 2009a, 115–22: Μεγάλη Μήτηρ Μηνὸς Ἀξιοττη|νοῦ· Μηνὶ Οὐρανίῳ, Μηνὶ Ἀρτεμι|δώρου Ἀξιοττα κατέχοντι Γλύ|κων Ἀπολλωνίου καὶ Μύρτιον Γλύ|(5)κωνος εὐλογίαν περὶ τῆς ἑαυτῶν | σωτηρίας καὶ τῶν ἰδίων τέκνων· | σὺ γάρ με, κύριε, αἰχμαλωτιζόμε|νον ἠλέησες. μέγα σοι τὸ ὅσιον, | μέγα σοι τὸ δίκαιον, μεγάλη ⟨ἡ⟩ νείκη, |(10)

> Great is the Mother of Meis Axiottenos! Glykon son of Apollonios and
> Myrtion daughter of (5) Glykon (offer this) praise (*eulogia*) to Meis
> Ouranios, Meis Artemidorou who rules over Axiotta, for their own sal-
> vation and that of their own children. For you had mercy on me, lord,
> when I was imprisoned. Great is your holiness, great is your justice, great
> is your victory, (10) great are your vengeances, great is the collective of
> the Twelve Gods founded beside you! I was imprisoned by Demainetos,
> the child of my brother, when I had neglected my own affairs and (15)
> had given you help as if you were my own child; but you locked me in
> and imprisoned me, as if I were not your paternal uncle, but a malefactor.
> Great, therefore, is Meis who possesses Axiotta! You gave me satisfaction
> (20), and I praise you. Year 142 [AD 57/8], day 2 of the month Panemos.

The 'speaker' throughout the text must be Glykon, paternal uncle to the
odious Demainetos. The wording of the inscription, with its direct sec-
ond-person addresses to the god and the malefactor ('you had mercy'; 'you
locked me in'), no doubt reflects the oral denunciation (and public shaming)
of Demainetos made by Glykon at the sanctuary of Meis at Axiotta. Why
Demainetos had treated his uncle so badly, we can only guess. From our perspective, the chief point of interest is the assumption that Demainetos' acts
of violence against Glykon were all the more outrageous precisely because
Glykon was his paternal uncle (twice emphasized in the text), who had cared
for Demainetos 'as if he were his own son'. One wonders whether Demainetos might have been orphaned, and taken in and raised alongside his cousins
by his paternal uncle, as his sentimentally and structurally 'closest' relative.

5.7 Summary and Conclusion (with Thoughts on Inheritance)

The main conclusions of this chapter can be summarized as follows.

(i)   In Roman Hieradoumia, deceased men and women of all ages were
      as likely to be commemorated by both nuclear and extended kin,
      or by extended kin alone, as they were by their nuclear family alone

μεγάλαι ⟨αἱ⟩ σαὶ νεμέσεις, μέγα σοι | τὸ δωδεκάθεον τὸ παρὰ σοὶ κα|τεκτισμένον. ἠχμαλωτίσθην |
ὑπὸ ἀδελφοῦ τέκνου τοῦ Δημαι|νέτου, ὅτι τὰ ἐμὰ προέλειψα καί |(15) σοι βοίθεαν ἔδωκα ὡς τέκνω·
| σὺ δὲ ἐξέκλεισές με καὶ ἠχμα|λώτισάς με οὐχ ὡς πάτρως, ἀλλὰ | ὡς κακοῦργον. μέγας οὖν ἐστι |
Μεὶς Ἀξιοττα κατέχων· τὸ εἶκα|(20)νόν μοι ἐποίησας· εὐλογῶ ὑμεῖν. | ἔτους ρμβ΄, μη(νὸς) Πανήμου
β΄. For the cult of Meis Artemidorou Axiottenos, see Ricl 2016; Malay and Petzl 2017, 135–54;
Chapter 8. In line 14, the precise force of ὅτι τὰ ἐμὰ προέλειψα is uncertain; Glykon must be
emphasizing the magnitude of the sacrifices he has made for his ungrateful nephew (in effect, 'I
gave up everything for you').

(48.6% of epitaphs erected by nuclear kin alone; 44.9% by nuclear and extended kin; 6.5% by extended kin alone). This stands in sharp contrast to commemorative practice in the western provinces of the Roman Empire, where deceased men and women were overwhelmingly likely to be commemorated by nuclear kin alone (75–90% of all civilian epitaphs). Foster-kin (foster-parents, foster-siblings, foster-children) appear among the commemorators in 26.7% of all epitaphs from Hieradoumia and in 52.3% of epitaphs which include non-nuclear kin of any type. Fosterage was, if not quite ubiquitous, at least an extremely widespread practice in the Hieradoumian household (see Chapter 6).

(ii) Men were overall more likely than women to be commemorated with their own tombstone (61.0% of tombstones for males; 39.0% for females). Unmarried females do not appear to be particularly under-represented (by comparison with unmarried males) in our surviving evidence; married women, by contrast, were considerably less likely than married men to receive their own tombstone. Our evidence strongly suggests that women typically married around the age of 16, while men seldom married before the age of 30.

(iii) Both married men and married women retained strong sentimental ties with their pre-marital kin after marriage. Pre-marital kin appear among the list of commemorators on around a third of all tombstones for married men and women (35.9% of tombstones for married women and 31.9% of tombstones for married men). In around one in eight cases, the deceased's own pre-marital kin took primary responsibility for the erection of the tombstone, even though the living spouse appeared among the list of commemorators (12.8% of tombstones for married women and 11.0% of tombstones for married men).

(iv) Married women tended to develop closer relations with their husband's family than married men did with their wife's family. The husband's kin appears among the commemorators in 16.4% of epitaphs for married women, while the wife's kin appears in only 7.3% of epitaphs for married men. The husband's brother, sometimes accompanied by his own wife and children, is a particularly frequent presence in epitaphs for married women; I have suggested that this may reflect a strong preference for patrilocal residence after marriage, such that several married brothers often ended up living together in their father's house.

(v) Unmarried males and females were more likely than married men and women to be commemorated by members of their nuclear family alone (55% of epitaphs erected by nuclear kin alone, compared with

43.8% for married men and women). When non-nuclear kin appear among the commemorators of unmarried males, there is a marked preponderance of paternal uncles: the relationship between the father's brother and his nephew is highlighted in some twenty-two epitaphs, compared to a mere six epitaphs which foreground the relationship between the mother's brother and his nephew. This pattern of avuncular commemoration mirrors the relationship between married women and their husband's brother noted in (iv).

(vi)   Both the kinship terminological system of Hieradoumia (which delineated the relationships between married women and their husband's family more precisely than the relationships between married men and their wife's family, and which also assimilated the grandfather to the father's brother) and our limited direct evidence for co-residential patterns tend to support the notion that married men typically resided with their father (if still living) and with their married brothers. Extended-family households were considerably more common in Hieradoumia than in most other parts of the Roman Empire, and tended to take the form of 'patriarchal' family households (several married sons co-residing with their father) or – at a later stage of the familial life cycle – *frérèche* households (several married brothers residing together).

This overall reconstruction of Hieradoumian family and household structure has the advantage of making sense of a large number of discrete aspects of funerary commemoration in the region. It helps explain why the inhabitants of Hieradoumia went in for relatively lengthy 'familial' epitaphs in the first place (Chapter 2): because the typical Hieradoumian household included numerous relatives outside the nuclear family, the inhabitants of the region developed locally distinctive norms of funerary commemoration to reflect the real shape of their families and households. It helps account for the unusually rich kinship terminology in use in Hieradoumia during the Roman imperial period (Chapter 4): the shape of the extended Hieradoumian household required a much more precise relational vocabulary (particularly for the wife's relations with her husband's kin) than was needed in regions characterized by nuclear family structures. Finally, it neatly explains some otherwise surprising patterns and preferences in the listing of extended kin in Hieradoumian epitaphs, most notably the prominence of the husband's brother in the commemoration of married women (Section 5.5), and of the father's brother in the commemoration of unmarried males (Section 5.6).

If this reconstruction is broadly correct, we would naturally expect to find that inheritance in Hieradoumia was partible rather than primogenitive. The evidence, although far from extensive, does indeed seem to point in that direction. A propitiatory inscription from the sanctuary of the 'Gods at Pereudos' is concerned with a testamentary bequest of a vineyard (τὰς ἀμπέλους ... τὰς ληγάτους) by a certain Hygie to three men: a pair of brothers, Apollonios and Eupelastos, as well as a man called Philippikos, who have each received a 'share' of the vineyard (τὰ λαχόντα μέρη τῶν ἀμπέλων). Hygie was almost certainly the mother of Apollonios and Eupelastos, and one wonders whether Philippikos might perhaps have been her daughter's husband.[113] A laconic votive inscription from a sanctuary of Meis Axiottenos records a vow offered to the god by a woman called Hermione, 'if I should receive my share (of an inheritance) from my mother' (ἐὰν παρὰ τῆς μητρὸς λήψομαι τὰ μέρη) – apparently not something that Hermione could count on.[114] More explicit is an extraordinary epitaph from a village in the Upper Tembris valley, some distance to the north-east of the core zone studied in these chapters, but in a region whose funerary epigraphy has many features in common with the epitaphs of Hieradoumia.[115]

> Aur. Onesimos and Stratonikos and Trophimas received the portions which were assigned to them, and let no-one make any further claim against anybody, either himself or through another. Aur. Papylos, son of Onesimos, and [*sc.* his wife] Appes, (set this up) while still living for their children Eugenios and Amias and for their grandchildren Epiktetos and Eugenia and for themselves. And their children Papylos and Amianos (also set this up) for their father and mother, and Ardemis and Amias and Trophime (also set this up) for their sweetest parents-in-law and brother-in-law, in memoriam. I, Aur. Papylos, bequeath the chest and the tools

---

[113] *SEG* 34, 1213 (Petzl 1994, no. 18); for the subsequent history of this family, see Section 5.6. For the circumstances of this inheritance, see further Chapter 8, Section 8.3 (a rather different interpretation in Chaniotis 2004a, 17–18). For joint inheritance between two brothers, compare perhaps *TAM* V 1, 231 (Petzl 1994, no. 35: Taza): two orphan brothers being swindled out of their inheritance (see further Chapter 9, Section 9.4).

[114] *SEG* 41, 1012. For female property ownership in Hieradoumia, Gordon 2016, 239.

[115] Beyond Hieradoumia, the largest concentration of extended familial tombstones from inner Anatolia comes from the Upper Tembris valley (most examples dating to the third or fourth century AD). As in Hieradoumia, *polis*-structures were thin or non-existent in the Upper Tembris region; the kinship terminology used in Upper Tembris epitaphs is notably richer than in more 'urbanised' parts of Phrygia, and there is clear evidence for extended family households of the 'patriarchal' type (Thonemann 2013c, 127–34). In contrast to Hieradoumian epitaphs (usually for individuals), Upper Tembris familial tombstones were generally set up for several family members at once.

and the portions which were assigned to me to Papylos and Amianos; out
of this I bequeath to Eutychiane and Appe thirty measures of *pyrokrithon*
(wheat mixed with barley), and I bequeath to my wife thirty measures and
a sheep.[116]

The first few lines of the inscription record a historic division of the family
property between three brothers, Onesimos, Stratonikos, and Trophimas.
The present inscription was set up by Onesimos' son Aur. Papylos, who
presumably recalls this original division of his grandfather's estate in order
to establish exactly what property he himself now has the right to dispose of
on his death. The estate itself, along with the family's strong box and all the
farm tools, he bequeaths to his two surviving sons, Papylos and Amianos,
no doubt with the expectation that they will divide it between them just as
his own father and uncles had done. Out of this property, he reserves three
smaller plots of land (the area of land sowed with thirty measures of cereal
seed) for his widow and for two unidentified women, probably his daughters or granddaughters (conceivably to serve as a dowry).[117]

There is nothing else quite like this in the funerary epigraphy of inner Anatolia, although it is clear that partible inheritance was quite normal elsewhere
in Roman Phrygia.[118] At any rate, if these kinds of inheritance arrangements
were also common in Hieradoumia, it is easy to see why married brothers
might often have chosen to continue living together in a *frérèche* household: co-residence was the best way of ensuring that one's paternal property
(house, vineyard, and arable land) remained intact and undivided.

---

[116] Anderson 1906, 212–14, no. 10 (*MAMA* X 272): Αὐρ. Ὀνήσιμος | κὲ Στρατόνικος | κὲ Τροφιμᾶς |
ἀπελάβοσα|(5)ν τὰ ἐπιβα|λόντα αὐτοῖ(ς) | μέρη· | κὲ μηδέπ[οτ]|ε μηδενὶ [ἐ]|(10)πενκάλο|ι μηδὲ
ἑαυτὸν | μηδὲ δι᾿ ἑτέ|ρου τινός. | Αὐρ. Παπύλος Ὀνησίμου | (15) κὲ Ἀππης τέκνυς Εὐγε|νίῳ κὲ
Ἀμιας κὲ ἐγγόνῳ | Ἐπικτήτῳ κὲ Εὐγενίᾳ | κὲ αὐτοῖ(ς) ζῶ(ν)τες, κὲ τὰ τέ|κνα αὐτῶν Παπύλος
|(20) κὲ Ἀμιανὸς πατρὶ κὲ μη|τρὶ κὲ Ἄρδε[μ]ις κὲ Ἀμιας | κὲ Τροφύ[μη ἐκ]υροῖς κὲ δ|αέρι
γλυ[κυτάτ]οι(ς) μνήμη(ς) | χάρι(ν). Αὐρ. Π[απύ]λος κατ(α)λίπω | (25) λάρκιον κὲ τὰ ἄρμενα
κὲ τὰ ἐπι|βαλόντα μοι μέρη Παπύλῳ | κὲ Ἀμιανῷ· ἐκκ τούτων καταλ(ίπω) | Εὐτυχιανῇ κὲ
Ἀππῃ πυ(ρο)κρι(θῶν) μέτρα | λ' κὲ τῇ συνβίῳ μου καταλίπω |(30) μέτρα λ' κὲ πρόβατον. See
further Thonemann 2013c, 131–2. In lines 7–8, where Anderson restores Ἄρδε[μᾶς] κὲ Ἀμίας
κὲ Τρόφυ[μος], the use of the kinship terms [ἐκ]υροῖς κὲ δαέρι ('husband's parents', 'husband's
brother') shows that all three commemorators must be female; hence my restoration.

[117] I previously suggested (Thonemann 2013c, 132) that these three *ad personam* bequests were an
annual 'pension' of thirty measures of cereal produce *per annum*. I now think it more likely
that the three women were granted plots of arable real estate, whose size could most usefully
be expressed in terms of the quantity of grain-seed required for sowing each year. Plots of arable land are often so defined in Hellenistic and Roman inscriptions: Thonemann 2009, 381–4.

[118] E.g. Akyürek Şahin 2006, 94, no. 4 (Ayvacık), a father and mother commemorated by their son
Philippos and three male grandchildren, 'the heirs of Appas' (οἱ Ἀππα κληρονόμοι), presumably Philippos' brother; cf. also 104, no. 20 (Bozüyük: οἱ Ἀπολλωνίου κληρονόμοι).

6 | The Circulation of Children

6.1 Ammia and Her Family

At some point in the late third century AD, a rural household in northern Phrygia suffered a cruel series of early deaths. The household patriarch Aurelius Marion, along with his son Titus, set up a fine tombstone for his deceased relatives, adorned with a series of five separate inscriptions of different types.[1] Like very many funerary monuments from the region, the tombstone takes the form of a false door topped with an arched pediment (hence the modern term 'doorstone' for this style of monument).[2] In the pediment, a young man and woman are depicted in deep relief; both have fashionable hairstyles, and the woman is shown wearing rich jewellery (pearl-shaped earrings and a triple choker-style necklace).[3] Each figure is accompanied by gendered objects, depicted in low relief to left and right: he is associated with a writing tablet, while she has her mirror, comb, wool basket, spindle, and distaff. At the very bottom of the stone, there is a careful depiction of a yoke of oxen pulling a scratch plough; although this family was rich enough to afford a fine marble tombstone, carved by one of the best sculptors of the region, they were still keen to represent themselves as a farming household (Figure 6.1).

The first inscription (I), carved in tiny letters on the writing tablet at the top left of the tombstone, reads simply 'This is the honour due to the dead'.[4] The upper moulding of the arched pediment bears the sculptor's signature (II), '*Euglyphis* Onesimos the sculptor made this'.[5] The third inscription, in prose, is spread across four lines on the lower moulding

---

[1] Waelkens 1986, 107–9, no. 252 (Upper Tembris valley, exact provenance uncertain).

[2] Waelkens 1986, with Lochman 2003, 147–83; Kelp 2008; Kelp 2013, 71–87; Kelp 2015.

[3] Masséglia 2013, 115–16.

[4] θνητοῖς ἡ χάρις αὕτη; cf. Waelkens 1986, 158, no. 396 (central Phrygia), θνητῶν τοῦτ' ἐστὶ τὸ δῶρον, and the very common Homeric formula τὸ γὰρ γέρας ἐστὶ θανόντων (examples collected by Merkelbach and Stauber, commentary to *SGO* III 13/07/02).

[5] Εὐγλύφις Ὀνήσιμος λατύπος ἐποίησε. The name Εὐγλύφι(ο)ς (literally 'good sculptor') is a nickname derived from Onesimos' profession; cf. Lambertz 1914, 116 n.2, 133–43; *SEG* 56, 1502 (Μολυβᾶς, 'lead-worker'). Onesimos can be associated with one of the major doorstone workshops of the Upper Tembris valley: Waelkens 1986, 88–93.

Figure 6.1 Epitaph of Apphia, Asklepiades and others, from the Upper Tembris Valley. Waelkens 1986, 107–9, no. 252 (İzmir Museum).

of the pediment and carries the basic information about who erected the tombstone and for whom (III): 'Aur(elius) Marion, for his own wife Apphia and for his son Asklepiades and for his *threptē* Ammia; and Titus, who is still living, for his mother and for his wife (*synbios*) Ammia and for his brother Asklepiades and for the baby who joined them for a few days – they set this up, in memoriam'.[6]

Then, wrapping around three sides of the door (top, right, and below), we have a highly emotional inscription, in prose with some hexameter rhythms (IV): 'If you wish to know, passer-by – here lies a young woman (*korē*) with her foster-brother (*syntrophos*) Asklepiades. In the middle (i.e. between them), they hold the baby. The father, in great grief, laid (the baby) to rest with his own hands. For neither did a stranger then work (this) evil on a stranger, nor did a neighbour show the evil eye to a neighbour, but it was Nemesis which thus hemmed in (the child), in whom his father had (already) recognised his own features'.[7] Finally, to the left of the door, there is a short imprecation in prose, cursing anyone who damages the tomb (V): 'If anyone brings a hand heavy with envy against the tomb, may he suffer similar disasters (i.e. to those that I have suffered)'.[8]

This is an extraordinary monument in all sorts of ways. There is little in Anatolian funerary epigraphy to compare with the pathos of this unnamed baby 'who joined them for a few days' (III) before dying along with its mother.[9] The verse text (IV) concludes with an unparalleled series of clauses, acknowledging that the baby's early death was neither the work of malevolent strangers nor of envious neighbours (a rare item of evidence for ancient peasant belief in the power of the evil eye), but merely of implacable fate.[10] There may be a distant echo of Psalm 15 in this passage, suggesting that the family may have been Christians.[11]

---

[6] Αὐρ. Μαρίων τῇ ἰδίᾳ συνβίῳ Ἀφφίᾳ κὲ Ἀσκληπιά|δῃ υἱῷ κὲ Ἀμμίᾳ τεθρεμμένῃ κ(ὲ) Τ(ί)τος ζῶν τῇ μητρὶ κὲ Ἀμ|μίᾳ συνβίῳ κὲ Ἀσκληπιάδῃ ἀδελφῷ κὲ βρεφίῳ τῷ προσ[γ]|ενομένῳ ἡμερῶν ὀλίγων ἀνέστησεν μνήμης χάριν.

[7] εἰ δὲ θέλις σὺ μαθῖν, παροδεῖτα, ὧδε κόρη κατάκειτι μετὰ συντρόφου Ἀσκληπιάδου· ἀνὰ μέσον τὸ βρέφος ἔχουσι· ὁ πατὴρ πολλὰ στενάχων ἰδίης παλάμης (i.e. ἰδίαις παλάμαις) κατέθετο· οὐδὲ γὰρ ξένος ξένωι κακὸν (so I read from the photograph; κανόνι Waelkens) τότ᾽ ἐποίει, οὐδὲ γίτων γίτονι ὄψιν ἐδείκνεν· οὕτω τότε ἡ Νέμεσις περιέστη ὃν ὁ πατὴρ τὰ προσόντα καθῖδεν. The final clause (ὃν... καθῖδεν) is very difficult, and I am not confident that my translation is correct. For 'rhythmic' prose of this kind, cf. e.g. Waelkens 1986, 116–17, no. 276 (*SGO* III 16/31/75: Upper Tembris valley); *MAMA* X 169 (*SGO* III 16/31/83: Appia).

[8] εἰ δέ τις προσοίσι χῖρα τὴν βαρύφθονον, τοιῆς περιπέσοιτο συνφορῆς. For curse-formulae of this type in northern Phrygia, cf. Strubbe 1997, Appendix 1, 285–8; Robert, *OMS* V, 715–18; *MAMA* XI 141 (Brouzos).

[9] Children in Roman Anatolia were not named at birth: see Chapter 5, Section 5.1.

[10] The most extensive ancient account of the evil eye is Plut., *Quaest. conv.* 680C–683B; the belief is also attested in the Gospels (Matthew 20:15; Mark 7:22). For a real-life case in Roman Egypt, see Bryen and Wypustek 2009; the phrase φθόνῳ περικλῖσαι in *P.Mich.* VI 423–4 is reminiscent of ἡ Νέμεσις περιέστη in our text. See further Russell 1982; Dunbabin and Dickie 1983; Dickie 1995.

[11] Compare Psalm 15:3: οὐδὲ ἐποίησεν τῷ πλησίον αὐτοῦ κακὸν καὶ ὀνειδισμὸν οὐκ ἔλαβεν ἐπὶ τοὺς ἔγγιστα αὐτοῦ. Christian epitaphs were widespread in northern Phrygia by the late third century: Mitchell 1993, II 37–43; Mitchell 2013. No other doorstones can be attributed with

But perhaps most striking of all is the family structure revealed by the two longest inscriptions on the stone (III and IV). Aurelius Marion and his wife Apphia had two sons, Asklepiades and Titus; they also raised a young woman, Ammia, as *syntrophos* ('foster-sibling') to the two brothers. In due course, Ammia married one of her foster-siblings, Titus. She seems to have died in the course of bearing Titus a child, which survived its mother by only a few days. Titus' brother Asklepiades – Ammia's foster-brother and brother-in-law – also seems to have died around the same time. Aurelius Marion and his surviving son Titus then erected a lavish tombstone for four deceased members of their family: Marion's wife Apphia, his son Asklepiades, his foster-daughter (and daughter-in-law) Ammia, and his unnamed grandchild.

In the poetic text on the lower part of the gravestone (IV) – composed, unlike the prose inscription (III), entirely from the perspective of the young widower Titus – we find some very unexpected emphases and silences. Titus' wife and foster-sister Ammia is the first to be mentioned ('here lies a young woman'), followed by his brother Asklepiades, whose position in the household is defined in relation to Ammia ('her *syntrophos*', not 'my brother'). Titus then turns to his deceased child, and describes placing the baby in the tomb with his own hands, between the bodies of its mother and paternal uncle. Remarkably, Titus' deceased mother Apphia is not mentioned in this poetic text at all – the primary focus is on Ammia, the family's former *threptē*, along with her foster-sibling and her baby. The pairing of Ammia and her brother-in-law Asklepiades is visually reaffirmed by the relief sculpture on the upper part of the stone, which shows the two young people side by side, decked out in their best 'Romanizing' dress. Indeed, from a casual glance at the portrait reliefs, the viewer would naturally assume that the tombstone marked the grave of an ordinary young *petit-bourgeois* married couple; the reality, distinctly more complex, only emerges from a close reading of the accompanying texts.

This remarkable monument gives us a rare insight into the social realities of fosterage in inner Anatolia. We have no way of knowing how Ammia originally entered the household of Aurelius Marion: as a foundling, as a house-born slave, as the orphaned daughter of a sibling or cousin, or simply as a neighbour's child raised for part or all of her childhood under a friend's roof. All that we can say for certain is that by the time she

certainty to the mason Onesimos, but the closest stylistic parallel to this monument, Waelkens 1986, 116–17, no. 276 (*SGO* III 16/31/75: Upper Tembris valley) was erected by a Christian family.

reached adulthood, any disparity of social status that may originally have existed between Ammia and her wealthy foster-family had been erased by their long intimacy. Aurelius Marion considered Ammia to be an appropriate marital partner for his own son, her foster-brother; she was buried alongside her other foster-brother (by now also her brother-in-law) and was depicted on their tombstone as his social peer and equal. Fosterage, in short, was both an integral and a highly complex component of family and household structure in Roman Asia Minor.

6.2 Terminology and Legal Status

As we saw in Chapter 5 (Section 5.2), fosterage was ubiquitous in Roman Hieradoumia; 26.7% of all 'familial' tombstones for individuals from Hieradoumia (181 of 677) include at least one foster-relative among those commemorating the deceased (either a foster-child, a foster-sibling, or a foster-parent). Omitting epitaphs erected only by members of the deceased's nuclear family, that proportion rises to 52.3% of the total (182 of 348 epitaphs erected by both nuclear and non-nuclear kin, or by non-nuclear kin alone). There is no reason to think that foster-relationships are significantly over-represented in our extant epitaphic evidence. We may be fairly confident that between a third and a half of all households in the region – and perhaps significantly more than that – reared at least one foster-child, whose sentimental relationship with his or her foster-family was intimate enough for him or her to be included on the family's tombstones.

Needless to say, no modern western society practises fosterage on anything like this scale. Fosterage in modern Britain is relatively unusual (touching less than 1% of children), since it tends to reflect extreme familial dysfunction of some kind: orphanhood, abandonment, abuse, or neglect. This was evidently not the case in Hieradoumia, where the circulation of children between households was a completely normal feature of family life. Still today, there are many parts of the world in which the circulation of children between families is the norm, not the exception: there are societies in contemporary sub-Saharan Africa and Oceania where rates of fosterage approach 100%.[12] Our conception of fosterage as a response to familial dysfunction – and, more generally, as something basically *atypical* – is simply not appropriate to the communities of the middle Hermos in antiquity.

[12] Bowie 2004, 4, 36, 56, 111.

This is worth emphasizing, since even the most careful studies of *threptoi* in Roman Anatolia have a tendency to assume that fosterage must reflect familial misfortune of some kind. In the words of one recent historian of fosterage in the Roman East, 'To study *threptoi* and their nurturers is to study the moral development of the Greeks and Romans and to see them at their best, as nurturers of abandoned infants, slave children, orphans, children sold by their parents – a host of unfortunate little creatures thrown on their mercy'.[13] This is, in my view, a modernizing misconception. At least in Hieradoumia, to study *threptoi* and their nurturers is simply to study the ordinary family going about its business.

The terminology of fosterage in Hieradoumia consists of a series of cognate nouns, adjectives, and participles derived from the verb τρέφειν, 'rear, nurse, feed'. Foster-parents are almost always designated with the aorist participle ὁ θρέψας (m.), ἡ θρέψασα (f.), οἱ θρέψαντες (pl.); in a single case, the foster-parents are described as οἱ τροφεῖς.[14] Foster-siblings are generally described as ὁ/ἡ σύντροφος (common gender).[15] The foster-child is usually called a θρέπτος (m.) or a θρέπτη (f.), although the neuter θρέμμα is found in a significant minority of cases, apparently always in the plural: compare υἱός (m.), θυγάτηρ (f.), τέκνον (n.) for natural children.[16] The perfect passive participle ὁ τεθραμμένος appears quite frequently, in its masculine, feminine, and neuter forms, while the aorist passive participle οἱ τραφέντες appears only once (in the plural).[17] The diminutive forms θρεπτάριον and θρεμμάτιον are also found occasionally.[18] The term τρόφιμος, often used of foster-children elsewhere in the Greek world, is virtually unattested in Hieradoumia (only two examples), perhaps because of the popularity in inland western Asia Minor of the personal names Trophimos and Trophimē.[19] The curious term υἱόθρεπτος ('*threptos*-son') appears in a single inscription from Philadelphia: most probably this is simply a synonym for

[13] Ricl 2009, an otherwise excellent article. Ricl's own research provides no support whatsoever for this poignant conception of *threptoi*.

[14] οἱ τροφεῖς: *TAM* V 1, 758. The term τροφεύς is common enough elsewhere in Asia Minor: e.g. *MAMA* IX 407; *SGO* III 16/23/11 (both Aizanoi); *MAMA* X 194 (Upper Tembris); *I.Kibyra* 162.

[15] Once apparently σ[ύνθ]ρεπτος (*TAM* V 1, 753).

[16] τὰ θρέμματα: e.g. *TAM* V 1, 176 (two females and a male); *TAM* V 1, 322, 663, 795, 822, etc.

[17] ὁ τεθραμμένος: e.g. *TAM* V 1, 25, 432, 433, 633, 786; *SEG* 32, 1231; 35, 1167. ἡ τεθραμμένη: e.g. *TAM* V 1, 379, 733, 772; *SEG* 38, 1229; τὰ τεθραμμένα (always in the plural): e.g. *TAM* V 1, 626, 683; *SEG* 32, 1226. οἱ τραφέντες: *SEG* 35, 1242 (Saittai).

[18] θρεπτάριον: *SEG* 40, 1037 (*SGO* I 04/13/02: Demirci). θρεμμάτιον: *I.Ephesos* 3287a (Kaystros valley).

[19] *SEG* 41, 1042; *Sardis* II 691 (Allahdiyen, territory of Sardis: in verse). For the personal names Trophimos, Trophimē and cognates in Hieradoumia, see *LGPN* V.A, *s.v.* (118 examples).

θρέπτος, although it is possible that the term refers to some specific category of foster-child.[20]

The terminology does not *in itself* reveal anything about the precise social or legal relationship between the 'rearer' or 'fosterer' (ὁ θρέψας) and his or her 'foster-child' (ὁ θρέπτος, ὁ τεθραμμένος). In western Asia Minor, the verb τρέφειν and its cognates were used of a wide variety of different kinds of relationships: a mother could be said to have 'reared' her natural child; an owner could be said to have 'reared' his or her home-born slave; a tailor could be said to have 'reared' his apprentice; a woman dedicated to the service of a goddess could describe the goddess as her 'rearer'; and one could be 'reared' (metaphorically) by one's native homeland or city.[21] As we will see in a moment, numerous epitaphs do in fact tell us something (either directly or indirectly) about the character of the relationship between particular *threpsantes* and their *threptoi*. But these relationships turn out to be so varied that any attempt to generalize about the legal status or social standing of 'the *threptos* in the Hieradoumian household' quickly runs into insuperable difficulties.[22] Fosterage demonstrably took several different forms: house-born slaves who were 'reared' by their masters, children of the élite who were raised by household slaves or professional child minders (either individuals or married couples), the orphaned children of close relatives who were taken in by uncles and aunts, and a whole variety of other kinds of quasi-kinship relationships. All these relationships involve the circulation of children between birth parents and foster-parents, but the precise character and purpose of that circulation demonstrably varied enormously from case to case.

Only in one very limited respect do we have reason to think that the relative socio-legal status of the foster-child and his foster-parent(s) might have affected the terminology used to describe their relationship. I know of no cases where a foster-child described as θρέπτος was demonstrably of higher social status than his foster-parents.[23] It is therefore possible that

---

[20] *TAM* V 3, 1798 (distinguished from τέκνον). Petzl compares *TAM* II 431 (Patara), τεκνόθρεπτοι ἀπελεύθεροι.

[21] Mothers for children: e.g. *TAM* V 2, 1326 (*SGO* I 04/03/01, Hyrkanis) μήτηρ δ' ἐκύησέ με [Χ]ρυσείν, ἥτις ἔθρεψεν, ἔθαψεν; for the common funerary tag '(s)he who reared me, buried me', cf. e.g. *I.Kios* 80; *I.Iznik* 1323; *IG* X 2, 1, 541 (Thessalonike); *SEG* 35, 1060 (Fréjus). Owners for slaves: *I.Smyrna* 543 (*SGO* I 04/01/45). Tailor for apprentice: *TAM* IV 1, 132 (*SGO* II 09/06/15: Nikomedeia), with Drexhage 2002. Cult-official for goddess: Malay and Petzl 2017, no. 158 (Thea Larmene, near Saittai). Homeland or city: *SEG* 40, 1037 (*SGO* I 04/13/02: Demirci, Μαιονίης θρέμμα); cf. e.g. *I.Kyzikos* 506 (*SGO* II 08/01/31); *SGO* I 06/02/28 (Pergamon); *SEG* 19, 840 (*SGO* IV 18/05/01: Pogla).

[22] Rightly emphasized by Nani 1943–1944, 46; Salsano 1998, 181.

[23] Already noted by Nani 1943–1944, 63–4; Levick and Mitchell, *MAMA* IX, p. lxvi n.4.

the specific term θρέπτος may have carried connotations of social dependency to a Hieradoumian ear. However, the phrase οἱ θρέψαντες was used indistinguishably of foster-parents of both higher and lower status than their foster-children. One might conjecture that if a deceased male was of higher status than his *threpsantes*, he would typically be commemorated in the form Μᾶρκον ἐτείμησαν Ἀρτεμᾶς καὶ Ἀπφίας οἱ θρέψαντες ('Artemas and Apphias, the *threpsantes*, honoured Marcus'), but if he was of lower status, he would typically be commemorated in the form Μᾶρκον ἐτείμησαν Ἀρτεμᾶς καὶ Ἀπφίας τὸν θρέπτον ('Artemas and Apphias honoured Marcus, their *threptos*').[24] Furthermore, in a couple of instances, the participle ὁ τεθραμμένος is used of a foster-child of significantly higher status than his foster-parents, and it is thus possible that τεθραμμένος was felt to be a more 'neutral' term of relationship than θρέπτος.[25] However, the fact that we are usually ignorant of the relative status of foster-parents and foster-children makes all this very difficult to demonstrate with any certainty.

The full social and legal range of attested foster-relationships in Hieradoumia (and elsewhere) can only be sketched here in briefest outline.[26] Once again, it is crucial to remember that in the overwhelming majority of cases where a foster-relationship is attested, we can say literally nothing about the relative social or legal status of the two parties. It is quite possible (indeed, in my view, probable) that many or most fosterage relationships were socially 'neutral', i.e. were contracted between families of broadly similar status, without the fostered child becoming in any sense legally dependent on his or her foster-parents (or *vice versa*). But in the nature of things, this is rather difficult to prove. At any event, the number of cases where we can say for certain that one or the other party was either socially or legally 'inferior' to the other is – relative to our total body of evidence for fosterage in Hieradoumia – pretty minuscule.

In a handful of instances, it is clear that a *threptos* was the slave or freedman of his or her *threpsantes*. So in an epitaph from the hill country west of Gordos, five named and several unnamed *thremmata* join in

---

[24] For the exercise of intelligent choice in the selection of 'grammatical perspective' for kinship terms in Hieradoumian epitaphs, see Chapter 2, Section 2.3.

[25] ὁ τεθραμμένος is evidently of higher status than his foster-parents in *TAM* V 1, 432 and 433; the same is probably also of the τεθραμμένοι in *TAM* V 1, 633 and 733. In *TAM* V 1, 786, one male is singled out as the deceased's τεθραμμένος (line 6), while some thirty-seven individuals describe the deceased as τὸν θρέψαντα; what distinction (if any) is intended is unclear.

[26] For more extended treatments, drawing also on material from other parts of Roman Asia Minor and beyond, see Cameron 1939; Nani 1943–1944; Levick and Mitchell, *MAMA* IX, pp. lxiv–lxvi; Ricl 2009.

commemorating a woman whom they address as their 'mistress' (τὴν αὐθέντριαν), which must surely mean 'owner'.[27] In an epitaph from Lyendos, a certain Chares son of Chares joined in burying his mistress (τῆς κυρίας μου), 'in whose memory I pour forth tears, since she left noble instructions concerning my manumission, which my *syntrophos* and my *threpsas* have fulfilled'; the *threpsas* and *syntrophos* here are evidently the husband and son of Chares' deceased owner.[28] In a verse epitaph from the territory of Sardis, a woman erects a tomb for herself and her *trophimoi*, 'on whom she had previously bestowed freedom'.[29] Perilous though it is to infer social status from personal names alone, it is at least striking to find a Hieradoumian *threptos* bearing the name Philodespotos, 'lover of his master', a characteristic slave name.[30] Similarly, a votive inscription from the region of Kula was erected by a certain Eutychis, the *threptē* of C. Iulius Aniketos of Pergamon; it is tempting to think that Eutychis might have been Aniketos' slave or freedwoman.[31] However, we can also point to cases where a relationship of fosterage is carefully distinguished from the owner–slave relationship: in an epitaph from Apollonioucharax, a deceased woman is commemorated separately by her *threpsantes*, her owners (*kyrioi*), and her parents, and in a Hieradoumian epitaph of uncertain provenance, a young man is commemorated by his siblings, his *syngeneis*, his *syntrophoi*, and his *familia* of slaves.[32]

Conversely, we also have a few examples of young men and women of relatively high social standing being reared by *threpsantes* who appear to be household slaves. Perhaps the clearest case can be found in the fifth book of the *Oneirocritica* of Artemidorus of Daldis, where he describes a young boy being handed over to a male slave for rearing after the death of the child's natural mother[33]:

---

[27] *TAM* V 1, 795.   [28] *TAM* V 1, 18.

[29] *Sardis* II 691 (second century AD: a high-status woman).

[30] *SEG* 48, 1432 (unknown provenance); note that Philodespotos does not carry the Aurelian *nomen*, unlike his co-*threptē* Aur. Zoe (who appears to be married, and is presumably of higher status than Philodespotos). For the name, see Robert 1969, 357–8; *MAMA* XI 138 (Pentapolis); cf. also *SGO* III 16/23/11 (Aizanoi: a *tropheus* Philodespotos). Similarly, a *threpsasa* at Saittai carries the 'slavish' name Banausis, 'working girl' (*SEG* 40, 1067); for the name, cf. *SEG* 57, 1232; *I.Ephesos* 3310. For the nomenclature of *threptoi* at Aizanoi, see Levick and Mitchell, *MAMA* IX, p. lxv.

[31] *SEG* 39, 1275 (AD 175/6).

[32] *SEG* 57, 1155; *SEG* 49, 1729. Levick and Mitchell argue that there was a separate, 'lower and unsung' class of *douloi* at Aizanoi, who seldom appeared on epitaphs (*MAMA* IX, p. lxvi). For slavery in Roman Hieradoumia, see Chapter 7, Section 7.1.

[33] Artemidorus 5.85 (trans. Hammond 2020).

A slave dreamt that he was given a boiled egg by his mistress, and that he threw away the shell and consumed the egg. His mistress happened to be pregnant at the time, and later gave birth to a little boy. She died in child-birth, and on the instruction of his mistress' husband the slave who saw this dream took over the baby and brought him up (ἀνεθρέψατο). This, then, was the sense in which the outer casing was dispensable as being of no value, and the inner content provided the dreamer with the means of sustenance.

The final clause may indicate that the rearing of the young boy may have been this slave's primary duty within his master's household.

In funerary epigraphy, a particularly striking example of slave-*threpsantes* comes from Nisyra in the Katakekaumene, where Polykarpos and Epiktesis, the 'rearers' of a wealthy young man called Lucius, seem to be two slaves belonging to Lucius' father's extended household.[34] An anal-ogous case can be found at Saittai, where a member of the local civic elite erected a tombstone for a man whom he describes as 'his father's freedman and his own *threpsas*'.[35] Similarly, in an epitaph from Hypaipa in the Kay-stros valley, two married sisters grant permission for the foster-parents/rearers of their children (τεκέων τρέφουσιν) to be admitted to the familial tomb, 'if anyone manumits any of them'.[36] A less certain case is an epitaph from Saittai, erected by a female member of the local civic elite, Octavia Aelia Artemidora, for her *threpsas* Glaukon; the onomastics clearly suggest that Glaukon was of lower social status than his foster-daughter, although we cannot be certain that he was actually unfree.[37]

There are also cases where the foster-child appears to be of very simi-lar status to his or her foster-parents and may even be a relative (e.g. an orphaned nephew or niece). In AD 230/1, a woman from the top reaches of the civic elite at Gordos, Aurelia Aelia Phoibe, paid for the construction of the portico of a bathhouse at the village of Hyssa near Gordos along with her *tropheis* T. Aelius Epaphrodeitos and Aelia Kallityche and her *syntro-phos* T. Aelius Alexandros. The onomastics strongly suggest that Phoibe's foster-parents, clearly persons of means, were also her relatives, perhaps

---

[34] *TAM* V 1, 432, lines 11–13; I assume that they are identical to the Polykarpos and Epiktesis of *TAM* V 1, 433, lines 12–14. For a (married) pair of imperial slaves as rearers of a child, cf. *SEG* 63, 992 (Gordos).

[35] *SEG* 31, 1018.

[36] *SEG* 55, 1288. The unnamed 'rearers' of the deceased's children were clearly unfree at the time the tomb was constructed. It is unclear precisely who the individuals referred to as ἀνθρώπων θρεπτικῶν in line 19 might be: this might be a general way of referring to foster-kin of all kinds (*threptoi, syntrophoi*, one's children's *threpsantes*, etc.).

[37] *SEG* 31, 1029 (AD 167/8).

her maternal uncle and aunt.[38] An undated epitaph from the region of Gordos was erected for the *threptos* Stratoneikos by his foster-parents, his foster-brother and foster-sister (the latter named Stratoneike), and by his 'brother-in-law' and 'sister's children', clearly in fact the husband and children of his *syntrophos* Stratoneike. It is likely enough that Stratoneikos – who was evidently treated as a full member of this particular family – was in fact a blood relative, perhaps taken in after the death of his own parents.[39]

6.3 Fosterage and Sentiment

This last example illustrates one highly important feature of the terminology used for foster-kin in Hieradoumia. When individuals had cause to refer to, say, the husband of their foster-daughter (*threptē*), or their mother's *syntrophos*, or their wife's foster-father (*threpsas*), these 'extended foster-relatives' were almost invariably designated with precisely the same terms that would normally be used of one's 'real' extended kin. Specifically, we have examples of women describing their husband's *threpsasa* as their 'husband's mother' (*hykera*)[40]; of men describing their wife's *threpsas* and *syntrophos* as their 'wife's father' and 'wife's brother' (*pentheros* and *pentheridēs*)[41]; of foster-parents referring to their *threptē*'s husband as their 'son-in-law' (*gambros*)[42]; of a *syntrophos*' wife or husband being referred to as 'sister-in-law' (*nymphē*) or 'brother-in-law' (*gambros*)[43];

---

[38] *TAM* V 1, 758; see further Chapter 10, Section 10.2. Phoibe is described as daughter of the centurion Aur. Iollas Ephesianos (perhaps already deceased) and as (maternal?) granddaughter of the *matrona stolata* Aelia Phoibe. For adoption and fosterage by the maternal grandfather or maternal uncle in the Greek world, see Bremmer 1983; Bremmer 2000.

[39] *TAM* V 1, 804. For a possible analogy, note the 'baby on the sibling's side' (παιδίον πρὸς ἀδελ(φοῦ/-φῆς) ἐτ(ῶν) α') being raised by his or her uncle's family in *I.Ephesos* 3804, II 11–19 (Chapter 5, Section 5.1, Declaration VI): in later life, this orphaned niece or nephew could well have been described as the family's *threptos* or *threptē*. For the extension of 'real' kinship terminology to extended foster-kin, see further below.

[40] *TAM* V 1, 765 (Gordos, lines 10–12: Flavia is Tryphon's wife); *I.Manisa* 522 (Apollonioucharax, lines 12–13: Apphias is Hesperos' wife).

[41] *TAM* V 1, 704 (Gordos, lines 10–13: Apollonios is clearly Ammias' husband).

[42] *SEG* 48, 1432 (unknown provenance: Trophimos is probably married to the *threptē* Aur. Zoe); *I.Manisa* 426 (unknown provenance, lines 9–11: Artemas is married to either Neike or Stratoneike). In *SEG* 32, 1226 (Saittai), γάνβρος = 'daughter's husband' in line 6, but γάνβροι = '*threptai*'s husbands' in line 9. Cf. also *TAM* III 1, 284 (Termessos): *gambros* = *threptē*'s husband.

[43] *Nymphe* = '*syntrophos*' wife': *I.Manisa* 292 (Saittai). *Gambros* = '*syntrophos*' husband': *SEG* 29, 1187 (Saittai, lines 4–6); *TAM* V 1, 804 (Gordos, line 6); contrast *TAM* V 1, 470a (ἡ πενθερὰ καὶ σύντροφος... κ[αὶ] ὁ ἀνὴρ αὐτῆς).

and of children referring to their mother's *syntrophos* as their 'mother's brother' (*mētrōn*).[44] That is to say, although the relations between immediate foster-kin (foster-siblings, *threptoi* and their foster-parents) were normally described with special terms indicating the foster-relationship, relations with 'extended' foster-kin (one's *syntrophos*' spouse and so forth) were assimilated to relations with one's 'true' extended kin (one's brother or sister's spouse). This use of 'true' kinship terms for extended foster-kin is worth emphasizing, since (so far as I know) servile extended-kin relationships in the Greco-Roman world were never assimilated to real extended-kin relationships in this way: you would not call your slave's wife your 'daughter-in-law'. Hence this particular Hieradoumian *façon de parler* can reasonably be taken as evidence for the sentimental assimilation of many *threptoi* and *syntrophoi* to the status of real children and siblings.

Epitaphs are not necessarily the first place to look for a realistic and objective view of kinsmen's sentiments towards one another.[45] Nonetheless, many texts do seem to attest a close sentimental relationship between foster-children and their foster-parents and foster-siblings. At a remote village in the hill country west of Gordos, a couple by the names of Tyche and Diokles set up an epitaph for their *thremma* Menophilos, 'since he loved his foster-parents even more than his own family' (ἐπὶ ἦν φιλόθρεψ ἀντὶ καὶ ἰδίων).[46] Numerous epitaphs for foster-children or other foster-relatives use the same terms of affection for the deceased as were regularly employed for real family members ('sweetest', 'dearest', 'beloved').[47] Perhaps most tantalizing of all is a votive inscription from Iaza, in which a couple by the names of Tatianos Glaukos and Ammiane set up a thank-offering to the god Meis Motyleites, 'having prayed continually for our first-born *threptē*; her name is Sabina, and may you save her ...' [the text breaks off].[48] Presumably Sabina was the eldest of several children being fostered by Glaukos and Ammiane, but the phrase 'first-born *threptē*' (θρεπτὴ γένει πρώτη) is nonetheless very striking. We seem, once again, to be dealing

---

[44] *TAM* V 1, 804 (Gordos, lines 7–8).

[45] For less harmonious relationships between *threptoi* and foster-parents, see *TAM* V 1, 492 (Petzl 1994, no. 44: Kollyda) and *SEG* 34, 1218 (Petzl 1994, no. 20: Pereudos), discussed further in Chapter 9, Section 9.6.

[46] *TAM* V 1, 815 (Kömürcü, AD 149/50).

[47] Ricl 2009, 105–6. But note the careful distinction of sentiments in *SEG* 55, 1344 (Nikaia): a twenty-five-year-old was 'faithful' (πίστος) to his foster-parents and 'affectionate' (φιλόστοργος) towards his parents. Presumably he was a slave or dependant of his foster-parents.

[48] *TAM* V 1, 457. Cameron 1939, 30, questions the sense of the phrase γένει πρώτη, here translated 'first-born'; his suggested alternative interpretation is (to my mind) considerably less likely. Cf. *RECAM* II 250 (a 'father and mother' for their *threptos*).

with a transferral of language normally used of one's natural children to a foster-child.

One of the more unusual items of evidence for sentimental relations between foster-kin is an epitaph from Iaza, dated to late summer AD 243, for a man who had formerly been the slave of his *syntrophos*[49]:

> Year 327 [AD 242/3], on the third day before the end of the month Hyperberetaios. Aur. Prokopton, having lived well, and having served well his *syntrophos* Tatianos (5) – who, on his death-bed, mindful of the goodwill which he [sc. Prokopton] held towards him, manumitted him through *vindicta* and left him with free-born status, and also left him the bequest (10) stipulated in his will – his parents Epineikos and Zenodote honoured Prokopton, and Preima (honoured) her *tethrammenos*, and Damianos (honoured) his father's *syntrophos*, and Aur. Romanus (15) his brother and his wife Tatias (honoured him), and his children Zenodote, Tatianos – also known as Prokopton – and Epineikos (honoured) their father, and Euphemia, Zenodote and Sokrates (honoured) their brother, (20) and Alexandros his uncle (honoured him), in memory.

The former slave Aur. Prokopton was evidently not a foundling: many of his family were still living at the time of his death, including both parents and four of his siblings. It is possible that his entire family was of servile status, though there is no way of knowing this for certain.[50] But what is particularly striking about the epitaph is the intimate relationship that seems to have persisted *both* between Prokopton and his natural kin *and* between Prokopton and his foster-kin (and former masters). After his death, Prokopton was commemorated (in this order) by his natural parents, his foster-mother, his foster-brother's son, and only then by other members of his own natural family (siblings, wife, children, uncle). Furthermore, although Prokopton named his daughter and his second son after his own

---

[49] *SEG* 35, 1167, with Salsano 1998 (*SEG* 48, 1453): ἔτους τκζ΄, μη(νὸς) Ὑπερβερτέ|ου γ΄ ἀ(πιόντος). Αὐρ. Προκόπτοντα | καλῶς ζήσοντα καὶ ὑπηρε|τήσ(α)ντα Τατιανῷ τῷ συντρό|(5)φῳ, ὃς μνημονεύσας ἣν ἔσχεν | εἰς ἐ(α)υτὸν εὔνοιαν τελευτῶν | κατέλιπε αὐτὸν ἐλεύθερον | εὐγενῆ διὰ βινδίκτων, κατέλι|πεν δὲ καὶ αὐτῷ καὶ ληγᾶτα τὰ ἐν |(10) τῇ διαθήκῃ δηλούμενα· ἐτείμησαν | Προκόπτοντα οἱ γονεῖς Ἐπίνει|κος κὲ Ζηνοδότη, κὲ Πρεῖμα τὸν τεθ|ραμμένον, κὲ Δαμιανὸς τὸν σύντρο|φον τοῦ πατρός, κὲ Αὐρ. Ῥωμανὸς ὁ |(15) ἀδελφὸς αὐτοῦ κὲ ἡ σύνβιος αὐτοῦ | Τατιας, κὲ τὰ τέ(κ)να τὸν πατέρα Ζηνο|δότη κὲ Τατιανὸς ὁ κὲ Προκόπτων | κὲ Ἐπίνεικος· Εὐφημία, Ζηνο|δότη κὲ Σωκράτης τὸν ἀδελφόν |(20) κὲ Ἀλέξανδρος ὁ πάτρως αὐτοῦ | μνείας χάριν.

[50] The onomastics of his family are not noticeably 'slavish'. Of Prokopton's six immediate kin, only his brother Aur. Romanus is recorded as bearing the Aurelian *nomen*, and Romanus is also listed separately from Prokopton's three remaining siblings. Is it conceivable that Romanus, like Prokopton – but perhaps unlike their parents and siblings – was a manumitted former slave?

parents, Zenodote and Epineikos, his first son was named after his own former owner and *syntrophos*, Tatianos. Of course, we do not know whether
the child Tatianos (also known as Prokopton, after his father) was born
before or after his father's manumission. Either way, the epitaph gives a
vivid picture of the close relations that Prokopton maintained with two
entirely separate families: his birth-kin, and the foster-kin to whom he was
(at least for a period) enslaved.

Was it socially acceptable for foster-siblings to marry? The question
is an important one, since *syntrophos*-marriage (or its absence) would
serve as a kind of litmus test of the extent to which foster-relationships
really were conceptually assimilated to natural kinship in Hieradoumia.
In fact, aside from the marriage between Ammia and Titus (discussed in
Section 6.1), I know of only two clear cases of marriage between *syntrophoi* anywhere in Roman Anatolia. At Termessos in southern Pisidia, a
certain Aurelius Achilleus set up a sarcophagus for himself, his wife, his
son Aurelius Konon, 'and my son's wife Ko[rkainē], my *threptē*'.[51] A long
verse epitaph from the modern village of Kurt Köy in the Upper Tembris valley, dating to the early fourth century AD, reveals that a Christian presbyter by the name of Aurelius Trophimos married his daughter
Ammia (apparently his sole child) to his *threptos* Telesphoros: 'my tomb
was built by my daughter Ammia and my *threptos* Telesphoros, to whom
I left my daughter Ammia as his wedded wife'.[52] This is not a very impressive haul, perhaps suggesting that marriages between *syntrophoi* were in
fact rather unusual. In Hieradoumia, I know of no certain cases of marriages between foster-siblings; we do have an example of a man marrying
the daughter of his foster-sister, but this is not a significant exception,
since marriages between uncles and nieces were perfectly common in
Roman Anatolia.[53]

---

[51] *TAM* III 1, 370.

[52] *SEG* 6, 137 (*SGO* III 16/31/93 A, verses 18–19); cf. also *MAMA* X 169, with *stemma* p. 55 (*SGO*
III 16/31/83). Aur. Trophimos as presbyter: *SGO* III 16/31/93 A, verse 3, with *BE* 2002, 342,
p. 701 (reading τὸν σοφίης ἐμὲ διδάσκαλ[ον] κὲ νόμον). It is striking that Trophimos chooses
to refer to Telesphoros as his foster-child (*threptos*) rather than as his son-in-law (*gambros*),
emphasizing Telesphoros' original position within his household.

[53] *TAM* V 1, 470a (Iaza); for uncle–niece marriage, Thonemann 2017a. Curiously, the deceased's
wife is not named on his epitaph, although his mother-in-law/foster-sister and her husband
are. An epitaph from Çal, in the middle Maeander valley, records the marriage of a man to his
relative's *threptē* (*SEG* 54, 1286); unfortunately, the exact relationship between the two men
is unclear. An epitaph from Aphrodisias (*SEG* 54, 1061) is interpreted by Chaniotis (*SEG, ad
loc.*) as evidence for the marriage of a man to his *threptos*' daughter (Φαυστεῖνα Ἀχιλλέως τοῦ
τροφίμου, ἡ γυνὴ αὐτοῦ), but it is preferable to see the woman as the granddaughter of a man
named Trophimos (i.e. τοῦ Τροφίμου).

6.4 Natal Parent and Foster-Parent

In light of the fact that a child could demonstrably develop close affective relationships with both his/her foster-parents and his/her natal parents, it is worth pausing on the relationships between the natal parents and foster-parents of the child, particularly in cases where the two pairs of parents were neither close kin nor of sharply different social status. In the light of the extraordinary rich and precise kinship terminology in use in Roman Hieradoumia (see Chapter 4), it would not be surprising if there were a specialized term for the relationship between natal parent and foster-parent, and I would like to suggest here that we do indeed know of a term which may connote that relationship: the term *synteknos*.[54]

The Greek word σύντεκνος only comes into widespread usage in the Byzantine period, when it denotes the relationship between the natal parent and the godparent – that is to say, a historically specific (Christian) form of 'co-parenthood'.[55] In a Christian epitaph of the fourth century AD from the Upper Tembris valley, a man describes the parents of his daughter's husband as his σύντεκνοι, and the term here clearly means 'parent of one's child's spouse', an analogous but slightly different form of 'co-parenthood'.[56] In both of these two senses, the term almost certainly has 'reciprocal' force (I am your *synteknos* and you are my *synteknos*), as in the cases of the morphologically similar Hieradoumian kinship terms σύνγαμβρος ('wife's sister's husband', WZH) and σύννυμφος ('husband's brother's wife', HBW).

The term σύντεκνος appears four times in epitaphs from Roman Hieradoumia. In no case does its sense emerge clearly from the context, but on the analogy of the later meanings of the term, it surely ought to denote 'co-parenthood' of some kind, and I think a strong case can be made that it denotes the relationship between natal parent and foster-parent. The four examples are as follows:

(1) Gordos, AD 108/9: epitaph of a married woman named Nia, erected by her husband, her son and daughter, her father, two female friends (Iulia and [- -]la), and two men and a women (Trophimos, Drusus, Iulia) who describe Nia as their *synteknos*.[57] There is no indication

---

[54] The evidence already collected by Thonemann 2019, 128–9.
[55] Macrides 1987; Rapp 1997, 300–4; Rapp 2016, 11–12.
[56] Gibson 1978, 76–9, no. 28 (*SGO* III, 16/31/88), with Tabbernee 1997, 394–401, no. 62.
[57] *TAM* V 1, 710. In lines 5–6, Ἰουλία […]λα probably represents two persons, since in Hieradoumia Ἰουλία is typically a free-standing personal name.

that Nia's children are already married, and hence *synteknos* is highly unlikely to signify 'parent of one's child's spouse'. However, it is quite possible that Nia's two children (Attinas and Ammin) were being reared or part-reared by foster-parents: if so, *synteknos* could easily denote the 'co-parenting' relationship between natal parent (Nia) and foster-parents (Trophimos, Drusus, Iulia).

(2) Gordos, AD 109/10: epitaph of a married man named Petraeites, erected by his wife, his co-freedman, his former master (perhaps), three male friends, a woman (Apphion) who describes Petraeites as her *synteknos*, his *threptos* Onesimos, and his neighbours.[58] There is no sign that Petraeites has any natural children, but he does have a foster-child (Onesimos); hence the term *synteknos* can again easily be taken as denoting the 'co-parenting' relationship between Onesimos' natal parent (Apphion) and his foster-parents (Petraeites and his wife).

(3) Gordos, AD 153/4: epitaph of a married man named Theogenes, erected by his parents, his brother, his wife, his brother's wife, three *syntrophoi*, a man and a woman (Florus and Soteriche) who describe Theogenes as 'son of their *synteknos*', and his wife's parents.[59] Once again, it is very easy to assume that Florus and Soteriche are the natal parents of one or more of Theogenes' *syntrophoi*, the children who were reared by Theogenes' own parents; hence Florus and Soteriche can correctly describe themselves as the *synteknoi* of Theogenes' parent(s).

(4) Iaza, AD 169/70 (Figure 6.2): epitaph of a woman named Iulia, apparently unmarried, erected by a long list of kin, beginning with her father and mother, and ending with (apparently) two couples (Soter and Pia, Eutychia and Asklepiades) who describe themselves as Iulia's *synteknoi*, followed by two named *syntrophoi*.[60] This text is somewhat more problematic, since Iulia does not seem to have either children or *threptoi* of her own. She does, however, have two *syntrophoi*, and hence it is quite plausible that the four listed *synteknoi* are the parents of her foster-siblings. If this is right, we would then be seeing the term *synteknos* being used in a 'classificatory' sense, of a relationship between two families created by the exchange of

---

[58] *TAM* V 1, 712, discussed further in Chapter 7, Section 7.1.

[59] *TAM* V 1, 725. The three *syntrophoi* appear in different parts of the epitaph; only one (Dionysios) is listed immediately before Florus and Soteriche, and I assume that he is their son. In line 4, restore Σωτηρ[ίχη] rather than Σωτήρ[ιχος].

[60] Thonemann 2019, 126–9, no. 6. Contrary to what I suggested there, I would now take all four persons listed in lines 11–12 to be Iulia's *synteknoi*: Σωτὴρ καὶ Πεία, Εὐτυχία καὶ Ἀσκληπιάδης.

Figure 6.2 Epitaph of Iulia, from Ayazören (Iaza). Thonemann 2019, no. 6.

children between them: so a term which strictly denotes the relationship 'natal parent – foster-parent' can be extended to cover the relationship 'natal parent – foster-sibling'. In practice, there is nothing problematic about this: we might compare the 'classificatory' usages of the terms *gambros* and *nymphē* in Hieradoumia, discussed in Chapter 4 (since the primary signification of *nymphē* is 'woman who enters a household by marriage', it can be used indiscriminately to refer to both the son's wife and the brother's wife).

If this argument is correct, then the occasional appearance of *synteknoi* in Hieradoumian epitaphs would further support the idea (see Section 6.2) that fosterage in the region was not a response to familial misfortune or dysfunction, but rather a mechanism which served to create strong horizontal ties between families by means of the circulation of children from one household to another. Indeed, although the specifically Christian institution of godparenthood did not exist in the Roman imperial period, the Byzantine use of the same term (*synteknos*) for the relationship between natal parent and godparent ought to alert us to the very similar social functions performed by ancient fosterage and medieval godparenthood: in both cases, we are dealing with an institution *parallel* to marriage, used (at least sometimes) as a way of making alliances between families.[61]

6.5 Reasons for Fosterage

In fact, we are seldom given any indication of why an individual child might have been handed over to foster-parents. Nor do we know whether foster-children would typically have resided in their foster-household throughout their childhood, or just for a few years (e.g. in infancy, or during one's teenage years, or whatever), as is often the case in other societies which practice extensive circulation of children between households.[62] Certainly, there is little reason to think that a majority (or even a significant minority) of *threptoi* were foundlings or orphans. In very many epitaphs for *threptoi* from Hieradoumia, the deceased is commemorated both by his or her natural parents and by his or her *threpsantes*, clearly showing that the natural parents were still living (and still sentimentally attached to their children) at the time when the child was passed to another couple for fostering.[63] The fosterage relationship clearly did not supersede or act as a substitute for relationships with one's natural kin; rather, a child's relationship with foster-parents and foster-siblings was typically *additional* to the relationship with his or her natural parents and siblings.

Only in a very few cases do we have reason to think that it was the death of a parent or parents which led to young children being handed over to foster-parents. An instance in Artemidorus' *Oneirocritica* was cited above;

---

[61] Davis 1977, 223–34, 236–8. Note in particular 237–8, on the Turkish and Syrian institution of 'milk-motherhood', a reasonably close analogy to what I understand to be the function of Hieradoumian fosterage. Cf. also Goody 1983, 196, for the analogy between fosterage and godparenthood.

[62] In Hieradoumia, the sentimental relationship with one's foster-parents persisted well into adulthood (see e.g. *TAM* V 1, 733; *SEG* 56, 1261), making it difficult to tell whether there was a typical age at which a child would be fostered out.

[63] Individuals commemorated by both natural parents and *threpsantes* (in that order): e.g. *TAM* V 1, 56; *SEG* 27, 783 (an eight-year-old); *SEG* 31, 1028 (an eighteen-year-old); *SEG* 32, 1225; *SEG* 32, 1230; *SEG* 40, 1089; *SEG* 48, 1433 (= *SEG* 51, 1685); *SEG* 49, 1560; *SEG* 49, 1712; *SEG* 56, 1261 (a twenty-six-year-old); perhaps *TAM* V 1, 137 (the fosterage relationship not certain). Individuals commemorated by both *threpsantes* and natural parents (in that order): e.g. *TAM* V 1, 150 (a fourteen-year-old); *SEG* 32, 1231; *SEG* 36, 1086; *SEG* 41, 1042; *SEG* 57, 1155.

perhaps the most explicit example in funerary epigraphy derives from Attaleia in northern Lydia[64]:

> Flavia Alexandreia set up this tombstone for her *threpsasa* Elpis, who left me, still a babe in (5) arms, before I had completed my first year. She departed the light of day aged twenty-(10)eight years, in haste, through love for her own children; and your husband's brother's wife reared me, whose name was Heliodora. The tombstone was erected by my father Flavius Ioul[eia]nos and (15) my *threpsas* [..]chylos, in memory. When Licinius Donatus was proconsul, on day 7 of the month Xandikos.

The foster-mother Elpis and her husband [..]chylos seem to have been of lower status than the foster-child Flavia Alexandreia and her family (who possessed Roman citizenship). Alexandreia's mother is not mentioned, suggesting that she may have died in childbirth or very early in her daughter's life. The 'foster-mother' (*threpsasa*) Elpis was presumably co-opted as wet-nurse to the little Alexandreia after her mother's death. It is poignant to learn that the twenty-eight-year-old Elpis had already lost at least two children of her own: in many pre-modern societies, wet-nurses tended to be women who had recently miscarried or whose child had died shortly after birth, and perhaps that was also the case here.

It is worth emphasizing that even in this rather atypical instance, 'fosterage' was not simply a matter of a well-off Roman citizen employing a poor wet-nurse to breast-feed his baby daughter, but involved a genuine transfer of the child from one household to another. Little Alexandreia also had a foster-father (*threpsas*), a certain [..]chylos, presumably Elpis' husband. The likelihood is that Alexandreia physically moved into the household of Elpis and [..]chylos, and in effect became a member of their own extended household. It is especially telling that, when the wet-nurse Elpis herself died, Alexandreia was passed on to another wet-nurse from Elpis' extended family, a certain Heliodora, [..]chylos' brother's wife. One wonders whether [..]chylos and his unnamed brother might have co-resided in an extended-family household of 'patriarchal'

---

[64] *TAM* V 2, 841 (*SGO* I 04/06/99): [Φ]λ. Ἀλεξάνδρεια Ἐλπίδ[ι] | θρεψάσῃ βωμὸν θέτο | τόνδε, ἥτις με ἔλιπεν | πάνυ νηπίαν ἐν κόλ|(5)ποις μήπως πληροῦσαν | ἔτος πρῶτον· αὐτὴ δ[ὲ ἔσ]πευσεν πρὸς παίδων | [ἰ]δίων φιλίαν προλιπο[ῦ|σα] φάος ὀκτὼ καὶ εἴκο|(10)[σι] ἐτῶν, ἐμὲ δ' ἔθρεψεν | [σ]ύννυνφος σή, ἧς οὔ[νο|μ]α Ἡλιοδώρα. τὸν βωμὸ[ν | ἀ]νέστησεν Φλ. Ἰουλ[..|.] νος ὁ πατήρ μου [σὺν |(15) τ]ῷ θρέψαντι μου [..|.]χύλῳ μνείας χ[ά]|ριν· ἀνθυ(πάτῳ) | [Λι]κινίῳ Δωνάτῳ, | [μη(νὸς)] Ξανδικοῦ ζ'. In *TAM* V 1, 150 (Saittai), a fourteen-year-old boy is commemorated by his foster-parents and his natural father, in that order: was he handed to foster-parents on the death of his mother? Note also the (orphaned?) baby reared by his/her uncle and aunt in *I.Ephesos* 3804, II line 16 (Chapter 5, Section 5.1, Declaration VI).

or *frérèche* type.[65] Alexandreia would, in that case, simply have been shunted across from one of the household's young women of child-rearing age (Elpis) to another (Heliodora).

There is no reason to think that either Elpis or Heliodora were in any sense 'professional' fosterers: the choice of Elpis and [..]chylos as foster-parents for the young Alexandreia was presumably a matter of timing and opportunity (a young bereaved mother becoming available for wet-nursing just as Alexandreia lost her own mother). However, some married couples are known to have had very large numbers of *threptoi*, suggesting that certain couples (not necessarily of low social status) may have specialized in the rearing of young men and women. So a certain Artemidoros of Maionia had three natural children and seven *threptoi*; Apollonios of Gordos had one natural son and eight *threptoi* (including two boys called Neikephoros and two girls called Moschion); Asklepides of Saittai had three natural children and eight *threptoi*, as did a woman called Harmonia from the hill country west of Gordos.[66] Most impressive of all is a man from the same village as Harmonia, who had at least one natural son, two step-daughters, and no fewer than thirty-eight *threptoi*: there is a certain aptness to the fact that his natural son carried the name Euxenos, 'Welcoming'.[67]

Outside Hieradoumia, another very likely case of professional fosterage emerges from a tombstone of uncertain provenance, perhaps from Phrygian Hierapolis (Pamukkale). This tombstone carries a relief depiction of a husband and his wife along with three boys and three girls, presumably their natural children; a further fourteen children, twelve females and two males, are depicted separately in a lower relief panel. The accompanying inscription tells us that Antonia Artemeis, a doctor (*iatreinē*), set up the tombstone for her husband, her children, and her *threptoi*.[68] It is tempting to wonder whether the large number of children reared by Antonia Artemeis (six of her own, and fourteen foster-children) might be connected to her profession as a doctor: might she perhaps have been a professional pediatrician?

6.6 Fosterage and Kinship in Hieradoumia

How does the unusual prevalence of fosterage in Roman Hieradoumia (unusual, that is, by Roman standards) connect to the other peculiarities of

---

[65] See Chapter 5, Sections 5.5 and 5.6.
[66] Artemidoros of Maionia: *SEG* 49, 1620. Apollonios of Gordos: *TAM* V 1, 764. Asklepides of Saittai: *SEG* 40, 1093. Harmonia: *TAM* V 1, 782 (Yayakırıldık).
[67] *TAM* V 1, 786 (Yayakırıldık); cf. n.25 above.   [68] *SEG* 52, 1862.

the kinship system of the region? As we saw in Chapter 4, the inhabitants of Roman Hieradoumia employed an unusually complex and precise terminology of kinship. Several specific categories of kin – the parents' siblings and their spouses, kin by marriage – were described with distinctive and unusual terms, hardly attested elsewhere in the Greco-Roman world (*daēr*, 'husband's brother'; *syngambros*, 'wife's sister's husband', etc.). This terminological richness is mirrored in the distinctive forms of Hieradoumian commemorative practice more generally (Chapter 2). Hieradoumian epitaphs typically describe the entire familial group involved in burying and commemorating the deceased; an ordinary epitaph might include a list of a dozen or more living family members, all of them precisely 'placed' in terms of their kinship or affective relationship to the deceased. Finally, as we saw in Chapter 5, extended multiple-family households were widespread in Hieradoumia; it appears to have been quite normal for married brothers to live together, along with their parents (if still living) and their own wives and children. At the end of Chapter 5, I suggested that these regionally distinctive features of Hieradoumian kinship might be connected: specifically, (a) that extended multiple-family households were in fact *unusually* common (by Greco-Roman standards) in Roman Hieradoumia; and (b) that the existence of these unusually large and complex households might have led to the emergence both of an unusually rich kinship terminology, and of unusually 'familial' commemorative practices, in the region.

We are now in a position to add another element to this hypothesis. I have argued in this chapter that fosterage – the circulation, temporary or (less often) permanent, of children between households – was unusually widespread in Roman Hieradoumia. A rough and ready survey of the relative prevalence of foster-kin in Hieradoumian epitaphs (see Chapter 5, Section 5.2) suggested that between a third and a half of all households in the region reared at least one foster-child. This should be seen as a minimum figure: the actual proportion of households with foster-children may have been still higher. These foster-children were of very varied social and legal status *vis-à-vis* their foster-parents. Some *threptoi* were slaves of their foster-parents, and some foster-parents were the slaves of their *tethrammenoi*'s natal parents, but it seems that very many (perhaps most) foster-relationships were between families of roughly similar standing. These *threptoi* and *syntrophoi* were, on the whole, well-integrated and valued members of their foster-households. They were frequently assimilated to real kin, to the extent that a woman could refer to her husband's foster-mother as her 'mother-in-law'. Marriage between foster-kin is hardly attested, perhaps suggesting that such marriages were regarded as, in effect, incestuous.

The prevalence of fosterage could well have been one of the reasons why the terminology of kinship in Hieradoumia continued to be so finely defined in a period when most Greco-Roman societies had moved to a simpler kinship terminological system. In a society like that of rural Hieradoumia, which practised extensive circulation of children (whether kin or non-kin) between what were often large and sprawling multiple-family households, it might well have been felt to be especially important to classify and distinguish one's familial relationships as precisely as possible. A young man or woman could easily have been co-resident with up to a dozen different categories of kin and foster-kin: parents, paternal uncles and their spouses, foster-siblings, grandparents, cousins, and so forth. In many cases – although the evidence is not as clear we should like – one's foster-siblings may *also* have been extended kin, if it is indeed the case that children were frequently fostered by their aunts and uncles (as apparently in the case of Aurelia Aelia Phoibe of Gordos, see Section 6.2). In a social system of this kind, a word like 'aunt' would have been so imprecise as to be effectively useless.

This concludes our description of the kinship system of Roman Hieradoumia. In Chapter 7, we will turn to look at other social groupings which play a prominent role in funerary commemoration, as a first step towards considering the relationship between kinship and household organization and the broader socio-political structure of the towns and villages of the region (the subject of Chapters 8–10).

7 | Beyond the Family

7.1 Neighbour, Cult Association, Friend: Social Solidarities

It is hardly surprising that the funerary epigraphy of Roman Hieradoumia tells us so much more about kinship groups, both nuclear and extended, than it does about other kinds of social ties. In most societies, and certainly throughout the ancient Greco-Roman world, funerary commemoration is typically the preserve of the deceased's family. Nonetheless, commemorating the dead in Hieradoumia was not purely a family matter: the epitaphs of the region in fact offer extraordinarily rich evidence for the involvement of extra-familial persons and social groups in funerary commemoration.

Which particular extra-familial social ties might have been most significant for the inhabitants of Hieradoumia depends a good deal on the social status (and gender) of the individuals concerned. Let us begin at the bottom of the social hierarchy, with persons of unfree status. It is certainly not necessarily the case that the social world of slaves in Roman Hieradoumia was significantly different from that of free men and women. An epitaph from Gordos, dated to spring AD 70, illustrates the point nicely: a certain Amerimnos was commemorated by his wife Helikonis, his son Amerimnos, his mother Terpousa, his grandmother Neikopolis, his siblings Alexandros, Demetria, and Terpousa, his foster-father Aigialos, his sister's husband Gamos, his relatives (*syngeneis*), and his fellow slaves (*syndouloi*).[1] Were it not for that single unexpected word *syndouloi*, we should never have guessed that Amerimnos was a slave: the shape of his extended family, and the manner of his funerary commemoration, are completely indistinguishable from those found among the free population at Gordos.[2] The similar case of Aur. Prokopton of Iaza (died AD 243) was discussed

---

[1] *SEG* 40, 1044.

[2] Familial epitaphs erected by δοῦλοι or οἰκέται are common throughout Asia Minor: e.g. *SEG* 41, 1094 (Kios); *I.Iznik* 204 (Nikaia); *I.Kibyra* 192, 296; *SEG* 55, 1488 (Phellos), citing numerous parallels at Olympos; note especially *TAM* II 967 (Olympos), where the δούλη Helenous, married with children, owns her own δούλη, Melinne, who is herself married with children! At Termessos, the burial of slave families was perfectly normal, but usually required their owners' permission: *TAM* III 1, Index XII, p. 351; also *SEG* 41, 1281, 1294, 1302; *SEG* 57, 1562.

in Chapter 6 (Section 6.3): the first half of Prokopton's epitaph describes his manumission by his *syntrophos* Tatianos, while the second half shows him being commemorated by his extended family in completely normal fashion (parents, foster-mother, foster-brother's son, siblings, wife, children, paternal uncle).[3] It is not hard to find other examples of slaves with perfectly ordinary families, commemorating and being commemorated in the typical Hieradoumian manner.[4]

Somewhat different, though I think only superficially so, is an epitaph from a large private estate at the village of Thermai Theseos (the 'Hot Springs of Theseus'), south of Silandos, owned by a non-resident elite family from Sardis. This tombstone, dated to summer AD 141, was set up by the '*collegium* of the *familia* of C. Iulius Quadratus which is in the village of Thermai Theseos in the district of Mokaddene', to commemorate an eight-year-old slave by the name of Epitynchanon; the final two lines of the inscription indicate that the boy's father and mother were responsible for preparing the tomb.[5] It is true that the group responsible for commemorating Epitynchanon were not his direct kin, but the slave-*collegium* to which he belonged. However, this does not show that Epitynchanon's immediate status peers (his fellow slaves) were in practice more significant to him than his kin group. Setting up a tombstone was expensive, and here the expense was shouldered by the *collegium* as a whole rather than the boy's parents.

Considerably more interesting is an epitaph from Gordos, dated to spring AD 110, which really does seem to attest an alternative pattern of social relations for at least some individuals from servile backgrounds.[6]

---

[3] *SEG* 35, 1167, with Salsano 1998 (*SEG* 48, 1453).

[4] *TAM* V 1, 782 (Yayakırıldık, AD 120/1): Isthmos, slave of Antistius Priscus (Ἴσθμος Ἀντιστίου Πρείσκου), for his wife, along with numerous other family members; *TAM* V 1, 37 (Silandos, AD 92/3): three slave siblings (δοῦλοι) for their parents; Robert, *Hellenica* VI, 117–22, no. 48 (Gordos, AD 263): epitaph of Serapis, erected by his wife, daughter, son-in-law, *despotēs*, 'closest friends', and other kin. Cf. also *TAM* V 1, 442 (Kollyda): dedication of Eutychos, slave *vilicus* of Iulia Tabilla (Ἰουλίας Ταβίλλης δοῦλος πραγματευτής: see Ehrhardt 1990), with his wife, on behalf of his son; *TAM* V 1, 692 (Gordos, under Domitian): a married δοῦλος ἀρκάριος; *TAM* V 1, 342 (Kollyda, AD 123): a δοῦλος with children; *TAM* V 1, 257 (Kula, AD 113/4): a married δούλη; *SEG* 63, 992 (Gordos, under Titus): a pair of imperial slaves set up a tombstone for their *threptē*, along with all their other *syngeneis*.

[5] *TAM* V 1, 71: κολλήγιον φαμιλίας Γ. Ἰουλίου Κουαδράτου τ[ὸ] ὃν ἐν Θερμαῖς Θησέως κώμη τῆς Μοκαδδηνῆς... προνοησαμένων... πατρός καὶ μητρός. On this estate, and the identity of the owner, see Chapter 10, Section 10.2. Married slaves are assumed in the sacred regulations of the cult foundation of Dionysios at Philadelphia (*TAM* V 3, 1539, lines 26–27: late Hellenistic).

[6] *TAM* V 1, 712 (Gordos). For the reading Πετραείτην in line 3, see *SEG* 48, 1439, and for the restoration Ἀντίστρατ||[ο]ς in lines 6–7 (*TAM*: Ἀντιστράτ[ι|ο]ς), see *LGPN* V.A, *s.v.* Ἀντίστρατος (2), also suggesting Ἀντιστρατ[ίδη]ς.

ἔτους ρϙδ΄, μη(νὸς) Δαισίου κ΄.
Κλαυδία Πελαγία ἐτείμη-
σε Πετραείτην τὸν ἑ-
αυτῆς ἄνδρα καὶ Εὔ-
5   τυχος τὸν συνεξε-
λεύθερον, Ἀντίστρατ-
[ο]ς τὸν ΟΙΚΕΤΟΝ, Διόδοτος, Ὁσιαν-
ός, Εὔφημος τὸν φίλον, Ἄπφι-
[ον] τὸν σύντεκνον, Ὀνήσι-
10   μος τὸν θρέψαντα καὶ ἡ γίτονες
τὸν συνεποκιανὸν καὶ οἱ
συνγαινῖς.
χαῖρε.

Year 194, Day 20 of the month Daisios. Claudia Pelagia honoured Petraeites, her husband, and Eutychos (honoured) his co-freedman; Antistratos (honoured) his *oiketos*;
Diodotos, Hosianos, and Euphemos (honoured) their friend; Apphion (honoured)
her *synteknos*; Onesimos (honoured) his foster-father; and his neighbours (honoured) their co-resident on the *epoikion*, and his relatives (honoured him). Farewell.

The group of individuals responsible for commemorating Petraeites is very
idiosyncratic by Hieradoumian standards. Petraeites' wife, Claudia Pelagia,
is listed first, followed by his 'co-freedman' (*synexeleutheros*), Eutychos,
clearly indicating that Petraeites was himself a former slave (as was, presumably, his wife Claudia Pelagia).[7] There then follows a man called
Antistrat[o]s, who describes Petraeites as his *oiketos* (*sic*). Earlier editors
corrected this term to *oikeios*, '(household) dependant', but we should
be cautious, since the term *oikeios* is scarcely attested in Hieradoumia.[8] I
would prefer to assume that this is an orthographic slip for *oiketēs*, 'slave',
or here rather '(former) slave'.[9] Next come three men, Diodotos, Hosianos,

---

[7] Note that Claudia Pelagia reappears, along with at least one slave ([δοῦλο]ς ἀρκάριος), among
the list of commemorators for another presumed freedman, Claudius Prokles, who died in the
following year: *TAM* V 1, 713 (Gordos, AD 111).

[8] οἰκε(ῖ)ον: Keil and Premerstein 1907, 75 no. 157, followed by Herrmann in *TAM* V 1. In
Hieradoumia, the term *oikeios* appears only in *SEG* 49, 1615 (Maionia, Hellenistic: a certain
Demophon commemorated by 15+ οἰκεῖοι, all males) and in *SEG* 62, 918, B13, and B31 (Gordos, AD 69/70: οἱ οἰκεῖοι apparently a catch-all term for the deceased's household). The term
also appears at Sardis, apparently meaning 'slaves' or 'dependants': *Sardis* VII 1, 163 (second
or third century AD: οἰκεῖοι of Herakleodoros and his heirs admitted to a tomb). Aristophanes
of Byzantium distinguished between *syngeneis*, kinsmen by blood, and *oikeioi*, kinsmen by
marriage (F263 Slater; cf. *Dig.* 38.10.10.1, Lat. *cognati* = Gr. συγγενεῖς), but this distinction is
not clearly attested in the epigraphy of Hieradoumia.

[9] οἰκέται are attested as co-commemorators of the deceased in another epitaph from Gordos,
TAM V 1, 702 (AD 37: οἱ συγγενεῖς καὶ οἰκέται); compare also *SEG* 40, 1044 (Gordos, AD 70:

and Euphemos, who describe Petraeites as their 'friend' (*philos*); a woman called Apphion, who describes Petraeites as her *synteknos* ('co-parent', probably indicating that she is the natural mother of Petraeites' *threptos*)[10]; and Onesimos, Petraeites' *threptos*. Finally, there are listed two groups of unnamed individuals, Petraeites' neighbours (*geitones*), who describe him as their *synepo(i)kianos* ('co-resident on the *epoikion*'), and a group of unspecified relatives (*syngeneis*).[11] To all appearances, Petraeites was a freedman residing on a substantial private estate (*epoikion*) at or near Gordos, owned by a Roman citizen family of Claudii.[12] In this distinctive social context, Petraeites' co-residents on the estate seem to have been sentimentally assimilated to his kin and foster-kin: his co-freedman, former owner, friends, and free or unfree neighbours on the *epoikion*.

Moving further up the social hierarchy, there is abundant evidence for the importance (at least for men) of social ties deriving from membership of small-scale cultic associations (*phratrai/phratreiai*, *symbiōseis*, *speirai*, *doumoi*).[13] Numerous familial epitaphs from Hieradoumia include one or more of these associations (or individual members thereof) among the commemorators of the deceased. So, for example, in the remote mountain villages to the west of Gordos, north of Şahankaya, three adult males were

οἱ συγγενεῖς καὶ σύνδουλοι), and *SEG* 49, 1729 (uncertain provenance: οἱ συγγενεῖς καὶ οἱ σύντροφοι καὶ ἡ φαμιλία). If a freedman can call his former master his *kyrios* (*TAM* V 1, 245), I see no reason why a man could not continue to call his freedman his *oiketēs*.

[10] On the meaning of *synteknos*, see Chapter 6, Section 6.4.

[11] The term συνεπο(ι)κιανός seems to be otherwise unattested, but compare *I.Miletupolis* 22 (II/I BC), οἱ κατοικοῦντες ἐν Ὀρνεεῖ… τὸν ἑαυτῶν συνκάτοικον.

[12] The term *epoikion* regularly means 'estate-village' in late Roman Egypt (Banaji 2007, 173–6; Konstantinidis 2015), but the term does not seem otherwise to appear in this sense in Asia Minor, where *epoikion* usually simply means 'building' (e.g. in the customs law of Asia, Cottier et al. 2008: §31, 36, 67, 71; also *I.Mylasa* 204, line 8; *I.Mylasa* 806, line 10). Elsewhere in Roman Asia Minor, privately owned estate-villages are sometimes called *chōria*: cf. e.g. *SEG* 35, 1272 (Lydia, unknown provenance) and *I.Kios* 107, both referring to δεσπόται τοῦ χωρίου (on the term *chōrion*, see further Thonemann 2007, 454–7).

[13] No sharp distinctions can be drawn between these different kinds of association (Petzl 1978a, 754; Naour 1985, 44–5; de Hoz 1999, 98–102; Ricl 2003, 92–3; Malay and Petzl 2017, 186). *TAM* V 1, 536 and 537 (Maionia, both dated to AD 171/2) demonstrate the simultaneous existence of two different cultic associations devoted to Zeus Masphalatenos and Meis Tiamou, one designated ἱερὸς δοῦμος, the other ἱερὰ συνβίωσις καὶ νεωτέρα; for another cultic *symbiōsis*, see *SEG* 35, 1264 (Thermai Theseōs, AD 151/2: [οἱ Ἡρ]ακλεῶται τὸν… συνβι[ωτήν]). At least some *phratrai* were also cultic associations, as shown by *TAM* V 1, 451 (Iaza, AD 28/9), a dedication set up by ἡ νεωτέρα φράτρα τοῦ Ἀσκληπίου; also *SEG* 49, 1623 (Nisyra, 48/7 BC: οἱ σημεαφόροι καὶ φράτορες). In only two cases can we demonstrate that a *phratra* or *symbiōsis* was *not* cultic in character: *TAM* V 3, 1519 (Yeşilova: a *symbiōsis* of carpet fullers); Malay and Petzl 2017, no. 193 (Maionia: a *phratra* of wagonners). In Artemidorus' *Oneirocritica* 4.44 (cf. 5.82), the terms *phratria/symbiōsis* are synonyms; in Hieradoumia, the form *phratr(e)ia* is attested only in *SEG* 35, 1162 (Kollyda).

commemorated by *speirai* along with close kin of the deceased.[14] The term *speira* usually denotes a Dionysiac religious association, and that is certainly also the case here, since in two of the three cases, the *speira* honoured the deceased in his capacity as *narthēkophoros*, 'fennel-stalk-bearer'.[15] In one case, the *speira* honoured the deceased both as *narthēkophoros* and 'village chief' (*prōtokōmētēs*), perhaps indicating that in this remote village (at or near modern Kömürcü), the cultic *speira* and the village community overlapped so much as to be effectively synonymous.[16]

In some cases, adult males were commemorated by more than one such association in company with the deceased's family. In one of the three epitaphs mentioned in the previous paragraph, an adult male was honoured by his family, his *speira,* and his *phratra*; in an epitaph from Iaza, a man was commemorated by his family, his sacred *doumos* (a kin-based cultic association), and his *phratra*.[17] In funerary contexts, such associations usually acted as anonymous collectives, but in a familial epitaph from Saittai, set up by a man's *symbiōsis* along with his family, we find sixteen members of the *symbiōsis* (not counting the deceased) listed by name.[18] In a few instances, tombstones for adult males were erected by specific named *symbiōtai* in company with their immediate and extended families: that is to say, individuals who were presumably *also* friends and neighbours of the deceased could choose to characterize their relationship in terms of shared membership of a *symbiōsis*.[19]

There is reason to think that some of these associations may have been structured by age classes. An epitaph found at Salihli, east of Sardis in the Hermos plain, but probably a *pierre errante* from Hieradoumia, is a tombstone for a man who died in AD 141/2 at the age of 22, erected by fourteen named

---

[14] *TAM* V 1, 806 (Yeğenoba), 817 (Kömürcü, AD 165/6), 822 (Kömürcü, AD 198/9). For the ancient village at Kömürcü, see further Robert 1963, 209–10, 321–2. Cf. also *I.Manisa* 354 (*SGO* I 04/25/04): a Dionysiac *thiasos* commemorates their *archēgos*, along with his family.

[15] Robert, *Hellenica* II, 131–2; cf. *SEG* 41, 1171 (Akmoneia).

[16] *TAM* V 1, 822, with L. and J. Robert, *BE* 1961, 427, and Schuler 1998, 235. For the term πρωτοκωμήτης, see further Kaplan 1992, 198–200. In the propitiatory inscription *SEG* 57, 1186 (Petzl 2019, no. 146: Kollyda, AD 205/6), two brothers appeal for forgiveness from their village (*katoikia*) and the local *hieros doumos*; the appeal seems to have been a single procedure, suggesting significant overlap between the two bodies: Chaniotis 2009a, 133–4.

[17] *speira* and *phratra*: *TAM* V 1, 806 (Yeğenoba). Sacred *doumos* and *phratra*: *TAM* V 1, 470a (Iaza, AD 96/7). On the term *doumos*, see Chapter 1, n.5.

[18] *TAM* V 1, 187 (Saittai, AD 95/6). It is notable that the *synbiōsis* paid for the tombstone: line 13, ἐκ τοῦ ἰδίου. Contrast *SEG* 32, 1230 (Saittai, AD 175/6), where the *synbiōtai* are listed as an anonymous collective after the deceased's family members.

[19] E.g. *TAM* V 1, 102 (Saittai, AD 111/2): wife, sons, and a single named συμβιωτής; *SEG* 41, 1042 (unknown provenance, AD 244/5): foster-father, father, and a single named συνβιωτής.

synhēlikes, 'age-mates'.[20] The 'age-mates' of this text were probably connected to the deceased through a formal association of some kind; at Synaos, just to the north of our region, a certain Trophimos was commemorated by a cultic association who described him as their 'age-mate [and] *phrator*' (συνήλικι… φράτορι).[21] Similarly, it is likely enough that the thirteen or fourteen named *philoi*, 'friends', of a certain Telemachos, who died at Saittai in AD 110/11, were co-members (perhaps an age class) of a formal association such as a *phratra* or *symbiōsis*.[22] Finally, although most of our evidence for these cultic associations pertains to adult males (both deceased and commemorators), at least some such associations also included women: at Kollyda, in AD 161/2, a cult statue of Dionysos was set up by an association dedicated to the cult of the Mother of the Gods, Meis Tiamou and Meis Petraeites, consisting of thirty-two men and twelve women.[23]

Many epitaphs, usually for men, but also for women, list individual 'friends' (*philoi*) of the deceased alongside familial commemorators.[24] In virtually all cases, it seems likely that these 'friends' are not close relatives of the deceased.[25] Many such 'friends' may in fact have been co-members of associations to which the deceased belonged, since both cultic associations and trade guilds often described their deceased members as *philoi*.[26] However, in at least some

---

[20] *I.Manisa* 266 (οἱ συνήλικες). A line missing from the transcription: in the middle of line 8, add Τειμοκράτης Τει|μοκράτου.

[21] *MAMA* X 382 (Yemişli, date uncertain).

[22] *SEG* 35, 1243, with Naour 1985, 44; similarly *TAM* V 1, 639 (Daldis), a tombstone erected by eleven or twelve named men for their *philos*. Cf. also *I.Manisa* 244 (uncertain provenance, AD 96/7), a tombstone erected for a φράτορα by thirteen named men: not necessarily the entire *phratra*, perhaps the deceased's age mates. A φιλόκαισαρ φρατρία near Maionia consisted of exactly fifteen men (Malay and Petzl 2017, no. 197, AD 114/5). See also Drew-Bear and Naour 1990, 1929–31 (*MAMA* XI 110).

[23] *TAM* V 1, 351 (οἱ καταλουστικοὶ Μητρ[ὸς θεῶν] καὶ Μηνὸς Τιαμου καὶ Μηνὸς Πετραείτου). It is notable that the association was devoted to both a female and a male deity; if there were all-female cultic associations devoted to female deities, they do not appear in our evidence. In *TAM* V 1, 434 (Nisyra, AD 194/5), a brother and sister were co-commemorated by a *symbiōsis*: but of course it may only have been the brother who was a member.

[24] E.g. *TAM* V 1, 210 (Tabala, AD 140/1: one *philos* + a man's extended family); *Sardis* II 667 (Bin Tepe, AD 149/50: one *philos* + a man's extended family); *TAM* V 1, 432 (Nisyra, AD 214/5: one *philos* + large extended family and dependents, for an eighteen-year-old man); *TAM* V 1, 710 (Gordos, AD 108/9: two female *philai* + a woman's extended family); *TAM* V 1, 712 (Gordos, AD 109/10: three *philoi* + others, for a freedman: see above); *SEG* 40, 1080 (uncertain provenance, AD 194/5: one *philos* + extended family for a twenty-three-year-old man). Tombstones erected by single friends alone: *TAM* V 1, 127 (Saittai, AD 241/2: Aur. Asklepides for his thirty-year-old *philos* Regillus); *SEG* 27, 785 (uncertain provenance, AD 256/7: Aur. Iulianus for his *philos* Aur. Diophantos); *SEG* 31, 1017 (Saittai: Aur. Alexandros for his *philos* Polychronios).

[25] But note *Sammlung Tatış* 62 (uncertain provenance, AD 120/1): Alexandros commemorates Petronianus, 'his own kinsman and blameless friend', τὸν ἴδιον συγγενῆ καὶ φίλον ἄμεμπτον.

[26] See below, n.37 and n.49.

instances, the term *philos* does seem simply to have denoted a personal friend of the deceased. A particularly nice example is a long epitaph from Nisyra for a ten-year-old boy called Dionysios, who was commemorated by four *philoi*, three male and one female, along with numerous members of his extended family (parents, siblings, uncles and aunts, six household slaves).[27] It is hard not to believe that these four 'friends' were precisely and only that, Dionysios' day-to-day companions. Furthermore, in an epitaph from Iaza for an adult man called Glykon Marcus, the commemorators included Marcus' sacred *doumos* (a kin-based cult association), a priest who describes Marcus as his 'co-*hierodoulos*', two *symbiōtai*, and a man who simply describes Marcus as his *philos*.[28] In light of the precision with which Marcus' associative ties are described elsewhere in this text, it seems reasonable to suppose that this *philos* was simply one of his personal friends.[29] Finally, at Gordos, in AD 263, a slave called Serapis was commemorated by his wife (a free woman), his daughter, his son-in-law, his master, 'and my closest friends (οἱ ἔγγιστοι φίλοι) and all my other relatives'.[30]

Unique in our evidence – so far as I know – is an epitaph from Kula, dated to winter AD 164/5, in which the priestess Onesime is 'honoured' (i.e. commemorated) by 'the gods' (Ὀνησίμην τὴν ἱέρειαν οἱ θεοὶ ἐτείμησαν). I take it that in practical terms the expenses of Onesime's burial and grave-stone were met from the revenues of the sanctuary at which she served, but it is nonetheless startling to find the gods acting alone as commemorators of this woman – did she perhaps have no other close living relatives?[31]

---

[27] *TAM* V 1, 433 (Nisyra, AD 183/4).

[28] *TAM* V 1, 483a (Iaza). I take it that Glykon Marcus had at some point in the past held the status of *hierodoulos* at a local sanctuary (see Chapter 8, Section 8.5) and had developed a friendly relationship with the life-priest of the sanctuary, who could thus describe him as his (sc. former) 'co-sacred slave'; see further J. and L. Robert, *BE* 1978, 435; Pleket 1981, 168–9. In *I.Manisa* 234 (unknown provenance, AD 50/1) a priestess is commemorated by her family and by the '*hieroi*', that is, the *hierodouloi* at the sanctuary over which she presided.

[29] Hieradoumian funerary epigrams frequently refer, in conventional terms, to the deceased's *philoi*: so a seventy-four-year-old man from Saittai was 'trusted by everyone and honoured by his *philoi*' (*TAM* V 1, 136 [*SGO* I 04/12/01]); two other men from Saittai left 'inextinguishable grief for all (their) *philoi*' (*TAM* V 1, 134 [*SGO* I 04/12/08]; *SEG* 34, 1222); and yet another man was 'everyone's *philos*, no-one's enemy' (*SEG* 41, 1043, uncertain provenance).

[30] Robert, *Hellenica* VI, 117–22, no. 48; for the provenance, *SEG* 48, 1440.

[31] *TAM* V 1, 282 (differently interpreted by Ricl 2003, 85); cf. perhaps *SEG* 40, 1077 (a nine-year-old boy, commemorated by his parents, 'honoured' by Apollo). A helpful point of comparison is Iulia daughter of Manios of Saittai, *kleidouchos* and *neōkoros* of Thea Larmene, who 'grew old as a virgin' in service of the goddess, describes the goddess as her 'foster-mother' (τῆς [θρ]εψάσης Λαρμηνῆς) and was eventually interred not in a village cemetery, but on a private field immediately facing the sanctuary: Malay and Petzl 2017, no. 158 (for the correct interpretation of this text, misunderstood by the first editors, see Chapter 10, Section 10.3).

7.2 Trade Guilds at Saittai

A distinctive group of sixty-five Hieradoumian epitaphs (for sixty-four individuals) were set up not by the deceased's kin, but solely by corporate bodies – typically trade guilds – to which the deceased belonged.[32] These 'corporate' epitaphs take exactly the same physical form as other familial tombstones from Hieradoumia (tapered pedimental *stēlai*, usually with a wreath above the inscription, either incised or in low relief) and follow the same basic textual conventions (date, 'honorific' formula with ἐτείμησεν, etc.). However, every element of the standard epitaphic format is, as it were, 'minimized' in this group: the *stēlai* tend to be physically small, the decoration is generally very simple (no examples of reliefs depicting the deceased), and the inscribed text offers only the most bare-bones information about the deceased. Here is a characteristic example, set up by the association of cobblers at Saittai for a certain Apollonides, dated to spring AD 153 (Figure 7.1)[33]:

> ἔτους σλζ΄, μη(νὸς) Ξανδικοῦ
> ι΄. ἡ πλατεῖα τῶν σκυτέ-
> ων ἐτείμησαν Ἀπολλω-
> νίδην β΄, ζήσανταν ἔτη
> 5   μζ΄.

Year 237 [AD 152/3], day 10 of the month Xandikos. The guild of the cobblers honoured Apollonides son of Apollonides, having lived for forty-seven years.

Virtually all surviving epitaphs of this type seem to derive from the immediate vicinity of the city of Saittai: two 'corporate' epitaphs with alleged provenances from towns to the west and south-west of Saittai (Gordos, Satala) are probably *pierres errantes*.[34] Epitaphs of this type are dated by month and year in all but two cases, and the age of the deceased is

---

[32] For earlier, incomplete collections of this material, see Dittmann-Schöne 2001, 194–204 (trade associations only); Harland 2014, 193–6; Uzunoğlu 2019. Sixty-five epitaphs for sixty-four individuals: Dionysios of Saittai received two separate tombstones from different guilds, both dated to 19 Peritios, AD 167/8: *TAM* V 1, 91: ἔτ(ους) σνβ΄, μη(νὸς) Περειτίου θι΄, οἱ περὶ τὸν Διόνυσον [πο]δάριοι Διονύ[σιον Ἐπαφροδείτου…]; *SEG* 33, 1018: ἔτους σνβ΄, μη(νὸς) Περειτίου ιθ΄, Διονύσιον Ἐπαφροδείτου ἐτείμησεν ἡ πλατεῖα ζή(σαντα) ἔτ(η) κε΄. See Thonemann 2017b, 192–4.

[33] *TAM* V 1, 79 (İcikler).

[34] *SEG* 40, 1045 (alleged provenance Gordos); *SEG* 49, 1683 (alleged provenance Satala). But in defence of the latter provenance, note the existence of a trade association very close to Satala, at the modern village of Yeşilova (*TAM* V 3, 1519, a *synbiōsis* of 'carpet-fullers', *psilagnaphoi*).

Figure 7.1 Epitaph of Apollonides, from İcikler. *TAM* V 1, 79.

almost always specified (with only two exceptions).[35] These Saittan 'corporate' epitaphs were erected over a period of a little less than a century, with the earliest text dating to AD 142/3 and the latest to AD 238/9.

Almost all of the individuals commemorated by corporate groups were adult males between the ages of 16 and 75. Four epitaphs for children are known, for a five-year-old girl and for boys aged six, nine, and eleven: these were probably children of members of the corporate groups concerned, rather than very young members of the associations in their own right.[36] The sixty-one indications of age at death in this group of epitaphs are tabulated

---

[35] Undated examples: *SEG* 29, 1200 (erected by οἱ πυθικοί); *SEG* 29, 1201 (erected by οἱ νεανίσκοι οἱ γυμναστικοί for τὸν νεανισκάρχην). Age not given: *TAM* V 1, 287 (probably from Saittai); *Sammlung Tatış* 34 (unknown provenance). The age is missing in *TAM* V 1, 91 and 146 (the stone broken below).

[36] *SEG* 55, 1310: a five-year-old girl, commemorated by a συνβίωσις; *SEG* 48, 1460 and *TAM* V 1, 84: boys of six and nine years old, commemorated by ἡ συνεργασία τῶν λινουργῶν; *SEG* 49, 1683: an eleven-year-old boy, commemorated by ἡ σύνοδος τῶν μουσικῶν. Children of association members: Dittmann-Schöne 2001, 28; Arnaoutoglou 2011, 271 n.46.

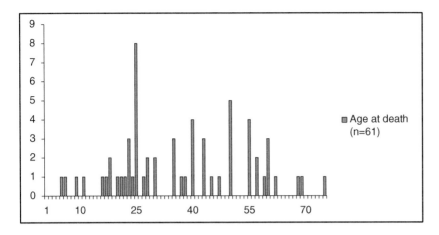

Figure 7.2 Age at death in 'corporate' epitaphs from Saittai (n = 61).

in Figure 7.2. We saw in Chapter 3 that Hieradoumian funerary epigraphy shows a pronounced tendency to 'round off' the age of the deceased to the nearest five years, a trend which becomes particularly prominent for older age groups. As Figure 7.2 indicates, this tendency to age-rounding is equally strong in epitaphs erected by corporate groups.

The majority of these epitaphs (thirty-seven out of sixty-five) were erected by manual trade associations, designated with the terms συνεργασία (21), ὁμότεχνον (6), πλατεῖα ('avenue, street', 6), and σύνοδος (2).[37] These various terms seem to be interchangeable, since we find (e.g.) the guild of linen workers (λινουργοί) designated in different epitaphs as a πλατεῖα, a ὁμότεχνον, and a συνεργασία.[38] There is some reason to think that the terminology of trade associations at Saittai became more standardized over time: all thirteen examples of ὁμότεχνα, πλατεῖαι, and σύνοδοι are of relatively early date (between AD 142/3 and AD 183/4), and συνεργασία is the only term found after AD 183/4 (nineteen of twenty-one examples dating between AD 183/4 and AD 233/4).[39] A total of nine (or perhaps ten) different professions are

---

[37] In one case, an association of wool workers is simply designated οἱ ἐριουργοί (*SEG* 48, 1462 = *SEG* 51, 1683); in another, a λινουργός is commemorated by his φράτορες φίλοι (*SEG* 49, 1673), presumably a way of describing his trade association. One epitaph (*SEG* 33, 1018) was erected simply by ἡ πλατεῖα, not further specified: probably this was a trade association of some kind. On the term πλατεῖα, see Robert 1937, 532–8; Naour 1983, 134; Zimmermann 2002, 34–7; Pont 2013, 130–8; Harland 2014, 159–66 (trade guilds associated with particular streets).

[38] Bakır-Barthel and Müller 1979, 166–7; Dittmann-Schöne 2001, 15–25; Zimmermann 2002, 23–45.

[39] Harland 2014, 195 correctly notes that the guild of cobblers/leather workers (σκυτεῖς) 'tended to identify itself as a "street" association' (πλατεῖα in four of five examples; ἡ σύνοδος

represented: linen workers (λινουργοί, 18 epitaphs), cobblers (σκυτεῖς, 5), wool workers (λανάριοι, 3; ἐριουργοί, 2),[40] fullers (γναφεῖς, 3), felt workers (πιλοποιοί, 1), weavers (ὑφαντεῖς, 1), flax workers (σιππινάριοι, 1), builders (τέκτονες, 1), and smiths (χαλκεῖς, 1).[41]

Most of these trades are connected with textile production. From the late Iron Age onwards, Lydia had been famous for its high-quality dyed textiles of both linen and wool, and it is reasonable to suppose that export-oriented textile production had been a central element of the Hieradoumian economy for many centuries before the Roman imperial period.[42] The extreme specialization of textile production at Saittai, with separate guilds connected with the working of wool and flax, and further dedicated guilds of fullers, weavers, linen workers, and felt workers, is a vivid indication of the central place that textile industries held in the local Saittan economy.[43] Whether or not the middle Hermos valley is 'naturally suited' to the production of textiles raises questions of geographic determinism which I cannot pursue here, but it is at least striking how much of our evidence for large-scale textile production in inland Asia Minor is concentrated in the middle Hermos and middle Maeander valleys – regions which could offer ample upland pasturage for flocks, well-watered valley floors for flax cultivation, perennial rivers for washing and fulling, thermal springs for dye-fixing, and easy connections by road and river to major export centres on the Aegean coast.[44] In the later Ottoman period, the major urban centres of the middle and upper Hermos (Uşak, Kula, Demirci, and Gördes) were all specialized rug-making towns.[45] One might note further the presence of dense forests of Valonia oak (*Quercus macrolepis*) in the middle and upper Hermos regions, whose acorn cups were traditionally used for tanning and

---

τῆσκυτικῆς [sc. πλατείας] in the fifth, *SEG* 29, 1183), but that is probably simply a reflection of the fact that the epitaphs set up by this guild are all early (between AD 147/8 and 173/4), rather than a distinctive form of guild organization.

[40] It is not clear whether the associations of λανάριοι (Latin *lanarii*) and ἐριουργοί were identical: Bakır-Barthel and Müller 1979, 176–8 think not (cf. Zimmermann 2002, 152). The three epitaphs erected by the association of λανάριοι date between 145/6 and 170/1, while the ἐριουργοί first appear in 192/3.

[41] For a comprehensive list of professions attested in Roman Hieradoumia and neighbouring regions, see Petzl 1999, 482–4. Note also the *phratra* of waggoners at nearby Maionia: Malay and Petzl 2017, no. 193.

[42] Greenewalt and Majewski 1980; Dusinberre 2003, 22–3; Roosevelt 2009, 70–1.

[43] Naour 1983, 133; Debord 1985, 355; Zimmermann 2002, 150–4. Large-scale textile exports from western Asia Minor in the Roman imperial period: Pleket 1998; Thonemann 2011a, 185–90; Benda-Weber 2013.

[44] Labarre and Le Dinahet 1996, 56. Against geographic determinism, Thonemann 2011a, 18–19.

[45] Quataert 1993, 134–60.

dyeing; in the early twentieth century, some 60,000 tons of valonia were exported annually from Smyrna.[46]

Of the remaining twenty-eight Saittan epitaphs erected by corporate groups, fourteen were set up by simple 'associations' (συμβιώσεις), not otherwise defined,[47] and three were erected by neighbourhood associations of uncertain type (ἡ γειτονία, ἡ γειτοσύνη).[48] Two epitaphs were set up by the deceased's 'friends' (οἱ φίλοι): most probably this term conceals either a trade association or a cultic *symbiōsis*, since all sorts of corporate groups described their members as 'friends' in their epitaphs.[49] More certainly cultic in character was an association of 'hymn-singers of Artemis', who set up an epitaph for their deceased priest.[50] Two epitaphs were erected by an association of musicians (ἡ σύνοδος/ὁ θίασος τῶν μουσικῶν), and a further two epitaphs by associations of *podarioi*, probably percussionists who accompanied mime performances.[51] Associations of *Chrysanthinoi* and *Pythikoi* are each attested by a single epitaph: the precise character of these associations is not clear, but both are probably also guilds of musicians, or perhaps athletes.[52] Still more mysterious is an association of *Kalokairoi*, associated in some way with 'good season' or 'summer'.[53] Finally, a

---

[46] Robert 1962, 309 n.4; Petzl 1978b, 251. Export from Smyrna: Stamp 1936, 97.

[47] In two cases, οἱ συμβιωταί: *SEG* 29, 1188 (*SEG* 49, 1665) and *SEG* 31, 1016. For *symbiōseis* as religious associations, see further above, n.13; for a trade association calling itself a *symbiōsis*, see *TAM* V 3, 1519 (Yeşilova: a *symbiōsis* of carpet fullers).

[48] On the character of these associations, see Pont 2013, 133–4 (unlikely to be clearly defined urban 'quarters').

[49] *SEG* 31, 1038 and *SEG* 49, 1735 (οἱ φίλοι τὸν φίλον); cf. *TAM* V 1, 287, ἡ συνβίωσις τὸν ἑαυτῶν φίλον; *SEG* 29, 1188 (*SEG* 49, 1665), οἱ συνβιωταὶ τὸν ἑαυτῶν φίλον; *SEG* 29, 1195, ἡ συνεργασία τῶν πιλοποιῶν τὸν φίλον; *SEG* 49, 1673, λινουργῷ φράτορες φίλοι; *TAM* V 1, 93, Χρυσάνθινοι οἱ φίλοι τὸν φίλον. For φίλος as 'member of association', see Herrmann 1962, 17 n.58; Bakır-Barthel and Müller 1979, 172. In western Lydia, cf. *TAM* V 2, 1087 (Thyateira), ἄνδρα φιλόφιλον (clearly erected by an association of some kind). For the adjective *philosymbiōtēs*, see Robert, *OMS* IV, 338 (also *Hellenica* XIII, 41 n.3, on the term *philophilos*).

[50] Οἱ ὑμνῳδοὶ τῆς Ἀρτέμιδος: Malay and Petzl 2017, no. 115; *Sammlung Tatış* 34 (correcting the reading of the date in line 2).

[51] μουσικοί: *SEG* 49, 1683 (for an eleven-year-old); *SEG* 55, 1311. Ποδάριοι: *TAM* V 1, 91 (οἱ περὶ τὸν Διόνυσον [πο]δάριοι); *TAM* V 1, 92 (ἡ σύνοδος τῶν νέων ποδαρίων). See Herrmann 1962, 16–17 (especially good on the designation νέοι); *BE* 1963, 234; Petzl 2005, 29–30.

[52] Χρυσάνθινοι: *TAM* V 1, 93 (cf. *TAM* V 3, 1524, for a *synodos* of [Χρυσά]νθινοι at Philadelphia); presumably associated with the *Chrysanthina* contest at Sardis: Herrmann 1962, 17; *BE* 1963, 234; Robert, *OMS* VI, 163–4. Πυθικοί: *SEG* 29, 1200, with Bakır-Barthel and Müller 1979, 178–80; cf. also *SEG* 35, 1236, in which a συνβίωσις commemorates a παράδοξος Πυθικὸς παγκρατιαστής.

[53] ἡ συνβίωσις τῶν Καλοκαίρων: Malay and Petzl 2017, no. 189 (from Karakoca, south of the Hermos, so perhaps not on Saittan territory); the same association seems to be attested in an inscription from Yeşilova, near Satala (*TAM* V 3, 1520: see Malay and Petzl 2017, p.187). The character of this association is wholly uncertain.

gymnastic association of young men commemorated their *neaniskarchēs* with an epitaph of 'corporate' type.[54]

The epitaphs set up by trade associations and other corporate groups almost certainly reflect the existence of co-operative burial-clubs at Saittai.[55] Burial-clubs connected with trade associations are attested elsewhere in Roman Asia Minor, notably in the (very laconic) regulations of a burial-club of flax workers at Smyrna.[56] Poorer men at Saittai, who were not confident that their family would be able to afford a funerary *stēlē*, subscribed to a burial-club linked to their trade association or other voluntary association, in order to be certain that they would receive proper burial.[57] Unlike elsewhere in the Roman world, it appears that members of these Saittan burial-clubs were not buried in collective tombs (such as the *columbaria* of the city of Rome), but were interred individually in good Hieradoumian fashion, each with their own distinct quasi-honorific grave *stēlē*. This of course would nicely account for both the extreme homogeneity of these corporate epitaphs and their generally 'minimalist' character (see above). We have at present no way of knowing whether there were specific grave-plots reserved for members of particular guilds at Saittai.[58]

There is a fascinating piece of evidence for Hieradoumian associations acting as burial-clubs in the *Oneirocritica* of Artemidorus, a native (at least on his mother's side) of Daldis in western Hieradoumia. In the fifth book of his *Oneirocritica*, Artemidorus recounts the following, purportedly real-life dream:

> A man dreamt that his *symbiōtai* and *phratores* suddenly presented themselves and said, 'Invite us round to your house and give us dinner', and he said, 'I don't have the money or the means to entertain you', and sent them away. On the next day he met with shipwreck, came into extreme danger, and barely escaped with his life. This outcome of his dream made sense and had its own logic. It is the custom for *symbiōtai* of those who have died to visit their homes and dine there, with the reception said to be hosted by the dead man, as a mark of the honour (τιμή) shown by his *symbiōtai* to the deceased. It made sense that he saved his life because he

---

[54] *SEG* 29, 1201: οἱ νεανίσκοι οἱ γυμναστικοὶ ... τὸν νεανισκάρχην.

[55] van Nijf 1997, 31–69; on Saittai in particular, Dittmann-Schöne 2001, 83–5.

[56] *I.Smyrna* 218; Dittmann-Schöne 2001, 164.

[57] The assumption that the decision to be buried by a trade association rather than one's kin was primarily determined by financial means is questioned by van Nijf 1997, 32–3; but see further below.

[58] Of the thirty-three epitaphs set up by associations whose provenance is known with certainty, twenty-five derive from the village of İçikler, immediately to the north of the urban centre of Saittai; the remaining eight stones derive from Uluköy (2), Encekler (2), Çayköy (2), Durasan (1), and Üşümüş (1).

did not stand them the reception. Their insistence and expectation of the reception signified the danger he was in: but it made sense that by his refusal he dispelled the danger. The shipwreck was signified by the lack of money which caused him to send his fellows away.

It is highly tempting to connect this passage with the specifically Hiera-doumian usage of the verb τειμᾶν (ἐτείμησεν/ἐτείμησαν) on funerary *stēlai*, including on those erected by *symbiōseis* and other corporate groups for their deceased members.[59]

There is some evidence that those Saittans who subscribed to burial-clubs were typically men of relatively modest means. Three of the men commemo-rated by the association of linen workers bore metronyms (Trophimos son of Apphia, Stratoneikos son of Eutychis, Stephanos son of Poleitike), probably implying that they were the children of free women and unfree men.[60] At least some members of these associations were of unfree status: a man commemo-rated by the Saittan association of builders was the slave of a wealthy Roman citizen (L. Octavius Pollio, probably from an Italian immigrant family), and a Saittan *synbiōsis* set up an epitaph for the steward (οἰκονόμος) of a Roman woman called Marcia.[61] Conversely, not all craftsmen at Saittai were depend-ent on burial-clubs for their funerary commemoration. In AD 201, a smith by the name of Kosmos was commemorated with a typical Hieradoumian 'familial' epitaph, set up by his wife, children, and brother.[62] There is no good reason to doubt that Kosmos belonged to the *synergasia* of smiths at Saittai. But unlike most Saittan craftsmen, he seems to have been a man of sufficient private wealth not to need to subscribe to the smiths' burial-club, and trusted in his wife and family to commemorate him appropriately.[63]

The size of Saittan associations seems to have varied widely.[64] In a Sait-tan epitaph dated to AD 96 (well before the main run of Saittan 'corporate'

[59] Artemidorus, *Oneirocritica* 5.82 (trans. Hammond 2020, adapted); Thonemann 2020, 120. The relevance of this passage for the corporate epitaphs of Saittai was first noted by Buresch 1898, 55; cf. Herrmann 1962, 14; Robert, *OMS* IV, 338.

[60] *SEG* 31, 1026; *SEG* 32, 1234; *SEG* 55, 1299. Many of the men commemorated by associations at Saittai are designated by their given name alone, without either parent's name. For metronymy indicating disparity between legal status of father and mother (rather than illegitimacy), see e.g. Tataki 1993; J. Price 2002.

[61] Slave of L. Octavius Pollio: *SEG* 29, 1186, with Bakır-Barthel and Müller 1979, 167–71; cf. *TAM* V 1, 85 (a freedman of the Octavii, commemorated by the association of *lanarii*). On the origins of the Octavii of Saittai, Thonemann 2017b, 190–2. *Oikonomos* of Marcia: *TAM* V 1, 88. See further Dittmann-Schöne 2001, 31–4; Zimmermann 2002, 93–100.

[62] *SEG* 48, 1463 (Κόσμον τὸν χαλκέα); cf. *SEG* 49, 1669 (AD 208/9), for the *synergasia* of smiths at Saittai.

[63] See also *SEG* 45, 1640 (probably from Saittai, AD 234/5), for the 'familial' epitaph of a certain Artemidoros, with a relief depiction of a smith at work.

[64] Dittmann-Schöne 2001, 29–30.

epitaphs), a certain Tryphon was commemorated by his *synbiōsis* along with his immediate family: sixteen *synbiōtai*, probably the entire membership of the association, are listed by name.[65] Similarly, in a Saittan epitaph dated to AD 111, one Telemachos was commemorated by fourteen named *philoi*, probably co-members of an association of some kind.[66] However, the Saittan guild of linen workers was evidently much larger than this, since in the stadium of Saittai, the whole of the front seven rows of one *cuneus* were reserved for linen workers, organized in their own *phylē* (see further below).[67]

We know relatively little of the functions of these various Saittan corporate groups outside the funerary sphere. At Thyateira, in western Lydia, we have some twenty honorific monuments erected by manual trade associations for their benefactors, mostly members of the local civic elite, but no such honorific texts are known from Saittai.[68] More positively, at a small village near Satala, in the far south-west of the territory of Saittai, we hear of a *synbiōsis* of carpet fullers (*psilagnaphoi*) building a *stoa* and *exedra* from their own funds, indicating that Saittan trade associations could – at least in remote parts of the city's territory – take on some of the functions normally performed by individual members of the civic elite.[69] It is likely enough that trade guilds at Saittai also performed cultic activities together: at nearby Maionia, we find a *phratra* of waggoners erecting an altar to Thea Andene and Meis Tiamou.[70]

Furthermore, as just noted, we do know that the members of at least one trade association, that of the linen workers (*linourgoi*), were organized in their own civic tribe (*phylē*) at Saittai. The organization of trade guilds into *phylai* is also attested at nearby Philadelphia, where we have evidence for *hierai phylai* of wool workers and cobblers.[71] The tribes attested at Saittai

---

[65] *TAM* V 1, 187.

[66] *SEG* 35, 1243 (not necessarily the entire membership of the association). Elsewhere in Hieradoumia, cf. e.g. *TAM* V 1, 537 (Maionia, AD 171/2), a ἱερὰ συνβίωσις (18 men); *SEG* 49, 1623 (Nisyra, 48/7 BC), οἱ σημεαφόροι καὶ φράτορες (27 men); *SEG* 35, 1162 (Kollyda), a *phratreia* (*c.* 8 men); *TAM* V 1, 351 (Kollyda, AD 161/2), οἱ καταλουστικοί of the Mother of the Gods, Meis Tiamou and Meis Petraeites (32 men, 12 women). See further n.22 above.

[67] Kolb 1990, 115–18 (*SEG* 40, 1063, nos. 36–40); van Nijf 1997, 232–4; Dittmann-Schöne 2001, 23–5, 76–9, 198–9; Zimmermann 2002, 39.

[68] Zimmermann 2002, 105–9; Arnaoutoglou 2011, 265–70.

[69] *TAM* V 3, 1519 (Yeşilova). Petzl attributes the inscriptions of Yeşilova to Philadelphia, but the village may instead have been on the territory of nearby Satala (itself a dependent *dēmos* of Saittai): note the very similar epitaphic formulae of *TAM* V 3, 1894 (Yeşilova) and *TAM* V 1, 604 (Satala).

[70] Malay and Petzl 2017, no. 193 (ἡ τῶν ἀμαξέων φράτρα).

[71] *TAM* V 3, 1490 (ἡ ἱερὰ φυλὴ τῶν ἐριουργῶν); 1491 (ἡ ἱερὰ φυλὴ τῶν σκυτέων); 1492 (ἡ φυλ[ὴ τῶν σκυ]τέων).

fall into three very different categories, those named after gods and heroes in the normal Greek civic manner (Asklepias, Apollonias, Dionysias, Herakleis), those made up of the inhabitants of outlying villages (the *Tamasaitēnoi* and *Satalēnoi*), and this anomalous tribe of the linen workers.[72] It seems likely enough that the *phylē* of the *linourgoi* was a later addition to an original group of 'normal' civic tribes at Saittai, part of a broader phenomenon of symbolic '*ordo*-making' in the cities of western Asia Minor during the Roman imperial period, whereby trade associations and other corporate groups took on the titulature (and some of the functions) of formal sub-divisions of the civic body.[73] We have no way of knowing whether other Saittan trade guilds were also organized as tribes, although the sheer number of epitaphs set up by the linen workers (eighteen, more than three times as many as the next 'largest' guild) suggests that theirs may have been by some distance the largest trade association at Saittai.

Private associations in the Greco-Roman world have sometimes been conceived as an institutional 'third space', situated between the individual and his/her immediate kin group on the one hand and the *polis* (or village, tribe, etc.) on the other.[74] The cultic and trade associations of Saittai seem to fit this model rather neatly. In the funerary sphere, Saittan associations acted as surrogate families in commemorating their deceased members: the tombstones that they commissioned took precisely the same physical form as Hieradoumian familial tombstones and employed identical textual conventions for commemorating the deceased. On these tombstones, the concepts of 'friendship' and 'co-membership of an association' were conceptually blurred; one's *synergastai* or *symbiōtai* could also be designated simply as one's *philoi*. At the same time, at least some Saittan associations were formally recognized as official subdivisions of the Saittan *polis*: the guild of linen workers formed a civic tribe at Saittai in their own right, and the same may have been true of other trade associations. We have already seen that there may have been a similar blurring of 'private' associations and 'political' institutions at the level of the Hieradoumian village: at Kömürcü, west of Gordos, the cultic *speira* and the village community seem to have been effectively indistinguishable one from the other (see Section 7.1).

---

[72] Kolb 1990 (*SEG* 40, 1063, with *SEG* 54, 1224). For the tribe Apollonias, see also *SEG* 57, 1208.
[73] van Nijf 1997, 20, 184–5 (*phylē* as 'a "title" adopted by professional associations in a bid for some form of political recognition'); also van Nijf 1997, 163–4 (cf. Tran 2006, 335), on '*ordo*-making' in Roman Asia Minor. For an analogous instance of 'titular appropriation' among trade associations, see *I.Milet* (VI 2) 939 (late second century AD): τὸ οἰκουμενικὸν καὶ σεμνότατον συνέδριον τῶν λινουργῶν (modelled on the titulature of athletic guilds).
[74] Kloppenborg 2016, referring to Rohde 2012.

7.3 Public Honour, Private Virtues

A final form of group membership reflected in the commemorative practices of Hieradoumia is that which derives from individuals' association with a larger political community, a *polis* or *dēmos* ('Gordos', 'Maionia', 'Saittai', etc.). As we saw in Chapter 2, Section 2.4, many epitaphs from the middle and upper Hermos valley take the form of hybrid public/private monuments, in which the deceased is commemorated ('honoured') both by his or her relatives and by his or her local community (which may or may not possess the formal status of a *polis*). Epitaphs of this kind are particularly common in the late republican and Julio-Claudian periods, and mostly derive from the western part of Hieradoumia, with a particular concentration of examples coming from the ancient towns of Gordos and Loros, the former located at modern Gördes in the upper Kum Çayı valley, the latter probably situated at or near Eğrit/Korubaşı, 15 km downstream of Gördes.[75]

Most of these hybrid public/private epitaphs tell us nothing about the precise character of the public honours for the deceased aside from the bare fact of their existence. So in an epitaph from Gordos, dating to spring AD 58, a certain Servilius was honoured by 'the *dēmos* of the Saittenoi and Publius Nonnius, for his wife's brother; Athes and Antiochis, for their brother', and so on, with a total of fourteen named relatives listed alongside the *dēmos* of Saittai.[76] Here, as is usual, the role of the *dēmos* in proceedings is left completely unclear: although the city or village seems almost always to have been named *before* the list of the deceased's relatives, as here, we have no way of telling what the *dēmos* actually contributed to the commemoration of the deceased.[77]

---

[75] The *dēmos* of Loros (for the name, Petzl 2018) passed six *post mortem* honorific decrees, four of them in conjunction with neighbouring *poleis*, between 45 BC and AD 37: *TAM* V 1, 775 (45 BC); *SEG* 57, 1176 (AD 5); *TAM* V 1, 702 (AD 37, with Iulia Gordos, quoted in Chapter 2, Section 2.4); *AE* 2012, 1478 (early first century AD, with Iulia Gordos); *TAM* V 1, 703 (uncertain date, with Iulia Gordos); *TAM* V 2, 1095 (uncertain date, with Thyateira). Most probably Loros was an autonomous *dēmos* without *polis*-status (Schuler 1998, 41–5); it may (but need not) have been linked to Gordos and/or Thyateira in a *sympoliteia* through some of this period. Loros seems to have been granted *polis*-status by Vespasian (*I.Ephesos* 13, I 7–8, Λορηναῖοι οἱ νῦν λεγόμενοι Φλαουιοπολεῖται): see *TAM* V 1, p.255. On the important new text *Sammlung Tatış* 37 (a corporate συγγένεια at Loros, 56/55 BC), see Chapter 10, Section 10.4.

[76] *TAM* V 1, 705 (photograph in Chapter 2, Figure 2.10). It is not clear why the *dēmos* of Saittai should have been named on a tombstone set up at Gordos. The earliest firm evidence for Saittai possessing *polis*-status dates to the reign of Hadrian (*RPC* III 2543–2544, with *RPC* online 2543A–B, 2544A–D), and it is possible that in AD 58 the Saittenoi were still in some way administratively dependent on the *polis* of Gordos.

[77] Other such 'minimal' examples, with bare mention of a *dēmos* at the head of a list of relatives: *TAM* V 1, 702 (AD 37: ὁ δῆμος ὁ Ἰουλιέων Γορδηνῶν καὶ ὁ Λορηνῶν δῆμος; similarly *TAM* V 1, 703, date unknown); *TAM* V 1, 704 (AD 76: ὁ δῆμος ὁ Ἰουλιέων Γορδηνῶν); *TAM* V 1, 604

Some hybrid public/private epitaphs give us a little more detail: a verse epitaph from an unknown city in the region informs us that the 'whole *polis*' participated at the funeral of a three-year-old boy, and we are sometimes told that the local *dēmos* has honoured the deceased with a golden wreath.[78] We are occasionally given some brief indication of the reasons why the individual had public honours conferred upon him/her: for instance, the tombstone of a certain Kleon of Gordos, dating to AD 12/13, records that 'the *dēmos* honoured Kleon son of Metrodoros for the sake of all his virtue', before moving on to a list of the family members who joined in commemorating their kinsman.[79]

There is no reason to doubt that these laconic indications of public honours are in fact based upon much longer *post mortem* honorific decrees passed by the political communities concerned. Such decrees were sometimes inscribed and erected at the deceased's tomb, as in the case of a fragmentary *post mortem* decree from Silandos, which concludes with the words: 'and let this decree be inscribed also on (the honorand's) future tomb on (a *stēlē* of) white marble, so that the recognition paid by the *dēmos* to its benefactors might be easy for all to see'.[80] In other instances, the full text of the posthumous honorific decree is incorporated into the epitaph proper, as in an epitaph from Iulia Gordos for a certain Attalos son of Menandros (Figure 7.3).[81] This epitaph begins as if it were a standard

---

(Satala, AD 156/7: ὁ δῆμος); *TAM* V 1, 626 (Daldis, AD 190: ἡ βουλὴ καὶ ὁ δῆμος); *TAM* V 1, 434 (*SGO* I 04/20/01, Nisyra, AD 194/5: ἡ πατρίς); *TAM* V 2, 1095 (*SGO* I 04/05/06, date unknown: ὁ δῆμος ὁ Λορηνῶν καὶ ὁ Θυατειρηνῶν); *TAM* V 1, 810 (Dağdereköy, date unknown: ὁ δῆμος); *SEG* 49, 1602 (territory of Maionia, date unknown: ὁ δῆμος); *TAM* V 2, 1062 and 1064 (Akçaalan, territory of Thyateira, date unknown: ὁ δῆμος).

[78] Public funeral: *Sammlung Tatış* 36, πᾶσα πόλις δὲ θανόντα προπέμψατο. Gold wreaths: *TAM* V 1, 775 (Loros, 45 BC: [ὁ δῆμο]ς στεφανοῖ... χρυσῶι στεφάνωι); *SEG* 57, 1176 (AD 5: ὁ δῆμος ὁ Λορηνῶν χρυσῷ στεφάνῳ); *TAM* V 3, 1894 (*SGO* I 04/24/12, Yeşilova, uncertain date: ὁ δῆμος ἐτείμησεν... χρυσῷ στεφάνῳ); a longer list of honours before the register of kin in *SEG* 57, 1157 (Gölmarmara, AD 8 or 62: ὁ δῆμος ἐτείμησεν ... χρυσῷ στεφάνῳ, κτλ.: see further below).

[79] *TAM* V 1, 701: ὁ δῆμος ἐτείμησεν Κλέωνα Μενάνδρο[υ] ἀρετῆς ἕνεκε πάσης. Compare e.g. *SEG* 40, 1098 (Axiotta, AD 80): the *katoikia* of the Axiottenoi, along with her husband and parents, honour a woman 'for the sake of her virtue and goodwill towards her husband <and> her incomparable devotion'; *I.Manisa* 51 (Çömlekçi, uncertain date): three villages honour Zosime, 'for the sake of her character and her household-management'. In *TAM* V 1, 743 (*SGO* I 04/10/05: second century AD), a young civic official of Gordos is honoured by his *patris* in his capacity as *oikonomos* of the *polis* and the *boulē*.

[80] *TAM* V 1, 48 (perhaps first century BC): [ἀ]ναγράψαι δὲ τόδε τὸ ψήφισμα καὶ [ἐπὶ τ]οῦ ἐσομένου μνημείου ἐν λίθωι λευκῶ[ι], κτλ.

[81] Ricl and Malay 2012, 80–6, no. 2 (*SEG* 62, 918). A very similar format is found in an earlier epitaph-*cum*-decree for another member of the same family, Ricl and Malay 2012, 73–80, no. 1 (*SEG* 62, 917: discussed further below), which also includes a two-line verse epigram inserted between the 'familial' epitaph and the civic decree. For similar examples from Kollyda and Iaza, see *TAM* V 1, 421 and 468b (*SGO* I 04/19/01).

Figure 7.3 Posthumous honours for Attalos son of Menandros at Gordos. *SEG* 62, 918, Fragment A (Manisa Museum).

Hieradoumian 'familial' tombstone, with the date of death (winter AD 69/70) and a list of relatives who joined in honouring the deceased. Six and a half lines in, the genre of the inscription changes abruptly: the next fifty lines consist of a verbatim quotation of a posthumous honorific decree of the city of Gordos, before the inscription returns to the original funerary genre for its final three lines, with a conventional curse formula against desecrators of the tomb.[82]

> (A) Year 154 [AD 69/70], Day 8 of the month Peritios. Tatias honoured Attalos her son, Kleon (honoured) his brother, Apphias her husband, Tatias her (5) father, Apphias her husband's brother, Galates his *syntrophos*. Proposed by the *stratēgoi* Demainetos son of Kleon, Apollonios son of Artemidoros, (10) Papias son of Apollonios, on the motion of Platon son of Agemachos, secretary of the *dēmos*: resolved by the *boulē* and the *dēmos* of the Ioulieis Gordenoi (15) and the Romans in business there. Since Attalos son of Menandros – a high-minded man, of the greatest nobility (inherited) from his father and his ancestors, a *dekaprōtos*, having fulfilled every (20) civic office and liturgy, as *agoranomos*, *stratēgos*, and *stephanēphoros*… [some clauses missing] (B) … in a manner useful to the *dēmos*, having set up a fine example of virtue and glory, being most eagerly (5) disposed towards his fellow-citizens, most sympathetic towards his relatives, and most perfectly disposed towards his brother Kleon, himself a *dekaprōtos* and a most honourable (10) representative of the *dēmos* in all its needs, and (displaying) what is worthy of the highest praise of all, sympathy towards his household – since he has now departed from life, through the work of the *daimōn* who tramples everything beneath his feet, (15) leaving the greatest grief and sympathy for his brother, mother, wife and daughter – and since it is fitting that those who have lived with such virtue and glory (20) towards their homeland should, first, receive praise for all their actions while still living, and receive appropriate care after their death, for this reason be it now resolved that the bath-houses and workshops should be closed (25) for his funeral, and that Attalos should be honoured with a gilded painted portrait, with a gold portrait and with a [marble] statue, and that he should be accompanied in his funeral procession by his homeland, and that this decree should be read out at his funeral (30) as a consolation for his household: 'The *dēmos* of the Ioulieis Gordenoi honoured Attalos son of Menandros, for the sake of his merit and his consummate virtue', and that this decree (35) should be inscribed on his tomb. If anyone wrongs this *stēlē* or inters another (here), let him not find favour with the goddess Thesmophoros.

---

[82] The north choir aisle of York Minster contains the memorial of Lora Burton Dawnay, Viscountess Downe (1740–1812). After listing her immediate relatives ('widow of John Dawnay … only child and heir of William Burton', etc.), the memorial shifts into quotation: 'For her character and other particulars, see the Gentleman's Magazine for May MDCCCXII, from which the following is an extract: A real, unpretending, and almost unconscious, good sense, and a firm desire to act right, on all occasions, to the best of her judgment, were her most distinguishing characteristics' – and so on in the same vein. I owe my knowledge of this wonderful monument to Noel Malcolm.

The decree 'embedded' in Attalos' epitaph belongs to a genre which is fairly widely attested in Roman Asia Minor, that of the so-called 'consolatory decree' (*psēphisma paramythētikon*), which confers posthumous honours on a deceased individual by way of consolation to his or her family.[83] The present decree describes Attalos' private and public virtues at length, and stipulates that the entire decree (or perhaps a one-line summary: the text is not entirely clear) is to be read out at Attalos' public funeral, 'as a consolation for his household (*oikeioi*)'. The text concludes with the provision that the decree should be inscribed on Attalos' tomb – which is, of course, the reason why this particular decree happens to survive at all. We might note that the decree includes, towards the end, a highly abbreviated 'honorific formula', summarizing in a single sentence the honours conferred on Attalos by the *dēmos* of Gordos: 'The *dēmos* of the Ioulieis Gordenoi honoured Attalos son of Menandros, for the sake of his merit and his consummate virtue'. No doubt many of the laconic summaries of public honours that appear on the familial tombstones of the middle and upper Hermos valley are in fact quotations of abbreviated 'honorific formulae' of this kind, drawn from lost *post mortem* consolatory decrees.[84]

The posthumous honours conferred on deceased men and women seem to have taken highly standardized forms throughout Hieradoumia. At Charakipolis, in 10 BC, a deceased woman called Tatia was honoured with a gold wreath, a bronze portrait, another life-size painted portrait, and a marble statue; exactly the same package of honours was conferred on a deceased general called Mogetes at Iaza, perhaps around 130 BC, and on a man named Stratonikos at Kollyda (uncertain date).[85] At Gordos, in the first century AD, deceased members of the civic elite were regularly honoured with a painted portrait, a gold portrait, and a marble statue (four examples, with minor variants)[86]; at Gölmarmara, in the early imperial

[83] Strubbe 1998, 59–75.

[84] E.g. *TAM* V 1, 688 (early first century AD), lines 20–21: ἐπιγραφὴν γεν[έσ]θαι ὅτι ὁ δῆ[μος τειμᾷ] Στρατ[ονίκην ἀρετῆ]ς ἕνεκ[εν πάσης], exactly the same wording as appears (without the accompanying decree) in *TAM* V 1, 701. Cf. also *SEG* 62, 917, lines 36–39.

[85] Charakipolis: *TAM* V 1, 678 (10/9 BC [*sic*; 9/8 BC *TAM*], not explicitly funerary); for this woman's family, see Chapter 5, Section 5.4. Iaza: *TAM* V 1, 468b (*SGO* I 04/19/01: perhaps an ancestor of the honorand of *SEG* 57, 1198 [Maionia, 16 BC]). Kollyda: *TAM* V 1, 374 (not explicitly funerary: marble column, probably the base of one of the honorand's portraits). For the adjective *teleios* = 'life-sized', Ma 2013a, 250.

[86] *TAM* V 1, 688 (early first century AD): painted portrait, marble statue; *SEG* 62, 917 (early first century AD): gold wreath, marble statue, painted portrait; *TAM* V 1, 687 (AD 76): painted portrait, gold portrait, marble statue; *SEG* 62, 918 (AD 69/70): gilded painted portrait, gold portrait, marble statue.

period (either AD 8 or AD 62), a young man was honoured posthumously with a gold wreath, a painted portrait in a gilt shield, and a marble statue.[87] At Gordos, we have three examples of members of the local elite being honoured with a public funeral: the city's bathhouses (*balaneia*) and workshops (*ergastēria*) were closed, the entire *polis* accompanied the funerary procession, and the posthumous decree in the deceased's honour was read out, by way of encouragement to other civic worthies.[88]

For our purposes, what is particularly remarkable about the *post mortem* honorific decree of the city of Gordos for the deceased Attalos is the consistent interweaving of Attalos' public and private virtues. Attalos, like his brother Kleon, served as an elected magistrate of the city of Gordos (*dekaprōtos, agoranomos, stratēgos,* and *stephanēphoros*) and was duly recognized by his fellow citizens in his capacity as civic benefactor. But the city's posthumous honours for him also encompassed his sentimental disposition towards his relatives, his brother in particular; the highest praise of all is reserved for Attalos' 'sympathy towards his household' (ἡ πρὸς τοὺς οἰκείους συνπαθία).[89] The decree for Attalos systematically conflates his private comportment towards his immediate and extended kinship group with his public conduct during his political career.

Similar ethical conflation between civic office holding and behaviour towards one's relatives is found in other extant *post mortem* honorific decrees from Gordos. In the early first century AD, the city conferred posthumous honours on Attalos' grandfather, also called Attalos (Figure 7.4).[90] The decree begins by praising his 'most manly and most trustworthy service' (ἀνδρηότατα καὶ πιστότατα ὑπηρετήσας) in his conduct of the various magistracies entrusted to him; in particular, during his tenure of office as *stratēgos*, 'when for many years the city's tax-register had been in disorder, he applied himself enthusiastically to the task, and through his careful oversight he set the register straight and returned it to the *dēmos*'. In the very next clause, we shift abruptly to the elder Attalos' attitude towards

---

[87] *SEG* 57, 1157.

[88] *TAM* V 1, 687, lines 20–25; *AE* 2012, 1478, lines 31–2; *AE* 2012, 1479, lines b23–35 (the fullest description). On public funerals, see further Herrmann 1995, 195–7; C. P. Jones 1999.

[89] Unless it is simply a matter of elegant variation, the decree seems to distinguish between Attalos' 'relatives' (*syngeneis*: B6) and his wider 'household' (*oikeioi*: B13, B31). This distinction is not found elsewhere in Hieradoumian epitaphs: for the term *oikeios* in Hieradoumia, see above, n.8.

[90] *SEG* 62, 917. *TAM* V 1, 688 is a *post mortem* honorific decree for Attalos' wife Stratonike, who is also praised specifically for her friendly attitude (φιλανθρωπότατα διατεθεῖσα) towards her daughter and son-in-law.

Figure 7.4 Posthumous honours for Attalos son of Dionysios at Gordos. *SEG* 62, 917 (Manisa Museum).

his children and grandchildren: 'he was a loving parent (φιλοτέκνως διακείμενος) to his daughter, sympathetic (συνπαθῶς) towards his son-in-law, and affectionately disposed (φιλοστοργία χρησάμενος) towards his daughter's children, living a life of devotion and loyalty (σπουδαῖον καὶ πιστὸν... βίον) towards his family (συνγενεῖς)'. Attalos' 'trustworthiness' in public life was matched by his 'life of loyalty' to his close kin group: in Greek, the two qualities are indicated with the same adjective, *pistos*.[91]

Likewise, in a *post mortem* honorific decree for a man called Theophilos son of Thyneites (late summer AD 76), the focus of the decree repeatedly shifts back and forth between Theophilos' household and the *polis* of Gordos as a whole.[92] 'Since Theophilos son of Thyneites, a man of the greatest nobility (inherited) from his ancestors, has shown all goodwill towards his homeland, has lived the life of a good household-manager (οἰκοδεσπότην ζήσας βίον), and has provided many benefits to his homeland through his tenure of the civic offices of *stratēgos* and *agoranomos* and his embassies to Rome, to Germany and to the Emperor, and since he was pleasant (προσαινής, i.e. προσηνής) towards his fellow citizens and sympathetic (συνπαθής) towards his wife, let it now be resolved to honour Theophilos, etc.' Perhaps the most startling element here is the praise of Theophilos for his exemplary household management, *oikodesposynē*: this classic private virtue is otherwise almost exclusively attributed to women, in both epitaphs and honorific inscriptions.[93]

7.4 An Imagined Social Order

The fact that extended kinship groups were responsible for the bulk of funerary commemoration in Roman Hieradoumia does not in itself tell us much about wider social structures in the region. At all places and times – with a few notable exceptions – the commemoration of the dead is a family affair.[94] In this chapter, we have seen that persons and groups outside the family were in fact (by comparison with other parts of the ancient world) strikingly *prominent* in Hieradoumian funerary epigraphy: there is no sign of this kind of 'commemorative participation' by friends, neighbours, cult associations, or trade guilds in the voluminous and discursive epitaphic

---

[91] For the quality of *pistotēs* in Greek inscriptions, see Robert, *OMS* II, 1060; *Hellenica* XIII, 36, 42.

[92] *TAM* V 1, 687.

[93] *oikodesposynē* as a female virtue in Roman Hieradoumia: *TAM* V 1, 688 (Gordos: posthumous honours for Stratonike, a καινὸν ὑπογραμμὸν οἰκοδεσποσύνης); *I.Manisa* 51 (Çömlekçi: posthumous honours for Zosime, ἐθῶν ἕνεκε καὶ οἰκοδεσποσύνης); *SEG* 48, 1428 (= *SEG* 51, 1684), a woman honoured for her ὑπερβάλλουσα οἰκοδεσποσύνη. See further Robert 1936, 110–11; Robert, *Hellenica* XIII, 34–5; *BE* 1974, 575. Another man is praised for his *oikodesposynē* in *SEG* 52, 1201 (Savaştepe, Mysia).

[94] The public commemoration of war-dead in fifth-century Athens and some neighbouring cities is a notable exception: e.g. Low 2003; Ferrario 2014, 25–52.

record from, say, Roman Lykia. Nonetheless, to reiterate a point made already (Chapter 4, Section 4.13), the fact that commemorative 'habits' in this region look different from practices elsewhere does not strictly prove that there was anything distinctive about the underlying dynamics of Hieradoumian society. But the choice of these particular commemorative habits does clearly mean *something*.

The funerary epigraphy of Roman Hieradoumia offers us a picture – a very partial picture – of an imagined social order. This social order is based first and foremost on highly complex and integrated extended kin groups; secondarily on small associative groups based on cult practice, residence, and profession (the cult association, neighbourhood, trade guild); and, to all appearances, only a very distant third on membership of a particular *polis*-community. But that picture may well be an illusion, generated by our exclusive focus thus far on epitaphic evidence. We would not, after all, necessarily expect a tombstone to tell us anything very much about the deceased's relationship to his or her native city. The question, then, is whether the unusually 'thick' social ties which seem to have existed within and between extended families, villages, cult associations, and trade guilds in Roman Hieradoumia might in fact have gone hand-in-hand with an unusually 'thin' or underdeveloped set of political institutions. In other words: did kinship networks, small cultic groups, and village communities in fact serve as a functional *alternative* to the *polis* in this region? Can we usefully conceive of Roman Hieradoumia as a 'kin-ordered society' rather than a '*polis*-ordered society'? This problem will be addressed head-on in the final chapter (Chapter 10). First, though, we should turn to look at our other chief category of evidence for the social structure of Roman Hieradoumia: the propitiatory inscriptions.

8 | Rural Sanctuaries

8.1 Gods, Villages, Village-Gods

As we saw in Chapter 7 – and as I will argue in more detail in Chapter 10 – the urban centres of Roman Hieradoumia (Saittai, Maionia, Daldis and others) were of relatively limited importance in structuring social life in the region. In no field of communal life is this as vividly clear as in that of the religious institutions of Roman Hieradoumia. Interactions between humans and gods in Hieradoumia typically took place not in towns but in the countryside, mediated through dozens of small rural sanctuaries scattered across the cultivated and wild landscape. Throughout the region – or at least in its eastern half (Chapter 2, Section 2.7) – these rural sanctuaries served as major sites of monumental self-representation by Hieradoumian families, cult associations, and village communities, both through the kinds of votive and dedicatory practices familiar from other parts of the Greco-Roman world, and through the locally distinctive medium of the inscribed propitiation-*stēlē*.

Very many of the gods of rural Hieradoumia were closely associated with particular village communities.[1] This emerges most vividly through the use of village 'ethnics' as cultic epithets or *epiklēseis*, a phenomenon which is certainly not unique to Hieradoumia, but which is notably widespread in this region: Meis Axiottēnos at Axiotta, Meter Tazēnē and the Theoi Tazēnoi at Taza, the Theoi Pereudēnoi at Pereudos, Apollo Nisyreitēs at Nisyra, the Theoi Neakōmētai at Nea Kome, and others.[2] In the dedicatory and propitiatory inscriptions of the region, these gods are often described as 'ruling as kings over' (βασιλεύοντες) or 'possessing' (κατέχοντες) the

---

[1] As we will see later on, several of these rural cults were also closely associated with particular descent groups: Chapter 10, Section 10.4.

[2] Axiotta: Ricl 2016; Malay and Petzl 2017, 135–6 (near Mağazadamları). Taza: Malay and Petzl 2017, 175–6 (Kavaklı). Pereudos: Malay and Petzl 2017, no. 186, with commentary (near Encekler). Nisyra: *TAM* V 1, pp. 132–6 (Saraçlar). Nea Kome: Petzl 1994, nos. 47 and 48; Petzl 2019, 16 (territory of Silandos?). In all of these cases, both village and deity are independently attested; there are many more examples where the existence of the village is inferred from the god's 'ethnic'. See de Hoz 1999, 39–41, 45–7, 50–2, 57–8.

villages from which they take their name. In the case of Meis Artemidorou Axiottenos, the god's 'rule' is known to have extended over several further villages in the vicinity of the god's chief sanctuary at Axiotta, including the villages of Tarsi, Perkon, Koresa, and Dorou Kome.[3] The notion of divine 'rule' is sometimes embedded in the god's cultic *epiklēsis*: in several texts from Hieradoumia, the god Meis carries the epithet *Tyrannos*, 'tyrant', and the deity Zeus Masphalatenos, worshipped at Maionia, is once described as the 'lord tyrant (*kyrios tyrannos*) Zeus Masphalatenos'.[4]

This vocabulary of 'possession', 'kingship', and 'tyranny' should not be taken too literally as a description of the relationship between god and village. there is no reason to think that the gods of rural Hieradoumia or their earthly representatives exercised any formal coercive authority over 'their' village communities.[5] Still, the underlying conception of gods as local 'kings' or 'tyrants' should not be dismissed as a mere *façon de parler*. As we will see, the gods of rural Hieradoumia were demonstrably recognized as having some traditional rights over the land and labour of 'their' villagers. There are also some striking indications in the propitiatory inscriptions of Hieradoumia that the gods could be conceptually assimilated to the secular ruling power, namely Rome. The 'council of the gods' is once described with the Latin loan-word *synatos*, and twice with the term *synklētos*, the standard Greek term for the Roman senate; structures within the sanctuary complexes seem sometimes to have taken their names from Roman public buildings (a 'basilica' and a 'praetorium').[6] Although the idea that the sanctuaries exercised formal 'temple justice' within the communities of rural Hieradoumia has long been exploded, the propitiation inscriptions

---

[3] Mitchell 1993, I 191; Petzl 1994, 64; Belayche 2005; Schuler 2012, 80–8, with Appendix III (95). For the various villages 'ruled' by Meis Artemidorou Axiottenos, Ricl 2016, 164.

[4] Meis Tyrannos in Hieradoumia: *TAM* V 1, 255 (Petzl 1994, no. 53: Kula); *TAM* V 1, 350 (Kollyda); *TAM* V 1, 536 (Maionia); Schwertheim 1975 (*BE* 1976, 628: uncertain provenance). Zeus Masphalatenos: *TAM* V 1, 537 (Maionia). The cult of Meis Tyrannos is attested in other parts of the Greek world (Pergamon, Athens, Thasos: Kielau 2016, 321–2), possibly as an 'export' from its original home in Hieradoumia; a putative Lydian origin for the Greek term *tyrannos* remains plausible but unproven (Högemann and Oettinger 2018, 47–51).

[5] In the wider Greek world, *polis*-deities are often conceived as 'possessing' or 'holding' (though not 'ruling as kings over') their *polis*: Schuler 2012, 80–8. The only Hieradoumian instance of deities 'possessing' a *polis* is *SEG* 57, 1187 (Petzl 2019, no. 144: 'Great Mother Anaeitis and Meis Tiamou and Meis Ouranios who possess Kollyda').

[6] *Synatos/synklētos*: Petzl 1994, no. 5, line 22 (Zeus or Meis is petitioned ὑπὸ τοῦ συνκλήτου); Petzl 2019, no. 165 (request for clemency from μεγάλην συνᾶτος καὶ σύνκλητον τῶν θεῶν); Potts 2019, 253. Basilica: Petzl 2019, no. 145. Praetorium: Petzl 1994, no. 5, lines 9–10 (surely a building within the sanctuary). Thus already Chaniotis 2009a, 143 ('assimilating the sacred buildings … with the secular buildings of Roman administration').

are suffused with the technical language of Roman court practice, and the gods are sometimes described in terms reminiscent of Roman judicial authorities (Meis Axiottenos is once described as an 'inescapable judge in heaven').[7]

The chief aim of this chapter is to draw out some of the structural tensions between the human communities of Hieradoumia and these rural sanctuaries, tensions which were strongly concentrated around land (Sections 8.3–8.4) and labour (Section 8.5).[8] The propitiatory inscriptions also inform us about structural tensions *within* those human communities, a separate topic which will be treated in Chapter 9.

8.2 Sacred Space in Roman Hieradoumia

Much remains uncertain about the physical appearance of rural sanctuaries in Roman Hieradoumia and their role within the settled landscape. It is not even clear whether Hieradoumian rural sanctuaries were typically situated within village settlements, or if they were usually located in the deep countryside, although the evidence does seem to point strongly to the latter. Two propitiatory inscriptions describe people 'going up' (ἀναβαίνειν, ἀνελθεῖν) to a sanctuary; one of these texts comes from the Hieradoumian sanctuary of Apollo Axyreos, securely located on a hillside above the left bank of the Demirci Çayı, between Saraycık and Gökveliler (Map 3) – a site which is indeed located 'above' the nearest ancient settlement, an unnamed

---

[7] Absence of formal 'temple-justice' in Hieradoumia: Chaniotis 1997, with discussion of judicial language, on which see further Harter-Uibopuu 2016 and Potts 2019, 241–74; note Petzl 2019, no. 142, line 9 (χωρὶς δόλου πονηροῦ = *sine dolo malo*). 'Inescapable judge in heaven': Petzl 2019, no. 137 (κριτὴς ἀλάθητος ἐν οὐρανῷ), with Chaniotis 2009a, 132–3. Everyday experiences of the Roman state in rural Anatolia were heavily dominated by the courts and penal system: Thonemann 2020, 202–5.

[8] The sanctuaries of rural Hieradoumia, like all sanctuaries in the Greco-Roman world, had a set of 'entry-regulations' enforcing ritual purity on worshippers. The only surviving set of 'entry-rules' from the region is *TAM* V 1, 530 (*CGRN* 211: Maionia, 147/6 BC); note also Malay and Petzl 2017, no. 1 (Thyateira, second century BC), with Parker 2018, and *TAM* V 3, 1539 (*CGRN* 191: Philadelphia, late Hellenistic). Many propitiatory *stēlai* record the punishments of persons who transgressed these purity rules, usually without further specification: e.g. Petzl 1994, nos. 6, 19 (entering 'one day too early'), 110, 112, 115, 116; Petzl 2019, no. 144. Sometimes the specific details of ritual impurity are given: e.g. entering the sanctuary while unwashed (Petzl 1994, no. 36), wearing dirty clothes (Petzl 1994, nos. 43 and 55), menstruating (Petzl 2019, no. 135), or (perhaps) without having observed sexual abstinence for the required number of days (Petzl 2019, no. 161). As these texts amply demonstrate, the 'entry-rules' of Hieradoumian rural sanctuaries show no meaningful local peculiarities compared with sanctuaries elsewhere.

katoikia lying some way to the north of the sanctuary, downhill and closer to the river.[9]

The sanctuary of Apollo Axyreos is one of several small rural sanctuaries in Hieradoumia whose precise locations have been fixed in recent years, although the physical relation between the sanctuary and the nearest settlement is seldom known with certainty. These include a sanctuary of Artemis Anaeitis and Meis Tiamou, 2 km to the east of the modern village of Esenyazı, in the southern Katakekaumene; a sanctuary of Meis Artemidorou Axiottenos, in the far north of the Katakekaumene, on the left bank of the Hermos near modern Mağazadamları; a sanctuary of Meter Tazene and Meis Petraeites near Kavaklı, further to the east near the confluence of the Hermos and the Selendi Çayı; and a remote hilltop sanctuary of Thea Larmene on the right bank of the Hermos, high above the confluence of the Hermos and the İlke Çayı on the peak of Yeşiloba Tepe (all marked on Map 3).[10] All of these sanctuary sites have produced abundant quantities of small inscribed *stēlai* and votive reliefs – at the sanctuary of Artemis Anaeitis and Meis Tiamou near Esenyazı, almost a hundred more or less fragmentary dedications and propitiatory *stēlai*, as well as (very unusually) a scrap of an inscribed hymn. Most of the sanctuaries have produced fragments of marble statuary (sometimes apparently statues of the gods themselves, sometimes of eagles or lions) and sacred 'furniture', particularly cylindrical or rectangular altars.

The best known of these Hieradoumian rural cult places is the hilltop sanctuary of Thea Larmene on Yeşiloba Tepe, partially excavated in 1995 by a team from Ege Üniversitesi in İzmir (Figure 8.1). This sanctuary must certainly have been situated at some distance from the nearest village settlement. The excavators identified four discrete structures within the sanctuary complex: a small temple building (*c.* 15–16m × 8.80m)

---

[9] 'Going up': Petzl 1994, no. 43 (Kula: ἀναβεβηκένε με ἐπὶ τὸν χōρον); Petzl 2019, no. 135 (sanctuary of Apollo Axyreos: ἀνελθεῖν ... ἐπὶ τὸν θεόν); I assume that the prepositional prefix is to be taken literally. For the location of the sanctuary of Apollo Axyreos, Malay and Petzl 2017, 129. It is unclear whether there was a village settlement closely associated with the hilltop sanctuary of Apollo Lairbenos, as perhaps implied by Petzl 1994, no. 112. The sanctuary of Apollo Lairbenos has been excavated, but not fully published: for a recent overview with good photographs, Scardozzi 2020, 265–75; the only site plans known to me are those published in *MAMA* IV, pp. 98–9.

[10] Malay and Petzl 2017, 69–70 (Artemis Anaeitis and Meis Tiamou: note that Esenyazı is placed too far to the south on the map); 135–6 (Meis Axiottenos, also Ricl 2016, 152–6); 175–6 (Meter Tazane and Meis Petraeites). On the sanctuary of Thea Larmene, see further below. For other rural sanctuaries in Hieradoumia and neighbouring regions whose approximate location is known, see Ricl 2003, 78 n.3.

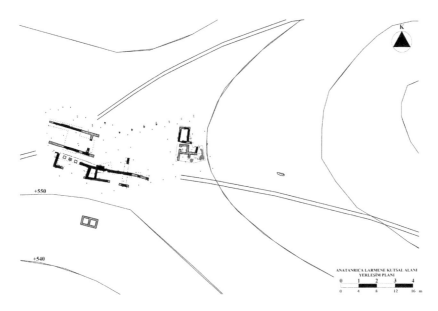

Figure 8.1 The sanctuary of Thea Larmene on Yeşiloba Tepe.

oriented roughly east-west, with a doorway at the east flanked by pro-
jecting antae; immediately to the south of the temple, a stoa-like structure at least 28.50 m in length, with a three-columned portico facing the
south wall of the temple; a small complex of rectilinear buildings some
20 m to the east of the temple, of uncertain function; and the remains
of a modest monumental *propylon* dedicated to the emperor Hadrian
(precise location uncertain), presumably giving access to the sanctuary
from the east.[11] Still further to the east, beside the road leading up the
sanctuary, is a small group of three niches cut directly into the rock
for the erection of *stēlai*, indicating that at least some inscribed monuments were set up outside the sanctuary complex proper; these might
have been tombstones rather than propitiatory or votive monuments,
since we know that at least one deceased sacred official was buried on
private land immediately outside the sanctuary to the east.[12]

---

[11] Akat 2009, 60–5 (temple), 66–71 (stoa), 72–79 (uncertain group of buildings); overall site plan,
   Levha 5 (an updated version of which is reproduced here, with corrections kindly provided
   by Sevgiset Akat Özenir, Figure 8.1); brief summary in Malay and Petzl 2017, 155–6. For the
   inscribed *propylon* architrave, Malay and Petzl 2017, no. 163 (AD 130/1). The complex of
   buildings to the east of the temple may have served as a residence for permanent sanctuary
   personnel, who included a female 'key-bearer and temple-warden' who served for life: Malay
   and Petzl 2017, no. 158.
[12] Akat 2009, 80–1. Burial of sacred officials on private land next to the sanctuary: Malay and
   Petzl 2017, no. 158 (misinterpreted by the first editors; see below, Chapter 10, Section 10.3).

Visualizing a little rural sanctuary like that of Thea Larmene requires something of an effort of imagination. The most vivid ancient description of a sanctuary of this kind appears in a delightful inscription discovered at İzmir in the late nineteenth century, now in the Epigraphical Museum in Athens, which gives a remarkably detailed 'tour' of a small rural sanctuary of the god Helios Apollo Kisauloddenos, probably located on the hill of Çaldağı in the lower Hermos valley, west of Sardis (Map 1):[13]

> Apollonios Sparos, son of Metrodoros, father of the deceased priest of Helios Apollo Kisauloddenos, Apollonios son of Apollonios Sparos, (5) dedicated to the god and the city the things constructed by him (i.e. his son), having received by decree (the right to) inscribe a list of them on a *stēle*. And they are as follows: The god himself, on a marble podium (*bēma*), and the table (*trapeza*) which stands next to the god, made of Lesbian stone, (10) which has sculpted griffin-feet; and in front of the table, a marble side-board (*abakēon*), for the use of those offering sacrifice; and a rectangular incense-burner (*thymiatērion*) made of Teian stone, with a burner (*peripyron*) made of iron; and a marble cult-statue (*agalma*) of Artemis (15) on a mill-stone base adjacent to it, and a cult-statue of Meis on a marble base, and a multi-coloured rectangular table, and a marble altar which has on it the eagle of Zeus; and a wooden shrine (*naos*) with a tiled roof, fitted with doors and a lock, (20) in which there are set up cult-statues of Pluto Helios and Kore Selene on a podium, dressed in robes, holding a wooden curtain-box (*pastēon*) in the shape of a shrine and a linen curtain; and by each of the entrance-ways an altar of Phocaean marble, and a gilded and upholstered (25) couch for the collection (?) and procession of the gods; and ground-floor rooms and a stoa constructed on top of them with a tiled roof, to serve as a residence for the sacred slaves (*hierodouloi*) and the worshippers of the god; and (30) the enclosure wall of the sanctuary, and the paving of the square with chips of marble, where the sanctuary was flat and on level ground; and eight iron weapons (*hopla*) lying next to the god, by way of decoration.

This sanctuary evidently had no real temple. It consisted of a walled sacred enclosure (*temenos*) with two entrances, each with an altar standing next to it. Within the enclosure, there may have been no stone buildings at all: the only free-standing structures mentioned in the text are a little wooden shrine with lockable doors and a tiled roof (probably very small, no more

[13] *I.Smyrna* 753. For the likelihood that this text is a *pierre errante* from Çaldağı, see Malay and Petzl 2017, 47–9. The identity of the 'city' mentioned in the inscription is uncertain (perhaps Hyrkanis). There is no room here to tackle all the glorious details of the text – note that in line 24 I take κλεῖν to be an idiosyncratic form of κλίνη, 'couch', rather than κλείς, 'key' (I do not see how one could upholster a key).

than a few metres square), and a set of single-storey rooms with a portico in front and a tiled roof, these too perhaps made of wood (picture something like a row of beach-huts). This building – apparently the largest roofed structure in the entire sanctuary complex – served as a kind of 'hostel' for the sacred slaves (*hierodouloi*) and worshippers wishing to stay overnight at the sanctuary; it is overwhelmingly likely that the stoa-like structure at the sanctuary of Thea Larmene (also the largest building on the site) was intended to perform a similar function.[14]

The 'god himself' – that is to say, the main cult statue of Apollo – stood in the open air, on a broad marble *bēma* or 'podium'. We should probably imagine this podium as being something significantly more substantial than a mere statue base, to judge from a propitiatory inscription from a Hieradoumian rural sanctuary of the god Meis Labanas, dated to winter AD 191/2 (Figure 8.2):[15]

> To Meis Labanas. Elpis belittled Meis Labanas and although she was unwashed, went up to his podium (*bēma*) (5) and explored the podium and his tablets (*tablai*). When the god demanded atonement, her heirs gave this in return, praising him. (10) Year 276 [AD 191/2], month Peritios. And to Meis Axiottenos – 'she has defiled my podium' – we give this in return, praising him.

The clear implication is that the god's 'podium' was something you could step up onto and explore (although this was probably not encouraged), and that it was cluttered with small votive *stēlai* and other dedications.[16]

Returning to the sanctuary of Apollo Kisauloddenos, the cult statue of Apollo was surrounded by various items of sacred 'furniture' (tables, incense burners, an altar) for the performance of sacrifices and other offerings, many of them made from different kinds of colourful stone: yellow

---

[14] On these *hierodouloi*, see Section 8.5.

[15] *SEG* 35, 1157 (Petzl 1994, no. 36): Μηνὶ Λαβανα· ἡ Ἐλπὶς | κατευτελίσασα Μῆνα | Λαβανα ἀκατάλουστος | οὖσα ἐπὶ τὸ βῆμά του ἀ|(5)νέβη καὶ ἠρεύνησεν τὸ | βῆμα καὶ τὰς τάβλας αὐ|τοῦ· ἐπιζητήσαντος τοῦ | θεοῦ οἱ κληρονόμοι εὐ|λογοῦντες ἀπέδωκαν. |(10) ἔτους σος΄, μη(νὸς) Περειτίου. | καὶ Μηνεὶ Ἀξειτηνῷ· | καταιμόλυνέ μου τὸ βῆμα· | εὐλογοῦτες ἀποδείδο|μεν. Note the enclitic possessive pronoun in line 4 (τὸ βῆμά του), as in modern Greek. The final three lines are inscribed in a different hand; Elpis' heirs evidently decided at some subsequent date that it was worth propitiating Meis Axiottenos as well as Meis Labanas (both of whom presumably had cult statues on the podium). Note the incised crescent moon above the text, widely used on Hieradoumian propitiation-*stēlai* as visual shorthand for Meis (see also Figures 8.3, 8.6, and 8.7).

[16] One of the more melancholy propitiation inscriptions records how a child (*paidion*) called Metrodoros inadvertently (ἀκουσίως) broke a small *stēlē* dedicated to the goddess, no doubt while exploring the *bēma* when he wasn't supposed to; the goddess demanded that he replace it (*TAM* V 1, 596; Petzl 1994, no. 78). For similar cases, see *TAM* V 1, 362, with Petzl 1994, IX (an anonymous person breaks a *pinakidion*); *TAM* V 1, 239 (an ox breaks a *stēllarion*).

Figure 8.2 Propitiatory *stēlē* of Elpis. *SEG* 35, 1157 (İzmir Museum).

Lesbian marble, black-and-red variegated Teian *africano*, Phocaean volcanic tufa. Nearby, and still in the open air, there stood further cult statues (presumably smaller ones) of two other deities, Artemis and Meis. The presence of multiple gods in this single sanctuary nicely accounts for the disconcerting way in which many of the Hieradoumian confession texts switch back and forth between addressing many gods and a single god: so worshippers will often acknowledge the power of all the gods worshipped in the sanctuary, before focusing down on the particular deity that they believe to be responsible for their punishment.[17] At the sanctuary of Apollo Kisauloddenos, there are also cult statues of two further deities, Pluto Helios ('sun') and Kore Selene ('moon'), locked away in a small wooden shrine. These two underworld deities pretty clearly 'correspond' to two of the heavenly deities worshipped in the sanctuary (Helios Apollo; the

---

[17] E.g. *TAM* V 1, 460 (Petzl 1994, no. 57): Trophime is punished by Meis Axiottenos alone; she addresses her request for forgiveness to Meter Tarsene, Apollo Tarsios, and Meis Axiottenos. See also de Hoz 1999, 81–6.

moon-god Meis), but it is fruitless to speculate when and why worshippers at this sanctuary might address themselves to the 'underworld' sun-god rather than the 'heavenly' sun-god.

We know very little about the character and frequency of human gatherings at these rural sanctuaries. A propitiatory inscription from a sanctuary of Meis Motylleites near Kollyda refers to a 'festival (*heortē*) of Meis Motylleites'; as we saw in Chapter 3, there is good reason to think that Meis Axiottenos may have had regular 'sacred days' on the twelfth day of the month, and it is possible that Day 18 and Day 30 of the month had particular significance in the cult of Zeus from the Twin Oaks on the territory of Saittai.[18] Some of these festivals seem to have involved the entire population of particular villages, to judge from another propitiation-*stēlē* from the sanctuary of Meis Motylleites, in which two brothers ask forgiveness both from the gods and from 'the village and the sacred *doumos*', who I take to have been present *en masse* at the sanctuary for the occasion.[19] No doubt these mass gatherings were often the occasion for public feasts, which could be laid on at the expense of priestly personnel: an inscription from a rural sanctuary of Zeus Targyenos in the Kaystros valley (some way to the south of Hieradoumia) describes how a newly appointed priestess of 'Hera and Zeus and all the gods' organized a one-day festival named 'Kaisarion' (i.e. a festival in honour of the emperor) at which 'she gave distributions of bread and wine to the village (*katoikia*) and to all those living nearby (*periplēsioi*), making the expenditure for this from her own dowry'.[20] We have some evidence for drinking parties (*oinoposia*) being held in sanctuaries, at least putatively in honour of the god.[21]

---

[18] Meis Motylleites: *SEG* 57, 1185 (Petzl 2019, no. 145): Μηνὸς Μοτυλλείτου ἱορτῆς γενομένης. 'Sacred days': Chapter 3, Section 3.3.

[19] *SEG* 57, 1186 (Petzl 2019, no. 146), with Chaniotis 2009a, 134.

[20] *SEG* 57, 1193 (Dibektaşı Mevkii, near Koloe, AD 259/60), lines 7–14: ἐποί|ησε μίαν ἡμέραν Καισ|άριον· ἡρτοδότησε καὶ |(10) ἐξεστοδότησεν τὴν | κατοικίαν καὶ τοῖς περι|πλήσι πᾶσι ποιήσασα τ|ὴν δαπάνην ἐκ τῆς ἰδία|ς προικός. On the sacred personnel attached to Hieradoumian rural sanctuaries, see Ricl 2003, 81–7; Section 8.5, and Chapter 10, Section 10.4.

[21] Petzl 1994, no. 1: Μείδων Μενάνδρου κρατῆρα | ἐποίει ἐπὶ τοῦ Διὸς τοῦ Τρωσου, 'Meidon son of Menadros did a mixing-bowl (*kratēr*) at the sanctuary of Zeus Trosou' – an odd but intuitive way of phrasing it, since the large mixing-vessel called a *krater* would typically only have been used at a gathering where several people were drinking together. An inscription from Mossyna in western Phrygia lists sixteen men who contributed small sums of money towards the making of a new cult statue and altar to Zeus Mossyneus, one of whom also paid for a 'wine-drinking' (*oinoposion*), probably a drinking party associated with the unveiling of the new statue (*MAMA* IV 265). See also Malay and Petzl 2017, no. 23 (Yeşilova in the Kogamos valley): a ritual *kratēr*, 55 cm in height and 76 cm in diameter, with an inscription on the rim bearing the name of a priest of the goddess Hekate, in whose sanctuary it must originally have stood.

Despite their physical isolation from village settlements, the sanctuaries of Roman Hieradoumia were closely integrated into everyday rural life, above all through their substantial agricultural landholdings. The wealthier sanctuaries managed large agricultural portfolios, including arable land, vineyards, sacred groves, and probably livestock as well. Quantifying the scale of these 'sacred lands', and their relative significance in the rural economy compared to peasant smallholdings and large private estates (discussed further in Chapter 10, Section 10.2), is quite impossible. All we can really say is that they were large enough to create significant social tensions, in cases when the gods' interests ran up against the interests of smallholders and the landless (see further below).

We have absolutely no reason to think that these sacred estates had existed since time immemorial.[22] On the contrary, we can see the property holdings of Hieradoumian rural deities being built up piecemeal, a field here and a vineyard there, through a patchwork of small 'voluntary' lifetime or testamentary gifts from worshippers – although, as we will see in a moment, the average Hieradoumian farmer might well have raised an eyebrow or two at the word 'voluntary'. The gods also engaged in some rather shadier forms of land acquisition. When a man or woman had been struck down with sickness for some minor sin and was seeking to soothe the god's anger, the god usually demanded no more than a public confession of guilt and the dedication of an inscribed *stēlē*. But in a few cases, I fear, the gods were only mollified on condition that the sinner hand over a particularly fruitful vineyard of theirs to the local sanctuary. We will shortly look at one particular group of gods – the *Theoi Pereudenoi*, at the village of Pereudos – who seem to have been especially shameless in exploiting the rituals of confession and propitiation to extort land from local smallholders.[23]

Some of the god's land was certainly worked directly by *hierodouloi* ('sacred slaves') attached to the sanctuary, whose status will be discussed later in this chapter (Section 8.5). Other plots – probably those located further away from the sanctuary – were put out on lease to local farmers.

---

[22] E.g. Ricl 2003, 81: 'As socio-economic organizations of great antiquity and conservatism, village shrines presumably preserved a structure based on that prevalent in Anatolia before Alexander ... they also "inherited" from their ancestors many obligations introduced in an earlier age, when a sanctuary's patrimony included both the lands in its possession and the people settled on them'. This seems to me quite wrong: see Schuler 2012, 67, 83–4, and Chapter 1, Section 1.3.

[23] For the 'Gods in Pereudos', see Herrmann and Varinlioğlu 1984 (*SEG* 34, 1210–1220). The location of Pereudos is not fixed with certainty, but seems to have been somewhere on or near the Encekler plateau, on the right bank of the Hermos west of the Selendi Çayı (Malay and Petzl 2017, 176, 181 n.151). For the ancient site at Encekler, see Naour 1983, 127–32.

This stands to reason, since the piecemeal accumulation of small plots must have created a very dispersed and incoherent pattern of sacred holdings. The clearest evidence for the leasing of sacred land in rural Hieradoumia is found in a propitiatory inscription dated to late summer AD 133[24]:

> Year 217 [AD 132/3], in the month Hyperberetaios. Stratonike daughter of Mousaios (5) received as a loan from Eutychis a *modinos* of wheat which was sacred to Axiottenos; she dragged out repayment until today (10), and was punished by the god in her right breast, and she has returned the complete amount along with the interest, having praised Axiottenos.

Eutychis – a woman – evidently holds a plot of arable land on lease from the local sanctuary of the god Meis Axiottenos. Eutychis has lent a small quantity of wheat grain grown on the god's land to her neighbour Stratonike (another woman). There is no indication that Eutychis did anything wrong in loaning the god's grain to her neighbour, or indeed that Stratonike was actually trying to defraud the sanctuary; but the god is a punctilious bookkeeper and expects his loans (and his accumulated interest) to be paid back in full and on time.

Once a field or vineyard had come into the gods' hands, by fair means or foul, it was, at least in theory, inalienable: it could not be 'deconsecrated' and sold in order to raise money for the sanctuary. This emerges from a fascinating and very unusual text from a sanctuary of Meis near Silandos, dated to winter AD 98/9, which is really a kind of hybrid between a propitiatory inscription and a sacred regulation[25]:

> Year 183 [AD 98/9], day 18 of the month Peritios. Meis 'from Attalos' [i.e. whose cult was founded by Attalos], having punished his own people on account of his own possessions, (proclaims) that it not be permissible (5) to anyone either to sell (his landed property) or to give it as security, but it shall be managed by his own people, and he shall receive from his own people as much as he demands. If anyone disobeys these instructions, in the (10) absence of the god's permission, he shall spend from his own property to propitiate him, along with Meis Labanas.

---

[24] *SEG* 39, 1277 (Petzl 1994, no. 63): ἔτους σιζ΄, μηνὸς | Ὑπερβερτα[ί]|ου. | Στρατονείκη Μουσαί|(5)ου δανισαμένη παρὰ | Εὐτυχίδος πυρῶν | μόδινον τῶν ἱερῶν | τοῦ Ἀξιοτηνοῦ καὶ πα|ρελκύσασα μέχρι σήμ|(10)ερον, κολασθεῖσα ὑπὸ | τοῦ θεοῦ κατὰ τοῦ δε|ξιοῦ μαστοῦ τὰ συν|αχθέντα σὺν τόκοις | ἀπέδωκεν εὐλογοῦ|(15)σα τῷ Ἀξιοττηνῷ.

[25] *SEG* 47, 1654 (Petzl 2019, no. 148): ἔτους ρπγ΄, μη(νὸς) Περειτίου | ιη΄. Μεὶς ἐξ Ἀττάλου κολά|σας ⟦ΑΣ⟧ τοὺς ἰδίους περὶ τῶν ἰ|δίων ὑπαρχόντων· ἵνα μηδεν[ὶ] |(5) ἐξὸν εἶναι μήτε πωλεῖν μή|τε ὑποθήκην τίθειν, ἀλλὰ ὑπὸ | τῶν ἰδίων οἰκονομεῖσθαι, καὶ ὅσα | ἐπιζητεῖ ἐκ τῶν ἰδίων γείνεσ|θαι αὐτῷ. ἐὰν δέ τις ἀπειθήσῃ χω|(10)ρὶς τῆς ἐκείνου συνχωρήσεος, | ἐκ τῶν ἰδίων δαπανήσας εἰλάσα|ται αὐτὸν μετὰ Μηνὸς Λαβανα. I largely follow Petzl's interpretation of the text (Petzl 1997, 70–5) in preference to that of Ricl (*SEG* 53, 1358).

It is pretty clear that there is some serious financial mismanagement of the god's property in the background here. The priests had sold a plot of the god's land or had pledged it as security for a loan, and this was promptly followed by some kind of collective disaster among the sanctuary's sacred officials (perhaps an outbreak of disease or suchlike). The priests interpreted this punishment as a 'communication' from the god, indicating the god's desire that his property should be managed in a more restricted way in future – a very rare case in which we can see Greek 'sacred law' emerging through a process of trial and error, as it were. It is striking that the text feels the need to specify that anyone breaching these norms in future will need to propitiate the god 'from his own property', without claiming the cost back from the sanctuary on expenses – one naturally wonders whether the priests might have been using the god's wealth as their own private slush fund.

8.3 The Acquisition of Land

The gods of Hieradoumia built up their estates through a mixture of cash purchases, voluntary gifts, semi-voluntary 'tithes' on inheritances and land sales, and forced expropriations masquerading as propitiations for sins. Of the first, little needs to be said. Some worshippers certainly donated substantial sums of money to the gods for the purchase of real estate, as in the following text from Dorylaion in northern Phrygia, which may in fact represent the initial 'start-up' fund of a new rural sanctuary[26]:

> To Zeus from the Cattle-Fold (*Zeus ex Aulēs*), the god who listens: the heirs of Papas and Gaios, on behalf of (5) Asklepiades, son of Damas, set this up in fulfilment of a vow – having given for the purchase/construction on Asklepiades' behalf of a sacred precinct (*temenos*), to the god (10) and the village, 2,010 Attic drachms, so that they might find the god forgiving.

There can be no doubt that many people gifted plots of land to the gods of their own free will (which is of course not to say that they did it for purely selfless motives). At Philadelphia, for instance, one Salvius dedicated to Meter Anaeitis 'the whole enclosure and the grove and the plants associated with it' – apparently a pre-existing walled garden, ready stocked with plants, which Salvius

---

[26] *SEG* 16, 753 (Petzl 2019, no. 153): Διὶ ἐξ Αὐλῆς ἐ|πηκόῳ θεῷ | οἱ Παπᾶ καὶ Γαΐου | κληρονόμοι ὑπὲρ Ἀσ|(5)κληπιάδου τοῦ Δα|μᾶ υἱοῦ εὐχὴν | τήνδε ἀνέστησαν, | δόντες καὶ τεμένους | ὑπὲρ αὐτοῦ τῷ θεῷ |(10) καὶ τῇ κώμῃ Ἀττικὰς | ͵β καὶ ι΄ | εἵνεκα εἵλωα ἔχιν τὸν | θεόν.

hands over wholesale to the goddess.[27] Likewise, at the village of the Pebaleis near modern Mazlıtepe, a hereditary priest of Zeus Keraunios donated a vineyard and a plot of arable land to the god, in order that the revenues from the land should be spent on sacrifices to Zeus[28]:

> …son of […]ios, the hereditary priest, additionally dedicated for the performance of sacrifice to Zeus Keraunios the vineyard (5) which goes by the name 'at the Watchpost', and the field at the Royal Folds, the one below the ditch which runs from the boundary of the land of the Pebaleis, (10) measuring roughly 20 *plethra*. The rights are to belong to those who will remain together (?).

The field being dedicated to the god is fairly substantial, about two hectares or five acres. It is far from clear who 'those who will remain together' (*symmenountes*) might be – it is possible that this is a periphrastic way of describing the sacred 'community' of *hierodouloi* who would have formed the main workforce on the god's land (see Section 8.5).

People could also leave plots of land to the gods in their wills, as for example in this epitaph from the modern village of Hamidiye, on the left bank of the Hermos near the ancient villages of Dima and Kerbia, dated to summer AD 105[29]:

> Year 189 [AD 104/5], day 3 of the month Loos. Apollophanes honoured his brother Pisides, and his wife Tatia (honoured) her husband. (5) As he ordered in his will: 'May Zeus be kind to my heir: transfer to Zeus as a gift (*dōrea*) the field and vines near Tillo'.

The epitaph includes a short verbatim quotation from Pisides' will, requiring his heir to hand over to Zeus a part of his own landed property, in order to procure the god's continued favour ('may Zeus be kind to my heir'). No doubt many such 'testamentary gifts' were entirely voluntary expressions of piety by the donors: in this particular case, I see no reason to doubt that Pisides freely decided to gift his field and vineyard to Zeus out of the goodness of his heart. But we can be quite certain that not all testamentary

---

[27] *TAM* V 3, 1547 (date uncertain), lines 5–9: τὴν περιοικοδ|ομὴν πᾶσαν κạ[ὶ] | τὸ ἄλσος καὶ τ[ὰ] | πρὸς {ΟΣ} αὐτ[ῷ] | ἔνφυτα πά[ντα].

[28] Malay and Petzl 2017, no. 199: [- -]ιου ὁ διὰ γένους ἱε|ρεὺς προσκαθιέρωσ|εν τῇ θυσίᾳ τῇ τοῦ Κερ|αυνίου Διὸς ἀμπέλο[υ]|(5)ς τὰς ἐπὶ τῇ Σκοπῇ καλο|υμένας [κ]α[ὶ] χώραν τὴν ἐπ[ὶ] | Βασιλικαῖς Μάνδραις, τ[ὴ]|ν ὑπὸ τὴν τάφρον τὴν ἀ|πὸ τοῦ Πηβαλέων περιο|(10)[ρ]ισμοῦ ὡς πλέθρων οὖσ|[α]ν εἴκοσι· ἔστω τὰ δ[ί]|καια τῶν συμμενο[ύ]|ντων.

[29] *SEG* 34, 1207: ἔτους ρπθ´, μη(νὸς) Λώου γ´. ἐτ[ί]|μησε Ἀπολλοφάνης τὸ[ν] | ἀδελφὸν Πισίδην κὲ | ἡ γυ|νὴ τὸν ἑαυτῆς ἄνδρα Τατ[ι]|(5)α· ὡς ἐν τῇ διαθήκη ἐκέλευ|σε· Δία εὐίλατον τῷ κληρο|νόμῳ, | κὲ δωρηὰν χώραν κὲ ἀμπ|έλους τῷ Διεὶ ἀνάφερε τὰ πρ|ὸς Τιλλω.

gifts to sanctuaries were quite as voluntary as this one was. Consider, for instance, the following text from the sanctuary of the 'Gods of Pereudos', probably somewhere on the Encekler plateau in the south-eastern part of the territory of Saittai, dating to autumn AD 198:[30]

> To the Gods of Pereudos, just as they demanded: the inheritance of Gaius Iounites, which his brother Glykon (5) hands over. A field with an oak tree on it, and the (other) trees with it, and the portion (*apomoira*) of the house, to the value of 75 *denarii*. Year 283 [AD 198/9], in the month Dios.

In terms of its genre and purpose, this little text is not easy to classify. It is not a propitiatory inscription: there is no sign that either Gaius Iounites or his heir have committed any sin which needs to be cancelled out. Nor is it really a votive dedication: there is no sign that Gaius Iounites had any intention of leaving a legacy to the Gods of Pereudos in his will. In fact, the thing looks suspiciously like a receipt. After the death of Gaius Iounites – no doubt a significant landowner at Pereudos – the Gods of Pereudos have insisted on receiving a 'tithe' on the dead man's estate. His brother and heir Glykon therefore feels grudgingly compelled to hand over a modest slice of his brother's agricultural land (a field with a few trees) as well as a 'portion' of his house, the latter apparently paid in the form of a cash equivalent. The text inscribed on stone is a bare record of this transaction, in language which makes it all too clear which of the two parties initiated this supposed gift ('just as the gods demanded').

Inheritances were not the only kinds of transactions affected. The Gods of Pereudos also claimed tithes of a similar kind on local property sales, to judge from a second inscribed 'receipt' from the same sanctuary[31]:

> … to Meis Labanas and Meis Petraeites in Pereudos: Ammia, daughter of Zenas of Ankyra, in respect of the house which (5) she bought from Ammia daughter of Kallimachos. I gave 72 *denarii*, just as the gods demanded, which was received by the priests Apollonios son of (10) Apollonios, Antiochos son of Antiochos, Glykon son of Publius.

[30] *SEG* 34, 1211: Θεοῖς Περευδηνοῖς, κα|θότι ἐπεζήτησαν· τὴν | τοῦ Γαΐου Ἰουνείτου κλη|ρονομίαν ἣν ἀποδίδει Γλύ|(5)κων ὁ ἀδελφὸς αὐτοῦ· τό|πον, ἐνόντα δρῦν καὶ τὰ | σὺν αὐτῷ δένδρα καὶ τὴν | ἀπόμοιραν τῆς οἰκίας ὡς | (δηνάρια) οε΄. ἔτους σπγ΄, μη(νὸς) Δείου. For a rather similar case, see *I. Manisa* 65 (Küpüler, AD 96): 'Asklas son of Zosimos left to Zeus Sabazios the inheritance which the heirs of Diodoros handed over' ([Ἀ]σκλᾶς Ζωσίμου κατέλιψε | [Δ]ιὶ Σαβαζίῳ κληρονομίαν | ἥντινα ἀπέδωκαν οἱ Διο|δώρου κληρονόμοι); the relation between Asklas and the heirs of Diodoros is unknown.
[31] *SEG* 34, 1219: [- -]ου Μηνὶ Λαβανᾳ καὶ Μη|νὶ Πετραείτῃ ἐν Περεύ|δῳ· Ἀμμία Ζηνᾶ Ἀνκυρα|νὴ ὑπὲρ τῆς οἰκίας τῆς |(5) ἠγόρασεν παρὰ Ἀμμίας | Καλλιμάχου ἔδωκα (δηνάρια) οβ΄,| καθὼς ἐπεσζήτησαν οἱ | θεοί, ἄτινα παρέλαβαν οἱ | εἱεροὶ Ἀπολλώνιος Ἀπολ|(10)λωνίου, Ἀντίοχος Ἀντιόχου,| Γλύκων Ποπλίου.

Once again, there is no sign that the housebuyer Ammia has any particular emotional investment in this transaction: she is neither atoning for a sin nor fulfilling a vow to the gods. It is just that the gods expect to take a certain percentage on all inheritances or sales of real estate, which for an indivisible property like a house is naturally commuted into a cash lump-sum – here 72 *denarii*, very close to the 75 *denarii* paid over by Glykon as a 'tithe' on the house he inherited from his brother.[32]

We certainly should not think of these 'tithes' to the gods as in any way mandated or enforceable by law. What they reflect, instead, is a conventional expectation that anyone receiving a sufficiently chunky inheritance would *of course* wish to hand over a certain portion of his land (or a cash equivalent) to his local gods. When these 'voluntary' gifts were not paid, the gods would begin with a very firm nudge, as apparently in the case of the inheritance of Glykon; if no gifts were forthcoming, the gods would then pursue the families concerned with vindictive tenacity, until they got what they wanted. The following two propitiatory *stēlai* from the sanctuary at Pereudos seem to reflect a prolonged tussle between the sanctuary and a local family over the payment of conventional dues on two properties, a house and a vineyard at Promiasse[33]:

> Apollonios bears witness to the Gods in Pereudos. When my mother cursed me, I asked the (5) gods, and I gave along with my brother Eupelastos 100 *denarii* for the house purchased from Myrmex, and I gave in return another 50 *denarii* for all the other (10) cut vines in Promiasse by the holm-oak. I asked the gods twice, I had good fortune and (15) I am grateful.

The precise situation here is somewhat obscure, but there has clearly been an acrimonious falling-out of some kind within the family.[34] A mother has cursed her son Apollonios, quite probably over some issue concerning the two properties mentioned here (an inheritance dispute of some kind is likely enough). At any rate, the brothers Apollonios

---

[32] I assume that the 72 *denarii* represents a 'tithe' of the cost of the house, rather than its total value; we have no way of judging how much a house might have cost in rural Hieradoumia. Note that although we have abundant evidence for shared ownership of land, we have (I think) no evidence for shared ownership of houses: compare Davis 1973, 158–9.

[33] *SEG* 34, 1212 (Petzl 1994, no. 17): Ἀπολλώνις θεοῖς τοῖς | ἐν Περεύδῳ μαρτύρειν· | ἐπεί με ἡ μήτηρ ἐπικατη|ράσετο, ἠρώτησα τοὺς |(5) θεοὺς καὶ ἔδωκα μετὰ τοῦ | ἀδελφοῦ Εὐπελάστου ὑ|πὲρ τοῦ στεγνοῦ (δηνάρια) ρ′ τοῦ | ἀγορασθέντος παρὰ Μύρ|μηκος, ὑπὲρ τῶν λυπῶν |(10) πάντων τομαίων ἀνπέλ|λων ἐν Προμιάσσῃ ἐπὶ τῇ | πρείνῳ ἀπέδωκα ἄλλα | δηνάρια ν′. δὶς ἠρώτησα τ|οὺς θεούς· ἐπέτυχα καὶ |(15) εὐχαριστῶ.

[34] For further discussion of intra-familial disputes, see Chapter 9, Section 9.6.

and Eupelastos consulted the gods at Pereudos ('how can we loosen this curse?') and were instructed to hand over to the sanctuary a tithe of 100 *denarii* on a house that they had recently purchased, as well as a smaller tithe of 50 *denarii* on a vineyard at Promiasse. Apollonios did so, and believed himself to have averted the gods' anger ('I had good fortune and I am grateful'). No such luck – shortly afterwards, Apollonios died unexpectedly, as we learn from a second inscription from the same sanctuary (Figure 8.3)[35]:

> The gods demanded the vines left in the will of Hygie daughter of Myrtos at Promiasse, in the place called (5) Lakoi, and the others on the hill-top; Eupelastos and the heirs of Apollonios and Philippikos son of Philippos hand them over, along with the full wine-jars and the rent. Each of (10) us have handed over our apportioned shares of the vines to the gods, because of the punishment indicated above. Year 284, month Daisios.

The gods at Pereudos had long had their eyes on the ill-fated vineyard at Promiasse, and they now see a golden opportunity to get their hands on the whole thing. The ownership of this vineyard was shared jointly between Apollonios, his brother Eupelastos, and a man called Philippikos (perhaps their brother-in-law); the three men had recently inherited it from a woman called Hygie, perhaps the mother of Apollonios and Eupelastos who was mentioned (unnamed) in the earlier inscription. Apollonios has now died, an event which is probably depicted in the relief sculpture at the top of the *stēlē*, showing a man reclining on a couch (the 'punishment indicated above', as the inscription puts it: Figure 8.3). The gods seem to have succeeded in persuading the surviving family members that Apollonios' death was a punishment for his earlier failure to pay his inheritance dues on the vineyard with sufficient promptness or enthusiasm. They therefore proclaim, in effect, that the entire vineyard should now be seen as 'morally forfeit', and demand its consecration to the gods in order to prevent further horrible consequences. The family, now thoroughly spooked, duly hand over the whole vineyard to the sanctuary, along with the full jars containing

---

[35] SEG 34, 1213 (Petzl 1994, no. 18): ἐπεζήτησαν οἱ θεοὶ τᾶς ἀν|πέλους τῆς Ὑγίης Μύρτου | τὰς [[ΑΝ]] ληγάτους ἐν Προμι|άσῃ τόπῳ λεγομένῳ Λά|(5)κοις καὶ ἄλας κορυφῆας· ἀπο|δίδουσιν σὺν ἐνκύθροις καὶ | φόρῳ Εὐπέλαστος καὶ οἱ Ἀ|πολλωνίου κληρονόμοι καὶ ὁ | Φιλιπικὸς Φιλίπου· ἕκαστος αὐ|(10)τῶν τὰ λαχόντα μέρη τῶν ἀν|πέλων παραδεδώκομεν τοῖς | θεοῖς διὰ τῆς προδιιλυυμέ|νης κολάσεως. | ἔτους σπδ΄, μη(νὸς) Δαισίου. See further Chapter 5, Section 5.7, on partitive inheritance. Note the incised crescent moon on the upper left of the *stēlē*, perhaps indicating that Apollonios' death was attributed to the god Meis.

Figure 8.3 Propitiatory *stēlē* of Eupelastos and others. *SEG* 34, 1213 (Uşak Museum).

that year's vintage, and the rent which they had received from the farmer who had been leasing the vineyard from them.

A broadly similar case of land-profiteering by the gods is recorded in a propitiatory inscription from a sanctuary of Meis Axiottenos at the modern village of Kalburcu, on the lower Selendi Çayı, just north of the Hermos[36]:

> To Meis Axiottenos. Since Glykon was punished in respect of his grandfather's lands, which Attalos – treating the god's lands with contempt – kept for his own profit, despising the gods at Nonnos. Glykon (now) hands

---

[36] *SEG* 57, 1222 (Petzl 2019, no. 142): Μηνὶ Ἀξιοττηνῷ· ἐπει|δὴ ὁ Γλύκων ἐκολάσθη ὑ|πὲρ παππικῶν ἐνγαίων, ἅ|τινα Ἄτταλος παρευχερί|(5)σας τὰ τοῦ θεοῦ ἔνγεα ἐν|επορεύσετο ἐξουθενή|σας τοὺς θεοὺς τοὺς ἐν Νον|νου· ἃ παραδίδει Γλύκων τῷ | θεῷ χωρὶς δόλου πονηροῦ |(10) δαπανήσ⟨ας⟩ πυ(ρῶν) κύ(πρους) δ<, οἴνου πρ(όχους) δ<· ἐλαίου κοτύλην συνεβάλε|το Μαρκία Ἀπφίας, τῆς ἀδελ|φῆς μου· ἐγένετο δὲ καὶ ἡ | προάπαρσις ἐξ ἐννεαφώνου, |(15) ἔτους σξε΄, μη(νὸς) Ἀρτεμε[ι]|σίου η΄. The relation between Attalos and Glykon is not explicitly stated: I take Attalos to be Glykon's father, but other interpretations are possible. For the 'nine-voice offering', see below, n.72.

over these lands to the god, without wilful deceit, paying four and a half *kyproi* of wheat, four and a half *prochoi* of wine; Marcia, daughter of my sister Apphia, added a *kotyle* of olive-oil. The propitiation was made with a nine-voice offering, in Year 265 [AD 180/1], on day 8 of the month Artemisios.

Here, the dispute seems to have run over two generations. When Glykon's grandfather died, he passed on his farm to his son Attalos, no doubt stipulating that Attalos might be wise to give a field or two to the local sanctuary. Attalos ignored this advice and kept the whole farm for his own profit; the god therefore decided that the farm was 'morally forfeit', just as with the vineyard at Promiasse. A generation later, Attalos' son Glykon suffered some unexpected disaster, and the god darkly reminded him of his father's failure to donate any of his inheritance to the sanctuary. Glykon was duly convinced to take the drastic step of handing over the entire farm to the god, along with various further symbolic offerings to help assuage the god's wrath.

The final case – from the same sanctuary of Meis Axiottenos at Kalburcu – is a still murkier affair: even by the standards of these laconic texts, the narrative of events is unusually compressed and allusive. Nonetheless, we are clearly dealing with a lengthy stand-off between the god and a local vineyard owner, an impressively bloody-minded character by the name of Apollonios[37]:

> Year 244 [AD 159/60], in the month Apellaios. Apollonios son of Apollonios spoke an immense word about Meis Axiottenos, and was punished. He (the god) ordered his relatives to erect (a statue of?) the god Meis Tiamou and Anaeitis. But when he (Apollonios) dragged out the time, and did not hand over the portions, he (the god) punished Apphia, so that he (Apollonios) would inscribe a *stēlē* and hand over the portions. And now he hands over the portion of the vines at Pagades, which he previously divided up with Claudius Milo, neighbouring the properties of Amyntas and Onesas. When Alexandros Murcus was priest.

I take it that Apollonios had received a demand to offer a 'tithe' to Meis Axiottenos concerning a vineyard at Pagades, which Apollonios had

---

[37] *SEG* 35, 1164 (Petzl 1994, no. 71), with the corrections of Petzl 1997, 76–7 (cf. Petzl 2019, 19–20): ἔτους σμδ΄, μη(νὸς) Ἀπελλαί|ου· Ἀπολλώνιος Ἀπολλω|νίου μεγαλορημονήσα|ς Μῆνα Ἀξιεττηνὸν καὶ |(5) ἐκολάσθη. ἐκέλευσεν | αὐτοῦ τοῖς ἰδίοις ἀναστ[ῆ]|σαι τὸν θεὸν Μῆνα Τιαμο[υ] | καὶ τὴν Αναειτιν. Παρελκύ|σαντος δὲ αὐτοῦ χρόνου (10) καὶ μὴ ἀποδιδόντος αὐτοῦ | τὰ μέρη ἐκολάϵετο τὴν Ἀπ|φίαν, ἵνα στηλογραφήσει κ[α]|ὶ τὰ μέρη παραδώσει· καὶ νῦν ἀ|ποδίδει τὸ μέρος τῶν ἀνπέ|(15)λων ἐπὶ ταῖς Παγάσι, ἃς ἐμερ[ί]|σετο πὸς Κλαύδιον Μίλωνα, γει|τονία Ἀμύντα καὶ Ὀνησᾶ. ἐπὶ | ἱερέως Ἀλεξάνδρου Μούρ|κου.

recently bought or inherited. In response, Apollonios 'spoke an immense word' about the god – that is to say, he politely, or not so politely, told the god where he could go – and was duly punished. The god then ordered Apollonios' relatives to set up a pair of images of the two chief gods of the sanctuary, presumably to propitiate the god's anger over Apollonios' first sin of 'immense speaking'. (Note that the gods already have the measure of Apollonios – rather than trying to persuade him directly, they decide to go after his more pliable relatives.)[38] Apollonios subsequently received a second demand to pay a tithe on the vineyard, and this time, rather than resorting to bad language, he simply 'dragged out the time', employing the timeworn peasant strategy of interminable foot-dragging. The god eventually lost his patience and punished a certain Apphia, perhaps Apollonios' daughter. At this point – as with the owners of the cursed vineyard at Promiasse – Apollonios finally threw in the towel and handed over his prized vines to the god.

As I am sure is all too obvious, the preceding discussion has involved a fair bit of filling in the blanks. In no text is it made absolutely explicit what kind of 'claim' on people's lands the sanctuary might have had, or on what basis the god might 'demand' a cash payment or the wholesale transfer of a vineyard or field to his possession. But even if some of the details are hazy, the overall picture is perfectly clear. The gods of rural Hieradoumia were ruthless and successful agricultural predators, who were quite prepared to exploit the rituals of confession and propitiation to build up their landed estates at their worshippers' expense. Although there was nothing legally binding about the customary rights which they claimed over land inheritances and sales, in practice these 'tithes' on land seem to have been effectively compulsory; people who refused to pay up could be persecuted by the gods even over multiple generations.

What is perhaps most startling about the texts collected here is the evident willingness of some Hieradoumian peasants to *resist* this encroachment on their property, through foot-dragging, evasion, and downright refusal to pay up. By definition, the propitiation-*stēlai* only inform us about those peasants whose resistance was eventually broken down by exemplary punishment; there must surely have been many more who successfully held the line against the gods' demands. Just as in the case of *hierodouloi* (discussed below), what we are seeing is a fundamental structural tension

---

[38] For this kind of 'strategy-switch' by the gods, compare e.g. *SEG* 57, 1224 (Petzl 2019, no. 125: Menophila fails to complete the propitiation; the god pursues her sister instead); *I.Manisa* 186 (Petzl 1994, no. 8: propitiation not performed; the god pursues the transgressors' *syngeneia*).

in the moral order of Hieradoumian rural society: a conventional expectation of 'giving the gods their due' perpetually running into widespread
and truculent non-compliance. As we will see, these underlying tensions
between sanctuaries and peasants over land-rights manifested themselves
in other spheres as well – particularly, it seems, in disputes over woodlands.

8.4 Trouble in the Sacred Grove

A particularly widespread feature of the landed property associated with Hieradoumian rural sanctuaries was the sacred grove, a patch of woodland marked
off for the god's exclusive use. In some cases, the sanctuaries may in fact have
been located within the grove itself: at a sanctuary on the right bank of the Hermos south of Saittai, the god Zeus was worshipped under the cult-title 'Zeus
from the Twin Oaks', presumably referring to two unusually large and impressive Valonia oaks near the place of worship.[39] These groves were numinous
places, far more closely associated with the gods' presence than the ordinary
productive agricultural plots owned by sanctuaries. In the extraordinary propitiatory inscription describing the persecution of the alleged poisoner Tatias
(Chapter 9, Section 9.6), we are told that her son Sokrates died as a result of a
freak accident which occurred 'when he was passing the entrance that leads off
into the grove (*alsos*)', no doubt a sacred grove belonging to Artemis Anaeitis
and Meis Tiamou.[40] That Sokrates' accident occurred just as he was passing
the way into the grove was taken as irrefutable proof that his punishment was
indeed the gods' work.

Local villagers were strictly forbidden from using these patches of woodland
for pasturage or other secular purposes, as we learn from a propitiation-*stēlē*
from a sanctuary near the village of Perkon (Figure 8.4); the accompanying
relief shows an adult man and woman standing to either side of a child, indicating that it was the sinners' son who was subjected to divine vengeance[41]:

---

[39] Petzl 1978b, 251; Hunt 2016, 244–9; cf. Güney 2020, for a Phrygian cult of 'Zeus of the cedar
tree'. On forests of Valonia oak in the middle Hermos region, see Robert 1962, 309 n.4. Today,
the largest surviving stretch of Valonia forest in the region lies just south of the İlke Çayı,
between the villages of Topuzdamları and Encekler.

[40] *TAM* V 1, 318 (Petzl 1994, no. 69), lines 17–18.

[41] *SEG* 38, 1236 (Petzl 1994, no. 7): ἐπὶ προήνγελαν οἱ θε|οὶ οἱ Περκηνῶν, Ζεὺς Ὀρεί|της εἰς
τὸ ἄλσος μὴ βόσχ|[ι]ν κτήνη, ἠπείθουσαν, ἐκό|(5)λασαν Εὐμένην β΄ τὸν υἱὸν | κὲ κατέθηκεν
ἰσοθάνατον. | ἡ δὲ ἐμὴ Τύχη ἐλπίδαν | ἔδωκε. μεγάλαι Νεμέσις | ἐν Περκῳ. I take it from the relief
that the elder Eumenes and his wife were the perpetrators, indicated by their raised right
hands; the gesture is widespread on Hieradoumian propitiatory monuments, probably
signifying acknowledgement of the gods' power.

Figure 8.4 Propitiatory *stēlē* of Eumenes. *SEG* 38, 1236 (Bergama Museum).

> Since the gods of the Perkenoi (and) Zeus Oreites pronounced that one
> must not graze cattle in the grove; they disobeyed; they (the gods) pun-
> ished (5) Eumenes son of Eumenes, the son, and made him like he was
> dead. But my Fortune gave hope. Great are the Nemeseis in Perkon!

Both in Hieradoumia and elsewhere, one of the commonest forms of
low-level rural impiety seems to have been the covert removal of timber
and brushwood from sacred groves or timber stands. Such, at least, is the
natural implication of the very large number of surviving sacred regulations from all parts of the ancient Greek world, often hedged round with
ferocious penalties, forbidding the cutting-down or removal of wood
from sacred groves. Here, for example, is a sacred regulation from fourth-
century BC Athens, unusual only in its slightly paranoid extension of the
prohibition to the collecting of dead leaves[42]:

---

[42] *IG* II² 1362 (*LSCG* 37). For further examples, see Sokolowski's commentary to *LSS* 81 (Samos);
Lupu 2005, 26–7; cf. Hunt 2016, 121–33.

The priest of Apollo Erithaseos pronounces and forbids – on his own behalf and that of the demesmen and the *dēmos* of the Athenians – that there be any cutting in the sanctuary of Apollo, or any carrying off of timber or green wood or firewood or fallen leaves from the sanctuary. If anyone is caught cutting or carrying off any of the forbidden things from the sanctuary, if the one caught is a slave, he will receive fifty strokes of the whip and the priest will hand him over, along with the name of his master, to the *basileus* and the *boulē*, according to the decree of the *boulē* and *dēmos* of the Athenians. If he is a free man, the priest and the demarch will fine him fifty drachms and hand over his name to the *basileus* and the *boulē*, according to the decree of the *boulē* and *dēmos* of the Athenians.

Timber poaching from sacred lands was clearly very widespread in Roman Asia Minor. The testament of Epikrates from Nakrason in northern Lydia, establishing a hero cult of his son Diophantos centred on a sacred grove, includes a clause stipulating 'Let no-one have the right to remove a tree from the grove, or to cut one down, on any pretext or contrivance'.[43] Likewise, a very fragmentary sacred regulation from a village in the Katakekaumene near Maionia reads simply 'Whoever offends against a tree, he will have to deal with the god's anger'.[44] A rather elliptical inscription from Neisa in Lykia, set up around AD 134, appears to be the confession of two woodcutters who had cut timber from a sacred grove and had been punished by the god[45]:

When Kilortes was high-priest. No-one has ever removed cut wood-poles from the woodland at Kartapis, but (5) only Artemes son of Hermaios, grandson of Apollonios, and Hermaios son of Hermaios, grandson of Theodotos, citizens of Nysa, who made a daring attempt to do so. Be of good fortune, (10) you who read this.

Two propitiatory inscriptions from Hieradoumia record the divine punishments which befell people who had cut down trees in groves belonging to the gods, or, more likely, who had lopped off useful-looking branches (cutting down a whole mature tree is a serious bit of work). The first comes from a sanctuary of Zeus Sabazios and Artemis Anaeitis

---

[43] Herrmann and Polatkan 1969, no.1, lines 74–76, with discussion at pp. 32–3: μηδέ τις ἐξουσίαν ἐχέτω | ἐκ τοῦ ἄλσους ἐξελεῖν δένδρον ἢ ἐκκόψαι ἐπὶ μηδεμιᾷ προφάσει ἢ πα|ρευρέσει.

[44] *TAM* V 1, 590: ὃς ἂν δένδρει | [πρ]οσαμάρτῃ, | κεχολωμένο|ν ἕξι τ[ὸ]ν θ(ε)ό[ν].

[45] *SEG* 57, 1667, as interpreted by Ricl 2012 (*SEG* 62, 1474): ἐπὶ ἀρχι(ερέως) Κιλορτου· | ἀπὸ τῆς ἐν Καρταπιδι ὕ|λης οὐδέιιοιε οὐδεὶς πρί|ωμα ἐξήγαγε ἴκρια, ⟨ἀ⟩λλὰ |(5) μόνοι Αρτεμης Ἑρμαίου | τοῦ Ἀπολλωνίου καὶ | Ἑρμαῖος δὶς τοῦ Θεοδότο|υ Νεισεῖς ἐπεχείρησαν. οἱ ἀναγεινώσκοντες |(10) εὐτυχεῖτε.

near Maionia; although the stone is now lost, we know that it bore above the inscription a sculptured image of three trees and a man raising his hand in prayer[46]:

> Year 320 [AD 235/6], day 12 of the month Peritios. Since I, Aur. Stratoneikos son of Stratoneikos, in ignorance cut trees of the gods Zeus Sabazios and (5) Artemis Anaeitis from the grove, having been punished, I made a vow, and I have set this up as a sign of gratitude.

Here, as in many other of the propitiatory texts, it is not quite certain whether Stratoneikos' claim of 'ignorance' (*agnoia*) is an attempt to exculpate his action (he did not know that the trees belonged to the gods), or whether it refers to his ignorance of the gods' power – that is to say, he cut the trees in full knowledge that they were sacred, but was not aware that the gods were so effective in hunting down and punishing transgressors.[47] The latter interpretation seems much more likely, to judge from a text from the sanctuary of Zeus from the Twin Oaks[48]:

> Great is Zeus from the Twin Oaks! Stratoneikos, son of Euangelos, because he was ignorant, cut an oak of Zeus *Didymeites* ('The Twin-One'), (5) and the god demonstrated his own power because of his lack of faith, and made him and his whole household like they were dead; and when he was saved from great danger, he set this up (10) in gratitude. And I pronounce, let no-one ever belittle his powers and cut an oak. Year 279 [AD 194/5], day 18 of the month Panemos.

Here, the perpetrator's 'ignorance' is pretty clearly synonymous with his 'lack of faith' and his 'belittling' of the god's powers – he knew perfectly well that the oak tree belonged to Zeus from the Twin Oaks, but decided to lop some branches off it anyway, with disastrous consequences for both him and his family. (We should note in passing – as already mentioned in Chapter 3, Section 3.6 – that this particular text is dated to early summer AD 195, a particularly terrible plague year in Hieradoumia, when many entire households must indeed have been brought 'close to death'.)

---

[46] *TAM* V 1, 592 (Petzl 1994, no. 76): ἔτους τκ΄, μη(νὸς) Περειτίου βι΄. Αὐρ. | Στρατόνεικος β΄, ἐπειδὴ κατὰ | ἄγνοιαν ἐκ τοῦ ἄλσου ἔκοψα | δένδρα θεῶν Διὸς Σαβαζίου καὶ |(5) Ἀρτέμιδος Αναειτις, κολασ|θεὶς εὐξάμενος εὐχαριστή|ριον ἀνέστησα.

[47] See the discussion in Chapter 2, Section 2.6.

[48] *TAM* V 1, 179b (Petzl 1994, no. 10), with Chaniotis, *EBGR* 2004, 98 (*SEG* 53, 1505): μέγας Ζεὺς ἐγ Διδύμων Δρυ|ῶν. Στρατόνεικος Εὐανγέ|λου διὰ τὸ ἀγνοεῖν αὐτὸν Δι|ὸς Διδυμείτου ἔκκοψε δρῦ|(5)ν, κὲ ἀναζητήσας ὁ θεὸς τὴν | ἰδίαν δύναμιν διὰ τὸ ἀπιστῖν | αὐτὸν κατέθηκεν ὁλοδουμε(ὶ) | ἰσοθανάτους, καὶ σωθεὶς ἐγ | μεγάλου κινδύνου εὐχαρισ|(10)τῶν ἀνέθηκεν. παρανγέλ|λω δέ αὐτοῦ τὰς δυνάμις μή | τίς ποτε κατευτελήσι καὶ | κόψει δρῦν. ἔτους σοθ΄, μη(νὸς) Πα|νήμου ηι΄.

It is in the nature of the propitiation inscriptions to present offences as the independent acts of single impious individuals. At least in the sphere of forest crime, that is very unlikely indeed to reflect reality. Here is another text from the sanctuary of Zeus at the Twin Oaks, this time recording the punishment of a man who purchased some sacred timber from the grove raiders[49]:

> Great is Zeus founded at the Twin Oaks and his powers! Since Menophilos bought sacred (5) timber, because of this he was punished by the god; and when he had suffered greatly, afterwards he ordered Menophilos, his son, to loosen his (10) father's responsibility. He pronounces to all men that one must not despise the god. He set up this testimony in Year 276 [AD 191/2], day 30 of the month Daisios.

This text gives us a fleeting glimpse of a much wider 'grey economy' focused around sacred woodlands.[50] The conscience-stricken Menophilos can no doubt stand for a much larger constituency of Hieradoumian peasants: those who might not rob a sacred grove themselves, but who were quite happy to pick up some good-quality timber on the quiet.

Not all of the Hieradoumian villagers who went crawling into the sacred thickets at dead of night were after timber or brushwood. Others were poachers, in search of one of the great delicacies of the Greco-Roman dinner table: doves, pigeons, or squabs for roasting. At many Hieradoumian rural sanctuaries, doves that roosted in the sanctuary or its associated woodland were regarded as sacred to the gods, with the strictest of bans on catching them for food. Doves and pigeons were sacrosanct in several Greek and Roman cults, and a few cities declared their entire pigeon population to be inviolable. At the city of Aphrodisias in Karia, we are told of civic laws 'which forbid anyone to catch, rear, chase off, or [- -] the doves in the city'[51]; similarly, when the Jewish philosopher Philo visited the Phoenician city of Askalon in the early first century, he saw 'an amazing number of pigeons at the junctions and on every building. When I asked the reason, they told me that it is unlawful to catch them, because their use (i.e. eating

---

[49] *TAM* V 1, 179a (Petzl 1994, no. 9): μέγας Ζεὺς ἐκ Διδύμων | Δρυῶν κατεκτισμένος καὶ | αἱ δυνάμις αὐτοῦ. ἐπεὶ | Μηνόφιλος ἠγόρασε ἱερὰ ξύ|(5)λα, διὰ τοῦτο ἐκολάσθη ὑπὸ | τοῦ θεοῦ, καὶ πολλὰ παθόν|τος αὐτοῦ μετὰ ταῦτα ἐκέ|λευσε Μηνοφίλῳ τῷ υἱῷ αὐ|τοῦ ῥοισάμενον τὴν τοῦ πα|(10)τρὸς αἰτίαν. παραγγέλλει | πᾶσιν ἀνθρώποις, ὅτι οὐ | δεῖ καταφρονεῖν το[ῦ θε]|οῦ. ἀνέστησε δὲ τὸ μαρτ[ύ]|ριον ἔτους σος΄, μη(νὸς) Δαισίου λ΄.

[50] Hunt 2016, 132.

[51] *IAph2007* 13.609: ψηφισμάτων ὄντων καθά κωλύεται συλλαμβάν[ειν] τρέφειν σοβεῖν [- - ἐ]ν τῇ πόλει τὰς [περιστερὰ]ς; see further Robert, *OMS* VII, 169–75; Brody 2001, 99–100.

Figure 8.5 Propitiatory *stēlē* of Diokles, from Kula. *TAM* V 1, 264.

them) has been forbidden to the city's inhabitants since ancient times. The animal has become so domesticated through lack of fear that not only does it come into people's houses, but even sits with them at table, and luxuriates in its immunity'.[52]

In rural Hieradoumia, sacred doves were evidently just as vulnerable to unscrupulous peasants as sacred trees were. Here is a short propitiatory inscription from the sanctuary of Zeus Sabazios and Meter Hipta near the village of Iaza (Figure 8.5)[53]:

> To Zeus Sabazios and Meter Hipta. Diokles son of Trophimos: because I snared the doves of the gods, I was punished in my eyes and I wrote up the virtue (of the gods).

This little *stēlē* bears the images of two doves in sculptural relief, as well as a depiction of the poacher's afflicted eyes – a kind of compressed visual

---

[52] Philo, *On Providence* 2.107.
[53] *TAM* V 1, 264 (Petzl 1994, no. 50): Διεὶ Σαβαζίῳ καὶ Μη|τρεὶ Εἵπτα. Διοκλῆς | Τροφίμου, ἐπεὶ ἐπεί|ασα περιστερὰς τῶν |(5) θεῶν, ἐκολάσθην ἰς | τοὺς ὀφθαλμοὺς καὶ | ἐνέγραψα τὴν ἀρετήν.

précis of the text's contents (sphere of transgression; sphere of punishment). The word for 'snare' (*piazein*) literally means 'squeeze' or 'throttle', a nice description of the way in which a noose snare catches a bird by the neck when it puts its head through the noose. Another poacher of sacred doves is known from the sanctuary of Apollo Lairbenos – the incorrigible slave 'Nick' (whose propitiatory *stēlē* is discussed in more detail below), whose long list of sins begins with the acknowledgement 'that I swore falsely about the doves', which I take to refer to the illicit trapping of sacred birds at or near the sanctuary of Apollo.

Perhaps the most tantalizing of all the propitiation-*stēlai* concerning landed property is a curious text from the sanctuary of Meis Axiottenos at the village of Tarsi, dated to early summer AD 201 (Figure 8.6)[54]:

> Year 285 [AD 200/1], the tenth day before the end of the month Panemos. To the Tarsian god (*Theos Tarsios*), the inexorable. Since Severus prevented the tree from being cut for garlands, the god demanded atonement for his sin. His foster-daughters Asiatike and Iuliane set this up, in gratitude.

The relief sculpture above the inscription shows a young tree (perhaps a cypress), with a man on the left cutting into the base of the trunk with an axe, while a second man – presumably Severus – stands on the other side of the tree, apparently trying to stop him. A crescent moon is depicted above the head of the axe-wielder, probably indicating that he is a human representative of the interests of the moon-god Meis. It is difficult to see on what grounds Severus might have tried to prevent the tree from being cut down if it belonged to the god, so it is best to assume that the god had in fact peremptorily demanded that Severus provide one of his *own* cypress saplings for the making of wreaths. Severus seems to have responded with an outright refusal, and one or more temple-servants therefore had to come along and cut down his young prize cypress by force. The description of the god as 'inexorable', combined with the fact that it was Severus' foster-daughters who eventually set up the *stēlē*, rather suggest that Severus suffered something very unpleasant indeed by way of punishment, perhaps an untimely death. In the absence of more context for this dispute, we are groping in the dark: it is perfectly possible that there is some prior history

[54] Cremer and Nollé 1988, 199–203, no. 1 (*SEG* 38, 1229; Petzl 1994, no. 4): ἔτους σπε΄, μη(νὸς) Πανήμου ι΄ ἀ(πιόντος). | Θεῷ Ταρσίῳ ἀλύτῳ· ἐπεὶ | ἐκώλυσεν ὁ Σεβῆρος τὸ | στεφάνωμα κοπῆναι, ἐ|(5)πεζήτησεν ὁ θεὸς τὸ ἁ|μάρτημα· ἀνέστησαν αἱ | αὐτοῦ τεθραμμέναι Ἀσια|τεικὴ καὶ Ἰουλιανὴ εὐχα|ριστοῦσαι.

Figure 8.6 Propitiatory *stēlē* of Asiatike and Iuliane. *SEG* 38, 1229.

which would make more sense of the god's demand (e.g. if the tree stood on a plot of land whose ownership was disputed, or if it lay on a boundary between sacred land and Severus' farm). But the implication certainly seems to be that the gods could lay claim to certain 'customary' rights over trees on other people's land, and that other landowners sometimes resisted these customary claims with bodily force.

Overall, the various types of 'forest crime' – the theft of timber or game from sacred groves, or simply the illicit use of these groves for animal pasturage – form one of the richest and most abundant categories of sinful behaviour in the Hieradoumian propitiation texts. From a broader historical perspective, there is nothing hugely surprising about this. Low-level struggles between peasants and landowners over access to forest resources are endemic in very many rural societies, partly as a result of the very widespread peasant conception of uncultivated woodland as a zone in which proprietorial rights do not or should not apply.[55] If there is a distinctive moral flavour to forest crime in rural Hieradoumia, it comes from the 'sacredness' of the stretches of woodland concerned. Poaching a pheasant or two from Mr Victor Hazell or lifting firewood from George I's royal forests is one thing; stealing oak wood from the god Zeus is, one might have thought, quite another. Still, the actual behaviour of Hieradoumian peasants seems not have been significantly constrained by the sacred character of these timber stands and flocks of doves. We can see here precisely the same kind of structural tensions between the sanctuaries and wider Hieradoumian rural society as we will see in a moment in the co-option of *hierodouloi* for the sanctuaries' workforce: a rural population whose submission to divine authority was always conditional at best and was always subject to rule-bending, foot-dragging, and (from time to time) outright non-compliance.

8.5 Labour: Hierodouloi

The Hieradoumian rural sanctuaries of Meis and other deities did have a small cadre of dedicated and specialized religious officials – priests, 'overseers' (*epimelētai*), 'temple-wardens' (*neōkoroi*) and others – some of whom served for life.[56] But a large part of the personnel attached to these sanctuaries were ordinary Hieradoumian villagers, who were required now and

---

[55] The literature is vast: e.g. Thompson 1975, esp. 130–8, 240–5; Scott 1985, 35, 265; Scott 1990, 189–95; Graham 2003 (all, however, discussing 'secular' woodlands).

[56] de Hoz 1999, 87–97; Ricl 2003, 81–7; for life-tenure, see e.g. *TAM* V 1, 484 (Iaza: husband and wife as priest and priestess, the former serving for life); *TAM* V 1, 490 (Iaza: hereditary priestess of Meis Axiottenos, serving for life); *SEG* 35, 1261 (Thermai Theseos: priest for 25 years); *SEG* 38, 1232 (priest of Apollo Tarsios who served for 86 years); Malay and Petzl 2017, no. 158 (*kleidouchos* and *neōkoros* of Thea Larmene, apparently serving for life). No doubt the many 'hereditary' priesthoods in Roman Hieradoumia were held for life: see Chapter 10, Section 10.4.

then by the god to come and perform service to the god for a fixed period of time (days, months, years: we simply do not know). During the period when a person was performing his or her fixed-term 'service' (*hypēresia*) in the sanctuary, he or she was classified as a 'sacred slave' or 'slave of the sanctuary' (*hierodoulos*), sometimes abbreviated to the bare *hieros*, 'sacred one'.[57] Sacred slaves are a fairly common presence in religious texts from Roman Hieradoumia, as for instance in the extraordinary propitiatory *stēlē* describing the devastation of a sanctuary during a rural festival of Meis Motylleites (discussed further below): a rioting mob 'beat up the sacred slaves and broke the statues of the gods, and no-one could save their skins, neither the gods nor the sacred slaves'. During their term of service, at least some *hierodouloi* lived in the sanctuary complex itself; as we saw in Section 8.2, the little sanctuary of Helios Apollo Kisauloddenos included a single-storey building with separate rooms to serve as residences for the sacred slaves, and the sanctuary of Thea Larmene on Yeşiloba Tepe included a long stoa-like building which was almost certainly intended to perform exactly the same purpose.

We certainly should not imagine these 'sacred slaves' as downtrodden serfs living in permanent bondage to the god. Many of them were in fact ordinary free Hieradoumian villagers, temporarily tied to the sanctuary for a fixed term of service.[58] Even the very rich could be compelled to spend periods as 'sacred slaves', as emerges from an unusually lengthy and lavish tombstone from the village of Iaza, for a well-off individual called Glykon Marcus.[59] This man is commemorated by at least seventeen named family members and friends, as well as his 'sacred *doumos*', the cult association to which he belonged; all of these family members and friends are said to have conferred 'gilded wreaths' on the deceased man (a minimum of twelve wreaths in total). In the middle of this lengthy epitaph, a certain 'Glykon the priest' is listed as one of the co-mourners, who describes the deceased as his 'fellow sacred slave' (*synhierodoulos* – a nice demonstration that priests could also be classed as 'sacred slaves'). Glykon Marcus must have spent a period of his life as a 'sacred slave' at a sanctuary near Iaza,

[57] Debord 1973; Debord 1982, 78–90; Scholl 1985 (Egypt); Ricl 2003, 87–91 (particularly clear and helpful); Caneva and Delli Pizzi 2015. The earliest Lydian example seems to be *TAM* V 2, 1253 (Hierokaisareia, 155/4 or 134/3 BC: dedication by οἱ ἐν Δοαρρηνης ἱερόδουλο[ι]).
[58] The 'consecration' of slaves or free children to the god through the procedure of *katagraphē*, abundantly attested at the sanctuary of Apollo Lairbenos (Ricl 2001; Dignas 2002, 238–41; Caneva and Delli Pizzi 2015, 173–5), may have created a permanent (or at least indefinite) state of dependence for the persons concerned; this procedure is not clearly attested in Hieradoumia proper.
[59] *TAM* V 1, 483a (Ayazören); cf. J. and L. Robert, *BE* 1978, 435; Pleket 1981, 168–9.

during which time he had struck up a sufficiently intimate friendship with the priest Glykon that the priest later joined in commemorating the man after his death.

What the service performed by the sacred slaves might have consisted of is never explicitly stated. I suspect that their main duty was to work the god's directly farmed landed property – his fruit trees and vineyards – perhaps especially at busy times of the agricultural year, but I cannot say I have any evidence to support this. Nor is it clear how the god or his priests chose the people to come and serve in the sanctuary – rather an annoying absence, in fact, since it makes a big difference to our understanding of the rural power-dynamics involved. At any rate, some villagers were clearly resentful of these peremptory demands for service, and several texts record the punishment of people who did not respond to the summons. At the village of Iaza, in spring AD 119, a woman called Trophime failed to come sufficiently quickly when asked, and was promptly driven mad by the god[60]:

> Year 203 [AD 118/19], day 6 of the month Artemisios. Since Trophime, daughter of Artemidoros Kikinnas, when called by the god to perform service (*hypēresia*), (5) was unwilling to come quickly, he punished her and made her insane; so she asked Meter Tarsene and Apollo Tarsios and Meis Artemidorou (10) Axiottenos who possesses Koresa, and he ordered me to inscribe the punishment on a *stēlē* and to register (*katagrapsai*) myself to the service (*hypēresia*) of the gods.

Not only is Trophime required to expiate her transgression in the usual way by a public confession of her delinquency and the erection of a *stēlē*; she is not even let off her period of sacred labour, but still has to register herself to the god's service for the prescribed period. Likewise, when a certain Chresimos was required to present himself at the sanctuary of Apollo Lairbenos, he failed to turn up on the appointed day, and one of his oxen was punished with sickness or death as a result[61]:

> Chresimos made a vow to Apollo Lyrmenos concerning the ox which had been punished, because of his being late and not being present, [on a] (5) clearly-written [*stēlē*...], having vowed, [...] he set up (?).

---

[60] *TAM* V 1, 460 (Petzl 1994, no. 57): ἔτους σγ΄, μη(νὸς) Ἀρτεμεισίου ϛ΄. ἐ|πὶ Τροφίμη Ἀρτεμιδώρου Κι|κιννᾶδος κληθεῖσα ὑπὸ τοῦ | θεοῦ ἰς ὑπηρεσίας χάριν μὴ |(5) βουληθοῦσα ταχέος προσελ|θεῖν, ἐκολάσετο αὐτὴν καὶ μα|νῆναι ἐποίησεν· ἠρώτησε οὖν Μη|τέρα Ταρσηνὴν καὶ Ἀπόλλωνα Τάρσι|ον καὶ Μῆνα Ἀρτεμιδώρου Ἀξι|(10)οττηνὸν Κορεσα κατέχοντα, | καὶ ἐκέλευσεν στηλλογραφη|θῆναι νέμεσιν καὶ καταγρά|ψαι ἐμαυτὴν ἰς ὑπερεσίαν | τοῖς θεοῖς.

[61] *MAMA* IV 286 (Petzl 1994, no. 113): [Χρ]ήσιμος Ἀπόλλωνι Λυ[ρμηνῷ] | εὐξάμενος ὑπὲρ τοῦ κολ[ασθέ]|ντος βοὸς διὰ τὸ ὑστε[ρηκέναι] | καὶ μὴ παραγεγον[έναι, ἐν στήλ]|(5)ῃ εὐσήμῳ [- -]|ων εὐξάμ[ενος - - ?ἀνέσ|τ]η̣σ̣εν [- -].

Similarly, in autumn AD 194, at the village of Pereudos, one Agathopous was punished with eye disease by the gods because 'the days were not fully paid'. It is possible that Agathopous failed to observe ritual purity for the appropriate number of days before entering the sanctuary, but the wording of his propitiatory *stēlē* makes it much more likely that he was ordered to work the god's lands for a fixed number of days and tried to 'cheat' the god by sloping off early[62]:

> Year 279 [AD 194/5], month Audnaios. When the gods in Pereudos demanded atonement from Agathopous, (5) because the days were not fully paid, they punished him in his eyes; and I praise them and give this in return.

Still, Trophime, Chresimos, and Agathopous could count themselves lucky: when one Apollonios failed to respond to the god's summons to 'reside in the house of the god' (almost certainly this same sanctuary at Pereudos), Meis brought about the death of his son and his granddaughter[63]:

> Great are Meis Labanas and Meis Petraeites! Since Apollonios – when a command was given to him by the god to reside in the house of the god – (5) when he disobeyed, (the god) slew his son Iulius and his grand-daughter Marcia, and he inscribed on a stele the powers of the gods, and from now on (10) I praise you.

Poignantly, the sculptural relief on the *stēlē* depicts Apollonios alongside his dead son and granddaughter, all raising their right hands in recognition of the terrible power of the gods (see Chapter 2, Figure 2.18).

There is some reason to think that the god sometimes co-opted people in this way to serve as higher religious officials, as priests or priestesses. We find this surprising, since we tend to regard priesthood as a vocation, not as a civic duty which anyone could be called on to perform (like modern jury service), but this was emphatically not the ancient way of thinking about things.[64] A text from the Upper Tembris valley seems to show a

---

[62] SEG 34, 1210 (Petzl 1994, no. 16): ἔτους σοθ′, μ(η)ν(ὸς) Αὐ|δνέου. Ἀγαθόποδα | ἐπὶ ἐπεζήτησαν οἱ | θεοὶ οἱ ἐν Περεύδῳ |(5) διὰ τὸ ἐνλιπέσθε ἡ|μέρας, ἐκολάσοντο εἰς | τοὺς ὀφθαλμοὺς καὶ 'γὼ | εὐλογῶν ἀποδεί|δω. For failure to maintain ritual purity for a prescribed period, cf. e.g. Petzl 1994, no. 19 (Markia enters the sanctuary 'one day too early'); Petzl 1994, no. 72 (Dionysios takes a sacred bath and does not 'keep to the period of days fixed by the goddess', cf. Petzl 2019, no. 163); Petzl 2019, no. 135 (Stratoneike enters the sanctuary while menstruating).

[63] SEG 35, 1158 (Petzl 1994, no. 37): μέγας Μεὶς Λαβανας καὶ Μεὶς | Πετραείτης. ἐπὶ Ἀπολλώνιος | οἰκῶν ἐ(ν) οἰκίᾳ τοῦ θεοῦ παραν|γελλομένῳ αὐτῷ ὑπὸ τοῦ θε|(5)οῦ, ἐπὶ ἠπίθησεν, ἀπετελέ|σετο αὐτοῦ Εἰούλιον τὸν υἱὸν | καὶ Μαρκίαν τὴν ἔκγονον αὐτοῦ, | καὶ ἐστηλογράφησεν τὰς δυνά|μ(ις) τῶν θεῶν καὶ ἀπὸ νῦν συ |(10) εὐλογῶ.

[64] Parker 2011, 48–57. In Classical Athens priests and priestesses could be appointed by lot from the entire citizen body (we do not know whether refusal was permitted); in the Hellenistic eastern Aegean, the sale of priesthoods was common.

woman being compelled, very much against her will, to act as priestess of
an unknown god or goddess[65]:

> With good fortune. Babou, daughter of Mamas, with her daughter Maeis.
> (5) When she received a demand from the divinity to become a priest-
> ess (*hiereia*), she did not respond; she received a demand a second time
> from the divinity, with great (10) compulsion and torture, and [became]
> an example for others coming to the place; she dedicated this in fulfilment
> of a vow, along with her (15) daughter – a vow on behalf of herself, and all
> her family, and the people that assemble (at the sanctuary), for the good.

In identifying potential candidates for co-option, the gods may well have
targeted the wealthier members of Hieradoumian society, who had the
resources to serve the god in a more munificent fashion. A fragmentary
text from the sanctuary of Apollo Lairbenos seems to show the god trying
particularly hard to co-opt a certain C. Antonius Apellas from Blaundos – a
Roman citizen, and so probably a man of higher social status than most of
the clientele of rural sanctuaries in western Asia Minor[66]:

> C. Antonius Apellas of Blaundos, having been punished by the god often
> and for many years because of his being unwilling to approach and partic-
> ipate in (5) the mysteries, although he was called on ...

Although the text breaks off at the crucial point, I strongly suspect that the
'calling' referred to in the last surviving line is a demand for Apellas to take
on some official role at the sanctuary; the same verb (*kaleisthai*) is used by
Trophime of Iaza when describing how she was called on by the god to
perform service.

It seems, finally, that people could voluntarily pledge their services to
the gods in gratitude for divine assistance or favour. A badly damaged
stēlē from the sanctuary of Meis Artemidorou at Axiotta introduces us
to a woman who committed a transgression of some kind, was punished
with eye sickness, and vowed that she would 'remain' at the sanctuary
and provide service to the god (or perhaps the god's mother: the text
is unclear), if he would only restore her to good health. The god duly

---

[65] *SEG* 47, 1751 (Petzl 2019, no. 151: Uyuz Tepe): ἀγαθῆ | τύχῃ· Βαβο|υ Μαμα ⟨σ⟩ὺν Μ|αιει
θυγατρί· ἐπιζ|(5)ητηθεῖσα ἱέρεια ὑπὸ τοῦ θείου ⟨κὲ⟩ μὴ ὑπο|κρεινομένη, πάλιν | ἐπιζη⟨τη⟩θεῖσα
ὑπὸ | τοῦ θείου μετὰ πολ|(10)λῆς ἀνάνκης κ⟨ὲ⟩ βασά|νων ἔκ⟨υτ⟩ο ⟨ὑ⟩πόδει⟨γ⟩μα | τῶν ⟨ἄλλ⟩ων
ἰς τὸν τό|πον, τήν τε εὐχὴν | ἀνέστησεν σὺν τῇ |(15) θυγατρὶ ΑΕΟΝ, τὴ|ν εὐχὴν ὑπὲρ ἑαυ|τῆς κὲ
τῶν ἰδίων πάντ|ων κὲ συνερχομ|ένου λαοῦ ἐπ᾽ ἀγα|(20)θῷ.
[66] *MAMA* IV 281 (Petzl 1994, no. 108): Γ. Ἀντώνιος Ἀπελ[λᾶ]ς Βλαυνδεὺς κο|λασθεὶς ὑπὸ τοῦ θεοῦ
πολλάκις καὶ | πολλοῖς χρόνοις διὰ τὸ μ(ὴ) βούλεσθε | [α]ὐτὸν ποσελθεῖν καὶ παρεστάναι |(5) τῷ
μυστηρίῳ καλούμενον ἐκ [- -].

did so, but the unfortunate woman showed insufficient promptitude in fulfilling her vow; Meis therefore decided to focus her mind by making her eyes sick again[67]:

> … for this reason she was punished in her eyes, and she vowed that if she was saved, she would remain with the god (or goddess) and erect a *stēlē*; (5) and when she dragged out the fulfilment of the vow, she was once again punished in her eyes, and she set up the *stēlē*. Year 202 [AD 117/18], in the month …

Considered in the round, these texts present several striking features. First, their sheer number: attempts to wriggle out of ritual service were clearly endemic in rural Hieradoumia. What is more, it seems pretty clear that the requirement of service in the sanctuary could not, in practice, be enforced by human means. That is not to say that a draft-dodger would not be looked down upon by his or her neighbours, or perhaps black-balled at the sanctuary; but ultimately the human administrators of the sanctuaries had no way to compel their rural neighbours to serve as *hierodouloi*, short of hoping that chance accidents would be interpreted as punishments for non-attendance. When a refusenik or foot-dragger was struck blind or mad, or saw his favourite ox fall sick, it was in the gods' interest to promote the idea that this was exemplary punishment for his failure to register himself as a sacred slave, thereby encouraging other Hieradoumian peasants to come quietly when called. The labour regime on the gods' lands ultimately depended not on coercion, but on collective subscription to a particular moral order of sin and punishment.

It is easy to see why people might have resisted the call to service. While serving as *hierodouloi*, they had to observe some pretty stringent restrictions on their behaviour. They were almost certainly required to live in the sanctuary, and it seems that they had to observe total sexual abstinence, even from their own spouses. At the sanctuary of Apollo Lairbenos, two people appear to have been punished by the god for having sex with their own husbands or wives while they were in this temporary state of 'sacred slavery'[68]:

---

[67] Malay and Petzl 2017, no. 131 (Petzl 2019, no. 164: Mağazadamları): [- – διὰ τ]οῦτο κολασ|θεῖσα [ὶς τ]ὰ ὄμματα εὔξατο, | ἐὰν σωθῇ, προσμεῖναι τ[ῇ/-ῷ θε]|ῷ καὶ στήλλην ἀναστῆ[σαι]·|(5) καὶ παρελκύσασα τ[ὴν εὐχὴν]| πάλι ἐκολάσθη τ[ὰ ὄμματα καὶ]| ἀνέστησε τὴ[ν στήλλην. ἔ]|τους σβ΄, μη(νὸς) [- -].

[68] Ramsay, *Phrygia* I, 150 no. 45 (Petzl 1994, no. 117): ΙΟΕΙΣ Ἀγαθημέ|[ρ]ου ἱερὰ βιαθῖσα | ὑπὸ αὐτοῦ κὲ ἡμά|ρτησα, στήκω κολ|(5)αθῖσα ἐπὸ τοῦ θε|οῦ· ἐπὶ ὃ κ⟨ὲ⟩ ἐστηλογ|ράφησεν παραγ|έλων μηδένα κα|ταφρονεῖ[ν τοῦ θεοῦ].

I, [...]eis, wife of Agathemeros, when I was a 'sacred one' (*hiera*) I was violated by him and I committed a *hamartia* – I stand punished by the god. In light of this, she inscribed a *stēlē*, proclaiming that no-one should despise the god.

This woman seems to have been compelled by her own husband Agathemeros to have sex with him while she was serving as a 'sacred slave' at the sanctuary; even though she only did so under compulsion (the verb used is *biazesthai*, effectively 'to be raped'), she still accepts responsibility for committing an 'error' in the eyes of the god. Rather similar is another text from the same sanctuary[69]:

I, Ape[...] son of Apollonios from Motella, acknowledge that I have been punished by the god, since I wished to stay with my wife; for this reason, I proclaim to everyone that no-one should despise the god, since he will have this *stēlē* to serve as an example – with his own wife Basilis.

It is not strictly certain that Ape[...] of Motella was a sacred slave trying to bend the rules, but it is difficult to think of any other circumstances in which 'staying with one's wife' (which I take to mean 'sleeping with her') could be classed as a transgression; sanctuaries did regularly require a short period of ritual abstention from sex before entry to the sanctuary, but that seems not to be what is going on here.[70] In the clause 'since I wished to stay with my wife', the Greek literally just says 'with a woman' (*meta gunaikos*: the Greek words for 'woman' and 'wife' are identical). In light of this potential ambiguity, Ape[...] subsequently had the final clause, 'with his own wife Basilis', added on to the bottom of the inscription, just to make it absolutely clear that it was not any old woman he had had sex with – a nice example of a repentant transgressor trying to minimize the seriousness of his act even in the act of acknowledging it.

This requirement of sexual abstinence for sacred slaves certainly underlies at least one, and perhaps two, of the *hamartiai* committed by an amiable Hieradoumian Don Juan by the name of Theodoros, who has left us one of the richest and most colourful of all the surviving propitiatory inscriptions. Theodoros' *stēlē* is both large and beautifully inscribed (although the

---

[69] *MAMA* IV 284 (Petzl 1994, no. 111): Ἀπε[- - Ἀπολλ]ωνίου | Μοτελληνὸς ἐξομολογοῦ|με κολασθεὶς ὑπὸ τοῦ θεοῦ, | ἐπεὶ ἠθέλησα μεῖνε μετὰ |(5) γυνεκός· διὰ τοῦτο οὖν πα|ρανγέλω πᾶσιν μ⟨η⟩δέ|να κα[τα]φ[ρονῖν] τῷ θεῷ, ἐπὶ | ἕξει τὴ[ν σ]τήλην ἐξον|πλάριον. – μετὰ τῆς |(10) εἰδ[ίας γ]υνεκὸς | Βα[σι]λίδος.

[70] Examples are legion: Parker 1983, 74 n.4; Parker 2018, 181. I take it that something of the kind is at issue in Petzl 2019, no. 161. The specified period of abstinence – at least for sex with a spouse – is never more than 2–3 days, and usually less.

Figure 8.7 Propitiatory *stēlē* of Theodoros. *SEG* 38, 1237 (Manisa Museum).

spelling and syntax of the inscription are idiosyncratic to say the least), strongly suggesting that he was a man of relatively ample means (Figure 8.7). After an excitingly varied sexual career, Theodoros was struck blind by the gods, to encourage him to mend his ways. His 'errors', punishment, propitiations, and eventual forgiveness are recounted in a kind of dramatic dialogue between Theodoros and the god (either Zeus or, more likely, Meis)[71]:

> Year 320 [AD 235/6], day 12 of the month Panemos. According to the instructions given by the gods, by Zeus and the great god of (5) Artemidoros:
>
> [Meis/Zeus]: 'I punished Theodoros in his eyes, because of the *hamartiai* he committed.'
>
> [Theodoros]: 'I had sex with Trophime, the slave-girl of Haplokomas, the wife of Eutyches, in the *praetorium*.' (10)
>
> [Meis/Zeus]: 'He takes away the first *hamartia* with a sheep, a partridge, a mole.'
>
> Second *hamartia*.
>
> [Theodoros]: 'But while I was a slave (*doulos*) of the gods in Nonou, I had sex with the *monaulia* Ariagne.'
>
> [Meis/Zeus]: 'He takes it away with a piglet, a tuna, a fish.'
>
> [Theodoros]: 'In the third *hamartia*, I had sex with the *monaulia* (15) Arethousa.'
>
> [Meis/Zeus]: 'He takes it away with a chicken, a sparrow, a pigeon, a *kypros* of mixed wheat and barley, a *prochos* of wine.'
>
> A *kypros* of wheat, pure, for the priests; one *prochos*.
>
> [Theodoros]: 'I took Zeus as my witness.'
>
> [Meis/Zeus]: 'See, I harmed him according to his acts, (20) and now he has appeased the gods and inscribed a *stēlē*, he has cancelled his *hamartiai*.'
>
> When he was asked by the council (of the gods):
>
> [Meis/Zeus]: 'I have compassion, if my *stēlē* is erected on the day I stipulated; you can open the prison, I release (25) the condemned man, now that a year and ten months have passed.'

To judge from the propitiatory offerings required of Theodoros, all three sexual escapades seem to have been more or less equally serious in

---

[71] *SEG* 38, 1237 (Petzl 1994, no. 5, with Petzl 2019, 11): ἔτους τκ΄, μη(νὸς) Πανήμου βι΄. | κατὰ τὸ ἐφρενωθεὶς ὑπὸ τῶν | θεῶν, ὑπὸ τοῦ | Διὸς κὲ τοῦ (crescent moon) μεγάλου Ἀρτεμι|(5)δώρου. ἐκολασόμην τὰ ὄματα τὸν | Θεόδωρον κατὰ τὰς ἀμαρτίας ἃς | ἐπύησεν. συνεγενόμην τῇ πε|δίσχῃ τῶ Ἁπλοκόμα, τῇ Τροφίμῃ, τῇ γυ|ναικὶ τῇ Εὐτύχηδος εἰς τὸ πλετώ|(10)ριν. ἀπαίρι τὴν πρώτην ἀμαρτίαν προβά|τῳ [[ν]], πέρδεικι, ἀσφάλακι. δευτέρα | ἀμαρτία· ἀλλὰ δοῦλος ὢν τῶν θεῶν τῶν | ἐν Νονου συνεγενόμην τῇ Ἀριάγνῃ τῇ | μοναυλίᾳ. ᾽παίρι χύρῳ, θείννῳ, ἐχθύει. τῇ |(15) τρίτῃ ἀμαρτίᾳ συνεγενόμην Ἀρεθούσῃ | μοναυλίᾳ. ᾽παίρι ὄρνειθει, στρουθῷ, περισ|τερᾷ, κύ(πρῳ) κρειθοπύρων, πρό(χῳ) οἴνου· κύ(προν) πυρῶν | καθαρὸς τοῖς εἰεροῖς, πρό(χον) α΄. ἔσχα παράκλητον | τὸν Δείαν. εἴδαι, κατὰ τὰ πυήματα πεπηρώκιν, |(20) νῦν δὲ εἰλαζομένου αὐτοῦ τοὺς θεοὺς κὲ στη|λογραφοῦντος ἀνερύσετον τὰς ἀμαρτίας. | ἠρωτημαίνος ὑπὸ τῆς συνκλήτου· εἴλεος εἶ|μαι ἀναστανομένης τῆς στήλλην μοι, | ᾗ ἡμέρα ὥρισα· ἀνύξαις τὴν φυλακὴν, ἐξαφίω |(25) τὸν κατάδικον διὰ ἐνιαυτοῦ κὲ μηνῶν ι΄ περι|πατούντων. The dialogic character of the text is well brought out by Chaniotis 2009a, 131–3; it is unclear which of the two gods is conceived as speaking.

the eyes of the gods.[72] But what precisely was it which made these liaisons so morally unacceptable? In the first case – Theodoros' dalliance with Trophime – it is probably relevant that the woman concerned was another man's wife: adultery with a married woman, even if she was a slave like Trophime, was very severely frowned upon in Roman Hieradoumia.[73] But I suspect that the real problem here was not Trophime's marital status (though that may well have been an aggravating factor), but the location of their fateful tryst – otherwise why bother to specify it? As a propitiation-*stēlē* from the sanctuary of Apollo Lairbenos shows, having sex in the sanctuary was an extremely serious offence in the eyes of the god.[74] It therefore seems to me very likely, as already suggested in Section 8.2, that the '*praetorium*' is in fact one of the buildings in the sanctuary complex.

It is the second and third 'errors' which chiefly interest us here. Both of the women concerned (Ariagne and Arethousa) are described with the term *monaulia*, a term which – annoyingly for us – can mean two quite different things, a 'solo flute-player' and a 'woman who is a sole householder'. It is hard to see why sex either with a professional flute player or with a sole householder should have been considered as especially awful, so Theodoros may in fact have included these descriptive terms in order to *mitigate* the seriousness of his *hamartia* (perhaps indicating that the women concerned were adult but unmarried). At least in the case of Ariagne, and perhaps with Arethousa too, I take it that Theodoros'

---

[72] Each of his three *hamartiai* was 'taken away' by means of what is called elsewhere a *triphōnon*, a 'three-voice offering', consisting of three animals (Petzl 1994, nos. 6 and 55; Petzl 2019, no. 131; a 'nine-voice offering' in Petzl 2019, no. 142); see Chaniotis 2009a, 137–8. We should therefore take θείννῳ, ἐχθύει in line 14 to be two separate animals rather than one ('a tuna-fish'). It is unclear whether the grain and wine listed as additional propitiatory offerings after the third *triphōnon* (lines 17–18) are specifically associated with the third sin alone; in Petzl 2019, no. 142 (see Section 8.3), the sinner apparently pays his 'nine-voice offering' in the form of nine measures of wheat/oil ('substituting' for the required animals?), and it is possible that that is also the case here.

[73] Cf. *TAM* V 3, 1539 (*CGRN* 191: 'entrance-rules' of a house-sanctuary at Philadelphia: late Hellenistic), lines 25–27: 'Apart from his own wife, a man will not seduce any other woman, whether free or enslaved, who has a husband.'

[74] *MAMA* IV 283 (Petzl 1994, no. 110): Αὐρήλιος | Σωτήρχος | Δημοστράτου Μοτελ|ηνὸς κολάθιν ἐπὸ τõ θε|(5)οῦ· παραγέλων πᾶσι μηδ|ὲ ἄναγον ἀναβῆτ' ἐπὶ τὸ χ|ωρίον, ἐπροκήσι ἢ κηνσ|ετε τὸν ὄρχις· ἐγὼ Γέ|α ἐκηνησάμην ἐπὶ τὸ χ|(10)ωρίον; 'I, Aurelius Soterchos son of Demostratos from Motella, was punished by the god. I proclaim to all not to go up to the place (*chōrion*) when impure, nor to swear a false oath, nor to move their balls; I screwed Gaia at the place.' I take it that the '*chōrion*' is the sanctuary itself, as in other texts from this temple (see below). The *stēlē* carries a depiction of a pair of legs and a pair of testicles, apparently visual shorthand for Soterchos' fateful journey up to the sanctuary to 'move his balls' with Gaia.

transgression primarily consisted in the fact that he had sex with these women 'while I was a slave of the gods in Nonou' – that is to say, while he was serving as a temporary *hierodoulos* at the sanctuary, and so was required to refrain from all sexual activity.

In the final lines of Theodoros' inscription, the god Meis (or perhaps Zeus) permits Theodoros to be released from 'custody' (*phylakē*) after a period of twenty-two months. What exactly this might mean is not clear. It seems very unlikely that Theodoros had literally been imprisoned for such a long period for a sequence of (in the grand scheme of things) rather minor sexual peccadillos, and so this may refer to the period over which he had been suffering from eye trouble, or (less likely) the period of his service as a *hierodoulos* at the sanctuary. Nonetheless, it was certainly possible for people to be physically compelled to remain at Hieradoumian rural sanctuaries by way of punishment, more likely as working servants of the god rather than literally 'imprisoned' in a dungeon. The clearest example appears in a propitiatory *stēlē* of uncertain provenance, erected by a woman whose name is missing at the start of the text[75]:

> [...] daughter of Apollonios was fettered in the sanctuary and punished by the gods (5), so that she might demonstrate their powers. Having made the payment, she appeased the gods, and inscribed a *stēlē* (10) and demonstrated their great powers, and from now on she praises them. When Metras was priest.

It is likely enough that this woman's 'fettering' is in fact a description of her punishment by the gods: she was caught out in a transgression of some kind, was 'sentenced' by the gods to a period of sacred service – literally or metaphorically in fetters – and after completing the designated period of labour on the gods' behalf, was required to set up a *stēlē* recording her punishment.

It is possible that a similar story of 'imprisonment' by the god underlies a tantalizing and very difficult text from the sanctuary of Apollo Lairbenos. I should emphasize that this text is an editor's nightmare: lettering, syntax, and spelling are all execrable, and it is often unclear what the stone actually says, let alone what it means. Even in my smoothed-out translation – which includes a fair bit of outright guesswork – the general scenario is very far

---

[75] *SEG* 41, 1038 (Petzl 1994, no. 33: Uşak Museum): [- -]ς Ἀπολλ[ω|νί]ου ἐνποδισθ[ῖ]|σα ἐν τῷ ναῷ ἐκο|λάσθη ὑπὸ τῶν θε|(5)ῶν, ἵνα ἀναδίξει | τὰς δυνάμις αὐ|τῶν. δαπανήσασα [ἰ]|λάσετο τοὺς θεοὺ[ς] | καὶ ἐστηλλογράφη|(10)σεν καὶ ἀνέδειξε | μεγάλας δυνάμις | αὐτῶν, καὶ ἀπὸ νῦν | εὐλογεῖ· ἐπὶ Μητρᾷ | [ἰ]ερέως.

from obvious. The repentant sinner is a man whose name starts Neik[…], whom it is difficult to resist nick-naming 'Nick'[76]:

> I, Neik[…], acknowledge that I swore falsely about the doves, and that I committed a transgression, and that I made an attempt against (5) the place (*chōrion*), and I stole a sheep from Demetrios' flock; and when the god instructed me not to give freedom to my master, I gave him freedom, having been impelled to it from all sides. (10) I was greatly punished by the god, and he appeared to me in dreams and said: 'Someone has taken my slave by the feet, even while he was sitting at my gates, and taken him away from there.' I proclaim (15) that no one should despise the god Helios Apollo, since he will have this *stēlē* to serve as an example.

If I understand the text correctly, Nick is a real slave, the property of the unnamed human 'master' (*kyrios*) mentioned about half-way through. Given the relatively trivial misdemeanours of most of the people who set up propitiatory inscriptions (wrongly counting off the prescribed days of ritual impurity, wearing dirty clothes, etc.), it is a relief to come across a real crook for once – Nick is a *bona fide* scoundrel, who absolutely had his divine punishment coming to him. He begins with a colourful list of transgressions he has committed: illicit fowling of the god's doves, and then lying about it under oath; sheep rustling; an attempted burglary of the sanctuary.[77]

But Nick's most serious transgression, or so he claims, was to have 'given freedom to my master', even after the god had ordered him not to. A slave emancipating his own master has a paradoxical air to it, and the easiest explanation is surely that Nick's owner was in a state of temporary 'unfreedom' at the sanctuary of Apollo Lairbenos. His owner might have been doing an ordinary term of service as a *hierodoulos*, but then it is difficult to see why he would have needed Nick to come and liberate him. Perhaps the best explanation is that Nick's owner was no less shady a character than Nick himself, and that he had been literally 'fettered' in the sanctuary as a punishment for something or other. If so, Nick's final and most drastic

---

[76] *MAMA* IV 279 (Petzl 1994, no. 106): Νεικ[- -] ὁμολογῶ | [περὶ] τῶ[ν] περιστερῶν | ἐπιωρκηκέναι με καὶ παραβε|[β]ῆχθαι καὶ 'πικεχειρηκέναι [ἐπὶ] |(5) τὸ χωρίον καὶ ἠρκέναι πρόβατον | τῶν Δημητρίου, καὶ παρανγ[είλα]ντός μοι τοῦ θεοῦ μὴ δίδιν | [τὴ]ν ἐλευθερίαν τῷ κυρίῳ μου | [πε]ριδιωκόμενος ἔδωκα. ἐκο|(10)λ[ά]σθην ὑπὸ τοῦ θεοῦ πολλὰ, | [κ]αὶ ὀνείροις μοι παρεστάθη καὶ | [εἶ]πεν· ποδῶν τις λαβὼν ἐμὸ[ν] | δοῦλον καὶ ἂν πύλας ἱζόμεν[ον] | καὶ κεῖθεν ἀνάξιν. παραν|(15)γέλλω μηδένα καταφρο|[νεῖν τῷ θ]εῷ Ἡλίῳ Ἀπ|[όλλωνος, ἐπεὶ ἕξει] τὴν στήλ|[ην ἐξεμπλάρι]ον.

[77] I take the term *chōrion* in line 6 to refer to the sanctuary, as also in *MAMA* IV 283, 285, and 289 (Petzl 1994, nos. 110, 112, and 116).

'error' was the effecting of a daring prison break – although, to be fair to him, Nick does claim to have been 'impelled to it from all sides' (in effect, 'my guvnor told me to do it'). At any rate, Nick's conscience was unable to bear up under the strain: he fell sick, the god Apollo appeared to him repeatedly in dreams raging at the loss of his prisoner, and eventually the whole story came out.

The expectation of service to the gods was evidently a significant source of tension between the sanctuaries and their worshippers. Although people in Roman Hieradoumia often broke the sanctuaries' purity rules and suffered for it, and although genuine wrongdoers – thieves, fraudsters, oath breakers – were subjected to dreadful punishments, there is no reason to think that anyone questioned the basic justice of the gods' vengeance in such cases. Quite the contrary: in most spheres of action, the gods did nothing more than uphold and enforce the basic moral and religious norms of rural Hieradoumian society. I take it that a man or woman who broke a purity regulation or poached wood from a sacred grove generally did so in the hope of getting away 'under the radar': there was no open repudiation of divine authority, and when something horrible happened as a result, they may well have accepted that they had got what was coming to them. But a refusal to act as *hierodoulos* was, I think, fundamentally different, because it necessarily constituted an open act of defiance. Someone who rejected a divine summons to serve as a 'sacred slave' must have been well aware that he or she was *publicly* challenging the god's authority – which makes it all the more striking that we have, relatively speaking, so much evidence for people doing exactly that.

This naturally raises the question of why the sanctuaries in fact chose to organize their labour regime in a manner which, in practice, seems so often to have led individuals to challenge the gods' authority. In most parts of the Greek world, sanctuaries managed their agrarian labour needs very differently, normally – so far as we can tell – by leasing out their agricultural land for others to farm (a phenomenon which is attested in Hieradoumia, but which seems not have been very widespread).[78] Why did the sanctuaries choose to depend on a workforce of co-opted *hierodouloi*, many of whom were demonstrably unwilling?

The answer must be that the social benefits of the system were taken as outweighing the risks. I suggest that the co-option of *hierodouloi* performed

---

[78] Dignas 2002, 28–30, 97–106; Horster 2010; Papazarkadas 2011, esp. 1–98; Rousset 2013. In Roman Hieradoumia, the only evidence for leasing of sacred land is *SEG* 39, 1277 (Petzl 1994, no. 63), discussed in Section 8.2.

much the same function as the use of the lot under the radical democracy at Classical Athens. Within a broadly egalitarian social system, the rotation of labour service among the rural population served (at least in principle) as a mechanism for promoting social harmony and integration. Rich though C. Antonius Apellas of Blaundos may be, he is not so high and mighty that he cannot be summoned to work on the lands of Apollo Lairbenos like any other peasant. On this hypothesis, the obligatory character of 'sacred slavery' served to reinforce the conceptual equality of members of the village community, a group of households which liked to see itself (whatever the reality might have been) as a community of peers. The 'fair' rotation of labour service between households can thus be seen as an institutional manifestation of a particular set of communitarian social values, most vividly seen in the extreme homogeneity of funerary commemoration in the region (the same kinds of tombstones used for slaves, free peasants, and members of the elite).[79] The tyrannical authority exercised by the gods of rural Hieradoumia over both land and labour – however much resistance and tension it may have led to in practice – can reasonably be seen as the logical corollary of an essentially non-hierarchical social structure. No one is entitled to special treatment.

8.6 Contestations

As we have seen in this chapter, the gods' claim to 'rule' the villages and villagers of Roman Hieradoumia (Section 8.1) was no mere metaphor. But in the spheres of both land rights and labour rights, the precise content and scope of this claim to rule was in a perpetual state of negotiation and struggle. The underlying moral norms may have been widely accepted ('this land is sacred to the god'; 'people ought to act as *hierodouloi* when asked'), but their practical application was another matter altogether. Some of the gods' specific claims were universally, if grudgingly accepted ('Pay a tithe to the god on your house-purchase'); others were accepted in principle, and quietly flouted in practice ('No poaching in the sacred grove'); others were resisted outright as unreasonable ('I require you to permit wreaths to be cut from your cypress tree').

Perhaps the most startling piece of evidence for the essentially unstable position of rural sanctuaries within the social structure of Roman

[79] More on this in Chapter 10.

Hieradoumia is a propitiatory inscription erected at a sanctuary near Kollyda in spring AD 198[80]:

> When a festival of Meis Motylleites was taking place, and when he was coming from the festival, a mob descended on the basilica bearing swords and sticks and stones, and they beat up the sacred slaves and broke the statues of the gods, and no-one could save their skins (?), neither the gods nor the sacred slaves. There was found among these men Onesimos Lathyros, and he was unable to escape (his punishment for) the battle; after years had passed, he was punished in the shoulder. And although he had no faith in the god, when he could not be cured by anyone, he was cured by the god. Then in a second punishment I was gripped by the soft parts for three days and three hours; and having been saved by the god, for my own part I praise him, and have dedicated this. Year 282 [AD 197/8], day 20 of the month Daisios.

Elsewhere in the Hieradoumian propitiation texts, 'impiety' towards the gods is a matter of individual foot-dragging and rule-dodging, occasionally escalating into an open stand-off over a piece of land. The situation here is quite different: an organized mob launch a concerted attack on a sanctuary during a festival, smashing the cult statues and beating up the *hierodouloi*. It is good to be reminded quite how little we really know of the texture of everyday life in Roman Hieradoumia. What sparked this riot? Who took part? Was this a common occurrence in rural Asia Minor? The answer is that we simply do not know; for us, this armed mob is like a strange leviathan suddenly and inexplicably emerging from the deep. In this chapter, we have at least seen some of the kinds of underlying social tensions which *could* have crystallized into this single act of collective violence; we might also recall the wider tendency in pre-modern societies for festivals to serve as occasions for the expression of lower-class discontent with the social order, sometimes spilling over into outright insurrection.[81]

As I remarked in Chapter 2, each of the propitiatory inscriptions of Hieradoumia opens a window onto a moment of social dysfunction of

---

[80] *SEG* 57, 1185 (Petzl 2019, no. 145): Μηνὸς Μοτυλλείτου ἰορτῆς γε|νομένης, ἐρχομένου αὐτοῦ ἀπὸ | τῆς ἰορτῆς συνῆλθεν ὄχλος ἐπὶ τ|ὴν βασιλικὴν ἔχοντες ξίφη καὶ ξύλα |(5) καὶ λίθους, συντρίψαντες τοὺς ἱερο|δούλους καὶ τὰ ἀφυδρίσματα τῶν θεῶν, | καὶ μηδενὶ χρῶμα τηρηθῆναι μήτε τῦ[ς] | θεοῖς μήτε τοῖς ἱεροδούλοις· εὑρε|θεὶς δὲ Ὀνήσμος Λάθυρος ἐν αὐτοῖς |(10) καὶ μὴ δυνηθεὶς τὴν μάχην ἀνακρ|οῦσαι διαγενομένων ἐτῶν ἐκολά|σθη ἰς τὸν ὦμον καὶ δυσαπιστῶν τῷ θε|ῷ καὶ ὑπὸ μηδενὸς δυνάμενος θαρα|πευθῆναι ἐ(θ)αραπεύθην ὑπὸ τοῦ θεοῦ· |(15) δευτέρᾳ οὖν κολάσει ἐδράχθην κατὰ | τῶν ἁπαλῶν ἐπὶ ἡμέρας τρεῖς | καὶ ὥρας τρεῖς· σωθεὶς οὖν ὑπὸ τοῦ θεοῦ | [κ]ατὰ τὸ ἐμὸν μέρος εὐλογῶν ἀνέθηκα. | ἔτους σπβ΄, μη(νὸς) Δαισίου κ΄.
[81] Forsdyke 2005.

some kind – a moment when the 'rules' of Hieradoumian rural society have been bent or broken in some way. In this chapter, we have explored the tensions which characterized relations between individuals (and occasionally groups) and the powerful rural sanctuaries of the region. As we have seen, these tensions seem to have been concentrated around questions of land rights, usufructs, labour, and the payment of conventional dues and perquisites of various sorts. In the following chapter, we will turn to look at a second category of antagonisms: interpersonal conflicts between neighbours and close family members.

9 | Village Society

One of the chief practical functions performed by the gods of Hieradoumia was that of 'mediation' in secular disputes between villagers. Many of the propitiatory inscriptions from the region describe appeals to the gods to intervene in interpersonal conflicts between neighbours and family members – often, but not always, conflicts on too minor a scale to be of interest to a secular court (suspected sheep-rustling and suchlike). As a result, the propitiation-*stēlai* provide us with an extraordinarily vivid picture of the everyday fault lines running through Hieradoumian village society, both between households and within households. These fault lines are the subject of the present chapter.

The precise form of divine mediation varied from case to case, but to judge from the narratives recorded on the propitiation-*stēlai*, a typical procedure seems to have been something like this. A controversy flares up in the village over a suspected crime – a handful of pigs go missing (Section 9.3); some money is stolen (Section 9.4); a young man goes mad, presumed poisoned (Section 9.6). Sometimes there is a prime suspect: Hermogenes appears to have more pigs in his yard than he did last month; Ammion is always short of money; everyone knows that Tatias dabbles in witchcraft. But the suspect noisily denies the charge, and nothing can be proved. At this point, when it is clear that the dispute cannot be satisfactorily resolved by human means, the village turns to its god or gods for help. One or more solemn rituals are performed at the village sanctuary, described in the propitiatory inscriptions as 'raising a sceptre' and 'depositing a *pittakion*' (more on these in a moment), indicating that the matter has been placed under the god's jurisdiction; the suspects may be required to swear an oath of innocence before the sceptre. The villagers then sit back to await the god's judgement. Sooner or later, the god inflicts some terrible punishment on the guilty party – sickness, death, or the death of a close family member. This disaster is regarded as settling the matter: the transgressor, or his or her surviving relatives, are required to erect a *stēlē* in the sanctuary recording both the crime and the punishment.

So much for the principle. In practice, things were not always as straightforward as that, because of the difficulty of actually *recognizing* the

284

god's act of vengeance when it occurred. My pig goes missing; I set up a sceptre; a few days later, my neighbour's daughter finally succumbs to a long-term illness. Is this the god's punishment at work, or is this just a tragic natural death? If my neighbour now owns up to the theft, all well and good; but if he continues to deny it (honestly or dishonestly), what is the village community to do? Annoyingly, our texts are seldom as informative as we should like on the practicalities of the 'social recognition of guilt'; nonetheless, as we will see in Section 9.3, we are not completely in the dark.

Before we turn to consider specific cases, let us take a brief look at the two chief rituals employed in rural Hieradoumia for placing a dispute under the god's jurisdiction: the erection of a sceptre (Section 9.1) and the deposition of a *pittakion* in a sanctuary (Section 9.2).

9.1 Raising a Sceptre

The ritual of 'raising a sceptre' seems to be unique to Roman Hieradoumia.[1] The sceptre is a very common attribute of the moon-god Meis and (less often) the goddess Anaeitis. When depicted in sculptural reliefs, the sceptre is generally of a similar height to the god or goddess, and sometimes – as in the sculpture shown in Figure 9.1 (*I.Manisa* 556) – seems to be topped with an unidentifiable small triangular or heart-shaped object (a pine cone?). The act of 'raising a sceptre' presumably involved setting up a replica of the god's sceptre in a sanctuary; we do not know whether these sceptres were available for hire from the sanctuary or whether people provided their own staffs for the purpose. The ritual served to place a matter under the god's authority, raising the stakes of exposure very dramatically for the transgressor.

So far as we know, sceptres were never erected 'against' particular individuals: the identity of the guilty party was left for the god to establish. Sceptres could also be erected 'pre-emptively', before crimes had taken place, as a way of warning off potential sinners. Several Hieradoumian epitaphs end with a clause warning the reader that one or more sceptres

---

[1] The ritual has been extensively discussed: Naour 1983, 119–22; Robert 1987, 362–7; Petzl 1994, 4–5; Chaniotis 1997, 363–9; Ricl 2003, 100–1; Gordon 2004, 185–7; Belayche 2008, 187–92; Chaniotis 2009a, 123–5; Petzl 2011b. *pace* Gordon and Chaniotis, there are no clear examples of sceptres being depicted in the hands of humans, either penitents or priests (thus correctly Rostad 2020, 20), though note the votive inscription *Sardis* II 451, set up to Meter Skepnou by a [σκ]ηπτροφόρος.

Figure 9.1 Dedication to Meter Anaeitis and Meis Tiamou, from Emre. *I.Manisa* 556 (Manisa Museum).

have been erected, guaranteeing dreadful punishment for any future tomb robber.[2] Here is a straightforward example, dating early in AD 92 – the tombstone of a girl named Tatia, erected by her mother and grandmother[3]:

> Year 176, the ninth day from the end of the month Peritios. Iole daughter of Hermophilos, the grandmother, honoured Tatia daughter of Artemidoros; Tryphaina, the mother, honoured Tatia her own daughter. Let no-one damage the memorial: Iole daughter of Hermophilos has laid a curse, by erecting sceptres concerning this matter.

---

[2] In addition to the three examples cited here, see *TAM* V 1, 160, 167a; *SEG* 32, 1222 (AD 27/8: the earliest known Hieradoumian reference to ritual sceptres); *SEG* 34, 1231; *SEG* 40, 1100. General discussion in Strubbe 1991, 44–5; Petzl 2011b.

[3] *SEG* 58, 1359 (uncertain provenance), with Petzl 2011b: lines 7–10, Ἰόλη | Ἑρμοφίλου ἐπηράσετο διὰ | τὸ ἐπεστάσθαι σκῆπτρα πε|ρὶ τούτου. It is notable that it is the deceased's grandmother, not her mother, who had primary responsibility for the erection of the tombstone and the sceptres; I know of no close analogies for this in Hieradoumia.

Often the sceptres are said to be associated with particular deities, as in the following tombstone, from Saittai, dated to autumn AD 93[4]:

> Year 178, day 4 of the month Dios. Ammias, his wife, and his sons Apollonios and Demophilos, honoured Pateres, as did Tryphaina his foster-daughter (*threptē*). In order that no-one may damage the *stēlē* or the tomb, they have set up sceptres of Axiottenos and Anaeitis.

In a few cases, the sceptres seem to be conceived as interchangeable with the gods themselves as agents of vengeance against wrongdoers, as in the following epitaph from Silandos, dated to early AD 123[5]:

> Year 207, day 8 of the month Dystros. Metras son of Zenas and Apphias daughter of Archaelaos honoured their son Apollonides, as did his brothers Archelaos and Metras and Zenas, and his wife Ammias, and his daughter Apphias. If anyone does any damage to this *stēlē*, may he find the twelve sceptres enraged!

It is hard to imagine that the family has literally set up twelve sceptres to protect the tomb, and the 'twelve sceptres' must here surely be a colloquial way of referring to the twelve gods of the Hieradoumian pantheon (sometimes referred to collectively as the *dōdekatheon*, 'The Twelve Gods', in Hieradoumian inscriptions).[6] This particular metaphorical turn of phrase ('sceptre' for 'god') is a very striking indication of the extent to which Hieradoumian villagers could identify the retributory power of sceptres with the power of the gods themselves.

9.2 Depositing a Pittakion

A second possible procedure was for the injured party to deposit a small inscribed bronze plaque called a *pittakion* in the sanctuary. These little plaques carried prayers for justice addressed to the gods, describing the crime or dispute, and appealing to the gods to punish the wrongdoer.[7] A single one of these *pittakia* has survived intact, and is now in the Musée

---

[4] *TAM* V 1, 172: lines 6–9, ἵνα μή τις προσαμάρτη τῆ | στήλη ἢ τῷ μνημείῳ, σκῆ|πτρα ἐπέστησαν τοῦ Ἀξ[ι]|οττηνοῦ καὶ Ἀναείτιδος. Compare the curse in *TAM* V 1, 173, an epitaph erected five years later by members of the same family: 'if anyone damages the tomb, may he find Axiottenos enraged' (εἰ δέ τις προσαμάρτη τῷ μνημείῳ, τεύξηται τοῦ Ἀξιοττηνοῦ κεχολωμένου).

[5] *SEG* 33, 1029: lines 8–10, ἴ τίς τι ταύτη προσαμάρτη τῆ στήλλη, | κεχολωμένων τύχοιτο τῶν δώδε|κα σκήπ⟨τρω⟩ν; near-identical formula in *SEG* 33, 1030 (same provenance).

[6] *SEG* 29, 1179 (with Strubbe 1997, 46–7, no. 51: epitaphic curse-formula from Saittai, invoking Axiottenos and the *dōdekatheon*); *SEG* 53, 1344 (Mağazadamları: Petzl 2019, no. 56): acclamation to Meis Axiottenos, 'great is the *dōdekatheon* founded beside you'; *SEG* 57, 1193 (Koloe: sacrifice to the Twelve Gods by a priestess); de Hoz 1999, 58, 83.

[7] Ricl 1991; Petzl 1994, 77; Versnel 2002, 48–56, 64–7; Chaniotis 2004a, 14–15; Petzl 2007; Chaniotis 2009a, 125–8. On prayers for justice, Versnel 1991 (with updates in Versnel 2010) remains fundamental; see now further Kotansky 2020.

Figure 9.2 *Pittakion* addressed to the Mother of the Gods. *SEG* 28, 1568 (Musées d'art et d'histoire de Genève, Inv. 020151).

d'Art et d'Histoire in Geneva (Figure 9.2). It is a small sheet of bronze, 8.1 cm by 5.5 cm, half a millimetre thick, with a hole in the top of the sheet for fixing it to a wall. The text incised on it reads as follows[8]:

> ἀνατίθημι Μητρὶ Θεῶν
> χρυσᾶ ἀπόλεσε [i.e. ἃ ἀπώλεσα] πάντα ὥ-
> στε ἀναζητήσηι αὐτ-
> ὴν καὶ ἐς μέσον ἐνε-
> 5   κκεῖν πάντα καὶ τοὺς
> ἔχοντες κολάσεσθα-
> ι ἀξίως τῆς αὐτῆς δυνά-
> μενος [i.e. δυνάμεως] καὶ μήτε αὐτ[ὴν]
> καταγέλαστον ἔσεσθ[αι].

I dedicate to the Mother of the Gods all the gold objects which I have lost, so that she may seek them out and bring them (5) all to light, and so that she may punish those who have them in a manner worthy of her power, and so that she (the goddess) may not be an object of mockery.

---

[8] Dunant 1978 (*SEG* 28, 1568), as corrected by Ricl 1991 (*SEG* 40, 1049). For a similar text – albeit inscribed on a *stēlē* rather than a *pittakion* – see *TAM* V 1, 362, with Petzl 1994, IX: ἔτους σμʹ, μη(νὸς) Αὐδ[ν]αίου. παραγράφε[ι] | Ἀπολλώνιος τὸ|ν βεβληκότα τὸ πι|(5)νακίδιον κ⟨α⟩ὶ ἠρκό|τα καὶ σύστορα τῇ | ἀπολείᾳ, 'Year 240 [AD 155/6], in the month Audnaios. Apollonios hands over (to the justice of the gods) the person who broke the little plaque, and whoever assisted him, and whoever is cognisant of the damage.'

The man or woman who wrote this plaque did not feel the need to give his or her name (which would anyway be known to the goddess): unlike the propitiation-*stēlai*, which are largely directed towards a human readership, this text's primary addressee is the goddess herself. Particularly striking is the twofold inducement, practical and reputational, offered to the goddess in order to encourage her to locate the thieves and punish them. The author begins by dedicating the missing gold objects to the goddess, thereby making them the goddess' own property; he or she concludes by, in effect, reminding the goddess that her reputation is at stake in recovering what has now been reclassified as sacred property. A purely secular crime is transformed into an offence against the gods, and the deity is placed under intense moral pressure to punish the offenders and recover 'her' treasures.[9]

These *pittakia* could, it seems, be directed against particular named individuals, to judge from the following propitiatory inscription from a sanctuary somewhere near Kula[10]:

> To Meis Axiottenos. Since Hermogenes son of Glykon and Nitonis daughter of Philoxenos abused Artemidoros (5) concerning (the) wine, Artemidoros deposited a *pittakion*. The god punished Hermogenes, and he appeased the god (10) and from now on he will exalt him.

Artemidoros has had some kind of falling-out 'concerning wine' with a man and a woman, Hermogenes and Nitonis. He has been on the receiving end of some verbal abuse or slanderous untruths (in Greek, *loidoria*) from Hermogenes and Nitonis: perhaps they have accused him of a theft that he had not in fact committed. Artemidoros has therefore deposited an inscribed *pittakion* in the sanctuary, which I take it would have said something like 'If I stole the wine, let me be destroyed by Meis Axiottenos; but if Hermogenes has accused me falsely, let the god punish him instead'. The god duly punished Hermogenes, who was therefore required to erect a propitiation-*stēlē* acknowledging that his verbal attack on Artemidoros

---

[9] For other instances of 'cession' of disputed objects to the god, see Section 9.4 (Apollonios' pig; a cloak stolen from a bathhouse); in general, Chaniotis 2004a, 16–19. Note also the dedication *I.Manisa* 171 (AD 177): 'I, Tatias, having purchased [...] and having been treated contemptuously, I ceded them to Meis Axiottenos, and he will do with them whatever he wants' ([Τα]τιὰς ἀγοράσασα |[...]α καταφρονουμε|[νη] ἐξεχώρησα αὐτὰ [Μ]ηνὶ Ἀξιοττηνῷ, ἅτινα πράξει ὡς ἂν θέλη). I take it that Tatias has been in some way defrauded in a purchase, and has dedicated the relevant objects to the god in order to encourage him to take vengeance on the seller; but the whole transaction is very obscure.

[10] *TAM* V 1, 251 (Petzl 1994, no. 60): Μηνὶ Ἀξιοττηνῷ. ἐπὶ | Ἑρμογένης Γλύκωνος | καὶ Νιτωνὶς Φιλοξένου | ἐλοιδόρησαν Ἀρτεμί|(5)δωρον περὶ οἴνου, Ἀρτε|μίδωρος πιττάκιον ἔ|δωκεν. ὁ θεὸς ἐκολά|σετο τὸν Ἑρμογένην, | καὶ εἰλάσετο τὸν θε|(10)ὸν καὶ ἀπὸ νῦν εὐδο|ξεῖ.

constituted 'abuse' or 'slander'. The *pittakion* deposited by Artemidoros served a broadly similar function to the surviving Geneva text: it served to 'raise the stakes' by inviting the god to punish the guilty party in a dispute which would otherwise have been just one man's word against another.

Whether the erection of a sceptre and the deposition of a written *pittakion* in the sanctuary were alternative procedures, or whether injured parties were typically expected to do both, is not wholly clear. A lengthy and fascinating text from the sanctuary of Artemis Anaeitis and Meis Tiamou at Esenyazı, discussed in Section 9.6, seems to imply that people could do both. A woman called Tatias has been accused of witchcraft against her son-in-law (who had gone mad), and hence she 'erected a sceptre and placed curses in the temple so as to prove her innocence against the rumour that she was implicated in the affair'. The 'curses' mentioned here were presumably inscribed on a *pittakion*, calling down divine vengeance on whoever was in fact responsible for her son-in-law's madness; as we will see, the process ended up rebounding spectacularly on Tatias herself.[11] Whether the erection of the sceptre and the deposition of the curses were conceived as doing slightly different things, or if they were two interdependent elements of a single process, we cannot say.

9.3 Trouble with Pigs

Villagers in Roman Hieradoumia fell out with one another over all sorts of things – the repayment of loans, thefts, false oaths, sexual misdemeanours, and so forth. But to judge from the surviving propitiatory inscriptions, most widespread and most acrimonious of all were disputes over animals. Much of the wealth of Hieradoumian farmers was in their livestock: working animals like donkeys and oxen; great flocks of sheep, reared for textile production at the specialized cloth towns of Saittai and Philadelphia; herds of pigs, these too perhaps reared primarily for export. Virtually the only native of the small Hieradoumian town of Saittai who is known to have

[11] *TAM* V 1, 318 (Petzl 1994, no. 69). For 'conditional self-cursing', see Versnel 2002, 65 (cf. Eidinow 2016, 212–23), who aptly compares a late Hellenistic (?) bronze *pittakion* from the temple of Demeter and Kore at Knidos, *I.Knidos* 147A: 'Antigone consecrates (this tablet) to Demeter, Kore, Plouton, all the gods and goddesses with Demeter. If I have given a potion to Asklepiades, or if I have considered in my soul doing any harm to him, or if I have called a woman to the sanctuary, paying her three *hemimnaia* so that she might take him from the living, then let Antigone be burned inside and go up to Demeter confessing what she has done, and may she not find Demeter kindly to her, but let her be tortured with terrible tortures. If anyone has spoken to Asklepiades against me, or if anyone has inducted the woman against me by giving her money, [text breaks off].'

resided abroad is a certain Aurelius Epiktetos, who died and was buried at the city of Sardis; appropriately enough, he was a pig trader (*choirenporos*).[12]

Livestock were entangled with Hieradoumian farmers' dealings with the gods in all sorts of ways. Farmers throughout the region regularly vowed to make offerings to the gods if their animals flourished: we hear, for instance, of a certain Diogenes, who 'made a vow to Zeus Peizenos concerning his ox, and did not fulfil it; his daughter Tatiane was punished in her eyes'.[13] Likewise, a man called Lucius 'swore a false oath concerning his flocks' and was duly punished in some way by the god Zeus Orkamanites.[14] A splendid votive *stēlē* from the sanctuary of the gods of Pereudos was erected by a certain Philippikos, having made a vow 'concerning my cattle'; the accompanying relief depicts a herd of eight cows or oxen, accompanied by a herdsman carrying a staff and leading one of the animals with a halter tied around its jaw (Figure 9.3).[15] The most lavish offering that a Hieradoumian smallholder could imagine making to the gods in gratitude for their help was one of his or her prize animals. In a moment of overenthusiastic piety, a woman called Tatiane 'vowed a bull to Meis Axiottenos on behalf of her siblings'; her prayer was answered, but Tatiane found herself unable to pay the bull, and received permission from the god to dedicate a votive *stēlē* with an image of a bull instead.[16] Conversely, animals could be punished

---

12. *Sardis* VII 1, 159. On pig commerce in inland western Asia Minor, Thonemann 2011a, 184–5, illustrating the tombstone of a swine merchant from Kolossai in southern Phrygia (*MAMA* VI 50). Conditions for pig-rearing in the middle Hermos region were particularly propitious, due to the presence of large stretches of oak forest (Robert 1962, 309), whose acorns make ideal pig feed.

13. *TAM* V 1, 409 (İbrahim Ağa Köy, Petzl 1994, no. 45): Διεὶ Πειζηνῷ Διογένη[ς] | εὐξάμενος ὑπὲρ τοῦ | βοὸς κὲ μὴ ἀποδούς, | ἐκολάσθη αὐτοῦ ἡ θυ|(5)γάτηρ Τατιανὴ ἰς τοὺς | ὀφθαλμούς· νῦν οὖν | εἰλασάμενοι ἀνέθη|καν.

14. *SEG* 33, 1120 (Uşak Museum, Petzl 1994, no. 103), lines 3–5: ἐφιώρκησε περὶ προβάτων. The term πρόβατα would normally refer to sheep, but the accompanying relief depicts a saddled horse or donkey below a bust of Zeus Orkamanites.

15. *SEG* 34, 1214 (Uşak Museum): Θεοῖς Περευδηνοῖς Φιλιππικὸς | εὐξάμενος μετὰ Βουνίωνος τοῦ | συντρόφου ὑπὲρ τῶν κτηνῶν καὶ | ἐπιτυχὼν εὐχαριστῶν ἀνέθηκεν. |(5) ἔτους τλβ΄, μη(νὸς) Λώου κ΄ ('Philippikos, having made a vow to the gods of Pereudos along with his *syntrophos* Bounion on behalf of his cattle, was successful, and dedicated this in gratitude. Year 332 [AD 247/8], day 20 of the month Loos'). Philippikos is depicted at the top of the *stēlē*, with one hand raised; the herdsman in the relief may be his *syntrophos* Bounion.

16. *TAM* V 1, 453 (Iaza, AD 235/6: Petzl 1994, no. 61): Μηνὶ Ἀξιοτηνῷ Τατιανὴ Ἐρ|μίππου εὐξαμένη ταῦρον ὑ|πὲρ ἀδελφῶν καὶ ἀκουσ|θεῖσα, μὴ δυνασθεῖσα δὲ |(5) ἀποδοῦναι ταῦρον ἠρώτη|σε τὸν θεόν, καὶ συνεχώρησε | ἀπολαβεῖν στήλλην. We have no way of knowing what the typical cost of an inscribed *stēlē* might have been (although see n.42 below: perhaps around 25 *denarii*?), but it was evidently significantly cheaper than a bull. This *stēlē* is in fact a relatively large one (0.88 m in height). For 'substitute' offerings of this kind, compare Pausanias 10.18.5 (I owe the reference to Jaś Elsner).

Figure 9.3 Votive *stēlē* of Philippikos. *SEG* 34, 1214 (Uşak Museum).

for the sins of their owners: one Chresimos 'made a vow to Apollo Lyrmenos concerning the ox which had been punished, because of being late and not being present' – that is to say, because of Chresimos' failure to serve as a 'sacred slave' at the sanctuary of Apollo Lairbenos.[17] We will meet in a moment a man who swore a false oath and was punished by the deaths of his ox and a donkey.

It is in the nature of sheep- and pig-rearing that animals spend a long time away from the direct supervision of their owners. In the early tenth century AD, the ascetic Luke the Stylite is said to have spent two years as a professional swineherd, hired at pay to look after all the pigs belonging to the little village of Lagaina in Phrygia; no doubt swineherds like Luke would take their herds of pigs up into the hills for weeks or even months on end, as some Turkish goatherds still do today.[18] As a result, there were abundant opportunities for 'confusion' over the ownership of particular animals. The clearest case is the following wonderful propitiatory inscription from a sanctuary of Meter Anaeitis and Meis Tiamou at the village of Azita, dated to AD 114/15[19]:

> Great is Meter Anaeitis who possesses Azita and Meis Tiamou and their powers! Hermogenes and Apollonios, the son of (5) Apollonios Midas – when three of the pigs of Demainetos and Papias from Azita strayed away from the Folds of Syros, and fell in with the flocks of Hermogenes and Apollonios, (10) then being shepherded by a five-year-old boy of theirs, they took them off inside; and when Demainetos and Papias came looking, they did not admit it, due to a certain enmity between them. (15) So the sceptre of the goddess and of the lord of Tiamos was set up, and when they still did not admit it, the goddess therefore showed her own powers.

---

[17] *MAMA* IV 286 (Petzl 1994, no. 113), lines 2–4: εὐξάμενος ὑπὲρ τοῦ κολ[ασθέ]|ντος βοὸς διὰ τὸ ὑστε[ρηκέναι]| καὶ μὴ παραγεγον[έναι κτλ. On sacred slaves at the sanctuary of Apollo Lairbenos and elsewhere, see Chapter 8, Section 8.5.

[18] Kaplan 1992, 40, 196, on the *Life of Luke the Stylite* ch. 9 (Delehaye 1923, 204); cf. Robert, *Hellenica* VII, 152–60; Chandezon 2003, 415–18.

[19] *TAM* V 1, 317 (Petzl 1994, no. 68). Μεγάλη Μήτηρ Αναειτις Αζι|τα κατέχουσα καὶ Μεὶς Τιαμου | καὶ αἱ δυνάμις αὐτῶν. Ἑρμογέ|νης καὶ Ἀπολλώνιος ὁ Ἀπολλω|(5)νίου Μίδου ἀπὸ Σύρου Μανδρῶν | πλαζομένων χοίρων τριῶν Δη|μαινέτου καὶ Παπίου ἐξ Αζι|των καὶ προσμιγόντων αὐτῶν | προβάτοις τοῦ Ἑρμογένου καὶ Ἀ|(10)πολλωνίου, παιδίου αὐτῶν βόσ|κοντος πενταετοῦς, καὶ ἀπαγα|γόντων ἔσω, ζητοῦντος οὖν τοῦ | Δημαινέτου καὶ τοῦ Παπίου οὐ|κ ὡμολόγησαν διά τινα ἀχαριστί|(15)αν. ἐπεστάθη οὖν τῆς θεοῦ τὸ σκῆ|πτρον καὶ τοῦ κυρίου τοῦ Τιαμου | καὶ μὴ ὁμολογησάντων αὐτῶν ἡ | θεὸς οὖν ἔδειξεν τὰς ἰδίας δυ|νάμις, καὶ ἱλάσοντο αὐτὴν τελευ|(20)τήσαντος τοῦ Ἑρμογένου ἡ γυνὴ | αὐτοῦ καὶ τὸ τέκνον καὶ Ἀπολλώνι|ος ὁ ἀδελφὸς τοῦ Ἑρμογένου, καὶ | νῦν αὐτῇ μαρτυροῦμεν καὶ εὐλο|γοῦμεν μετὰ τῶν τέκνων. |(25) ἔτους ρϙθ′. It is unclear whether Αζιτα (also in *TAM* V 1, 318, discussed below) is a variant of Αξιοττα, or a different village altogether.

> And now that Hermogenes has died, (20) his wife and his son and Apollonios, the brother of Hermogenes, have appeased the goddess, and now we bear witness to her and praise her, along with our children. (25) Year 199.

Demainetos and Papias (perhaps brothers) were the owners of a herd of pigs, who were kept – at least some of the time – at a place called *Syrou Mandrai*, the 'Folds of Syros' (*mandra* is a generic term for an enclosed byre, sty, or fold).[20] Three of their pigs somehow made it out through the fencing and got themselves mixed up with a flock of sheep owned by the brothers Hermogenes and Apollonios, which was being looked after at this moment by a five-year-old boy (perhaps, but not necessarily, a slave).[21] When the flock with its three supernumerary pigs returned home at sunset, Hermogenes and Apollonios cheerfully took the pigs for themselves. Worse, when Demainetos and Papias came knocking at the door next day ('You often pasture your sheep up near Syrou Mandrai – have you seen our pigs?'), Hermogenes and Apollonios flatly denied all knowledge. Thus stymied, Demainetos and Papias dramatically escalated the issue by setting up sceptres at the village sanctuary of Anaeitis and Meis Tiamou, and apparently requiring Hermogenes and Apollonios to take a public oath that they did not steal the pigs ('they still did not admit it'). Shortly afterwards, one of the two suspects, Hermogenes, died suddenly; the surviving brother, Apollonios, threw in the towel and admitted that it was in fact they who had the pigs all along.

From the perspective of the wider village community, the 'social recognition of guilt' was pleasingly straightforward in this case. Two men were accused of a crime; they denied it; one of them was struck dead; the other confessed. I see no reason to doubt that Hermogenes and Apollonios were indeed the guilty parties in this case, and that Apollonios' confession was prompted by the holy terror induced by his brother's death, probably combined with intense social pressure (not least from his own family) in the wake of Hermogenes' 'punishment'. Nonetheless, the text remains an unusually fascinating one, because even in the very act of owning up to his sin, Apollonios has evidently taken great care to structure the whole narrative in a manner designed to minimize his culpability. Hermogenes and Apollonios did not raid the Folds of Syros: the pigs wandered off by themselves. It was not Hermogenes and Apollonios who

---

[20] Robert 1962, 80.

[21] The use of small children as swineherds was common in antiquity and the Byzantine world; St Ioannikios of Bithynia is said to have looked after his parents' pigs from the age of seven (Kaplan 1992, 196; Talbot 2018).

picked up these wandering pigs: it was their shepherd, a five-year-old boy, whose age is no doubt specified in order to minimize his personal responsibility ('he didn't know any better'). Apollonios does not deny that he received the pigs and subsequently concealed them, but he is very keen to emphasize that he did not strictly *steal* them in the first place. Then, when he comes to the critical point – the brothers' bare-faced denial that they knew anything about the pigs – he is careful to reassure us that this was not a gratuitous bit of criminality, but was inspired and justified by a longer-term relationship of 'enmity' (*acharistia*, literally 'lack of goodwill/gratitude' or 'absence of reciprocity') between the two families. Apollonios is perfectly willing to make a public confession that he has acted dishonestly and impiously: he accepts the justice of his brother's death. But he is also most eager for the village to recognize that he has not acted *dishonourably*. He may have received and concealed another man's pigs, but he is not just a common thief. His action, or so he insists, has to be understood in context, as part of a long-term vendetta between the two families.

The resolution of this case was, in the end, socially pretty straightforward. But this was not always so. Sometimes, divine punishment might not be forthcoming at all, making it effectively impossible for the village community to assign guilt. This appears to have been the case in a second episode of suspected pig-rustling, described (not, it must be said, as clearly as we might like) in a propitiatory inscription from the sanctuary of Apollo at the village of Tarsi, near Silandos (Figure 9.4).[22]

> When a pig belonging to Apollonios was lost, in Year 217, a sceptre of Apollo Tarsios was erected concerning the affair; and when no-one confessed beside the sceptre, (5) later it was found at (the farm of) Alexandros Tasilas. The priest persuaded Apollonios that he (the priest) should receive the pig, judging that a period of time exceeding the stipulated (10) number of days had elapsed; but he (Apollonios) drove off the pig (for himself), and the god demanded that Tatia, wife of Apollonios, should inscribe on a *stēlē* the powers of the god. Year 239.

---

[22] *SEG* 57, 1182 (*Sammlung Tatış* 23; Petzl 2019, no. 141), with Gordon 2016, 245–6: ἐπεὶ ὗς ἀπόλετο Ἀπολλωνίου | ἔτει σζι', περὶ τούτου σκῆπτρον ἐ|φέστη Ἀπόλλωνος Ταρσίου· καὶ μη|δενὸς ὡμολογήσαντος παρ' αὐτό, |(5) ἐξ ὑστέρου εὑρεθεὶς παρὰ Ἀλεξάν|δρῳ Τασιλα· πείσαντος τοῦ ἱερέως | προσλαβέσθαι τὸν ὗν τὸν Ἀπολλώ|νιν, ἐπιγνοὺς, ὅτι ἐντὸς τῆς προθεσ|μίας τῶν ἡμερῶν, ὧν ὑπεξειρημέ|(10)νων ἦσαν, ὑπερχρόν⟨ι⟩ον ἦν, ἀπελάσαν|τος τὸν ὗν ὁ θεὸς ἐπεζήτησε στηλ|λογραφῆσαι τὰς δυνάμεις τοῦ θεοῦ | Τατίαν γυναῖκα τοῦ Ἀπολλωνίου. | ἔτους σλθ'.

Figure 9.4 Propitiatory *stēlē* of Tatia, from Köleköy. *SEG* 57, 1182 (collection of Yavuz Tatış, Turkey, inv. 2049).

The first chapter of the story is reasonably clear. Apollonios' pig goes missing, and he sets up a sceptre in an attempt to persuade the thief to come forward, without success ('no-one confessed'). Some time later, the pig turns up at the farm of Alexandros Tasilas. The studiously neutral language of these first few clauses is well worth noting: the pig 'was lost', and subsequently 'it was found'. It seems pretty clear that

Alexandros Tasilas *neither* suffered divine punishment *nor* confessed to the crime: the pig had indeed turned up in his own yard, but there was no way of showing that he had deliberately stolen it from Apollonios ('it must have just wandered off'). This created a serious problem for the community in resolving the dispute. The priest of Apollo Tarsios seems to have tried to seek a compromise between the two parties: Alexandros Tasilas clearly could not be permitted to keep the pig, but too much time had elapsed since the setting up of the sceptre for Apollonios to be able to reclaim the animal. The priest therefore suggested that the pig should now be considered forfeit to the god.[23] In the face of this, Apollonios seems (not unreasonably) to have blown his top: after all, the point of the whole process was to get his pig back. Apollonios therefore forcibly reclaimed his pig and stomped off home, against the priest's strong professional advice. Apollonios – we may infer – subsequently died, probably as a result of a leg injury (the *stēlē* carries a sculpted image of a leg above the inscribed text: Figure 9.4), and his death was apparently understood as punishment for having cheated the god out of the pig.

The most startling thing about the whole saga is the extraordinary expanse of time that elapsed between the original loss of the pig and Apollonios' final punishment: a total of twenty-two years ('Year 217' to 'Year 239', AD 122/3 to 154/5). It is hard to imagine that the period between the loss and the rediscovery of the pig can have been anything like this long: the priest speaks of a stipulated number of 'days' having elapsed, not 'years'. We can therefore be pretty sure that most of these twenty-two years elapsed *after* Apollonios' row with the priest. I take it that with Apollonios' public flouting of the god's authority, the 'social recognition of guilt' was settled: Apollonios had put himself in the wrong in the eyes of this small community, and so his punishment by the god was now only a matter of time. As a result, even though Apollonios lived on for another two decades or so (!), his eventual death could still plausibly be taken as a belated punishment for his disrespect to the gods many years earlier, and was commemorated as such by his widow.

---

[23] The syntax here is extremely unclear. I have followed Herrmann and Malay 2007, 94, in assuming that the priest argued that the pig should be forfeit to the sanctuary (taking the nominative ἐπιγνούς as an error for the genitive ἐπιγνόντος), since that seems to me to make the best sense of Apollonios' subsequent 'transgression'; Ricl 2011, 148 suggests that the priest recommended that Alexandros should be allowed to keep the pig, which is also possible. Petzl 2019, 36–7 suggests that the priest persuaded Alexandros that Apollonios should be permitted to take back his pig; this seems to me considerably less likely.

A third multi-stage dispute over livestock is narrated in a lengthy propitiatory inscription from the village of Iaza. The top of the stone is missing, and so we do not know which deity inflicted the punishment.[24]

> … Hermogenes Valerius, son of Apollonios, gave satisfaction to Kaikos son of Kaitron concerning his flock. On this matter, it was decided that Hermogenes should swear (5) that he had not abandoned (?) Kaikos' flock. So Hermogenes, because he was unaware, swore in the god's name. The god showed his own powers and punished Hermogenes (10) and laid a penalty on him, by slaying his livestock, an ox and a donkey. When Hermogenes still did not obey, he (i.e. the god) slew his daughter; then he (Hermogenes) annulled his oath. Apphias and her children (15) Alexandros, Attalos, Apollonios, Amion – we set up the *stēlē* and inscribed on it the powers of the god, and from now on we praise him.

Something unfortunate has happened to a flock of sheep owned by a man named Kaikos, and one Hermogenes Valerius is suspected of being responsible. What exactly Hermogenes is accused of having done is far from clear: he is made to swear that he has not 'abandoned' or 'delivered up' Kaikos' flock (the Greek verb is *prodidonai*), whatever that means. Hermogenes is clearly a landowner himself (he owns his own ox and donkey), and so it is unlikely that Kaikos had hired him as his shepherd; perhaps the two men regularly pastured their sheep together, and Hermogenes was believed to have taken insufficient care of Kaikos' animals. At any event, Hermogenes was required to 'give satisfaction' to Kaikos by taking an exculpatory oath, publicly swearing in the god's name that he is innocent of the charge. (I assume it was the priests who required him to do so, though it is possible that a secular court was involved.) Hermogenes is said to have sworn the oath 'because he was unaware' – that is to say, because he was unaware how ruthlessly and effectively the gods pursue those who swear false oaths, not because he was 'unaware' of having done anything wrong.[25]

At this point, a familiar sequence of events unfolds. First two of Hermogenes' animals die, his ox and his donkey. Hermogenes was evidently

---

[24] *TAM* V 1, 464 (Iaza: Petzl 1994, no. 34), with Harter-Uibopuu 2016: [- - - - - -]ω Ἑρμογένης Ἀπολωνί|ου Βαλέρι(ο)ς γενόμενος εἰκανοδ|ότης Καΐκου Καιτρωνος περὶ προ|βάτων ὧν ἐκρίθη ὁμόσε τὸν Ἑρ|(5)μογένην μὴ προδεδωκένε τὰ | πρόβατα τὰ Καείκου· ἀγνοήσας οὖ|ν ὁ Ἑρμογένης ὤμοσεν τὸν θεὸ|ν· ὁ θεὸς ἀνέδιξεν τὰς εἰδίας δυν|άμις καὶ ἐκόλασεν τὸν Ἑρμογένην |(10) καὶ ζημίας αὐτῷ ἐπόησεν ἀποκτί|νας αὐτῷ τὰ κτ⟨ή⟩νη, βοῦν κὲ ὄνον· ἀπιθ|οῦντος δὲ τοῦ Ἑρμογένου ἀπέκτινεν α|ὐτοῦ τὴν θυγατέραν· τότε ἔλυσεν τὸ|ν ὅρκον. Ἀφιὰς καὶ τὰ τέκνα αὐτῆς Ἀλέ|(15)ξανδρος, Ἄτταλος, Ἀπολ⟨ώ⟩νιος, Ἄμιο|ν ⟨ἐ⟩στήσομεν τὴν στήλην καὶ ἐνεγράψομε|ν τὰς δυνάμις τοῦ θεοῦ καὶ ἀπὸ νῦν εὐλ|ογοῦμεν.

[25] A different – to my mind less likely – interpretation in Chaniotis 1997, 367 (followed by Gordon 2004, 193). For my interpretation of ἄγνοια, see Chapter 2, Section 2.6.

unmoved; he stuck to his original story and denied that the gods had anything to do with the death of his animals ('No, no, the donkey was already ill'). The community seems to have been unable to take any further action at this stage: his guilt was not yet 'socially established', as it were. Only when his daughter also died unexpectedly was Hermogenes finally obliged to confess that he had sworn falsely, and that he was indeed responsible for the 'abandonment' of Kaikos' flock. It appears that Hermogenes himself may have died shortly afterwards, since the propitiatory *stēlē* was eventually set up not by him, but by other members of his family (probably his wife and surviving children).

Taken together, these last two stories – the god's inconvenient failure to punish Alexandros Tasilas, followed by the twenty-one-year postponement of Apollonios' punishment; Hermogenes' initial refusal to attribute any significance to the death of his animals – beautifully illustrate what for us seems like the most obvious problem with the Hieradoumian system of 'divine mediation' in intra-village disputes. Sooner or later, *everyone* suffers a family tragedy of some kind – so how can one tell the difference between divine vengeance and random strokes of misfortune? Of course, once Hermogenes has actually confessed his sin, the deaths of Hermogenes' ox and donkey can retrospectively be recognized as a 'first' manifestation of divine vengeance; but until he does so, it is always open to Hermogenes to argue that the animals might just have died of natural causes.

In fact, I would suggest, this apparent 'problem' is in fact central to the functioning of the whole system. The villagers of rural Hieradoumia were perfectly well aware that they could not reliably distinguish between a freak death and an act of divine vengeance on the basis of observation alone. Hence no disaster ever constituted decisive proof of guilt in and of itself, but was always interpreted in the light of a prior social judgement. If a man was widely regarded as the innocent party in the dispute, I take it that he would tend to be given the benefit of the doubt if his donkey died. Conversely, if a man was widely suspected of being guilty, his neighbours would watch him like hawks until a corroborating act of divine vengeance occurred – and such an act could *always* be identified sooner or later, even if (as in the case of Apollonios) it took more than twenty years to do so. This does not mean that the gods are minor or incidental actors in the process: their act of vengeance remains absolutely central to the moral narrative. But the assignment of guilt was necessarily a social process, ultimately dependent on the consensus of human actors: priests, family members, and no doubt the wider village community.[26]

---

[26] This point is well brought out by Eidinow 2016, 220–3.

9.4 Burglars

Petty larceny is a recurring theme of the Hieradoumian propitiation-*stēlai*. As well as the livestock disputes recounted in the previous section, and the timber rustling described in Chapter 8, we also hear of several straightforward acts of burglary: thefts of money, documents, and precious objects of various kinds. On the whole – with one exception – the goods stolen tend to be of relatively low value: four silver coins, a cloak, three pigs, a single gemstone. This may indicate that only minor acts of criminality were entrusted to the gods' judgement, with more serious crimes being dealt with by secular authorities from the nearest city. Alternatively – and I think more plausibly – it could well reflect the real contours of criminal behaviour in rural Hieradoumia. We might recall the list of thefts confessed by the petty criminal Neik[- -] (Chapter 8, Section 8.5), all of which seem to have been on a very small scale: trapping sacred doves near the sanctuary of Apollo Lairbenos; an attempted burglary of the sanctuary; stealing a sheep belonging to a certain Demetrios.[27] For unscrupulous persons, living in tight-knit villages of a few dozen farming families with relatively few movable possessions, the opportunities for self-enrichment were, quite simply, limited.

The most substantial theft known to us from Roman Hieradoumia is described in a votive inscription from Kula, dated to spring AD 114[28]:

> Year 198 [AD 113/14], month Daisios. Rhodia, slave of Flavia Menogenis, (set this up to) Meter Aliane in fulfilment of a vow concerning the stolen (5) silver, 412 *denarii*, of Agathon her husband, from [...] – (stolen) from the granary, and found in the possession of Crescens, foster-son (*threptos*) of Alkimos and (10) Ekloge.

The text is accompanied by a sculptural relief depicting a jar, suggesting that the stolen money was stored in a pot. Agathon had apparently concealed a pot containing his life savings in a granary (perhaps that of Flavia Menogenis?), where it had been discovered and stolen by Crescens. It may be significant that Flavia Menogenis – owner of Rhodia, and probably of Agathon also – is known to us from other sources as one of the largest landowners in the Kula region.[29] One wonders whether Agathon and Rhodia (no doubt workers on Menogenis' estate) might have been saving their *peculium* in order to purchase their freedom.

[27] *MAMA* IV 279 (Petzl 1994, no. 106).
[28] *TAM* V 1, 257, with Petzl 2007: ἔτους ρϙη′, μη(νὸς) Δαισίου. Ῥοδία | Φλαουίας Μηνογενίδος | δούλη Μη[τ]ρὶ Ἀλιανῇ εὐ|χὴν ὑπὲρ τοῦ κλαπέντος |(5) ἀργυρίου (δηνάρια) υιβ′ Ἀγάθωνος | τοῦ ἀνδρὸς αὐτῆς ἐκ ΛΑ|ΝΑΠΟΣΤΩΝ ἐκ τοῦ σειτοβο|λείου καὶ εὑρεθέντος παρὰ | Κρήσκεντι τῷ | Ἀλκίμου καὶ Ἐκ|(10)λογῆς θρεπτῷ.
[29] *TAM* V 1, 274, with Malay and Petzl 2017, no. 200 (esp. p.203); Chapter 10, Section 10.2.

At any event, other recorded thefts in Roman Hieradoumia were on a far less dramatic and consequential scale. Low-level pilfering does in fact seem to have been fairly widespread, often perpetrated by close relatives and neighbours. In a text dated to spring AD 103 from a sanctuary of Meis Axiottenos, a certain Alexandros finds that he has been robbed of four *denarii* – not a trifling sum, but not one's life savings either. He appeals to the god Meis, here hailed as an 'all-seeing judge in heaven', to investigate the matter[30]:

> Year 187, day 12 of the month Daisios. Great is Meis Ouranios Arte-
> midorou who possesses Axiotta and his power, an all-seeing (5) judge
> in heaven, to whom Alexandros son of Sokrates resorted concerning
> the theft already described. Ammion, wife of Diogas, in concert with
> her daughter Meltine, stole four *denarii* from her own (10) husband's
> brother; when they were made to take an oath, they swore (falsely); the
> god killed her/them. Great, then, is the god! … (remaining text missing).

Alexandros clearly already suspected his sister-in-law and his niece of the theft, but was unable to prove it. He therefore compelled them to take an exculpatory oath in the sanctuary of Meis Axiottenos, which was then followed by the death of one or both of the women. We have good reason to think that married brothers in Roman Hieradoumia sometimes lived together (Chapter 5), but we have no way of knowing whether that was the case here. The fact that Ammion stole money from her brother-in-law does indicate that horizontally extended family groups did not normally pool their family wealth.

Small-scale theft from sanctuaries (as attempted by the slave Neik[- -] at the sanctuary of Apollo Lairbenos) may well also have been an everyday occurrence, to judge from a short propitiatory inscription dated to spring AD 216, from the sanctuary of Apollo Axyreos near Saittai[31]:

> Year 300, the twelfth day of the month Xandikos. Because of the error
> (*hamartēma*) which they committed against the god – and they (5) stole
> some glass vessels and other dedications – Melite and Makedon were
> punished by the god; their parents asked (10) Apollo Axyreos on their
> behalf; they asked, they dedicated this in gratitude.

---

[30] *SEG* 57, 1158 (Petzl 2019, no. 137), with Gordon 2016, 240–1: ἔτους ρπζ΄, μη(νὸς) Δαισίου βι΄· | Μέγας Μεὶς Οὐράνιος | Ἀρτεμιδώρου Ἄξιοττα | κατέχων καὶ ἡ δύναμις αὐτοῦ, κρι|(5) τῆς ἀλάθητος ἐν οὐρανῷ, εἰς ὃν | κατέ(φ)υγεν Ἀλέξανδρος Σωκράτο[υ] | ὑπὲρ κλοπῆς τῆς προδηλουμένης· | Ἄμμιον, Διογᾶ γυνή, ἔχουσα θυγα|τέρα Μελτίνην ἦραν ἰδίου δ|(10)αέρος (δηνάρια) δ΄· ὀρκιζόμεναι ὤμοσαν· | [ἀ]πέκτεινεν ὁ θεός· μέγας ὦν ὁ θ||[εός - - -]ΙΑΝΤΩΝΥ[- - -].

[31] *SEG* 37, 1737 (Petzl 1994, no. 22, with the correction proposed by M. Ricl, *SEG* 53, 1349): ἔτους τ΄, μη(νὸς) Ξανδικο|ῦ δωδεκάτη. διὰ τὸ ἁ|μάρτημα, τὸ ἐποίη|σαν ἐπὶ τῷ θεῷ, καὶ ἔκ|(5)λεψαν εἰάλιν α κὲ ἕτ|ερά τινα τὰ κίμενα, κο|λασθέντα ὑπὸ τοῦ θε|οῦ ἡ Μελίτη καὶ ὁ Μακ|εδών, ἠρώτησαν οἱ γονῖς |(10) ὑπὲρ αὐτῶν Ἀπόλλωνα Α|ξυρον· ἠρώτησαν, εὐχαρι|στοῦν τες ἀνέθηκαν.

One naturally wonders whether Melite and Makedon (perhaps, but not necessarily, siblings) might have been children; that would nicely explain why it was their parents who set up the *stēlē* on their behalf.

A more interesting example of 'everyday' theft is found in an inscription from the village of Tarsi, dating to AD 164/5 (Figure 9.5)[32]:

> Great is Meis Axiottenos who rules as king over Tarsi! Since a sceptre was set up, if anyone steals anything from the bath-house – when a cloak (*himation*) was stolen (5), the god was enraged at the thief and made him bring the cloak to the god after a time, and he acknowledged (the god's power). So the god ordered through an angel that the cloak be sold (10), and to write up his powers on a *stēlē*, Year 249.

The opening lines of the text show that a sceptre had been set up pre-emptively at the local sanctuary of Meis Axiottenos, in order to warn people off stealing things from the village bathhouse – a broadly similar procedure, as we have already seen, to that described in several tombstones from the region (the pre-emptive erection of sceptres to warn off grave robbers). This text is, I think, unique among the surviving propitiation-*stēlai*, in that neither the thief nor the victim is named; nor is there any indication that the thief has suffered any exemplary punishment. The most likely explanation is that the identity of the thief was not in fact known. I take it that the stolen cloak simply reappeared one morning in the sanctuary: the thief had no doubt slipped in quietly to leave the cloak in a prominent place, probably in front of the sceptre or the statue of Meis Axiottenos, as represented in the accompanying relief sculpture (here, Figure 9.5: the cloak is depicted at the god's feet, next to his sceptre).

This caused a procedural problem for the village community. The god had, in one sense, done his work admirably: the cloak was returned, and the thief had therefore (in a sense) acknowledged the god's power, by dint of returning the cloak. However, it remained the case that no one in the village knew the identity of the thief, nor whether he had been punished or not, making the final stage in the process (the erection of a propitiatory *stēlē*) logistically problematic. As a result, the sanctuary personnel consulted the god *via* an angel on the best way to proceed. (How this was done in practice is totally unclear: perhaps the angel communicated with the priest through a dream.)

---

[32] *TAM* V 1, 159 (Petzl 1994, no. 3, with further bibliography in Petzl 2019, 10): Μέγας Μεὶς Ἀξιοττηνὸς Ταρσι βα|σιλεύων. ἐπεὶ ἐπεστάθη σκῆ|πτρον, εἴ τις ἐκ τοῦ βαλανείου τι | κλέψι· κλαπέντος οὖν εἱματίου |(5) ὁ θεὸς ἐνεμέσησε τὸν κλέπτην, | καὶ ἐπόησε μετὰ χρόνον τὸ εἱμά|τιον ἐνενκῖν ἐπὶ τὸν θεὸν καὶ ἐ|ξωμολογήσατο. ὁ θεὸς οὖν ἐκέλευ|σε δι᾽ ἀνγέλου πραθῆναι τὸ εἱμά|(10)τιν καὶ στηλλογραφῆσαι τὰς δυ|νάμεις. ἔτους σμθ´.

Figure 9.5 Propitiatory *stēlē* dedicated to Meis Axiottenos, from Köleköy. *TAM* V 1, 159.

The god suggested that the cloak should be sold, rather than returned to its owner, and – I take it – that the profit from the sale of the cloak should be used to pay for a *stēlē* describing the affair. The relief sculpture on the *stēlē* nicely encapsulates the whole transaction: in the upper register, the god holding his sceptre, with the cloak lying at his feet; in the lower register, the anonymous thief, arms raised in recognition of the god's power.[33]

A more serious act of domestic theft is described in a curious propitiatory inscription from the village of Taza, on the south bank of the Hermos near the modern village of Kavaklı, dating to winter AD 210/211[34]:

> Year 295, day 8 of the month Peritios. To Meis Petraeites and Meis Labanas. Metrophanes and Flavianus, sons of Philippikos, were left (5) as orphans by their parents, and some men from the village plotted against them, and secretly took written documents and other copies from their house; (10) and when they were subjected to seizure by their creditors, the village of the Tazenoi was outraged, and set up a sceptre against those who had dared to act wickedly against them; the god then demanded atonement and (15) punished and destroyed those who had plotted against them. The god demanded that they inscribe a *stēlē* [and praise] his powers, that …

Despite the loss of the final lines of the inscription, the general situation seems clear enough. Various documents have gone missing from the house of a pair of orphaned brothers, apparently leading to the seizure and imprisonment of the orphans by their creditors. The village community was 'outraged' by the undeserved fate of these young people, and set up a sceptre to encourage the god to intervene. The god then punished the thieves with death. At first sight, we seem to have here a straightforward case of an entire village mobilizing in support of some of their most vulnerable members: when the orphans were unable to act on their own behalf, it was the village community as a whole which acted by setting up a sceptre against the malefactors and hunting them down.

There is, however, a rather peculiar aspect to this text, which might reasonably lead us to doubt that we have the whole story. As in the bathhouse text discussed above, the supposed thieves are left unnamed: they are simply

---

[33] Belayche 2008, 187–8; Chaniotis 2012, 224–9.
[34] *TAM* V 1, 231 (Petzl 1994, no. 35), with Chaniotis 2004b, 248: ἔτους σϞε′, μη(νὸς) Περειτίου η′.|
Μηνὶ Πετραείτῃ καὶ Μηνὶ Λα|βάνῃ. Μητροφάνης καὶ Φλαβια|νὸς οἱ Φιλιππικοῦ
καταλειφθ|(5)έντες ὑπὸ τῶν γονέων ἐν ὀρ|φανείᾳ καὶ ἐνίων ἀνθρώπων ἐ|πιβουλευσάντων αὐτοῖς
ἐκ τῆ[ς]| κώμης καὶ ἀρόντων ἔνγραφα καὶ ἕτε|ρα εἴδη ἐκ τῆς οἰκίας αὐτῶν λα|(10)θραίως καὶ
περισυρομένων αὐτῶν | ὑπὸ δανιστῶν ἡ Ταζηνῶν κατοι|κία ἀδοξήσασα ἐπέστησε τὸ | σκῆπτρον
τοῖς κακῶς εἰς αὐτοὺς τ[ολ]|μήσασιν καὶ ὁ θεὸς ἐξεζήτησεν [καὶ]| (15) ἐκολάσετο καὶ διέφθειρε
τοὺς [ἐπι]|βουλεύσαντας αὐτοῖς. ὁ θεὸς [οὖν | ἐπεζήτ]ησε στηλλογραφῆσα[ι εὐ|λογοῦντας τὰ]ς
δυνάμις, ὅτι [- | -]. ΤΗΣ[- -].

described as 'some men from the village'. It is true that the closing lines of the inscription are missing, but on other propitiatory *stēlai*, the name of the transgressor is invariably given at the head of the text, in line with the normal function of these *stēlai* as extremely public avowals of guilt and repentance. It is difficult to know quite what to make of this. The analogy of the bathhouse theft ought to make us wonder whether the identity of the document thieves might not in fact have been firmly established by the village community; and if their identity was not known, then evidently their 'punishment' cannot have been objectively verified. Did the village perhaps simply take the god's word for it (transmitted somehow through his sanctuary personnel) that the thieves had been punished and the case was closed?

At any event, it is quite clear that the primary function of this text is radically different from that of our other surviving propitiation-*stēlai*. The central 'actor' is not the transgressor, making a public avowal of personal guilt, but the village community, reassuring itself that it has done all it can in the face of a major collective moral crisis ('the village of the Tazenoi was outraged'). Reading between the lines, one wonders whether the real story here might in truth be the effective *abandonment* of a pair of orphans by the village community. As in all pre-modern societies, many children in Roman Hieradoumia must have lost their parents before reaching adulthood; but the characteristic domestic structures of rural Hieradoumia – the multiple-family household, and the regular circulation of children between households (Chapters 5 and 6) – would normally have served to 'cushion' young children from the impact of early parental death. Orphans typically remained part of their grandparents' or uncle's household, and/or would be brought up by *threpsantes* (either kin or non-kin). That is to say, if Metrophanes and Flavianus really did end up as isolated and vulnerable to fraud and seizure as this text suggests, then that must reflect a disastrous *failure* of their wider kin group and neighbours to live up to the normative 'rules' of the Hieradoumian kinship system. When the hapless boys were seized by their creditors, their fellow villagers – profoundly embarrassed by this failure of collective care – attempted to 'save face' by postulating the existence of unnamed thieves who were responsible for the children's plight. But we are visibly far into the realms of speculation, and other explanations are no doubt possible.

9.5 Loans

A third major category of low-level secular disputes to appear in the propitiatory inscriptions is that of attempts by creditors to reclaim money from their debtors. There is no indication that professional moneylenders are involved in any of these cases, and it seems that we are generally dealing with small-scale loans between neighbours – that is to say, the kind of 'informal' loans whose repayment might be particularly difficult to enforce at law. We have already met the two women, Stratonike and Eutychis, who fell out over a loan of wheat grain[35]:

> Year 217 [AD 132/3], in the month Hyperberetaios. Stratonike daughter of Mousaios received as a loan from Eutychis a *modinos* of wheat which was sacred to Axiottenos; she dragged out repayment until today, and was punished by the god in her right breast, and she has returned the complete amount along with the interest, having praised Axiottenos.

As we saw in Chapter 8, Eutychis was clearly leasing a plot of arable land from the sanctuary of Meis Axiottenos; she lent a modest quantity of grain to a neighbour, who failed to repay it on time, and was duly struck down with a breast illness by the god. Exactly how small the loan was depends on what we think the Greek word *modinos* represents. The Roman dry unit known as the *modius* is a mere 8.62 litres, which seems implausibly small for a grain loan, and so I suspect that Stratonike has in fact borrowed a *medimnos* of grain (a Greek dry measure representing around 52–54 litres, though the precise volume varied from region to region and over time) – still not a large quantity, but conceivable as a very short-term emergency loan in a period of dearth (the equivalent of roughly two weeks' consumption for a family of four or five, with a normal value of around 5–6 *denarii*).[36]

A broadly similar 'neighbourly' loan, this time of cash, is described in another inscription from a sanctuary of Meis Axiottenos[37]:

> Great is Meis Artemidorou who possesses Axiotta and his power! Since Tatia daughter of Neikephoros from Mokada made a loan of money to (5) Gaios and his wife Apphia from Mokada, saying 'I make this loan [...]'. Then Gaios defrauded her; and Tatias, having been defrauded, called down the god (10) upon him. And so, great [- -] Gaios [- -] money [- -].

A married couple from the village of Mokada have borrowed money from a woman from the same village; the lender, Tatia (or Tatias), appears to

---

35 *SEG* 39, 1277 (Petzl 1994, no. 63); Chapter 8, Section 8.2.

36 For the figures, Rathbone 2014; Rathbone and von Reden 2015.

37 *TAM* V 1, 525 (Petzl 1994, no. 79): Μέγας Μὶς Ἀρτεμιδώρου Ἀξ[ι|ο]ττα κατέχων καὶ ἡ δύνα|μις αὐτοῦ. ἐπὶ Τατια Νεικηφό|ρου Μοκαδδηνὴ ἐδάνεισε Γα|(5)[ἴ]ῳ καὶ Ἀφφιᾳ τῇ γυναικὶ αὐτοῦ Μ[ο|κ]αδδηνοῖς χαλκὸν προειποῦσα |[.]ΤΗ.ΡΟΝ δανίζω· ὁ Γάϊος οὖν ἐχρ[ε|οκ]ό(π)ησεν αὐτήν· ἡ Τατιας οὖ[ν χρε|οκ]οπ(η)θ(ε)ῖσα ἐπεκαλέσετ[υ κατ᾽ αὐ|(10)τοῦ τὸ]ν θεόν. μέγας οὖ[ν – | – τ] ὸν Γάϊον καὶ Ε[- | – χ]αρκὸν Ο[- -].

have attached a specific condition to the loan, perhaps 'I make this loan [on daily interest]'.[38] One might have thought that, when the husband refused to repay the loan, Tatia could simply have taken him to court. The fact that she did not do so presumably shows that this was an 'informal' loan between neighbours, whose terms (perhaps including the harsh requirement of daily interest) could not be legally enforced. Tatia was therefore reduced to the nuclear option of appealing directly to the god in order to recover her money, with unpleasant consequences for Gaios. One does wonder whether it might be significant that female lenders were involved in both of these cases: were women particularly prone to making 'informal' loans?

A slightly different situation seems to be envisaged in a lengthy text from the modern village of Ayvatlar, dated to spring AD 119, also concerned with the non-repayment of a cash loan[39]:

> [Great is Meter Atimis and Meis Tiamou who rules over…] and [his] power! Apollonios […] to Apollonios, […] 40 *denarii*. Then, when Apollonios (5) asked for the cash back from Skollos, he swore by the gods listed above that he had paid back the complete sum owed within the specified period. But since Skollos had not kept (10) faith with him, Apollonios handed the matter over to the goddess. So when Skollos was punished by the gods, in the form of death, after his death atonement was demanded by the (15) gods; so Tatia, his daughter, loosened his oaths, and now, having appeased them, she praises Meter Atimis and Meis Tiamou. Year 203 [AD 118/19], day 15 of the month Xandikos.

Skollos has borrowed a fairly substantial sum of money, 40 *denarii*, from one Apollonios. When Apollonios attempted to recover his money – quite possibly in court, but certainly in a public context of some kind – Skollos responded by swearing an exculpatory oath in the names of the gods Meter Atimis and Meis Tiamou, to the effect that he had in fact *already* paid the loan back on time.[40] Precisely as in the case of the exculpatory oath sworn by Hermogenes Valerius when accused of 'abandoning' Kaikos' flock (discussed above), this

---

[38] Restoring ἡμερο{ν}δανίζω in line 7 (M. Ricl: *SEG* 53, 1347).

[39] *TAM* V 1, 440 (Petzl 1994, no. 54): [- - -]ων καὶ ἡ δύ|[ναμις αὐτοῦ - -] Ἀπολλώνιος |[- -]ΤΟ· Ἀπολλωνί|ῳ [- - χαλκ]οῦ (δηνάρια) μ´· εἶτα ἀπα[ι]|(5)τοῦντος τοῦ Ἀπολλωνίου τὸν χαλ|κὸν παρὰ τοῦ Σκόλλου ὤμοσε τοὺς | προγεγραμμένους θεοὺς ἰς προ|θεσμίαν ἀποδοῦναι τὸ συνα|χθὲν κεφάλαιον· μὴ τηρήσαντος |(10) αὐτοῦ τὴν πίστιν παρεχώρησεν | τῇ θεῷ ὁ Ἀπολλώνιος· κολασθέν|τος οὖν τοῦ Σκόλλου ὑπὸ τῶν θε|ῶν ἰς θανάτου λόγον μετὰ τὴν τ[ε]|λευτὴν αὐτοῦ ἐπεζητήθη ὑπὸ τ[ῶν]|(15) θεῶν· Τατιας οὖν ἡ θυγάτηρ αὐτοῦ | ἔλοισε τοὺς ὅρκους καὶ νῦν εἰλα|σαμένη εὐλογεῖ Μητρὶ Ατιμιτι | καὶ Μηνὶ Τιαμου. ἔτους σγ´, μη(νὸς) | Ξανδικοῦ ει´.

[40] Thus, correctly, Harter-Uibopuu 2016, 69; a different, in my view less likely interpretation in Chaniotis 2004a, 16–17 (Skollos *promises* to pay back the loan).

left Apollonios without any further options for legal redress, and so he put the matter in the hands of the goddess Meter Atimis, no doubt by depositing a *pittakion* in the sanctuary. Some time later, Skollos died, and Apollonios succeeded in persuading the sanctuary personnel and Skollos' surviving daughter Tatia that Skollos' death was a sure-fire indication that he had sworn falsely. Whether Tatia also repaid the loan at this point, we do not know.

Two further incomplete texts are almost certainly concerned with the non-repayment of loans and the punishments that followed. A very fragmentary text from the modern village of Karaoba near Iaza preserves only isolated words ('he … faith … but … punished … and he returned … the complete sum … saved … example … he set up'), but the sequence of thought is clear enough: someone failed to 'keep faith' (*pistis*) with his creditor, was punished by the god, returned the complete sum that was owed (*kephalaion*), and was thereby saved from death.[41] Rather clearer is a text dating to spring AD 223, from the vicinity of the modern village of İbrahimağa, of which only the final lines survive[42]:

> … when the gods demanded atonement, his sons Erasistratos and Sperkyllos and Alexandros restored the 25 *denarii*, twofold, so that the *stēlē* might be made from this money. Year 307 [AD 222/3], month Panemos.

The basic situation here seems to be very similar to that in the Ayvatlar text (Apollonios' loan of 40 *denarii* to Skollos). The unnamed father of these three men has taken out a loan of 25 *denarii*; he has died without repaying it, and his death has been interpreted as punishment by the god for his attempt to cheat his creditor. His sons are therefore required to repay twice the sum that was owed, a nice instance of the imposition of quasi-judicial 'damages' by the god (in this instance, double the principal).[43] I take it that 25 *denarii* were returned to the creditor, and the remaining 25 *denarii* were spent on the *stēlē*, though the text is not quite explicit about this.

9.6 Trouble at Home

As already noted in Chapter 2, the Hieradoumian propitiation texts offer a useful counterpoint to the eirenic and normative picture of rural kinship

---

[41] *TAM* V 1, 443 (Karaoba: Petzl 1994, no. 26).

[42] *TAM* V 1, 510 (Petzl 1994, no. 46): ἐπ[ιζητησά]ντων τῶν [θ]ε[ῶν] | ἀπέδωκαν οἱ υἱοὶ αὐτοῦ Ἐρασί|στρατος καὶ Σπερκύλλος καὶ Ἀλέ|ξανδρος τὰ εἰκοσιπέντε (δηνάρια) δι|(5)πλᾶ, ἵνα ἐξ αὐτῶν γενήσεται | ἡ στήλλη. ἔτους τζ΄, μη(νὸς) Πανήμου.

[43] Potts 2019, 249.

structures offered by the funerary epigraphy of the region. Epitaphs – pre-
dictably enough – offer a strongly idealized picture of extended family
groupings; only very occasionally do we receive hints (and never anything
more than that) of intra-familial tensions or dysfunction.[44] The propitiatory
inscriptions, by contrast, are a mine of information on disputes between
close kin, sometimes quite remarkably violent and acrimonious. In Chapter 5, we met Glykon son of Apollonios from Axiotta, who set up a 'eulogy'
to Meis Axiottenos after being rescued by the god from confinement by his
own nephew: 'I was imprisoned by Demainetos, the child of my brother,
when I had neglected my own affairs and had given you help as if you were
my own child; but you locked me in and imprisoned me, as if I were not
your paternal uncle, but a malefactor'.[45] Similarly, earlier in this chapter,
we met Ammion and her daughter Meltine, who together stole four *denarii*
from Ammion's husband's brother Alexandros (Meltine's paternal uncle);
when the two women were accused of the theft, they both swore a false oath
of innocence, and one or both of them were accordingly slain by the god as
punishment for both the original theft and their subsequent perjury. It is
mildly surprising that Glykon and Alexandros (who clearly suspected his
sister-in-law from the outset) chose to involve the gods in the first place;
but what is really startling is the fact that both men subsequently chose to
commemorate the affairs with a *stēlē* which made the family relationship
absolutely explicit (Glykon was imprisoned by 'the child of my brother',
ἀδελφοῦ τέκνου; Ammion stole the money 'from her own husband's
brother', ἰδίου δαέρος). In both cases, one might have expected that family honour would have discouraged Hieradoumian villagers from washing
their dirty household linen in public like this, but clearly not. The mere fact
that people were prepared to drag their own close relatives' names through
the mud in this way is striking testimony – among other things – to the
heat which family quarrels could generate.

The number of texts concerned with intra-familial disputes is too small
to give us any statistically robust data on which relationships were most
likely to 'break down'. However, it is very striking that the overwhelming

---

[44] 'The writer of an epitaph should not be considered as saying nothing but what is strictly true.
Allowance must be made for some degree of exaggerated praise. In lapidary inscriptions a man
is not upon oath.' Boswell, *Life* ed. Hill and Powell 1934, III 407. Dysfunction: e.g. *TAM* V 1,
682 (Charakipolis: AD 161/2): the mother and father have divorced, and the natural father
is tucked away at the end of the list of relatives commemorating the deceased, significantly
'below' the step-father. See further Chapter 5, Section 5.4.

[45] *SEG* 53, 1344 (Petzl 2019, no. 56); Chapter 5, Section 5.6.

majority of attested family conflicts (six out of eight, on my count) were cross-generational disputes between older women and their sons, sons-in-law, and foster-sons (or in one case, foster-daughter), a pattern which is sufficiently clear and consistent to suggest that we might be dealing with an intrinsic structural fault line within the Hieradoumian household. Four of the six relevant texts are concerned with women cursing their own children or foster-children, as follows:

> Apollonios bears witness to the gods in Pereudos. When my mother cursed me, I asked the gods, and I gave along with my brother Eupelastos 100 *denarii* for the house purchased from Myrmex, and I gave in return another 50 *denarii* for all the other cut vines in Promiasse by the holm-oak. I asked the gods twice, I had good fortune and I am grateful.[46]

> To the gods of Pereudos. Iulia cursed her own *threptē* Onesime, and having received nothing (?), was investigated (?); and the gods came down on her, and from now on I praise them. Year 294 [AD 209/10].[47]

> Year [.]09, day [.] of the month Peritios. Theodote [cursed] her *threptos* Glykon, because he raised his hands against her and harmed her, and when both she and Glykon died, the god demanded atonement from […], her grandson, and he fulfilled it and from now on he praises him.[48]

> Great are the gods who possess Nea Kome! Year 231 [AD 146/7]. Menophila was enraged by her son Polychronios, and made a vow to the gods, that she might receive satisfaction. And when he was punished and appeased the gods, he (the god) ordered her to inscribe the powers of the gods on a *stēlē*.[49]

The immediate 'triggers' for the breakdown of relations between these women and their children or foster-children are rather varied: in the first case, the unnamed mother's curse seems to have been prompted by some kind of familial dispute over land (most probably a question of inheritance); in the second, Iulia's motivations are unclear; in the third, Theodote was

---

[46] *SEG* 34, 1212 (Petzl 1994, no. 17), discussed further in Chapter 8, Section 8.3.

[47] *SEG* 34, 1220 (Petzl 1994, no. 20): Θεοῖς Περευδηνοῖς· Ἰου|λία ἐπαρασαμένη θρε|πτῆ ἰδίᾳ Ὀνησίμῃ καὶ | μηδὲν λαβοῦσα ἠρω|(5)τήθη· καὶ οἱ θεοὶ μετέ|βησαν ἰς αὐτήν, καὶ ἀπὸ | νῦν εὐλογῶ· ἔτους σϘδ΄. I do not know what the phrase μηδὲν λαβοῦσα ἠρωτήθη means; nor is it quite clear whether the gods' punishment fell on Iulia or Onesime.

[48] *TAM* V 1, 492 (Petzl 1994, no. 44): ἔτους [.]θ΄, μη(νὸς) Πε[ρειτίου.΄]| Θεοδότη Γλύκω[νι ἐπηράσατο(?)]| θρεπτῷ, ἐπιδὴ ἀράμ[ενος]| τὰς χῖρας αὐτῆ ἐκα[κώσα]|(5)το, κὲ ἀποθανούσης[αὐτῆς]| κὲ τοῦ Γλύκωνος ὁ [θεὸς]| ἐπεζήτησεν παρὰ [- - -]| τοῦ ἐκγόνου αὐτῆς, [καὶ ἀπέ]|δωκε καὶ ἀπὸ νῦν ε[ὐλογεῖ]. See further Gordon 2004, 195–6.

[49] *SEG* 38, 1233 (Petzl 1994, no. 47): μεγάλοι θεοὶ Νέαν Κώμην κατέχοντες·| ἔτους σλα΄· Μηνοφίλα | ὑπὸ Πολυχρονίου τοῦ υἱοῦ χολιασθεῖσα καὶ τοῖς |(5) θεοῖς ἐνευξαμένη ἰς τὸ | εἰκανοποιηθῆναι αὐτὴν, | καὶ κολαοθέντος αὐτοῦ | καὶ εἰλασαμένου τοὺς θεοὺς, ἐκέλευσεν αὐτὴν |(10) στηλλογραφῆσαι τὰς δυνά|μεις τῶν θεῶν.

responding to physical violence performed against her by her *threptos*; and in the fourth, we are simply told that Menophila was 'enraged' by her son. Nonetheless, the basic pattern is strikingly consistent: in each case, the curse is performed by an adult woman against a child or foster-child (three male and one female). It is not clear whether the act of cursing a younger relative was seen as ethically problematic in and of itself; the woman performing the curse is sometimes (but apparently not always) punished by the god.[50]

In none of these four cases can we be certain whether the woman's husband was still alive at the point when her relationship with her children and foster-children turned sour. But I strongly suspect that in each case we are dealing with widows – older women whose former position of authority over their children and foster-children has been sharply diminished by the death of their husband, and whose instrumental 'usefulness' to the wider household in both productive and reproductive terms might be increasingly contested. That familial disputes might often have revolved around the position of older women within the household receives some confirmation from a second recurrent category of problematic relationship, between married men and their wives' mothers. A short propitiatory inscription from the sanctuary of Apollo Axyreos reads as follows (Figure 9.6)[51]:

> Trophimos son of Apollonios neglected his wife's mother Ammia, and he loosened the gods' anger and inscribed a *stēlē*; he dedicated this to Apollo Axyreos, in gratitude.

Once again, we cannot be sure that Ammia is a widow; but it is hard to see that Trophimos' 'neglect' of Ammia (whatever 'neglect' means in this context) would have constituted a moral fault if he had not had a duty of care towards her, which is surely most likely to have arisen through the death of her husband. A second case of (alleged) dysfunctional relations between an older woman and her son-in-law emerges from one of the best known of all the propitiatory inscriptions of the region, erected in the sanctuary of Artemis Anaeitis and Meis Tiamou near Esenyazı in early summer AD 157[52]:

---

[50] Other curses performed by older women in Hieradoumia: *TAM* V 1, 318 (quoted and discussed below): Tatias deposits curses in the temple; *SEG* 58, 1359, with Petzl 2011b: Iole lays curses on her granddaughter's tomb (see Section 9.1).

[51] *SEG* 42, 1082 (Petzl 1994, no. 21): Τρόφιμος υ(ἱὸς?) Ἀπ[ολ]|λωνίου Ἀμμίαν τ[ὴν]| πενθερὰν παρῖδ[ε(?)]| κὲ ἐθυμολύτησε |(5) κὲ ἐστηλογρά[φη]|σε· Ἀπόλλωνι Αξ[υρῳ | εὐχ]αριστῶν ἀ[νέθη|κεν].

[52] *TAM* V 1, 318 (Petzl 1994, no. 69): ἔτους σμα′, μη(νὸς) Πανήμου β′. | Μεγάλη Ἄρτεμις Ἀναει|τις καὶ Μεὶς Τιαμου. ἐπὶ | Ἰουκοῦνδος ἐγένετο ἐν |(5) διαθέσι μανικῇ καὶ ὑπὸ πάν|των διεφημίσθη ὡς ὑπὸ | Τατιας τῆς πενθερᾶς αὐ|τοῦ φάρμακον αὐτῷ δεδόσ|θαι, ἡ δὲ Τατιας ἐπέστησεν |(10) σκῆπτρον καὶ ἀρὰς ἔθηκεν | ἐν τῷ ναῷ ὡς ἱκανοποιοῦ|σα περὶ τοῦ πεφημίσθαι αὐ|τὴν

Figure 9.6 Propitiatory *stēlē* of Trophimos. *SEG* 42, 1082 (Ege Üniversitesi).

Year 241, day 2 of the month Panemos. Great is Artemis Anaeitis and Meis Tiamou! Since Iucundus fell into a (5) state of madness, and it was rumoured among everyone that a potion had been given to him by his mother-in-law Tatias; and Tatias erected (10) a sceptre and placed curses in the temple so as to prove her innocence against the rumour that she was implicated in the affair – the gods placed her in (15) a state of punishment, which she did not escape. Likewise, when her son Sokrates was passing the entrance that leads off into the grove, holding a vine-pruning hook (20), it fell from his hand onto his foot, and so he died through a

ἐν συνειδήσι τοιαύτῃ, | οἱ θεοὶ αὐτὴν ἐποίησαν ἐν |(15) κολάσει ἣν οὐ διέφυγεν· ὁ|μοίως καὶ Σωκράτης ὁ υἱός | αὐτῆς παράγων τὴν ἴσοδον | τὴν ἰς τὸ ἄλσος ἀπάγουσαν | δρέπανον κρατῶν ἀμπελοτό|(20)μον, ἐκ τῆς χειρὸς ἔπεσεν | αὐτῷ ἐπὶ τὸν πόδαν καὶ οὕ|τως μονημέρῳ κολάσει ἀ|πηλλάγη. μεγάλοι οὖν οἱ θε|οὶ οἱ ἐν Ἀζιττοις· ἐπεζήτησαν |(25) λυθῆναι τὸ σκῆπτρον καὶ τὰς | ἀρὰς τὰς γενομένας ἐν τῷ | ναῷ, ἃ ἔλυσαν τὰ Ἰουκούνδου | καὶ Μοσχίου, ἔγγονοι δὲ τῆς | Τατιας, Σωκράτεια καὶ Μοσχᾶς |(30) καὶ Ἰουκοῦνδος καὶ Μενεκρά|της κατὰ πάντα ἐξειλασάμενοι | τοὺς θεοὺς καὶ ἀπὸ νοῖν εὐλογοῦ|μεν στηλλογραφήσαντες τὰς δυ|νάμις τῶν θεῶν. The bibliography is huge: see especially Chaniotis 2004a, 11 14; Chaniotis 2009a, 122–5; Eidinow 2016, 218–23; Gordon 2016, 246–7; Kotansky 2020, 150–1.

punishment which took effect in the course of a single day. Great, therefore, are the gods in Azitta! They demanded that (25) the sceptre should
be loosened, as well as the curses deposited in the temple; they were loosened by the children of Iucundus and Moschion, the grandchildren of
Tatias, Sokrateia and Moschas (30) and Iucundus and Menekrates, having
appeased the gods in all respects; and from now on, having inscribed a
stēlē, we praise the powers of the gods.

Once again, it seems very likely that Tatias is a widow, perhaps an elderly
widow; she appears to have four adult grandchildren by her daughter Moschion (Sokrateia, Moschas, the younger Iucundus, and Menekrates), who
take on responsibility for the erection of the *stēlē*. In this case, the family
dispute seems to have had a wider 'public' dimension from the outset:
the fact that Iucundus' mental illness was rumoured 'by everyone' (ὑπὸ
πάντων) to have been caused by his mother-in-law's use of magic surely
implies that bad relations between the two were already a matter of widespread public knowledge in the village of Azitta. Whatever the facts of the
matter might have been, the story follows a perfectly coherent logic in terms
of kin-relations. Tatias has two children, a daughter (Moschion) and a son
(Sokrates); her relations with her daughter's husband are known to be bad,
and so the village community pins the guilt on Tatias when he falls sick;
Tatias' guilt is apparently corroborated by the death of her *other* child, her
son; it is the children of her *daughter* who ultimately endorse this narrative
by erecting the propitiation-*stēlē*. The overall narrative is 'satisfying' from the
perspective of the wider community because it reflects the reality of a social
system characterized by patrilocal residence – a pattern suggested, as we saw
in Chapter 5, both by the 'lop-sidedness' of Hieradoumian kin-terminology
and by the broad patterns of funerary commemoration of married persons.
In this system, the son, married or unmarried, will tend to remain 'closer' to
the mother than the married daughter does, and the son-in-law will tend to
have a relatively 'distant' relationship with his wife's mother.

In this propitiatory inscription, then, we can see an intersection between
two *different* fissures running through the Hieradoumian extended kin
group: the unstable position of older women, particularly widows, vis-à-
vis younger family members, particularly men; and the relative structural
weakness of the relationship between a married man and his wife's parents.
This particular case may have been unusual only in the magnitude of suspi-
cion which developed – tragically – across those two fault lines.

As already noted, the frankness with which the villagers of Roman Hieradoumia were willing to describe (and monumentalize) the transgressions
of their own close family members, including those arising from 'private'

intra-familial disputes of various kinds, is deeply remarkable. Whether this terrifying candour was prompted by individual religiosity ('we ought to do it'), social pressure ('the neighbours expect it'), or priestly authority ('the god demands it') is, of course, unknowable. But there are some indications that individual families went to great lengths to avoid having their disgrace commemorated for posterity. An extraordinary propitiatory inscription from Kollyda in the Katakekaumene dating to winter AD 205/6 seems to describe an attempt by two brothers to *interrupt* their father halfway through the anticipated four-step cycle of transgression, punishment, propitiation, and bearing witness to the god's powers (Figure 9.7)[53]:

```
       ἔτους υϟ', μη(νὸς) Περιτίου. Ἀμμι-
       ανὸς καὶ Ἑρμογένης Τρύφω-
       νος πάρισιν ἐρωτῶντες το-
       ὺς θεοὺς Μῆνα Μοτυλλίτ-
5      ην καὶ Δία Σαβάζιον καὶ Ἄρτε-
       μιν Αναειτιν καὶ μεγάλην συ-
       νᾶτος καὶ σύνκλητον τῶν θε-
       ῶν, ἐρωτῶντες τὴν κατοικία[ν]
       καὶ τὸν ἱερὸν δοῦμον, ἵνα ἐλέ-
10     ου τύχωσιν, ἐπὶ ἐκολάσθη[σ]-
       αν οὗτοι, ὅτι τὸν πατέρα ἐκρά-
       τησαν ἐξομολογούμενον
       τὰς δυνάμις τῶν θεῶν, καὶ ἐλη-
       μοσύνην μὴ λαβόντος τοῦ πα-
15     τρὸς αὐτῶν, ἀλλὰ ἀποτελεσθέ-
       ντος αὐτοῦ· μή τίς ποτε παρευ-
       τελίσι τοὺς θεούς· διὰ τὰς π[ρ]-
       ώτας προγραφὰς αὐτοῦ ἔγρα[ψ]-
       αν καὶ ἀνέθηκαν εὐλογοῦντε[ς]
20     τοῖς θεοῖς.
```

Year 290, in the month Peritios. Ammianos and Hermogenes son of Tryphon are present, entreating the gods, Meis Motylleites and Zeus Sabazios and Artemis Anaeitis and the great senate and council of the gods, and entreating the village and the sacred *doumos*, that they should receive forgiveness, since they have been punished, because they overpowered their father while he was acknowledging the powers of the gods, and their father did not receive pity, but perished. 'Let no-one ever belittle the gods': because of his first written declaration, they have written and dedicated this, praising the gods.

---

[53] *SEG* 57, 1186 (Petzl 2019, no. 146), with Chaniotis 2009a, 131–4; Chaniotis 2012, 217–18.

Figure 9.7 Propitiatory inscription of Ammianos and Hermogenes, from Gölde (Kollyda). *SEG* 57, 1186 (Manisa Museum).

Tryphon had clearly committed a transgression of some kind, and had gone on to suffer some misfortune which convinced him that he was being punished by the gods for his misdemeanour. But while he was in the act of acknowledging the power of the gods, and perhaps after submitting some kind of preliminary written deposition (the 'first written declaration' mentioned in the final lines), he was physically prevented from doing so by his two sons. It is difficult to know how we should imagine this in practice, but clearly the point is that the act of propitiation was left incomplete as a result of Tryphon's sons' intervention, no doubt made in order to protect the family's honour.[54] Tryphon subsequently died, an event depicted in the fragmentary relief above the inscription, which shows a male figure with his legs crumpled beneath him, perhaps being crushed under a boulder or attacked by a wolf (here, Figure 9.7).[55] As a result, the two sons were subjected to a very public humiliation before the entire village and the cult association who worshipped at the sanctuary (the 'sacred *doumos*' – probably in effect co-extensive with the village population), in the course of which they were required to beg forgiveness both from the gods and from their neighbours for their attempt to prevent the cycle of justice and reparation from taking its course. As so often, the cover-up – honourably motivated though it was – proved to be more damaging than the original crime.

This is an extreme case of what could well have been a more widespread reluctance to incur the disgrace of ending up in Petzl's *Beichtinschriften*. We have several examples of people who were punished by the god for a *hamartia* of some kind, but then delayed or 'dragged out' (παρέλκειν) the inscribing and erecting of the propitiatory *stēlē* which they had had demanded of them. It is true that the inhabitants of Hieradoumia were not, in general, notably prompt in fulfilling their vows to the gods.[56] But some cases of 'delayed propitiation' may well result specifically from an attempt to avoid the dishonour of having one's transgression immortalized on stone. Consider, for instance, the following text, dated to spring AD 203[57]:

> To Zeus from the Twin Oaks. Menophila, daughter of Asklepiades, having been punished by the gods, vowed a *pinax* ('tablet'); she dragged (5) out the time and did not give it; the god demanded a *stēlē* from her sister Iulia, who had made the vow along with her; she gave it in gratitude (10) to the god. Year 287, on day 30 of the month Daisios.

[54] The regular 'Day 12' festival at the sanctuary; the priest proclaims 'Who wishes to acknowledge the power of the gods?'; Tryphon steps forward, 'I bear witness that …'; his sons grab him from behind, 'Shut up, Dad!'.

[55] For wolf attacks in Roman Asia Minor, see *MAMA* I 286, the tombstone of a young shepherd from eastern Phrygia who was 'torn apart by wolves' (λακισθέντος ὑπὸ λύκων); Nollé 2005, 63.

[56] Instances of divine punishment resulting from unfulfilled vows are very numerous, suggesting that 'foot-dragging' was rife in this sphere: Petzl 1994, nos. 45, 62, 65, 101; Petzl 2019, nos. 129, 132 (?), 139, 152, 171.

[57] *SEG* 57, 1224 (Petzl 2019, no. 125): Διεὶ ἐγ Διδύμων Δρυῶν· | Μηνοφίλα Ἀσκληπιάδου | κολασθεῖσα ὑπὸ τοῦ θεοῦ εὔξατο πίνακα· ἐχρο|(5)νούλκησε καὶ οὐκ ἀπέ|δωκε· συνευξαμένης | τῆς ἀδελφῆς Ἰουλίας ἐ|πεζήτησε ὁ θεὸς στήλ|λην, ἣν ἀπέδωκε εὐχαρισ|(10)τοῦσα τῷ θεῷ. ἔτους σπζ´, μη(νὸς) | Δαισίου λ´.

Menophila has been punished for some unspecified transgression (apparently in the form of a leg injury, to judge from the accompanying relief, which depicts a right leg), and the god has required her to dedicate a small inscribed 'tablet' in the sanctuary. Menophila has persistently put off doing so, and so the god has approached her sister instead and 'raised the price' by demanding a *stēlē* instead of a *pinax*. We might note that Iulia – like the sons of Tryphon in the text quoted above – has nonetheless loyally protected the family honour by continuing to leave it unclear what her sister had actually done to prompt the punishment in the first place.[58]

Over the last two chapters, we have looked at various kinds of everyday conflict in Hieradoumian rural society: between humans and gods, over land tenure, land use, and labour; between humans and other humans (both within and between families), over livestock, theft, money, and other things. The propitiatory inscriptions represent the material trace of the settling of these conflicts by the parties involved and their village communities. An act of social dysfunction occurs (a theft, a quarrel, a suspected poisoning); an unexpected disaster befalls a man or woman's family; the disaster is recognized as a punishment resulting from the original transgressive act; the transgressor propitiates the god's anger through a public avowal of his or her misdeeds. As I argued in Section 9.3, it is crucial to remember that within this system, the causal connection between transgression and divine punishment was always and necessarily in the eye of the beholder. The judgement that human disaster x (usually sickness or death) represented a divine punishment for human action y was always, in the last resort, a *social* judgement, handed down in the form of a negotiated consensus between the community and the transgressor (or the deceased transgressor's family) about what had gone wrong and why.

We can therefore usefully think of the ritual procedure described in the propitiatory inscriptions as a normative filter through which low-level local disputes could pass, without the need for an appeal to higher legal authorities. By categorizing a theft or an act of violence as a transgression against the village's gods, the village community could neatly sidestep the need to involve the *polis* or the Roman state in the resolution of local problems. In other words, this particular ritual system can be seen as (among other things) an adaptive mechanism for *keeping the state at arm's length*.[59]

---

[58] Similar examples in Petzl 1994, no. 8 (propitiatory offerings not performed; the god exacts them from the transgressors' *syngeneia*); Petzl 2019, no. 164 (reiterated punishment of a woman until she erects the required *stēlē*); cf. also *SEG* 35, 1164 (Petzl 1994, no. 71, with Petzl 2019, 19–20), discussed above, Chapter 8, Section 8.3.

[59] For habits of state-resistance in inner Anatolia, Thonemann 2013b.

As we saw in Chapter 2 (Section 2.7), the practice of erecting propitiatory *stēlai* emerged only in the Flavian period, and we really have no good reason to think that the ritual procedure described on these *stēlai* had been in use in Hieradoumia for hundreds of years before that. It may well be no coincidence that it was precisely in this period (the late first century AD) that much of Hieradoumia was for the first time carved up into contiguous *polis*-territories, under the legal authority of 'artificial' new urban centres like Saittai and Silandos (Chapter 10, Section 10.1). That is to say, it is quite possible that the ritual system of dispute resolution described in the propitiatory inscriptions is not some fossilized relic of immemorial Anatolian antiquity, but a pragmatic situational response to the experience of increased state penetration into the lives of rural Hieradoumian communities in the early Roman imperial period.

This concludes our discussion of the second major commemorative practice of Roman Hieradoumia, the erection of propitiatory *stēlai* in rural sanctuaries. It remains only for us to draw together the threads of the preceding chapters into a synthetic picture of the Hieradoumian social order in the first three centuries AD; this will be attempted in the final chapter.

10   City, Village, Kin-Group

The cumulative impression left by the first nine chapters of this book may well have been that the village and its various residential and associative subgroupings – above all cultic and kin-based – were the only forms of social order that mattered in Roman Hieradoumia. As we shall see in this final chapter, that would be to oversimplify things a bit. By the mid-second century AD, the human communities of the middle Hermos valley had been organized into around ten *poleis* with (we assume) clearly defined contiguous territories. These 'cities' had at least a modest level of monumental urban infrastructure, were equipped with many of the characteristic civic institutions of the Greek *polis*, and at least in some cases served as nodes of industrial intensification, a phenomenon seen most clearly in the case of the 'textile-town' of Saittai. As was the case everywhere in the eastern Roman Empire, these cities were dominated by a small class of indigenous landowning civic elites, many of whom possessed Roman citizenship. I have no doubt that there were people who were proud to be citizens of the *polis* of Daldis, who enthusiastically participated in the worship of Zeus Polieus or Apollo Mystes at Daldis, and who competed for the honour of holding a civic magistracy at Daldis with as much enthusiasm as any member of the civic elite at Miletos or Pergamon.[1]

Nonetheless, in my view, such people – the wealthy, the Romanized, the urban – were relatively few, and the influence of the new cities on the wider social structure of the region was limited. In the small villages of rural Hieradoumia where most of the population resided, formal subordination to one or other of the new *poleis* created in the early imperial period did not, I think, impinge much on day-to-day life. In the various overlapping webs of interrelation which linked people and families together, public and official relationships between male *polis*-citizens, both horizontal and vertical, were of relatively minor significance.[2] The residential and social networks that mattered were on a smaller scale: the village (*kōmē, katoikia*), the

---

[1] See Thonemann 2020, 103–23, on the image of the *polis* in Artemidorus of Daldis' *Oneirocritica* (presumably based as much on Ephesos as on Daldis).
[2] Le Roy Ladurie 1978, 262.

neighbourhood (*geitonia*), the local cult association (*phratra, doumos*), the little groups of worshippers who made their way, once or twice each month, up the slopes of Yeşiloba Tepe to the remote hilltop sanctuary of Thea Larmene (Chapter 8). Some of these pre-existing associative groups were certainly *appropriated* by the new *poleis* of the region: as we will see, the *polis* of Saittai had a civic tribe named after the outlying village of Satala, almost 40 km to the south-west of the urban settlement, and the god Meis Axiottenos – whose chief cult centre was at Mağazadamları, 11 km to the south of Saittai across some extremely rough terrain – was claimed by the Saittans as one of their chief *polis* deities.[3] None of this should deceive us into thinking that the average inhabitant of the villages of Satala or Axiotta necessarily had any meaningful emotional or practical investment in 'his' or 'her' *polis*.

In this final chapter, we will look first at the actual evidence, such as it is, for *polis*-institutions in Roman Hieradoumia (Section 10.1), before turning to the 'anatomy' of the urban and land-holding elites of the region in the first three centuries AD (Section 10.2). We will then return to the villages of Hieradoumia, for a final attempt at mapping out what I take to be the structure of relations between villages, cult associations, and extended kin groups (Sections 10.3 and 10.4). I conclude with a few thoughts on the notion of Roman Hieradoumia as a 'kin-ordered society' and its implications for our understanding of local cultures in the broader Greco-Roman world (Section 10.5).

10.1 Civic Life in Roman Hieradoumia

As we saw in Chapter 1, several of the small towns of the middle and upper Hermos valley (Map 2) received *polis*-status in the early Roman imperial period. Maionia seems to have been the first to do so, at some point before 16 BC; Kadoi was described as a *polis* by Strabo, writing in the later Augustan period; and Gordos certainly possessed *polis*-status by spring AD 37 at the latest.[4] Daldis must have received *polis*-status in the early Flavian period, to judge from her dynastic name Flavia Caesarea Daldis (or

---

[3] Satala a *phylē* of Saittai: *SEG* 40, 1063, nos. 12–14. Before the discovery of the relevant inscribed stadium seats at Saittai, Peter Herrmann had (quite reasonably) assumed that Satala was an independent *polis* or *dēmos*, and set the south-western limit of Saittan territory a good 20 km to the north-east of Satala (*TAM* V 1, pp. 194–5 and map) – a nice illustration of the essentially arbitrary character of the *polis*-territories of Roman Hieradoumia. Meis Axiottenos as 'civic deity' at Saittai: Ricl 2016, 161 n.53, 165–7.

[4] Maionia: *SEG* 57, 1198. Kadoi: Strabo 12.8.12. Gordos: *TAM* V 1, 702.

Flaviopolis Daldis), which appears first on coins struck under Vespasian.[5] Civic coin-issues show that Silandos and Bagis possessed *polis*-status by the reign of Domitian, Saittai by the reign of Hadrian, and Tabala by the reign of Antoninus Pius.[6] Kollyda, which never struck its own coinage, certainly also possessed the status of a *polis*, apparently by AD 85.[7] In the Flavian *conventus*-list from Ephesos, the inhabitants of Loros appear as the 'Lorenaioi, now called Flaviopoleitai', suggesting that Loros enjoyed *polis*-status in the Flavian period; a second-century epitaph from Karayakup, in the Kum Çayı valley north of Daldis, is dated 'according to the calendar of the Charakipolitai', implying that this community too possessed *polis*-status.[8]

By the mid-second century AD, then, around ten towns in the region must have possessed the formal status of a *polis*. What is rather less clear is how much institutional and social change was actually involved in the 'transformation' of formerly non-*polis* communities into *poleis*, and how much impact this change of status might have had for the organization and self-perception of the human communities of the middle Hermos valley. The new Roman-period *poleis* of Hieradoumia may have served as a major focus of collective activity and collective loyalty for their citizens and residents; or they may instead have been largely administrative abstractions, like modern British electoral constituencies, which played only a limited role in the lives of the inhabitants of the region. As Stephen Mitchell has put it[9]:

> Although none of these cities has been excavated, hardly any developed into a genuinely prosperous urban centre with important public buildings and a flourishing urban upper class and civic culture. Only Saittai, which was an important centre for the commercial production of textiles, and Iulia Gordus seem to have emerged as urban centres of any significance; the others are hardly to be distinguished from the larger villages of the same area ... Only an arbitrary decision about status, designed

---

[5] *RPC* II 1324–1326; in the Flavian *conventus*-list from Ephesos, they are listed as Φλαουιοκαισαρεῖς Δαλδιανοί (*I.Ephesos* 13, lines I.10–11).

[6] Silandos: *RPC* II 1350–1355. Bagis: *RPC* II 1357–1358. Saittai: *RPC* III 2543–2544, with *RPC* online 2543A–B, 2544A–D. Tabala: *RPC* IV.2, 2859 and 11013 (temp.). The earliest use of the ethnic Σαϊττηνός dates to AD 122/3 (*TAM* V 1, 148), but the large number of (Ti.) Claudii attested at Saittai may point towards *polis*-status already in the Julio-Claudian period: *TAM* V 1, 118, 168d; *SEG* 31, 1018 and 1021; *SEG* 33, 1012; *SEG* 35, 1242; *SEG* 57, 1208 and 1210.

[7] Kollyda a *polis*: *TAM* V 1, 333 (οἱ κατὰ πόλιν ἄρχοντες); doubted by Schuler 2012, 95. The ethnic Κολλυδεύς appears in Malay and Petzl 2017, no. 180 (autumn AD 85), and in *SEG* 32, 1212 (undated); in two dedications of the late Hellenistic period, individuals are described as τῶν ἐκ Κολλύδων (*SEG* 49, 1598; *SEG* 54, 1216).

[8] Loros: *I.Ephesos* 13, I 7–8. Charakipolis: *TAM* V 1, 683. See further Habicht 1975, 73–4.

[9] Mitchell 1993, I 176–81 (quote from 180–1); cf. Thonemann 2013b, 24–37, on Phrygia.

for administrative convenience, will have ordained a difference between *katoikiai* like Lyendos, Ariandos, Apateira and the Teirenōn katoikia and *poleis* like Bagis, Maeonia, Tmolus, and Hypaepa.

Demonstrating the *absence* of a thriving sphere of civic politics in the Roman-period *poleis* of the middle Hermos valley is evidently a pretty tall order. A paucity of extant civic documents, and an apparent absence of monumental urbanism (although excavation could well show this absence to be illusory), can in themselves hardly be taken to indicate an underdeveloped civic culture.[10] Nonetheless, certain 'negative' features of our evidence for *polis*-institutions in the region are worth emphasizing. Fines for tomb violation are not a common feature of the region's epitaphs, and when they do appear, fines are almost always payable to the village (*katoikia, kōmē*) and/or to the imperial fisc, rather than the nearest *polis*.[11] Civic archives are attested only at Gordos and Saittai; there are no Hieradoumian instances of copies of epitaphs being deposited in *polis*-archives, a practice which is widespread in western Lydia (Thyateira, Hierokaisareia, Hyrkanis, Magnesia).[12] Very few persons chose to highlight their *polis*-citizenship on their tombstones, and civic status-designations such as *bouleutēs* almost never appear in funerary contexts.[13] More generally, the epitaphs, propitiatory *stēlai*, and other private religious inscriptions of Roman Hieradoumia are

---

[10] At Saittai, a large Roman-period stadium is still visible today, along with the ruins of some substantial public buildings, but the overall size of the urban centre is hard to gauge: Robert, *OMS* I, 424–5; Herrmann 1962, 12–14; Kolb 1990; Umar 2001, 291–9. An epistyle fragment survives from a tetrastyle temple of Aphrodite at Saittai, also depicted on the city's coins: Malay and Petzl 2017, no. 111, with *RPC* VI 4443 (temp.); VII.1 224; VIII ID 20227. The epigraphy of Gordos and Maionia clearly shows that the cities had a substantial monumental infrastructure: see below, nn. 23 and 26.

[11] Fisc and village: *TAM* V 1, 608 (the Iouddēnōn katoikia); *TAM* V 1, 776 (Gordos, with Robert, *Hellenica* VI, 100). Village only: *SEG* 49, 1684 (near Satala). Fisc and *polis*: only *TAM* V 1, 665 (Daldis). Fisc only: e.g. *TAM* V 1, 741, 743 (Gordos); *TAM* V 1, 637, *I.Manisa* 355, and *SEG* 29, 1161 (Daldis); Thonemann 2019, no. 7 (Iaza). See Mitchell 1993, I 187–8.

[12] Gordos: *TAM* V 1, 758 (donation of the *peristōon* of a bathhouse). Saittai: *SEG* 40, 1064 (donation of water supply [?]). Civic archives in western Lydia (a selection only): e.g. *TAM* V 1, 1050 (Thyateira), 1293 (Hierokaisareia), 1386 (Magnesia); *SEG* 49, 1584 (Hyrkanis). *TAM* V 1, 670, assigned by Herrmann to Daldis, is better attributed to Hierokaisareia or the Ioulieis Maibozanoi.

[13] *Polis*-citizenship and status designations on Hieradoumian tombstones: *TAM* V 1, 168c (Σεττηνός); *TAM* V 1, 739 and *TAM* V 3, 1851 (a Γορδηνὸς βουλευτής in each case); *TAM* V 1, 759 (a married couple, Γορδηνοί); *SEG* 40, 1094 (Σιλανδεύς); *SEG* 40, 1095 (ἄρχοντα πρῶτον τὸ γ′ καὶ στεφανηφόρον τῆς Μαιόνων πόλεως); *SEG* 40, 1100 (Τα⟨βαληνός⟩); Thonemann 2019, no. 7 (Μαίων); perhaps *TAM* V 1, p.200, B.6 (Δ⟨αλ⟩διανή (?)). *Polis*-ethnics are rather more common in private religious texts (e.g. *TAM* V 1, 148, 185, 202, 240; *SEG* 33, 1144; *SEG* 57, 1173; Malay and Petzl 2017, no. 158) and, naturally, on epitaphs of persons who died abroad (e.g. *Sardis* VII 1, 165, a woman Ταβαλὶς κατοικοῦσα ἐν Σάρδεσι). For a *bouleutēs* of Daldis honoured at Philadelphia, see *TAM* V 3, 1511 (M. Aur. Peios, also on coins of Daldis under Valerian and Gallienus).

extremely homogeneous in their physical form and language (Chapter 2, Sections 2.1–2.4); in the absence of a clear provenance, it is usually impossible to assign stones to a particular city.[14] None of these negative features in themselves necessarily tell us much, but cumulatively they are at least suggestive.

Turning to more positive evidence for *polis*-institutions, our richest evidence for civic institutions comes from Iulia Gordos and Maionia. Gordos has produced the largest concentration of civic decrees in the region, with posthumous honorific decrees for one Attalos and his wife Stratonike (early Julio-Claudian period), for their grandson Attalos (AD 69/70, translated in Chapter 7, Section 7.3), and for a certain Theophilos son of Thyneites (AD 76).[15] That the activities of the *boulē* and *dēmos* at Gordos in the early imperial period seem to have been restricted to the passing of honorific decrees is not in itself particularly significant (the same was true in very many cities of the Greek world in this period); more striking and unusual is the fact that collective political activity at Gordos seems to have consisted *solely* in the funerary commemoration of elite individuals.[16] It may be significant that none of these four inscribed decrees were found at the urban centre of Gordos, but all come from sites on the city's rural territory, perhaps implying that elite individuals tended to be buried near their home villages or estates; likewise, almost all of the hundreds of epitaphs attributed to Saittai were found at outlying villages, rather than at the urban centre itself.[17]

Three of these four posthumous decrees of Gordos honour politically active male citizens, and thus provide some evidence for the range of civic offices and liturgical activities at early imperial Gordos. The decree-prescripts show that the chief executive magistrates were a college of three *stratēgoi*, supported by a 'secretary of the *dēmos*'. The elder Attalos held the office of *stratēgos* (among other unspecified magistracies), in which capacity

---

[14] The onomastics of the region are also very homogeneous: the only example known to me of a personal name restricted to a single *polis* is the name Thyneites at Gordos (below, n.54).

[15] *SEG* 62, 917 (Attalos); *TAM* V 1, 688 (Stratonike); *SEG* 62, 918 (Attalos the younger); *TAM* V 1, 687 (Theophilos). Other public documents from Gordos include honorific *stēlai* for the emperor Trajan (*TAM* V 1, 697: *dēmos* only), a civic *stephanēphoros* (*TAM* V 1, 698: *boulē* and *dēmos*), and a private individual (*TAM* V 1, 699: unnamed *phylē*). The last two texts may be funerary. *SEG* 57, 1177 (honours by *boulē*, *dēmos* and *neoi* for two lampadarchs) is surely to be attributed to Thyateira rather than Gordos.

[16] Compare *TAM* V 1, 66 (the *patris* weeps for a young man deceased at Silandos); *SEG* 35, 1233 (*SGO* I 04/12/09, AD 148/9: the 'whole *dēmos*' grieves over a young man at Saittai); *Sammlung Tatış* 36 (unknown provenance: the 'whole *polis*' participates in the funeral of a three-year-old boy).

[17] *SEG* 62, 917–918 were found at Tüpüler, *TAM* V 1, 687 between Gördes and Oğuldurak, *TAM* V 1, 688 at Kayacık. Saittai: Robert, *OMS* I, 423.

he tidied up the city's tax registers.[18] The younger Attalos acted as *agoranomos*, *stratēgos*, and *stephanēphoros*, this last perhaps being the eponymous magistracy at Gordos (although it does not appear in decree prescripts)[19]; both he and his brother Kleon were *dekaprōtoi*, members of the city *boulē* with special responsibility for tax collection on behalf of the Roman state.[20] Theophilos similarly held the offices of *stratēgos* and *agoranomos*, and went on more than one embassy to the emperor on the city's behalf. We later hear of two further financial officials at Gordos, the *logistēs* and *oikonomos*, responsible for managing the city's public accounts.[21] The prevalence of financial magistrates of one kind or other in the city's roster of officials is noteworthy: the collection of taxes and management of the tax register on behalf of the Roman state seem to have loomed large among the civic duties of the local elite at Gordos. We know that the population of Gordos was divided into civic tribes, but none of the tribes' names are known, and it is unclear how significant they were for *polis*-life.[22] The decree for the younger Attalos specifies that the 'bath-houses and workshops' at Gordos are to be closed during Attalos' funeral, and a group of building inscriptions attest the construction of a *stoa* at private expense around AD 180, some of the columns of which were paid for by the year's *agoranomos*.[23]

Turning to Maionia, the only known decree of the city is a lengthy and rhetorically elaborate decree of 16 BC in honour of a civic benefactor called Kleandros (Chapter 1, Figure 1.8), resolved by the *boulē* and *dēmos* on the proposal of the *stratēgoi* and the secretary of the *dēmos*, and dated by the provincial high priest of Roma and Augustus, the civic *stephanēphoros* and priest of Roma, and the civic priest of Zeus Olympios.[24] Civic liturgies at Maionia are attested in a building inscription dated to AD 154/5, recording the restoration (by the city's first archon) of a 'sun-room', probably in

---

[18] The office of *stratēgos* last appears at Gordos AD *c.* 139–144 (*RPC* III 1248–1249, 1257, 9322, 9939); it may then have been replaced by a college of *archontes* (first attested AD *c.* 161–169, *RPC* III 1251, 3105, 8319); cf. *TAM* V 1, 693 (AD 177–180). An *archōn* already in *TAM* V 1, 701 (*SGO* I 04/10/03: AD 12/13), line 14; but since the text is in verse, this may not be the official title of his office.
[19] The office of *stephanēphoros* is otherwise attested at Gordos only in *TAM* V 1, 698.
[20] Office of *dekaprōtos*: Samitz 2013. The decree for the younger Attalos (AD 69/70) is the earliest attestation of the office in the province of Asia.
[21] *Logistēs*: *TAM* V 1, 693 (AD 177–180); for civic *logistai* in Hieradoumia, cf. *TAM* V 1, 517 (Maionia); *TAM* V 1, 650 (Gölmarmara); Dmitriev 2005, 193–4. *Oikonomos*: *TAM* V 1, 743 (*SGO* I 04/10/05); on this office, Robert, *Hellenica* XI–XII, 229–30 (discussing *I.Smyrna* 761, 771–772).
[22] Only in *TAM* V 1, 699 (honorific inscription set up by an unnamed φυλή).
[23] 'Bath-houses and workshops': *SEG* 62, 918, lines B 23–25; bathhouses alone in *SEG* 62, 917, lines 31–32. Stoa: *TAM* V 1, 693–695.
[24] *SEG* 57, 1198.

a bathhouse, funded from the *summa honoraria* given by a civic *logistēs*.[25]
Various fragments of monumental epistyles and other building inscriptions indicate that Maionia had several large public buildings, including at least one *propylon* and a stoa dedicated to Zeus Olympios.[26] In the high imperial period, the leading civic magistrate at Maionia simultaneously held the offices of archon (or first archon) and *stephanēphoros*; the offices of eirenarch and *agoranomos* are also attested at the city.[27]

Elsewhere in Hieradoumia, the evidence for *polis*-institutions is considerably more scanty. From Saittai, we have only a single *post mortem* honorific decree, which may well antedate the community's elevation to *polis*-status, as well as two honorific statue bases for civic magistrates and benefactors; the better preserved of these two bases (not certainly from Saittai) honours a man who had acted as prytane, agonothete, *stephanēphoros*, and 'first *stratēgos*'.[28] Saittai is the only city in the region other than Gordos for which civic tribes are attested, some named after deities (Apollonias, Asklepias, Dionysias, Herakleis), others after outlying villages on Saittan territory (the *Tamasaitēnoi* and *Satalēnoi*), others after trade guilds (a 'tribe of linen-workers').[29] At Daldis, aside from a single 'hybrid' public/private funerary monument, only three public documents survive: an honorific base for a certain [P]yrrhos who paid for a bathhouse and its water supply at Daldis, as well as acting as priest, *stephanēphoros*, agonothete, and ambassador to the emperors; a very fragmentary honorific text for an ambassador and grain distributor; and the

---

[25] *TAM* V 1, 517, as explained by J. and L. Robert, *BE* 1963, 221. For the *logistēs* at Maionia, see also *TAM* V 1, 515; elsewhere in Hieradoumia, *TAM* V 1, 650 (Gölmarmara) and *TAM* V 1, 693 (Gordos); see Dmitriev 2005, 193–4.

[26] Epistyles: *TAM* V 1, 518 (*propylon*), 519–521. Stoa of Zeus Olympios: *SEG* 49, 1599. Uncertain building: Malay and Petzl 2017, no. 194 (Severan). Tetrastyle and hexastyle temples dedicated to uncertain deities are depicted on Antonine coins of Maionia: *RPC* IV.2 1227, 3780 (temp.).

[27] Simultaneous tenure of offices of (first) archon and *stephanēphoros*: *TAM* V 1, 553 (undated); *SEG* 40, 1095 (AD 211/12: epitaph of a man who was first archon three times and *stephanēphoros*); *RPC* IX 725–727 (Aur. Apphianos β', first archon for the second time and *stephanēphoros*). The stephanephorate could be held by a husband and wife simultaneously: *TAM* V 1, 542 (the husband also on coins, *RPC* IV.2 1300 (temp.), under Antoninus Pius). Other civic offices: *SEG* 57, 1171 (AD 125, the village of Iaza honours Philippikos, three times archon, twice eirenarch, *agoranomos*); for the attribution of Iaza to the territory of Maionia, Thonemann 2019, 130.

[28] *Post mortem* decree: *TAM* V 1, 705 (AD 58, erected at Gordos). Honorific bases: *TAM* V 1, 78 (very fragmentary); *SEG* 50, 1194 (honours for M. Aur. Attinas Valentillianus, perhaps a relative of the Saittan mint-magistrate M. Aur. Attinas, under Elagabalus, *RPC* VI 4434–4436, 10905). For the *stephanēphoros* as eponym at Saittai, Malay and Petzl 2017, no. 111 (temple dedicated to Aphrodite and the Antonine emperors).

[29] Known largely from inscriptions on the seats of the stadium, Kolb 1990 (*SEG* 40, 1063, with *SEG* 54, 1224); also *SEG* 57, 1208 (honorific inscription set up by the tribe Apollonias). On the φυλὴ λινουργῶν, see Chapter 7, Section 7.2.

base of a statue of Hadrian, erected by an archon college of three men, headed by a man who simultaneously held the offices of priest of Zeus Polieus, archon for the second time, *neōkoros* of the emperor, and priest of the goddess Roma.[30] From Silandos, the only known public document seems to be an honorific inscription for a certain C. Iulius Aelianus (probably identical to a mint-magistrate under Severus Alexander) who served as high priest, *stephanēphoros* and agonothete.[31] From Tabala, we have an honorific *stēlē* erected by the city's *gerousia* for a pair of civic benefactors (no offices mentioned) and a fragmentary list of annual magistrates, showing that Tabala had a formal *cursus* of civic magistracies, with pairs of men serving over three successive years as *agoranomoi*, *archontes*, and *ekdikoi*.[32]

It is difficult to detect any clear patterns in this rather miscellaneous evidence. Leaving aside the cities' chief magistrates and eponyms (usually the archon, *stephanēphoros*, or *stratēgos*, often held in tandem with a civic priesthood), the cities of Roman Hieradoumia seem to have made do with a relatively small roster of civic offices. The *agoranomos* appears at several cities, as does the agonothete, indicating (as we would expect) that most of the cities in the region held regular civic games and festivals.[33] Financial officials also appear reasonably regularly (*dekaprōtoi*, *logistai*, *oikonomoi*), as do magistrates appointed for the management of public works (*ergepistatai*).[34] The most surprising 'missing persons' are the gymnasiarch and other gymnasium officials, to the best of my knowledge nowhere attested in the region.[35]

---

[30] Private/public funerary monument: *TAM* V 1, 626 (*boulē* and *dēmos*, AD 190). Pyrrhos: *SEG* 29, 1157. Fragmentary text for ambassador: *SEG* 29, 1158. Hadrian: *SEG* 29, 1156; for simultaneous tenure of the first archonship and priesthood of Zeus Polieus at Daldis, see also *TAM* V 1, 621. A temple dedicated to Apollo Mystes is depicted on coins of Daldis (*RPC* VII.1 200). A posthumous honorific base from Gölmarmara for Menekrates, 'great doctor and philosopher', *logistēs*, *stratēgos*, gymnasiarch, prytane, and agonothete (*TAM* V 1, 650) should be attributed to Hierokaisareia or the Ioulieis Maibozanoi rather than Daldis.

[31] *SEG* 57, 1221; cf. *RPC* VI 4451–4453 (surely the same man).

[32] *Gerousia* honours: *TAM* V 1, 194. List of magistrates: *SEG* 49, 1685 (better attributed to Tabala than Silandos).

[33] At Gordos, the term *agōnothessia* appears on a bronze coin-issue struck under Valerian (*BMC Lydia* 98, no. 46); agonistic types seem otherwise to be absent from the coins of the region. Note that we have a small group of gladiatorial monuments from Saittai (*TAM* V 1, 138–140), as well as evidence that the great pantomime artist Tib. Iulius Apolaustos performed and was honoured at Saittai (Slater 1995).

[34] *Ergepistatai* appear at Daldis (*TAM* V 1, 620), Bagis (?) (*TAM* V 1, 3), and Maionia (*TAM* V 1, 517).

[35] A gymnasiarch at Gölmarmara, just outside our region (*TAM* V 1, 650: Hierokaisareia or the Ioulieis Maibozanoi). There were *paides*, *ephēboi*, *neoi*, *paideutai* and cavalry at late Hellenistic Gordos (*TAM* V 1, 700, with Robert, *Hellenica* VI, 89–91); there may have been an ephebate at Saittai (*SEG* 35, 1233 [*SGO* I 04/12/09], line 14), unless the term here simply means 'young man'.

The evidence for monumental public buildings in urban centres is relatively scanty, although public bathhouses are attested at Gordos, Maionia, and Daldis, and temples are depicted on the coins of Daldis, Maionia, and Saittai. The low volume of surviving public epigraphy of all kinds produced by the *poleis* of Hieradoumia (particularly after the Julio-Claudian period) is worth emphasizing, particularly in light of the extremely abundant funerary and religious epigraphy of the region; this was demonstrably a region in which the private epigraphic habit was strong, and the public epigraphic habit (at least at the *polis*-level) was weak.

What for me is most striking about this material is the extraordinary level of *duplication* of these institutions to be found at the level of the village, whose 'public' epigraphy is at least as abundant in volume as that produced by *polis*-communities.[36] We have good evidence for annually appointed village financial magistrates (*brabeutai*, *logistai*, and *tamiai*), mirroring those at polis-level.[37] Many Hieradoumian villages had their own *agōnothetai*, with responsibility for the organization of village *agōnes*: at the village of Kollyda in the Katakekaumene, in autumn AD 44, we find a village agonothete honoured by around ten named individuals (perhaps a sub-village cultic association?); an inscription of the first century AD from the village of Hamidiye in the northern Katakekaumene shows an agonothete being honoured by the *dēmos*, here presumably the local village community (perhaps Dima or Kerbia: Map 3).[38] Most strikingly of all, two decrees from the remote village of Parloai, south-east of Gordos in the highlands between the Demrek Çayı and Kum Çayı rivers, show the village community honouring an 'agonothete of Tiberius Caesar *divi filius* Augustus' in spring AD 25 and subsequently (after AD 41) an 'agonothete of Tiberius Claudius Nero Germanicus Caesar'.[39] This small village clearly organized its own local *agōnes* in honour of the Roman imperial house; as two further texts from Parloai demonstrate,

---

[36] Thus, correctly, Schuler 1998, 262–5 and 290, who interprets this duplication as the result of imitation of *polis*-institutions by villages; but in Hieradoumia the village institutions *precede* the emergence of cities.

[37] E.g. *TAM* V 1, 234 (unknown village near Kula: annual *brabeutēs*); *TAM* V 1, 515 (village near Maionia: annual *logistēs* and *brabeutēs*); *SEG* 49, 1622 (Nisyra: annual *brabeutai* and *tamiai*). See Schuler 1998, 238–40 (*brabeutai*: perhaps agonistic), 243–7 (financial magistrates); Müller and Wörrle 2002, 213–14 (*brabeutai*).

[38] Kollyda: *TAM* V 1 376 (Kollyda was almost certainly not yet a *polis* at this point). Hamidiye: *TAM* V 1 487. Two further inscriptions from the vicinity of Hamidiye show us two villages operating as a single political unit, οἱ ἐν Διμοις καὶ Κερβιοις κάτοικοι (*TAM* V 1, 488–489), and it is possible that the *dēmos* of *TAM* V 1, 487 is the collective *dēmos* of Dima and Kerbia.

[39] Malay and Tanrıver 2016, nos. 3 and 5. The nomenclature of Claudius is idiosyncratic, perhaps suggesting that no. 5 dates very shortly after his accession.

the imperial cult at Parloai was also served by a 'priest of Apollo and the Caesars/Augusti'.[40] Many villages had their own secular public buildings and amenities, paid for by wealthy villagers or nearby estate owners.[41] A large village on the territory of Philadelphia, on the fringe of the Katakekaumene on the northern flank of the Kogamos valley, had its own aqueduct, whose construction was overseen by two members of the village *gerousia*, as well as a 'double stoa' paid for by the village headman (*kōmarchēs*: a Roman citizen).[42] Several villages had their own bathhouses, including the villages of Tarsi east of Saittai (where the theft of a cloak from the village bathhouse is described in a propitiatory inscription), Kapolmeia south-east of Philadelphia, and Hyssa near Gordos, where a bathhouse stoa was donated to the village by a member of a local family of equestrian rank.[43] Some villages had their own *agora*, and villages certainly competed for the right to hold regular monthly 'market-days': in an inscription from the village of Tetrapyrgia in the Katakekaumene, the proconsul of Asia grants the village the right to hold a market day on Day 15 of each month, 'especially since none of all the other villages in [or "near"] Maionia hold a market on that day of the month'.[44] In short, there is little reason to think that the cities of Roman Hieradoumia were able to provide many distinctive 'services' to their outlying rural communities which the larger villages were not quite capable of providing for themselves.

---

[40] Malay and Tanrıver 2016, no. 2 (spring 5 BC), ἱερῆα τοῦ Ἀπόλλωνος καὶ τῶν Καισαρήων (wrongly understood by the editors as 'priest of the temples of Augustus'); no. 4 (autumn AD 18), ἱερῆ τοῦ Ἀπόλλωνος καὶ τῶν Σεβαστῶν. For village associations dedicated to the imperial cult, compare Malay and Petzl 2017, no. 195 (Emre, summer 18 BC), the 'sacrificers of the Caesars who gather at Spalmasis at (the temple of) Zeus Ariou' (οἱ θυσιασταὶ τῶν Καισαρήων οἱ συνηγμένοι ἐν Σπαλμασει παρὰ τῷ Διὶ τῷ Ἀρίου). Cf. also Malay and Petzl 2017, no. 197 (Emre, summer AD 115: a *philokaisar phratria* of fifteen men); *SEG* 48, 1445 (an association of *Philokaisareioi* at Maionia). In *SEG* 57, 1220 (first century AD: honours for an asiarch and sebastophant), I would restore the honouring body as a village association dedicated to the imperial cult, οἱ κατ[οικοῦντ]ες ἐν Μορει Καισάρ[ειοι], 'the Caesar-worshippers living at Morei'; cf. *IGR* IV, 1348 (Tmolos), οἱ ἐν [- - Κ]αισαριασταί. On the imperial cult in villages of inland western Asia Minor, S. R. F. Price 1984, 81–6.

[41] Schuler 1998, 255–62.

[42] *TAM* V 3, 1430 (aqueduct: 12/11 BC) and 1431 (stoa: AD 166/7). The ancient name of the village (at modern Kemaliye) is unknown; in the early third century AD, the villagers petitioned the Roman emperor to prevent itinerant soldiers from extorting money, goods or labour from the village (*TAM* V 3, 1417).

[43] Tarsi: *TAM* V 1, 159 (Petzl 1994, no. 3); see Chapter 9, Section 9.4. Kapolmeia: *TAM* V 3, 1523. Hyssa: *TAM* V 1, 758 (AD 230/1); for the donor, see n.57.

[44] Village *agora*: *TAM* V 3, 1522. Market days: *TAM* V 1, 230 (Nollé 1982, 59–86; *TAM* V 3, 1422: AD 253/4), esp. lines 13–15, μ[ά]λιστα μ[η]δεμίας ‖[?πασῶν] τῶν κατ[ὰ] τὴν Μαιον[ί]αν φθ[αν]ουσῶν |(15)[κωμῶν τ]αυτῇ τῇ ἡμέρᾳ ἀγό[ρε]ιον ἀγούση[ς]. Whether 'Maionia' here refers to the city or to the wider region (the Katakekaumene?) is unclear.

10.2 The Roman Citizen Elite

The character of *polis*-life in Roman Hieradoumia must have been largely determined by the small group of elite families who provided the cities with their *bouleutai*, civic magistrates, and public benefactors. Given the extreme homogeneity of the Greek onomastics of the region (innumerable instances of Apollonios, Dionysios, Menekrates, Apphia, Tatia, etc.), it is in practice usually only possible to identify these elite families across multiple generations when they possess Roman citizenship.

It is difficult to judge what proportion of the office-holding class in the cities of the middle Hermos region possessed Roman citizenship before AD 212. A rough-and-ready index is provided by magistrates named on the cities' bronze coinages: of sixty-nine individuals named on the imperial bronze coinages of Gordos, Daldis, Maionia, Saittai, Silandos, and Tabala, around half (thirty-five) carry a Roman gentilician; the rest either have no gentilician or (for coins struck after AD 212) bear only the *nomen* 'Aurelius'. But Roman citizens are probably under-represented in these numbers: it is quite possible – and in a few cases demonstrable – that some magistrates chose not to advertise their Roman citizenship on their coins.[45] As we will see shortly, evidence for large-scale landholding in Roman Hieradoumia is more or less exclusively confined to Roman citizens.

In absolute terms, Roman citizens make up only a very small minority of persons attested in the epigraphy of Hieradoumia prior to AD 212.[46] A tiny number of Roman citizens are attested in Hieradoumia in the late republican period, all of whom are presumably Italian immigrants or their freedman: Publius Pactumeius, who appears in a list of twenty-seven members of a phratry who set up a dedication to Apollo and Artemis at Nisyra in 48/7 BC; C. Iulius C.f. Rufus, honoured for unspecified services by a village community near Maionia in 37/6 BC; and Cn. Antius Apollonios (no doubt a freedman), who set up a tombstone for his wife Tertia Vigellia in (probably) 23/2 BC.[47] In later periods, the overwhelming majority of

[45] The *archon* Agathephoros on coins of Tabala under Severus Alexander was almost certainly a member of the family of the L. Pomponii (see below). Several magistrates with Roman citizenship chose to omit their *nomen* on some of their issues: e.g. the magistrate (Octavius) Artemidoros at Saittai under Commodus (the *nomen* present on *RPC* IV.2 1394–1395, 2853, 8137, 11125, absent on 1397–1399).

[46] Note Gordon 2004, 180, on the particular paucity of Roman citizens in the propitiatory inscriptions of the region.

[47] Pactumeius: *SEG* 49, 1623. Rufus: *SEG* 49, 1597. Antius and Vigellia: *SEG* 48, 1428 (= *SEG* 51, 1684); since the provenance is unknown, the date ('Year 63') could represent either 23/2 BC or 33/4 AD. Other Vigellii – probably all Italian *negotiatores* or their freedmen – are attested at Philadelphia

people with Roman citizenship carry imperial *gentilicia* (and usually *prae-nomina*: C. Iulii, Ti. Claudii, T. Flavii, P. Aelii).[48] It is occasionally possible to identify persons as the descendants or freedmen of Italian immigrants on the basis of relatively unusual *gentilicia*; I have argued elsewhere that the half-dozen (L.) Octavii attested on coins and epitaphs at Saittai in the second century BC can ultimately be traced back to the Italian landowner L. Octavius Naso, known to have owned a large estate near Apollonis in northern Lydia in the early first century BC.[49] There is known to have been an organized community of Roman *negotiatores* at Gordos in the 60s and 70s AD, and this no doubt accounts for the striking density of Roman cit-izens with non-imperial *gentilicia* at first- and second-century Gordos.[50] An unpublished inscription from the village of Kastollos in the Katakeka-umene, now in the Uşak Museum, shows that there was a community of resident Romans there too.[51]

The epigraphic evidence should warn us against assuming that this small group of Roman citizens in Hieradoumia formed a sharply distinct 'upper' social stratum, separate from the wider population of the region.[52]

---

and Sardis in the late republican period: *TAM* V 3, 1692 (C. Vigellius, first century BC); *Sardis* II 587 (M. Vigellius Asiatikos, I BC – I AD); *Sardis* II 629 (M. Vigellius Rufus, 15 BC: in Latin).

[48] A selection only (all with the *praenomen*): C. Iulii: *TAM* V 1, 688; *SEG* 55, 1303; *SEG* 57, 1221; *Sammlung Tatış* 11. Ti. Claudii: *TAM* V 1, 301 and 342; *SEG* 31, 1018 and 1021; *SEG* 35, 1242; *SEG* 57, 1208 and 1201. T. Flavii: Malay and Petzl 2017, no. 200. P. Aelii: *TAM* V 1, 2 and 694.

[49] Thonemann 2017b, 190–2: L. Octavius Glyptos (died AD 108/9); Octavius Cimber (mint-magistrate under Hadrian); Octavius Polykleitos (died AD 145/6); L. Octavius Pollio (owner of a slave who died AD 165/6); Octavia Aelia Artemidora (erected a tombstone for her *threpsas* in AD 167/8); Octavius Artemidorus (mint-magistrate under Commodus). L. Octavius Naso: Cic., *Ad Q. fr.* I.2 (SB 2), 10–11 (59 BC).

[50] *Negotiatores* at Gordos: *SEG* 62, 918 (Gordos, AD 69/70): ἔδοξεν τῇ Ἰουλιέων Γορδηνῶν βουλῇ καὶ τῷ δήμῳ καὶ τοῖς πραγματευομένοις Ῥωμαίοις; *TAM* V 1, 687 (Gordos, AD 75/6): ἔδοξεν τῇ βουλῇ καὶ τῷ δήμῳ τῷ Ἰουλιέων Γορδηνῶν καὶ τοῖς παρ' ἡμῖν πραγματευομένοις Ῥωμαίοις; cf. also *TAM* V 1, 802 (Yeğenoba, just west of Gordos, AD 63/4): ἔδοξε δη[μο]κατοίκοις [τοῖ]ς [ἐν – -] καὶ Ῥωμαίο[ις]. Non-imperial *gentilicia*: *SEG* 62, 917 (L. Antonius Euphron, civic *stratēgos*, early first century AD); *TAM* V 1, 705 (P. Nonnius, Helvia Prima, Servilius: AD 57/8); *TAM* V 1 745 (P. Cluvius Euphemos: date uncertain); *TAM* V 1, 782 (Antistius Priscus, a slave owner at Yayakırıldık, AD 120/1); *TAM* V 1, 693 (M. Antonius Alexandros Apphianos, *logistēs* and asiarch, late 170s AD). Note also Malay and Petzl 2017, no. 17 (P. Velitius Thyneites Fonteianus and Livia Valeria: Korubaşı/Eğrit, mid-160s AD).

[51] On display in the Uşak Museum in 2011: an honorific *stēlē* for a Roman citizen, described as '[saviour] and benefactor', erected by [οἱ ἐν Κ]αστωλλῶι κατοικοῦν[τες Ῥωμαῖοί] τε καὶ Ἕλληνες; a very similar formula on a statue base from the village of Naeis (?) near Blaundos, dated to AD 88 (Filges 2006, 331, no. 17: οἱ ἐν Ναει κατοικοῦντες Ῥωμαῖοί τε καὶ [Ἕλληνες]); cf. Thonemann 2010, 169–70; Thonemann 2013b, 29–31.

[52] I have discussed elsewhere the striking marginality of Roman culture and institutions in the *Oneirocritica* of Artemidorus of Daldis (Thonemann 2020, 191–212), who may have acted as mint-magistrate at Daldis in the Severan period (ibid., 10–11).

On the contrary, there seems to have been no particularly strong demarcation between the Romanized 'elite' and ordinary well-off farmers in the region.[53] Epitaphs for Roman citizens generally use the same distinctively Hieradoumian 'familial' formulae as epitaphs for non-citizens, and there is abundant evidence for intermarriage between citizens and non-citizens.[54] More importantly, epitaphs erected by or for persons who demonstrably belonged to the Romanized civic elite of the region are often indistinguishable in physical form and decorative elaboration from those erected by 'ordinary' Hieradoumian rural families. The most striking example known to me – striking because of its sheer banality – is the perfectly ordinary little tombstone erected at Saittai by Sossia Philia and her son P. Sossius Charikles for her deceased husband, Aelius Theon, which both in form and content is completely indistinguishable from a thousand other epitaphs erected by modest Hieradoumian rural families (Figure 10.1); a couple of decades later, Sossius Charikles would go on to act as first archon and mint-magistrate at Saittai.[55] Similarly conventional in both physical form and content is the epitaph of Tryphon son of Bithys, first archon for the third time and *stephanēphoros* at the *polis* of Maionia.[56]

Perhaps the most telling indication of the relatively modest character of the Romanized elite is the fact that we know of only *two* local families of equestrian rank from the whole of Hieradoumia, who may in fact have been closely related to one another. At Saittai, we find a certain 'Aur. Ael(ius) Attalianos, the son, *eques*, asiarch' acting as archon and mint-magistrate under Gordian III (AD 238–244); a couple of decades later, we find a certain 'Aur. Ael(ius) Phoibos, *eques*, kinsman of senators' as archon and mint-magistrate at Gordos (AD 253–268). The latter individual must be the son or brother of Aur. Aelia Phoibe, 'daughter of the centurion Aur.

---

[53] As at Montaillou: Le Roy Ladurie 1978, 14–18.

[54] Ordinary epitaphic formulae: e.g. *SEG* 40, 1066 (undated); *SEG* 48, 1428 (23/2 BC or AD 33/4); *TAM* V 1, 705 (AD 57/8); Malay and Petzl 2017, no. 17B (AD 167/8). Intermarriage: e.g. *TAM* V 1, 549 (Maionia, AD 81/2: Statilius Setianus a συγγενής of a local non-Roman family); Malay and Petzl 2017, no. 17 (P. Velitius Thyneites Fonteianus: 'Thyneites' is an epichoric name, only attested at Gordos (Robert, *Hellenica* VI, 93): see *LGPN* V.A, *s.v.* Θυνίτης, to which add *RPC* IV.2 8319 (temp.), the archon Ἰουλιανὸς Θυν(ίτης)).

[55] *TAM* V 1, 109: ἔτ(ους) σνδʹ, μη(νὸς) Ξανδικοῦ ιγʹ. | Σοσσία Φίλα Αἴλ. Θέω|να τὸν γλυκύτατον | ἄνδρα καὶ Π. Σόσσιος Χα|(5)ρικλῆς τὸν πατέρα ἐτείμη|σαν ζήσαντα ἔτη μγʹ ('Year 254 [AD 169/70], (Day) 13 of the month Xandikos. Sossia Phila honoured Ael(ius) Theon, her sweetest husband, and P. Sossius Charikles honoured his father, having lived for forty-three years'). For Saittan bronzes minted by Sos(sius) Charikles under Septimius Severus, Caracalla, and Elagabalus, see e.g. *BMC Lydia* 221, nos. 50 and 51; *GM Winterthur* 3880, 3893; *Naumann* 34 (09/08/15), 681.

[56] *SEG* 40, 1095 (AD 211).

Figure 10.1 Epitaph of Aelius Theon, from İcikler. *TAM* V 1, 109.

Iollas Ephesianos, granddaughter of the *matrona stolata* Aelia Phoibe', who donated a bathhouse stoa to the village of Hyssa near Gordos in AD 230/1.[57] To the best of my knowledge, no other Aurelii Aelii are attested anywhere in Hieradoumia, and it is obviously tempting to suppose that Attalianos and Phoibos (and Phoibe) were in fact members of the same solitary Hieradoumian equestrian family.

The wealth of the Romanized civic elite (such as it was) was no doubt based on the ownership of landed estates in the middle Hermos valley. We know of around half a dozen local estate-owning families in the region; as we would expect, all of these families possessed Roman citizenship. At Saittai, we have the epitaphs of the *oikonomos* of a certain Marcia (AD 194/5) and the *saltarius* of Septimius Iollas (AD 242/3), a man who also appears as first

---

[57] Attalianos: *RPC* VII.1, 219–220, 224–5, 228–9, with Bakır-Barthel and Müller 1979, 173–5. Phoibos: *TAM* V 1, p.226. Phoibe: *TAM* V 1, 758. Equites and senators are almost totally absent from Artemidorus' *Oneirocritica*: Thonemann 2020, 207–8.

archon and asiarch on coins of Saittai struck under Philip I (AD 244–249).[58]
An estate near the village of the Pebaleis, near Mazlıtepe south-west of Kula,
seems to have been owned in succession by a certain T. Flavius Thrasymachos and his daughter Flavia Menogenis in the late first and early second
century AD.[59] Near Nisyra, we have the epitaph of the slave *actor* (*pragmateutēs*) of a woman named Iulia Tabilla, and a fragmentary votive inscription
from Kula was erected by the slave *actor* of another woman, this time a high
priestess.[60] Another estate near Nisyra in the mid-first century AD seems to
have belonged to a certain Ti. Claudius Machatas, interred – very unusually
for the region – in a large and lavish sarcophagus, discovered at Kula.[61]

Perhaps the most striking case of a local estate-holding family derives
from the very small *polis* of Tabala, in the far east of the Katakekaumene.
Only four magistrates appear on the bronze coinage of Tabala (Antoninus
Pius – Gordian III): the priest Menophantos, under Antoninus Pius[62]; the
priest L. Pom(ponius) Marcus, under Commodus and Septimius Severus[63];
and a pair of magistrates, the priest P(omponius?) Fronto and the *archon*
Agathephoros, who appear together on coins under Severus Alexander.[64]
Virtually the only surviving public document of Tabala is a decree of the
gerousia dating to AD 140/1 in honour of L. Pomponius Agathephoros and
his homonymous son, and we can therefore be reasonably confident that
the mint-magistrate and *archon* Agathephoros under Severus Alexander
also belonged to this Tabalan family of L. Pomponii.[65] An unprovenanced
dedication in the Manisa Museum was set up by a certain Onesimos, estate
manager (*pragmateutēs*) of Pomponius Marcus; the estate holder must
surely be identical to the late second-century Tabalan mint-magistrate

[58] Marcia: *TAM* V 1, 88. (Aur.) Septimius Iollas: *SEG* 57, 1213, with *RPC* VIII ID 20224–20227
(ἐπὶ Αὐρ. Σεπ. Ἰόλλα ἄρχ. Αʹ υἱοῦ ἀσιάρ.).

[59] T. Flavius Thrasymachos: Malay and Petzl 2017, no. 200 (honorific). Flavia Menogenis: *TAM*
V 1, 274 (honorific, with the corrections of Malay and Petzl 2017, p.203); *TAM* V 1, 257
(dedication by her slave, AD 113/14).

[60] Iulia Tabilla: *TAM* V 1, 442. High priestess: Thonemann 2019, no. 2.

[61] *TAM* V 1, 439 (honours for Machatas at Dora, AD 23/4); *TAM* V 1, 594 (a freedman of
Machatas at Sandal); *TAM* V 1, 301 (sarcophagus of Ti. Claudius Machatas and his wife Flavia
Apphia, at Kula). It is not certain that all three inscriptions refer to the same individual.

[62] *RPC* IV.2 1525–1526, 2859, 2920, 11013, 11557–11558 (temp.).

[63] Commodus: *RPC* IV.2 10834 (temp.), Λ. Πομ(πωνίου) Μάρκου ἱερέως; *RPC* IV.2 1531–2, 11559
(temp.), Λ. Μάρκου. Septimius Severus: *Coll. Wadd.* 5300; *SNG Von Aulock* 3194; *CNG E-Auction*
224 (16/12/09) 390, Π. Μάρκου or Λ. Π. Μάρκου. Treated as two separate men by *TAM* V 1, p.65,
followed by *LGPN* V.A *s.v.* Μᾶρκος (**125–126**).

[64] *RPC* VI 4459–4462 (temp.). The reverse of *RPC* VI 4462 (temp.) was previously read as ἐπ(ὶ)
Π. Φρόντων(ος) κ(αὶ) Ῥεκ() Ἀγαθηφόρου ἀρχ(όντων) (*TAM* V 1, p.65); I prefer to read ἐπ(ὶ)
Π. Φρόντων(ος) ἱερέ(ως) κ(αὶ) Ἀγαθηφόρου ἄρχ(οντος). The *pi* may represent Π(ομπωνίου) or
Π(ομπωνίων).

[65] *TAM* V 1, 194.

L. Pomponius Marcus.[66] This single estate-holding family of L. Pomponii are the only known Roman citizens at Tabala before AD 212; the combination of numismatic and epigraphic evidence suggests that they may have exercised a near-monopoly over public affairs in their small city.[67]

The local land-owning families discussed in the last two paragraphs were not the only large-scale estate holders in the middle Hermos region. There were certainly imperial estates in Hieradoumia, though they do not seem to have been particularly extensive: we know that there was a group of imperial estates around Philadelphia, which may have extended into the Katakekaumene, and there must have been a further cluster of imperial estates around Gordos, as is clear from the presence there of imperial slaves acting as *arcarii* and *dispensatores* of imperial revenues.[68] Probably more important than these imperial holdings were the private estates of non-resident elite families from the large nearby cities of Sardis and Philadelphia. The clearest example of a major 'outside' landowner of this kind in rural Hieradoumia is a certain C. Iulius Quadratus, owner of a large slave-run estate at the village of Thermai Theseos, on the right bank of the Hermos south of Silandos. Quadratus is known from the epitaph of an eight-year-old boy erected by 'the *collegium* of the *familia* of C. Iulius Quadratus at Thermai Theseos' (dated to AD 140/1) and from a dedication to Asklepios erected by his freedman Attikos, 'for the health and salvation of his master C. Iulius Quadratus' (from Kula, dated to AD 145/6).[69] This landowner C. Iulius Quadratus has previously been supposed to be a member of the great Pergamene senatorial family of the Iulii Quadrati, but this is almost certainly wrong.[70] A recently published series of honorific inscriptions from Sardis have revealed the existence of a major civic benefactor at Sardis in the first century AD by the name of C. Iulius Quadratus

---

[66] *I.Manisa* 323: Ὀνήσιμος Πονπωνίου Μάρκου πραγματευτής. For estate managers (usually of slave status) in Hieradoumia and elsewhere, see Ehrhardt 1990; Thonemann 2019, 124.

[67] The only other known public documents from Tabala (leaving aside the late Hellenistic document *SEG* 53, 1360, on which see Chapter 1) are a dossier of correspondence to the *archontes*, *boulē*, and *dēmos* of Tabala from Pertinax and the proconsul of Asia (AD 193), concerning abuses by Roman soldiers passing near the town (*SEG* 38, 1244; Hauken 1998, 203–14), and a list of annual magistrates from AD 150–155 (*SEG* 49, 1685, from Thermai Theseos: better attributed to Tabala than Silandos). For small cities dominated by single families, see Thonemann 2011a, 218–27 (Herakleia under Salbake); cf. Thonemann 2013b, 32–4 (Blaundos).

[68] Philadelphia: *TAM* V 3, 1871 (an *adiutor procuratorum regionis Philadelphenes*); also *TAM* V 3, 1418 (imperial estate village at Ağa Bey Köyü, east of Philadelphia). Gordos: *TAM* V 1, 692 and 713 (δοῦλοι ἀρκάριοι under Domitian and Trajan); *TAM* V 1, 745 (a bilingual epitaph for an *Augg(ustorum) verna disp(ensator)*); cf. also *SEG* 63, 992 (a married pair of imperial slaves, under Titus).

[69] *TAM* V 1, 71 (κολλήγιον φαμιλίας), 245 (dedication to Asklepios).

[70] Herrmann and Polatkan 1969, 47–9; Leschhorn 1993, 322–3; Mitchell 1993, I 161.

Machairion.[71] This man also served as high priest and *stephanēphoros* at Maionia, perhaps around the turn of the era.[72] It is surely better to assume that the major Hieradoumian landowner C. Iulius Quadratus is an Antonine-period descendant of this Sardian elite family, part of whose wealth was no doubt based on their landed interests in eastern Hieradoumia.[73]

A second major non-resident landowning family, this time of Philadelphian origin, is also known to have possessed land around Thermai Theseos. In a fragmentary honorific inscription from Tabala, an anonymous slave honours 'Curtia Iulia Valentilla *hypatikē*, his owner, who entrusted to him the care of the construction of the bathhouse and the buildings on the site'.[74] This inscription was almost certainly brought to Tabala from nearby Thermai Theseos, where the remains of a large Roman-period bathhouse are still visible today (Figure 10.2); a verse dedication to Attis at Thermai Theseos was erected by one 'Valentilla', presumably the same woman.[75] Curtia Iulia Valentilla *hypatikē* is also attested in an honorific inscription from Kula, in which she is described as daughter of Crispus and Demo; her daughter appears in a later dedication from Kula, erected by a slave 'for the health and salvation of his owner Curtia Flavia Archelais Valentilla *hypatikē*'.[76] Both of these women were certainly natives of Philadelphia, where several other members of the family are attested, including the husband of Curtia Iulia Valentilla (and father of Curtia Flavia Archelais Valentilla), the *consularis* T. Fl. Archelaos Claudianus.[77] This Philadelphian consular family evidently

---

[71] *Sardis* II 339–341. The two men named Iulius Machairion (father and son) of *Sardis* II 350, high priests of Asia in the late first or early second century AD, are presumably descendants.

[72] *TAM* V 1, 544, [οἱ ἐν Μαι]ονίᾳ τῇ πό[λει κατοικοῦντες ἐ[τείμησαν] Γάϊον Ἰούλι[ον Μαχαιρί]ωνος υἱὸν [- c.8 -] Μαχαιρίω[να]. In his commentary on *Sardis* II 339, Petzl notes that [Κουαδρᾶτον] is too long for the lacuna, but the name *Quadratus* is often rendered Κοδρᾶτος in Greek (e.g. *TAM* V 1, 553), and [Κοδρᾶτον] fits the lacuna perfectly.

[73] The name Machairion is unattested outside Sardis and Hieradoumia, and it is tempting to suppose that Claudius Machairion, archon and mint-magistrate at Saittai under Hadrian (*RPC* III 2543, 2543A, 2543B), is also a relative of this Sardian family: Thonemann 2017b, 190.

[74] *TAM* V 1, 209.

[75] *TAM* V 1, 73 (*SGO* I 04/15/01). Petzl 1996, 8–11, plausibly suggests that the unprovenanced verse inscription *SEG* 31, 1658 (*SGO* I 04/15/02; cf. Busch 1999, 281–2), in which 'Valentilla' and a bathhouse are mentioned, may also derive from Thermai Theseos.

[76] *TAM* V 1, 273; *SEG* 46, 1496.

[77] Curtia Iulia Valentilla: *TAM* V 3, 1645 (referring to Philadelphia as 'her sweetest fatherland'). Her mother, 'Haruspicia Demo *hypatikē*': *TAM* V 3, 1465. Her sister, 'Priscilla *hypatikē*, daughter of Demo': *TAM* V 3, 1466. Her husband, 'T. Fl. Archelaos Claudianus *hypatikos*': *TAM* V 3, 1461 (perhaps identical to a *legatus Augusti* in Hispania, *PIR*[2] F 214); his freedman, *TAM* V 3, 1911. Another Curtia Valentilla at Philadelphia, probably not identical to Curtia Iulia Valentilla: *TAM* V 3, 1467. It is conceivable that the 'village of Archelaos' somewhere in Hieradoumia (attested in a dedication of AD 161/2) might be part of a large estate owned by this family: Schwertheim 1975, with *BE* 1976, 628.

Figure 10.2 Remains of a bath complex at Thermai Theseos (Emir Kaplıcaları, Şehitlioğlu).

owned large estates in the eastern part of the Katakekaumene, in broadly the same region as the estates of the Iulii Quadrati of Sardis.

Another Sardian elite family is known to have been heavily involved in civic politics in the small towns of Hieradoumia, and it is likely enough (though not strictly demonstrable) that they were also major landowners in the middle Hermos region. Several members of the *gens Stlaccia* are attested as civic notables at Sardis in the second century AD, of whom one, Ti. Claudius Stlaccius Niger, seems also to have acted as first archon and priest of Zeus Polieus at Daldis.[78] Other wealthy Stlaccii are attested at both Gordos (a mint-magistrate and archon T. Fl. Stlaccius Cel(er), under Caracalla) and Maionia (a civic benefactor Stlaccius, under Marcus Aurelius; P. Claudius Stlaccius Quadratianus, uncertain date), and in both cases, it seems

---

[78] Sardis: *Sardis* VII 1, 43 (*I.Manisa* 39: Ti. Claudius Stlaccius); *Sardis* VII 1, 61 (Stlaccius Niger); *Sardis* VII 1, 77 (*SEG* 36, 1091: Arruntius Maternus Anullinus Stlaccianus); *Sardis* II 384 (Ti. Claudius Stlaccius Niger); *Sardis* II 477 (L. Fl. Stlaccius the sophist, also in *SEG* 61, 1004); see further Petzl 2016. Daldis: *TAM* V 1, 621, where we should surely restore Νί[γρου Στ]λακκίου in lines 4–5 (the remainder of this inscription is extremely difficult).

very likely that we are dealing with members of the Sardian civic elite with landed interests on the territories of several small Hieradoumian *poleis*.[79]

Finally, it is possible (but far from certain) that a Pergamene family of Iulii also owned estates in the region of Kula. In AD 123/4, a *koinon* of *neoi Herakleotai* at or near Kula erected an honorific inscription for 'their benefactor, A(ulus) Iulius Aneiketos', a name which is attested at Pergamon in the second century.[80] A generation later, in AD 175/6, a certain Eutychis, *threptē* of 'C. Iulius Aneiketos of Pergamon', set up a dedication to Meis Axiottenos; this man is also attested as having set up dedications to Meis Axiottenos and the 'Holy and Just Divinity' in his own right.[81]

Overall, the strong impression left by our evidence is that of a very small Romanized citizen elite, of relatively modest resources and limited geographic horizons. Each *polis* had a few well-off landowning families who turn up suspiciously often as leading civic magistrates (the L. Octavii at Saittai, the L. Pomponii at Tabala), but there is little sign that many of these families were active on a wider stage than their native *polis*. Almost no families of equestrian rank are known (perhaps only a single family of Aurelii Aelii, with interests at Gordos and Saittai), and only three individuals from the region (all from Saittai) are known to have served as asiarchs.[82] A handful of rich families from Sardis and Philadelphia (and perhaps Pergamon) owned estates in the region, and there is reason to think that members of these 'outsider' families occasionally held civic offices in the cities of Hieradoumia. All of this makes a pleasing fit with the picture sketched out in Section 10.1, of a region characterized by rather limited urban development and monumental infrastructure, with relatively simple civic institutions. As a result (we may infer) of the unusually late emergence of *poleis* in the region, the wealthier families of the region never developed into a

---

[79] T. Fl. Stlaccius Cel(er): *BMC Lydia* 96, no. 39. Maionia: *TAM* V 1, 542 (Stlaccius, AD 163–165); *TAM* V 1, 553 (P. Cl. Stlaccius Quadratianus, perhaps a relative of the Sardian Iulii Quadrati).

[80] *I.Manisa* 36; Aulus Iulius Aneiketos at Pergamon, *IvP* II 590 (undated).

[81] *SEG* 39, 1275 (dedication of Eutychis to Meis Axiottenos, AD 175/6); *SEG* 28, 929 (dedication of C. Iulius Aneiketos to Theion Hosion kai Dikaion); *TAM* V 1, 253 (dedication of C. Iulius Aneiketos with his wife Iulia Tyche to Meis Axiottenos), probably all from the region of Kula.

[82] Saittan asiarchs: Aur. Ae(lius) Attalianos, *RPC* VII.1 219–220, 224–5, 228–9 (Gordian III); Aur. Sep(timius) Iollas, *RPC* VIII ID 20224–20227 (Philip I); ΚΑΦ (?) Syllas, *CNG* 92 (23/06/04), 76; *Naumann* 52 (02/04/17), 1240; *Leu Web Auction* 6 (09/12/18), 476 (Gallienus: his *gentilicia* uncertain). The *logistēs* and asiarch M. Antonius Alexandros Apphianos of *TAM* V 1, 693 (Gordos, *c.* AD 180) may not have been a native of Gordos; the asiarch Ti. [Claudius/ Iulius] Damas honoured in *SEG* 57, 1220 (near Silandos: first century AD?) was almost certainly not a local.

true indigenous urban elite, and the *polis* therefore remained a distinctly marginal phenomenon in the social and economic life of the middle Hermos valley. As the funerary epigraphy of the region so vividly illustrates, the social structure of the region was – by the standards of the wider Greek world in the Roman imperial period – remarkably 'flat' and undifferentiated, and there seems to have been no strong divide between urban and village cultures. An urbanized world, in short, this was not.

10.3 The Village as Collective Agent

The dominant extra-familial social unit in Roman Hieradoumia was beyond all doubt the village (*kōmē, katoikia*). By the second century AD, the great majority of the hundreds of *kōmai* and *katoikiai* of the middle Hermos valley were formally assigned to the territory of one or other of the *poleis* of the region, but it is very much more difficult to say in which spheres of life (aside from tax collection) this 'subordination' might have had a meaningful impact.[83] We know that two villages on the territory of Saittai, the *Tamasaitēnoi* and *Satalēnoi*, were organized as Saittan civic tribes, but this cannot have been the case for all the villages on the territory of Saittai (the number of villages is just too large). At Maionia, a public document of some kind (*c.* AD 300) was subscribed by 'the *epimelētēs* and the other heads of households (*oikodespotai*) and the *kōmarchoi*', perhaps suggesting some formal role for village chiefs (*kōmarchoi*) in *polis*-level decision-making.[84]

Our clearest evidence for independent self-governance by village communities derives from the village of Kastollos in the Katakekaumene, in the far north-east of the territory of Philadelphia[85]:

ἐν Καστωλλῷ κώμῃ Φιλαδελφέων γενομένης ἐκκλησίας ὑπὸ τῆς γερουσίας
καὶ τῶν λοιπῶν κωμητῶν πάντων καὶ βου-
λευσαμένων αὐτῶν διελέσθαι τὸν ὑπά[ρ]-
5   χοντα αὐτοῖς ἀγρὸν ἐν τοῖς ἰδίοις ὅροις
[τ]όπῳ τῷ λεγομένῳ Ἀγάθωνος Μάνδραις

---

[83] The Flavian *conventus*-list from Ephesos implies that many villages and *ethnē* in rural Lydia and Phrygia retained some administrative independence from *poleis*: Habicht 1975, 67; Schuler 1998, 221.

[84] *SEG* 54, 1218B; on *komarchoi* and other terms for 'village headmen', Schuler 1998, 233–8.

[85] *TAM* V 1, 222; *TAM* V 3, 1415. On this village, see further above, n.51 (resident Romans at Kastollos).

[ὄ]ντα ὀρινόν, ἐφ᾽ ᾧ πάντες οἱ κωμ[ῆτα]ι

- - - - - - - - - - - - - - - - - -

At Kastollos, village of the Philadelphians, when an assembly was held by the *gerousia* and all the other villagers, and they resolved to divide up the plot of land which belongs to them (and is) within their own boundaries, at the place called 'Folds of Agathon', being mountainous land, on condition that all the villagers ...

Although Kastollos was administratively dependent on the *polis* of Philadelphia (a 'village of the Philadelphians'), it evidently had its own clearly defined village territory, over which the village community was sovereign. Decisions about this territory (here apparently involving the division of a stretch of common pastoral land into discrete plots for cultivation) were taken by a village assembly, seemingly involving the entire male population of the settlement. Kastollos had its own *gerousia* (a council of 'village elders'), and perhaps other annual magistrates; as we have already seen, many Hieradoumian villages had a roster of local magistrates (including *agōnothetai* and financial officials) hardly less developed than that of the smaller *poleis* of the region.

It is impossible to reconstruct the pattern of landholding in and around villages like Kastollos in any detail. As we have seen, parts – perhaps substantial parts – of the agricultural land of Hieradoumia were carved up into large private estates, whether owned by local elites or by rich outsiders from Sardis or Philadelphia; the larger estates may have been organized around 'estate-villages' (Thermai Theseos is the clearest example) inhabited by persons, free or unfree, who had no proprietary rights over their agricultural land.[86] The gods also owned significant landed estates, at least some of which was leased out for cultivation to individual farmers.[87] But the strong cumulative impression given by the propitiatory inscriptions of the middle Hermos region is that small peasant holdings were the norm in most village communities, and that land could be disposed of by testament, divided, or (more rarely) sold according to the wishes of the individual peasant landholder (Section 8.3).[88] It is striking to find, for instance, that the field immediately to the east of the sanctuary of Thea Larmene on Yeşiloba Tepe was privately owned and that the 'key-bearer and temple-warden' of

---

[86] On Thermai Theseos, see Section 10.2. In *Sardis* II 318, we learn that the village of the Arillēnoi, in the plain of Sardis north of Lake Gygaia, 'belonged' as an ancestral possession to a certain Asinius Rufus, no doubt a wealthy member of the civic elite at Sardis (lines 47–48, [ἡ Ἀριλ]ληνῶν κώμη προσήκουσά μοι ἐ(κ) προγόνων): see Schuler 1998, 220–1.

[87] The only clear evidence is *SEG* 39, 1277 (Petzl 1994, no. 63), discussed in Chapter 8, Section 8.2: lease of an arable plot belonging to Meis Axiottenos.

[88] Mitchell 1993, I 161. On inheritance, see also Chapter 5, Section 5.7.

the goddess had to seek permission from the landowner to be interred on his land: evidently private peasant smallholdings could run right up to the very entrances of sanctuary complexes.[89]

Nonetheless, this general picture of large-scale private landholding does need to be qualified in one important respect. As we saw in Chapter 8, there is abundant evidence that the village-gods of Roman Hieradoumia expected to receive conventional 'tithes' on inheritances and land sales in the region. This normative expectation must reflect an underlying set of 'communitarian' or mutualist assumptions about the character of the village community as a whole: its members did not see themselves as atomized and autonomous individuals, free to dispose of their assets as they saw fit. This mutualist ethos is neatly illustrated by a propitiatory inscription from the village of Nea Kome on the territory of Silandos, which tells us that 'Kallistos made a vow to the Theoi Neakometai, and when he achieved the object of his vow, he disposed of it just as he wished, without involving the village (ὡς ἠθέλησεν αὐτὸς ἄτερ τῆς κατοικίας)'; Kallistos was duly punished by the god.[90] We have no idea precisely what the independent-minded Kallistos actually did or failed to do, but it seems clear that the village community expected to have a say in the disposition of the assets gained by Kallistos as a result of his successful vow. Similarly, villages could expect to receive a portion of fines or fees imposed by the gods on individual members of the village community: in a propitiatory inscription from an unknown village in the northern Katakekaumene, the god Meis Axiottenos imposes a 'ransom' (presumably payable in cash) on the transgressor, a third of which is to be paid to the gods, a third to the village, and a third to the priests.[91]

The votive and propitiatory epigraphy of Roman Hieradoumia demonstrates very clearly that villages conceived of themselves as unitary 'institutional actors'. Dedications to the gods were often erected by village communities as collective acts, as for instance in the case of a dedication from the village of Nisyra in the Katakekaumene, 'To Zeus Seleukios and

---

[89] Malay and Petzl 2017, no. 158: ἔταξε κατὰ τὴν τῆς θεοῦ πρόνοιαν κατέναντι τοῦ ναοῦ τεθῆναι ... σὺν γνώ[μη Διο]νυσίου τοῦ ἐνκτήτορος, 'she stipulated, in accordance with the providence of the goddess, that she should be interred opposite the temple, with the consent of the possessor Dionysios'. The inscription was understood by the first editors as referring to the erection of a statue or altar; but in Hieradoumian inscriptions, the verb τεθῆναι is invariably used of burial (e.g. *TAM* V 1, 637, 653, 670, 800). Note the presence of three slots cut into the bedrock just to the east of the presumed location of the *propylon* beside the main road leading up to the sanctuary (Akat 2009, 80–1), conceivably a small burial plot for sacred officials.

[90] Petzl 1994, no. 48, text in Petzl 2019, 16 (AD 146/7).

[91] *SEG* 49, 1720 (Petzl 2019, no. 133: AD 168/9), with Gordon 2004, 183 n.28. On 'ransoms', see Chapter 2, n.77.

the Fruit-Giving Nymphs, the village of the Nisyreis (set this up) for the freedom from harm and the fruit-bearing of their crops, in response to a divine command'.[92] In Chapter 9, we looked at a rather mysterious propitiatory inscription from the sanctuary of Meis Petraeites at the village of Taza, dating to winter AD 210/211, in which 'some men from the village' (ἀνθρώπων … ἐκ τῆς κώμης) are said to have plotted against a pair of orphaned boys, in the face of which 'the village of the Tazenoi was outraged' (ἡ Ταζηνῶν κατοικία ἀδοξήσασα): once again, the point of interest is the conception of the village as a single (in this case moral) agent.[93]

The solidarity of the village was further cemented by what were evidently extremely strong overlaps between village communities and worshipping groups. As we saw in Chapter 8, the gods of Roman Hieradoumia were very often conceived as being associated with particular villages (the Theoi Pereudēnoi at Pereudos, Apollo Nisyreitēs at Nisyra, and so forth) or clusters of villages (the several villages over which Meis Axiottenos is described as 'ruling': Axiotta, Koresa, Tarsi, Perkon, Dorou Kome), and in such cases, it is very likely that the worshipping community was precisely co-extensive with the village population. This is more or less explicit in a propitiatory inscription from a sanctuary of Meis Motylleites near Kollyda, in which a pair of brothers are said to have sought forgiveness both from the gods and from 'the village (κατοικία) and the sacred association (ἱερὸς δοῦμος)'; it is hard not to think that the *katoikia* and the *doumos* are in effect one and the same body, the collective body of worshippers gathered at the sanctuary of Meis Motylleites for a festival.[94] A similar picture is presented by an honorific inscription from the village of Halokome north of Saittai, in which two village benefactors (who appear to have paid for a public building of some

---

[92] *TAM* V 1, 426 (May/June AD 229, at the start of the growing season): [Δ]ιὶ Σελευκίῳ καὶ Νύμφαις | Καρποδοτείραις ἡ Νισυρέων | κατοικία ὑπὲρ τῆς ἀβλαβείας | καὶ τελεσφορίας τῶν καρπῶν |(5) κατ' ἐπιταγήν; for parallels, Schuler 2012, 67–76. Similarly e.g. *TAM* V 1, 193 (consecration of a statue of Zeus Sabazios by the village of Koloe), 489 (dedication of a statue of Meter Leto by the villages of Dima and Kerbia, 'by divine command'), 609 (dedication to 'the divine god' by the village of the *Basileis*); *I.Manisa* 184 (dedication to Theios Megistos by the village of the Odenoi 'for its salvation'); Malay and Petzl 2017, no. 117 (dedication to Apollo Axyreos by two men 'with the village'); Malay and Petzl 2017, no. 186 (Petzl 2019, no. 169: the village of Pereudos and outlying inhabitants propitiate the gods).

[93] *TAM* V 1, 231 (Petzl 1994, no. 35); see Chapter 9, Section 9.4.

[94] *SEG* 57, 1186 (Petzl 2019, no. 146: AD 205/6), with Chaniotis 2009a, 134: ἐρωτῶντες τοὺς θεοὺς Μῆνα Μοτυλλίτην καὶ Δία Σαβάζιον καὶ Ἄρτεμιν Αναειτιν καὶ μεγάλην συνᾶτος καὶ σύνκλητον τῶν θεῶν, ἐρωτῶντες τὴν κατοικία[ν] καὶ τὸν ἱερὸν δοῦμον, ἵνα ἐλέου τύχωσιν. That the individual acts of propitiation which took place at rural sanctuaries were mass public events is indicated by the occasional depiction of 'crowds' in the relief sculptures on propitiatory *stēlai*: Robert 1987, 365–6; Belayche 2008, 190–2; Chaniotis 2009a, 140. See further Chapter 9, Section 9.6.

kind) are honoured by 'the *katoikia* of the Halokometai and the *thiasos*', with the stipulation that they are to be crowned both at meetings of the *thiasos* and at sacrifices to all the gods performed by the village community.[95] Likewise, in an epitaph from the remote village of Kömürcü, north-west of Gordos, a Dionysiac cult association (*speira*) joins a family grouping in commemorating 'their fennel-stalk bearer (*narthēkophoros*) and village headman (*prōtokōmētēs*)', phraseology which strongly implies that the Dionysiac *speira* and the village were in fact one and the same community seen from 'secular' and 'sacred' perspectives (with the village headman also serving as a leading figure in the local Dionysiac cult).[96]

10.4 Villages and Kin Groups

One of the most delicate problems in the social morphology of Roman Hieradoumia is that of the relationship between the extended kin group and the village community. It is quite evident that both forms of social organization (kin group and settlement group) were of profound importance for the inhabitants of the region, in both practical and ideological terms. But how the two structures fitted together is very far from clear.[97] Could an extended kin group be distributed across several villages (one brother living with his household in Iaza, another in Nisyra)? How common was intermarriage between people in different villages, and what were the consequences for the solidarity of particular village communities? Should we a picture a given village as being made up of a cluster of clearly *distinct* kin groups, waltzing around one another in an ever-changing pattern of marriage alliances, interest groups, and factions, like the half-dozen leading *domus* of Le Roy Ladurie's Montaillou; or is each village better considered as a *single* large and ramified *syngeneia*, without clear dividing lines separating one lineage from another?

---

[95] *TAM* V 1, 144 (Hüdük): [ἡ] Ἀλωκωμητῶν κατοικία καὶ ὁ θίασος … [ἐ]ψηφίσαντο [στ]εφα[νοῦσ]θαι αὐτοὺς διὰ γένους ἐ[ν – -] θιάσῳ καὶ ταῖς πάντων [- -] θεῶν θυσίαις. For the conferral of wreaths by villages at village sacrifices, compare *SEG* 57, 1219, from the village of Morei near Silandos (45/4 BC): στεφανοῦσθαι αὐτὸν ἐν ταῖς δημοτελῆ θυσί[αις] διὰ γένους, 'let him and his descendants be crowned at the sacrifices performed at public (i.e. village) expense'; similarly *SEG* 49, 1622 (Nisyra, late Hellenistic).

[96] *TAM* V 1, 822 (AD 199): ἡ σπεῖρα τὸν ναρθηκοφόρον κὲ πρωτοκωμήτην.

[97] The most detailed analysis of this kind known to me for any ancient society is the study of kin groups and Attic demes by Humphreys 2018, II 773–1211: note, for example, the rich studies of lineage–deme dynamics for Sounion (950–9), Thorikos (991–1000), Athmonon (1056–67: particularly interesting), Halai Aixonides (1083–97), Aphidnai (1141–50), Rhamnous (1158–77) and Anaphlystos (1199–1206).

I cannot say I have any clear answers to these questions, and progress is rendered difficult by the extreme repetitiveness of Hieradoumian onomastics (innumerable examples of Demetrios, Dionysios, Apollonios, Artemidoros), which makes it effectively impossible to trace particular lineages *between* texts.[98] However, a few inscriptions do provide us with helpful leads. Perhaps most suggestive of all is a recently published decree from the small settlement of Loros in the middle Kum Çayı valley, dated to summer 55 BC, honouring a certain Demetrios for his services as agonothete (the annual official presiding over a set of games).[99] The inscription is badly worn and difficult to read, but the opening lines are clear enough (Figure 10.3):

[ἔ]τους λ΄, μηνὸς Γορπιαίου ἐν Λορῳ· ἔδο-
[ξ]εν τοῖς περὶ Ἀττίναν Μενεκράτου[ς]
[σ]υνγενεῖσιν· ἐπεὶ Δημήτριος Ἀρτεμιδώρου ἀνὴρ καλὸς καὶ ἀγαθὸς γενόμενο[ς]
5 [ἐν τ]ῷ[ι] ἐν[εστ]ῶτι ἔτει ἀγωνοθέτης ΜΕ[.]
[.......] σ[υ]νγενέου ἐτέλεσεν πάντα
τὰ καθήκοντα κατὰ τὸν [ἀ]γῶνα, κτλ.

Year 30, in the month Gorpiaios, at Loros. Resolved by the kinsmen (*syngeneis*) around Attinas son of Menekrates. Since Demetrios son of Artemidoros, a fine and good man, having become *agōnothetēs* [- -] of the kinship-group in the current year, performed all the customary things concerning the games, etc.

As the resolution formula shows, the body which honoured Demetrios was a group of 'kinsmen' (συγγενεῖς), organized around or presided over by a named individual, Attinas son of Menekrates, presumably the senior living member of this *syngeneia*. This group of *syngeneis* was resident at (but apparently not coextensive with) the settlement of Loros, and they celebrated their own annual games (*agōnes*) in honour of a deity whose name would have been given in lines 5–6 of the text: the god appears to have carried the epithet συγγένε(ι)ος, '(god) of the kinship-group'.[100] The '*syngeneis* around Attinas son of Menekrates' were evidently a clearly defined corporate body within the larger village community at Loros, with their own corporate cult, *agōnes* and agonothete. They were also organized in a

[98] I take the opportunity to note one suggestive connection: the presence of the name Χαμάσων, unattested elsewhere, in two families which controlled hereditary priesthoods at the neighbouring villages of Nisyra and Iaza (*TAM* V 1, 433 and 449).
[99] *Sammlung Tatış* 37, with Petzl 2018.
[100] In light of the crescent moon depicted on the *stēlē*, the god Meis seems likely: in lines 5–6, I have wondered about restoring ἀγωνοθέτης Μη[νὸς θεοῦ] σ[υ]νγενέου. For gods associated with particular kin groups, see further below.

Figure 10.3 Honorific decree for Demetrios, from Loros. *Sammlung Tatış* 37 (collection of Yavuz Tatış, Turkey, inv. 2159).

sufficiently formal and structured way that they could pass decrees in honour of their members, on the model of larger political bodies.

For our purposes, it clearly matters a good deal whether this *syngeneia* was a 'true' kinship group, whose membership was (at least in principle) defined by traceable and verifiable kin connections to the eponymous Attinas, or whether it was instead a formal political subdivision of the wider *dēmos* of Loros (like the *phylai* of Greek *polis*-communities), which just happened to be designated by a term ultimately derived from the vocabulary of kinship.[101] The former seems to me overwhelmingly likely to be the case, for the simple but (to my mind) compelling reason that

---

[101] Elsewhere in the Greek world, *syngeneiai* only appear as corporate decree-making bodies in Hellenistic Karia. These Karian *syngeneiai* probably originated as 'true' kin-based organizations (local 'clans' associated with particular sanctuaries, as at fourth-century Sinuri), but by the later Hellenistic period they seem all to have mutated into 'fictive' kin-units, fully integrated into the political structure of Karian *poleis* (as at late Hellenistic Mylasa, where *syngeneiai* were non-kin-based segments of civic *phylai*). See Bresson and Debord 1985; Williamson 2016.

this association of *syngeneis* has *no collective name*. Were they a 'civic' subdivision of the *dēmos* of Loros, they would have been called the '*syngeneia* of Attinas' or the '*syngeneia* of the Attineis'. But no – they are simply the '*syngeneis* around Attinas son of Menekrates', defined by their relation to a single living individual. Attinas is, I take it, the 'patriarch' of the extended family group; when Attinas dies, they will become the '*syngeneis* around someone else'. Given the early date of this text (55 BC), it is worth noting that the personal name Attinas seems to have been particularly widespread in Mysia: it is quite possible that the '*syngeneis* around Attinas' are descendants of a group of second-century Mysian settlers at Loros, still organized as a distinct corporate body within the village a century later.[102]

Another 'unnamed' group of kinsmen acting as a corporate body can be found in a slightly later votive inscription from the village of Tetrapyrgia in the eastern Katakekaumene. Here, in autumn 4 BC, the 'kinsmen dwelling at Tetrapyrgia' (οἱ ἐν Τετραπυργίᾳ κατοικοῦντες συνγενεῖς) set up a votive *stēlē* to Zeus Keraunios, bearing relief images of an ox and a goat, presumably indicating that the *stēlē* was erected in fulfilment of a vow concerning the safety of the villagers' livestock.[103] Just as at Loros, this institutionalized group of *syngeneis* has no collective name. But in this case, unlike at Loros, the 'kinsmen' at Tetrapyrgia appear be *identified* with the population of the village: in the epigraphy of late Hellenistic and Roman Asia Minor, the phrase οἱ ἐν [village name] κατοικοῦντες, 'those dwelling at *x*', is invariably used of the entire village community.[104] It therefore appears that the villagers of Tetrapyrgia self-identified as a single extended kin group: village and *syngeneia* were perceived as strictly homologous entities.

Further evidence for the institutionalization of kin groups within village communities comes from the frequent association of rural cults with a particular family lineage. In an honorific inscription from Iaza (Figure 10.4), dating to summer AD 224, a local cult association (the 'sacred *doumos*')

---

[102] Of ninety-five instances of the name Ἀττίνας, thirteen are from Hieradoumia and twenty-seven from Mysia (*LGPN* V.A, s.v. Ἀττίνας); note especially *TAM* V 1, 690, a 'Kleon son of Attinas' as ἡγέμων Μυ[σῶν] under Eumenes II. Cf. Robert 1963, 211; Catling 2004–2009, 405–7.

[103] Malay and Petzl 2017, no. 203: ἔτους κζ´, μη(νὸς) Δείου ϛ´. | οἱ ἐν Τε|τραπυργί|ᾳ κατοικοῦν|(5)τες συνγε|νεῖς | Διὶ Κεραυνίωι εὐχήν. For votive inscriptions for the safety of livestock, see Schuler 2012, 76–9, with catalogue at 93–4. The same cult is attested in Malay and Petzl 2017, no. 199 (a hereditary priest of Zeus Keraunios).

[104] Schuler 1998, 33–6.

Figure 10.4 Honours of a sacred *doumos* for Aurelius Glykon, from Ayazören (Iaza). *TAM* V 1, 449.

honours a priest of Artemis Anaeitis, 'the goddess of the kinship-group' (τῆς συνγενικῆς θεοῦ):[105]

    ἔτους τη', μηνὸς Πανήμου ιη'.
    ὁ ἱερὸς δοῦμος ἐτείμησαν Αὐρ.
    Γλύκωνα Διονυσίου τὸν ἐκ προ-
    γόνων ἱερέων πρῶτον Ἀρτέμι-
5   δος Αναειτις τῆς συνγενικῆς
    θεοῦ σὺν καὶ Διονυσίῳ τῷ υἱῷ αὐτοῦ
    κὲ Χαμάσωνι τῷ ἐκγόνῳ αὐτοῦ διὰ
    τὴν ἰς τοὺς θεοὺς θρησκείαν καὶ
    τὰς ἰς τὸν δοῦμον πολλὰς εὐερ-
10 γεσίας καὶ τετελεκότα κὲ τελοῦντα.

[105] *TAM* V 1, 449: in the pediment, a standing goddess of the 'Artemis Ephesia' type; in a recessed panel, three standing figures of uncertain sex (probably Glykon, his son, and his grandson). Compare perhaps *I.Iznik* 1130, a dedication to Διὶ συνγενικῷ, although this may refer to Zeus' capacity as god of kinship more generally. A fragmentary propitiatory inscription from Saittai may also refer to the deity of a kinship group: *TAM* V 1, 151 (Petzl 1994, no. 23: perhaps Μῆ[να θεὸν συ]νγενικόν?).

Year 308 [AD 223/4], day 18 of the month Panemos. The sacred *doumos* honoured Aur(elius) Glykon, son of Dionysios, descended from priestly ancestors, first (priest) of Artemis Anaeitis, the goddess of the kinship-group, along with his son Dionysios and his grandson Chamason, because of his service towards the gods and his many benefactions to the *doumos*, both those he performed in the past and those he continues to perform.

Here we have a clear case of a deity (Artemis Anaeitis) who is conceived as having a particularly close association with a kin group (she is described as *syngenikē theos*, 'goddess of the *syngeneia*'). It is therefore hard not to suppose that the 'sacred *doumos*' which honoured Glykon was in fact a kin-based organization: here and elsewhere in Roman Hieradoumia, the term *doumos* may well be a semi-technical term for an extended *syngeneia* operating in its capacity as a worshipping group.[106] It therefore comes as no surprise to find that the priesthood of Artemis Anaeitis at Iaza is a hereditary one, passing from father to son within a single family line. Hereditary priesthoods are of course perfectly common elsewhere in the Greco-Roman world, but they do seem to have been especially widespread in the villages of Roman Hieradoumia, offering some support for the idea that many village cults may have been closely associated with particular kin groups.[107]

One further feature of the relation between kin groups and village deities should be tackled briefly here, although its significance is very hard to pin down with any precision. As we have seen, several of the rural gods of Roman Hieradoumia carry cultic *epiklēseis* (epithets or 'by-names') derived

[106] The term *doumos* sometimes unambiguously denotes a 'kinship group' or 'family' (Neumann 2002, with Chaniotis, *EBGR* 2004, 98 and *SEG* 53, 1505), rendering it highly like that the 'sacred *doumoi*' of Hieradoumia were primarily kin-based associations. See Chapter 1, n.5.

[107] E.g. Malay and Petzl 2017, no. 112 (Saittai, AD 81: a hereditary priest of Zeus at the village of the Spelmenoi); Malay and Petzl 2017, no. 199 (area of Kula: hereditary priest of Zeus Keraunios, probably the same cult as that attested at Tetrapyrgia, above); *TAM* V 1, 432–3 (Nisyra: two 'younger priests' of an unnamed deity, no doubt priesthoods transmitted within the family); *TAM* V 1, 490 (Hamidiye: hereditary life priestess of Meis Axiottenos); perhaps *TAM* V 1, 241 (Kula: priesthood of Artemis, perhaps held by father and daughter). Life tenure of priestly office may indicate that the post is hereditary: *TAM* V 1, 484 (Iaza); *SEG* 35, 1261 (Thermai Theseos); *SEG* 38, 1232 (Saittai: Apollo Tarsios); Malay and Petzl 2017, no. 158 (Thea Larmene). For hereditary priesthoods elsewhere in Lydia, see e.g. Malay and Petzl 2017, no. 16 (Zeus Mesdianos, SE of Thyateira, *c.* 148 BC); *SEG* 49, 1572 (Zeus Sabazios, Kidoukome near Hierokaisareia, late Hellenistic); *TAM* V 2, 1229 (Zeus, (N)Akokome near Apollonis, 28/7 BC); in south-west Phrygia, *MAMA* IV 265 (Zeus Mossyneus); *MAMA* IV 302bis (Asklepios). At the village of the Thamoreitai, north of Sardis, we can see a son succeeding his father as hereditary priest of Zeus Driktes: *Sardis* II 666: death in AD 93 of Metrodoros, priest διὰ γένους of Zeus Driktes; *Sardis* II 318, his son Metras still in office as priest διὰ γένους of Zeus Driktes in *c.* AD 136.

from the name of the village where the cult was based: so the chief sanctuary of Meis Axiottenos was located at Axiotta, Apollo Nisyreites was particularly associated with the village of Nisyra, and so on. We also find several examples of cultic *epiklēseis* which derive from the name of a human, generally (and surely correctly) taken to be either the founder of the cult or the person who received the epiphany which led his community to establish the cult.[108] In many instances, the deity is known only by his proper name and the name of the presumed cult founder, as for instance in the case of the cult of 'Meis from Attalos' (Μεὶς ἐξ Ἀττάλου) at Silandos, or 'Meis from Diodotos' (Μεὶς ἐγ Διοδότου) in two Hieradoumian propitiatory inscriptions of uncertain provenance.[109] More problematic is the example of the cult of Meis Axiottenos, with its centre at the village of Axiotta near modern Mağazadamları, since this cult is associated with three *different* named individuals: the god can be identified as Meis Axiottenos 'of/from Artemidoros' (the best-attested case: around twenty instances), Meis Axiottenos 'from Epikrates' (three instances, all from Kollyda), and as Meis Axiottenos 'from Apollonios' (one instance, from Kula).[110] I take it that an original cult of Meis Axiottenos at Axiotta, probably founded by a certain Artemidoros, was subsequently 'replicated' at several other nearby villages: so Epikrates would be the founder of a 'branch' sanctuary of the god at Kollyda, and Apollonios the founder of another branch sanctuary somewhere else.[111] It is likely enough that the priesthoods of these cults continued to be closely associated with the linear descendants of the eponymous cult founder (or 'transferrer'), but I cannot say there is any clear evidence for this.

---

[108] The key text is *SEG* 56, 1434 (late second century AD): the cult of 'Great Zeus of Menophilos' near Aizanoi founded by the villagers of Daokome on the nineteenth day of the month Loos, after Menophilos was 'struck terribly with amazement' ([κ]ατεπλήχθη δε[ινῶς]): perhaps an epiphany, or a divine punishment, or even a lightning strike (cf. *TAM* V 2, 1108). The best discussion of these 'personal' cults is now Parker 2017, 113–19.

[109] Meis from Attalos: Petzl 2019, no. 148. Meis from Diodotos: Petzl 1994, nos. 51 and 52 (the latter now *TAM* V 3, 1631). More examples of this type listed by de Hoz 1999, 41–2, 47; Ricl 2016, 159–60; cf. also Malay and Petzl 2017, no. 107 (cults of Meter). On the problematic case of 'Anaeitis from Metro', see Petzl 2019, no. 132, with commentary. The character of the epithet 'Petraeites' carried by Meis in several inscriptions is unclear: morphologically it ought to derive from the name of a village ('Petra': de Hoz 1999, 39 n.221), but it is once combined with the village-*epiklēsis* 'Axiottenos' (Petzl 1994, no. 38). Πετραείτης is attested as an anthroponym at Gordos (*TAM* V 1, 712, with *SEG* 48, 1439), but there are other cases of anthroponyms in the region deriving from local village toponyms (e.g. Βευδεινός, discussed by H. Malay in his commentary on *I.Manisa* 234).

[110] Μεὶς (ἐξ) Ἀρτεμιδώρου: Ricl 2016, 157–8 (listing the various versions of the *epiklēsis*), with Malay and Petzl 2017, nos. 123–127, 129. Μεὶς Αξιοττηνὸς ἐξ Ἐπικράτου: *TAM* V 1, 343–5. Μεὶς Αξιοττηνὸς ἐξ Ἀπολλωνίου: *TAM* V 1, 253.

[111] The phenomenon is attested elsewhere, e.g. the 'branch sanctuary' of Helios Apollo Lairbenos at Eibeos on the territory of Sebaste (see my commentary to *MAMA* XI 70).

As will be obvious to the reader, the evidence for the 'institutionaliza-tion' of kin groups in the villages of Roman Hieradoumia is dispersed and ambiguous. The decree of the '*syngeneis* around Attinas' at Loros is, at pres-ent, the only absolutely clear case of an extended kin group operating as a quasi-political decision-making body. It is telling that this decree dates to the mid-first century BC, when the old Attalid *koina* in the region (the Mysoi Abbaeitai and the 'Maionians in the Katakekaumene') may well have ceased to exist, but before the creation of the first Hieradoumian *poleis* (first Maionia in the early Augustan period, followed shortly afterwards by Gor-dos and Kadoi). That is to say, the Loros text dates to a period when 'political' institutions across Hieradoumia may have been unusually thin; it is quite possible that all sorts of odd quasi-political forms may have sprouted up in the small towns and villages of the region in the last years of the Republic.

Nonetheless, when set alongside the extraordinarily rich evidence for the importance of extended kin groups in the social organization of Hier-adoumia in the first three centuries AD (Chapters 4 and 5), the material discussed here necessarily has a significance quite disproportionate to its small volume. It shows that the large and ramified kin groups which are so prominent in the epitaphic evidence from the region were not purely 'pri-vate' or sentimental networks of related households, but that they could, on occasion, form distinct 'segments' of larger residential communities (towns and villages), with an independent institutional existence of their own, par-ticularly in the sphere of religious life. In smaller villages, as at Tetrapyrgia, kin groups could be coextensive with the village community ('the *syngeneis* dwelling at Tetrapyrgia'); in larger villages, such as Loros and Iaza, they oper-ated as sub-village corporate units (the '*syngeneis* around Attinas' at Loros; the kin-based 'sacred *doumos*' who worshipped their *syngenikē theos* Artemis Anaeitis at Iaza). That many rural priesthoods were monopolized by par-ticular family groups is not in itself an unusual phenomenon, but there are (to my knowledge) no analogies elsewhere for the multiple 'familial' cults of Meis Axiottenos at different villages of the region. Kin group, worship-ping group, and village community: these, not the *polis*, were the three chief organizing principles of the social order in Roman Hieradoumia.

10.5 The Hyacinth Stone

For what it's worth, I am glad that I was not born into a small Hieradoumian village in the second century AD. Like you, I am a child of the open society, and I take certain personal freedoms for granted. I expect my neighbours and kin to respect my individual dispositions and wishes; I do not expect to have my spouse, profession, or domestic arrangements chosen for me by my father or his brothers or my wider *syngeneia*. The tight-knit communitarian families and villages of rural Hieradoumia had no interest in granting those kinds of freedoms to their sons and daughters.

The affairs of rural families in Roman Hieradoumia – including what might seem to us to be purely intra-familial affairs – were governed by a rigorous communal ethical code, patrolled and overseen by the village community, and enforced by the gods.[112] As the content of the propitiatory inscriptions shows all too clearly, everyone in the village made it their business to know everyone else's business, and to pass judgement on it. It is hard not to be repelled by the scapegoating and persecution of unpopular and marginal members of the community (think of poor Tatias the witch), or by the unforgiving Hieradoumian moral doctrine of collective familial responsibility, sanctioned and enforced by the gods, under which the wider *syngeneia* was treated as liable for the faults of individual family members.

The sexual norms of rural Hieradoumia were particularly rigorous and uncompromising. Men or (especially) women who failed to conform to these norms could find themselves ostracized by both family and village in the most humiliating and public fashion.[113] This was what happened to Iulia, daughter of Kosmos[114]:

> μέγας {Μ} Μὶς Τιαμου Ἀρ⟨τε⟩μιδώρου
> Ἀξιοττα κατέχων καὶ ἡ δύναμις αὐ-
> τοῦ· Ἀ⟨φ⟩φιας συνέθετο γάμου κοινω-
> νίαν, Γάϊς Ἰουλίαν Κόσμου θυγατέραν,
> 5 [ἥ]τις οὐκ ἐτήρησε τὴν πίστιν τ-
> ῷ Γαείῳ, ἀλλ' ἐξήμαρτεν. μέγα-
> ς οὖν ΟΠΩΝ ὁ θεός· ἐκόλασεν αὐτή-
> [ν - - - - - - - -]. ϹΙΙΑΙΕΜΙϹ[- - - -]Λ
> -

---

[112] Mitchell 1993, I 189–95; Gordon 2004; Chaniotis 2004b, 245–53.

[113] Men got off more lightly: the sexual escapades of Theodoros (Petzl 1994, no. 5: Chapter 8, Section 8.5) were punished only because they breached sacred regulations (sex in the sanctuary complex; sex while a *hierodoulos*), not because they were extra-marital. Note the different language used of men's and women's sexual transgressions in *TAM* V 3, 1539 (Philadelphia): married male transgressors are simply barred from the sanctuary; married female transgressors are castigated as being 'full of familial defilement' (μύσο[υς] ἐμφυλίου πλή[ρ]η).

[114] *SEG* 57, 1159 (Petzl 2019, no. 138). Gordon 2016, 241, takes the breach of faith to be Apphias', not Iulia's.

Great is Meis Tiamou Artemidorou who rules Axiotta and his power! Apphias concluded a marriage-alliance (whereby) Gaius (was to marry) Iulia, the daughter of Kosmos. She (Iulia) did not preserve her faith towards Gaius, but transgressed. Great, then, is the god! He punished her ...

We do not know what 'sin' Iulia committed, but we can have little doubt that another man was involved – someone whom she preferred to Gaius, the husband selected for her by the matchmaker Apphias. Whatever punishment the god inflicted on her, it can scarcely have been worse than the public humiliation of having her sexual transgression proclaimed before a great audience of fellow villagers and family at the sanctuary of Meis at Axiotta, and subsequently immortalized on stone for all to see.

That is not to say that no one in Roman Hieradoumia dreamed of another kind of social order, one in which a man or woman might *keep to oneself*.[115] Perhaps the most haunting of all the stories that we can tell about the people of rural Hieradoumia is the tragedy of Apphia, the daughter of Glykon, described in a propitiatory inscription from the sanctuary of Meis at Axiotta.[116]

Μηνὶ Ἀρτεμιδώρου Ἀξιοτηνῷ
Συντύχη Θεογένου· εὑρόντος αὐτῆς Θεογένου τοῦ ἀνδρὸς λιθάριον ὑα-
κίνθιον, εἶτα κειμένου αὐτοῦ ἐν τῇ οἰκίᾳ
5　αὐτῆς ἐκλάπη τὸ λιθάριον, καὶ ζητούσης
αὐτῆς καὶ βασανιζομένης ἐπεύξατο
Μηνὶ Ἀξιοττηνῷ περὶ αὐτοῦ ἵνα αὐτὴν
ἱκανοποήσι, καὶ εὑρέθη κατακεκαυμένον
καὶ ἠφανισμένον, ἐνδεμένον ἐν λινου-
10　δίῳ ὑπὸ τοῦ κλέπτου τεθειμένον ἐπὶ
τὸν τόπον, οὗ ἔκειτο ὁλόκληρον. οὕτως
τε ἐπιφανεὶς ὁ θεὸς ἐν μιᾷ καὶ τριακοσ-
τῇ τὴν κλέψασα⟨ν⟩ καὶ τοῦτο πυήσασα⟨ν⟩ Ἀπφίαν
Γλύκωνος οὖσαν παρθένον διέρηξε·
15　περικρυβούσης τε αὐτῆς τὴν δύναμιν τοῦ
θεοῦ διὰ τὸ ἠρωτῆσθαι ὑπὸ τῆς μητρὸς

[115] Lévi-Strauss 1969.
[116] *SEG* 37, 1001 (Petzl 1994, no. 59). I largely follow the reconstruction of events by Chaniotis 1990, 127–31, plausibly (if speculatively) elaborated by Ogden 2009, 243–4, no. 233; see also Gordon 2004, 192; Chaniotis 2004a, 20, 22; Gordon 2016, 249. For 'hyacinth stones', Lightfoot 2003, 444. Lines 23–25 are inscribed in a different hand, perhaps added at the time of the ritualised erection of the *stēlē*: compare Chapter 3, Section 3.3 on the addition of dates to propitiatory *stēlai* once the appropriate day is fixed, and the *addendum* of the final three lines of *SEG* 35, 1157 (Petzl 1994, no. 36; here, Chapter 8, Figure 8.2).

τῆς παρθένου, ἵνα σειγήσι, καὶ ὁ θεὸς τοῦτο ἐνεμέσησε, ὅτι οὐκ ἐξεφάντευ-
σε οὐδὲ ὕψωσε τὸν θεὸν ἡ Συντύχη. διό-
20   τι ἐποίησεν αὐτὴν ἐπὶ τέκνου Ἡρακλεί-
δου ἐτῶν ιγ΄ νέμεσιν ἐπὶ τὸν τόπον αὐτοῦ
στῆσαι, ὅτι τὸ τῶν ἀνθρώπων μᾶλλον ἐπό-
ησεν ἢ τοῦ θεοῦ. *vac.* Συντύχη Ἀπολλωνίου
θυγάτηρ καὶ Μελτίνης ἡ προγεγραφοῦ-
25   σα τὴν νέμεσιν.

Syntyche, wife of Theogenes, (dedicated this) to Meis Artemidorou Axiottenos. Theogenes, her husband, found a hyacinth stone, and then the stone was stolen (5) while it was lying in her house. While she was searching for it, and was being inter-rogated (or: was tormented with worry), she offered a prayer to Meis Axiottenos about the stone, in order that he might give her satisfaction. The stone was then found, burned and disfigured and wrapped in a linen cloth, (10) having been put back by the thief in the place where it was kept while it was still undamaged. The god then made an epiphany on the thirty-first day, and 'broke' Apphia daughter of Glykon, the one who had stolen the stone and done all this, who was still a *parthenos* (young girl/virgin). (15) But Syntyche tried to conceal the god's power, since she had been asked by the *parthenos*' mother to keep silent. And the god punished this act, because Syntyche did not make known the god's intervention or exalt the god. Therefore (20) he made her set up this record of the divine punishment at his sanctuary, on account of her son Herakleides, thirteen years old, because she had taken more account of human interests than the interests of the god. – It is Syntyche, daughter of Apollonios and Meltine, who has written up in public (25) the divine punishment.

A precious gemstone is discovered by chance by Theogenes, and then goes missing from his house. Theogenes' wife Syntyche is suspected of theft; she denies all knowledge, and swears an oath to prove her innocence. Then the stone mysteriously reappears, 'burned and disfigured', indicating that someone has attempted to use the stone for magical purposes. Thirty-one days later, an epiphany of the god Meis occurs, revealing the true iden-tity of the thief: an unmarried girl from a neighbouring household named Apphia, perhaps in her early or mid-teens.[117] The epiphany took the form of an act of divine violence against Apphia, whose precise character is

---

[117] For typical age at marriage in Hieradoumia, see Chapter 5, Section 5.3. The description of Apphia as a *parthenos* may indicate that she was still a virgin, or (depending on how we interpret the events described here) that she still belonged to the age-class of 'young girls' (Chaniotis 2016).

left frustratingly unclear: the god is said to have 'broken' her ('killed' her? 'deflowered' her? 'injured' her?).[118] But the god's anger was chiefly directed not at the unfortunate Apphia, but the woman Syntyche, who was persuaded by Apphia's unnamed mother to hush up the whole affair. The god therefore took his revenge in some way on Syntyche's thirteen-year-old son Herakleides (killing him?), because Syntyche 'had taken more account of human interests than the interests of the god'.[119] As a result, Syntyche is finally compelled to reveal the whole sad story to the village community.

The general outline of events is clear enough, although it may be no coincidence that the text – or rather the drafter of the confession, perhaps Syntyche herself – becomes ambiguous and evasive at precisely those points where clarity would (for us) be most helpful.[120] How confidently we choose to fill in the blanks is a matter of personal taste. The most likely scenario is that we are dealing with the oldest story of all, an illicit teenage love affair. The girl Apphia is accidentally made pregnant by the boy next door, the thirteen-year-old Herakleides. The children steal a precious stone from Herakleides' father, and employ a dangerous magical technique (burning the stone near Apphia's vagina?) to try to induce an abortion. This fails, and a month later, Apphia falls dangerously ill, or dies, or simply reveals the truth about her pregnancy to her family. The two children's mothers agree to try to keep the affair quiet, in order to protect the two families' honour – 'an unusual glimpse into the world of village women, where neighbourly solidarity (against men, and in this case, the temple) was of central importance in the management of daily life'.[121] The women did not succeed: it seems that Herakleides, too, was subject to some kind of divine punishment. Syntyche, the mother who had rashly sworn an oath of ignorance, is left to confess the whole business at the sanctuary of Meis Axiottenos, before a full assembly of her fellow villagers.

A bleak story. And yet perhaps we should not be too hard on the villagers of Axiotta. Few human societies, in any place or time, have looked

---

[118] The verb is διαρρήγνυμι, for which the sense 'kill' is attested but rare (*DGE* s.v. 2); the normal sense is 'tear apart', 'rend asunder'.

[119] The specification of Herakleides' age may indicate his age at death, or may be introduced by Syntyche to exculpate him as being 'under-age'; cf. *SEG* 37, 1737 (Petzl 1994, no. 22: parents propitiate the gods on their children's behalf); *SEG* 37, 1000 (Petzl 1994, no. 58: a husband addresses the god on his wife's behalf, because she was 'not yet of age', μήπω οὖσα ἐνῆλιξ).

[120] Gordon 2004, 179: 'the "artlessness" [of these accounts] is as much as anything else a textual device, which permits strategic silences, tacit self-exculpations'. Not really now not any more.

[121] Gordon 2004, 192.

on pre-marital teenage pregnancies with a particularly forgiving eye. And if, amidst this melancholy sequence of events, we choose to fix our attention on the 'confessor' Syntyche, rather than the 'transgressors', Apphia and Herakleides, we can only be struck by the risks which Syntyche chose to run in the name of interfamilial solidarity and friendship. Syntyche and the mother of Apphia really did do their best to protect their children, even after the worst was known – and even though, for Syntyche, it meant knowingly taking 'more account of human interests than the interests of the god'. The stern and unbending sexual and social mores of the Hieradoumian family may have left little space for individual choice or personal preferences; but the Hieradoumian village was, in the end, a place where neighbours and kin *looked out for one another*.

In this book, I have tried to describe what I believe ought to be understood as a fundamentally kin-ordered society. The people of the middle Hermos valley classified their relatives with a kinship terminology vastly richer and more precise than is known from any other part of the Greco-Roman world (Chapter 4). They also commemorated their kin in a highly distinctive manner, with tombstones that listed numerous members of the deceased's extended family – aunts and uncles, sisters- and brothers-in-law, nieces and nephews – who shared in the 'honouring' of the dead (Chapter 2). From these 'familial' epitaphs, we can reconstruct the typical household structures of the region, characterized by patrilocal residence after marriage, and co-residence of several married brothers both with one another and their parents ('patriarchal' and *frérèche* extended-family households: Chapter 5). The circulation of children between households during early childhood was an absolutely standard feature of family life in the region: 'fosterage' was not, as it is today, a mechanism for dealing with the early death of parents, or familial dysfunction more generally (Chapter 6).

Beside and beyond these broad and ramified kinship networks (including networks of foster-kin), the people of Hieradoumia were also linked together in networks based on small-scale cultic associations (some of which were certainly based on kin groups), trade guilds, and more informal groups of friends, neighbours, and fellow villagers (Chapter 7). All of these associative groups were bound by sufficiently close sentimental ties that they participated, from time to time, in funerary commemoration of their members, usually alongside kin groups. The wider political community – the *polis* – was also an occasional participant in funerary ritual for elite individuals. But as we have seen in this final chapter, although around ten small *poleis* existed in the middle Hermos valley during the Roman imperial period, these towns and political communities were of relatively limited significance for the social organization of Roman Hieradoumia or the collective identities of its inhabitants. This was fundamentally a village society, organized around sprawling extended kin groups (*syngeneiai*), whose interpersonal relations were governed by a strict ethical code enforced by the family, the village, and ultimately by the local gods who 'ruled' over particular villages and kinship groups (Chapter 8).

The empirical basis of this 'big picture' is furnished by two large groups of epigraphic monuments, familial epitaphs and propitiatory inscriptions. I have suggested that these two categories of monuments can usefully and productively be set into dialogue with one another. In both form and content, these two different groups of monuments are expressions of a single, distinctively Hieradoumian idea of social order. What we have here, in fact, is a classic practical illustration of the concept of 'artistic volition' – the expression of a unitary local *Weltanschauung* through very different commemorative media. Naturally, it is hard to say whether extended rural families in Roman Hieradoumia were really quite as solid and harmonious as the tombstones represent them as being. The point is that both the familial epitaphs and (in a very different way) the propitiation-*stēlai* should be seen as *epigraphies of desire*: expressions of an imagined ideal state of affairs, where every family is large, tight-knit, and honourable; where village communities stick together; where even the most disastrous breakdown of relations between men and gods can always be repaired, so long as the transgressor's *syngeneis* are willing to pull together to set things right.[122]

Perhaps the communitarian and mutualist ethos which underlay Hieradoumian village society was not that unusual in the ancient world.[123] Although the ancient city looms large in our historical imagination, the Greco-Roman world was not, on the whole, a world of cities. Only some 5 per cent of the inhabitants of the Roman Empire at its peak lived in urban centres.[124] Our conception of the culture and values of 'the ancient world' is disproportionately based on the texts and material evidence left behind by this small and atypical group of city-dwellers. On the basis of urban evidence, it is easy to misrepresent Greco-Roman society in its generality as highly differentiated, sharply stratified, and obsessed with status and rank; kinship studies are, on the whole, not that prominent in the wider historiography

---

[122] Riegl 1901, 215. As Elsner 2006 rightly emphasizes, it is the centrality of *desire* to Riegl's concept of artistic volition that imbues this conception of the relation between material culture and social reality with its peculiar heuristic power.

[123] Compare Thonemann 2013b and 2013c (Phrygia).

[124] Woolf 2020.

of the Greco-Roman world.[125] But for the vast silent rural masses, things may well have been very different. In most places and times, we simply do not have the evidence to judge: the villagers of Aitolia, Sardinia, and Norfolk never developed the admirable habit of erecting voluble and discursive tombstones and propitiatory inscriptions. Roman Hieradoumia is, I believe, the *only* non-urban society in the Greco-Roman world whose kinship system, social structure, and village ethics can be described at the fine-grained level of detail attempted in this book. We perhaps ought not to be too surprised to find that at Nisyra and Axiotta, different values held sway.

Here in the hill country, among the vineyards and the slow-moving herds, from the late Republic to Late Antiquity, the experience of one generation was very much like that of the last. This was, for good and ill, a society in which everyone *knew where they belonged.* Not many outsiders moved in, and not many people moved away from home. There were some rich people in the middle Hermos valley, and there were slaves; but the rich were not all that rich, and slaves lived in large extended kin groups which looked very much like the families of the free population. Children were raised in big households – often in *several* big households – and were cherished and nurtured by their biological parents, by their uncles and aunts, and by their beloved *threpsantes*. One quiet summer afternoon, the teenagers Apphia and Herakleides made love in the hay-loft. Women were supported by robust networks of neighbours and kin: their natal family, their husband's brothers' wives, their friends. Men sat beneath the oak trees. People grew old, and were cared for, and died. Not a great deal happened.

> And out over Thoon above Bully Thrumble the high lord hanging holy under heaven. And Crom asleep in the ground.[126]

---

[125] Although there are signs of change: see e.g. Rawson 2011; Huebner 2013; Humphreys 2018.
[126] Garner 2003, 158.

References

Akat, S. (2009) *Anatanrıça Larmene Kültü*. Unpublished PhD thesis, Ege Üniversitesi, İzmir.

Akıncı Öztürk, E., Baysal, H. H. and Ricl, M. (2015) 'A new attestation of the cult of Zeus Trossou in a public inscription from the upper Maeander river valley (Çal Ovası)', *Gephyra* 12, 191–8.

Akyürek Şahin, E. (2006) 'Phrygia'dan yeni Zeus Bronton adakları', *Arkeoloji ve Sanat* 122, 98–124.

Alexandridis, A. (2018) 'Funerary containers from Roman Sardis', in *Sculpture in Roman Asia Minor: Proceedings of the International Conference at Selçuk, 1st–3rd October 2013*, ed. M. Aurenhammer. Vienna, 265–80.

Anderson, J. G. C. (1899) 'Explorations in Galatia cis Halym', *The Journal of Hellenic Studies* 19, 34–134, 280–318.

(1906) 'Paganism and Christianity in the upper Tembris Valley', in *Studies in the History and Art of the Eastern Provinces of the Roman Empire*, ed. W. M. Ramsay. Aberdeen, 183–227.

Arnaoutoglou, I. (2011) 'Craftsman associations in Roman Lydia: A tale of two cities?', *Ancient Society* 41, 257–90.

Aubrichs, W. (2007) 'Germanic and Gothic kinship terminology', in *The Ostrogoths from the Migration Period to the Sixth Century*, eds S. J. Barnish and F. Marazzi. Woodbridge, 143–82.

Bagnall, R. S. and Frier, B. W. (2006) *The Demography of Roman Egypt*. Paperback edition, with Supplement. Cambridge.

Baker, P. and Thériault, G. (2005) 'Les Lyciens, Xanthos et Rome dans la première moitié du Ier s. a. C.: Nouvelles inscriptions', *Revue des Études Grecques* 118/2, 329–66.

Bakır-Barthel, S. and Müller, H. (1979) 'Inschriften aus der Umgebung von Saittai (II)', *Zeitschrift für Papyrologie und Epigraphik* 36, 163–94.

Balland, A. (1981) *Fouilles de Xanthos, Tome VII: Inscriptions d'époque impériale du Létôon*. Paris.

Banaji, J. (2007) *Agrarian Change in Late Antiquity*, revised edition. Oxford.

Bean, G. E. (1971) *Journeys in Northern Lycia 1965–1967*. Vienna.

Bean, G. E. and Mitford, T. B. (1965) *Journeys in Rough Cilicia in 1962 and 1963*. Vienna.

(1970) *Journeys in Rough Cilicia 1964–1968*. Vienna.

357

Belayche, N. (2005) '"Au(x) dieu(x) qui règne(nt) sur…": *Basileia* divine et fonctionnement du polythéisme dans l'Anatolie impériale', in *Pouvoir et religion dans le monde romain*, eds A. Vigourt, X. Loriot, A. Bérenger-Badel and B. Klein. Paris, 257–69.

(2006) 'Les stèles dites de confession: une religiosité originale de l'Anatolie impériale?', in *The Impact of Rome on Religious, Ritual and Religious Life in the Roman Empire*, eds L. de Bois, P. Funke and J. Hahn. Leiden and Boston, 66–81.

(2008) 'Du texte à l'image: les reliefs sur les stèles "de confession" d'Anatolie', in *Image et religions*, eds S. Estienne, D. Jaillard and C. Pouzadoux. Naples, 181–94.

(2012) '"Un châtiment en adviendra". Le malheur comme signe des dieux dans l'Anatolie impériale', in *La raison des signes. Présages, rites, destin dans les sociétés de la Méditerranée ancienne*, eds S. Georgoudi, R. Koch Piettre and F. Schmidt. Leiden and Boston, 319–42.

Belfiore, E. S. (1992) *Tragic Pleasures: Aristotle on Plot and Emotion*. Princeton, NJ.

Benda-Weber, I. (2013) 'Textile production-centres, products and merchants in the Roman province of Asia', in *Making Textiles in Pre-Roman and Roman Times: People, Places, Identities*, eds M. Gleba and J. Pásztókai-Szeőke. Oxford and Oakville, 171–91.

Bernand, É. (1969) *Inscriptions métriques de l'Égypte gréco-romaine*. Paris.

(1999) *Inscriptions grecques d'Hermoupolis Magna et de sa nécropole*. Cairo.

Blažek, V. (2001) 'Indo-European kinship terms in *-Hter', in *Grammaticus: Studia linguistica Adolfo Erharto quinque et septuagenario oblata*, eds. O. Šefcik and B. Vykypel. Brno, 24–33.

Boulay, T. (2014) *Arès dans la cité. Les poleis et la guerre dans l'Asie Mineure hellénistique*. Studi Ellenistici 28. Pisa and Rome.

Bowie, F. (ed.) (2004) *Cross-Cultural Approaches to Adoption*. London and New York.

Bradley, K. (2000) 'Fictive families: Family and household in the *Metamorphoses* of Apuleius', *Phoenix* 54, 282–308.

Bremer, J. M. (1969) *Hamartia. Tragic Error in the Poetics of Aristotle and in Greek Tragedy*. Amsterdam.

Bremmer, J. N. (1983) 'The importance of the maternal uncle and grandfather in archaic and classical Greece and early Byzantium', *Zeitschrift für Papyrologie und Epigraphik* 50, 173–86.

(2000) 'Fosterage, kinship, and the circulation of children in ancient Greece', *Dialogos* 6, 1–20.

Bresson, A. (1991) *Recueil des inscriptions de la pérée rhodienne (pérée intégrée)*. Paris.

(2012) 'Painted portraits and statues: Honors for Polystratos at Phrygian Apameia', in *Stephanèphoros: De l'économie antique à l'Asie Mineure*, ed. K. Konuk. Bordeaux, 203–20.

Bresson, A. and Debord, P. (1985) 'Syngeneia', *Revue des Études Anciennes* 87, 191–211.

Brixhe, Cl. (1987) *Essai sur le grec anatolien au début de notre ère*, Nouvelle édition. Nancy.

(1999) 'Du Lycien au Grec: lexique de la famille et de la société', in *Langues en contact dans l'antiquité: Aspects lexicaux*, eds A. Blanc and A. Christol. Nancy and Paris, 81–105.

(2001) 'Individu, langue et communauté sociale: à propos des confessions païennes du Moyen Hermos', in *Norma e variazione nel diasistema greco. Atti del Quarto Incontro Internazionale di Linguistica Greca*, eds C. Consani and L. Mucciante. Alessandria, 101–18.

(2013) 'The personal onomastics of Roman Phrygia', in *Roman Phrygia: Culture and Society*, ed. P. Thonemann. Cambridge, 55–69.

Brody, L. R. (2001) 'The cult of Aphrodite at Aphrodisias in Caria', *Kernos* 14, 93–109.

Broughton, T. R. S. (1951–1986) *The Magistrates of the Roman Republic* (3 vols). New York.

Broux, Y. and Clarysse, W. (2009) 'Two Greek funerary stelae from Lydia and the Antonine plague', *Tyche* 24, 27–33.

Bryen, A. Z. and Wypustek, A. (2009) '*Gemellus*' evil eyes (P.Mich. VI 423–424)', *Greek, Roman and Byzantine Studies* 49, 535–55.

Buckler, W. H., Calder, W. M. and Cox, C. W. M. (1925) 'Asia Minor, 1924. II. – Monuments from Cotiaeum', *Journal of Roman Studies* 15, 141–75.

Buresch, K. (1898) *Aus Lydien: epigraphisch-geographische Reisefrüchte*. Leipzig.

Busch, S. (1999) *Versus Balnearum: Die antike Dichter über Bäder und Baden im römischen Reich*. Stuttgart and Leipzig.

Busine, A. (2005) *Paroles d'Apollon: Pratiques et traditions oraculaires dans l'Antiquité tardive (IIe–VIe siècles)*. Leiden and Boston.

Calder, W. M. (1910) 'A journey round the Proseilemmene', *Klio* 10, 232–42.

Cameron, A. (1939) 'ΘΡΕΠΤΟΣ and related terms in the inscriptions of Asia Minor', in *Anatolian Studies Presented to William Hepburn Buckler*, eds. W. M. Calder and J. Keil. Manchester, 27–62.

Caneva, S. G. and Delli Pizzi, A. (2015) 'Given to a deity? Religious and social reappraisal of human consecrations in the Hellenistic and Roman East', *Classical Quarterly* 65, 167–91.

Catling, R. W. V. (2004–2009) 'Attalid troops at Thermon. A reappraisal of IG IX 1² (1) 60', *Horos* 17–21, 397–439.

Chandezon, Chr. (2003) *L'élevage en Grèce (fin V^e-fin Ier s. a.C.). L'apport des sources épigraphiques*. Bordeaux.

Chaniotis, A. (1990) 'Drei kleinasiatische Inschriften zur griechischen Religion', *Epigraphica Anatolica* 15, 127–34.

(1995) 'Illness and cures in the Greek propitiatory inscriptions and dedications of Lydia and Phrygia', in *Ancient Medicine in Its Socio-Cultural Context*, eds H. F. J. Horstmanshoff, P. J. van der Eijk and P. H. Schrijvers. Amsterdam and Atlanta, II, 323–44.

(1997) 'Tempeljustiz im kaiserzeitlichen Kleinasien: Rechtliche Aspekte der Beichtinschriften', in *Symposion 1995*, eds G. Thür and J. Vélissaropoulos-Karakostas. Cologne, Weimar and Vienna, 353–84.

(2002) 'Foreign soldiers – Native girls? Constructing and crossing boundaries in Hellenistic cities with foreign garrisons', in *Army and Power in the Ancient World*, eds A. Chaniotis and P. Ducrey. Stuttgart, 99–113.

(2004a) 'Under the watchful eyes of the gods: Aspects of divine justice in Hellenistic and Roman Asia Minor', in *The Greco-Roman East: Politics, Culture, Society (YCS 31)*, ed. S. Colvin. Cambridge, 1–43.

(2004b) 'Von Ehre, Schande und kleinen Verbrechen unter Nachbarn: Konfliktbewältigung und Götterjustiz in Gemeinden des antiken Anatolien', in *Konflikt (Heidelberger Jahrbücher 48)*, ed. F. R. Pfetsch. Heidelberg, 233–54.

(2009a) 'Ritual performances of divine justice: The epigraphy of confession, atonement, and exaltation in Roman Asia Minor', in *From Hellenism to Islam: Cultural and Linguistic Change in the Roman Near East*, eds H. M. Cotton, R. G. Hoyland, J. J. Price and D. J. Wasserstein. Cambridge, 115–53.

(2009b) 'Acclamations as a form of religious communication', in *Die Religion des Imperium Romanum. Koine und Konfrontationen*, eds H. Cancik and J. Rüpke. Tübingen, 199–218.

(2012) 'Constructing the fear of gods: Epigraphic evidence from sanctuaries of Greece and Asia Minor', in *Unveiling Emotions: Sources and Methods for the Study of Emotions in the Greek World*, ed. A. Chaniotis. Stuttgart, 205–34.

(2016) 'The age of a parthenos: A new epitaph from Aphrodisias', in *Vir Doctus Anatolicus: Studies in Memory of Sencer Şahin*, eds B. Takmer, E. N. Akdoğu Arca and N. Gökalp Özdil. Istanbul, 200–5.

Chankowski, A. S. (2010) *L'éphébie hellénistique*. Paris.

Chantraine, P. (1999) *Dictionnaire étymologique de la langue grecque, avec un Supplément*. Paris.

Chin, M. and Lazar, L. (2020) 'Antipatros of Derbe, Akmoneia and Rome in a notebook of William Mitchell Ramsay', *Philia* 6, 42–52.

Cline, R. (2011) *Ancient Angels: Conceptualizing Angeloi in the Roman Empire*. Leiden and Boston.

Clinton, K. (2005) *Eleusis. The Inscriptions on Stone IA: Text*. Athens.

Cohen, G. M. (1995) *The Hellenistic Settlements in Europe, The Islands, and Asia Minor*. Berkeley, Los Angeles, and Oxford.

Colvin, S. (2004) 'Names in Hellenistic and Roman Lycia', in *The Greco-Roman East: Politics, Culture, Society (YCS 31)*, ed. S. Colvin. Cambridge, 44–84.

Cottier, M., Crawford, M. H., Crowther, C. V., Ferrary, J.-L., Levick, B. M., Salomies, O. and Wörrle, M. (2008) *The Customs Law of Asia*. Oxford.

Cremer, M.-L. and Nollé, J. (1988) 'Lydische Steindenkmäler', *Chiron* 18, 199–214.

Curbera, J. (2013) 'Simple names in Ionia', in *Personal Names in Ancient Anatolia*, ed. R. Parker. Oxford, 107–43.

Davis, J. (1973) *Land and Family in Pisticci*. London.

(1977) *People of the Mediterranean*. London.

Debord, P. (1973) 'L'esclavage sacré: état de la question', in *Actes du colloque 1971 sur l'esclavage*. Besançon, 135–50.

(1982) *Aspects sociaux et économiques de la vie religieuse dans l'Anatolie gréco-romaine*. Leiden.

(1985) 'La Lydie du nord-est', *Revue des Études Anciennes* 87/2, 345–58.

Debord, P. and Varinlioğlu, E. (2001) *Les hautes terres de Carie*. Bordeaux.

Déléage, A. (1945) *La capitation du bas-empire*. Macon.

Delehaye, H. (1923) *Les saints stylites*. Brussels.

Dickie, M. W. (1995) 'The fathers of the church and the evil eye', in *Byzantine Magic*, ed. H. Maguire. Washington DC, 9–34.

Dignas, B. (2002) *Economy of the Sacred in Hellenistic and Roman Asia Minor*. Oxford.

Dittmann-Schöne, I. (2001) *Die Berufsvereine in den Städten des kaiserzeitlichen Kleinasiens*. Regensberg.

Dmitriev, S. (2005) *City Government in Hellenistic and Roman Asia Minor*. Oxford.

Drew-Bear, T. (1972a) 'Deux décrets hellénistiques d'Asie Mineure', *Bulletin de Correspondance Hellénique* 96, 435–71.

(1972b) 'Some Greek words: Part II', *Glotta* 50, 182–228.

(1978) *Nouvelles inscriptions de Phrygie*. Zutphen.

(1979) 'The city of Temenouthyrai in Phrygia', *Chiron* 9, 275–302.

(1984) 'Une épigramme de Phrygie', in *Sodalitas: Scritti in Onore di Antonio Guarino* I. Naples, 439–56.

Drew-Bear, T. and Naour, Chr. (1990) 'Divinités de Phrygie', *ANRW* II.18/3, 1907–2044.

Drew-Bear, T., Thomas, C. M. and Yıldızturan, M. (1999) *Phrygian Votive Steles*. Ankara.

Drexhage, H.-J. (2002) 'Zum Berufsbild und den Lebensverhältnissen des *rhaptès* Euphras aus Nikomedia', *Laverna* 13, 69–80.

Dunant, C. (1978) 'Sus aux voleurs! Une tablette en bronze à inscription grecque du Musée de Genève', *Museum Helveticum* 35, 241–4.

Dunbabin, K. M. D. and Dickie, M. W. (1983) 'Invida rumpantur pectora: The iconography of Phthonos/Invidia in Graeco-Roman art', *Jahrbuch für Antike und Christentum* 26, 7–37.

Duncan-Jones, R. P. (1977) 'Age-rounding, illiteracy and social differentiation in the Roman Empire', *Chiron* 7, 333–53.

(1990) *Structure and Scale in the Roman Economy*. Cambridge.

(1996) 'The impact of the Antonine Plague', *Journal of Roman Archaeology* 9, 108–93.

Dusinberre, E. R. M. (2003) *Aspects of Empire in Achaemenid Sardis*. Cambridge.

Edmondson, J. (2005) 'Family relations in Roman Lusitania', in *The Roman Family in the Empire*, ed. M. George. Oxford, 183–229.

Ehrhardt, N. (1990) 'Eine neue Grabinschrift aus Iconium', *Zeitschrift für Papyrologie und Epigraphik* 81, 185–8.

Eidinow, E. (2016) *Envy, Poison, and Death: Women on Trial in Classical Athens.* Oxford.

Elliott, C. (2016) 'The Antonine Plague, climate change and local violence in Roman Egypt', *Past & Present* 231, 3–31.

Elliott, C. B. (1838) *Travels in the Three Great Empires of Austria, Russia, and Turkey* (3 vols). London.

Elsner, J. (2006) 'From empirical evidence to the big picture: Some reflections on Riegl's concept of *Kunstwollen*', *Critical Enquiry* 32, 741–66.

Elsner, J. and Lorenz, K. (2012) 'The genesis of iconology', *Critical Enquiry* 38, 483–512.

Faraone, C. A. (1992) *Talismans and Trojan Horses: Guardian Statues in Ancient Greek Myth and Ritual.* New York and Oxford.

Feissel, D. (1983) *Recueil des inscriptions chrétiennes de Macédoine (BCH Supplément 8).* Paris.

Ferrario, S. B. (2014) *Historical Agency and the 'Great Man' in Classical Greece.* Cambridge.

Filges, A. (2006) *Blaundos. Berichte zur Erforschung einer Kleinstadt im lydisch-phrygischen Grenzgebiet.* Tübingen.

Finley, M. I. (1977) *The World of Odysseus,* second edition. London.

Fıratlı, N. and Robert, L. (1964) *Les stèles funéraires de Byzance gréco-romaine.* Paris.

Fischer-Bovet, C. (2014) *Army and Society in Ptolemaic Egypt.* Cambridge.

Flemming, R. (2018) 'Galen and the Plague', in *Galen's Treatise Περὶ Ἀλυπίας (De indolentia) in Context,* ed. C. Petit. Leiden, 219–44.

Forsdyke, S. (2005) 'Revelry and riot in Archaic Megara: Democratic disorder or ritual reversal?', *The Journal of Hellenic Studies* 125, 73–92.

Foss, C. (1987) 'Sites and strongholds of northern Lydia', *Anatolian Studies* 37, 81–101.

Fraser, P. M. (1977) *Rhodian Funerary Monuments.* Oxford.

Gagné, R. (2013) *Ancestral Fault in Ancient Greece.* Cambridge.

Gamkrelidze, T. V. and Ivanov, V. V. (1995) *Indo-European and the Indo-Europeans: A Reconstruction and Historical Analysis of a Proto-Language and a Proto-Culture* (2 vols). Berlin and New York.

Garner, A. (2003) *Thursbitch.* London.

Gates, H. P. (1971) *The Kinship Terminology of Homeric Greek.* Baltimore, MD.

Gauthier, P. (1989) *Nouvelles inscriptions de Sardes II.* Geneva.

Gibson, E. (1978) *The "Christians for Christians" Inscriptions of Phrygia.* Ann Arbor.
    (1981) 'The Rahmi Koç collection. Inscriptions. Part VIII, a cinerary chest from Sardis', *Zeitschrift für Papyrologie und Epigraphik* 42, 215–16.

Ginzburg, C. (1989) 'From Aby Warburg to E. H. Gombrich: A problem of method', in *Clues, Myths and the Historical Method,* translated by J. and A. Tedeschi. Baltimore, MD, 17–59.

Godelier, M. (2011) *The Metamorphoses of Kinship*, translated by N. Scott. London and New York.

Goltz, A. and Hartmann, U. (2008) 'Valerianus und Gallienus', in *Die Zeit der Soldatenkaiser*, ed. K.-P. Johne. Berlin, I, 223–95.

Gombrich, E. H. (1960) *Art and Illusion: A Study in the Psychology of Pictorial Representation*. London.

Goody, J. (1969) *Comparative Studies in Kinship*. London.

(1983) *The Development of the Family and Marriage in Europe*. Cambridge.

Gordon, R. (2004) 'Raising a sceptre: Confession-narratives from Lydia and Phrygia', *Journal of Roman Archaeology* 17, 177–96.

(2016) 'Negotiating the temple-script: Women's narratives among the "confession-texts" of western Asia Minor', *Religion in the Roman Empire* 2, 227–55.

Graham, H. (2003) 'Policing the forests of pre-industrial France: Round up the usual suspects', *European History Quarterly* 33/2, 157–82.

Greenewalt, C. H. Jr. and Majewski, L. J. (1980) 'Lydian textiles', in *From Athens to Gordion: The Papers of a Memorial Symposium for Rodney S. Young*, ed. K. DeVries. Philadelphia, 133–47.

Güney, H. (2020) 'A new Zeus-epithet found in northeast Phrygia: Zeus of the cedar tree', *Journal of Epigraphic Studies* 3, 49–60.

Günther, W. (1975) 'Ein Ehrendekret post mortem aus Aizanoi', *Mitteilungen des deutschen archäologischen Instituts. Abteilung Istanbul* 25, 351–6.

Habicht, Chr. (1975) 'New evidence on the province of Asia', *Journal of Roman Studies* 65, 64–91.

(2003) 'Peter Herrmann', *Gnomon* 75, 474–9.

Hagel, S. and Tomaschitz, K. (1998) *Repertorium der westkilikischen Inschriften*. Vienna.

Haldon, J., Elton, H., Huebner, S. R., Izdebski, A., Mordechai, L. and Newfield, T. P. (2018) 'Plagues, climate change, and the end of an empire: A response to Kyle Harper's *The Fate of Rome* (2): Plagues and a crisis of empire', *History Compass* 16/12, https://doi.org/10.1111/hic3.12506.

Hallmannsecker, M. (2022) *Roman Ionia: Constructions of Cultural Identity in Western Asia Minor*. Cambridge.

Hamilton, W. J. (1842) *Researches in Asia Minor, Pontus and Armenia* (2 vols). London.

Hammond, M. (2020) *Artemidorus: The Interpretation of Dreams*. Oxford.

Hanfmann, G. M. A. (1983) *Sardis from Prehistoric to Roman Times*. Cambridge, MA, and London.

Hanfmann, G. M. A. and Waldbaum, J. C. (1975) *A Survey of Sardis and the Major Monuments Outside the City Walls*. Cambridge, MA, and London.

Harland, P. A. (2014) *Greco-Roman Associations: Texts, Translations and Commentary II. North Coast of the Black Sea, Asia Minor*. Berlin.

Harper, K. (2008) 'The Greek census inscriptions of Late Antiquity', *Journal of Roman Studies* 98, 83–119.

(2011) *Slavery in the Late Roman World, AD 275–425*. Cambridge.

(2015) 'A time to die: Preliminary notes on seasonal mortality in late antique Rome', in *Children and Family in Late Antiquity: Life, Death and Interaction*, eds C. Laes, K. Mustakallio and V. Vuolanto. Leuven and Walpole, MA, 15–34.

(2017) *The Fate of Rome: Climate, Disease, & the End of an Empire*. Princeton and Oxford.

(2018) 'Integrating the natural sciences and Roman history: Challenges and prospects', *History Compass* 16/12, https://doi.org/10.1111/hic3.12520.

Harter-Uibopuu, K. (2016) 'Hermogenes und die πρόβατα des Kaikos (TAM V 1, 464)', *Philia* 2, 63–71.

Hauken, T. (1998) *Petition and Response: An Epigraphic Study of Petitions to Roman Emperors 181–249*. Bergen.

Heberdey, R. and Kalinka, E. (1897) *Bericht über zwei Reisen im südwestlichen Kleinasien*. Vienna.

Heineke, C., Niedermann, S., Hetzel, R. and Akal, C. (2016) 'Surface exposure dating of Holocene basalt flows and cinder cones in the Kula volcanic field (Western Turkey) using cosmogenic ^{3}He and ^{10}Be', *Quaternary Geochronology* 34, 81–91.

Herrmann, P. (1959) *Neue Inschriften zur historischen Landeskunde von Lydien und angrenzenden Gebieten*. Vienna, reprinted in Herrmann 2016, 3–35.

(1962) *Ergebnisse einer Reise in Nordostlydien*. Vienna.

(1972) 'Überlegungen zur Datierung der «Constitutio Antoniniana»', *Chiron* 2, 519–30.

(1985) 'Sühn- und Grabinschriften aus der Katakekaumene im archäologischen Museum von Izmir', *AnzWien* 122, 248–61; reprinted in Herrmann 2016, 103–17.

(1993) 'Inschriften von Sardeis', *Chiron* 23, 233–66.

(1995) Γέρας θανόντων: Totenruhm und Totenehrung im städtischen Leben der hellenistischen Zeit', in *Stadtbild und Bürgerbild im Hellenismus*, eds M. Wörrle and P. Zanker. Munich, 189–97; reprinted in Herrmann 2016, 671–84.

(2016) *Kleinasien im Spiegel epigraphischer Zeugnisse: Ausgewählte kleine Schriften*, ed. W. Blümel. Berlin and Boston.

Herrmann, P. and Malay, H. (2007) *New Documents from Lydia*. Vienna.

Herrmann, P. and Polatkan, K. Z. (1969) *Das Testament des Epikrates und andere neue Inschriften aus dem Museum von Manisa*. Vienna.

Herrmann, P. and Varinlioğlu, E. (1984) 'Theoi Pereudenoi. Eine Gruppe von Weihungen und Sühninschriften aus der Katakekaumene', *Epigraphica Anatolica* 3, 1–18, reprinted in Herrmann 2016, 81–101.

Hill, G. B. and Powell, L. F. (1934) *Boswell's Life of Johnson* (4 vols). Oxford.

Hin, S. (2013) *The Demography of Roman Italy: Population Dynamics in an Ancient Conquest Society, 201 BCE–14 CE*. Cambridge.

Högemann, P. and Oettinger, N. (2018) *Lydien: Ein altanatolischer Staat zwischen Griechenland und dem Vorderen Orient*. Berlin and Boston.

Horster, M. (2010) 'Religious landscape and sacred ground: Relationships between space and cult in the Greek world', *Revue de l'histoire des religions* 227/4, 435–58.

de Hoz, M.-P. (1999) *Die lydischen Kulte um Lichte der griechischen Inschriften (Asia Minor Studien 36)*. Bonn.

(2006) 'Literacy in rural Anatolia: The testimony of the confession inscriptions', *Zeitschrift für Papyrologie und Epigraphik* 155, 139–44.

Huebner, S. (2013) *The Family in Roman Egypt*. Cambridge.

Hughes, J. (2017) *Votive Body Parts in Greek and Roman Religion*. Cambridge.

Humphreys, S. C. (2018) *Kinship in Ancient Athens: An Anthropological Analysis* (2 vols). Oxford.

Hunt, A. (2016) *Reviving Roman Religion: Sacred Trees in the Roman World*. Cambridge.

Isager, S. (2016) 'The necropolis outside the Myndos Gate in Halikarnassos: Five inscriptions', in *Death and Burial in Karia (Halicarnassian Studies VI)*, eds. E. Mortensen and B. Poulsen. Odense, 120–33.

Jannoray, J. (1946) 'Inscriptions delphiques d'époque tardive', *Bulletin de Correspondance Hellénique* 70, 247–61.

Jones, A. H. M. (1928) 'Inscriptions from Jerash', *Journal of Roman Studies* 18, 144–78.

Jones, C. P. (1999) 'Interrupted funerals', *Proceedings of the American Philosophical Society* 143/4, 588–600.

Kantor, G. (2016) 'Local law in Asia Minor after the constitutio Antoniniana', in *Citizenship and Empire in Europe 200–1900: The Antonine Constitution after 1800 Years*, ed. C. Ando. Stuttgart, 45–62.

Kaplan, M. (1992) *Les hommes et la terre à Byzance du VIe au XIe siècle*. Paris.

Kaygusuz, I. (1984) 'Funerary epigram of Karzene (Paphlagonia): A girl raped by the Goths?', *Epigraphica Anatolica* 4, 61–2.

Keil, J. and Premerstein, A. von (1907) *Bericht über eine Reise in Lydien und der Südlichen Aiolis*. Vienna.

(1911) *Bericht über eine zweite Reise in Lydien*. Vienna.

(1914) *Bericht über eine dritte Reise in Lydien und den Angrenzenden Gebieten Ioniens*. Vienna.

Keil, J. and Wilhelm, A. (1915) 'Vorlaufiger Bericht über eine Reise in Kilikien', *Jahresheft des Österreichischen Archäologischen Instituts* 18, Beibl., 1–60.

Kelp, U. (2008) 'Das Phänomen der Türfassaden in Phrygien. Zu lokalen Identitäten anhand einiger Grabtypen römischer Zeit', in *Neue Funde und Forschungen in Phrygien*, eds. E. Schwertheim and E. Winter. Bonn, 69–91.

(2013) 'Grave monuments and local identities in Roman Phrygia', in *Roman Phrygia: Culture and Society*, ed. P. Thonemann. Cambridge, 70–94.

(2015) *Grabdenkmal und lokale Identität: Ein Bild der Landschaft Phrygien in der römischen Kaiserzeit (Asia Minor Studien 74)*. Bonn.

Kielau, S. (2016) 'Zwei Ton-Matrizen für den Mondgott Men aus dem Bereich der Wohnstadt von Pergamon', in *Man kann es sich nicht prächtig genug vorstellen,*

Festschrift für Dieter Salzmann zum 65. Geburtstag, eds H. Schwarzer and H.-H. Nieswandt. Münster, 315–25.

Kiourtzian, G. (2000) *Recueil des inscriptions grecques chrétiennes des Cyclades*. Paris.

Klingenberg, A. (2014) 'Die "Iranische Diaspora". Kontext, Charakter und Auswirkung persischer Einwanderung nach Kleinasien', in *Mobilität in den Kulturen der antiken Mittelmeerwelt*, eds E. Olshausen and V. Sauer. Stuttgart, 309–24.

Kloppenborg, J. S. (2016) *Review of Private Associations and the Public Sphere*, eds V. Gabrielsen and C. A. Thomsen (Copenhagen, 2015), BMCR 2016.07.02.

Kolb, F. (1990) 'Sitzstufeninschriften aus dem Stadion von Saittai (Lydien)', *Epigraphica Anatolica* 15, 107–18.

Kölligan, D. (2012) 'Regular sound change and word-initial */i/- in Armenian', in *Laws and Rules in Indo-European*, eds P. Probert and A. Willi. Oxford, 134–46.

Konstantinidis, G. (2015) 'A reconsideration of *epoikion* in Byzantine Egypt', Βυζαντιακά 32, 23–38.

Kontorini, V. (1993) 'La famille de l'amiral Damagoras de Rhodes: contribution à la prosopographie et à l'histoire rhodiennes au Ier s. av. J-.C.', *Chiron* 23, 83–99.

Kotansky, R. D. (2020) 'A silver votive plaque with a judicial prayer against slander', *Greek, Roman and Byzantine Studies* 60, 139–57.

Labarre, G. and Le Dinahet, M.-Th. (1996) 'Les métiers du textile en Asie Mineure de l'époque hellénistique à l'époque impériale', in *Aspects de l'artisanat du textile dans la monde méditerranéen*. Lyon and Paris, 49–116.

Laes, Chr. (2011) *Children in the Roman Empire: Outsiders Within*. Cambridge.

Laes, Chr. and Strubbe, J. (2014) *Youth in the Roman Empire. The Young and Restless Years?* Cambridge.

Laffi, U. (1967) 'Le iscrizioni relative all'introduzione nel 9 a.C. del nuovo calendario della provincia d'Asia', *Studi classici e orientali* 16, 5–98.

Lajtar, A. and Petzl, G. (2003) 'Eine lydische Familie aus der zweiten Hälfte des 3. Jahrhunderts n. Chr.', *Epigraphica Anatolica* 36, 45–50.

Lambertz, M. (1914) 'Zur Ausbreitung des Supernomen oder Signum im römischen Reiche, II', *Glotta* 5, 99–170.

Le Camus, É. (1896) *Voyage aux sept églises de l'Apocalypse*. Paris.

Le Roy Ladurie, E. (1978) *Montaillou: Cathars and Catholics in a French Village 1294–1324*, translated by B. Bray. London.

Leschhorn, W. (1993) *Antike Ären: Zeitrechnung, Politik und Geschichte im Schwarzmeerraum und in Kleinasien nördlich des Tauros*. Stuttgart.

Lévi-Strauss, C. (1969) *The Elementary Structures of Kinship*, translated by J. H. Ball, J. R. von Sturmer and R. Needham. London.

Lightfoot, J. L. (2003) *Lucian: On the Syrian Goddess*. Oxford.

Lo Cascio, E. (ed.) (2012) *L'impatto della 'peste Antonina'*. Bari.

Lochman, T. (2003) *Studien zu kaiserzeitlichen Grab- und Votivreliefs aus Phrygien*. Basel.

Low, P. (2003) 'Remembering war in fifth-century Greece: Ideologies, societies, and commemoration beyond democratic Athens', *World Archaeology* 35, 98–111.

Lupu, E. (2005) *Greek Sacred Law: A Collection of New Documents (NGSL)*. Leiden and Boston.

Ma, J. (2013a) *Statues and Cities: Honorific Portraits and Civic Identity in the Hellenistic World*. Oxford.

(2013b) 'The Attalids: A military history', in *Attalid Asia Minor: Money, International Relations, and the State*, ed. P. Thonemann. Oxford, 49–82.

MacMullen, R. (1986) 'Frequency of inscriptions in Roman Lydia', *Zeitschrift für Papyrologie und Epigraphik* 65, 237–8.

Macrides, R. (1987) 'The Byzantine godfather', *Byzantine and Modern Greek Studies* 11, 139–62.

Maiuri, A. (1925) *Nuova silloge epigrafica di Rodi e Cos*. Florence.

Malay, H. (1985) 'The sanctuary of Meter Phileis near Philadelphia', *Epigraphica Anatolica* 6, 111–25.

(1999) *Researches in Lydia, Mysia and Aeolis*. Vienna.

Malay, H. and Petzl, G. (2017) *New Religious Texts from Lydia*. Vienna.

Malay, H. and Ricl, M. (2006) 'Some funerary inscriptions from Lydia', *Epigraphica Anatolica* 39, 49–83.

(2019) 'Two new Hellenistic inscriptions from Lydia and Aiolis', in *Epigraphische Notizen: Zur Erinnerung an Peter Herrmann.*, ed. K. Harter-Uibopuu. Stuttgart, 45–60.

Malay, H. and Tanrıver, C. (2016) 'The cult of Apollo Syrmaios and the village of Parloai near Saittai, north-eastern Lydia', in *Between Tarhuntas and Zeus Polieus: Cultural Crossroads in the Temples and Cults of Graeco-Roman Anatolia*, eds M.-P. de Hoz, J. P. Sánchez Hernandez and C. Molina Valero. Leuven, 171–84.

Mallory, J. P. and Adams, D. Q. (2006) *The Oxford Introduction to Proto-Indo-European and the Proto-Indo-European World*. Oxford.

Marek, Chr. (1993) *Stadt, Ära und Territorium in Pontus-Bithynia und Nord-Galatia*. Tübingen.

Martin, D. B. (1996) 'The construction of the ancient family: Methodological considerations', *Journal of Roman Studies* 86, 40–60.

Masséglia, J. (2013) 'Phrygians in relief: Trends in self-representation', in *Roman Phrygia: Culture and Society*, ed. P. Thonemann. Cambridge, 95–123.

Masson, O. (1987) 'L'inscription d'Éphèse relative aux condamnés à mort de Sardes', *Revue des Études Grecques* 100, 225–39.

(1993) 'Les "Mysiens" de Lilaia', *Revue des Études Grecques* 106, 163–67.

Matthews, R. and Glatz, C. (2009) *At Empire's Edge. Project Paphlagonia Regional Survey in North Central Turkey*. London.

Meissner, T. (2006) *S-Stem Nouns and Adjectives in Greek and Proto-Indo-European*. Oxford.

Melchert, H. C. (1994) *Anatolian Historical Phonology*. Amsterdam and Atlanta, GA.

Meriç, R. (2018) *Hermus (Gediz) Valley in Western Turkey: Results of an Archaeological and Historical Survey*. Istanbul.

Michels, C. (2019) 'Aizanoi zwischen Pergamon und Bithynien und die Instrumente von Kommunikation und Kontrolle', *Geographia Antiqua* 28, 31–46.

Michon, E. (1906) 'Stèles funéraires phrygiennes', *Mémoires de la société nationale des antiquaires de France* 66, 27–46.

Mikalson, J. D. (1975) *The Sacred and Civil Calendar of the Athenian Year*. Princeton, NJ.

Mitchell, S. (1993) *Anatolia: Land, Men, and Gods in Asia Minor* (2 vols). Oxford.

(1999) 'The Administration of Roman Asia from 133 BC to AD 250', in *Lokale Autonomie und römische Ordnungsmacht in den kaiserzeitlichen Provinzen vom 1. bis 3. Jahrhundert*, ed. W. Eck. Munich, 17–46.

(2010) 'The Ionians of Paphlagonia', in *Local Knowledge and Microidentities in the Imperial Greek World*, ed. T. Whitmarsh. Cambridge, 86–110.

(2013) 'An epigraphic probe into the origins of Montanism', in *Roman Phrygia: Culture and Society*, ed. P. Thonemann. Cambridge, 168–97.

(2018) 'Dispelling Seleukid phantoms: Macedonians in western Asia Minor from Alexander to the Attalids', in *The Seleukid Empire, 281–222 BC: War Within the Family*, ed. K. Erickson. Swansea, 11–36.

Mitchell, S., Niewöhner, P., Vardar, A. and Vardar, L. E. (2021) 'Church building and wine making east of Ankara: Regional aspects of Central Anatolia in the Early Byzantine period', *Gephyra* 21, 199–229.

Müller, H. and Wörrle, M. (2002) 'Ein Verein im Hinterland Pergamons zur Zeit Eumenes' II', *Chiron* 32, 191–235.

Nani, T. G. (1943–1944) 'ΘΡΕΠΤΟΙ', *Epigraphica* 5–6, 45–84.

Naour, Chr. (1980) *Tyriaion en Cabalide: épigraphie et géographie historique*. Zutphen.

(1981) 'Inscriptions du Moyen Hermos', *Zeitschrift für Papyrologie und Epigraphik* 44, 11–44.

(1983) 'Nouvelles inscriptions du Moyen Hermos', *Epigraphica Anatolica* 2, 107–41.

(1985) 'Nouveaux documents du Moyen Hermos', *Epigraphica Anatolica* 5, 37–76.

Neumann, G. (1961) *Untersuchungen zum Weiterleben hethitischen und luwischen Sprachgutes in hellenistischer und römischer Zeit*. Wiesbaden.

(1979) *Neufunde lykische Inschriften seit 1901*. Vienna.

(1987) 'Zur Verwandtschaftsbezeichnung *ἰανατηρ', *Glotta* 65, 33–7.

(1992) 'Sprachwissenschaftliche Erläuterungen zu den epichorischen Namen', in *Epigraphische Forschungen in Termessos und seinem Territorium II*, eds. B. İplikçioğlu, G. Çelgin and A. Vedat Çelgin. Vienna, 26–33.

(1999) 'ΔΟΥΜΟΣ: Belege, Bedeutung, Herkunft, Etymologie', in *Linguisticum: Festschrift für Wolfgang P. Schmid*, ed. E. Eggers. Frankfurt am Main, 345–53.

(2002) 'Ein neuer Beleg für ΔΟΥΜΟΣ', *Historische Sprachforschung* 115, 57–8.

Niewöhner, P. (2007) *Aizanoi, Dokimeion und Anatolien. Stadt und Land, Siedlungs- und Steinmetzwesen vom späteren 4. bis ins 6. Jh. n. Chr.* Wiesbaden.

(2013) 'Phrygian marble and stonemasonry as markers of regional distinctiveness in Late Antiquity', in *Roman Phrygia: Culture and Society*, ed. P. Thonemann. Cambridge, 215–48.

van Nijf, O. M. (1997) *The Civic World of Professional Associations in the Roman East*. Amsterdam.

Nilsson, M. P. (1962) *Die Entstehung und religiöse Bedeutung des griechischen Kalenders*, second edition. Lund.

Nishiura, H. and Kashiwagi, T. (2009) 'Smallpox and season: Reanalysis of historical data', *Interdisciplinary Perspectives on Infectious Diseases* 2009, 59135, https://doi.org/10.1155/2009/591935.

Nollé, J. (1982) *Nundinas instituere et habere: Epigraphische Zeugnisse zur Einrichtung und Gestaltung von ländlichen Märkten in Afrika und in der Provinz Asia*. Hildesheim.

(2005) 'Boars, bears and bugs: Farming in Asia Minor and the protection of men, animals, and crops', in *Patterns in the Economy of Roman Asia Minor*, eds S. Mitchell and C. Katsari. Swansea, 53–82.

(2010) 'Beiträge zur kleinasiatischen Münzkunde und Geschichte 10: Kadwenische Münzbilder', *Gephyra* 7, 71–126.

Oesterheld, C. (2008) *Göttliche Botschaften für zweifelnde Menschen: Pragmatik und Orientierungsleistung der Apollon-Orakel von Klaros und Didyma in hellenistisch-römischer Zeit*. Göttingen.

(2014) 'La parole salvatrice transformée en remède perpétuel: L'oracle d'Apollon de Claros rendu à la ville de Hiérapolis en Phrygie', in *Le sanctuaire de Claros et son oracle*, eds J.-C. Moretti and L. Rabatel. Lyon, 211–26.

Ogden, D. (2009) *Magic, Witchcraft, and Ghosts in the Greek and Roman Worlds*, second edition. Oxford.

Osborne, R. and Rhodes, P. (2017) *Greek Historical Inscriptions 478–404 BC*. Oxford.

Özgen, İ. and Öztürk, J. (1996) *Heritage Recovered: The Lydian Treasure*. Istanbul.

Panofsky, E. (1939) *Studies in Iconology: Humanistic Themes in the Art of the Renaissance*. New York.

(1981) 'The concept of artistic volition', translated by K. J. Northcott and J. Snyder, *Critical Inquiry* 8/1, 17–33.

Papazarkadas, N. (2011) *Sacred and Public Land in Ancient Athens*. Oxford.

Parker, R. (1983) *Miasma: Pollution and Purification in Early Greek Religion*. Oxford.

(2011) *On Greek Religion*. Ithaca and London.

(2017) *Greek Gods Abroad: Names, Natures, and Transformations*. Oakland, CA.

(2018) 'The new purity law from Thyateira', *Zeitschrift für Papyrologie und Epigraphik* 205, 178–83.

Patlagean, E. (1977) *Pauvreté économique et pauvreté sociale à Byzance, 4ᵉ – 7ᵉ siècles.* Paris and The Hague.

Petzl, G. (1978a) 'Vier Inschriften aus Lydien', in *Studien zur Religion und Kultur Kleinasiens: Festschrift für Friedrich Karl Dörner,* eds S. Şahin, E. Schwertheim and J. Wagner. Leiden, II 745–61.

(1978b) 'Inschriften aus der Umgebung der Saittai (I)', *Zeitschrift für Papyrologie und Epigraphik* 30, 249–76.

(1990) 'Epigraphische Funde aus Lydien', *Epigraphica Anatolica* 15, 49–72.

(1994) 'Die Beichtinschriften Westkleinasiens', *Epigraphica Anatolica* 22.

(1995) 'Ländliche Religiosität in Lydien', in *Forschungen in Lydien (Asia Minor Studien 17),* ed. E. Schwertheim. Bonn, 37–48.

(1996) 'Neue Inschriften aus Lydien (I)', *Epigraphica Anatolica* 26, 1–29.

(1997) 'Neue Inschriften aus Lydien (II)', *Epigraphica Anatolica* 28, 69–79.

(1999) 'Lydien in der späteren Kaiserzeit: Wirtschaft, Gesellschaft und Religion im Spiegel der Inschriften', in *XI Congresso Internazionale di Epigrafia Greca e Latina, Roma, 18–24 Settembre 1997: Atti.* Rome, II 473–88.

(2003) 'Peter Herrmann (22.05.1927–22.11.2002)', *Zeitschrift für Papyrologie und Epigraphik* 144, 105–7.

(2005) 'Neue Inschriften aus Lydien (V)', *Epigraphica Anatolica* 38, 21–34.

(2007) 'Göttliche Hilfe bei Verlust', in *Scripta Anatolica: Hommages à Pierre Debord,* ed. P. Brun. Bordeaux, 331–8.

(2010) 'Beobachtungen zu einer Grabstele aus Nordostlydien', in *Studies in Greek Epigraphy and History in Honor of Stephen V. Tracy,* eds G. Reger, F. X. Ryan and T. F. Winters. Bordeaux, 293–300.

(2011a) 'Klage der Menschen – Klage der Götter. Aspekte der kleinasiatischen Beichtinschriften', in *Klagetraditionen: Form und Funktion der Klage in den Kulturen der Antike,* ed. M. Jaques. Fribourg and Göttingen, 63–81.

(2011b) 'Keine Szepter an Gräbern', *Zeitschrift für Papyrologie und Epigraphik* 177, 123–6.

(2016) 'Zu zwei Inschriften aus Sardis', *Zeitschrift für Papyrologie und Epigraphik* 200, 239–46.

(2018) 'Zu einem Ehrenbeschluss aus Loros (oder Loron) in Lydien', *Epigraphica Anatolica* 51, 164–6.

(2019) 'Die Beichtinschriften Westkleinasiens: Supplement', *Epigraphica Anatolica* 52, 1–105.

Pleket, H. W. (1981) 'Religious history as the history of mentality: The "believer" as servant of the deity in the Greek world', in *Faith, Hope and Worship: Aspects of Religious Mentality in the Ancient World,* ed. H. S. Versnel. Leiden, 152–92.

(1998) 'Models and inscriptions: Export of textiles in the Roman Empire', *Epigraphica Anatolica* 30, 117–28.

Pont, A.-V. (2013) 'Les groupes de voisinage dans les villes d'Asie Mineure occidentale à l'époque impériale', in *Groupes et associations dans les cites grecques (IIIe siècle av. J.-C. – IIe siècle apr. J.-C.)*, eds P. Fröhlich and P. Hamon. Geneva, 129–56.

Popescu, E. (1976) *Inscripțiile grecești și latine din sec. IV-XIII descoperite în România*. Bucharest.

Potts, J. (2017) 'Corpora in connection: Anatomical votives and the confession stelai of Lydia and Phrygia', in *Bodies of Evidence: Ancient Anatomical Votives Past, Present and Future*, eds J. Draycott and E.-J. Graham. London and New York, 20–44.

   (2019) *Confession in the Greco-Roman World: A Social and Cultural History*. Unpublished DPhil thesis, University of Oxford.

Price, J. (2002) 'On Jewish metronymics in the Graeco-Roman period', *Zutot* 2, 10–17.

Price, S. R. F. (1984) *Rituals and Power: The Roman Imperial Cult in Asia Minor*. Cambridge.

Purcell, N. (2013) 'On the significance of East and West in today's "Hellenistic" history: Reflections on symmetrical worlds, reflecting through world symmetries', in *The Hellenistic West: Rethinking the Ancient Mediterranean*, eds J. R. W. Prag and J. Crawley Quinn. Cambridge, 367–90.

Quataert, D. (1993) *Ottoman Manufacturing in the Age of the Industrial Revolution*. Cambridge.

Ramsay, W. M. (1888a) 'Antiquities of southern Phrygia and the border lands (III)', *American Journal of Archaeology* 4, 263–83.

   (1888b) 'Laodiceia Combusta and Sinethandos', *Mitteilungen des Deutsches Archäologisches Instituts. Abteilung Athen* 13, 233–72.

Rapp, C. (1997) 'Ritual brotherhood in Byzantium', *Traditio* 52, 285–326.

   (2016) *Brother-Making in Late Antiquity and Byzantium. Monks, Laymen, and Christian Ritual*. Oxford.

Rathbone, D. (2014) 'Mediterranean grain prices c. 300 to 31 BC: The impact of Rome', in *Documentary Sources in Ancient Near Eastern and Greco-Roman Economic History*, eds H. D. Baker and M. Jursa. Oxford, 289–312.

Rathbone, D. and von Reden, S. (2015) 'Mediterranean grain prices in classical antiquity', in *A History of Market Performance. From Ancient Babylonia to the Modern World*, eds R. van der Spek, B. van Leeuwen and J. L. van Zanden. London, 149–235.

Rawson, B. (2011) *A Companion to Families in the Greek and Roman Worlds*. Malden, MA.

Rhodes, P. J. and Osborne, R. (2003) *Greek Historical Inscriptions 404–323 BC*. Oxford.

Rice, E. E. (1986) 'Prosopographika Rhodiaka', *Annual of the British School at Athens* 81, 209–50.

Ricl, M. (1991) 'Meonsi πιττάκιον u Zenevi?', in *Greek–Roman Antiquity in Yugoslavia and on the Balkans*, eds P. H. Ilievski and V. Mitevski. Skopje, 201–6.

(1997) 'CIG 4142: A forgotten confession-inscription from north-west Phrygia', *Epigraphica Anatolica* 29, 35–43.

(2001) 'Donations of slaves and freeborn children to deities in Roman Macedonian and Phrygia: A reconsideration', *Tyche* 16, 127–60.

(2003) 'Society and economy of rural sanctuaries in Roman Lydia and Phrygia', *Epigraphica Anatolica* 35, 77–101.

(2009) 'Legal and social status of *threptoi* and related categories in narrative and documentary sources', in *From Hellenism to Islam: Cultural and Linguistic Change in the Roman Near East*, eds H. M. Cotton, R. G. Hoyland, J. J. Price and D. J. Wasserstein. Cambridge, 93–114.

(2011) 'Observations on a new corpus of inscriptions from Lydia', *Epigraphica Anatolica* 44, 143–52.

(2012) 'Sacrilege in a sacred forest? New interpretation of a recently published inscription from Lycia', *Belgrade Historical Review* 3, 25–9.

(2016) 'The cult of Meis Axiottenos in Lydia', in *Between Tarhuntas and Zeus Polieus: Cultural Crossroads in the Temples and Cults of Graeco-Roman Anatolia*, eds M.-P. de Hoz, J. P. Sánchez Hernandez and C. Molina Valero. Leuven, 151–69.

Ricl, M. and Malay, H. (2012) 'Two new decrees from Iulia Gordos and Lora', *Epigraphica Anatolica* 45, 73–87.

Riegl, A. (1901) *Die spätrömische Kunst-Industrie nach den Funden in Österreich-Ungarn*. Vienna.

Robert, L. (1936) *Collection Froehner I: Inscriptions grecques*. Paris.

(1937) *Études anatoliennes. Récherches sur les inscriptions grecques de l'Asie Mineure*. Paris.

(1962) *Villes d'Asie Mineure: études de géographie ancienne*, seconde édition. Paris.

(1963) *Noms indigènes dans l'Asie Mineure gréco-romaine*. Paris.

(1966) *Monnaies antiques en Troade*. Geneva and Paris.

(1969) 'Les inscriptions', in *Laodicée du Lycos: Le Nymphée. Campagnes 1961–1963*, ed. J. des Gagniers et al. Québec and Paris, 247–389.

(1987) *Documents d'Asie Mineure*. Athens and Paris.

Robert, L. and Robert, J. (1954) *La Carie, Tome II: Le plateau de Tabai et ses environs*. Paris.

Roberts, B. W. and vander Linden, M. (2011) 'Investigating archaeological cultures: Material culture, variability, and transmission', in *Investigating Archaeological Cultures*, eds B. W. Roberts and M. vander Linden. New York, Dordrecht, Heidelberg and London, 1–21.

Rohde, D. (2012) *Zwischen Individuum und Stadtgemeinde: Die Integration von Collegia in Hafenstädten*. Mainz.

Rojas, F. (2019) *The Pasts of Roman Anatolia: Interpreters, Traces, Horizons*. Cambridge.

Roosevelt, C. H. (2009) *The Archaeology of Lydia, from Gyges to Alexander*. Cambridge.

(2019) 'The inhabited landscapes of Lydia', in *Spear-Won Land: Sardis from the King's Peace to the Peace of Apamea*, eds A. M. Berlin and P. J. Kosmin. Madison, WI, 145–64.

Rostad, A. (2020) *Human Transgression – Divine Retribution. A Study of Religious Transgressions and Punishments in Greek Cultic Regulation and Lydian-Phrygian Propitiatory Inscriptions ('Confession Inscriptions')*. Oxford.

Rousset, D. (2013) 'Sacred property and public property in the Greek city', *The Journal of Hellenic Studies* 133, 113–33.

Russell, J. (1982) 'The evil eye in early Byzantine society', *JÖB* 32/3, 539–48.

Sallares, R. (2002) *Malaria and Rome: A History of Malaria in Antiquity*. Cambridge.

Saller, R. P. (1987) 'Men's age at marriage and its consequences in the Roman family', *Classical Philology* 82, 21–34.

(1994) *Patriarchy, Property and Death in the Roman Family*. Cambridge.

Saller, R. P. and Shaw, B. D. (1984) 'Tombstones and Roman family relations in the principate: Civilians, soldiers and slaves', *Journal of Roman Studies* 74, 124–56.

Salsano, D. (1998) 'Manumissio vindicta in ambiente provinciale: problemi e proposte', *Chiron* 28, 179–85.

Samitz, Chr. (2013) 'Die Einführung der Dekaproten und Eikosaproten in den Städten Kleinasiens und Griechenlands', *Chiron* 43, 1–61.

Sargın, Y. (2020) 'Akhisar Müzesi'nden yeni yazıtlar', *Cedrus* 8, 519–29.

Scardozzi, G. (2020) *The Territory of Hierapolis in Phrygia: An Archaeological Guide*. İstanbul.

Scheidel, W. (1991/1992) 'Zur Angabe des Lebensalters in den römischen Grabinschriften Österreichs', *Römisches Österreich* 19/20, 143–59.

(1992) 'Inschriftenstatistik und die Frage des Rekrutierungsalters römischer Soldaten', *Chiron* 22, 281–97.

(1996) *Measuring Sex, Age and Death in the Roman Empire: Explorations in Ancient Demography*. Ann Arbor.

(2001a) 'Roman age structure: Evidence and models', *Journal of Roman Studies* 91, 1–26.

(2001b) *Death on the Nile: Disease and the Demography of Roman Egypt*. Leiden.

(2003) 'Germs for Rome', in *Rome the Cosmopolis*, eds C. Edwards and G. Woolf. Cambridge, 158–76.

(2007) 'Roman funerary commemoration and the age at first marriage', *Classical Philology* 102, 389–402.

(2012a) 'Physical well-being', in *The Cambridge Companion to the Roman Economy*, ed. W. Scheidel. Cambridge, 321–33.

(2012b) 'Epigraphy and demography: Birth, marriage, family, and death', in *Epigraphy and the Historical Sciences*, eds J. Davies and J. Wilkes. Oxford, 101–29.

Scholl, R. (1985) 'ΙΕΡΟΔΟΥΛΟΙ im griechisch-römischen Ägypten', *Historia* 34, 466–92.

Schuler, Chr. (1998) *Ländliche Siedlungen und Gemeinden im hellenistischen und römischen Kleinasien*. Munich.

(2005) 'Die griechischen Inschriften von Phellos', *MDAI(I)* 55, 250–69.

(2012) 'Inscriptions and identities of rural population groups in Roman Asia Minor', in *Epigraphy and the Historical Sciences*, eds J. Davies and J. Wilkes. Oxford, 63–100.

(2019) 'Lycian, Persian, Greek, Roman: Chronological layers and structural developments in the onomastics of Lycia', in *Changing Names: Tradition and Innovation in Ancient Greek Onomastics*, ed. R. Parker. Oxford, 195–216.

Schürr, D. (1999) 'Gräko-lykisch πιατρα', *Die Sprache* 41/1, 24–38.

Schwertheim, E. (1975) 'Ein neues Weihrelief für Men und seine Mutter aus Lydien im Museum von Izmit', *MDAI(I)* 25, 357–65.

Scott, J. C. (1985) *Weapons of the Weak: Everyday Forms of Peasant Resistance*. New Haven and London.

(1990) *Domination and the Arts of Resistance: Hidden Transcripts*. New Haven and London.

(2009) *The Art of Not Being Governed: An Anarchist History of Upland Southeast Asia*. New Haven and London.

Segre, M. and Pugliese Carratelli, I. (1949–1951) 'Tituli Camirenses', *Annuario della Scuola Archeologica di Atene n.s.* 11–13, 141–318.

Sekunda, N. V. (1985) 'Achaemenid colonization in Lydia', *Revue des Études Anciennes* 87, 7–30.

Sewell-Rutter, N. J. (2007) *Guilt by Descent: Moral Inheritance and Decision Making in Greek Tragedy*. Oxford.

Shaw, B. D. (1987) 'The age of Roman girls at marriage: Some reconsiderations', *Journal of Roman Studies* 77, 30–46.

(1996) 'Seasons of death: Aspects of mortality in imperial Rome', *Journal of Roman Studies* 86, 100–38.

(2006) 'Seasonal mortality in imperial Roman and the Mediterranean: Three problem cases', in *Urbanism in the Preindustrial World: Cross-Cultural Approaches*, ed. G. R. Storey. Tuscaloosa, 86–109.

Slater, W. J. (1986) *Aristophanis Byzantii Fragmenta*. Berlin and New York.

(1995) 'The pantomime Tiberius Iulius Apolaustus', *Greek, Roman and Byzantine Studies* 36, 263–92.

Spawforth, A. (2001) 'Shades of Greekness: A Lydian case study', in *Ancient Perceptions of Greek Ethnicity*, ed. I. Malkin. Cambridge, MA, 275–300.

Staab, G. and Petzl, G. (2010) 'Vier neue Epigramme aus Lydien', *Zeitschrift für Papyrologie und Epigraphik* 174, 1–14.

Stamp, L. D. (1936) *Asia: A Regional and Economic Geography*, third edition. London.

Stern, S. (2012) *Calendars in Antiquity: Empires, States & Societies*. Oxford.

Sterrett, J. R. S. (1888) The Wolfe Expedition to Asia Minor. Papers of the American School of Classical Studies at Athens 3.

Stinton, T. C. W. (1975) '*Hamartia* in Aristotle and Greek tragedy', *Classical Quarterly* 25, 221–54.

Strubbe, J. H. M. (1991) '"Cursed be he that moves my bones"', in *Magika Hiera: Ancient Greek Magic and Religion*, eds C. A. Faraone and D. Obbink. Oxford, 33–59.

(1994) 'Curses against violations of the grave in Jewish epitaphs of Asia Minor', in *Studies in Early Jewish Epigraphy*, eds J. W. van Henten and P. W. van der Horst. Leiden, 70–128.

(1997) *APAI EΠITYMBIOI. Imprecations against Desecrators of the Grave in the Greek Epitaphs of Asia Minor. A Catalogue. IGSK* 52. Bonn.

(1998) 'Epigrams and consolation decrees for deceased youths', *L'Antiquité classique* 67, 45–75.

Swoboda, H., Keil, J. and Knoll, F. (1935) *Denkmäler aus Lykaonien, Pamphylien und Isaurien*. Brünn.

Szemerényi, O. (1977) 'Studies in the Kinship Terminology of the Indo-European Languages, with special references to Indian, Iranian, Greek and Latin', *Acta Iranica* 16 (*Textes et Mémoires VII: Varia 1977*), 1–240.

Tabbernee, W. (1997) *Montanist Inscriptions and Testimonia. Epigraphic Sources Illustrating the History of Montanism*. Macon, GA.

Talbot, A.-M. (2018) 'Childhood in middle and late Byzantium', in *Childhood in History. Perceptions of Children in the Ancient and Medieval Worlds*, eds R. Aasgaard, C. Horn and O. M. Cojocaru. London and New York, 240–56.

Tataki, A. B. (1993) 'From the prosopography of ancient Macedonia: The metronymics', in *Archaia Makedonia* V. Thessaloniki, III 1453–71.

Thompson, E. P. (1975) *Whigs and Hunters: The Origin of the Black Act*. London.

Thonemann, P. (2004) 'Review of *Inscriptiones Graecae IX I² 4: Inscriptiones insularum maris Ionii*', *Classical Review* 54, 215–18.

(2007) 'Estates and the land in late Roman Asia Minor', *Chiron* 37, 435–78.

(2009) 'The estate of Krateuas', *Chiron* 39, 363–93.

(2010) 'The women of Akmoneia', *Journal of Roman Studies* 100, 163–78.

(2011a) *The Maeander Valley: A Historical Geography from Antiquity to Byzantium*. Cambridge.

(2011b) 'Eumenes II and Apollonioucharax', *Gephyra* 8, 19–30.

(2013a) 'The Attalid state, 188–133 BC', in *Attalid Asia Minor: Money, International Relations, and the State*, ed. P. Thonemann. Oxford, 1–47.

(2013b) 'Phrygia: An anarchist history, 950 BC–AD 100', in *Roman Phrygia: Culture and Society*, ed. P. Thonemann. Cambridge, 1–40.

(2013c) 'Households and families in Roman Phrygia', in *Roman Phrygia: Culture and Society*, ed. P. Thonemann. Cambridge, 124–42.

(2015) 'The calendar of the Roman province of Asia', *Zeitschrift für Papyrologie und Epigraphik* 196, 123–41.

(2017a) 'Close-kin marriage in Roman Anatolia', *Cambridge Classical Journal* 63, 143–66.

(2017b) 'Three notes on Lydian Saittai', *Philia* 3, 188–96.

(2019) 'New inscriptions from the Middle Hermos', *Philia* 5, 122–37.

(2020) *An Ancient Dream Manual: Artemidorus' The Interpretation of Dreams*. Oxford.

(2021) *Lucian, Alexander or The False Prophet*. Oxford.

Todd, E. (2011) *L'origine des systèmes familiaux, Tome I. L'Eurasie*. Paris.

Tran, N. (2006) *Les membres des associations romaines. Le rang social des collegiati en Italie et en Gaules sous le Haut-Empire*. Rome.

Umar, B. (2001) *Lydia: Bir Tarihsel Coğrafya Araştırması ve Gezi Rehberi*. Istanbul.

Uzunoğlu, H. (2019) 'Zwei neue Grabsteine als Belege für den Leinenverein (συνεργασία τῶν λινουργῶν) aus Saittai', *Olba* 27, 501–16.

Versnel, H. S. (1991) 'Beyond cursing: The appeal to justice in judicial prayers', in *Magika Hiera: Ancient Greek Magic and Religion*, eds C. A. Faraone and D. Obbink. Oxford, 60–106.

(2002) 'Writing mortals and reading gods: Appeal to the gods as a dual strategy in social control', in *Demokratie, Recht und soziale Kontrolle im klassischen Athen*, ed. D. Cohen. Munich, 37–76.

(2010) 'Prayers for justice, east and west: New finds and publications since 1990', in *Magical Practice in the Latin West*, eds R. L. Gordon and F. Marco Simón. Leiden and Boston, 275–354.

Vlassopoulos, K. (2007) *Unthinking the Greek Polis: Ancient Greek History Beyond Eurocentrism*. Cambridge.

Waelkens, M. (1986) *Die kleinasiatischen Türsteine. Typologische und epigraphische Untersuchungen der kleinasiatischen Grabreliefs mit Scheintür*. Mainz am Rhein.

Watson, P. A. (1995) *Ancient Stepmothers: Myth, Misogyny and Reality*. Leiden, New York and Cologne.

West, M. L. (1978) *Hesiod: Works and Days*. Oxford.

(1999) 'Ancestral curses', in *Sophocles Revisited. Essays Presented to Sir Hugh Lloyd-Jones*, ed. J. Griffin. Oxford, 31–45.

Wiegand, Th. (1905) 'Inschriften aus Kleinasien', *MDAI(A)* 30, 323–30.

Wilgaux, J. (2006) 'Les évolutions du vocabulaire grec de la parenté', in *Parenté et société dans le monde grec de l'antiquité à l'âge moderne*, eds A. Bresson, M.-P. Masson, S. Perentidis and J. Wilgaux. Bordeaux, 209–34.

Wilhelm, A. (1901) 'Ψήφισμα Ἀθηναίων', *AE* 1901, 49–57; reprinted in *Abhandlungen und Beiträge zur griechischen Inschriftenkunde* II. Leipzig, 1984, 13–17.

(1911) 'Neue Beiträge zur griechischen Inschriftenkunde, I. Teil', *SB Wien* 166/1; reprinted in *Akademieschriften zur griechischen Inschriftenkunde, Teil I*. Leipzig, 1974, 19–82.

(1921) 'Neue Beiträge zur griechischen Inschriftenkunde, VI. Teil', *SB Wien* 183/3, 1–79; reprinted in *Akademieschriften zur griechischen Inschriftenkunde, Teil I*. Leipzig, 1974, 294–370.

Williamson, C. G. (2016) 'A Carian shrine in a Hellenising world: The sanctuary of Sinuri, near Mylasa', in *Between Tarhuntas and Zeus Polieus: Cultural Crossroads in the Temples and Cults of Graeco-Roman Anatolia*, eds M.-P. de Hoz, J. P. Sánchez Hernandez and C. Molina Valero. Leuven, 75–99.

Woods, R. I. (2007) 'Ancient and early modern mortality: Experience and under-
    standing', *Economic History Review* 60, 373–99.

Woodward, A. M. and Ormerod, H. A. (1909/10) 'A journey in south-western Asia
    Minor', *Annual of the British School at Athens* 16, 76–136.

Woolf, G. (2020) *The Life and Death of Ancient Cities*. Oxford.

Wörrle, M. (2009) 'Neue Inschriftenfunde aus Aizanoi V: Aizanoi und Rom I', *Chi-
    ron* 39, 409–44.

Zanker, P. (1993) 'The Hellenistic grave stelai from Smyrna: Identity and self-image
    in the polis', in *Images and Ideologies: Self-Definition in the Hellenistic World*,
    eds A. W. Bulloch, E. S. Gruen, A. A. Long and A. Stewart. Berkeley, Los Ange-
    les and London, 212–30.

Zgusta, L. (1964a) *Kleinasiatische Personennamen*. Prague.
    (1964b) *Anatolische Personennamensippen*. Prague.

Ziegler, R. (1993) *Kaiser, Heer und städtisches Geld*. Vienna.

Zimmermann, C. (2002) *Handwerkervereine im griechischen Osten des Imperium
    Romanum*. Mainz.

Index